SMALL BUSINESS
MANAGEMENT

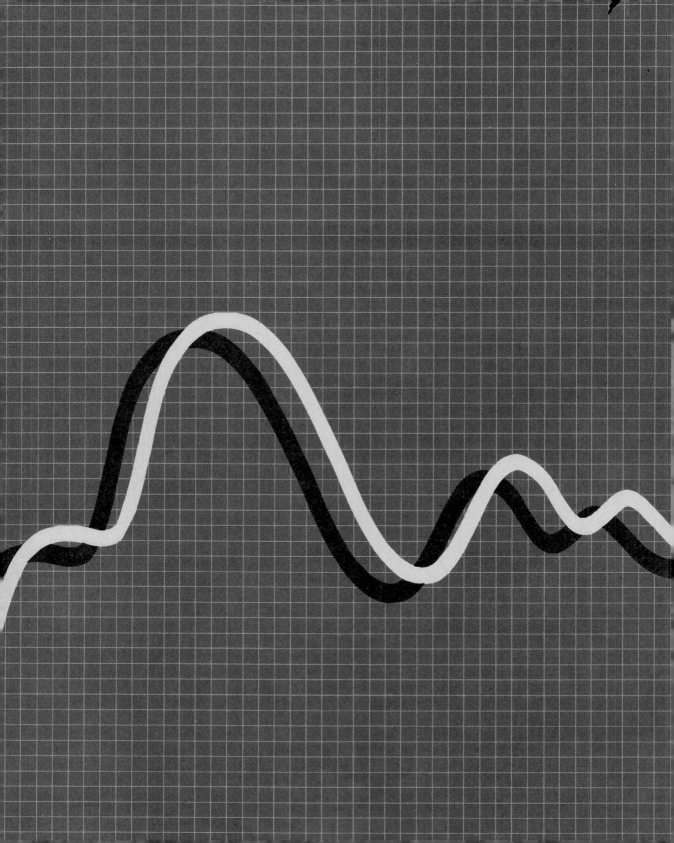

SMALL BUSINESS MANAGEMENT

A GUIDE TO ENTREPRENEURSHIP

Second Edition

Nicholas C. Siropolis

Cuyahoga Community College

Houghton Mifflin Company   Boston

Dallas   Geneva, Ill.   Hopewell, N.J.

Palo Alto   London

Dedicated to: Shirley, my mother, and my sister, Helen

All photos in this text, unless otherwise noted, are by Karabinus & Associates, Inc. Interior art rendered by Omnigraphics.

Printed in the U.S.A.

Library of Congress Catalog Card Number: 81-82561

ISBN: 0-395-31732-0

CONTENTS

v

CHAPTER TWO
THE ENTREPRENEUR 27

CHAPTER THREE
SMALL BUSINESS AND
INDUSTRY 52

PART TWO / STARTING A NEW VENTURE **79**

CHAPTER SEVEN
LEGAL ASPECTS 165

CHAPTER EIGHT
LOCATION 197

PART THREE / MANAGING THE ONGOING VENTURE 287

PREFACE

This book is for those men and women who someday may go into business for themselves and for those who are already in business for themselves but who wish to strengthen their entrepreneurial and managerial skills. It is designed expressly for courses and programs called Small Business Management, Starting a New Venture, and the like, offered by two-year community and technical colleges and four-year colleges and universities.

Although many colleges require an Introduction to Business course as a prerequisite, others do not. This means that for some students a course in entrepreneurship—or small business management—will be their first and perhaps only exposure to the business world. For this reason, the text is written in such a way that the material can be grasped by students having little or no background in business.

The text covers the entire spectrum of entrepreneurship, ranging from the business plan to computers, from marketing research to social responsibilities. Coverage of these subjects and others is deep enough to challenge students and ensure a working knowledge. To excite the student's interest, the text makes wide use of graphics and true-to-life examples. Equally important, the text is written in a style that invites enthusiastic reading and study.

Thanks to the suggestions of reviewers as well as of professors who used the first edition, we made many changes in this second edition, among them the addition of major sections on financial analysis and computers. We also rewrote most topics to update them and to make them more comprehensive. As in the first edition, we have strived to supply a textbook that reflects the letter and spirit of the entrepreneurial tradition, a textbook that is teachable and readable, content-rich and stimulating. We have also strived to convey to students the conviction that entrepreneurship is a vitally important endeavor.

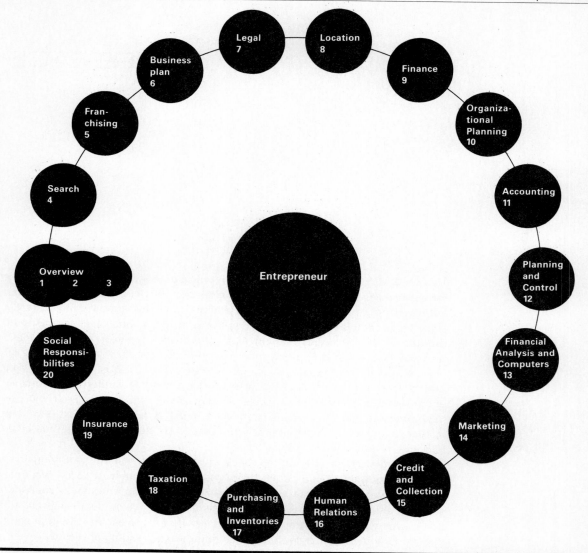

The book is divided into three parts. The first three chapters give an overview of entrepreneurship. The next seven chapters discuss the problems of launching a new venture, and the remaining ten chapters deal with the problems connected with managing an ongoing venture. Each of the twenty chapters contains two short cases, and one comprehensive case. (See the chapter guide above.)

The sixty cases are based on actual experiences of entrepreneurs and people in small business. The comprehensive cases describe how the entrepreneurs began their ventures, how they progressed with them, and the directions in which they are moving with their ventures. These cases have financial statements, including ones that show how the entrepreneurs financed their ventures at the start. Many of the cases also show examples from business plans used by the entrepreneurs. Students generally like the case method of instruction because it focuses, not on memorization, but on thinking through true-to-life business problems and opportunities.

Finally, we invite your comments and criticisms. That way, we can better provide you with materials that lend themselves to the teaching and learning of entrepreneurship. We sincerely appreciate your suggestions.

ACKNOWLEDGMENTS

This book is by no means the work of one person. Many have contributed to its development. Let me mention just a few:

☐ The entrepreneurs who gave so freely of their time and energies to supply me with case material.
☐ The faculty and staff at Cuyahoga Community College, who enabled me to create an accredited curriculum devoted to entrepreneurship. I am especially indebted to Darl Ault, Elizabeth Boyer, Mildred Brown, John Coleman, Walter Johnson, Kenneth Killen, Kermit Lidstrom, Joseph Malone, Robert Parilla, George Plavac, Robert Sexton, Richard Shapiro, Booker Tall, and Lowell Watkins.
☐ The Greater Cleveland Growth Association, where I first got the idea to create an entrepreneurship curriculum. In particular, I am indebted to Melvin Roebuck, with whom I have had a long professional relationship. Others that I am indebted to are Michael Benz, John Robinson, and Ramesh Shah.
☐ The Small Business Administration, which never failed me in my numerous requests for help. In particular, I am grateful to Eleanor Bozik, S. P. Fisher, Hudson Hyatt, and Norman McLeod.
☐ Vincent Panichi of John Carroll University and Ciuni and Panichi, Inc., who so generously helped me with updating the chapter on taxation.
☐ Reviewers whose numerous criticisms were so creatively helpful to me. I am especially indebted to Carol Eliason, American Association of Community and Junior Colleges; Don F. Gadbury, Hillsborough Community College and senior vice president, Flagship Bank of Tampa; Harry Goldman, Los Angeles Valley College and president, Self-employment Advisory Foundation; Robert C. Grau, Cuyahoga Community College; Julius Grossman, Mohawk Valley Community College; Roy R. Grundy, College of DuPage; James L. Hyek, Los Angeles Valley College; and Martha R. Smydra, Macomb County Community College.

To all of these men and women and their organizations, my heartfelt thanks.

Nicholas C. Siropolis

PART ONE

AN OVERVIEW
OF SMALL BUSINESS

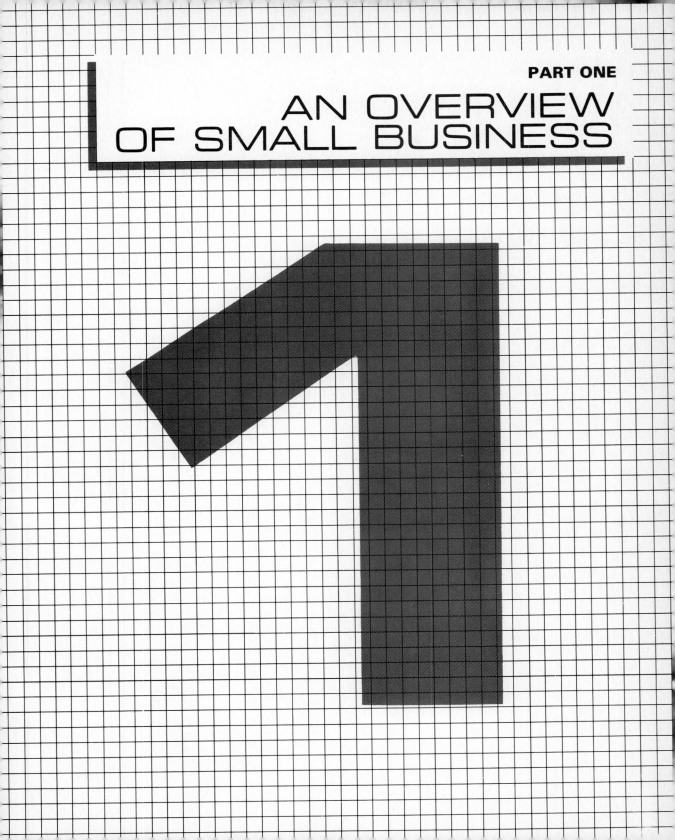

CHAPTER ONE

SMALL BUSINESS IN A FREE ENTERPRISE SOCIETY

questions for mastery

why is the study of small business important?

how is small business defined?

what is the role of small business in our economy?

what is the relationship between small business and big business?

why do small businesses succeed or fail?

If America is to be civilized, it must be done by the business class.

Alfred North Whitehead

S mall business enjoys a tradition of infinite variety and solid achievement. It thrives everywhere. So vital is small business that few, if any, parts of our economy could go on without its products and services. Small business is also a civilizing influence, rising above dollars and cents to enrich the lives of men and women the world over.

PLACE OF SMALL BUSINESS IN HISTORY

In the vast sweep of human history, small business has received scant attention. Few historians have bothered to record its contributions to society, even though the first known piece of writing appeared more than 4,000 years ago. It described how bankers loaned money at interest.[1] Since then, small-businesspersons have spent countless hours pouring out products and services to benefit the consumer.

Small business flourished in almost all ancient cultures. The Arabs, Babylonians, Egyptians, Jews, Greeks, Phoenicians, and Romans excelled at small business. Their products and services, however, were often shoddy and slipshod. Consumers often were cheated and defrauded. The result was that small businesses became objects of scorn.

Into this controversy stepped Hammurabi, King of Babylon. In 2100 B.C., he drafted a code of three hundred laws to protect consumers and small-businesspersons, especially against fraud. Carved on marble columns 8 feet high, the original code now resides at the Louvre Museum in Paris, though much of it has been erased by time. A sampling of Hammurabi's laws follows:

> If outlaws hatch a conspiracy in the house of a wineseller and she does not arrest them and bring them to the palace, that wineseller shall be put to death.
>
> If a builder has built a house for a man and does not make his work perfect; and the house which he has built has fallen down and so caused the death of the householders, that builder shall be put to death.[2]

These two laws underscore the truth of the saying that "the more times change, the more they stay the same." Indeed, the need to protect consumers from business and business from consumers is as vital today as in Hammurabi's time. Note that the first law deals with businesswomen and their social responsibilities toward government.

SMALL BUSINESS IGNORED

Although crowded with achievement, small-business history has never fired the public mind. Greek and Roman historians virtually ignored small business. In their view, ideas and military deeds were the stuff of history. Yet it was largely through small business that civilization was spread to all four corners of the then-known world. Small businesses brought to the have-nots such

1. Edward C. Bursk, *The World of Business* (New York: Macmillan, 1963), I, 2.
2. G. R. Driver and John C. Miles, *The Babylonian Laws* (Oxford: The Clarendon Press, 1955), II, 83.

things as Babylonian astronomy and Greek philosophy, the Jewish calendar and Roman law.

In the centuries that followed, even the Roman Catholic church held small-businesspersons in low esteem. The church branded retailers as sinners because they did nothing to improve a product; yet they charged a higher price than did the maker of the product. And, until the nineteenth century, the church often spoke against the practice of charging interest on loans.

Although now held in higher esteem than ever before, small business remains overshadowed by professions such as medicine and law. In her classic history of businesses big and small, Miriam Beard points out:

> Physicians are now wrapped in such dignity that the public forgets how recently they occupied the status of barbers. Lawyers have climbed from the solicitor-family relation to a solemn eminence. . . . Not so the businessman; he still struggles on, unfathered and unhallowed. He is his own ancestor, and, usually, his memory does not reach back even to the last business crisis.[3]

A CHANGE IN IMAGE

Today, however, small business enjoys more esteem and prestige than ever before. Educators, journalists, and politicians alike have begun to underscore its achievements and opportunities, its promise and problems. Perhaps the best measure of its new-found prestige was the White House Conference on Small Business held in 1980. Called at the urging of President Jimmy Carter, this conference brought together 1,683 delegates from all 50 states, most of them small-businesspersons. At the conference, they:

☐ Defined and analyzed their problems and opportunities.
☐ Proposed how the federal government could best help them solve those problems and pursue those opportunities.

This conference likely never would have happened but for the "rising tide in the spirit of individual enterprise in America. . . ."[4] Later in the chapter, we will discuss more deeply both the spirit and the proposals of the conference.

DEFINITIONS OF SMALL BUSINESS

Small business defies easy definition. Typically, we apply the term *small business* to so-called mom-and-pop stores such as neighborhood groceries and restaurants, and we apply the term *big business* to such giants as Du Pont and General Motors. But between these two extremes fall businesses that may be looked upon as big or small, depending on the yardstick and cutoff point used to measure size.

3. Miriam Beard, *A History of the Business Man* (New York: Macmillan, 1938), I, 1.
4. White House Commission on Small Business, *Report to the President: American Small Business Economy: Agenda for Action* (Washington, D.C.: U.S. Government Printing Office, April 1980), p. 9.

There are a number of common yardsticks:

☐ **Total assets** The total cash, inventory, land, machinery, and other resources held by a business.
☐ **Owners' equity** The total investment made by investors. For example, in a corporation, investors would generally be the shareholders who buy stock; creditors would generally be those who either lend money or supply credit.
☐ **Yearly sales revenues**
☐ **Number of employees**

Each yardstick has its points. But *number of employees* has more in its favor than any of the others. Among other things, this yardstick is:

☐ **Inflation proof** It is unaffected by changes in the purchasing power of the dollar.
☐ **Transparent** It is easy to see and understand.
☐ **Comparable** It allows good comparisons of size between businesses of the same industry.
☐ **Available** It is easy to get from businesses.

If we accept number of employees as the yardstick of size, what should the cutoff point be? We believe it should be 500, mainly because this is the number recommended by the U.S. Department of Commerce and widely used by Chambers of Commerce. So in this textbook, we will call a business small if it employs fewer than 500 persons, unless noted otherwise.

Almost all definitions require some qualification. Ours is no exception. To qualify as small, a business not only should employ fewer than 500 persons but should also be:

☐ **Independently owned** It should not be part of another business.
☐ **Independently managed** Small-businesspersons should be free to run their businesses as they please.

The second qualification rules out many franchises. One of the hardy myths about franchising is that owners work for themselves. Often, that is not so. In many franchises, the true boss is the franchisor, not the franchisee. In fact, an investor who buys a franchise must often live up to numerous contractual obligations, such as keeping certain store hours, paying monthly fees to the franchisor, and preparing monthly performance reports.

Let us now look at some other definitions of small business, namely those laid down by the U.S. Small Business Administration (SBA). This federal agency was created by the U.S. Congress in 1953 to help small business thrive. To meet this goal, the SBA offers programs that have already helped hundreds of thousands of small businesses to upgrade their managerial skills and to borrow money.

For businesses seeking loans, the SBA has drawn up definitions of smallness to fit virtually every industry. A partial list appears in Exhibit 1-1. Note the

EXHIBIT 1-1

SBA Standards of Smallness for Selected Industries

Manufacturers	Employing Fewer Than
Aircraft	1,500 persons
Calculating machines	1,000
Household vacuum cleaners	750
Men's and boys' clothes	500
Macaroni and spaghetti	250

Retailers	Earning Sales of Less Than
Mail order houses	$7.5 million a year
Grocery stores	7.5
Automobile agencies	6.5
Variety stores	3.0
Radio and television stores	2.5

Wholesalers	Earning Sales of Less Than
Paints and varnishes	$22.0 million a year
Tires and tubes	22.0
Groceries	14.5
Sporting goods	14.5

Source: "SBA Rules and Regulations," *The Code of Federal Regulations* (Washington, D.C.: U.S. Government Printing Office, October 5, 1978), Section 121.3–10.

SBA's use of different yardsticks and cutoff points. Exhibit 1-2 condenses the definitions into broad industry groups.

These definitions are by no means hard and fast, and they can be relaxed in exceptional cases. In 1966, for example, the SBA classified American Motors as small to enable the company to bid on certain government contracts. At the time, American Motors ranked as the nation's sixty-third largest manufacturer, with 32,000 employees and sales revenues of $991 million. The SBA justified its judgment by applying a seldom-used test of smallness—namely, that a business qualifies as small if it does not dominate its industry. American Motors easily met that test.

Note in Exhibit 1-1 that many of the SBA's definitions really cover medium-sized businesses. For example, a manufacturer employing 1,000 persons probably has sales revenues in excess of $50 million a year. Few laypersons would view such a business as small.

THE BRIGHT SIDE OF SMALL BUSINESS

Returning to our earlier, simpler definition of a small business as one that employs fewer than 500 persons, let us now place this number in focus. How many businesses are that small? How many persons does small business employ?

EXHIBIT 1-2

Industry Group	Yearly Sales Revenues (millions of dollars)	Number of Employees
Wholesaling	9.5 to 22.0	—
Services	2.0 to 8.0	—
Retailing	2.0 to 7.5	—
Manufacturing	—	250 to 1,500

As shown in Exhibit 1-3, more than 99 percent of the nation's 14 million businesses are small—even if we define a small business as one that employs fewer than 100 rather than 500. The total of 14 million businesses includes farms, franchises, and professional firms.

Clearly, small business is a vital force in the economy. Further evidence of its vitality is the fact that small business employs 58 percent of the nation's workforce.[5]

FINANCIAL PERFORMANCE

In terms of sheer numbers, then, small business far outstrips big business. But how well are small businesses doing? Are they falling behind, keeping pace with, or moving ahead of big business? These questions are hard to answer with precision.

Even so, the evidence suggests that small business outdoes big business. Some proof appears in Exhibit 1-4. Note that, on the average, small manufacturers earn a higher return on owners' equity than do big manufacturers. In other words, for each dollar they put in, small-business investors earn more

EXHIBIT 1-3

Percentage of Businesses	Number of Employees Fewer Than
88.9%	10 persons
94.7	20
99.2	100
99.9	500

Source: U.S. Department of Commerce, *Enterprise Statistics* (Washington, D.C.: U.S. Government Printing Office, 1977), Series ES77-1, Table 5, p. 142.

5. U.S. Small Business Administration, *Facts About Small Business* (Washington, D.C.: U.S. Government Printing Office, 1980), p. 3.

EXHIBIT 1-4

Comparison of Financial Performance

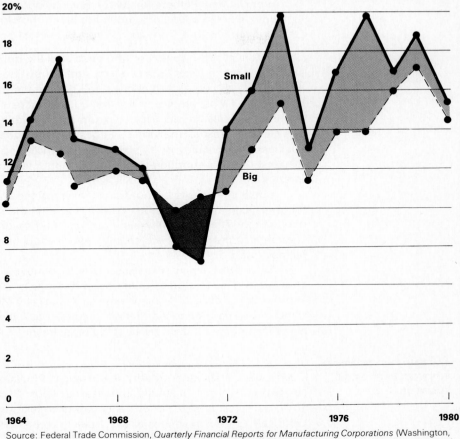

Return on owners' equity

Since 1964 small manufacturers have consistently outperformed big manufacturers.

Source: Federal Trade Commission, *Quarterly Financial Reports for Manufacturing Corporations* (Washington, D.C.: U.S. Government Printing Office, 1964–1980), Table 5.

than do big-business investors. Although we lack hard data showing why small manufacturers do better, we can offer these two major reasons:

☐ In many industries, small business can respond more quickly and at less cost than big business to the quickening rate of change in products and services, processes and markets.

☐ Small business has become more attractive to talented, individualistic men and women.

We lack similar data comparing the performance of small and big business in nonmanufacturing industries such as retailing, services, and wholesaling. But we believe, for the reasons given earlier, that small businesses in these industries are also doing well.

INNOVATION

Small business sparks our economy. Often creative and resourceful, small-businesspersons tend to be mavericks. They are likely to:

☐ Cut prices when others follow the price leader
☐ Innovate when others are content to sit on their hands
☐ Reject suggestions from competitors to set just one price

Often, it is the mavericks who push back the frontiers of knowledge. Ideas are their stock in trade. In fact, study after study shows that major inventions are as likely to come from either small businesses or individuals as from big businesses. "Most studies show that . . . size adds little to research intensity and may actually detract from it in some industries."[6] An example bears this out. General Electric, the world's largest electrical manufacturer, credits small businesses with many of its product ideas, including the invention of electric toasters, ranges, refrigerators, dishwashers, vacuum cleaners, and deep freezers.[7]

Small businesses or individuals invented the stainless steel razor blade, the transistor radio, the photocopying machine, the jet engine, and the quick photograph. Their ingenuity also gave us the helicopter, power steering, the automatic transmission, air conditioning, cellophane, and even the 19-cent ballpoint pen.

Since 1953, small businesses have accounted for half of all major inventions, according to studies made by both the U.S. Department of Commerce and the U.S. Office of Management and Budget.[8] Moreover, a study by the National Science Foundation found that small businesses produce 24 times as many inventions for each research dollar as many of the biggest businesses.[9]

INVENTIVENESS OF BIG BUSINESS

Clearly, we are all better off for the presence of millions of small businesses in our economy. Their ingenuity enriches our lives. Of course, big business enriches our lives as well. For evidence, we need look no further than DuPont. In 1980, half its sales revenues of $13.7 billion came from chemicals that did not even exist 15 years before. That is a dazzling record.

The very size of many big businesses, however, may discourage innovation. For example, "An auto industry with millions of dollars invested in great stamping dies to turn out steel bodies has no incentive to embrace the technology of plastics."[10]

Big business seldom suppresses invention (ideas) and innovation (application of ideas). But it is impossible for every new invention to be put straight

6. Leonard Weiss, quoted in Mark J. Green, *The Closed Enterprise System* (New York: Bantam Books, 1972), pp. 22–23.
7. Theodore K. Quinn, *Giant Business: Threat to Democracy* (New York: Exposition Press, 1953), p. 116.
8. U.S. House of Representatives Committee on Small Business, *Future of Small Business in America* (Washington, D.C.: U.S. Government Printing Office, August 1979), p. 7.
9. U.S. Senate Committee on Small Business, *Small Business and Innovation* (Washington, D.C.: U.S. Government Printing Office, June 1979), p. 42.
10. Jerry S. Cohen and Morton Mintz, *America, Inc.* (New York: Dial Press, 1971), p. 49.

into production just because it outdoes a current product. Big business must wait until new ways and new products are so superior that the changeover can be made without a steep rise in price. If we could start from scratch, we doubtless could have a much better automobile than we have. But the scrapping of entire automobile plants is too far-fetched even to think about.

DEPENDENCE OF BIG BUSINESS ON SMALL BUSINESS

Our economy depends on small business for much more than invention and innovation. For one thing, small business employs tens of millions of men and women. For another, it sells to consumers most of the products made by big manufacturers.

In addition, it provides big business with many of the services, supplies, and raw materials it needs. General Motors, for example, buys from 37,000 suppliers, most of whom are small. Why? Because big business cannot supply them as cheaply as small business. Some of the products and services that small business can supply more cheaply are:

☐ Products and services whose sales volume is small
☐ Products and services that demand close personal contact with customers
☐ Products and services that must meet the customer's unique specifications

SMALL BUSINESS CREATES JOBS

In the popular view, it is not small business but big business that creates most new jobs. This view is false. Professor David L. Birch of the Massachusetts Institute of Technology has found that between 1969 and 1976:

☐ Small businesses with 20 or fewer employees created 66 percent of all new jobs in the nation. In New England alone, such businesses created 99 percent of all new jobs. But—
☐ Middle-sized and big businesses created few new jobs.[11]

These results are striking, based as they are on data files of 5.6 million businesses. In Professor Birch's words, "It appears that the smaller corporations . . . are aggressively seeking out most new opportunities, while the larger ones are primarily redistributing their operations."[12]

Another study found that small, young, high-technology businesses create new jobs at a much faster rate than do older, larger businesses.[13] High-technology businesses, such as chemistry and electronics, require a high degree of scientific or engineering knowledge in order to succeed. Their ability to create jobs quickly is dramatized in Exhibit 1-5.

Still another measure of small-business vitality is the increasing number of businesses formed each year since 1960. New business incorporations crossed the 500,000 mark for the first time in 1979.[14] This number is roughly

11. David L. Birch, *The Job Generation Process* (Cambridge, Massachusetts: M.I.T. Program on Neighborhood and Regional Change, 1979), p. 8.
12. Ibid.
13. U.S. Department of Commerce, *Recommendations for Creating Jobs Through the Success of Small Innovative Businesses* (Washington, D.C.: U.S. Government Printing Office, March 1980), p. 88.
14. Alfred L. Malabre, Jr., "Tracking a Trend," *The Wall Street Journal,* March 12, 1980, p. 40.

EXHIBIT 1-5

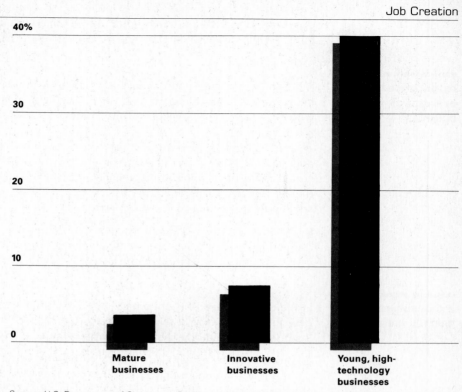

Average yearly growth of jobs

40%

30

20

10

0

Mature businesses

Innovative businesses

Young, high-technology businesses

Young, high-technology businesses create jobs at a much higher rate than do mature businesses.

Source: U.S. Department of Commerce, *Recommendations for Creating Jobs Through the Success of Small, Innovative Businesses* (Washington, D.C.: U.S. Government Printing Office, March 1980), p. 88.

triple the number in the early 1960s. However, this total covers mature as well as newly founded businesses:

☐ Mature businesses born as either sole proprietorships or partnerships that incorporated later
☐ New businesses that incorporated at birth

THE DARK SIDE OF SMALL BUSINESS

Financial performance and innovation, responsiveness and job creation form the bright side of the picture. In contrast, the dark side reflects the problems unique to small business. Many small businesses die in their infancy. In fact, of the 500,000 new businesses born each year in the United States, only half live as long as 18 months and only one in five lives as long as ten years.[15]

Why so high a death rate? Perhaps the chief reason is ease of entry. In fact, it is often easier for men or women to go into business for themselves than to find an employer. No law stops them from choosing themselves as boss. And they may choose almost any line of business they like best. They may have 20 years of experience in that line or none at all. They may do a textbook job of researching their markets or plunge in with no information at all. They may be millionaires or penniless. Yet, regardless of their qualifications, freedom of opportunity guarantees them the right to launch their own venture.

But, as economists often point out, freedom of opportunity means not only the freedom to succeed but also the freedom to fail. Failure to see this reality often causes untold stress, trauma, and tragedy.

SURFACE CAUSES OF FAILURE

Should we somehow screen would-be small-businesspersons before the marketplace does its own screening? No. The right to make wrong choices lies at the heart of our economic system. Without this right, initiative and incentive would soon dry up and our free enterprise system would then cease to be free.

What are some of the reasons so many fledgling businesses die? What do experts like Dun & Bradstreet identify as the cause of business failure? *Bad management.* Dun & Bradstreet has more than a century of experience in reporting on the financial health of businesses. In fact, they keep up-to-date credit ratings on 3.5 million businesses, and so they are uniquely qualified to judge why small businesses fail. They have found that businesses fail for the very same reasons year after year. The reasons are listed in Exhibit 1-6 and charted in Exhibit 1-7. Note that the first four reasons add up to bad management. All told, 92 percent fail because of bad management.

According to Dun & Bradstreet, bad management often is evidenced by such problems as heavy operating expenses or slow-paying customers, a poor location or competitive weaknesses, inventory difficulties or excessive fixed assets.

Impressive as these statistics may be, pointing an accusing finger at bad management, the fact remains that the real reason so many businesses die young is ease of entry. That is the chief cause, and bad management is merely the effect.

ARE SMALL-BUSINESS FAILURES REALLY FAILURES?

Though widely accepted, the failure rates quoted earlier may be open to question. In the words of Professor Albert Shapero of Ohio State University:

> The fact is that no one knows the startup rate or the failure rate. In fact, we don't even know what "failure" means. Do we mean bankruptcy? But

15. These statistics are "rough estimates" made by Dun & Bradstreet in 1969 and reported in *The Wall Street Journal* on April 10, 1969. These estimates probably still hold true today. (Author's communication with Dun & Bradstreet, Inc., New York, June 1980.)

EXHIBIT 1-6

Percentage of Business Failures	Cause of Failure	Explanation
44%	Incompetence	Lack of fitness to run the business—physical, moral, or intellectual
17	Lack of managerial experience	Little, if any, experience managing employees and other resources before going into business
16	Unbalanced experience	Not well rounded in marketing, finance, purchasing, and production
15	Inexperience in line	Little, if any, experience in the product or service before going into business
1	Neglect	Too little attention to the business, due to bad habits, poor health, or marital difficulties
1	Fraud or disaster	Fraud: misleading name, false financial statements, premeditated overbuy, or irregular disposal of assets. Disaster: fire, flood, burglary, employees' fraud, or strike (some disasters could have been provided against through insurance)
6 / 100%	Unknown	

Source: The first two columns are from *The Business Failure Record* (New York: Dun & Bradstreet, Inc., 1981), p. 12.

many people go out of business without declaring bankruptcy, working like hell to settle every debt even though they have to close the doors of their business.

Others close because their owners reach retirement age and have no one to turn the company over to. Still others shut down because they're bored. Are these business failures?

And is failure really failure? Many heroes of business failed at least once. Henry Ford failed twice. Maybe trying and failing is a better business education than going to a business school that has little concern with small business and entrepreneurship.[16]

BIG-BUSINESS GROWTH Still another worrisome statistic is big business's share of the nation's economic pie. According to the Federal Trade Commission (FTC), the nation's top two hundred manufacturers boosted their share of manufacturing assets to 60 percent in 1972 from 48 percent in 1950.[17]

16. Albert Shapero, "Numbers That Lie," *Inc.,* May 1981, p. 16.
17. U.S. Department of Commerce, *Statistical Abstract of the United States* (Washington, D.C.: U.S. Government Printing Office, 1978), p. 576.

EXHIBIT 1-7

Surface Reasons Why Businesses Fail

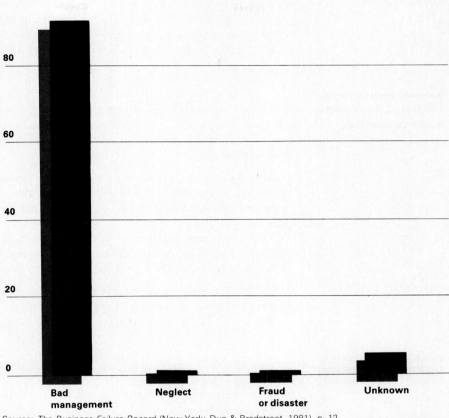

Percentage
of all
failures

100%

80

60

40

20

0

Bad
management

Neglect

Fraud
or disaster

Unknown

Bad management accounts for almost all failures.

Source: *The Business Failure Record* (New York: Dun & Bradstreet, 1981), p. 12.

That comes to a stunning 25 percent increase in concentration of assets in 22 years. We can only conclude that small businesses, at least in manufacturing, are finding it harder and harder to compete against big businesses.

Perhaps the main reason for the failure of small businesses to keep pace with the growth of big businesses is their inability to handle increased managerial demands. It is one thing to manage a shop of 10 employees and quite another to manage a shop of 100. With only 10 employees, small-businesspersons generally have visual control over everyone and everything under them.

But once their business grows to, say, 100 employees, small-businesspersons must rely on more sophisticated ways to plan and control their business. Unfortunately, they often lack the managerial skills to recognize, hire, and tap the talents they need to survive and grow.

In contrast, presidents of billion-dollar corporations are more likely to be professional managers. Skillful in the best and latest managerial tools, they orchestrate the talents of dozens of knowledgeable workers to solve problems and pursue opportunities.

Although the FTC's analysis focuses on manufacturing, similar trends toward concentration are apparent in both wholesaling and retailing. For example, the fifty largest retail businesses owned 32 percent of all retail assets in 1977.[18]

MINORITIES AND WOMEN IN SMALL BUSINESS

Historically, minorities and women have always played a disproportionately small role in small business. Although they have made some progress, they have a long way to go before they participate in small business to the full extent of their dreams and goals. For example:

☐ Blacks own only 1.7 percent of the nation's 14 million businesses. Yet they make up 11 percent of the total population. What is more, their businesses account for less than 0.1 of one percent of the total yearly sales volume in the nation.[19]

☐ Women own only 5.0 percent of the nation's businesses. Yet they make up 51 percent of the total population. Like the blacks, they account for less than 0.1 of one percent of the total yearly sales volume.[20]

Similarly, statistics for Hispanics and Native Americans also show that their share of the business world is disproportionately low.

THE FUTURE OF SMALL BUSINESS

The future looks bright. Small business will probably hold its strong position in the economy because of:

☐ Its ability to generate new ideas, new products, and new services that benefit consumers
☐ Its ability to create new jobs
☐ Big business's increasing dependence on small business for supplies, services, and raw materials
☐ Rising individualism among the young. More and more, business school graduates prefer to work for themselves rather than somebody else.

18. U.S. House of Representatives Committee on Small Business, *Future of Small Business in America* (Washington, D.C.: U.S. Government Printing Office, August 1979), p. 15.
19. "Business," *Black Enterprise* (February 1980), p. 55.
20. U.S. Department of Commerce, *Selected Characteristics of Women-Owned Businesses* (Washington, D.C.: U.S. Government Printing Office, October 1980), p. 1.

These observations lack statistical support. We do not have a crystal ball that peers into the future, but small business will probably continue to spark progress in our economy.

It is unlikely, however, that small-business failures will slow down. The example of successful small businesses will continue to attract the unqualified as well as the qualified in increasing numbers. As our population expands, we can expect a steady rise in the total number of small businesses.

THE IMPORTANCE OF EDUCATION

Our economy is likely to continue to become more scientific and therefore more complex. The rising flood of new knowledge, new managerial tools, and new managerial lifestyles will make obsolete many managerial practices as well as many products and services. So small-businesspersons will have to be better prepared to master change. Colleges and universities have already begun to meet this need. In fact, according to a survey by Professor Karl H. Vesper of the University of Washington, 137 universities offered courses in launching new businesses in 1978, up from 8 universities ten years before.[21]

Too, the SBA will continue to help small business with its many programs to upgrade skills and lend money. State and local governments will play an increasingly creative role, especially in stimulating inventions and their development into strong, healthy businesses that provide jobs.

Help will also come from an unexpected quarter: big business. In fact, some big businesses already are helping finance small businesses. Others are likely to follow suit. But their interest will be limited largely to small businesses with big brains—that is, high-technology companies that promise to grow at a fast rate. Such high-risk companies usually have a new product or service that promises to make a major breakthrough in the marketplace. Some spectacular examples in the past were Xerox, Sony, and Polaroid.

The future will also see the rise of small business as a new and unified political force at the local, state, and federal levels. One likely result is the passage of laws and policies that encourage risk taking and innovation by small business. At the federal level, small business has already won some recognition as a political force, as described below.

THE WHITE HOUSE CONFERENCE ON SMALL BUSINESS

In 1980 small business made history at the White House Conference. Small-businesspersons from all over the country came together to speak as one voice about their problems and opportunities. Until recently, "small business in the nation's political dialogue had been treated as a motherhood and apple pie issue. Everyone was for it but few policymakers took it very seriously, and its problems were left to the care of a small government agency. . . ."[22]

21. Quoted by David E. Gumpert, "Future of Small Business May Be Brighter than Portrayed," *Harvard Business Review,* July–August 1979, p. 176.
22. James Morrison, *Small Business: New Directions for the 1980s* (Washington, D.C.: The National Center for Economic Alternatives, 1980), p. iii.

This attitude has changed dramatically. In fact, the White House Conference might never have happened but for the newly widespread belief that small business is a seedbed for innovation and growth, productivity and new jobs. More and more, national leaders are seeking out small business to help cure such national ills as energy needs and urban blight. At the White House Conference, small-businesspersons responded in a can-do spirit by drafting for the president a series of 60 recommendations covering 12 issues:

1 Capital formation	7 Inflation
2 Economic policy	8 Innovation and technology
3 Education and management assistance	9 International trade
4 Energy	10 Minorities in business
5 Federal procurement	11 Veterans in business
6 Government regulations	12 Women in business

These 12 issues grew out of information amassed at 57 forums held in every state. Attended by 25,000 small-businesspersons, the entire process took 18 months. Task forces of experts then distilled this information into a series of logical recommendations.

The last step was the conference in Washington, where small-businesspersons debated and amended, deleted and added—to come up with their final 60 recommendations to the president. In the words of the conference report:

When the final conference sessions ended, it was with a solid sense of achievement and a determination to keep building upon their new-found unity. Many delegates now are enthusiastically organizing ways to continue pressing their interests at state as well as federal levels. If Small Business can keep that momentum going, the 1980 Conference may come to be regarded as the birthplace of a new political force in the nation.[23]

SUMMARY

Small business had its crude beginnings more than 40 centuries ago in the civilization of the eastern Mediterranean. Although crowded with achievement, small-business history has never captured the public mind, at least not to the extent that law and medicine have. But this gap is narrowing as small business begins to win recognition as a creative force in our economy.

Small business is at the center of modern society, touching all our lives. Few if any parts of our economy could run without its endless flow of products and services. More important, its ingenuity sparks invention and innovation. In fact, studies show that major ideas and inventions are as likely to come from small business as from big business. Riding a wide wave of creativity, small business will continue to spawn new products and new services to benefit consumers.

23. The White House Commission on Small Business, *Report to the President: America's Small Business Economy: Agenda for Action* (Washington, D.C.: U.S. Government Printing Office, April 1980), p. 42.

Of the nation's 14 million businesses, 99 percent qualify as small; that is, they employ fewer than 500 persons. About 500,000 new businesses are born each year, but half die within 18 months. The main reason for so high a death rate is the ease with which unqualified people may start new businesses.

Contrary to popular opinion, small business is more than holding its own against big business. One study shows that, on the average, small manufacturers are more profitable than big manufacturers.

The future of small business looks bright. In ever-increasing numbers, men and women will make their careers in small business. And they will be better prepared to make the most of their opportunities, thanks largely to better education and better help from the many groups devoted to giving small business a helping hand.

Small business is fast becoming a political force at the local, state, and federal levels. One likely result is the passage of laws and policies to spur the birth and growth of small business.

DISCUSSION AND REVIEW QUESTIONS

1 Write a short paragraph indicating what you believe you are likely to get out of a course in small business management.
2 Should small business be as highly regarded as medicine and law? Why?
3 Does small business dominate the business world? Why?
4 Define these terms: *small business, return on owners' equity, invention, innovation, high-technology companies, freedom of opportunity, ease of entry.*
5 On the basis of your own observations, is small business thriving or declining? Justify your answer.
6 What guarantees the existence of small business?
7 Why, on the average, are small manufacturers more profitable than big manufacturers?
8 Why do so many small businesses fail in the first few years of their existence? Explain fully.
9 Why was the U.S. Small Business Administration created by Congress?
10 Why is small business becoming an increasingly strong voice in political circles?
11 Should all men and women be screened before they go into business for themselves? Why?
12 How does the definition of small business used in this textbook differ from the SBA's definitions? How did you define a small business before you read this chapter?
13 Should small-businesspersons be concerned with political forces and their effects? Why?
14 How does small business serve as a barrier against monopoly?
15 Why is the study of small business especially vital for those who plan to launch their own venture?

Margaret Ware Kahliff views with pride one of her latest achievements. She took over an ailing plastics company and improved its performance dramatically. Thanks to her, after-tax profits leaped from $7,000 to $115,000 annually in just three years. But sales revenues rose only slightly, from $1.4 million to $1.6 million a year.

Mrs. Kahliff is now wondering how best to increase her revenues at a time when raw materials are so hard to come by.

BACKGROUND

Mrs. Kahliff caught the entrepreneurial fever from her father. He owned and managed a furniture store, a hardware store, and a funeral home in an Arkansas hamlet of 1,500 called Charleston.

Her father was a compulsive achiever. Besides managing three businesses at once, he served on the school board and ran the Methodist Sunday School. "He expected us to achieve, so we all did," says Mrs. Kahliff. And, indeed, they did: one brother, Carroll Bumpers, now heads two Greyhound subsidiaries in Phoenix, Arizona; another brother, Dale Bumpers, became a United States senator from Arkansas; and Mrs. Kahliff heads a plastics company employing 102 persons. Speaking of her father's influence, Mrs. Kahliff says, "If we kids made a 'B' in some subject and not an 'A,' father wanted to know how come? He never talked about money, but he talked about integrity and character."

Mrs. Kahliff recalls that her father once said, "There's nothing worse than an empty-headed woman who talks all the time. I know we're never going to get you to stop talking, so we had better train your mind." She proceeded to train her mind at the College of the Ozarks. And in 1970, the college bestowed upon her an honorary doctorate of humanities in recognition of her many achievements in business.

CREATES VENDING MACHINE VENTURE

Mrs. Kahliff launched her first entrepreneurial venture at age 14, when she produced her own radio program. Later she helped finance her college education by singing at a public dance hall—until her father found out and stopped her. "To think you'd use God's gift at a public dance hall," he told her.

Soon after college, she married a small businessman who received a Dr Pepper franchise in a town 1,000 miles from Arkansas. The franchise failed. Out of need, Mrs. Kahliff decided to go into business for herself with her husband's help. The business she chose was vending machines. The year was 1950. And she began with just $300 of her own savings and a $1,000 bank loan. Her beginning balance sheet appears in Exhibit 1A-1.

On this shoestring, Mrs. Kahliff parlayed one vending machine in 1950 into 500 vending machines by 1960. Her revenues soared from zero to $3.5 million a year. She credits this success to "knowledge, knowledge, and knowledge."

Balance Sheet (July 1, 1950)

Assets			Equities		
Cash	$ 100		Bank loan	$1,000	
Vending machine	1,000		Owner's equity	300	
Other assets	200				
Total assets	$1,300		Total equities	$1,300	

When Mrs. Kahliff went into the vending-machine business, she knew nothing about it. A friend of hers had told her in passing that the "coming thing in vending machines was cups not bottles." After sounding out vending-machine suppliers and local bankers, she decided to plunge into the business.

To learn about the business, she talked to suppliers and attended sales seminars. She also took courses in accounting and marketing. "I was like a sponge, soaking up all the knowledge I could," says Mrs. Kahliff.

SELLS VENTURE

She did so well she paid off all of her husband's debts. And later she merged her business into a giant conglomerate—Servomation, Inc.—for 47,000 shares of common stock.

Meanwhile, she divorced her first husband and married William Kahliff, who had started his own plastics company during World War II.

Although she no longer headed her own business, Mrs. Kahliff did not lose her habit of winning. She soon became group president at Servomation. And by her third year there, her division ranked second in profitability among the company's 200 divisions.

About that time, her second husband died. She inherited his business lock, stock, and barrel—with all shares of company stock now in her name. She was now head of one company and group president of another. And she found herself working 80 hours a week and sometimes more.

This grueling work schedule all but overwhelmed her. She continued to do well at Servomation. But she soon found it physically impossible to oversee the affairs of Majestic Molding. As a result, the company began to flounder. In just one year, net profits plunged from $40,000 to $7,000. And it looked as though the company would soon find itself awash in red ink. Worse yet, the company was now so cash-poor it could not pay its bills on time.

ACCEPTS NEW CHALLENGE

Drastic problems call for drastic solutions. So, Mrs. Kahliff quit her job at Servomation to devote her full time to Majestic Molding. She soon found that her husband had picked the wrong man to succeed him as company president. His successor was a chemical engineer who had been with the company for three years.

Although competent as an engineer, he knew little about running a plastics business. "One of his first acts," says Mrs. Kahliff, "was to abolish paid lunch hours. That, on top of his inability to get along with his workers, destroyed morale. Within three months, we had a union in the plant."

By mutual agreement, the engineer soon left. Mrs. Kahliff then took over the day-to-day operations of the business. Overnight she began to put into practice the knowledge she gained running her own vending-machine business and managing a division for a conglomerate.

"How well you do depends largely on how well the people under you do," says Mrs. Kahliff. Looking around her, she soon found that the engineer was not the only nonperformer. Such persons were everywhere, and they were gradually replaced. In fact, of the ten managerial employees she inherited, just one still works for her. She now has 102 employees, most of them hand-picked. "I test and interview almost every job applicant," she says. "I can't afford to be wrong."

In just three years, Mrs. Kahliff worked a minor miracle, reversing the downward trend of profits dramatically, as shown in Exhibit 1A-2.

Her success became the talk of the town. She soon found herself in demand as a luncheon speaker. And she accommodated them by talking on "How to Get to the Top in a Man's World." Today, speaking requests flood in at such a high rate that she accepts only one in ten requests.

Besides turning over the work force, what other changes did Mrs. Kahliff make to earn such high marks for competency? For one thing, she put in several big business practices:

☐ A cost-accounting system, including a chart of accounts, to keep daily tabs on costs and leaks. "How can you price a product unless you know, to the penny, what it would cost to make?" says Mrs. Kahliff.

☐ Tuition-free education to all employees who take courses in high school or in college. "I've had as many as 16 employees in school at one time at my expense," says Mrs. Kahliff. "I won't promote anyone unless they prepare themselves for a better job."

☐ A sharp separation between line and staff work. In fact, she carries this separation to extremes by placing her plant not under one manager but under two—each with equal but separate responsibilities and authorities. "I don't want the production manager to buy raw materials and still take a

---

EXHIBIT 1A-2

Majestic Molding Company, Inc.

Year	Sales Revenues	Net Profits
1976	$1,400,000	$ 7,000
1977	1,450,000	27,000
1978	1,510,000	91,000
1979	1,620,000	115,000

physical count," says Mrs. Kahliff. "That's wrong." Says Mrs. Kahliff of her organizational chart, "I keep changing it at least once a year."

She took one look at her production process and decided to change that, too. Molding machines and raw materials were scattered helter-skelter throughout the plant. "It was messy and dirty," she says. Today, production is clean and orderly, flowing in a straight line from raw material storage through production and finally into finished-product inventory. (See Exhibit 1A-3.)

Mrs. Kahliff also modernized her plant, replacing old molding machines with the latest models. And she added a recycling process that all but eliminates waste. "We don't throw away anything," says Jack Kulasa, who is in charge of purchasing and inventory control.

MAKES SWEEPING CHANGES

Majestic Molding Company, Inc.

EXHIBIT 1A-3

Shop Floor

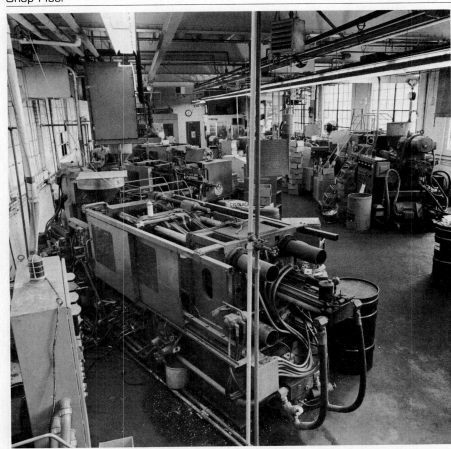

With her employees' welfare in mind, Mrs. Kahliff installed an exhaust system to cut air pollution and she initiated a safety program to keep employees safety-conscious. Soon after, a government representative enforcing the Occupational Safety and Health Act inspected the plant and gave it a clean bill of health. The inspector told Mrs. Kahliff upon completing his rounds, "This is one of the finest plastic injection molding plants I have had the privilege of visiting."

Of course, these sweeping changes took money, mostly hers. When she took over, the company's coffers were all but empty. She pumped $300,000 of her own money into the company. In addition, she borrowed $100,000 to enlarge the plant.

Motivated more by challenge than by money, Mrs. Kahliff draws a salary of just $35,000 a year. "I'm interested more in building up my equity in the business than drawing a big salary," says Mrs. Kahliff. One of her personal goals at this time is to build up a million-dollar equity. She is just $50,000 shy of that goal.

Has she set any long-range goals? No. "I've been too busy surviving to think about where we should be five years from now," says Mrs. Kahliff. "But now that the company is on its feet, I'm going to think about the future, especially about ways to create more customers." **MARKETING**

Today, her plant makes two kinds of products. One kind is called proprietary, meaning products made to the company's own design for sale directly to wholesalers or retailers. One such product is the Majestic Duck, a decorative piece for the home, office, or garden.

The other kind is called secondary, meaning products made to the design of other manufacturers. Into this category fall such diverse products as snowmobile wheels, shower knobs, tape cartridges, and football cleats—all made to order and all made to customer design.

Tape cartridges account for 38 percent of the company's revenues, up from 3 percent in 1971. This heavy dependence on one customer, which happens to be giant RCA, worries Mrs. Kahliff.

Today, products made for other manufacturers supply 75 percent of the company's revenues, while products made to Majestic's own design account for only 25 percent of revenues.

For both types of products, Mrs. Kahliff's marketing mix consists almost solely of word-of-mouth advertising. She employs no salespersons, nor does she advertise. But recently she hired an advertising agency to draw up flyers promoting the Majestic Duck. Nearly all her customers are repeat customers, landed by her late husband. "We've managed to keep them because we produce a quality product and deliver on time," says Mrs. Kahliff.

One of her biggest problems has been the short supply of raw materials. It seems that, under pressure from federal agencies, oil refineries no longer remove benzene from gasoline. And since resin is made from benzene, one of the company's most important raw materials is in short supply. RCA cartridges, for example, are made from resin.

1 What is Mrs. Kahliff's most pressing problem? Why? How would you suggest
she solve it?
2 Comment on Mrs. Kahliff's attitude toward goal setting.
3 Comment on Mrs. Kahliff's marketing strategy.
4 Is Mrs. Kahliff more an entrepreneur than a manager? Explain.
5 What should Mrs. Kahliff do now?

CASE 1B   **ADAM SMITH***

Following are selected excerpts from a cover story about free enterprise that appeared in *Time* magazine:

> In [Adam] Smith's† view, the great motivator of economic activity is "the uniform, constant, and uninterrupted effort of every man to better his condition"—or, bluntly, self-interest. Only this drive moves men to produce the goods that society needs.
>
> As [Adam Smith] put it: "It is not from the benevolence of the butcher, the brewer, or the baker, that we expect our dinner, but from their regard to their own interest. . . ."
>
> Self-interest expresses itself as the drive for profit and produces that great marvel, the self-regulating market. If consumers are free to spend their money any way they wish—and businessmen can compete uninhibitedly for their favor—then capital and labor will flow "naturally" . . . into the uses where they are most needed.
>
> If consumers want, say, more bread than is being produced, they will pay high prices and bakers will earn high profits. Those profits will lure investors to build more bakeries. If they wind up turning out more bread than consumers want to buy, prices and profits will fall and capital will shift into making something that consumers need and desire more—shoes, perhaps.
>
> Thus the businessman seeking only his profit is "led by an invisible hand to promote an end which was no part of his intention"—the common good. . . .
>
> [Adam Smith's] system was designed to enthrone not the businessman but the consumer. . . . he advocated complete laissez-faire.‡ Government, he said, should stop trying to regulate trade, cease all intervention in the market, and let free competition work its wonders.

1 Is the above an accurate description of the operation of today's economy?
Does today's economy differ? If so, how?
2 Identify at least one flaw in Adam Smith's system.

---

* Source: "Cover story: Can Capitalism Survive?" *Time,* July 14, 1975, p. 53. [Reprinted by permission from *Time,* the Weekly Newsmagazine; copyright Time, Inc. 1975]
† Adam Smith was a Scottish philosopher who wrote the classic, *The Wealth of Nations,* in 1776. In it, he describes how a free economy works.
‡ *Laissez faire* is a French phrase meaning "letting people do as they please without intervention."

A councilman in a major city was bemoaning the high death rate of small businesses in his district. "Empty store fronts invite vandalism," said the councilman.

"There should be a law against inexperienced people going into business for themselves," continued the councilman. "To be a lawyer, you must pass a bar exam. Otherwise, you can't practice law. Why can't we have the same kind of thing for would-be businesspeople?"

How would you answer the councilman? **QUESTION**

CHAPTER TWO

THE ENTREPRENEUR

questions for mastery

what is an entrepreneur?

what are the main traits of successful
entrepreneurs?

what is the difference between
entrepreneurship and management?

what are the problems of minorities and
women as entrepreneurs?

what are the rewards and hazards of being
an entrepreneur?

Every man has business and desire,

such as it is.

William Shakespeare

Successful men and women come from backgrounds so broad and complex that analysis of what it takes to create a successful business has been imprecise. Experts often try to pinpoint those traits that favor success and those that do not. But most have only been able to conclude that good managers run successful small businesses and poor managers run unsuccessful ones.

Some scholars, however, have researched the matter meaningfully, to help answer such elusive questions as these: What kinds of men and women are likely to found successful businesses? Can business success be taught? If so, how?

DEFINITION OF ENTREPRENEURS

Today, we take for granted the meaning of the word *entrepreneur.* It suggests spirit, zeal, ideas. But we tend to apply the word loosely to describe anyone who runs a business—for example, to the person who presides over General Motors or owns a corner fruit stand, or the person who owns a McDonald's franchise or hawks magazine subscriptions from a home telephone.

In the past, the word *entrepreneur* enjoyed a purer, more precise meaning. It described only those who created their own business. In fact, the *American Heritage Dictionary* defines an entrepreneur as "a person who organizes, operates, and assumes the risk for business ventures," as did Henry Ford.

HENRY FORD, ENTREPRENEUR

Mr. Ford created his first two businesses in 1899 and 1901 to make racing cars. In one car, he raced 90 miles an hour, a feat unheard of at that time. He became a celebrity overnight, and his success led him to believe there was a barrel of money in the business. Unfortunately, there was not; both companies later folded.

Clearly, Mr. Ford mistook his market. The racing car market was too small. Next, he turned his energies to putting the world on wheels. In 1903, at age 40, Mr. Ford raised $28,000 and began the Ford Motor Company, this time to make a car for the masses. The philosophy underlying his venture has been described as follows:

> A car for the multitude . . . large enough for the family . . . a car to lift farm drudgery off flesh and blood and lay it on steel and motor.[1]

Mr. Ford met his goal by 1908, when he built the cheap and sturdy Model T automobile. It revolutionized our way of life. Priced as low as $260, the Model T soon crowded out the horse and buggy. It also tore down the walls between city and farm. In short, it changed the face of the land. Today, superhighways thread the continent, and one hundred million cars spell freedom to pursue almost any way of life.

1. *Ford at Fifty* (New York: Simon & Schuster, 1953), p. 104.

What kind of man was Henry Ford? Above all, he had a burning desire to succeed. Success itself meant more to him than the field in which he achieved it. That may also account for his many other interests, ranging from airplanes and rubber plantations to American furniture and car racing.

A resilient man, Mr. Ford was a two-time loser before he became a winner. He reveled in risk taking, in trying something new and making it work. Himself never more than a tinkerer and mechanic, he was brilliantly intuitive. He had an uncanny ability to search out the mass market. And he saw that the best way to reach such a market was by selling cars at less than $500, at prices low enough to fit the consumer's pocketbook. It was this vision that brought about the mass production of cars.

PURE ENTREPRENEURS

Like Henry Ford, pure entrepreneurs also launch their own ventures from scratch. They nurse them into lusty businesses by dint of hard work and idea-getting ability. They display an instinct for opportunity and a sense of timing. They quicken the development of our economy. And they seem motivated not merely by profit but also by the "desire to found a private dynasty, the will to conquer in a competitive battle, and the joy of creating."[2]

As a nation, we often put pure entrepreneurs like Mr. Ford on a pedestal. Novelists and economists alike glorify them. The Horatio Alger tales, for example, dramatize the entrepreneurial habit of winning through hard work and education. And economists credit the pure entrepreneur with pushing our economy ahead in giant steps. Some well-known examples of other pure entrepreneurs appear in Exhibit 2-1.

In this textbook, therefore, we define pure entrepreneurs as men and women who create a venture from the raw materials of their own ideas and hard work. Others, of course, may also qualify as entrepreneurs, but not as pure ones. These others would include:

☐ Those who take over a business after the founder retires, dies, or sells out—but who continue to build and innovate
☐ Those who run a franchise independently of the franchisor

ENTREPRENEURSHIP AND THE ENTREPRENEUR

Let us pause here to distinguish between the terms *entrepreneur* and *entrepreneurship*. Although in this textbook we regard entrepreneurs mostly as those who launch new ventures, entrepreneurship is far more widely practiced—among old businesses as well as new ones, among big businesses as well as small ones. In the words of Professor Nathaniel H. Leff, "Entrepreneurship is the capacity for innovation, investment, and expansion in new markets, products, and techniques."[3]

2. Joseph A. Schumpeter, *The Theory of Economic Development,* trans. Redvers Opie (Cambridge, Mass.: Harvard University Press, 1934).
3. Quoted by Office of Economic Research, The New York Stock Exchange, *Economic Choices for the 1980s* (January 1980), p. 9.

EXHIBIT 2-1

		Well-Known Examples of Pure Entrepreneurs
Entrepreneur	**Product**	**Comment**
Thomas Alva Edison		The hardest won of Mr. Edison's 1093 patents was invention of the bulb that would light up the world. He also fathered the motion picture and recording industries.
Miles Lowell Edwards		Mr. Edwards, a retired engineer, and Albert Starr, a heart surgeon, worked together to integrate pumping technology and the human heart. Their artificial valve now helps tens of thousands of hearts to keep pumping.
Benjamin Franklin		Almost 200 years after Mr. Franklin glued together two sets of spectacles, no one has been able to improve the basic design of bifocal lenses.
Whitcomb L. Judson		Mr. Judson nearly went bankrupt selling his new zippers because they tended to pop open unexpectedly. An electrical engineer refined the idea, and the business eventually was named Talon, Inc.

These entrepreneurs had life-improving ideas and made them work. They all began small.

Source: Adapted from an SBA exhibit at the National Geographic Society in Washington, D.C. (May 1980).

This definition means that an entrepreneur is at work whenever someone takes risks and invests resources to make something new, or to design a new way of making something that already exists, or to create new markets.

MANAGEMENT AND ENTREPRENEURSHIP

Nor is entrepreneurship the same thing as management. The first job of the manager is to make a business perform well. The manager takes given resources—such as manpower and money, machines and materials—and orchestrates them into production. In contrast, the first job of the entrepreneur is to bring about change on purpose. As Economist Irving Kristol has suggested:

> More and more, chief executives refer to themselves as "managers," sometimes even "professional managers." Well, if that indeed is what they are . . . then they are wildly overpaid. A good executive . . . is above all an energetic and shrewd entrepreneur, seeking out—no, creating—

new opportunities for profitable economic transactions. It is only the possession of this talent . . . that justifies the high salaries they receive.[4]

ENTREPRENEURIAL TRAITS

Henry Ford is not a typical entrepreneur. In fact, no two entrepreneurs are precisely alike. In the words of Professor Peter F. Drucker, noted author-lecturer-consultant:

> Some are eccentrics, others painfully correct conformists; some are fat and some are lean; some are worriers, some relaxed; some drink quite heavily, others are total abstainers; some are men of great charm and warmth, some have no more personality than a frozen mackerel.[5]

Though taken out of context, Professor Drucker's words underline the futility of painting a word picture of the typical entrepreneur. Precious little is known about entrepreneurs, about the kinds of men and women who go into business for themselves. How do they get started? Why do they do it?

Is it because, in Henry David Thoreau's phrase, they "lead lives of quiet desperation" and desire something new and different? Are they society's rejects who "instead of becoming hobos, criminals, or professors make their adjustment by starting their own business"?[6]

To be sure, many seek escape from boring, dead-end jobs. This is especially true of those who in their middle years face up to the fact that they will never climb to the executive suite, write a Broadway play, or make a million dollars. They feel frustrated and ponder the possibility of a new career—perhaps entrepreneurship.

EXAMPLE

Five years ago, Fletcher Waller was toiling 14 hours a day as a Bell and Howell vice-president in Chicago. "I loved sailing," he says, but he could never get his boat out. So, at 52, he quit his job and started his own business—renting boats and teaching sailing to overworked executives. Mr. Waller's income is now less than his former income tax, but he laughs at *Who's Who* for dropping him, extols the magic effect on his marriage. "Why," he says, "we fell in love."[7]

∎

Or are entrepreneurs overachievers, drawn to the challenge of creating their own venture rather than escaping from previous failure? Studies at Harvard University and Massachusetts Institute of Technology found that entrepreneurs are not likely to come from the pool of society's rejects. In fact,

---

4. Irving Kristol, "Business vs. the Economy," *The Wall Street Journal,* June 26, 1979, p. 18.
5. Peter F. Drucker, *The Effective Executive* (New York: Harper & Row, 1966), p. 22.
6. Orvie F. Collins and David G. Moore, quoted by Patrick R. Liles, *New Business Ventures and the Entrepreneur* (Homewood, Ill.: Richard D. Irwin, 1974), p. 2.
7. "Second Acts in American Lives," *Time,* March 8, 1968, p. 39. [Reprinted by permission from *Time, The Weekly Newsmagazine;* copyright Time Inc. 1968.]

entrepreneurs enjoy a "generally higher than average level of success in their previous employment."[8]

This finding suggests that it is not outside pressures that force successful people to become entrepreneurs. If they decide to go into business for themselves, they usually do so for good reasons. They may prefer not to be ciphers in somebody else's business, or they may want to exploit an invention themselves. Society's rejects, however, often go into business for the wrong reasons, with outside pressures playing a strong role. They may decide to go on their own only after being demoted, passed up, or fired. Not that they all fail. Many succeed, sometimes spectacularly.

EXAMPLE

An unemployed paperhanger in Hammond, Indiana, one day in 1939 invented a large, boxlike machine that could simultaneously freeze and dispense ice cream. He sold the rights to a manufacturer in Illinois. This merger produced the first Dairy Queen, and by 1981 there were nearly 5,000 outlets all across America.[9]

■

Clearly, men and women become entrepreneurs for a variety of reasons. However, their desire for self-expression appears to be a common thread. This desire helps explain why more than half of all the nation's wage earners prefer to work for themselves rather than somebody else.[10] Yet few become entrepreneurs. In fact, most overachievers choose to work for somebody else. Why?

Perhaps most are dreamers, sitting on a cloud with their feet dangling in air. A more likely reason is that their horizons are defined by monthly mortgage payments and broken washing machines. Many cannot give up their jobs without risking their home life. Besides, how can they sacrifice pensions and company-paid insurance? So, early on, they become emotionally incapable of taking that fateful first step—unless forced to do so by the loss of a job, for example.

KEY ENTREPRENEURIAL TRAITS

Of the men and women who do become entrepreneurs, why are so few successful? As mentioned in Chapter One, many new businesses die in infancy. In fact, half die within 18 months of birth. What is it, then, that makes for success instead of failure? Can we pinpoint the key traits of successful entrepreneurs? If we could, then we might predict what kinds of men and women are most likely to succeed as entrepreneurs.

To begin with, successful entrepreneurs are likely to be overachievers. Like Henry Ford, they burn with the desire to excel. In his landmark study of

---

8. Herbert A. Wainer and Paul V. Tiplitz, master's theses at Massachusetts Institute of Technology, 1965, quoted by Patrick R. Liles, *New Business Ventures and the Entrepreneur*, p. 3.
9. Daniel J. Boorstin, *The Americans: The Democratic Experience* (New York: Random House, 1973), pp. 431–432 (updated).
10. The Gallup Report (Princeton, N.J.: The Gallup Organization, July 1979), p. 1.

entrepreneurs, Professor David C. McClelland of Harvard University found that they are likely to do well if they are also: [11]

- ☐ Reasonable risk-takers
- ☐ Self-confident
- ☐ Hard workers
- ☐ Goal setters
- ☐ Accountable
- ☐ Innovative

These traits defy sharp separation. Each trait shades off into the others like the colors of a spectrum. Just as it is impossible to tell where red shades into orange, so it is with these traits.

SUCCESSFUL ENTREPRENEURS ARE REASONABLE RISK TAKERS

Any new business poses risks for entrepreneurs. They may succeed or fail, and lacking a crystal ball, they cannot foresee which it will be.

For protection, entrepreneurs are likely to take the middle ground. How? For one thing, they shun ventures in which the odds are stacked high against them. One such situation is the automobile industry. Few entrepreneurs, for example, would try to come up with a pollution-free automobile to vie with Detroit's billion-dollar automobile industry, because their chance of success would border on zero.

At the same time, most entrepreneurs shun a sure thing, because the satisfaction from such a task would be too small to justify the effort. Entrepreneurs are not likely to be found performing routine chores like sorting buttons or grinding coffee.

However, even though entrepreneurs generally choose ventures that fall between these two extremes, they tend to go in the direction of high risk. They are likely to prefer ventures in which risk of failure is high but not too high. Why? Because they recognize that they are more likely to gain both satisfaction and success from tasks that fit their own skills. That is what makes them reasonable risk takers. Like mountain climbers who test their abilities against a terrain that matches yet stretches their knowledge and experience, entrepreneurs are reasonable adventurers. The following entrepreneur, for example, vied with General Motors by staying out of its way:

EXAMPLE

George Barris customizes and builds cars. He began 30 years ago on a $900 budget and today boasts a multi-million-dollar showroom plant in Los Angeles. Mr. Barris's major market is the very rich, the film and television industry, and companies that can use his cars for promotional purposes.

11. David C. McClelland, *The Achieving Society* (Princeton, N.J.: Van Nostrand, 1961).

Dick Martin of "Laugh In" is about to pick up his Italian-made mink-carpeted Stutz. Mr. Barris has lacquered it in his own color: gold mirage. The cost is $35,000.[12]

■

Contrary to popular belief, entrepreneurs generally avoid ventures that are pure gambles. They would rather depend on themselves than on Lady Luck. There is no way, for example, to influence the roll of a pair of dice—unless, of course, they are loaded. Entrepreneurs prefer to shape events by their own actions. They want to make things happen rather than let them happen.

SUCCESSFUL ENTREPRENEURS ARE SELF-CONFIDENT

Entrepreneurs believe in themselves. They have confidence that they can outdo anyone in their field. They tend not to accept the status quo, believing instead that they can change the facts. Often, they believe the odds are better than the facts would justify—as did the old New York Yankees. Their winning habits once dazzled the world of sport. But they often won with mediocre ballplayers, prompting sportswriters to say: "Those pinstripe uniforms convince a ballplayer that he's better than he ought to be." That captures, in part, the essence of what makes the entrepreneur tick.

SUCCESSFUL ENTREPRENEURS ARE HARD WORKERS

Few persons in our society work harder than entrepreneurs. The long hours logged by many big-business executives are legendary, too. But entrepreneurs seem to put in even longer hours, driven by their desire to excel.

According to one study, top executives work an average of 60 hours a week. Although we lack similar data on entrepreneurs, it is likely that they work even longer, especially during the first few years. Only when their venture is firmly rooted in the marketplace do they taper off. But even then, entrepreneurs tend to be compulsive workers, especially when a crisis flares up. Mentally, they rarely are away from their office. In her study of hard workers, Dr. Marilyn Machlowitz of Yale University found that:

During the New York City power blackout in 1977, many entrepreneurs still worked compulsively. Despite radio warnings to stay home, they had gone to work, often to find that they had to walk up 20 to 30 flights of stairs because the elevators were down.[13]

Dr. Machlowitz also found that it is a mistake to assume that hard workers never have any leisure. "They have reversed the relationship that America has with work. It is far better to live for the 50 weeks a year that you work than for the 2 weeks you are off."[14] To Winston Churchill, hard workers were "fortune's favorite children whose work and pleasures are one."

12. Adapted from "Custom-Car Maker on Coast Thrives by Diversifying," *New York Times,* March 19, 1972, p. I-66.
13. Janet Gardner, "A Workaholic—and Happy That Way," Cleveland *Plain Dealer,* March 14, 1980, p. 1-D.
14. Ibid.

Not that entrepreneurs always work harder. They do so only when their own skills can shape events. If a situation lacks challenge, they leave it alone.

SUCCESSFUL ENTREPRENEURS ARE GOAL SETTERS

Psychologists often define happiness as striving toward meaningful goals, not necessarily the achievement of those goals. This definition of happiness fits many entrepreneurs. Happiest with goals in front and not behind them, they rarely feel that they have arrived.

To entrepreneurs, merely choosing a new, meaningful goal is self-renewing. Planning and carrying out the steps needed to reach the goal are stimulating. And the result is often the opening of a door that leads to still another goal—as in the following example:

EXAMPLE

A college drop-out, Joseph Hrudka twice won the National Hot Rod Association championship. He observed that drag racing is tough on gaskets, and he soon found himself making his own reusable ones. In 1965, at 26, he set up his own business to make gaskets for hot rodders. The gaskets were an instant success. Seven years later, Mr. Hrudka caught the eye of W. R. Grace & Company and was bought out for $17.7 million. Mr. Hrudka's share was $12 million.

Did he retire? No. He set new goals for himself and started two new, unrelated businesses: Bike Products Company and Rupco Industries, Inc.[15]

Entrepreneurs like Mr. Hrudka are compulsive achievers. Once they have met a goal, they lose interest in further effort in that area because it gives them little, if any, sense of achievement. Only if challenged do they work hard.

SUCCESSFUL ENTREPRENEURS ARE ACCOUNTABLE

Entrepreneurs generally want full credit, or full discredit, for their success or failure. Steady feedback on their performance enables entrepreneurs to remain accountable. To measure the performance, entrepreneurs may use any one of several yardsticks, among them return on investment and rate of profit growth. These yardsticks, of course, may cut two ways, giving proof not only of success but also of failure.

And what they measure is profitability, for it is profits that best tell entrepreneurs how well they are doing in the marketplace. However, profits really serve as a yardstick of performance, not as a goal. In the words of Marvin Bower, a management consultant:

Profits are really a measure of the competitive value of a company's contribution to users, distributors, and the public. And, it is only by maximizing that contribution that a company can maximize its profits. In other words, concentrate on things that produce a profit rather than on

15. Adapted from "Faces Behind the Figures," *Forbes,* November 1, 1972, p. 76.

profit itself. Perhaps using profit as a measure instead of a goal is a distinction without a difference. Maybe so. But it is a useful distinction to guide the thinking of entrepreneurs.[16]

Profits play another role, as a reward for successful risk taking. Entrepreneurs deserve some return (profits) on their investment, just as individual savers deserve some return (interest) on their savings accounts. Entrepreneurs, moreover, deserve a higher return because they risk failure, whereas individual savers usually do not.

SUCCESSFUL ENTREPRENEURS ARE INNOVATIVE

To the lay mind, innovation is generally the most distinctive entrepreneurial trait. As exemplified by Henry Ford, entrepreneurs tend to tackle the unknown; they do things in new and different ways; they weave old ideas into new patterns; they offer more solutions than alibis.

In practice, however, the role of the entrepreneur often differs from the role of the innovator. Although innovation may be vital to being entrepreneurial, it becomes entrepreneurial only when carried into production to benefit consumers. For example, although Americans invented the transistor, it was mostly the Japanese who benefited from making, selling, and adapting the transistor to new products.

DEVELOPING ENTREPRENEURS

This profile of the successful entrepreneur gives only a partial answer to the question, What makes the entrepreneur tick? A more rounded answer requires a look at the social origins of entrepreneurs.

Psychologists say that entrepreneurs are likely to come from families in which parents set high standards for their children's performance, encourage habits of self-reliance, and avoid being strict disciplinarians.

But what determines how parents set standards? Why do some parents stress achievement and others not? Probably because their social or ethnic group believes in it. For example, persons of Jewish background have been known to make every sacrifice to give their children an education. In fact, Judaism stresses education and achievement.

The need to achieve crops up in all ethnic groups, but more so in some than in others. For example, Armenians and Chinese, Greeks and Jews tend to become entrepreneurs. Other minority groups have lagged as entrepreneurs. The main reasons are easy to pin down. For one, minority groups—blacks especially—have long held business in low esteem:

> More often than not, many Negro businessmen are a symbol of frustration and hopelessness rather than an example of achievement, success, and leadership. As a result, "business" is not a polite word in the Negro

16. Marvin Bower, *The Will to Manage* (New York: McGraw-Hill, 1966), pp. 62–63.

community, and Negro parents tend to discourage their children from pursuing business careers either as employees or as entrepreneurs.[17]

Too, minority groups have lacked business skills and attitudes, mainly because they have had little exposure to the ways of business. Historically, the plight of minorities has prevented the development of such skills and attitudes. The plantation system in the South, for example, offered blacks no experience with money, no incentive to save, and no idea of progress—none of the experiences that would prepare them for urban living.

Small wonder, then, that their share of the business world has been so small. Just how small is apparent from the statistics cited in Chapter One: Blacks own just 1.7 percent of the 14 million businesses in the nation, even though they account for 11 percent of the population.

SOME PROGRESS

There are signs, however, that blacks may soon be entering the entrepreneurial world in record numbers. Attitudes toward business and entrepreneurship are beginning to change dramatically. Take this headline that appeared in a monthly magazine devoted to blacks in business:

Black Students Are Bullish on Business[18]

As recently as 1965, black college students overwhelmingly preferred to major in either the liberal arts or education. No more. As borne out by Exhibit 2-2, they now prefer business administration and the sciences in increasing numbers. Although these statistics cover 41 black colleges, students at other colleges and universities show similar trends toward business and the sciences. To cite one dramatic example, in 1950 the Harvard Business School had just two black students; in 1980, there were 66.

EXHIBIT 2-2

Black Students Favor Business and the Sciences

Course of Study	1976	1979
Business Administration	16.7%	21.5%
Engineering and Computer Sciences	6.9	11.0
Sociology	10.2	9.5
Education	14.4	9.0

Source: United Negro College Fund, "Black Students Are Bullish on Business," *Black Enterprise,* February 1980, p. 52.

17. Robert B. McKersie, "Vitalize Black Enterprise," *Harvard Business Review,* September–October 1968, p. 90.
18. United Negro College Fund, "Black Students Are Bullish on Business," *Black Enterprise,* February 1980, p. 52.

Barriers are dissolving for groups long denied equal access to entrepreneurial opportunities. Women, for example, are heading for business careers in record numbers. A survey by the University of California and the American Council on Education found that women students majoring in business mushroomed from 3 percent in 1966 to 17 percent in 1980.[19]

Similar data on other disadvantaged groups—Hispanics and Native Americans in particular—are unavailable. Even so, some progress seems to be taking place, although not as dramatically as in the case of blacks and women. Community colleges, especially, have pioneered educational programs to help bring Hispanics and Native Americans into the nation's economic mainstream—as they have done with blacks and women.

This new pool of minority managers and entrepreneurs will expand, helped along not only by educational institutions but by the federal government as well.

EXAMPLE

Federal policy in the 1980s is likely to encourage the creation and development of minority businesses that stand the best chance of becoming large and economically significant. This change in policy is likely because of the fact that, despite massive federal help since 1965, the nation's 400,000 minority businesses have average sales revenues of only $40,000 a year.[20]

INDIVIDUAL VERSUS GROUP ACHIEVEMENT

So far, our discussion of entrepreneurs has centered on the individual achiever at the expense of group achievers. This emphasis is natural, mainly because most psychological research stresses the individual achiever. Another reason is that team spirit seems to be out of fashion, even in athletics. Yet there is impressive evidence that some men and women achieve more as members of a group than they do as individuals. In the words of one psychologist:

> In spite of the theories of psychologists, administrators, and educators, our society does not run on individual achievement alone. I fear that our beliefs that it does have led us to assume that people who can't cut the mustard on their own initiative can't cut it at all.[21]

In some circumstances, entrepreneurs may achieve more when they work as a group rather than as individuals. And such group effort often helps individuals to overcome their fear of failure or kindle their desire to achieve.

19. "Record Number of Freshmen Heading for Business Careers," Cleveland *Plain Dealer,* January 20, 1980, p. 8-A.
20. Richard F. America, "How Minority Business can Build on Its Strength," *Harvard Business Review,* May–June 1980, p. 116.
21. Alvin F. Zander, "Team Spirit vs. the Individual Achiever," *Psychology Today,* November 1974, p. 68.

REWARDS AND HAZARDS OF ENTREPRENEURSHIP

In general, entrepreneurs like nothing better than the psychological satisfaction of being their own boss. Esteemed by friends and relatives alike, their self-image mirrors that esteem.

Financially, successful entrepreneurs often outdo big-business executives. Rather than save money or dabble in stocks, entrepreneurs are likely to plow profits back into their venture to keep it growing. They are often more interested in seeing their equity in the business increase than in drawing a big monthly paycheck.

These are the chief rewards of entrepreneurship. But what of the hazards? Launching a new venture always carries some risk of failure. There is no such thing as a perfectly safe investment. As a rule, the riskier the venture, the greater the profit potential. If the entrepreneur succeeds, profits may be high; if not, life savings may be lost.

For some, failure is tragic; to others, it is an opportunity to begin anew. Henry Ford, for example, failed twice before he successfully launched Ford Motor Company. Ralph Waldo Emerson wrote, "Valor consists in the art of self-recovery." Even so, many men and women cannot take failure in their stride; it shatters their ego, dulls their drive, weakens their will. With each such tragedy, society loses also.

ON SELF-ANALYSIS

Libraries overflow with books that tell bosses how best to pick their workers. But, for some reason, writers fail to offer any advice on how best to pick oneself as boss. Yet this decision is of first importance. In the words of Louis L. Allen:

> The man who begins a small business has *selected himself* to run the show . . . In almost every case I have seen, the man who has done this selecting is neither qualified by training and inclination nor by objective reasoning to make such a judgment. This, more than any single ingredient in a small business, accounts for the high rate of failure. . . .
>
> When a man picks himself as "the boss" he has made a fateful choice— one on which the fortunes of his enterprise will rise or fall.[22]

In Arthur Miller's Pulitzer Prize-winning play *Death of a Salesman,* the widow of Willy Loman asks her son, Biff, "Why did he do it? Why did he kill himself?" Biff replies, "Poor guy, he never knew who he was."

Like Willy Loman, few would-be entrepreneurs look long and hard at themselves, mainly because there is so little to measure themselves by, except for some checklists. But these are so trivial that few aspiring entrepreneurs would take them seriously. One checklist, for example, asks about neatness, cleanliness, clothing, mannerisms, breath, posture, height, and weight.

22. Louis L. Allen, *Starting and Succeeding in Your Own Business* (New York: Grossett & Dunlap, 1968), pp. 8–9.

EXHIBIT 2-3

In each pair of statements, circle the one you agree with.

1 **a.** Promotions are earned through hard work and persistence.
  b. Making a lot of money is largely a matter of getting the right breaks.
2 **a.** Many times the reaction of teachers seems haphazard to me.
  b. In my experience, I have noticed that there is usually a connection between how hard I study and the grades I get.
3 **a.** The number of divorces indicates that more and more men and women are not trying to make their marriages work.
  b. Marriage is largely a gamble.
4 **a.** When I am right I can convince others.
  b. It is silly to think that one can really change another person's basic attitudes.
5 **a.** In our society, a man's future earning power depends on his ability.
  b. Getting promoted is really a matter of being luckier than the next guy.
6 **a.** I have little influence over the way other people behave.
  b. If one knows how to deal with people, they are really quite easily led.
7 **a.** Sometimes, I feel that I have little to do with the grades I get.
  b. The grades I make are the results of my own efforts; luck has little or nothing to do with it.
8 **a.** People like me can change the course of world affairs if we make ourselves heard.
  b. It is only wishful thinking to believe that one can influence what happens in society at large.
9 **a.** A great deal that happens to me is probably a matter of chance.
  b. I am the master of my fate.
10 **a.** Getting along with people is a skill that must be practiced.
  b. It is almost impossible to figure out how to please some people.

Clearly, such questions fail to help the would-be entrepreneur evaluate himself or herself as a potential entrepreneur. But there is a test, brief and to the point, that we recommend highly. Appearing in Exhibit 2-3, this test has ten pairs of statements. For each pair, circle the one you agree with. This description of the test is purposely sketchy. You will see why when your instructor analyzes your responses.

SUMMARY

Most men and women would like to go into business for themselves, but few do. Of those who do, few succeed. Even so, becoming a successful entrepreneur is not impossible. The odds favor the man or woman who is an overachiever. Such people are also likely to be:

- ☐ Reasonable risk takers
- ☐ Self-confident
- ☐ Hard workers
- ☐ Goal setters
- ☐ Accountable
- ☐ Innovative

Entrepreneurs inspired the energy that spans the American continent. It was entrepreneurs like Henry Ford who pushed our economy ahead in giant steps.

Entrepreneurs spring from every walk of life, and each ethnic group boasts its own successful entrepreneurs. But some ethnic groups tend to have more entrepreneurs than others. For example, Armenians and Chinese, Greeks and Jews tend to go into business for themselves. But other minority groups and women tend not to, mainly because until recently most entrepreneurial opportunities were closed to them.

Other social factors also appear to influence entrepreneurial success. Psychologists say that entrepreneurs are likely to have parents who set high standards for their children's performance, encourage habits of self-reliance, and avoid being strict disciplinarians.

The chief reward of entrepreneurial success is the satisfaction of a job well done, reflected especially in a profitable performance. The chief hazard is entrepreneurial failure, which may shatter the ego and destroy life savings.

Evaluating oneself as an entrepreneur is an important task, aided in this chapter by a special test.

DISCUSSION AND REVIEW QUESTIONS

1 In what ways are entrepreneurs necessary to the health and growth of our economy?
2 Do you agree that franchisees are not pure entrepreneurs? Why?
3 Write a paragraph on the traits of an entrepreneur you know well.
4 Define the terms *entrepreneur, reasonable risk taker, gamble, accountability, profit, entrepreneurship, management.*
5 What is it in men and women that responds so deeply to the call of entrepreneurship?
6 Which entrepreneurial trait do you believe is most necessary for success? Why?
7 What are the rewards and hazards of entrepreneurship?
8 How do entrepreneurs and managers differ?
9 Why do so few men and women actually become entrepreneurs, even though most of them say they would prefer to work for themselves rather than for someone else?

10 Do you agree that profits are *not* a goal of doing business? Explain, using an example.

11 Are innovators necessarily also entrepreneurs? Explain, using an example.

12 In what ways do the six entrepreneurial traits overlap?

13 How can parents influence entrepreneurial behavior in their children?

14 Why are there so few entrepreneurs among minority groups and women?

15 Why is education so vital to entrepreneurial success?

Mark and Helen Weaver began their silk-printing venture in 1978. Their venture lost money in 1980, although sales revenues approached $100,000. "I'm not a smashing success yet," says Mr. Weaver, "but then again, I'm satisfied. In fact, I think I can double or triple sales in two years by expanding out of my plant into retailing."

To do that, though, Mr. Weaver may have to quit his job at Lubrizol Corporation. He has two years to go before he can "legally" retire and still get his pension benefits. Says Mr. Weaver, "I'm not sure what to do, how best to balance my desire for inner peace against my retirement benefits."

BACKGROUND

There was little in the Weavers' background to indicate they would someday become entrepreneurs. Both began their business careers at the same rayon manufacturing company, where Mr. Weaver worked as a chemist and Mrs. Weaver as a laboratory technician.

Shortly after they met there in 1950, they married and soon expanded their family to include two sons. One job change later found Mr. Weaver working as a project engineer for Lubrizol Corporation, a large chemical manufacturer with revenues of $902 million in 1980. Mrs. Weaver also changed jobs to work for a large department store selling children's apparel.

At Lubrizol, Mr. Weaver rose from project engineer to warehousing manager. In 1977, after 22 years with the company, Mr. Weaver suddenly realized that he would rise no higher. He was now 49 years old.

"I saw for the first time that I would never become a vice president," says Mr. Weaver. "Lubrizol is a great company to work for, but you've got to be a chemical engineer or a chemical researcher to get anywhere in the company. The top executives are mostly from one engineering school. So I began to look around."

In his search for a better job, Mr. Weaver soon found that his age worked against him. "Who wants to hire a 49-year-old?" says Mr. Weaver. Blocked off in one direction, he began to overflow with ideas in another. "Overnight, I made up my mind to go into business for myself. Just like that! Of course, I first talked it over with my wife and, without a moment's hesitation, she said yes. In fact, she even offered to quit her job at the department store where she enjoyed nine years of seniority. Working as a team, we just knew we couldn't fail."

CHOICE OF INDUSTRY

For weeks, Mr. Weaver pondered what kind of industry to go into. When he was in his twenties, he had often thought about someday opening his own restaurant. He had moonlighted for five years at a drive-in restaurant, working at every job, including cook and dishwasher. But after watching so many restaurants fail, he had concluded long ago that a restaurant would be "too big a gamble. They're too faddist. They're popular for five years, then they go under."

Then, opportunity beckoned. As president of the Little League Baseball League in his hometown, Mr. Weaver observed that the printing on the players' uniforms kept peeling off. So he approached the sporting goods retailer who had sold them the uniforms to find out why.

The retailer told Mr. Weaver that he was having a terrible time getting high-quality silk printing on T-shirts. "It came to me right there and then," says Mr. Weaver, "that if he was having trouble, then other sporting goods retailers had the same problem also. Wow, that very moment my thoughts jelled!"

In the next breath, Mr. Weaver asked the retailer a question: "Would you buy silk printing from me if I guarantee its quality?" "You better believe I would," replied the retailer. "I'll not only buy from you—if you guarantee the quality—but I'll also give you a guaranteed sales contract each year. If I buy less than the guarantee, I'll pay you the difference. And, if I buy more than the guarantee, I'll still pay you the difference. You can't lose. Now, what do you think of a deal like that?"

"You just put me in business," laughed Mr. Weaver. "Would you put your offer in writing?" The retailer did, although he left out any mention of a guaranteed sales contract.

A LEARNING EXPERIENCE

Of course, the Weavers now had themselves a problem: How and where to launch their new silk-printing venture? They knew nothing about silk printing. In fact, they had never seen it done before.

Undaunted, the Weavers spent "every spare second" for a month reading and studying every article and book they could find about the art of silk printing. Here, the public library proved to be especially helpful.

After absorbing all they could, they then leafed through the Thomas Register to get the names of local suppliers of silk-printing equipment. "We had to start somewhere," says Mr. Weaver. "I was sure that suppliers would help us get started if it meant we'd be customers."

And that is precisely what happened. Armed with the letter of intent from the sporting goods retailer, the Weavers landed a supplier who:

☐ Suggested how best to design a silk-printing plant
☐ Specified precisely what pieces of equipment the Weavers would need
☐ Suggested that they hire a "22-year-old who knows silk printing inside out"

"The supplier gave us quite an education," says Mr. Weaver. "So, just two weeks after talking to him, we took out a second mortgage on our house, borrowed $40,000 from the bank, and ordered the equipment from the supplier. We never even looked at another supplier." To justify the $40,000 loan, the Weavers gave the bank the statement that appears in Exhibit 2A-1.

IN BUSINESS AT LAST

It was now March 1978. One month later, the Weavers leased 1,000 square feet of space in an industrial park zoned for light manufacturing. "We first looked for an abandoned gas station, but we couldn't find one that was suitable, so we settled on an industrial park," says Mr. Weaver.

Justification for $40,000 Loan as

Presented to the Bank

☐ We request a loan of $40,000.
☐ Our minimum operating expenses per year will be:

$ 8,000	Operating expenses
7,200	Loan payments
6,000	Lease payments
3,000	Utilities
3,000	Miscellaneous expenses
500	Insurance premiums
$27,700	Total operating expenses

☐ Necessary business volume to break even:

$$\text{Breakeven volume} = \frac{\$27,700 \text{ total expenses per year}}{\$1.50 \text{ sales price per unit}}$$

$$= 18,470 \text{ units per year}$$
$$= 1,540 \text{ units per month}$$
$$= 70 \text{ units per day (assuming 22 business}$$
$$\text{days per month)}$$

The breakeven volume above can be achieved by the Weaver family, so no salary is necessary.

☐ There is no apparent competition in Lake County.
☐ The purchased equipment can produce 475,200 units per year, requiring 10 employees at $4.00 an hour.
☐ Expected volume the first year is 90,000 units, or sales of $135,000. This sales figure is attainable because of a handshake agreement with Koenig Sporting Goods to sell them at least 60,000 units per year at $1.50 per unit.

At the same time, they hired the "silk-printing expert" the supplier had recommended. By July 4, "everything was in place," and the Weavers opened for business. Their beginning balance sheet appears in Exhibit 2A-2.

When they began, the Weavers had just the retailer's letter of intent and *no* customers. Mr. Weaver continued to work days at his old job. Mrs. Weaver, on the other hand, quit her job with the department store to become the new venture's manager. They named their venture Weaver Screen-Print.

With overhead costs to cover, the Weavers' chief worry was how best to go about marketing their services. "We had to get customers in a hurry," says Mr. Weaver, "or else we'd run out of cash. So I thumbed through the Yellow Pages and worked up a list of every sporting goods store in the county—44 in all. Then I began paying a few of them a visit, cold."

Beginning Balance Sheet (July 4, 1978)

Assets		Equities	
Cash	$13,800	Accounts payable	$ 1,000
Printing supplies	2,000	Mortgage loan	40,000
Office supplies	500	Owners' equity	1,500
Plant equipment	24,000		
Prepaid rent	1,200		
Other	1,000		
Total assets	$42,500	Total equities	$42,500

View of Screen-Print Process

The Weavers' first customer was a yacht club that wanted this message emblazoned across each of 48 T-shirts:

Cruizin

Boozin

Snoozin

With that order, and Mr. Weaver's after-hour visits to prospective customers, business began to pick up. By the end of 1978, the Weavers "managed to break even." Word had spread that they guaranteed their performance, a rarity in the industry.

This strategy did, indeed, give the Weavers a competitive edge. So much so that the large sporting goods retailer followed through on his original promise to sign a guaranteed sales contract. By the fall of 1980, Mr. Weaver was landing one-half of all prospective customers he visited on his monthly round of sales calls. "If only I had more time," says Mr. Weaver, "I just know I could get many more customers." Financial statements for 1980 appear in Exhibits 2A-4 and 2A-5. The seasonality of their sales is shown in Exhibit 2A-6.

Now that their revenues are approaching $100,000 a year, the Weavers are "taking stock of our business. We've grown so fast that we have to pause and see where we want to be, two or three years down the road," says Mr. Weaver. Looking back, the Weavers believe their three years in business have been "highly rewarding."

TAKING STOCK

They do regret one thing, however. A competitor sued the Weavers for printing on T-shirts the logo, "Cleveland, You've Got to Be Tough!" The competitor claimed it had the copyright for the message, suing the Weavers for $500,000. In its suit, the competitor asked the U.S. District Court to "seize all plates, molds, and matrices used for marking the shirts and any T-shirts stored" by the Weavers.

As it turned out, the suit was settled quietly out of court for just $29.75. "Would you believe," says Mr. Weaver, "that they sued us for $500,000 over an order on which we made just $29.75?" But they ended up paying legal fees of $2,000.

To achieve revenues of nearly $100,000 a year, the Weavers had to expand their original idea of doing only direct printing on T-shirts. They also began to do transfers, promotional printing, and sewing of decals and numbers—all on T-shirts, uniforms, and jackets.

Weaver Screen-Print

EXHIBIT 2A-4

1980 Income Statement

Sales revenues		$91,600
Operating expenses		
Salaries and wages	$39,400	
Materials and supplies	18,900	
Utilities	7,900	
Rent	7,800	
Professional fees	5,300	
Depreciation	5,300	
Payroll taxes	3,500	
Interest	2,200	
Office supplies	800	
Property tax	700	
Freight	500	
Insurance	400	
Miscellaneous	200	92,900
Operating loss		$ 1,300

Balance Sheet (December 31, 1980)

Assets			Equities		
Assets			**Equities**		
Current assets			Liabilities		
Cash	$ 2,900		Note payable	$50,000	
Accounts receivable	8,080		Payroll taxes	830	$50,830
Supplies inventory	2,300	$13,280			
Fixed assets			Owners' equity		(1,650)
Printing equipment	$35,820				
Automobile	2,590				
Improvements	380				
Office equipment	130				
	38,920				
Less: accumulated depreciation	3,100	35,820			
Deposit		80			
Total assets		$49,180	Total equities		$49,180

"We now offer a complete service," says Mr. Weaver. To meet the demand for expanded services, the Weavers had to expand their shop space from 1,000 to 3,500 square feet. It cost them $34,000 to buy the latest silk-printing equipment. "I'm always looking for ways to invest in equipment of the latest technology," says Mr. Weaver. "Our competitors don't. Their equipment is so old it's held together by baling wire. Our equipment is one of the major reasons our quality is so good."

A CRITICAL TIME

The Weavers believe this is a critical time in the life of their venture. It is now the spring of 1981. They are convinced they can double or triple revenues, if only they had the time to market their services. "I'm really in a puzzle," says Mr. Weaver. "With more time, I'm sure I could do a better job of selling. The only time I've got is after hours, when I'm done working at my other job at Lubrizol. I'm not sure whether to quit or not. I have just two years to go before I can retire legally and receive the pension benefits I'm entitled to."

The Weavers lack a marketing plan. "We don't need one," says Mr. Weaver. "Ours is a seat-of-the-pants operation. We just go from day to day; and so far, things have worked out well. I'm a do-it-yourselfer. I even put in all the equipment myself. My wife and I never needed legal help to get started. We just went ahead and did it. We're equal partners, she and I. Nothing's on paper, and we like it that way.

"Our business philosophy may be summed up in one word: trust. We trust our employees, and they trust us. We also trust our customers, and they trust us. That's the Japanese way." Mr. Weaver once spent two years in Tokyo with the U.S. Army.

Seasonality

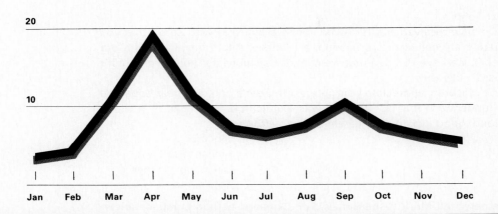

Percentage of yearly revenues (vertical axis: 30%, 20, 10)

Horizontal axis: Jan Feb Mar Apr May Jun Jul Aug Sep Oct Nov Dec

OPTIMISTIC OUTLOOK

To double or triple revenues, the Weavers are giving "serious thought" about expanding into retailing. "We might set up a dummy store in the city," says Mr. Weaver. "We could sell T-shirts with standard prints like the Superman logo and cartoon characters like Peanuts and Popeye. The exposure would be great."

To carry off such an expansion, the Weavers are counting heavily on their reputation as high-quality silk printers. Their quality has been so high that they have rarely lost a customer. "Even the few customers we lost have referred others to us," says Mrs. Weaver. She says the keys to their success are:

☐ Fast service, just one-week delivery for custom work
☐ The best equipment available
☐ Guaranteed performance
☐ Good, loyal employees

QUESTIONS

1 What are the strengths of Weaver Screen-Print? Its weaknesses?
2 Comment on the Weavers' justification for a $40,000 loan (see Exhibit 2A-1).
3 Should Mr. Weaver quit his job with the Lubrizol Corporation and devote full time to his venture? Why or why not?
4 How well has Weaver Screen-Print performed financially? What questions does your financial analysis raise?
5 Outline a step-by-step plan for the Weavers to follow before launching the expansion they are now considering. In doing so, focus on the questions they should answer before making the decision.

For the past six years, John Vitt has pursued his desire to own a Zero's fast-food franchise. Zero's, Inc. has 450 franchised outlets, mostly in the East and Midwest. These outlets sell mostly hamburgers, french fried potatoes, and milk shakes. Mr. Vitt is 49 years old. In January 1982 he received this letter from a Zero's executive:

Dear John:

We have received and reviewed your work history with Zero's that you pursued in your desire to become a licensee. After consulting with our people, we have decided that we cannot now consider you favorably for a Zero's license.

We sincerely appreciate your interest in Zero's and sincerely hope you will understand that our decision was a difficult one to make.

John, good luck in your career-seeking efforts.

Sincerely,
Richard R. Rhine
Licensing Manager
Zero's, Inc.

The news left Mr. Vitt speechless. For six years, he had pursued, single-mindedly, his goal to own a Zero's franchise. To prepare himself for the franchise, he had taken the following steps:

☐ He moonlighted for five years at a Zero's franchise in Syracuse, learning all he could about fast-food service.
☐ He studied small business management at a local community college for six years, eventually earning a two-year associate degree. He made the dean's list every quarter.
☐ He made three trips to Zero's headquarters in Philadelphia for interviews.
☐ He had amassed personal assets worth $135,000 and owed no one.

"I'm really at a loss why they turned me down," says Mr. Vitt. "I'm a good family man, active in civic affairs, a churchgoer, and a union steward. Everybody looks up to me, even my five children. And I also have a little business on the side, as a plasterer. I know it wasn't the money, because I could've scraped together the $60,000 cash required for a franchise."

A Zero's brochure contains the following profile of a typical franchisee:

The entrepreneur awarded a Zero license gains the prestige of operating under a nationally known reputation and of receiving strong corporate support.

Our selection process focuses on matching the right place with the right person. We know what kind of person will get along well in which community—and we place him where his chances for success will be best.

Our licensees enthusiastically accept the responsibility of a 10-year license and a 10-year lease on a Zero's restaurant. They eagerly become active in community affairs. All are on-the-job owners. Some have a restaurant background; but most come from backgrounds as diverse as chemistry and the army, law and professional football. In fact, about 85 percent have never been connected with the food industry before.

Our licensees are good decision makers with the ability to recruit, train, and motivate the 20 to 40 full- and part-time employees that work for them.

1 What should Mr. Vitt do now?
2 Why did Zero's turn down Mr. Vitt's application for a franchise?
3 Could Mr. Vitt make a go of a Zero's franchise? Why?

CASE 2C

Robert Bartik is organizing a venture to make small, lightweight fiberglass sailboats. To help finance his venture, Mr. Bartik has approached a venture-capital firm. Along with his plans for the venture, Mr. Bartik gave the firm a profile of himself. The following is excerpted from the profile.

Profile of Robert Bartik

Job Experience 1977–81	Empire Chemical Corporation Plant manager. Supervises 57 employees. Responsible for production of such chemical products as polyester resin and polyhydric alcohols.
1967–77	Buckeye Chemical Industries, Inc. Senior chemical engineer. Responsible for the design of new chemical processes, including processes to produce urea and ammonium nitrate.
Education 1963–67	University of Idaho Bachelor of science degree in chemical engineering. Graduated magna cum laude. Editor of weekly newspaper. Organized mock political convention. Elected to four honor societies.
Interests	Boating, bridge.
Personal	Married, 2 children 36 years old

If you worked for the venture-capital firm that Mr. Bartik approached, would you judge him to have entrepreneurial potential? Explain.

CHAPTER THREE

SMALL BUSINESS AND INDUSTRY

questions for mastery

**how do products and services flow between
manufacturers, wholesalers, retailers,
services, and consumers?**

how are products and services classified?

**where are the most promising
entrepreneurial opportunities?**

**how vital is it to keep up with the
knowledge explosion?**

what may the world be like in the year 2000?

> **No profit grows where there is no
> pleasure taken; in brief, Sir, study
> what you most affect.**
>
> **William Shakespeare**

E ntrepreneurs energize our economy, thriving in almost every industry. Entrepreneurial opportunities, however, are greater in some industries than in others. To better spot those opportunities, we will examine in this chapter four major industry groups and their relationships to one another and to the consumer.

MAJOR INDUSTRY GROUPS

Before we look at each industry group in some detail, let us first define them briefly.

☐ **Manufacturing** Manufacturers convert raw materials into product. This product may then be sold to another manufacturer, to be used as raw material for still another product. Or it may be sold unchanged to wholesalers, retailers, or even directly to consumers. An example is the manufacture of nylon stockings, parachutes, and toothbrushes out of coal, air, and water.

☐ **Wholesaling** Wholesalers are middlemen between manufacturers and retailers. The popular view of the wholesaler as someone who sells at big discounts off list price is incorrect. Rather, wholesalers buy product from manufacturers, store it, and then sell it either to retailers or to consumers. As it passes from the manufacturer to the wholesaler and then to the consumer, the product stays unchanged but the wholesaler provides services to the retailer, such as fast delivery or credit financing, that enhance the value of the product. An example is the wholesaler who stores a farmer's fruit and vegetables for resale to a wider market of grocers than the farmer could economically reach.

☐ **Retailing** Retailers buy product from either wholesalers or manufacturers and sell it to consumers. Retailers in turn add value to the product by offering services to the consumer such as personal attention, wide selection, or credit terms. An example is the department store that sells consumers a host of products ranging from toothpaste to shirts to home computers.

☐ **Services** Service firms do not deal in a product. Instead, they sell personal skills to manufacturers, wholesalers, and retailers as well as to consumers. An example is the tax preparer who guides taxpayers through Form 1040.

Note in Exhibit 3-1 how these four industry groups differ in terms of personnel and money, materials and machines. As a rule, manufacturing businesses are the hardest to establish and services are the easiest. To make toothpaste, for example, the entrepreneur must invest not only in personnel but also in raw materials and machines. To prepare tax forms, however, entrepreneurs need only invest in their own training and perhaps some reference material; they can run their business out of a storefront or even from their home.

In Exhibit 3-2, note how manufacturers, wholesalers, and retailers link together to serve consumers. Tubes of toothpaste, for example, may move

EXHIBIT 3-1

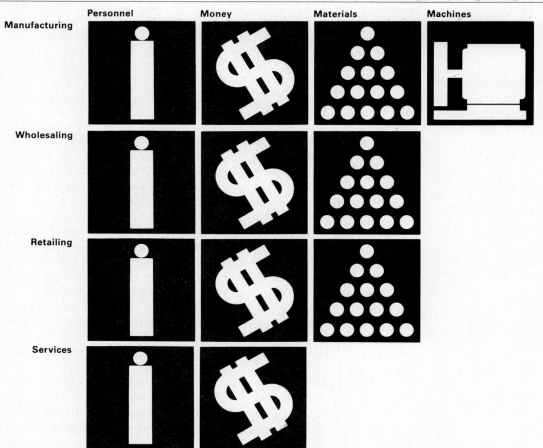

Of course, the differences are by no means as sharp as shown here. In fact, industry groups often overlap and blur together. One example is the laundry industry, which uses equipment like washing machines and presses; yet it is a *service* and not a manufacturing industry.

EXHIBIT 3-2

Flow of Products and Services Between Industry Groups

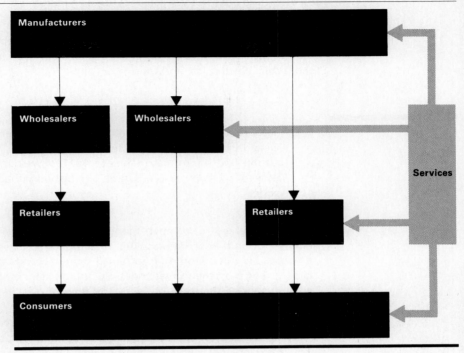

from manufacturers to drug wholesalers and finally to drug stores where consumers may buy them. Men's suits may move directly from garment makers to men's shops. Note, also, that services reach out to all industry groups as well as to consumers.

MANUFACTURING

Manufacturing, more than any other industry group, lends itself to bigness. And for good reason. Because of the investment required in equipment, energy, and raw materials, it takes much more money just to start a manufacturing venture. Automobile manufacture, for example, calls for millions of dollars of investment and hundreds of workers before the first automobile can roll off the assembly line.

Such requirements shut out most entrepreneurs. True, Henry Ford began on a shoestring of just $28,000. But today, it is all but impossible to begin from scratch in competition with giants like Ford Motor Company. Just how strongly does big business dominate the world of manufacturing? The nation's top 500 manufacturers account for:

☐ Two-thirds of the total sales revenues generated by manufacturers
☐ Three-fourths of the total number of employees in manufacturing

Even so, many entrepreneurs do well in manufacturing. It is not uncommon for entrepreneurs to outdo big business in such innovative industries as chemicals, electronics, and toys.

In pocket calculators, entrepreneurs are doing well against such giants as Texas Instruments and Hewlett-Packard. In fact, entrepreneurs brought out the first pocket calculators in 1971. It was only after calculators became a runaway success that big business began making their own models.
∎

With generally so much money at stake, the risks are much greater in manufacturing than in wholesaling, retailing, or services. But, often, so are the rewards. It is not uncommon for small manufacturers to earn more than a 20 percent return on their investment. Such high returns, however, tend to favor those industries that turn out a steady flow of new ideas and new products. They expect change, and they help it happen.

Not change, but tradition dominates such old industries as sawmills and bakeries, clothing and machine tools. These industries tend to be marginal, with many businesses just breaking even. Few entrepreneurs are drawn to such industries, although they seem to offer opportunities because they are ripe for change.

In the early 1950s, one entrepreneur saw opportunity in an old industry's problems. He began his own business to make machinery for the sawmill industry. He chose the sawmill industry because it had changed little since the Civil War and there was ample room for innovation. He modernized the design of sawmill machinery, offering sawmill operators equipment tailored to their specific needs. His strategy was to sell machinery unavailable from any other manufacturer.

The success of his strategy is evident in the growth of his business from just 3 employees to 104 when he sold out.
∎

Such entrepreneurial success often attracts the attention of big business. Most big businesses are aware of the innovations that flow from small manufacturers. In fact, Ford Motor Company and many others have set up special departments to find innovative manufacturers, either to buy into or to buy out. On both sides, a buy-out may be favorable.

☐ For a big business, it may be a way to invest profits or to diversify into something new.

☐ For the entrepreneur, it may be a way to retire or to realize capital gains.

The purchase of small businesses by big business does not always benefit the consumer, however.

Until the 1950s, hundreds of textile entrepreneurs made cotton and woolen fabric of almost every conceivable color, style, and weave. If garment makers failed to find what they wanted at one textile mill, they could go to another mill in search of style and elegance. Today, such variety and competition no longer exist. A handful of big businesses has bought out almost all small mills and converted them to focus on the manufacture of fabrics made from manmade fibers like nylon and polyester. Because such fibers lend themselves to mass production of the same style, color, and weave, consumers now find similar clothes in virtually every store.

In general, manufacturing offers more opportunities for innovation than any other industry. As discussed later, retailing ranks last.

WHOLESALING

Small business dominates wholesaling. In fact, businesses with fewer than 100 employees account for nearly 80 percent of the number of employees in wholesaling. This high percentage stems from the fact that wholesalers are mostly caretakers; so they need fewer employees for a given volume of business than do manufacturers or retailers.

As caretakers, wholesalers buy product in bulk from manufacturers, store it in a place convenient to retailers, and then sell it as retailers call for it. Besides having fewer employees, a wholesaler usually has fewer customers, although most tend to be large-volume, repeating customers.

Entrepreneurs who try their hand at wholesaling normally do so only after a long apprenticeship. It takes time to master the subtleties of negotiating low purchase prices, winning the confidence of retailers, and anticipating their needs. There are few instant wholesalers.

Often, wholesaling is a balancing act in which the entrepreneur is either calming the feathers of a retailer whose promised goods fail to arrive or chasing after suppliers who fail to deliver. Despite the frenzy, many entrepreneurs prosper, especially those few who innovate.

Entrepreneurs have opened specialty pharmaceutical houses that deliver prescription items to druggists four times a day. Such fast service enables druggists to eliminate inventories of slow-moving drugs.

Exhibit 3-3 shows how small business dominates not only wholesaling but also retailing and services. Note, however, that small business accounts for less than 20 percent of the total employment in manufacturing.

RETAILING

As shown in Exhibit 3-3, small businesses with fewer than 100 employees account for more than 50 percent of all employees in retailing. Most of them have fewer than five employees. Moreover, there are hundreds of different kinds of retailers, ranging from wig shops to automobile agencies, from custard stands to department stores.

Although sometimes called the nation's biggest small business, retailing nonetheless has spawned some giant businesses. Two examples are department-store chains like Sears and J. C. Penney. Big chains also stand out among groceries, restaurants, and variety stores.

Even so, small retailers are holding their own. Almost as many men and women, for example, work in small grocery stores as in large chains like A&P.

Some entrepreneurs do quite well in retailing, such as the innovative entrepreneurs who start discount drug stores and convenience food stores that open at 8 A.M. and close at midnight. As a rule, however, there is little innovation here, with retailers following traditional ways of doing business. Few retailers pursue innovation with regularity, as do manufacturers in growth industries like chemicals and electronics.

EXHIBIT 3-3

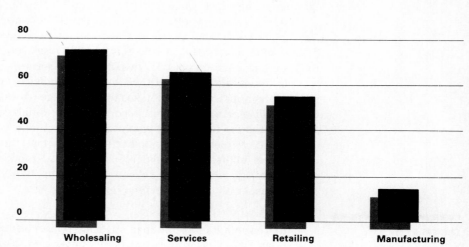

Small Business Employment by Industry Group

Percentage of total employment

Businesses with fewer than 100 employees account for most of the employment in wholesaling, services, and retailing.

Source: U.S. Department of Commerce, *Enterprise Statistics* (Washington, D.C.: U.S. Government Printing Office, 1977), E372-1, Table 5, p. 142.

Specialty shops are especially attractive to retailing entrepreneurs because such shops enable them to focus their resources in depth on a narrow segment of the market rather than spread those resources too thinly over a wider spectrum. For example, a retailer may sell suits styled only for men taller than 6 feet 2 inches, but in doing so, may offer a broader selection and better fit than the department store with which it competes.

Many entrepreneurs go into retailing with an eye to multiplying one store into many as quickly as possible. They do so chiefly by selling franchises to investors. That way, entrepreneurs can expand without putting up too much of their own money. Franchising often is a shortcut to growth.

EXAMPLE

Schlotzky's Sandwich Shops sell only one product, a hodgepodge of meats, cheeses, and marinade known as the Schlotzky sandwich, which was developed by husband-and-wife Donald and Dolores Dissman in Austin, Texas. Since the Dissmans began to franchise the concept, the number of Schlotzky Sandwich Shops has increased rapidly: to 155 stores in 1980, from 1 in 1976.[1]

SERVICES

Of all the industry groups, services generally are the easiest to go into. Many can be run from a home or a storefront office. Examples are telephone-answering services and management consulting firms. Such businesses require little, if any, investment.

Other services, such as motels and professional athletic teams, require much more investment. For example, new professional football franchises go for as much as $25 million.

Like retailing, the different kinds of services number into the hundreds, ranging from shoeshine parlors to car rental agencies, from marriage counselors to brain surgeons. Services are the fastest growing part of our economy. If we count all the men and women who work for nonprofit organizations, services today account for more than 50 percent of the nation's total work force. Ours is the first economy in history in which services dominate.

Services hold a magnetic attraction for the entrepreneur. Unlike retailing, services are open to innovation. And no other industry group offers entrepreneurs a higher return on their investment in time. Often, they can do it independently, without having to work with others. That is why they are drawn to such fields as computer services and the law, accounting and management consulting.

EXAMPLE

A pioneer in personal computing, Portia Isaacson of Richardson, Texas, foresaw the trend toward widespread business use of microcomputers.

1. Adapted from "Growing as Fast as They Can," *Venture,* February 1981, p. 22.

She felt confident enough in 1976 to gamble on opening one of the nation's earliest computer stores.

In 1980 Ms. Isaacson left retailing and founded her own technology forecasting and consulting firm—Future Computing. Her firm specializes in product and strategic planning for clients who include leading computer and electronics equipment manufacturers and retailers.[2]

■

Like retailing, services lend themselves to franchising; and for many kinds of services, franchising is the least costly way to expand. For example, one employment agency founded in Cleveland grew in four years from 1 outlet to 32, simply by selling franchises in other Midwest cities.

Big business offers little threat to the survival of small service businesses. The greater threat is posed by the consumer who turns do-it-yourselfer. In some cases, entrepreneurs fight back by creating new, hard-to-copy services. Beauty shops, for example, have created hair styles that defy imitation by do-it-yourselfers.

So far, we have talked about retailing and services as if they were separate industry groups that do not overlap. This is not always so, as borne out by these examples:

☐ Professional football teams sell not only entertainment but also foot-long hot dogs and 98-page programs featuring player rosters and photographs.
☐ Motels sell not only a night's lodging but also razor blades and steak-and-potato dinners.
☐ Service stations sell not only gasoline and motor oil but also such services as fixing flat tires and balancing wheels.

The lines separating services from other industry groups often overlap and blur and it is sometimes hard to classify businesses into such neat categories as manufacturing, wholesaling, retailing, or services.

SERVICES NOT NORMALLY CLASSIFIED AS SUCH

So far, we have discussed only those industries that are normally classified as services. But there are other industries that may also fall into this category, such as communication, construction, finance, insurance, real estate, transportation, and utilities—even though the federal government treats them separately.

For our purposes in examining the nature of various industries and their accessibility to entrepreneurs, we will group these industries under services. They logically belong there, although it could be argued that construction and utilities also qualify under manufacturing. For example, a carpenter may translate an architect's drawings (services) into a two-story house (manufacturing).

2. Adapted from "Spotlight: Portia Isaacson," *Output,* April 1981, p. 54.

Building the house also requires other craftspeople who put in plumbing and electrical wiring (services).

Such communications media as magazines, newspapers, television, and radio are dominated by big business. Their very nature limits opportunities for new ventures. But so great is their lure that some entrepreneurs try their hand at starting, say, a new magazine featuring hot-rod cars or a new suburban newspaper featuring local happenings. Consider this example.

EXAMPLE

In 1953, Hugh Hefner hocked his furniture for $600, scraped together $10,000 more, and started his own magazine. Its name? *Playboy.* The first issue in 1953 sold 54,000 copies. By 1980, *Playboy* had a circulation of 5,700,000 and sales revenues of $363 million.
■

CONSTRUCTION

Most construction contractors are small. And contrary to popular opinion, small business is the nation's biggest builder. This is especially true among electrical, painting, and plumbing contractors. Big business is not absent from the construction industry, however. For example, giant general contractors build skyscrapers like the Prudential Tower in Chicago or blast through mountain ranges to build superhighways like the Pennsylvania Turnpike.

General contracting holds the greatest attraction for pure entrepreneurs in construction, mostly because of the challenges it offers. For example, they may take an architect's plans for a domed football stadium, translate them into hundreds of materials, and then contract out the construction work to dozens of subcontractors.

Subcontracting also attracts the entrepreneur, often because it requires little investment beyond tools and skill. A painting subcontractor, for example, need only invest in a pickup truck, a ladder, a brush, and some cans of paint.

Construction also attracts entrepreneurs because it appeals to their desire for creative satisfaction. Carpenters building a hencoop, for example, get a deeper satisfaction from their work than someone tightening bolts on an assembly line. When the hencoop is finished, it often belongs more to the carpenter than to the person who hired him or her, continuing to bring pleasure long after the job is completed.

FINANCE

Finance, too, is dominated by small business. Most of the nation's 14,500 commercial banks are small. Almost every town has one. But banking also has its giants. In 1980, San Francisco's Bank of America had assets of $112 billion, more than the combined holdings of all the small banks in the country. Note how humbly the Bank of America began:

In 1904, Amadeo Peter Giannini opened his first branch in a remodeled saloon. His bank catered to the needs of the little person and to small business. As they grew rich, so did his bank. Today, the Bank of America is the world's biggest bank.

■

Commercial banking no longer has much attraction for entrepreneurs. It is too hard to get into. Federal and state laws often require entrepreneurs to raise as much as $2.5 million before opening their doors for business. Even so, many entrepreneurs do make their mark in finance, but in such other areas as venture capital, stock brokerage, mortgage lending, finance companies, and investment banking.

Of these, venture capital has perhaps the strongest appeal for entrepreneurs. In their view, what could be more creative fun than to risk money on a new idea or a new product? Note the difference between banks and venture-capital firms:

☐ Banks rent money.
☐ Venture-capital firms risk money.

Venture-capital firms seek out new enterprises, especially those backed by new ideas and keen talent. Banks, on the other hand, avoid them because by law they cannot take chances with their depositors' money.

INSURANCE

This industry's statistics boggle the mind. Insurance is the nation's greatest reservoir of money, with more than $430 billion in assets. The industry's 1,900 companies have sold policies totaling an astronomical $3.2 trillion. Few of the companies are small.

There are, however, tens of thousands of insurance agents who represent insurance companies and sell policies. All are independent small-business-persons.

Insurance holds some attraction for the entrepreneur, but not much. The entrepreneurs who do well usually sell group life insurance or group medical insurance. Group policies enable organizations to insure each of their workers for far less than the cost of insurance for an individual.

REAL ESTATE

A popular form of investment, real estate has grown into a $110 billion-a-year industry. Servicing it are more than 130,000 real estate firms. Most of them are small, with just a handful of employees. Such firms normally work as finders. For example, if a family wants to sell their house, the real estate agent's job is to find them a buyer.

Entrepreneurs, however, generally prefer commercial rather than residential sales. And they are likely to go in not as brokers but as developers. For example, the explosive growth of shopping centers after World War II was mostly the work of entrepreneurs. More than 22,000 shopping centers now dot the country, with 500 new ones sprouting up each year.

TRANSPORTATION

Like the insurance industry, transportation is made up almost entirely of big businesses. The reason is obvious: it takes millions of dollars just to establish a railroad or an airline. A few small businesses have been successful in transportation, such as taxicabs and helicopter short-hop services.

The opportunity that entrepreneurs are exploring in transportation has been opened up by the combination of suburban sprawl, the energy crunch, and inadequate mass transit. Entrepreneurs are filling the gap with door-to-door autobus service. That involves picking up passengers, taking them to work or to shopping centers, and then returning them home.

UTILITIES

This is the only industry that almost entirely shuts out the entrepreneur. Utilities are monopolies in virtually every community. Gas, electric, and telephone companies are closely controlled and regulated by state laws which also give utilities the exclusive right to serve a community.

A LOOK AT THE FUTURE

What will tomorrow be like? What products and services will consumers want 10 or 20 years from now? Which industries will lend themselves to entrepreneurial adventure?

Looking into the future is high art. Knowledge is now exploding so fast that industry leaders must look 5, 10, or 20 years ahead just to keep up. They can ill afford to sit on their hands.

In fact, our store of knowledge is doubling every five years, or several hundred times faster than in the 1920s. By contrast, in the Stone Age, the knowledge of primitive human beings doubled every 100,000 years.[3]

Futurism itself has become a growth industry for entrepreneurs. The Library of Congress, which has its own futures research group, has estimated that there are nearly 100 small firms devoted to some aspect of futures research. In fact, one such firm has already helped more than 500 government and corporate clients to peer into the future.[4]

Futurists foresee a world far different from today's. Some of their predictions about the year 2000 follow.

3. Martin Levin, "Phoenix Nest," *Saturday Review,* June 22, 1968, p. 4.
4. Paul Dickson, "The Future Revised," *Northwest Orient Magazine,* January 1979, p. 10.

ON PEOPLE

The nation's population will stop growing, peaking at 270 million. Cities and suburbs will cluster together to form so-called megalopolises. For example, the coastal strip between Boston and Washington will become as one city, with little farmland in between. Such megalopolises will be home for 8 out of 10 persons. Many men and women will work at home, using the instant communication of television to keep in touch with their employers.

ON TRANSPORTATION

Two dramatic changes will begin to take place in transportation. One will be the production of automobiles powered by electricity. The other will be the design of hovercraft that ride on cushions of air.

ON FOOD

Beef consumption will lessen as frogmen raise fish in a network of underwater pens. These underwater farmers will then grind their nutrition-rich crop into a variety of foods. The magic of chemistry will impart flavors to please any palate—from garlic to champagne, from mustard to beefsteak.

ON SHOPPING

Today's supermarkets will diminish in number as homemakers begin shopping by video phone. These phones will enable homemakers to scan, price, and order groceries without leaving their kitchens. This practice will spread to other retailing industries, especially to department stores and drug stores.

ON INFORMATION

Because of a computer smaller than a thumbnail, called the microprocessor, the world seems to be on the eve of a revolution that will change the life of every man, woman, and child on earth. A marvel of technology, this computer can process mountains of information with lightning speed. It most likely will cause these changes to take place by the year 2000:

☐ Electronic books will begin to replace printed books.
☐ Computers will do much of the work now being done by physicians and lawyers, teachers and accountants.
☐ Electronic mail will replace much of the postal service.
☐ Robots will run much of the machinery now run by humans.

Too, libraries and filing cabinets will begin to give way to computers capable of performing feats of memory now unheard of. These storehouses of information will be at the fingertips of every man or woman who wants it—they will simply dial a coded number from their home.

Computers that listen and respond to human speech may also become widespread by the year 2000. Such computers could give entrepreneurs access to large data bases through the telephone network. They could provide for the control of complex machines by vocal command and make possible sophisticated devices for the handicapped. They could also be helpful in the day-to-day control of business operations.

EXAMPLE

Consider a conversation between a computer and its users concerning the inventory of a warehouse. The computer "knows" how many of each item are on hand and where each article is stored. Its data base also lists costs and suppliers.

The users have questions that the computer can answer, at least in principle, such as, "Do we have any blue pencils in stock?" The users also have things to say that the computer can profitably "understand," such as, "There is no more room in bay 13."[5]

■

ON WORK

The number of working men and women will drop from 40 percent today to 30 percent. The drudgery of manual labor, the monotony of clerical work, and the dullness of assembly lines will be borne by versatile computers. The computer will also invade the executive suite, replacing many middle managers.

With the arrival of the computer age, lifestyles will also change sharply. For example, the average person will spend his or her life span of 75 years as follows: one-third getting educated, one-third working at a job, and one-third enjoying retirement.

Many families will be independently wealthy. Thanks to government benefits, even nonworking families will be well off. Median family income will approach $20,000 a year (in 1980 dollars).

ON MEDICINE

Science and medicine will combine their talents to all but free the world of bacterial and viral disease. Artificial hearts and lungs will be within everyone's reach. Pocket radar will enable the blind to see and the deaf to hear. Chemical therapy will cure the mentally retarded.

ON THE ENVIRONMENT

A garbage-disposal revolution is also in the offing. Consider that we make more garbage in a year than we do steel. By law, every municipality will have to recycle all of its garbage. One benefit will be the burning of combustible materials to produce electrical energy.

Almost everyone likes to play the game of future. We are no exception. Although forecasts such as this one must be taken with a grain of salt, they do hint at answers to this key question: In what industries lie the best opportunities for entrepreneurial adventure in the future?

5. Stephen E. Levinson and Mark Y. Liberman, "Speech Recognition by Computer," *Scientific American,* April 1981, p. 64.

There is no way to answer this question with military precision. We can only guess. But it seems that entrepreneurs will be drawn to those industries prepared to ride strong upward trends in:

☐ Affluence and leisure
☐ Individualism
☐ Urbanization
☐ Technology

We will take up each of these trends in the next chapter, when we deal with the search for a venture.

SUMMARY

Although small business thrives in almost every industry, it is stronger in some than in others. The requirements of each industry group—the initial financial investment and personnel, materials, and equipment—determine just how strong the presence of small business is. In terms of number of employees, small business dominates three of the four major industry groups: wholesaling, retailing, and services. It is less strong in manufacturing, mostly because of the large sums of money needed just to get started.

Entrepreneurial opportunities abound in virtually every industry. In any industry, small businesses are most successful when they are innovators. In manufacturing, for example, small businesses compete well in high-technology industries such as chemicals and electronics. Services, because of their ease of entry, attract many entrepreneurs and are the fastest growing part of our economy.

Life in the year 2000 will differ sharply from life today. The knowledge explosion will continue to spark change at an accelerating rate, thanks largely to the remarkable versatility of the computer.

DISCUSSION AND REVIEW QUESTIONS

1 Which industry group appeals most to you? Why?
2 Do you agree that entrepreneurial opportunities will broaden in the future? Why?
3 Why have service industries grown so rapidly?
4 Define the terms: *manufacturing, wholesaling, retailing, services, venture capital, futurism, megalopolis.*
5 What is the difference between venture capital and bank loans? Which is better for the entrepreneur? Why?
6 Why do manufacturing industries generally lend themselves to big business?
7 Why may some old industries like textiles be attractive to entrepreneurs?

8 Which of the four major industry groups—manufacturing, retailing, services, or wholesaling—is likely to attract the innovative entrepreneur? Explain.

9 Is there always a sharp distinction between retailing and services? Explain.

10 Comment on the reasonableness of our forecast for the year 2000.

11 What do manufacturers, wholesalers, retailers, and services have in common? In what ways do they differ, giving your own examples?

12 Many consumers believe that restaurants are a service business. Is this true? Explain.

13 Identify and briefly describe some of the dramatic changes that have taken place in your community in the past five years. How have these changes influenced entrepreneurial opportunities?

14 Should every entrepreneur be a futurist? Why? How do you plan to keep up with the knowledge explosion?

15 Is it reasonable to call the age we live in the computer age? Explain.

CASE 3A

When he came to this country from Greece, Steve Caloudis owned only the clothes on his back and spoke not a word of English. Today, he owns three restaurants that ring up sales revenues of $2.1 million a year.

His success has caught the eye of shopping center developers throughout the state. "They want me because of my record," says Mr. Caloudis. "It's a good feeling, but I'm not sure I should keep expanding. I'm happy with what I've got."

BACKGROUND

To Mr. Caloudis, hard work is a way of life. "Work is a habit, and I've never grown out of it," says Mr. Caloudis. Indeed, he began working when he was 12, selling apricots and grapes to tourists in Greece. When he was 18, Mr. Caloudis left Greece for New York City, where he hired on as a dishwasher at seven dollars a week. His hours were from 6 A.M. to 6 P.M., six days a week.

Mr. Caloudis continued to work in restaurants and bars, mostly as a waiter. His objective was to learn the restaurant business "inside out." To meet that objective, he often "did a lot of extra work for nothing." For example, he worked with the chef, the bartender, the cleaning crew—on his own time, without pay.

His appetite for work paid off. He finally became manager of one of the city's biggest downtown restaurants.

That turned out to be his last promotion, for Mr. Caloudis decided to go into business for himself. He was sure he was ready and he had saved $11,000. After looking around for a month, he zeroed in on a 40-seat coffee shop that was for sale.

HIS FIRST VENTURE

The owner wanted $25,000 for the shop. But before he would buy, Mr. Caloudis wanted to assure himself that he could make a go of the business. For a week, he stood 12 hours a day outside the coffee shop, asking customers just one question: "What attracts you to this location?"

Although his family thought $25,000 was too much to pay for a coffee shop, Mr. Caloudis felt strongly that he was buying "clientele and not salt shakers and coffee cups." He was sure that if he upgraded the menu and gave customers "more of a variety," he could double revenues in a year.

He bought out the owner for $25,000, making no attempt to negotiate a lower purchase price. His beginning balance sheet appears in Exhibit 3A-1.

To swing the $15,000 loan, Mr. Caloudis had the help of his wife, Mary, who did the banking for the advertising agency she worked for. When he applied for the loan, the Caloudis name was already familiar to the bank.

Mary Caloudis helped her husband in still another way. An attorney was teaching business law at a local college. One of his students was Mrs. Caloudis. When she told him about her husband's plans to go into business for himself, the attorney offered to incorporate the business at a small fee. The attorney

Ted's Restaurant, Inc.

Balance Sheet (July 1, 1965)

Assets			Equities		
Cash	$	500	Bank loan		$15,000
Equipment		2,000	Owner's equity		10,500
Goodwill		23,000			
Total assets		$25,500	Total equities		$25,500

still counsels Mr. Caloudis on all legal matters—though now, of course, at his usual fee.

The restaurant was a quick success. In fact, soon after Mr. Caloudis took over, patrons began lining up outside at 11:15 A.M. for lunch. Word had spread that he had enlarged the menu, improved the service, and that he called each customer by name. Revenues soared (see Exhibit 3A-2).

A SECOND RESTAURANT

Mr. Caloudis's success soon drew the attention of shopping center developers. Impressed by the restaurant's performance, the owner of Southgate shopping center told Mr. Caloudis: "I have a place for you in Southgate. You'd be a good tenant for us."

Again, his family was skeptical about the idea. After all, he was making a lot of money where he was. So why move? "My family told me I was overextending myself financially," says Mr. Caloudis.

True to form, he went against their opinion. He estimated it would cost $120,000 just to install equipment, fixtures, and furniture. "When you go into a shopping center, all you get is four walls and a ceiling," says Mr. Caloudis. "The rest is up to you." Unwilling at the time to sell his other restaurant, he had to look elsewhere for money to finance his new venture. So, he sold his house for $40,000 and borrowed $80,000 from a bank, using as collateral the market value of his other restaurant.

Ted's Restaurant, Inc.

Year	Sales Revenues	Notes
1964	$ 35,000	Under former owner
1965	60,000	Under Mr. Caloudis
1966	110,000	
1967	190,000	Seating capacity expanded from 40 to 86 seats
1968	190,000	

When it opened in 1969, the new restaurant was not a runaway success—as his first restaurant had been. "I never stopped to think about whom to cater to," says Mr. Caloudis. "I was too busy running the other restaurant and also setting this one up. In fact, I was putting in an 18-hour day."

The problem of "whom to cater to" now took up most of Mr. Caloudis's time. To solve the problem, he talked to customers, other businesspersons, and his wife. From these talks, he found that the shopping center drew its shoppers mostly from middle-income families. So he decided to change his image:

☐ He changed the restaurant's name from Ted's to Teddi's. Why? Because Ted's suggests the image of a truck stop.

☐ He upgraded the quality of the menu. "People wanted home-cooked meals," says Mr. Caloudis. So he added meals with a foreign flavor.

Despite these changes, revenues failed to go up until 1971, when Mr. Caloudis borrowed $30,000 to carpet the restaurant and to change from an open to a closed kitchen. "That improved the atmosphere," says Mr. Caloudis. "You can't offer broiled Florida scampis and champagne to customers with an open kitchen staring them in the face." His revenues picked up immediately (see Exhibit 3A-3).

In 1973, opportunity knocked again. This time, the developer of the Parmatown shopping center asked Mr. Caloudis to become a tenant. Despite his family's opposition, Mr. Caloudis said yes, but only after the developer agreed to help finance the $200,000 cost of the new restaurant. "The only way to get ahead is to use other people's money," says Mr. Caloudis. His new restaurant was an instant success, as shown in Exhibit 3A-4.

Mr. Caloudis's success soon moved another shopping center developer to ask him to take over a bankrupt restaurant in Richmond Mall. Its owners had gone under after just six months of business.

Teddi's Restaurant at Southgate

Year	Sales Revenues	Notes
1969	$300,000	Restaurant is opened
1970	300,000	Foreign meals added
1971	310,000	Open kitchen changed to closed kitchen
1972	375,000	
1973	375,000	
1974	465,000	Cocktail lounge and party room added

Teddi's Restaurants, Inc.

Sales Revenues: 1974–1978

Year	Southgate	Parmatown
1974	$465,000	—
1975	510,000	—
1976	525,000	$450,000
1977	550,000	465,000
1978	610,000	510,000

The bankrupt owners offered Mr. Caloudis the equipment and furnishings for $25,000. After inspecting the restaurant, Mr. Caloudis estimated it would take another $175,000 to make it over to his own taste.

Again, his family thought it would be a mistake for him to buy another restaurant. "You'll lose everything," they told him, but Mr. Caloudis went ahead anyway. To make a long story short, he again succeeded. In fact, it took just three years for this restaurant to catch up with the other two (see Exhibit 3A-5).

A newspaper reporter recently asked Mr. Caloudis: "What's the secret to all this success?" The reply: "We've learned what the public wants. They like family-type, home-cooked meals—along with the right price, plus good service and a clean establishment."

CREDITS WIFE FOR SUCCESS

Mr. Caloudis knows that he probably never would have made it without his wife, Mary. "She's been by my side for 17 years," says Mr. Caloudis. Working as a team, they still put in 12-hour days. And being fully involved has paid off for both.

Shopping center developers still beat a path to Mr. Caloudis's door, seeking him as a tenant. They always come away impressed with his grasp of details. For example, he keeps in his head such financial details as these:

☐ Payroll costs as a percentage of revenues, broken down by restaurant and by month for the past two years
☐ Sales revenues and before-tax profits, broken down by restaurant and by year for the past 17 years

Teddi's Restaurants, Inc.

Sales Revenues: 1979–1981

Year	Southgate	Parmatown	Richmond
1979	$635,000	$515,000	$415,000
1980	720,000	580,000	510,000
1981	760,000	705,000	660,000

His strong memory helps him spot trends and danger signals quickly. "That's why my restaurants have never had a losing month," says Mr. Caloudis. "I always know where I stand and where I'm going. You can't get along without figures in a business like mine."

Indeed, he is one of the most efficient restaurateurs in the state. In 1981, out of every sales dollar, 10 cents was left over as profit (see Exhibit 3A-6). Compared to the industry average of 4 cents, it becomes obvious that Mr. Caloudis is a rare manager indeed.

ORGANIZATION

Mr. Caloudis receives almost all the profits himself. No outsider owns a single share of stock. Of the 1,500 shares outstanding, he owns 1,400 shares and his daughter 100. Yet his business is organized as a Subchapter S corporation, which permits as many as 25 shareholders.

In addition to this corporation, Mr. Caloudis owns four others. The Subchapter S corporation serves as the management company, while the others serve as operating companies (see Exhibit 3A-7).

To help him run all five corporations, Mr. Caloudis relies on just three persons: his wife, daughter, and son-in-law. They hold all the key positions. "It's all in the family," says Mr. Caloudis. His organizational chart appears in Exhibit 3A-8.

Altogether, Mr. Caloudis employs 190 persons. "I hire the best," says Mr. Caloudis. "My turnover is low compared to other restaurants. Only 12 percent a year. If I hire cheap employees, my costs are going to go up. That's why I go after the best."

CONTROLLING PERFORMANCE

He controls his employees' performance by setting standards and rewarding them if they do well. "Your employees have to know what you expect of them," says Mr. Caloudis, "and they appreciate knowing. I pay them well." For example, he pays his dishwashers five dollars an hour. Mr. Caloudis himself was paid only 10 cents an hour to wash dishes when he first came to this country. "How dimes have changed," he says in jest.

EXHIBIT 3A-6

Teddi's Restaurants, Inc.

Item	1981 Breakdown per Sales Dollar	
Sales revenues		$1.00
Costs		
Food	$0.42	
Overhead	0.26	
Labor	0.22	0.90
Profit		$0.10

Corporate Structure

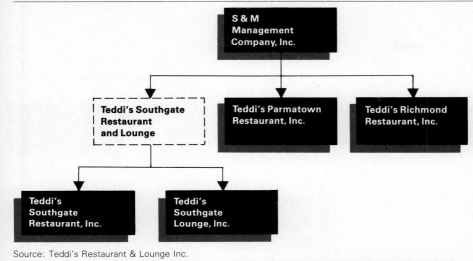

Source: Teddi's Restaurant & Lounge Inc.

Mr. Caloudis also believes in treating his employees humanely. "In a capitalistic system, we have to learn to share. I even lend employees up to $300 each, without interest. And I never get mad when they make mistakes. Self-respect is important. I know every one of my 190 employees by name. They know I mean it when I say, 'How are you?' I even have a policy that my managers cannot fire an employee without first consulting me. I don't like the word 'fire.' It's bad for morale." Employees enjoy such fringe benefits as a pension plan, profit-sharing, medical insurance, paid vacations, and business-interruption insurance.

Mr. Caloudis is especially proud of his management team. Every manager came up through the ranks, working at jobs ranging from dishwasher to chef. "We develop our own managers," says Mr. Caloudis. One example is his daughter. She started when she was just 12 years old. Now 24, she is treasurer of the business.

SETS GOALS

Looking back, Mr. Caloudis says: "I knew what I wanted to do, and I did it. My record speaks for itself. And my credit is triple-A. Nobody asks me when I'm going to pay. Instead, they ask how much do I want." He has never submitted his financial statements to Dun & Bradstreet, the national credit-rating firm. "I don't need them," says Mr. Caloudis. A recent income statement appears in Exhibit 3A-9.

Looking ahead, Mr. Caloudis has set a goal of $5.0 million in revenues by 1986, up from $2.1 million in 1981. To reach that goal, he may have to add two restaurants. Yet he has second thoughts about further expansion. For one thing, his family opposes the idea of "expansion for expansion's sake." For

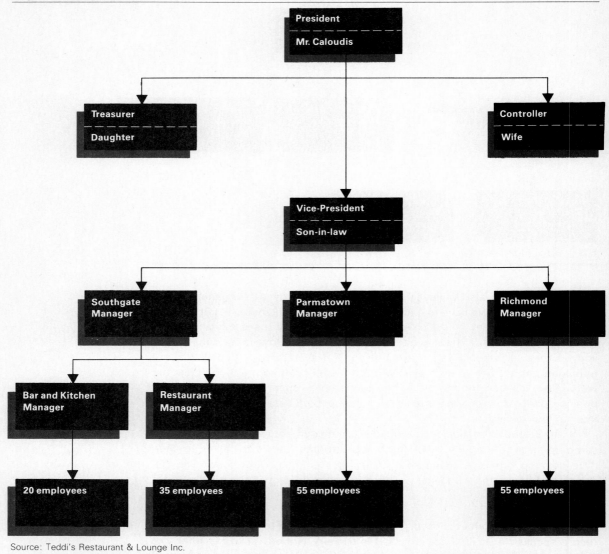

President
Mr. Caloudis

Treasurer
Daughter

Controller
Wife

Vice-President
Son-in-law

Southgate
Manager

Parmatown
Manager

Richmond
Manager

Bar and Kitchen
Manager

Restaurant
Manager

20 employees

35 employees

55 employees

55 employees

Source: Teddi's Restaurant & Lounge Inc.

Sales revenues		$2,125,000
Cost of goods sold		861,000
Gross profit		$1,264,000
Operating expenses		
Payroll	$468,000	
Office*	164,000	
Rent	119,000	
Payroll taxes	49,000	
Depreciation	47,000	
Utilities	38,000	
Interest	36,000	
Supplies	36,000	
Advertising	33,000	990,000
Operating profit		$ 274,000

* Includes such expenses as accounting, entertainment, insurance, legal, office payroll, telephone, and travel.

another, Mr. Caloudis, now 53 years old, has been training his son-in-law and daughter to take over.

But Mr. Caloudis continues to feel pressures to expand. In the past month alone, two shopping center developers have asked him to set up restaurants in the centers they are now building. One will be the largest shopping center in the state, with 260 shops.

Photographs of one of Mr. Caloudis's restaurants appear in Exhibit 3A-10.

QUESTIONS

1 If you were Mr. Caloudis, would you expand again? Explain.
2 Comment on how Mr. Caloudis has organized his business.
3 What accounts for Mr. Caloudis's success?
4 Comment on Mr. Caloudis's attitude toward his employees.
5 Looking at Exhibit 3A-9, how would you adjust the income statement to arrive at a better estimate of profit?

CASE 3B   ELLEN WAGNER

At age 33, Ellen Wagner wants to shift careers. She now works as a certified public accountant (CPA) for a large auditing firm. "The pay is good," says Miss Wagner. "And I get to meet a lot of top executives, but I'm tired of looking at numbers all day long. It's getting to me. I want to do something new and different."

Outside and Inside Views of One Restaurant

Source: The Cleveland Press, Cleveland, Ohio.

So one day Miss Wagner called up her accounting professor at the University of Michigan for advice. "I'm not sure where to start," began Miss Wagner. "But I've made up my mind to give up the accounting profession. I'm just not cut out for it. It's too confining. Does that shock you?"

"No," replied the professor. "Tell me, do you have any idea what you'd like to do?"

"That's why I'm calling," said Miss Wagner. "I thought you might give me some guidance. As a CPA, I've audited the books of a lot of entrepreneurs. I really admire them. One of my clients, for example, started with just one employee to make electronic gadgetry. And would you believe, in just 13 years, he has expanded to 270 employees. He built his business with his own two hands, literally. It must give him a lot of satisfaction."

"Is that what you'd like to do, go into business for yourself?" asked the professor.

"Yes, I would," replied Miss Wagner. "But all I know is accounting. How do you suggest I start?"

"Well," said the professor, "why don't you look at some of the fragmented industries. You know, industries like real estate where no single firm has more than, say, 1 percent of the total market. Fragmented industries are generally inefficient and could use someone of your talents. Another point about fragmented industries is that they're usually easy to go into. They often require little beginning capital."

"Thanks for the advice," said Miss Wagner. "Real estate sounds like a good place to start. I have only $22,000 in stocks and savings, so I can't think too much about going into other industries, especially manufacturing. Besides, I'm not mechanically inclined. I can't even fix a leaky faucet. You know, it's a good thing I'm still single."

The idea of going into some aspect of the real estate industry intrigued Miss Wagner. She vaguely recalled reading in *The Wall Street Journal* that industry leaders see the development of franchises as a revolution in real estate. "You know, someday there'll be a McDonald's of the real estate world," said Miss Wagner, "and it could be me."

QUESTIONS

1 What should Miss Wagner do now?
2 Do you think the professor's advice was sound? Why or why not?

CASE 3C   JOSEPH ADAMLE

Joseph Adamle's first venture was a Kool-Aid stand when he was nine years old. "I made five dollars a week at it," remembers Mr. Adamle.

It is now two ventures and 16 years later. The ventures were a laundry pick-up service at college and a house-painting business in the summer. "I made enough to pay my way through college," says Mr. Adamle. "In fact, I graduated with $2,400 in my savings account."

In college, Mr. Adamle majored in accounting, earning a C+ average. "Now that I'm out," says Mr. Adamle, "my goal is to be worth a million by the time I'm 30—and I don't care what field I make it in."

QUESTION

What would you advise Mr. Adamle to do? Explain.

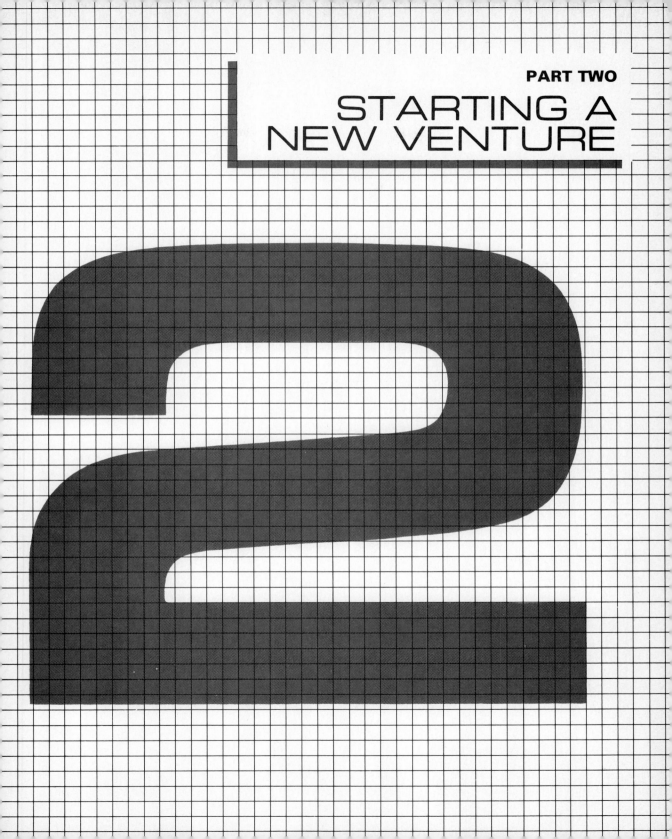

PART TWO

STARTING A
NEW VENTURE

2

CHAPTER FOUR

SEARCH FOR A NEW VENTURE

questions for mastery

why is it important to answer the question
"what business am I in?" thoughtfully and
precisely?

what are the specific industries that are
likely to prosper in the future?

what are the two major ways of going into
business for oneself?

how does one evaluate the financial worth
of a business?

how does one patent an invention?

Let us watch well our beginnings,
and results will manage themselves.

Alexander Clark

As the saying goes, "a thousand-mile journey begins with but a single step." So must a new venture. The first step may be the decision to become an entrepreneur. And the next step may be to choose a product or service. Then the would-be entrepreneur must decide whether to:

☐ Buy an existing business, or—
☐ Start from scratch

This chapter focuses on these two ways of going into business—after first dealing with choice of product or service. This chapter also explains how to evaluate a venture and how to deal with the problems of patenting an idea.

CHOICE OF PRODUCT OR SERVICE

Early on, the entrepreneur must answer this question: What business should I be in? This may seem an absurd suggestion. "If there's one thing I know," said one entrepreneur, "it's what business I'm going into." Often entrepreneurs *think* they know what business they have chosen without closely analyzing their choice. To show why, let us look at this example:

EXAMPLE

Joseph Vosmik started a business selling and renting boats. He thought he was going into the marina business. But when he got into trouble and asked for outside help, he learned that he was not really in the marina business. Instead, Mr. Vosmik was in several businesses. He was in the restaurant business with a dockside cafe—serving meals to boating parties. He was also in the real estate business—buying and selling lots up and down the coast. And he was in the boat-repair business—buying parts and calling in a mechanic to help him.

The fact was that Mr. Vosmik was trying to be all things to all people. With this approach, he was spreading himself thin.

Before he could make a profit, Mr. Vosmik had to decide *what* business he really was in and concentrate on it. After much study, he saw that his business was really a recreation shopping center. From that point on, profits began to flow.[1]

A vital first step for would-be entrepreneurs is to define their business with precision and brevity. In this regard, Robert Townsend, a former board chairman of Avis Rent-A-Car Corporation, had this to say:

We defined our business as "renting and leasing vehicles without drivers." This let us put the blinders on ourselves and stop considering the acquisition of related businesses like motels and travel agencies. It also

1. Adapted from U.S. Small Business Administration, "Business Plan for Retailers," *Small Marketers Aid No. 150* (Washington, D.C.: U.S. Government Printing Office, 1973), p. 3.

showed us that we had to get rid of some limousine and sightseeing companies that we already owned.[2]

Choosing a product or service requires entrepreneurs to look closely at their own skills and at industry trends to see how well they mesh. As mentioned in Chapter Three, it is most likely that entrepreneurs will be attracted to those industries that will capitalize on the upward trends in affluence and leisure, individualism, urbanization, and technology. Let us now look at these trends, one by one.

AFFLUENCE AND LEISURE

Ours is truly an affluent society and it is likely to be even more affluent by the year 2000. The gap between the haves and the have-nots will narrow, not only in the United States but also abroad. And, as affluence grows, so will leisure time. Which industries are likely to seize on this upward trend? Let us name just a few:

☐ Recreation and travel
☐ Banking and stock brokerages
☐ Real estate
☐ Luxury and specialty goods
☐ Education
☐ Health spas and beauty salons
☐ Restaurants
☐ Sporting goods and hobbies
☐ Performing arts and entertainment
☐ Publishing

INDIVIDUALISM

More and more, men and women will choose to work for themselves rather than for someone else. With more leisure time, they may choose to moonlight by setting up their own business as a sideline. Many will work out of their homes. Industries most likely to benefit from this trend include:

☐ Law
☐ Management consulting
☐ Accounting and tax preparation
☐ Mail order
☐ Telephone answering services
☐ Computer programming
☐ Financial services

URBANIZATION

Many more persons will be living in urban areas by the year 2000, and consumers will be more sophisticated in their buying habits. They will seek the

2. Adapted from Robert Townsend, *Up the Organization* (New York: Alfred A. Knopf, 1970), p. 129.

highest quality products and services. The following industries will probably benefit from increased consumer sophistication:

- ☐ Equipment rental
- ☐ Pet shops
- ☐ Day care centers
- ☐ Housing construction
- ☐ Fashion clothing, gourmet foods, and boutiques
- ☐ Home computers, electronic gadgetry, and stereo systems

TECHNOLOGY

The nation's laboratories will continue to invent new gadgets, new machines, new products. Many of these will be so complex as to defy servicing by do-it-yourselfers. So strong growth is foreseen in many service industries, including:

- ☐ Plumbing
- ☐ Television and appliance repair
- ☐ Electronics servicing
- ☐ Auto repair
- ☐ Lawn care

Too, the fast growth of technology will attract many entrepreneurs to manufacturing. As inventors come up with new products, the need for entrepreneurs to make and market them will intensify. Most new products will spring from such industries as:

- ☐ Chemicals
- ☐ Environmental control and energy-saving equipment
- ☐ Computers, automated machines, and electronics
- ☐ Medical equipment
- ☐ Office equipment

GENERAL OUTLOOK

From now until the year 2000, more entrepreneurial opportunities than ever before can be expected. Competition surely will be keener, but it will be so healthy as to stimulate the birth of new ventures.

This optimism must be tempered, however, by the knowledge that some industries are rapidly passing out of the hands of small business into those of big business—as seems to be happening with small computers. Trends toward bigness are bound to affect many areas of manufacturing, some areas of retailing and wholesaling, and a few areas of services. However, new entrepreneurial opportunities will more than offset such trends.

Big business will continue to stimulate small business growth. Many big businesses, for example, find that it pays to farm out such work as building maintenance and computer services. Many also find that it does not pay to have more than a skeleton staff in marketing research, public relations, and other services that may be hired as needed.

After choosing a product or service and making sure that the choice fits their skills and desires, entrepreneurs must decide whether to buy an existing business or to start a business from scratch.

Lawyers and bankers often advise entrepreneurs to buy out a business rather than start from scratch. The reason is that existing businesses are much less risky. The odds are better because an existing business, if successful, has already:

☐ Proven its ability to draw customers at a profit
☐ Established healthy relationships with bankers, suppliers, and the community

The track record of an existing business surpasses the guesswork required to evaluate the prospects of a business begun from scratch. But past records never eliminate risk. "Any fool can buy a business," said Royal Little, the former president of Textron. "The question is whether the business you buy will be successful." [3]

Mr. Little points up the sticky problem of evaluating a business to buy. To help resolve this problem, entrepreneurs should follow a procedure like the one in Exhibit 4-1. Note that we have already covered the first step in the procedure: the choice of product or service; we will discuss the remaining steps below.

UNDERSTANDING A SELLER'S MOTIVES

Sellers commonly hide their true motives for selling. They often give good rather than real reasons for selling. Some owners, seeing that technology may soon outdate their product or service, will offer such good reasons as they want to retire to California or they want to teach small business management at a local college. In most cases, though, fear underlies their desire to sell:

☐ Fear about the financial future of their business and family
☐ Fear that because they are company-rich though cash-poor, wealth built up over a lifetime would be lost
☐ Fear that technology, once simple, is now too complex to cope with
☐ Fear that the product or service is outdated[4]

Owners rarely express their fears; instead they hide them and stress the good reasons for selling. So buyers must search out the real reasons. Otherwise, they may lack any basis for deciding whether they can solve the problems of the business to be acquired. Among the valid business reasons why owners may want to sell are:

---

3. James H. Perry, *Acquisition-Merger Study* (Wilmington, Del.: Atlas Chemical Industries, December 13, 1963), p. 25.
4. Adapted from Myles L. Mace and George G. Montgomery, *Management Problems of Corporate Acquisitions* (Boston: Division of Research, Harvard Business School, 1962), pp. 37–56.

EXHIBIT 4-1

Deciding Whether to Buy an Existing Business

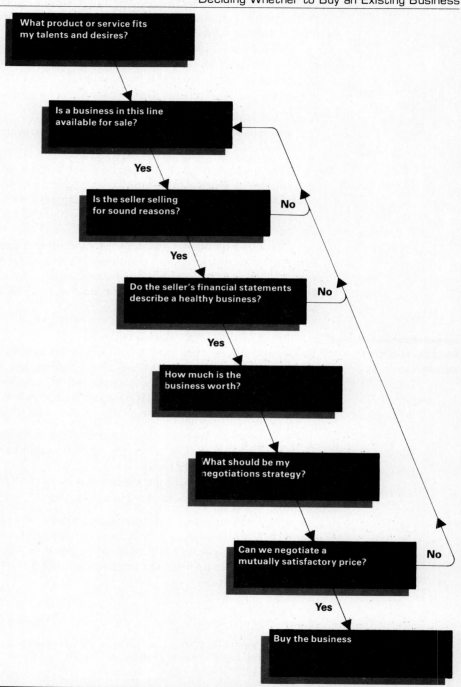

☐ **Personal and career reasons** Owners may wish to convert their holdings in a family-held business to cash.

☐ **Management succession** Owners may doubt the ability of younger men and women in the business to carry on profitably in the future.

☐ **One-person management** Owners may realize that their business is getting too big for them and that, because of their own managerial shortcomings, they cannot continue to strengthen the business themselves.[5]

EVALUATING FINANCIAL ASPECTS OF A BUSINESS

Let us now turn to the equally important problem of evaluating the financial aspects of a business. Financial evaluation raises the following questions:

☐ How healthy is the seller's business?
☐ How profitable has it been?
☐ How much is it worth?

Role of financial statements To help answer such questions, buyers should begin with the seller's financial statements. Many buyers accept blindly any financial statements bearing an accountant's signature. But remember that an accountant works chiefly as an advisor. Accountants may make suggestions but they cannot stop sellers from using any accounting method that best serves their own purposes.

The idea that businesspersons may more or less select the profit level of their business may seem a bit novel. But that is precisely what owners have the right to do. Few owners habitually juggle their books, but there are many ways by which profits can legally be overstated or understated. For example:

☐ Inventories may be accounted for in a half-dozen ways, each affecting profits differently.
☐ Assets such as machines and buildings may be written up or down in value.
☐ Depreciation may be speeded up or slowed down.

One buyer, speaking from bitter experience, said:

We have studied companies for months before making an acquisition. We have made audits, sent in our controller, paid attention to every financial detail—or so we thought. In each case we found out something after we took over that we did not know before the deal was closed. Some of the differences between what we thought we were buying and what we did buy were major. We have learned. But this we believe sincerely. Financial statements *don't* really answer any questions, they just allow you to ask them.[6]

The problems are especially severe in small family-owned businesses. Here, accounting practices tend to vary widely. Owners may take, for example, every possible deduction to cut taxes. They may use the fastest depreciation

5. Adapted from Mace and Montgomery, pp. 37–56.
6. Mace and Montgomery, p. 184.

allowances permitted by the Internal Revenue Service. And they may expense rather than capitalize their costs.

Auditing The buyer's first step in evaluating the financial aspects of a business should be to find out what adjustments should be made to the seller's financial statements. To do that, the buyer should get the seller's income statements and balance sheets for, say, the past five years. These statements show, at least on paper, the seller's financial health as well as profitability. Armed with these statements, the buyer should now examine, with a dentist's doubtful eye, such information as:

☐ Bills owed by customers—to make sure they are collectible
☐ Inventories—to make sure of their existence and their quality
☐ Equipment—to make sure every piece of equipment works and is not held together by baling wire
☐ Bank loans, bills owed to suppliers, and other debts—to make sure payment can be made
☐ Leases, licenses, franchises, and contracts—to make sure they can be transferred
☐ Public records—to make sure the seller is the titleholder of record, has no tax liens against the property, has no outstanding product warranties, has no payments due under purchase contracts, and the like

To carry out this audit, the buyer normally needs the help of two professionals: an accountant and a lawyer. Their services are indispensable. Although the fees of such professionals are high, their knowledge may spare the buyer the pain of buying the wrong business. Their judgment is by no means flawless, yet they reduce the odds of making the wrong choice.

SETTING A PRICE

Having thoroughly examined and questioned the financial records of a business, the buyer may now tackle the problem of pricing it. Any one of several methods may be used.

Capitalizing profits The method of *capitalizing profits* assumes that the entrepreneur, or buyer, is really buying a series of yearly profits when purchasing a business. It requires that entrepreneurs ask themselves: What am I willing to pay for the chance to earn a certain profit each year for, say, the next 10 years? To clarify the meaning of this question, let us go through this example:

EXAMPLE

Suppose a buyer estimates that a bookstore will earn $10,000 a year after taxes for the next 10 years. What should the buyer pay the seller for this opportunity? To answer this question, the buyer should first estimate what return to expect on the investment. Let us assume that she expects a 10 percent return on investment, after income taxes. Why does she expect 10 percent?

- ☐ Because the buyer has other opportunities that will return at least that much; or
- ☐ Because the buyer simply wants that much return even though the next best opportunity may be a bank that returns 5½ percent on savings; or
- ☐ Because it is the seller's current return on owners' equity

We can now arrive at the purchase price by capitalizing the buyer's estimate of average yearly future profits:

$$\$10,000 = 10\% \times \text{Purchase price}$$
$$\text{Purchase price} = \$10,000 \div 10\%$$
$$= \underline{\$100,000}$$

Capitalizing profits is a popular method, although it often gives misleading results. For one thing, buyers may estimate after-tax profits in any one of several ways, among them:

- ☐ *Last* year's profits only
- ☐ The average yearly profits for the *past* five years
- ☐ The average yearly *projected* profits for the next five years, estimated on the basis of past profits
- ☐ The average yearly *projected* profits for the next five years, based on the buyer's belief that his or her superior managerial skills will boost profits

The first two ways have little to recommend them in logic because they fail to take into account any changes that will occur as a result of the transfer of ownership. Although the third way does suggest that the future will be different, only the fourth method recognizes the key role of the entrepreneur. Generally, entrepreneurs buy a business only if convinced their managerial skills will improve the performance of the business.

Personal return With the capitalizing profits method, we looked at return on investment only from the business's viewpoint. Another method would be to look at return only from the perspective of the buyer's personal gain. This method stresses the cash flow—or its equivalent—that the buyer would earn by buying a business. The *personal return* method assumes that the entrepreneur stands separate and apart from the business and its profits.

The capitalizing profits method relates after-tax profit to total investment. But it is a flawed estimate of return in that entrepreneurs often invest little of their own money. It is often useful to think of return more as a personal return on just the entrepreneur's own investment. Following are some of the ways that entrepreneurs may earn a return on their investment:

- ☐ Perquisites, meaning such fringe benefits as an automobile, season tickets to football games, and the like
- ☐ Dividends and interest
- ☐ Salary

A seller offers her toy-making business to an entrepreneur for $100,000. After some study, the entrepreneur estimates that his yearly personal return would be:

$24,000 salary
  4,000 perquisites
  2,000 interest on long-term loan
$30,000 total personal return (cash flow or its equivalent)

Now let us assume that $100,000 is the seller's firm price for the business and that the entrepreneur plans to finance the purchase price in this way:

☐ $20,000 cash sale of stock to himself, keeping 60 percent of the business for himself
☐ $60,000 cash sale of stock to others, giving them just 40 percent of the business
☐ $20,000 long-term loan from the entrepreneur to the business

Now what would the entrepreneur's personal return on his investment be? His return may be estimated as follows:

Personal return = $30,000
Personal investment = $40,000 (including loan)

$$\text{Personal return on investment} = 75\% \text{ a year} \left(\frac{\$30,000}{\$40,000} \times 100 \right)$$

So far, discussion has focused on two evaluation methods. *Capitalizing profits* stresses after-tax profits expressed as a percentage of total business investment. *Personal return* stresses the entrepreneur's personal return expressed as a percentage of personal investment. Let us now describe one more method of evaluating a business.

Book value *Book value* is the fastest way to price a business. The buyer need only look at the seller's book value on the latest balance sheet. Book value is the difference between what a business possesses (assets) and what it owes (liabilities).

But this method is full of pitfalls, because it tells the buyer nothing about the true worth of a business. For example, a business may have a book value of $100,000 and still be worthless—because its assets are incapable of creating customers at a profit.

Even so, book value does offer a good beginning from which to estimate a purchase price. Remember, however, that the entrepreneur is really buying profitability and not assets such as land, buildings, and machines.

NEGOTIATING A PRICE

When entrepreneurs have estimated what to pay for a business, they have only just begun. They must now get down to the nitty-gritty of negotiating a price with the seller. Unless buyer and seller are of like mind, there may well be a wide gap between what the buyer believes the business is worth and what the seller believes it is worth.

Negotiations are rather like a game of chess. The buyer must think out a strategy, anticipate the seller's reactions, and develop effective countermoves all in advance. It is an intellectual exercise. In thinking out their strategy, buyers should begin by looking at numbers such as these:

☐ Ceiling price—meaning what the business is worth today with new and superior management
☐ Best price—meaning what the business is worth today with current management
☐ Book value—meaning what the business is worth today on paper

Sellers, of course, will come up with their own numbers. For reasons of sentiment if not greed, sellers are likely to inflate the asking price. For the buyer, no matter how well prepared, it is hard to see through such a practice.

Although negotiations may turn on numbers, the buyer must also look closely at the seller's human side. The seller may, for example, seek ironclad assurances that:

☐ The business name, which often is also the seller's name, will continue after the sale
☐ Certain employees, especially relatives, will enjoy continued job security
☐ Product or service quality will continue to be improved

It is the buyer's job to tell which human factors matter most to the sellers. They may balk unless convinced the buyer will meet such nonfinancial demands. Remember, sellers usually come from sturdy stock. They molded the business in their own image, and probably spent much of their life doing so. Often, they see the business as a personal monument. So it is only wise that the buyer should weigh the human aspects of the business with the financial aspects, as shown earlier in Exhibit 4-1.

However, human aspects do have their price. For example, if the buyer agrees to keep nonworking relatives on the payroll, there is a cost connected with such a concession. The buyer naturally should negotiate a lower purchase price to offset the added cost.

Even after all this give-and-take, buyer and seller may still be miles apart on price. Their ability to agree hinges on their skills at the negotiating table and on how they see each other's strengths and weaknesses.

STARTING FROM SCRATCH

This is the road traveled by the pure entrepreneur, for whom founding and molding a business poses a much greater challenge than taking over an existing business. Pure entrepreneurs seek a business that is truly their own creation, not somebody else's. They crave the creative satisfaction that comes from planting an idea and then making it grow into a strong and sturdy business.

To be sure, the risks are also greater. As mentioned earlier, newborn ventures are less likely to succeed than takeovers. With a takeover, there are records to give some idea of how healthy and profitable the business is. But, with a new venture, the best an entrepreneur can do is guess at what the profits will be. It may be intelligent guesswork, but it is guesswork nonetheless. There are some practical reasons why entrepreneurs may prefer to begin from scratch, among them:

☐ To avoid the ill effects of a prior owner's errors
☐ To choose their own banker, equipment, inventories, location, suppliers, and workers—without being hamstrung by commitments and policies made by the previous owner
☐ To create their own customers, loyal to them and not to somebody else

How does the entrepreneur evaluate the prospects of a new venture? According to the SBA, the first condition for business success is:

. . . the existence of a real, and not merely an apparent, business opportunity. This means that his venture must sell a product or a service needed and desired by consumers. It also means that his venture must draw enough customers who will buy at a price high enough and at a volume high enough to make a profit.[7]

To do that, entrepreneurs must study their market to estimate such things as total market, share of market, and sales revenues. This is difficult, even for businesses the size of General Motors and Du Pont, let alone the small entrepreneur. Still, it must be done.

With a takeover, entrepreneurs have past records that may tell them, for example, what the sales revenues were during the past five years. And more important, records may tell them whether revenues are going up, standing still, or going down. From such information, entrepreneurs may then predict their yearly revenues by assuming that revenues will either:

☐ Follow past trends; or—
☐ Outdo past trends

But when starting from scratch, entrepreneurs must put in a lot of effort to get information about their markets. Before estimating their revenues, for example, entrepreneurs should answer such questions as these:

☐ Who are my customers?
☐ Where are they?
☐ How many of them are there?
☐ What percentage will buy from me?
☐ At what price will they buy my product or service?
☐ In what quantities will they buy?

7. Adapted from U.S. Small Business Administration, *Success and Failure Factors in Small Business* (Washington, D.C.: U.S. Government Printing Office, 1964), p. 37.

Getting answers to these and related questions is called marketing research. As discussed in Chapter Six, marketing research probably is the most important step in the preparation of a business plan. More will be said about this tool in that chapter as well as in Chapter Eight on location and Chapter Fourteen on marketing.

INVENTION AND THE ENTREPRENEUR

Many entrepreneurs are also inventors. Often, such entrepreneurs must decide whether to apply for a patent, which would give them the exclusive right to their invention. Patenting a product, however, takes time and money. So before launching a new venture, entrepreneurs should weigh this cost against the possible benefits. To do that, they should answer such questions as these:

☐ Is my product patentable?
☐ Do I need or desire patent protection?
☐ How do I go about getting such protection?
☐ If I do get a patent, can I keep competitors from circumventing it?

To answer such questions, entrepreneurs should hire a patent attorney. Although entrepreneurs can get a patent themselves, the patenting process is so complex that they would be wise to leave it to a patent attorney. Summarized below are some guidelines prepared by the Patent, Trademark and Copyright Research Institute of George Washington University, guidelines that every inventor-entrepreneur should follow.

THE PATENTING PROCESS

Assume that an entrepreneur has invented a new hydraulic bumper device that absorbs automobile collisions up to 30 miles an hour. The law says that, to be patentable, the device must be new, useful, and "unobvious." If the new device appears to meet these standards, the entrepreneur should take the following steps:

Make a record The entrepreneur should fix the time the device was invented, for this may have to be proved later. The entrepreneur should also write out a description of the hydraulic bumper device and illustrate it with sketches. Finally, the description and illustrations should be signed and dated in the presence of knowledgeable witnesses.

Be sure the invention is practical The entrepreneur should learn enough about the automobile market to make sure there is some chance that the device will be used. Can it be made more cheaply than others on the market? Does it involve engineering problems for the manufacturer? Entrepreneurs should avoid saddling themselves with a patented product that will not create customers at a profit.

Get a patent attorney The entrepreneur should seek out an attorney from the *Directory of Registered Patent Attorneys and Agents*[8] which lists patent attorneys by state and city.

Have a search made The entrepreneur should ask the patent attorney to get copies of existing patents on hydraulic bumper devices that might stop the entrepreneur from getting a patent.

Prepare an application If the search suggests that this hydraulic bumper device is the first of its kind, the entrepreneur should now ask the patent attorney to prepare the formal application for a patent. The application must include:

- ☐ A petition, which is a request for a patent, addressed to the Commissioner of Patents of the U.S. Department of Commerce.
- ☐ The specification, which describes the entrepreneur's hydraulic bumper device, explains how it works, and describes how it is constructed.
- ☐ The claims of patentability, which define the entrepreneur's invention. Such claims are intended to tell how the hydraulic bumper device differs from all other such devices not only on the market but disclosed in patents, magazines, and other publications.
- ☐ An oath, which the entrepreneur signs before a notary public. The oath requires the entrepreneur to swear that he believes himself to be the first and sole inventor of this hydraulic bumper device.

The patenting process is complex, costly, and time-consuming. In fact, it takes an average of two years from the time the entrepreneur files the application with the Commissioner of Patents until the patent is received. And should the entrepreneur's patent application conflict with another patent, it may take much longer than two years.

Once the patent is granted, the entrepreneur has the "right to exclude others from making, using, or selling the invention throughout the United States."[9] Such patent rights last 17 years. After the patent expires, anyone may make, use, or sell the hydraulic bumper device without the entrepreneur's permission. The 17-year term may not be extended except by special act of Congress.

Meanwhile, competitors may try to design around the invention. To succeed, and thus avoid infringing on the entrepreneur's patent, a competitor need only eliminate a single element of the entrepreneur's patent claims.

PROBLEMS IN THE PATENT SYSTEM

When the Congress created the patent system in 1790, the system was designed "to encourage citizens to invent and to disseminate information on their inventions throughout the new nation for its overall good."[10]

8. This directory is available from the Superintendent of Documents of the U.S. Government Printing Office in Washington, D.C. 20402.
9. U.S. Department of Commerce, *Patents* (Washington, D.C.: U.S. Government Printing Office, 1972), p. 24.
10. Theodore L. Bowes, "Help for the Patent System," *NAM Reports,* March 18, 1974, p. 6.

Recently, the patent system has come under strong fire. Some federal judges, for example, believe that patents work against the public good. The Antitrust Division of the U.S. Department of Justice seems to share that view. They seem to be saying that monopolies are bad; and since patents are monopolies, patents are bad.

We believe otherwise. Without the incentive to invent, talented entrepreneurs are less likely to channel their creative energies into new products. In the words of Intellectual Property Owners, Inc.:

> The purpose of the patent system is to encourage inventions and their marketing by granting patent holders exclusive rights to their patentable products or processes. These rights are being subverted by a growing clash between the nation's patent and antitrust laws.
>
> There is a growing acceptance that patent use should be tested by antitrust law criteria—a viewpoint which severely and unnecessarily limits the manner in which a patent holder can control his property.
>
> Certain members of the judiciary and the U.S. Department of Justice . . . have succumbed to this interpretation, thus seriously eroding the patent incentive.[11]

How serious is this erosion of the patent incentive? One study for the U.S. Department of Commerce suggests that the incentive both to invent and innovate has slowed down dramatically. The following statistics show that many men and women have, indeed, lost their desire to invent:

☐ The number of patents granted yearly to Americans has dropped 21 percent since 1971.
☐ By contrast, the number of U.S. patents granted to foreigners has tripled.[12]

Whatever the reasons for this 21 percent drop, there is a strong need to restore the inventive spirit. At stake is a patent system that has encouraged entrepreneurs such as Jack Ryan to create new products. One of his inventions is a device that makes guns safe for policemen:

> A high percentage of all policemen who are shot are shot with their own guns, maintains Jack Ryan. "Public officers are inhibited because they're afraid their guns will be taken away."
>
> Given that problem, Mr. Ryan, inventor of the Barbie Doll . . . , came up with an ingenious solution: a safety device contained in an electronically coded ring on the shooter's third finger. "The gun cannot be fired unless the ring is touching the grip of the gun," says Mr. Ryan.
>
> Mr. Ryan, a transplanted New Yorker who lives in Los Angeles, also is the creator of numerous walking toys, Hot Wheels, an electric shaver for women, a hair dryer, and an all-weather bicycle braking system.[13]

11. Ibid.
12. Editorial, "American Ingenuity," Cleveland *Plain Dealer,* November 16, 1979, p. B-6.
13. "Barbie's Creator Makes Guns Safe," *People,* September 15, 1975, p. 50.

Would-be entrepreneurs may go into business for themselves in one of two ways: either by buying an existing business or by starting a business from scratch. But before choosing one or the other, entrepreneurs must first select a product or service. They must ask themselves the critical question: What business should I be in?

An intelligent answer requires entrepreneurs to look closely at their strengths and desires as well as at industry trends to see how well they mesh. Aspiring entrepreneurs must be attuned to these trends to better prepare themselves for the opportunities ahead.

Buying an existing business poses fewer risks than starting a venture from scratch. An existing business boasts a track record. A buyer may look at balance sheets, count inventories, inspect equipment, and observe customer traffic.

To price an existing business, prospective buyers may use personal return on investment or business return on investment as a yardstick of the business's worth. They may also use the book value of a business to arrive at a price, but book value is generally only a good starting point because it fails to take into account the business's potential to generate profits.

Once entrepreneurs have set a price, they must then engage in the delicate art of negotiation, taking into account both the financial and human needs of the seller.

To pure entrepreneurs, starting from scratch has the greater appeal. They prefer to pick their own product or service, their own location, workers, suppliers, and so on.

Many entrepreneurs double as inventors of products. Before launching their ventures, such entrepreneurs should decide carefully whether to patent their inventions. The patenting process is complex, costly, and time-consuming and usually requires the help of a patent attorney.

DISCUSSION AND REVIEW QUESTIONS

1 Why might you, as a would-be entrepreneur, prefer to buy an existing business rather than start from scratch?
2 Why does the seller of a business often give good rather than real reasons for wanting to sell?
3 Would you consult with an attorney and an accountant before buying a business? Why or why not?
4 Define these terms: *audit, capitalizing profits, perquisites, personal return on investment, business return on investment, book value, marketing research.*
5 Which is a better yardstick of investment worth, personal return on investment or business return on investment? Why?

mundane, to say the least. True, I was doing what I like best, taking photographs, but the psychic satisfaction just wasn't there.

"Nobody seemed to care about quality. It was annoying to work for bosses whose standards were so much lower than mine. There I was, a college graduate, reduced to taking photographs of stuff like broken hardware, test rigs, and new electronic instrumentation for TRW's advertising brochures. The pay was good, but I just couldn't stand it."

Against the advice of his family, Mr. Karabinus quit his job with TRW. "When I told my boss that I was quitting," says Mr. Karabinus, "he told me how sorry he was to see me leave. I reminded him that I had done the same kind of photographic work for 12 years. Just think, I had one year's experience 12 times over. That's not growth. Then, my boss reminded me that TRW had once laid off everybody else in my department but me. That's how much they thought of me and my work.

FINALLY BREAKING AWAY

"To go it alone, I knew my family had to support my decision completely, without compromise. They did, eventually, although at first they tried hard to discourage me from striking off on my own. But, after 12 years of leading a compromised life, there was no alternative for me. They saw that it was now or never for me." The year was 1974.

When he opened his doors for business in 1974, Mr. Karabinus was so cash-poor that he had to borrow all his start-up costs—$6,000 at 9 percent interest. "It was a five-year signature loan," says Mr. Karabinus. "I didn't even have to mortgage my house. I'm sure the bank was impressed by my ability to earn money—if I really had to—to pay off the loan. They trusted me." His beginning balance sheet appears in Exhibit 4A-1.

IN BUSINESS FOR HIMSELF

Two problems, besides financing, were (1) where best to locate and (2) how best to organize legally. After talking with a friend of his who was also an entrepreneur, Mr. Karabinus decided to locate in the basement of his home, until "my sales volume justified my moving away to larger quarters." He also decided to form a sole proprietorship, because "it's a lot simpler than forming a corporation."

Karabinus & Associates, Inc.

EXHIBIT 4A-1

Beginning Balance Sheet (April 15, 1974)

Assets		Equities	
Cash	$1,400	Accounts payable	$ 500
Photographic supplies	1,100	Long-term loan	6,000
Camera equipment	3,600	Owner's equity	0
Office equipment	300		
Other	100		
Total assets	$6,500	Total equities	$6,500

With $3,600 worth of camera equipment in his basement, Mr. Karabinus was fully equipped to satisfy customers in need of photographic services. "Of course, I never told the prospective clients I approached that my studio was next to the washer in my basement," says Mr. Karabinus. "If I had, they would have labeled me an amateur and not a professional. Believe me, image is important."

Indeed, for the first few months he spent almost all his time "beating the bushes," explaining his photographic services. He soon found that his experience at TRW worked against him. "There, all I did was industrial photography," says Mr. Karabinus. "When prospective clients asked me what experience I had, they questioned my ability to do photographic art rather than straight industrial stuff." He had defined his business in this way: **DEFINING HIS BUSINESS**

> To create photographic art for clients who do creative work, such clients as advertising agencies, public relations firms, and architectural design firms

Mr. Karabinus was bent on "creating photographic art rather than simply taking photographs. I wanted to do unusually creative things for clients, translating their words into visual images that evoke feelings. In a real sense, I saw myself as an interpreter, an artistic interpreter at that."

After six months of being on his own, Mr. Karabinus landed only one client. The client was an architect friend of his who needed photographs taken of several ice rinks that he had designed. His income from that one job was $753.10. "It's a good thing my wife was working," says Mr. Karabinus, "or I would have been on the bread line or out driving a taxicab at night. A big part of my problem was that I knew nothing about business. I never took a single course in small-business management when I was in college."

A professor friend of his recommended that he enroll in a small-business program at a local college. He did so, taking all six courses devoted to small-business management. "That helped a lot," says Mr. Karabinus. "The case studies really opened my eyes, gave me direction." **TURNAROUND**

One of the things he learned was the value of having a "thought-through marketing strategy. I had my priorities all wrong. I never sat down and figured out how best to attract clients." When he finally did, he came up with this strategy:

☐ To spend one-third of my time seeking new clients, mostly by visiting them sight unseen and armed with a sample portfolio of my best photographic art

☐ To update my list of existing and prospective clients each quarter, focusing on architectural firms and advertising agencies, public relations firms and downtown retail stores.

☐ To offer clients a broader range of services by forming an informal partnership with someone knowledgeable in advertising

☐ To project an image of professionalism by incorporating my business and by moving into more spacious quarters downtown

☐ To guarantee my performance, offering to do a job over if I fail to satisfy a client's needs

This strategy seemed to work. Two years later, in 1976, revenues increased from almost zero to $19,000; and, in 1977, revenues tripled, to $57,000. "I thought I was on my way," says Mr. Karabinus. "But, since 1977, my sales have been on a roller coaster ride."

☐ Revenues and profits since 1976 are graphed in Exhibit 4A-2.

☐ Condensed income statements appear in Exhibit 4A-3.

☐ A detailed income statement for 1980 appears in Exhibit 4A-4.

Mr. Karabinus is unsure why his "sales curve hasn't kept moving onward and upward. I'm doing all the things my professors told me to do. One thing I

PROBLEM ANALYSIS

Karabinus & Associates, Inc.

EXHIBIT 4A-2

Sales Revenues and Profits by Year

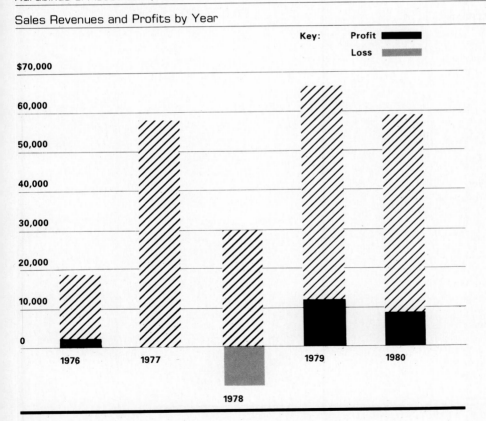

Key: Profit ▬▬ Loss ▨▨

Karabinus & Associates, Inc.

Condensed Income Statements (1976 through 1980)

	1976	1977	1978	1979	1980
Sales revenues	$19,170	$57,970	$30,240	$66,720	$58,730
Cost of sales	11,430	27,470	12,620	27,470	21,750
Gross profit	$ 7,740	$30,500	$17,620	$39,250	$36,980
Operating expenses	6,290	30,270	27,770	26,990	28,020
Operating profit	$ 1,450	$ 230	($10,150)	$12,260	$ 8,960

Karabinus & Associates, Inc.

Detailed Income Statement (1980)

Sales revenues		
Laboratory services	$20,160	
Advertising	19,210	
Commercial	10,090	
Industrial	3,670	
Materials	1,530	
Architectural	1,220	
Miscellaneous	2,850	$58,730
Cost of sales		21,750
Gross profit		$36,980
Operating expenses		
Salaries and benefits	$ 7,830	
Supplies	4,790	
Rent	4,410	
Maintenance	2,500	
Travel and entertainment	2,220	
Interest	2,130	
Professional services	1,510	
Utilities	1,190	
Insurance	750	
Dues and seminars	560	
Licenses	100	
Advertising	30	
Depreciation	0	28,020
Operating profit		$ 8,960

remember came from my small-business professor. He kept stressing the importance of finding a niche in the marketplace, offering clients what your competitors aren't. That's why I guarantee performance on a no-questions-asked basis.

"In an industry like mine, competition is fierce. Everybody thinks he's an expert. Anybody with a $199.50 camera can set up shop and call himself a professional photographer. It's these amateurs who muddy the waters. Most people don't realize the years it takes to be a true professional." See Exhibit 4A-5 for the quality of Mr. Karabinus's work.

One avenue that Mr. Karabinus has recently pursued is an "informal partnership" with an advertising agency run by Jeffrey Wershing. The agency is now located in a corner of the same suite of rooms that Mr. Karabinus occupies.

"Working with Jeff is an ideal arrangement," says Mr. Karabinus. "I've expanded my market. I can now say to a prospective client that if you want an advertising brochure done, I can do the *whole* thing for you—the photographic art, the layout, the written word, everything. Believe me, the advertising industry can be lucrative; its potential is limitless. For example:

A competing photographer working for an advertising agency recently shot two rolls of 35-mm film. He charged the agency $9,000 for just a half hour of shooting. After deducting the cost of the model and the set, his income was $4,000. Set-up time, however, took a week.

"Other photographers I know in town get as much, if not more. But it takes time to get yourself established. Now that I'm in partnership with an advertising agency, I'm sure that I'll land more clients, especially those willing and able to pay $9,000 for just a half hour of shooting." Turn to Exhibit 4A-6 for a description of a typical job for a client.

Another recent change is the hiring of Chrissie Spuhler. Her duties include manning the receptionist desk, keeping the books, and keeping after slow-paying customers. "I hired her because she's a self-starter," says Mr. Karabinus. "She doesn't have to be told what to do. I'm away so much I needed somebody just to watch the shop."

Although his books are now up-to-date, Mr. Karabinus rarely looks at them. "I'm just too busy getting jobs and then getting them done," says Mr. Karabinus. He vows to "change my attitude and do some hard planning. I should have a budget but I keep putting it off. If my old professor ever saw how I run my little business, he would have cardiac arrest."

1 Comment on Mr. Karabinus's entrepreneurial and managerial qualities.
2 What questions would you raise after analyzing Mr. Karabinus's financial statements?
3 Comment on the quality of Mr. Karabinus's marketing research and his marketing plan.

4 Would you invest in Mr. Karabinus's venture? Why?

5 If Mr. Karabinus came to you for advice on how best to boost sales, what would you suggest he do now? Why?

Karabinus & Associates, Inc.

Examples of Karabinus Quality

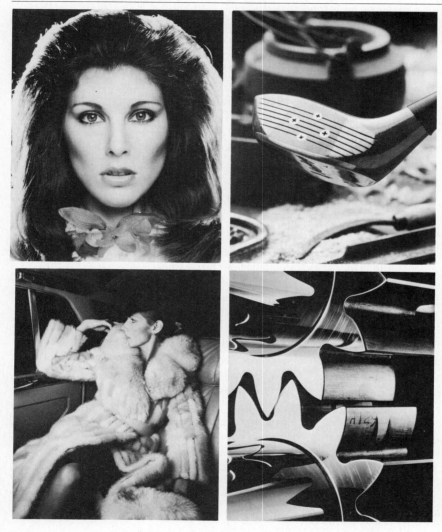

Description of a Typical Photographic Assignment

A typical job begins with the client seeking out a photographer, either with a layout in hand specifying the photographs to be taken, or with an idea in mind. In essence, the client seeks a photographer who can contribute creatively to the client's concept. One such job is described below, in Mr. Karabinus's own words:

> The job called for a fashion spread to be shot on location. My client's art director already had a location chosen but wanted to confer with me before going ahead.
>
> The location was a small, private museum-to-be, not yet ready to be opened to the public. It had fire engines, old cars, farm buildings, a general store, and a work shop stocked with antiques.
>
> The next step was to select the live models, and set the date. Because of conflicts in scheduling, my client and I chose to shoot the job on a weekend.
>
> The amount of preparation is awesome on a shoot like this. Everything that might be needed must be packed and brought with you. Everything from coffee pots and lunch meat to clothes pins and masking tape. For this particular job, we even brought an auxiliary power unit to run the strobes so we could shoot at night in the woods.
>
> We started at 8 A.M. and got back about 11 P.M. About six hours were spent actually taking pictures. I then processed the film and made contact proof sheets.
>
> Next came the long process of selecting the best photographs. I then sized the photographs to fit the proportions of the layout that my client and I had worked out jointly. The advertising copy was then set in the selected type face.
>
> Last, upon the client's approval, I sent the layout to the engraver for separations. Color keys were pulled for client approval, and the final run was made. All told, 100,000 copies of the layout were printed.

CASE 4B

GUS DuPREA SHOE STORE*

In January 1981, Gus DuPrea, a shoe salesman for a big department store in Chicago, was discussing his future with the sales manager of a shoe manufacturer. Mr. DuPrea confided:

> I'm unhappy. I'm making a living, but I spend $400 a week to live and this doesn't leave anything to put away. My wife and I aren't getting any

*Source: Case prepared by Alan S. Marcus of Taylor Business Institute in New York City.

younger. I've been in this store 17 years now. I'd like to have my own store, be my own boss. Do you know of any shoe stores for sale?

The sales manager told Mr. DuPrea of a store in Elko, Indiana, whose owner wanted to sell out:

The man is retiring to Florida as soon as he can find a customer. He has already sold his other properties in town. His name is Tom Watkins, and he's been in Elko all his life. He has the only shoe store there; about all the town can handle. Tom serves the townspeople and the majority of farmers for about 10 miles around.

The nearest towns are Fisher and Attumwa, both about 17 miles away, and about the same size as Elko. It's a growing area—about a 10 percent rise in population every decade. There are a few small new industries in Elko.

Tom told me about the store a couple of months ago. You could buy it for $40,000 in cash. Tom says there is no point in saying how much he earns from the store. He'll give anyone all the facts and let him see for himself that, with the lower cost of living in Elko, there's enough in it to make a good living and still put a little aside.

A week later, Mr. DuPrea drove to Elko and visited the store. It was not fancy, but he told his wife later, "it's a nice store. It sure looked good compared to the other stores in Elko."

Elko is the Umbagawa county seat. The townspeople number 1,776 and make up one-third of the population of the trading area. Most business activities there center on servicing the food industry. The town has two canneries, shippers, a flour mill, farm machinery dealers, and food stores.

All stores in Elko are open from 8:00 A.M. to 5:00 P.M. on Monday, Tuesday, and Thursday. Stores are open till 1 P.M. on Wednesdays, except during the fishing season, when they are closed on Wednesdays. Fridays and Saturdays are late nights, with stores staying open until 9:00 P.M.

The store is located on a busy corner of town. It has two display windows. The larger one, on Main Street, faces most of the everyday shopping traffic. Mr. Watkins usually had about 25 pairs of shoes in this window.

Soon after they met, Mr. Watkins gave Mr. DuPrea these figures:

Inventory at original retail	$50,400
Average fixed expenses	$ 9,600 per year
Store fixtures	$ 8,000
Average gross margin	35%
Expenses variable with sales	12%
Average turnover per year	2.5

Mr. Watkins took Mr. DuPrea around town and found a house for sale in a suitable neighborhood. On the level that Mr. DuPrea planned to live, he thought he could get by on $1,200 a month in Elko.

Mr. Watkins said he was so well-known that he did not have to advertise.

A credit check later disclosed that Mr. Watkins did indeed have an unusually good reputation.

When he returned to Chicago, Mr. DuPrea figured that his total assets could be converted into $48,000 in cash if necessary.

1 What should Mr. DuPrea do?
2 What range of income and personal savings is Mr. DuPrea likely to receive from the store?
3 Imagine that you are an experienced retailer and an old friend of Mr. DuPrea. Assuming that you know as much about the offer as Mr. DuPrea, what questions would you raise?

CASE 4C   **VIKING, INC.**

Ollie Ness has organized a new venture to make antipollution equipment for the chemical, oil, and steel industries. To finance his venture, Mr. Ness has raised $300,000 by selling stock to friends, $200,000 by borrowing from a bank (long-term), and by investing $50,000 himself. In exchange for that sum of money, he received 60 percent ownership of the new venture. The remaining shareholders, who invested $300,000, received 40 percent ownership.

Mr. Ness expects to draw a salary of $30,000 the first year and to pay dividends of $5,000 that year. He values the use of a company car and other perquisites at $4,000 a year. He expects a net profit of $50,000 the first year.

1 What is Mr. Ness's personal return on investment the first year?
2 What is the business return on investment?
3 Which of these two estimates of return is the better measure of Mr. Ness's performance? Explain.

CHAPTER FIVE

FRANCHISING

questions for mastery

how important is franchising to the economy?

what are the different kinds of franchising systems?

what are the advantages and pitfalls of franchising?

how valuable is a lawyer's help in evaluating a franchise opportunity?

how does one best evaluate a franchise opportunity?

Help me with knowledge . . .

Robert Browning

I n Chapter Four we discussed two major ways of going into business for oneself: either to start from scratch or to buy out an existing venture. A third major way is to buy a franchise.

Today, few business topics spark more controversy than franchising. Opinions about its place in the economy differ sharply: some see franchising as the last frontier of the would-be entrepreneur, and others see it as a fraud. Neither of these two extreme views is correct—the truth lies somewhere in between. This chapter will try to put franchising in proper perspective.

HISTORY OF FRANCHISING

Contrary to popular opinion, franchising did not begin with the boom of fast-food franchises like McDonald's in the 1950s. In fact, there is little that is new about franchising. Its beginnings date back to the early 1800s. However, it was in 1898 that modern franchising got its first push, when General Motors began franchising dealerships. Still alive and well today, their franchise system boasts 12,000 dealers scattered throughout the country. Here is how franchising works:

EXAMPLE

> The franchised new-car dealer signs a contract with one of the car manufacturers to serve as its representative in an area. The franchised dealer then sells only that line of new cars—Buicks, for example. In some areas, the franchisee may have a double franchise and sell, say, Gremlins made by American Motors as well as Buicks made by General Motors.
> ■

Similar franchise systems were created by Rexall in 1902 and Howard Johnson in 1926—as were many oil, grocery, motel, and fast-food franchises during those years. So great has been its growth that most industries have already been touched by franchising. According to the National Federation of Independent Business, about 10 percent of the nation's 14 million businesses now run under some kind of franchise agreement. And as shown in Exhibit 5-1, franchising accounts for 32 percent of all retail sales.

DEFINITION OF FRANCHISING

There is no one best definition of franchising. Borrowed from the French, *franchising* originally meant being free from slavery. Today, it has several other meanings, depending on the industry. Some persons even call franchising an industry, as if it were a product or service. But a typical franchise is simply an agreement between seller and buyer—an agreement that permits the buyer (franchi*see*) to sell the product or service of the seller (franchi*sor*). The International Franchise Association defines it this way:

> A franchise is a continuing relationship between the franchisor and the franchisee in which the sum total of the franchisor's knowledge, image, success, manufacturing, and marketing techniques are supplied to the franchisee for a consideration.

EXHIBIT 5-1

Importance of Franchising

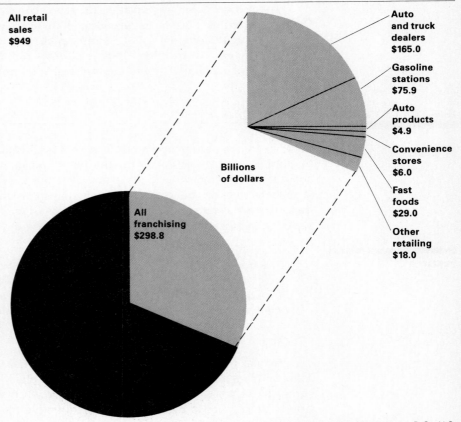

All retail
sales
$949

Billions
of dollars

All
franchising
$298.8

Auto
and truck
dealers
$165.0

Gasoline
stations
$75.9

Auto
products
$4.9

Convenience
stores
$6.0

Fast
foods
$29.0

Other
retailing
$18.0

In 1980, franchising accounted for an estimated 32 percent of all retail sales.

Source: U.S. Department of Commerce, *Franchising in the Economy: 1978–1980* (Washington, D.C.: U.S. Government Printing Office, 1980), p. 12.

The franchisee thus gets a ready-made business. And therein lies the appeal of franchising. The franchisee does not have to build up a business step by step as must the entrepreneur who starts from scratch. Rather, the franchisee's business is established overnight. And it probably will be a carbon copy of all the others in the franchise chain.

For a fee, the typical franchisee gets expert help that would otherwise be too costly or beyond reach—such help as:

☐ Marketing strategy, with special emphasis on advertising
☐ Initial employee and management training
☐ Store design and equipment purchasing
☐ Standardized policies and procedures
☐ Centralized purchasing with savings
☐ Continued management counseling

☐ Location selection and advice
☐ Negotiation of leases
☐ Financing

In essence, franchising thrives because it merges the incentive of owning a business with the management skills of big business. And personal ownership is one of the best incentives yet created to spur hard work.

Franchising may benefit not only the franchisee but also the franchisor. For example, it may enable the franchisor to grow rapidly by using other people's (the franchisee's) money. That is largely how giant franchisors like McDonald's and Baskin-Robbins have mushroomed into billion-dollar businesses in so short a time.

THE STRENGTH OF FRANCHISING

The International Franchising Association predicts that franchising will soon become the dominant form of retailing. Franchising also is strong in services, and to a lesser degree, in manufacturing. The following statistic from the U.S. Department of Commerce underscores its role in the economy: in 1980, there were 488,000 franchises with sales revenues estimated at $338 billion.[1]

Until recently, the word *franchising* was synonymous with fast-food outlets like McDonald's and Chicken Delight. But today franchising has invaded most industries. Name a product or service, and chances are there is someone who franchises it. Even old-line companies like Sears or Montgomery Ward have joined the ranks of franchisors. These two companies have franchised 1,800 small-town catalogue order outlets since the mid-1960s.

Some idea of franchising's role in the economy may be gained from a partial list of blue-chip franchisors:

☐ Hertz car rental agencies and General Motors dealerships
☐ Exxon service stations, Goodyear Tire distributorships, and AAMCO transmission shops
☐ Holiday Inn motels and Ralston Purina restaurants
☐ Coca-Cola bottling plants

Franchises are offered in industries as different as art galleries and shoe-repair shops, dating bars and home computers. Franchising has even spread to services for weight watching and bed-wetting control.

KINDS OF FRANCHISING SYSTEMS

Franchise systems take many forms. These systems are by no means limited to such chains as McDonald's and Holiday Inn. For example, franchise systems may exist between:

1. "Franchising Opportunities for the Entrepreneur," *Venture,* November 1980, p. 54.

☐ Manufacturer and manufacturer
  Manufacturer and wholesaler
  Manufacturer and retailer
☐ Wholesaler and wholesaler
  Wholesaler and retailer
☐ Retailer and retailer
☐ Services and services

Let us look first at franchise systems between manufacturer and manufacturer. Suppose a chemical manufacturer patents a new way to make ammonia. Because this process cuts the cost of ammonia manufacture by, say, 20 percent, other chemical manufacturers may want to use it. So the chemical manufacturer who invented the process may license the others to use it. The license would give them the right to use the new process in return for a fee called a *royalty.* In this case, the licensor is really the franchisor; the licensee is the franchisee.

Another franchise system might be between manufacturer and retailer. The best example of such a system is that between automobile manufacturers and retail automobile dealerships. Still another example is service stations, which lease space and sell gasoline and oil bought under contract from oil refiners like Exxon. Franchise systems between manufacturer and wholesaler, wholesaler and wholesaler, and wholesaler and retailer operate in a similar way.

However, retail and service franchise systems like McDonald's or Holiday Inn differ markedly from manufacturer or wholesaler systems because the franchisee is really an extension of the franchisor. In such chains, each franchise resembles a company outlet, the main difference being that the franchisor invested the franchisee's money to create the outlet instead of its own money.

In contrast, with a manufacturer-to-manufacturer franchising system, franchisees are relatively autonomous. Such franchisees are all but free to do as they please. Policies and procedures may be of their own making; even the shop and equipment may be of their own design. That would not be the case with such service-to-service franchise systems as McDonald's.

MYTHS OF FRANCHISING

THE MYTH OF INSTANT WEALTH

The fast growth of franchising has spawned a number of myths. Perhaps the most popular one is the promise of instant riches. Get-rich-quick schemes abound. Many prey on lower-income men and women looking for a way to become rich without having to work for someone else. Take this example:

I could tell this was no ordinary Corvette. The body was covered with blue and yellow velvet. The interior was finished floor-to-roof with blue and yellow fur. Two men in flashy double-knit suits leaned against the car's long hood and snagged lunchtime passersby as they crossed an intersection in downtown Washington.

"How would you like to be able to afford a car like this?" one of the men asked me. "Sure," I answered. "Great. Give me a call," he said, and produced a card that read: "Above-average earnings for the average person. Put yourself in the successful 2%. Opportunities unlimited."[2]

These two men were franchisees of Koscot Interplanetary, Inc., selling mink-oil-based cosmetics. For $5,000, Koscot would sell an investor a distributorship. The investor could then earn money in one of two ways:

☐ Hire a sales force to sell Koscot cosmetics door-to-door
☐ Sign up other investors at $5,000 each, keeping a $2,650 commission

The two men had chosen the second way as the easier path to riches. The trouble with such a scheme is that somebody inevitably gets hurt. It benefits the few franchisees who get in early, but hurts those who get in later.

The foregoing example is extreme. But it does dramatize how unethical operators may take in the innocent with overblown promises of instant riches. And it does show why franchising sometimes swirls with controversy. As the Bank of America points out:

> To its protagonists, franchising is the last frontier of independent businesspeople and the most dynamic distribution method for bringing goods and services to market ever devised.
>
> To its severest critics, it is a fraudulent gimmick to separate the small investor from his funds—and worse.[3]

THE MYTH OF INDEPENDENCE

Another myth is that franchisees are independent businesspersons. In many cases, this simply is not so. Franchisees generally are not free to run their business as they see fit, as mentioned earlier. They often are hamstrung by the franchisor's policies, standards, and procedures. Nor do franchisors encourage their franchisees to improve the way they do business. The Bank of America says:

> The best franchisee, as far as many franchisors are concerned, is someone who is smart enough to understand and operate the system, but not smart enough to try to improve on it.
>
> One franchisor describes the ideal franchisee as the sergeant type— midway between the general who gives the orders, and the private who merely follows them. People who want their own business to escape taking orders from others frequently see franchising as the answer. They are subsequently frustrated by their lack of autonomy. For example:

2. Rudy Maxa, "Products Prove Second to Selling Right to Sell," Cleveland *Plain Dealer,* January 1, 1973, p. 6-B.
3. Reprinted with permission from Bank of America, NT&SA, "Franchising," *Small Business Reporter,* Vol. 9, No. 9, Copyright 1975, 1978. This report is currently out of print.

□ The paper work involved in preparing sales records and reports may be as extensive as that required of a paid manager of a chain outlet.

□ Inventory mix may be spelled out without regard to customer preferences.

□ The franchisee may dislike the franchisor's advertising campaign but have no say in the matter.[4]

EVALUATING A FRANCHISE OPPORTUNITY

In a real sense, franchisees do not start from scratch. When they buy a franchise, entrepreneurs generally receive a ready-made business. And all they need do is follow the franchisor's instructions on how best to do business. Instructions cover a host of details including:

□ What product or service to sell
□ How to sell it
□ How to control costs
□ What reports to prepare
□ How long to stay open each day

Nevertheless, before buying a franchise, entrepreneurs should first make sure that their decision to become a franchisee is sound. Outlined in Exhibit 5-2 is a step-by-step procedure that entrepreneurs should follow. Searching out likely franchises is, of course, the first step. The next step, having to do with self-analysis, is especially critical. It calls for entrepreneurs to match their skills and desires to the franchise opportunity, by answering such questions as these:

□ Do I really believe in the franchisor's product or service?
□ Do I really want to be that kind of person, do that kind of work, run that kind of franchise?

CHECKLIST

These questions are just a beginning. To do a thorough job of analyzing a franchise opportunity, entrepreneurs should next go through a checklist like the one in Exhibit 5-3. This checklist of 25 questions may spare the entrepreneur the pain of making the wrong decision, or of being victimized by unkept promises—as was this franchisee:

Until 1970, Caleb Moberly was the colonel in charge of all military payrolls for the Air Force. Still he wondered "whether I could run a business of my own." It cost him $30,000 and more work than he had ever done before to find out.

Mr. Moberly and his wife opened a United Rent-All equipment center in a fast-growing suburb of Denver in October 1971. For the first year and a half, they worked seven days a week from 8 A.M. until 6 P.M. They now take occasional days off, but, he says, "you never get the work done."

4. Ibid., p. 3.

EXHIBIT 5-2

Procedure for Evaluating Franchise Opportunities

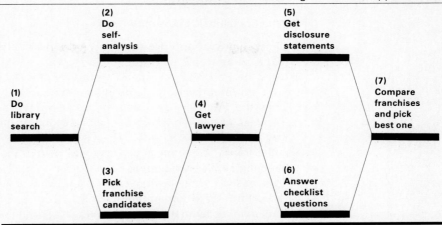

Yet it's not the hard work that bothers him—even if their income this year of nearly $30,000 strikes him as inadequate—because he expects to sell out for a profit of over $100,000 within a year and go back to playing golf. He frowns at the memory of promises he says were broken by the franchisor.

"At first I didn't get the help I was told I'd get," he says. "The coordinator they sent to help me get started was completely inept." The company failed to deliver all the items for their inventory by the time the store opened, Mrs. Moberly complains.

They find United Rent-All better to work with now. "They have an excellent system for keeping track of what is in stock and how much is earned on each item, and their public image is good," they say.[5]

These entrepreneurs might have avoided the problem of unkept promises had they gone through a checklist like the one in Exhibit 5-3. Fortunately, their franchise later prospered. But often, franchisees make costly mistakes in judgment. The entrepreneur's best defense against such mistakes is the checklist.

GETTING DISCLOSURE STATEMENTS

To evaluate a franchise opportunity, entrepreneurs should ask the franchisor for its *disclosure statement*. A priceless tool, this statement should enable the entrepreneur to answer many of the questions posed in the checklist. It should also enable the entrepreneur to:

☐ Compare one franchise with another
☐ Understand what to expect from the franchisor
☐ Estimate the risks and costs involved

5. Michael Creedman, "A Franchise Is a Hard Way to Get Rich," *Money*, September 1973, p. 36.

EXHIBIT 5-3

On the Franchise Opportunity Itself

1 Did your lawyer approve the franchise contract after he studied it paragraph by paragraph?
2 Does the franchise call upon you to take any steps which are, according to your lawyer, unwise or illegal in your state, county, or city?
3 Does the franchise give you an exclusive territory for the length of the franchise or can the franchisor sell a second or third franchise in your territory?
4 Is the franchisor connected in any way with any other franchise companies handling similar merchandise or services?
5 If the answer to the last question is yes, what is your protection against this second franchisor organization?
6 Under what circumstances and at what cost can you pull out of the franchise contract?
7 If you sell your franchise, will you be paid for your goodwill, or will the goodwill you have built into the business be lost by you?

On the Franchisor

1 For how many years has the franchisor been in business?
2 Does the franchisor have a reputation for honesty and fair dealing among the local entrepreneurs holding its franchise?
3 Has the franchisor shown you any certified figures indicating exact net profits of one or more going franchises, which you *yourself* checked with the franchisee?
4 Will the franchisor help you with:
   (a) A management training program?
   (b) An employee training program?
   (c) A public relations program?
   (d) Merchandising ideas?
   (e) Financing?
5 Will the franchisor help you find a good location for your franchise?
6 Is the franchisor adequately financed so that it can carry out its stated plan of financial help and expansion?
7 Is the franchisor a one-man company or a larger company with a trained and experienced management team—so that there would always be an experienced person as its head?
8 Exactly what can the franchisor do for you which you cannot do for yourself?
9 Has the franchisor investigated you carefully enough to assure itself that you can successfully operate one of their franchises at a profit both to them and to you?

EXHIBIT 5-3 (cont.)

On You—the Franchisee

1 How much equity capital will you need to buy the franchise and operate it until your sales revenues equal your expenses?
2 Where are you going to get the equity capital you need?
3 Are you prepared to give up some independence of action to get the advantages offered by the franchise?
4 Do *you* really believe you have the ability, training, and experience to work smoothly and profitably with the franchisor, your employees, and your customers?
5 Are you ready to spend much or all of the rest of your business life with this franchisor, offering its product or service to your public?

On Your Market

1 Have you made any study to find out whether the product or service which you propose to sell under franchise has a market in your territory at the prices you will have to charge?
2 Will the population in your territory increase, remain static, or decrease over the next five years?
3 Will the demand for the product or service you are considering be greater, about the same, or less in five years?
4 What competition exists in your territory for the product or service from nonfranchise firms and franchise firms?

Source: U.S. Department of Commerce, *Franchise Opportunities Handbook* (Washington, D.C.: U.S. Government Printing Office, July 1980), p. xxix.

All franchisors are now required by federal law to provide disclosure statements to entrepreneurs in each state. The law requires that such statements give detailed information on 20 subjects, a sampling of which follows:

☐ The financial statements of the franchisor
☐ A description of the lawsuits in which the franchisor and its officers, directors, and management personnel have been involved
☐ Information about the initial franchise fee and other initial payments that are required to obtain the franchise
☐ A description of the involvement of any celebrities or public figures in the franchise
☐ A list of the names and addresses of other franchisees
☐ A complete statement of the basis for any profit claims made to the franchisee, including the percentage of existing franchises that have actually achieved the profits that are claimed

Entrepreneurs should rely on a lawyer to get through the fine print of the franchisor's disclosure statement. It would be a mistake for entrepreneurs to assume that the statement tells everything there is to know about the franchisor. Nor will it necessarily tell all about the consequences of signing a franchise contract.

So it is vital for entrepreneurs to get the help of a lawyer familiar with the legal workings of franchising. Such lawyers can also inform entrepreneurs fully about their legal rights before signing the franchise contract. Equally important, lawyers can advise entrepreneurs about their legal obligations to the franchisor. But perhaps the lawyer's most creative role is to suggest changes in the contract that would better serve and protect the entrepreneur's interest. According to the U.S. Department of Commerce:

> At the very least, you should be certain that every promise you consider important made by the franchisor and its representative is stated clearly in writing in the franchise contract. If such promises do not clearly appear in the contracts you sign, you may have no legal remedy if they are not kept; and you may be legally obligated to comply with your own continuing obligations under the franchise contract.[6]

THE FRANCHISE CONTRACT

The contract is the backbone of any franchisor-franchisee relationship. Failure to understand its fine print may cause the entrepreneur grief and heartache later on. It is especially critical to ask the question: Under what conditions may the entrepreneur pull out of the franchise contract and what would it cost to pull out?

Entrepreneurs should make sure they understand what they stand to lose or gain if they should decide to pull out or if the franchisor should decide to cancel the franchise contract. Typically, franchisors reserve the right to cancel a franchise contract if the franchisee:

☐ Fails to reach revenue goals
☐ Tarnishes the image of other outlets by giving poor service to customers
☐ Fails to provide required weekly or monthly progress reports to the franchisor

Other, though less precise, reasons for canceling a contract include:

☐ The franchisee's failure to work hard and for long hours
☐ The franchisee's failure to work smoothly with the franchisor
☐ The franchisee's misuse of the franchisor's name and equipment

Typically, franchise rights run one to five years, with options to renew. An exception is McDonald's, which sells for $300,000 the right to operate a franchise at a specific site for 20 years. When the contract expires, the franchisee must put up *another* $300,000 or so to continue operating at the same site.

6. U.S. Department of Commerce, *Franchise Opportunities Handbook* (Washington, D.C.: U.S. Government Printing Office, July 1980), p. xxvii.

Unlike McDonald's, some franchise rights run indefinitely—but generally the contract has a clause that gives either the franchisor or the franchisee the right to cancel on 30 to 60 days' notice.

SELLING AN EXISTING FRANCHISE

A problem could arise, however, if the franchisee should decide to sell out before the contract runs out. Such a sale generally cannot be carried out without the franchisor's approval. This seems a distinct drawback of franchising, as explained below:

> The right to sell or transfer the franchise determines whether or not a franchisee is truly an independent owner of a business, or merely an affiliate within a chain. Contract provisions should reflect your rights to build a profitable business and then sell it on the open market. The reputable company will do everything to protect its trademarks, patents, and uniquely developed services, but it should not—and must not—deprive you of the right to sell or transfer *your* business.[7]

Another sore point is the price at which a franchisee may be forced to sell the franchise, either to another entrepreneur or back to the franchisor. The franchisor often forces the franchisee to sell at a price lower than its value to a prospective buyer. For example, a franchise may be worth $50,000 more than its book value to a prospective buyer. Who deserves the gain of $50,000 if the franchise is sold, the franchisor or the franchisee?

Franchisors may claim it was their image that generated the $50,000 gain. Franchisees may counter that it was their hard work that created all that gain. To avoid such a problem, entrepreneurs should make sure they have the right to sell the franchise at the highest possible price and that they can pocket the entire selling price. McDonald's has an enlightened attitude in this regard:

> In 1980, a franchisee sold his McDonald's restaurant for $500,000. Its value on the books was about $100,000. The franchisee got to keep the entire capital gain of $400,000. McDonald's had an interesting though imprecise way of estimating the purchase price of the franchise. They took the most recent year's revenues and multiplied by half.

FRANCHISOR'S TRAINING PROGRAM

Perhaps the most critical question to consider in evaluating a franchisor relates to the franchisor's training program. Reputable franchisors like McDonald's and Baskin-Robbins provide intensive training programs, including on-the-job training at an existing outlet. Some franchisors even provide refresher training after the franchisee has been operating for some time.

The main goal of these training programs is to supply entrepreneurs with the management skills they need to run a franchise profitably. Without such training, the typically inexperienced franchisee is likely to flounder and fail. So

7. Robert M. Dias & Stanley I. Gurnick, *Franchising: The Investor's Complete Handbook* (New York: Hastings House, 1969), p. 89.

entrepreneurs should make sure their franchise contract tells precisely how and where training will take place. McDonald's, for example, provides a three-step training program:

☐ **Instruction at a training school** McDonald's has a $2 million school called Hamburger University near Chicago. After a three-week cram course in how to run a franchise profitably, franchisees receive a degree in *Hamburgerology*. Courses cover everything from how to mop the floor to how to post a ledger.

☐ **Instruction at an existing franchisee's site** McDonald's has every new franchisee spend at least one week with an established franchisee. While there, the new franchisee works at every job, from sweeping the parking lot to waiting on customers.

☐ **Instruction at own site** McDonald's provides franchisees with an experienced instructor to tide them over the rough edges of start-up. The instructor works side by side with the franchisee for at least one week—or until such time as the instructor is sure the franchisee can go it alone.

COSTS TO THE FRANCHISEE

Entrepreneurs should be sure to take pains to estimate what a franchise would cost. Often, franchisors fail to tell entrepreneurs the full story. A franchisor may say, for example, that "all you need is $10,000 to buy a wall-cleaning franchise." But, the $10,000 may cover just the right to use the franchisor's trade name and way of doing business. Hidden may be such costs as equipment, lease deposits, and even the signs needed to open the franchise—not to mention the money to finance inventory or to finance customers who buy on credit.

Entrepreneurs may avoid such problems by preparing a business plan, as discussed in Chapter Six. The cash budget, a key part of the business plan, will identify all cash costs, including the franchise fee, working capital, building and equipment costs, and royalties:

☐ **The franchise fee** This gives the franchisee the right to do business at a specific address or in a specific territory. Depending on the franchise, this fee may range from zero to millions of dollars. As mentioned earlier, McDonald's charges a fee of $300,000.

☐ **Working capital** This covers the money needed to buy inventory, pay salespersons, make lease payments, and the like until customers buy and pay up.

☐ **Building and equipment costs** The entrepreneur may pay for these in full or in part. Some franchisors lease both building and equipment to the franchisee, thus sparing the entrepreneur the need to make a large initial cash outlay. McDonald's, for example, charges a leasing fee of 8.5 percent of revenues.

☐ **Royalties** These generally range from zero to 15 percent of revenues. In return for the royalty payment, the franchisee may get such services as advertising, financial statements, and management advice. McDonald's, for example, charges a royalty of 3 percent on revenues. Thus a franchisee with yearly revenues of $800,000 pays McDonald's $24,000 a year in royalties.

As with any other venture, financing a franchise may pose problems if an entrepreneur has little savings. Typically, the reputable franchisor wants the entrepreneur to put up at least half the money needed to get started, as equity capital. Often, the entrepreneur will try to raise the money needed from savings, relatives, and friends. To do that, the entrepreneur may sell stock to them or borrow from them to buy stock in his or her own name. The remaining half may be borrowed from a commercial bank, often with the franchisor as co-signer of the note.

FRANCHISE OPPORTUNITIES FOR MINORITY PERSONS

Until the mid-1960s, there were few minority franchisees. For example, of the 30,000 retail automobile dealerships existing in 1967, only one was owned by a black. This picture has changed dramatically. By 1980, there were more than 200 minority dealerships, most of them black-owned and prospering.

Similar gains have been made in other industries, thanks to a more enlightened attitude toward minority franchisees. In fact, more than 850 franchisors have declared that their franchises are open to all would-be entrepreneurs, regardless of race.[8] McDonald's, for example, had 220 black franchisees in 1980. There were none in 1968.

It is vital, however, not to mistake progress for arrival. Minorities have a long way to go before they own their proportionate share of franchises. To help speed things along, the federal government has been pushing franchising as a good way to improve the economic lot of minorities. Franchising offers special promise to minority men and women with little money and little experience, enabling them to have their own business with the backing of big-business practices.

SUMMARY

Franchising plays a vital role in our economy and may soon become the dominant form of retailing. It also is prominent in services and, to a lesser degree, in manufacturing. Currently, franchising is growing at a rate of 10 percent a year and shows few signs of slowing down significantly.

Franchising thrives because it combines the incentive of personal ownership with the management and technical skills of big business. To the entrepreneur, franchising offers a short-cut to growth. The entrepreneur gets a ready-made business virtually overnight without having to build a business slowly, step by step. To the franchisor, franchising offers quick expansion. The franchisor grows by letting franchisees finance its growth through the sale of franchises.

8. U.S. Department of Commerce, *Franchise Opportunities Handbook* (Washington, D.C.: U.S. Government Printing Office, June 1979), p. xiii.

The rapid growth of franchising has attracted dishonest as well as honest franchisors. Get-rich-quick schemes abound. Such schemes generally promise instant riches with little work, the freedom of being one's own boss, and little initial investment.

Before buying a franchise, entrepreneurs should do a thorough job of evaluating a franchise opportunity, following a procedure like this one:

☐ Do a self-analysis, matching personal skills and desires to the franchise opportunity
☐ Get legal advice to review contracts and protect one's interests
☐ Answer the checklist questions with the help of disclosure statements from prospective franchisors
☐ Select the most promising franchisor
☐ Negotiate a franchise contract

DISCUSSION AND REVIEW QUESTIONS

1 Explain the myths of franchising.

2 How would you evaluate a franchise opportunity?

3 Identify some franchising abuses and suggest ways to correct them.

4 Define these terms: *franchise, franchisor, franchisee, disclosure statement, franchise fee, working capital, royalties.*

5 What accounts for the rapid growth of franchising?

6 Is the franchisee an entrepreneur? Explain fully.

7 Why might you prefer to be a franchisee rather than start from scratch or buy out an existing business?

8 Why should would-be franchisees work closely with a lawyer before committing themselves to a franchise?

9 Is franchising limited to fast-food services like McDonald's? Explain.

10 Why is the franchise contract the backbone of any franchisor-franchisee relationship?

11 Why does franchising offer a good way for minorities to go into business for themselves?

12 What should a franchisor's management training program consist of to be of most benefit to the franchisee?

13 Assume you are the franchisee of a pet shop. Somebody offers to buy the shop at twice its book value. In your opinion, should you or the franchisor reap the benefit of the difference between what the franchise is worth to the buyer and its worth on the books? Explain.

14 What are some of the reasons a franchisor may cancel a franchise contract?

15 Name the different kinds of franchising systems and describe how they differ.

CASE 5A

TACO LUKE FRANCHISE AND PUERTO RICAN

ECONOMIC DEVELOPMENT CORPORATION

After only six months in business, this fast-food franchise made a before-tax profit of $18,900 on sales revenues of $79,300. This record is a source of pride to:

☐ Adelanio Matos, the franchisee
☐ Luke Owens, the franchisor
☐ Hector Suarez, who heads the Puerto Rican Economic Development Corporation

It took them three years to launch the franchise—three years measured in miles of red tape, acres of paper, and dozens of meetings. "If I had it all to do over again, I'm not sure I would," says Mr. Owens.

But bolstered by this success after a previous failure, Mr. Owens looks forward to selling similar franchises in New York City, where 900,000 Puerto Ricans live.

BACKGROUND

Mr. Owens is an unlikely entrepreneur. Until 1966, football was his passion. He played for 10 years as a professional, mostly with the St. Louis Cardinals. His performance earned him a spot as defensive tackle on the Associated Press All-Pro Team four times.

But in his ninth season, as he turned 30, Mr. Owens suddenly realized that he would soon be washed up as a player. The thought struck a chill in his heart. "I was an old man at 30," says Mr. Owens. "I knew my days with the Cardinals were numbered. So I had to do some hard thinking about what to do with the rest of my life. I owed it to my wife and kids."

At the time, many professional football players were buying fast-food franchises. "It seemed the thing to do," says Mr. Owens. "So I thought I'd look into a McDonald's franchise." At the end of the 1965 season, he visited their headquarters in Elk Grove, Illinois to see about buying a franchise.

McDonald's turned him down. "They wanted $46,000 for a franchise in St. Louis," says Mr. Owens. "I had $27,500 to put down and I could've borrowed the rest. But I never got to first base. They seemed surprised I was black."

Undaunted, Mr. Owens visited other franchisors, including Arby's, Burger Chef, Chicken Delight, and Red Barn. All turned him down. "I couldn't find anybody to take my money," says Mr. Owens.

One lesson he had learned from football was how to come back from defeat. "I was down but not out," says Mr. Owens. "I saw that I'd have to make it on my own. But I lacked experience. I had never sold milk shakes and hamburgers, much less run a business."

His luck turned when he met two Chicago entrepreneurs, Bruce Kirk and David **OPPORTUNITY KNOCKS**
Roosevelt. Mr. Roosevelt was the great-grandson of Theodore Roosevelt, the
nation's president from 1901 to 1909. They had started a fast-food business in
Oklahoma City called Senor Taco, serving Mexican food only. Although not yet
successful there, they were already planning to sell franchises to investors like
Mr. Owens.

"I told Dave Roosevelt I'd like to learn about the business first," says Mr.
Owens. "He said OK. So I went down to Oklahoma City for two and a half
weeks, at my own expense, to learn all I could about selling tacos. I thought it
was a real opportunity for me."

Impressed with Mr. Owens's desire and talents, the two entrepreneurs
agreed to sell him a franchise. The agreement called for them to finance both
the building and the equipment and for Mr. Owens to pay a franchise fee of
$10,000. So, in 1967, one year after he quit professional football, Mr. Owens
was busy selling tacos as a franchisee.

Then Mr. Owens found himself in trouble: Mr. Kirk was killed in a plane crash **DISASTER STRIKES**
and Mr. Roosevelt was drafted into the infantry and packed off to Vietnam.
With no one to look after the Senor Taco parent company, it went under.

After the shock wore off, Mr. Owens moved fast to pick up the pieces. He
talked to Mr. Kirk's wife, offering to buy the assets of the defunct parent
company. It took three years and $3,200 of legal fees before he finally worked
out a deal suitable to all parties—not only to bill collectors and bankers but
also to Mrs. Kirk and Mr. Roosevelt. The final price was $14,500. And part of
the deal was a change in name, to Taco Luke. "That was a great feeling," says
Mr. Owens. "I was finally my own man." The year was 1971.

But during those three years of negotiating his freedom, Mr. Owens was
knocked to his knees by events beyond his control. In the summer of 1968, race
riots broke out that left in their wake 11 persons dead and parts of the city
ravaged by fire. "Before the riots, half my customers were black and half were
white," says Mr. Owens. "But after the riots, I lost all my white customers. I
knew right then that I'd be swallowed up."

Revenues dropped steadily as even blacks began to stay away:

I watched the area change to a low-level street life. I saw things I never
imagined I'd see: shootings, muggings, murders, rapes, killings, dope
pushers, pimps, contract people, after-hour gamblers. You name it, I saw
it. But it's a funny thing: I met some fair-minded blacks who looked up to
me and liked my image as a clean guy. I was someone different to these
low-life persons. And I tried to help those who let me. I found that many
of them had good minds but were misdirected. In fact, I think some of
them might have become managers if their energies had been channeled
elsewhere.

Now on the edge of failure, Mr. Owens began to make plans to pull up
stakes and go elsewhere. Neighboring fast-food franchises were having similar
problems. On Mr. Owens's block were Burger Chef, Mahalia Jackson, and
McDonald's. "They were all hurting," says Mr. Owens. "The rumor was that

McDonald's was doing a million dollars of business *before* the riots and less than half that *after* the riots. So I just had to get out—but how?''

The answer came one steamy Sunday afternoon. Business was especially slow that day, causing Mr. Owens to feel depressed and weary. But not for long. One of his customers happened to be Hector Suarez, who headed the Puerto Rican Economic Development Corporation (PREDC), described in Exhibit 5A-1. They struck up a conversation, and Mr. Owens casually said that he ''had lots of problems and wished he had a way out.'' ''I've got a way out,'' offered Mr. Suarez. ''You'll hear from me in a week or so.'' When Mr. Suarez called Mr. Owens, his first words were, ''Let's make a deal.''

That call marked the beginning of a new lease on life for Mr. Owens. ''I just knew in my bones it would work out,'' says Mr. Owens. ''Hector was as sincere a guy as I've ever met. Would you believe we picked a site the day he phoned me? That's how fast we moved.'' The site was a busy intersection in the middle of the city's Puerto Rican district.

Mr. Owens had now come full circle. All along, he had wanted to put a franchise in the city's near-west side, which is almost all white—even before he opened his first outlet on the east side, which is almost all black. ''I couldn't sell my good points to bankers,'' says Mr. Owens. ''They were worried because I was black. They thought I'd bring blacks in from the ghetto. So they wanted me to locate in the black ghetto. And I went along with them, even though I knew blacks didn't know too much about Mexican food. That's one of the reasons I didn't do well in the ghetto.''

So Mr. Owens and Mr. Suarez joined hands to put up a Taco Luke franchise. There was little doubt in their minds that it would succeed. After all,

---

Taco Luke Franchise

EXHIBIT 5A-1

Brief Description of Puerto Rican Economic Development Corporation

The Puerto Rican Economic Development Corporation (PREDC) was formed in November 1969 and incorporated under state law as a nonprofit organization in February 1970. Its tax-exempt status was granted under Section 501c of the Internal Revenue Code.

PREDC is governed by a board of 26 trustees, representing 80 percent of the city's Puerto Rican leadership. This board meets every two weeks, with an average attendance of 16 trustees a meeting.

PREDC was born out of a concern for the economic future of the city's 22,000 Puerto Ricans. Survey after survey had shown that this community lagged far behind other ethnic groups, especially in new-business starts and employment.

Moreover, urban blight has stripped the community of much-needed shopping services. Empty store fronts are eyesores everywhere.

It is PREDC's goal to reverse urban blight by creating jobs and entrepreneurial opportunities throughout the Puerto Rican community.

there were 22,000 Puerto Ricans within a half mile of the corner site they had chosen—and most of them enjoyed eating tacos.

Equally important, Burger King wanted the site. "When I heard that, I just knew it had to be a good site," says Mr. Owens. "They're tops at marketing research. So, in a way, their research helped me, because now I wouldn't have to make a fancy market survey."

NEEDS A BUSINESS PLAN

Not so. Mr. Owens and Mr. Suarez soon found they could not move their venture to first base without a business plan. Banks, the Chamber of Commerce, and the SBA all asked for such a plan. And, of course, a key part of it is a market survey. "That really upset me," says Mr. Owens. "They just wouldn't accept the fact that Burger King had already done such a survey. My Lord, I didn't know the first thing about doing such a survey, much less about putting a plan together."

His frustration was short-lived, thanks to a college student, Angelo Lupo. A marketing major, Mr. Lupo had volunteered his services through VISTA (Volunteers In Service To America). When Mr. Lupo offered to work up a business plan for the proposed Taco Luke franchise, Mr. Owens was skeptical. "I thought he was one of those college guys with a crew-cut, white socks, wing-tipped black shoes—and a white sheet over his arm. But to my surprise he was a hip guy and very brilliant."

Mr. Lupo began working on the business plan "with jet-like energy." His life soon became a busy round of meetings and interviews to get answers to such questions as these:

☐ What sales revenues is the franchise likely to generate in its first year of operation?
☐ How soon is the franchise likely to break even?
☐ How much would it cost to buy the corner lot, raze the abandoned building on it, construct a building, put in a parking lot, and buy fixtures and equipment?
☐ What is the best way to finance these costs?
☐ Who is the person likely to do the best job of running the franchise?

RESEARCHING THE MARKET

High on the list of Mr. Lupo's priorities was to get a marketing research study done. He asked the Chamber of Commerce for help. They responded by assigning their marketing consultant, Dr. William Trombetta, to do the study. "This study had to come first," says Mr. Lupo, "because it's the revenue forecast that tells you how big a building to put up, how much working capital you'll need, how many people to hire, and a host of other things."

To forecast revenues, the marketing consultant borrowed procedures worked out by the Chicago Development Corporation. These procedures are designed to help establish small businesses in low-income areas, and they focus on such things as these:

☐ The number of families in each census tract located in the proposed franchise's trading area (see Exhibit 5A-2)
☐ The median family income in each census tract

Taco Luke Franchise

o 100 households

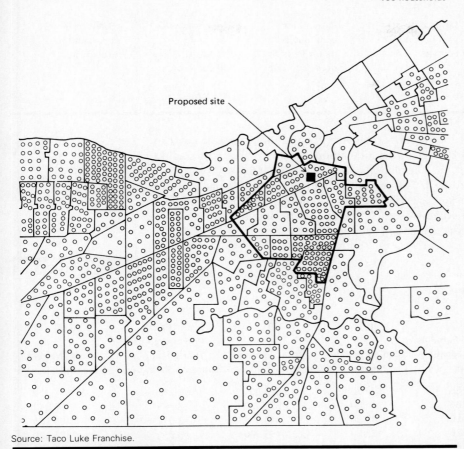

Proposed site

Source: Taco Luke Franchise.

Trading area around proposed franchise site as shown by census tracts. The assumed trading area of the facility is outlined by a dark line, based on a five-minute driving-time radius from the proposed retail site.

☐ The median percentage each family spends eating out

☐ The percentage of total expenditures for food that families are *likely* to spend buying tacos and other Mexican food at the proposed franchise

The idea was to multiply the four factors to produce a sales revenue forecast (see the model in Exhibit 5A-3).

It was no problem for the consultant to get this information. Information on the number of families in each census tract came from a local newspaper's marketing and research department. Information on median family income came from the *United States Census of Population and Housing* at the public library. And information on what percentage of a family's income is spent on food came from a report published by the U.S. Department of Labor, also available at the library.

Model for Estimating Sales Revenues

| Number of families in census tracts | × | Median income of families in census tracts | × | Percentage of family's income spent on eating out | × | Percentage of family's food expense likely to be spent at franchise | = | Sales revenue forecast for franchise |

Armed with all this information, the consultant put his desk calculator to use and came up with $4,250,000 as the total amount that families in the trading area spend on eating out. His calculations appear in Exhibit 5A-4.

Now came the hard part. The consultant had to estimate what share of the total food dollar the franchise was *likely* to get. More or less picking a figure out of the air, he settled on 5 percent. So he forecast revenues of $210,000 for the proposed franchise for its first year of operation.

Estimate of Market Potential

(A) Census Tracts in Trading Area	(B) Number of Families in Each Census Tract	(C) Median Family Income	(D) Total Gross Income—(B × C)	(E) Percentage of Yearly Income Spent on Eating Out	(F) Total Market Potential—(D × E)
C-9	1,788	$7,630	$ 13,650,000	3.9%	$ 530,000
C-5	1,484	7,800	11,580,000	3.9	450,000
B-7	1,395	8,490	11,840,000	3.9	460,000
C-8	1,376	8,550	11,760,000	3.9	460,000
C-6	1,163	6,180	7,190,000	3.3	240,000
B-6	1,115	8,040	8,970,000	3.9	350,000
B-8	1,088	8,230	8,960,000	3.9	350,000
D-1	1,004	7,360	7,380,000	3.3	240,000
C-7	992	6,660	6,610,000	3.3	220,000
C-4	936	7,960	7,500,000	3.9	290,000
D-9	820	8,800	7,220,000	3.9	280,000
C-2	410	7,580	3,110,000	3.9	120,000
D-6	305	8,250	2,520,000	3.9	100,000
B-5	304	8,280	2,520,000	3.9	100,000
C-3	202	4,160	840,000	6.7	60,000
Total	14,382		$111,650,000		$4,250,000

Not entirely satisfied with this textbook approach, the consultant went on to **VERIFIES FORECAST** verify the forecast by making an on-the-spot traffic study with Mr. Lupo's help. In fact, Mr. Lupo stood on the corner for seven straight days in December to count:

☐ The number of pedestrians by the hour
☐ The number of passing cars by the hour

Based on this study, the consultant came up with a revenue forecast lower than his earlier one: $155,000 versus $210,000. How he got the $155,000 is explained in Exhibit 5A-5.

The consultant also looked at the quality of competing fast-food franchises in the area. He found that the only serious competition would come from a six-stool coffee shop and a stand-up sub shop. In contrast, Mr. Owens's original outlet on the east side competed with such giants as Burger King, Mahalia Jackson, and McDonald's—"all this in a black area. But on the near west side, the area's Puerto Rican flavor would surely enhance the chances that an ethnically related outlet would succeed." Return-on-investment calculations appear in Exhibit 5A-6.

Taco Luke Franchise

EXHIBIT 5A-5

Forecast of Sales Revenues from On-the-Spot Survey

A. Key assumptions*	
Average purchase by customers	$1.00
Drive-in ratio	0.5%
Walk-in ratio	1.2%
B. Pedestrian flow at proposed site	
Number of pedestrians per day	2,120
Walk-in ratio	1.2%
Walk-in trade per day	250 (2,120 × 0.12)
C. Vehicular flow at proposed site	
Number of vehicles per day	19,500
Drive-in ratio	0.5%
Drive-in trade per day	100 (19,500 × 0.005)
D. Student flow at proposed site	
Number of students at high schools	3,040
Assumed drop-in ratio	2.5%
Student trade per day	75 (3,040 × 0.025)
E. Forecast of sales revenues	
Walk-in trade	250
Drive-in trade	100
Student trade	75
Average purchase	$1.00
Number of days per year	365
Forecast of revenues	$155,000†

* These assumptions come from Mr. Owens's experience at his original outlet on the east side.
† $1.00 × 365 (250 + 100 + 75) = $155,000

While this marketing study was underway, Mr. Lupo was spending most of his time on a nagging question every banker had asked him: What would it cost to start up the business?

The answer: $138,000. It took him nine months to make that estimate with the help of architects, realtors, and lawyers. The $138,000 would be invested as follows:

$ 82,500 for purchasing the corner lot, razing two old
         buildings, and putting in a paved parking lot
  50,000 for constructing a building and buying equip-
         ment, fixtures, and furniture
   5,500 for working capital
$138,000

With the marketing and investment aspects in hand, Mr. Lupo was able to piece together the rest of the business plan. When he completed the plan, it weighed more than a pound. "I never knew there was so much red tape around," says Mr. Lupo. "I filled out enough forms to last a lifetime."

Mr. Lupo carried five copies of his business plan to the SBA, with whom he had been in touch from the day he began work on the plan. Within five months, the SBA agreed to make the $124,200 loan called for by the plan, at 5½ percent interest. The rest, or $13,800, would be invested by members of the Puerto Rican community. The SBA requires that at least 10 percent of a new venture's total capitalization come from private investors—hence the need for seed money.

"Anthony Delfine deserves a lot of credit for getting us the loan," says Mr. Owens. "He was a loan specialist for the SBA, helping minority entrepreneurs get on their feet. Without Tony's help—and Angelo Lupo's—I wouldn't have made it."

But a year later, in 1973, the venture ran into a snag. Dealings with unskilled construction contractors led to spiraling costs in materials and labor. Mr. Lupo now estimated it would take another $29,500 to complete the project. At first, the SBA refused to approve the cost overrun. But after some discussion, the SBA approved it.

Taco Luke Franchise

EXHIBIT 5A-6

Estimated Return on Investment

A. Forecast of yearly revenues	$155,000
B. Operating profit ratio	5.0%*
C. Operating profit (A × B)	$7,750
D. Total investment	$138,000
E. Return on investment (C ÷ D)	6% a year

* Industry average

When the project was finally completed in May 1974, the Taco Luke franchise opened with the balance sheet shown in Exhibit 5A-7. A photograph of the franchise appears in Exhibit 5A-8.

The franchise opened in a splash of ceremony. The mayor praised the Puerto Rican community for its efforts at self-improvement. But few of the hundreds who attended the ceremony were aware of the sweat and heartache that had preceded it. Few knew that three long years had passed since the first meeting between Mr. Owens and Mr. Suarez until the opening of the franchise. "If I had it all to do over again, I'm not sure I would," says Mr. Owens. "It wasn't easy."

The man Mr. Suarez chose to run the franchise is Adelanio Matos. Once a grocer, Mr. Matos owns the franchise and the equipment, leasing from PREDC the building and grounds. Mr. Matos's income statement after six months in business appears in Exhibit 5A-9.

As the franchisor, Mr. Owens gets 4 percent of revenues from Mr. Matos. In turn, Mr. Owens donates one-fourth of his franchise fee to PREDC for use in other community projects. "It's the least I can do," says Mr. Owens. "They're such great people, and they helped me when nobody else would."

Bolstered by his success here, Mr. Owens plans to sell the franchise to investors in other cities with large Puerto Rican populations. Especially appealing is New York City, with 900,000 Puerto Ricans.

1 Identify the obstacles that Mr. Owens had to overcome when he first sought to become an entrepreneur in 1966. In your opinion which obstacles still remain today?
2 Why did Mr. Owens succeed?
3 Comment on the paperwork that is needed in order to qualify for a loan from the SBA.
4 What are Mr. Owens's prospects for expanding his franchise into other Puerto Rican communities? If you were Mr. Owens, how would you go about it?
5 Comment on the franchise's performance to date.

Taco Luke Franchise

EXHIBIT 5A-7

Balance Sheet (May 6, 1974)

Assets			Equities	
Current assets			Bank note	$150,750
Cash	$ 4,000			
Inventory	1,000	$ 5,000	Owners' equity	16,750
Fixed assets				
Land	$82,500			
Building	69,500			
Equipment	10,000	$162,000		
Organization costs		500		
Total assets		$167,500	Total equities	$167,500

Exterior View of Restaurant

Income Statement (May 6, 1974 to November 1, 1974)

Sales revenues		$79,300
Cost of goods sold		
Food purchases	$36,400	
Ending inventory	100	36,300
Gross profit		$43,000
Operating expenses		
Wages	$11,300	
Rent	2,800	
Franchise fee	2,000	
Insurance	1,700	
Salaries	1,500	
Supplies	1,000	
Utilities	900	
Taxes	700	
Interest	500	
Depreciation	500	
Repairs	400	
Telephone	200	
Commissions	200	
Advertising	200	
Licenses and permits	100	
Lease improvements	100	24,100
Operating profit		$18,900

Ron Schultz was a life insurance salesman, modestly providing for his wife and two sons. They lived in a quiet urban neighborhood on the tight budget that many families with a limited income find necessary.

At 42 years of age, Mr. Schultz was seeking to enter a new field—one that would enable him to increase his income. One opportunity he looked at was a franchise with one of the nation's biggest automatic-transmission repair services. Investigation revealed a fast-growing market with little competition:

☐ New-car dealers were equipped to repair only the one make of transmission they sold. Because of their high overhead, their transmission-repair prices ran high.
☐ Neighborhood garages farmed out their transmission-repair work to small shops that varied sharply in quality and cost.

The potential was clear. But Mr. Schultz was bothered by his lack of a mechanical background. The franchisor's intensive training program was designed to overcome just such doubts. Spanning four weeks, the program ran 48 hours a week and covered such subjects as pricing, employee recruiting, advertising, customer service, supervision, and cost controls.

The program's objective was to familiarize the franchisee with all aspects of the transmission-repair business—with emphasis on *managing* transmission specialists rather than doing the actual mechanical work.

At the franchisor's suggestion, Mr. Schultz picked several names at random from a list of their franchisees. He visited each one at his convenience. Each franchisee seemed pleased with his own business. And each one urged Mr. Schultz to seek his own franchise with the parent company.

Further investigation indicated that the site for the new franchise could be right in Mr. Schultz's area. The tentative site boasted 40,000 registered automobiles within a 30-minute drive.

The initial cash investment for this franchise was $70,000. And the franchisor was ready to help Mr. Schultz raise the money. The $70,000 investment would cover such items as:

☐ Initial rental and parts inventory
☐ Special tools and outdoor signs
☐ Workbenches and office supplies

Continuing help offered by the franchisor included monthly conferences for all area franchisees to review sales progress and business proficiency.

The requirements Mr. Schultz had to meet—besides his initial $70,000 investment—were a strong desire to earn money and a knack for communicating with people.

---

[*]Source: Case prepared by the SBA.

1 What should Mr. Schultz do?
2 What advantages do you see in the franchisor's offer?
3 What disadvantages do you see in the offer?
4 What added information would you advise Mr. Schultz to get?

CASE 5C   **ANTHONY WILLIAMS**

Anthony Williams wants to own a franchise. "I don't care what kind of franchise I go into," says Mr. Williams, "just so I'm the owner. Believe me, I've been around a lot and learned a lot. I've poured steel, washed dishes, clerked at supermarkets, peddled papers, tended bar. You name it, I've done it. Of course, now I've got a steady job driving a truck for the Post Office. Been at it for eight years."

Mr. Williams is 39 years old, married, with four children. Like others in his neighborhood, he is heavily mortgaged and buys often on the installment plan—all the time betting that paychecks will keep coming in week after week.

A graduate of a local community college, Mr. Williams recalls what a professor once told him. "Franchising," said the professor, "is ideal for entrepreneurs who lack experience. Franchisors teach you all you have to know." And Mr. Williams remembers to this day the professor's statement that 99 percent of all McDonald's franchisees had *no* prior experience in the restaurant industry.

Assume that Mr. Williams has come to you for advice. What would you tell   **QUESTION**
him to do?

CHAPTER SIX

DEVELOPING A BUSINESS PLAN

questions for mastery

why write a business plan?

how do you prepare a business plan?

can a business plan be versatile?

why is it important to get the facts and make sound assumptions?

what is the difference between operating plans and financial plans?

If we are true to plan, our statures touch the skies.

Emily Dickinson

W ould-be entrepreneurs need to prepare a business plan as an essential step in bringing their ideas for a product or service to the reality of a flourishing venture. Planning requires entrepreneurs to *anticipate*:

☐ The potential market for their venture
☐ The potential costs of meeting the demands of that market
☐ The potential pitfalls in organizing the operations of the venture
☐ The early signals they will use to alert them of progress or setbacks

The business plan is a rigorous exercise, based on facts, that provides the underpinnings for a successful venture.

NEED FOR PLANNING

Planning is decision-making; that is, deciding what to do, how to do it, and when to do it. It is vital for business success. As one businessman puts it:

> Planning is so important today that it occupies a major part of the time of some of the most respected men in business . . . Planning allows us to master change. It forces us to organize our expectations and develop programs to bring them about.
> Planning is a most effective way to draw out the best in all of us—our best thinking, our best interests and aims—and to enable us to develop the most efficient way of achieving our maximum growth.[1]

The very act of preparing a business plan forces entrepreneurs to think through the steps they must take—from the moment they decide to go into business for themselves through the moment they open for business to the moments they are actively engaged in business.

A ROAD MAP FOR ENTREPRENEURS

In many ways, the business plan resembles a road map, telling entrepreneurs how best to get from A to Z. Entrepreneurs may think: Why should I spend my time drawing up a business plan? The answer is simply that they cannot afford not to. A complex economy such as ours demands such a plan:

> Time was when an individual could start a venture and prosper provided he was strong enough to work long hours and had the knack for selling at prices above what materials or product had cost him. Small stores, grist mills, livery stables, and blacksmith shops sprang up in many cross-road communities as Americans applied their energy and native intelligence to settling the continent. Today, this native intelligence is still important. But, by itself, the common sense for which Americans are famous will not ensure success in a small business. Technology, the

1. Harold Blancke, quoted in Marvin Bower, *The Will to Manage* (New York: McGraw-Hill, 1966), p. 46.

marketplace, and even people themselves have become more complicated than they were 100, or even 25, years ago.

Today, common sense must be combined with new techniques in order to succeed in the space age. Just as one would not think of launching a manned space capsule without a flight plan, so one should not think of launching a new business without a business plan.[2]

OUTSIDE PRESSURES

The idea of a business plan is hardly new. Big business has long been turning them out yearly by the thousands, especially for marketing new products, buying out an existing business, or expanding into foreign markets. But what is new is the growing use of such plans by entrepreneurs. Outside pressures now force them to develop their businesses on paper before investing time and money in a venture that may have little chance of success.

Outside pressures flow mainly from creditors and investors whom the entrepreneur may approach for money. Most of them ask for a business plan before entertaining a request for money. These outside pressures are healthy:

☐ Entrepreneurs benefit because a business plan makes them better appreciate what it may take to succeed.
☐ Investors and creditors also benefit because a business plan gives them better information on which to decide whether to help finance the entrepreneur.

How many entrepreneurs actually prepare a formal business plan? Probably fewer than 5 percent. The remaining 95 percent plan in less structured ways. Some may do it entirely in their heads, for example, and others may simply write notes on the backs of old envelopes.

PARTS OF A BUSINESS PLAN

What should a business plan cover? It should be a thought-through and objective analysis of both personal abilities and business requirements for a particular product or service. It should define strategies for such functions as marketing and production, organization and legal aspects, accounting and finance. A business plan should answer such questions as:

☐ What do I want and what am I capable of doing?
☐ What are the most workable ways of achieving my goals?
☐ What can I expect in the future?

There is no single best way to begin. What follows is simply a guide and can be changed to suit individual needs. Exhibit 6-1 suggests to entrepreneurs

2. U.S. Small Business Administration, "Business Plan for Small Manufacturers," *Management Aid No. 218* (Washington, D.C.: U.S. Government Printing Office, 1973), p. 3.

EXHIBIT 6-1

Step No.	Description of Steps	Completion Date*	Comments
1	Decide to go into business for your-self.		
2	Analyze your strengths and weak-nesses, paying special attention to your business experience, business education, and desires. Then answer this question: Why should I be in business for myself?	Third week	
3	Choose the product or service that best fits your strengths and desires. Then answer these questions: What is unique about my product or service? How do I know it is unique? What will my product or service do for customers? What will it not do? What should it do later but does not now do?	Fourth week	
4	Research the market for your prod-uct or service, to find answers to such questions as these: Who are my customers? Where are they? What is their average in-come? How do they buy? At what price? In what quantities? When do they buy? When will they use my product or service? Where will they use it? Why will they buy it? Who are my competitors? Where are they? How strong are they? What is the total market potential? Is it growing?	Seventh week	
5	Forecast your share of market if pos-sible. Then forecast your sales rev-enues over a three-year period, bro-ken down as follows: First year—monthly Second year—quarterly Third year—yearly	Eighth week	

EXHIBIT 6-1 (cont.)

Step No.	Description of Steps	Completion Date*	Comments
	Next, answer this question: Why do I believe my sales-revenue forecast is realistic?		
6	Choose a site for your business, then answer this question: Why do I prefer this site to other possible sites?	Eighth week	
7†	Develop your production plan, answering such questions as these: How big should my plant be? How should my production process be laid out? What equipment will I need? In what size? How will I control the waste, quality, and inventory of my product?	Tenth week	
8	Develop your marketing plan, answering such questions as these: How am I going to create customers? At what price? By what kinds of advertising and sales promotion? Through personal selling? How?	Tenth week	
9	Develop your organizational plan, answering this question: What kinds of talent will I need to make my business go? Draw up an organizational chart that spells out who does what, who has what authority, and who reports to whom.	Twelfth week	
10	Develop your legal plan, focusing on whether to form a sole proprietorship, a partnership, or a corporation; and then explain your choice.	Twelfth week	
11	Develop your accounting plan, explaining the kinds of records and reports you need and how you will use them.	Twelfth week	

EXHIBIT 6-1 (cont.)

Step No.	Description of Steps	Completion Date*	Comments
12	Develop your insurance plan, answering this question: What kinds of insurance will I need to protect my venture against possible loss from unforeseen events?	Twelfth week	
13	Develop your financial plan by preparing such statements as these: A three-year cash budget, showing how much cash you will need before opening for business; and showing how much cash you expect will flow in and out of your business, broken down as follows: First year, monthly Second year, quarterly Third year, yearly An income statement for the first year only Balance sheets for the beginning and ending of the first year A profitgraph (breakeven chart), showing when you will begin to make a profit Then determine how you will finance your business and where you expect to raise money.	Fifteenth week	
14	Write a cover letter summarizing your business plan, stresssing its purpose and its promise.	Sixteenth week	

* See note in Exhibit 6-2.
† This step applies only to those entrepreneurs who plan to go into manufacturing. Otherwise, it should be omitted.

the steps that they may take to prepare a business plan as well as the time it may take to complete each step.

Exhibit 6-2 shows how all 14 steps in Exhibit 6-1 tie together. It is apparent from the exhibit that certain key steps cannot be taken until earlier steps are completed. For example, entrepreneurs cannot research their market (Step 4), unless they first choose a product or service (Step 3). And they cannot prepare a marketing plan (Step 8), unless they first research their market (Step 4), forecast their revenues (Step 5), and choose a site (Step 6).

The guidelines in Exhibits 6-1 and 6-2 are tailored to new ventures. They are, however, also applicable to the following situations:

☐ Buying an existing business—perhaps omitting Steps 3, 8, 9
☐ Expanding an existing business—perhaps omitting Steps 1, 2, 3, 10
☐ Floating additional shares of common stock—perhaps omitting Steps 1, 6, 10
☐ Borrowing money from a commercial bank—perhaps omitting Steps 1, 6, 10

As they follow the guidelines in Exhibits 6-1 and 6-2, entrepreneurs should keep complete notes. They should document all facts, back all assumptions, and give the authority for all opinions. Otherwise, entrepreneurs may lack credibility with investors and creditors.

EXHIBIT 6-2

Flow Diagram Showing How Steps in Business Plan Relate

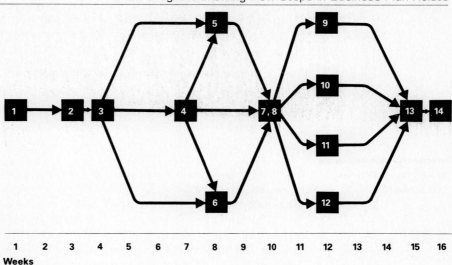

Shown here at 16 weeks for illustrative purposes. Clearly, the time it takes to prepare a business plan may take less or much more than 16 weeks, depending on the complexity of the venture.

| 1 | 2 | 3 | 4 | 5 | 6 | 7 | 8 | 9 | 10 | 11 | 12 | 13 | 14 | 15 | 16 |

Weeks

By answering the guideline questions in Exhibit 6-1, entrepreneurs can prepare a thoughtful and effective business plan. To use the guidelines well, however, they will need to get facts, opinions, and judgments. The following suggestions may be helpful.

STEP 1: DECIDING TO GO INTO BUSINESS

The decision to go into business requires little fact finding. It is recommended, however, that entrepreneurs take the self-analysis test offered in Chapter Two.

STEP 2: ANALYZING ONESELF

Analysis of personal strengths and weaknesses also requires little fact finding. Entrepreneurs may simply sit down and list their strengths, paying special attention to their business experience and education. On another sheet of paper, they may list their weaknesses. Next, they should analyze their readiness to start their own business.

When analyzing their strengths and weaknesses, entrepreneurs should be honest with themselves. It is often hard for them, as for others, to see their own shortcomings.

STEP 3: CHOOSING A PRODUCT OR SERVICE

This is a critical step. As a rule, it is foolish for entrepreneurs to choose a product or service they know little about. A bad choice will severely weaken their chance of success. It is possible they might learn from their mistakes, but that could be costly. Still, some entrepreneurs do go into an entirely unfamiliar field and succeed. The general rule, however, is for entrepreneurs to pick a product or service they:

☐ Know intimately because they have worked with it for years
☐ Are convinced will grow at a rate faster than that of the economy as a whole
☐ Can get excited about

It is also vital that entrepreneurs develop precise answers to these two questions:

☐ What is unique about my product?
☐ What does it offer customers that competing products do not offer?

STEP 4: RESEARCHING THE MARKET

Research is perhaps the most critical step of all. Entrepreneurs should spare no expense in their quest for facts. The more they know about their markets, the greater their chance of creating customers at a profit.

Too often, entrepreneurs do a poor job in this vital area, tending to rely on hearsay instead of facts and thus lacking even the foggiest idea of how best to reach the customer. Many new ventures fizzle into oblivion because entrepreneurs fail to get the basic information they need to move products out of their hands and into those of customers.

In quest of facts, the logical place to begin is with the question: Who are my customers?

Entrepreneurs who sweep their market with a glance and decide, "Every one of the city's million persons will want my product," are taking a casual approach that can only hamper their later efforts to define a strategy to reach their market.

Instead, entrepreneurs should get facts on where customers live and shop, their average income, how they buy, at what price, why they buy, and so on. This is a tall order; but the information is not only necessary, it is also obtainable.

To get such information, entrepreneurs should begin with their local Chamber of Commerce. The Chamber can tell entrepreneurs what facts are available, either at hand or buried in government statistics. Trade associations are equally fruitful sources; they offer mountains of information, often at no cost. Virtually every industry has such an association. After collecting facts already unearthed by others, entrepreneurs should then leave their desks and do some fact finding on their own.

EXAMPLE

Let us assume an entrepreneur plans to open a computer service for small businesses only. As part of her business plan, the entrepreneur needs to estimate the total *market potential* for such a service. *Market potential* is the total dollar value of computer services now purchased by small businesses in the marketing area. To estimate market potential, the entrepreneur should begin by talking to prospects. She may choose about 25 small-businesspersons at random and visit each one to get answers to such questions as:

☐ Will you buy my computer service at competitive hourly rates, if I promise my service will be quicker and better suited to your needs? If not, why?
☐ How much does your present computer service charge you?

Armed with such information, the entrepreneur may now estimate her total market potential in this way:

a Average hourly charge = $40.00
b Average number of hours per week of service time used by small businesses = 5
c Number of small businesses in sample = 25
d Number of small businesses in marketing area = 1,000
e Number of weeks in year = 52
f Yearly market potential (a × b × d × e) = $10,400,000

Besides estimating market potential, the entrepreneur should also look at her competition, getting answers to such questions as these:

☐ Who are my competitors?
☐ Where are they?

☐ How strong are they?
☐ What kinds of computer services do they offer?

To answer the first two questions, the entrepreneur should thumb through the Yellow Pages and visit each computer service to get a feeling for the scope of their operations. Then, on an area map, she should pinpoint their locations.

Answers to the questions about competitors' strengths and services should come from the entrepreneur's banker, who has access to a copy of each competitor's Dun & Bradstreet report. These reports offer insights into a competitor's financial strength, credit rating, and line of computer services.

∎

The process of fact finding described in the example is usually called marketing research. We will discuss this vital tool more fully in Chapters Eight and Fourteen.

STEP 5: FORECASTING SALES REVENUES

After estimating the market potential for their selected business, entrepreneurs should next estimate what share of that market they can reasonably expect to gain. They must do so by making realistic assumptions that take into account the number and size of competitors and the amount of time it will take them to achieve their goals. Entrepreneurs then need to express their expected market share in terms of sales revenues. A good rule of thumb is to estimate sales revenues over a three-year period, broken down as follows:

☐ First year—monthly
☐ Second year—quarterly
☐ Third year—yearly

These revenue figures are key estimates because they are the basis for almost all other figure estimates that the entrepreneur must make. It is vital, therefore, that revenues be estimated in a realistic way and not picked out of the air.

EXAMPLE

For her computer service, the entrepreneur might now estimate her share of market (or revenues) as follows:

a Total market potential = $10,400,000
b Number of competitors = 19
c Number of competitors *plus* entrepreneur = 20
d Share of market (a ÷ c) = $520,000 a year

Next, the entrepreneur should estimate how long it will take her to reach that revenue level. A realistic estimate might be three years.

∎

It bears repeating that revenue forecasts must qualify as intelligent guess-work. Unless armed with such forecasts, the entrepreneur lacks a realistic target to aim for and cannot plan such expenditures as the following:

☐ Buying or leasing such long-lived assets as buildings, equipment, or land
☐ Buying inventories and supplies
☐ Hiring employees
☐ Financing customers, who may pay their bills in one, two, or more months

Revenue forecasts must be based on assumptions as well as facts; the accuracy of a revenue forecast hinges largely on the accuracy of the assumptions that support it.

STEP 6: CHOOSING A SITE

Entrepreneurs usually have some idea, from the very start, of where best to locate their business. California, for example, may be preferred because of its climate. Or a hometown location may be preferred because life-long friendships may enable the entrepreneur to raise money and draw customers more readily than in a town of strangers.

Wise entrepreneurs, however, balance personal preference with business logic. Because the two rarely mesh perfectly, entrepreneurs must often compromise:

EXAMPLE

If he is going into chemical manufacture, the entrepreneur may have to locate his plant hundreds of miles from where he prefers to live. The chemistry of his process may require 10 pounds of raw materials to make 1 pound of chemical product, suggesting to the entrepreneur that he should locate close to suppliers in order to cut transportation costs.

Suppliers, customers, or financial support may determine regional loca-tions. Equally important is location within a city or neighborhood. Too often, entrepreneurs jump at the first vacancy that comes along, rather than base their choice on the results of their marketing research. Location is a critical decision that can mean the difference between success or failure. We will discuss location in greater detail in Chapter Eight.

STEP 7: DEVELOPING A PRODUCTION PLAN

The need for a production plan applies only to entrepreneurs who intend to manufacture a product. Neither wholesaling, retailing, nor services generally call for a production plan. In preparing such a plan, perhaps the most critical question an entrepreneur should answer is: How big should my plant be? The estimate should be in volume of product per year and should flow logically from the revenue forecast. General practice is to use the third-year forecast, or even the fifth-year forecast, to size a plant. However, entrepreneurs may find that a five-year forecast often stretches too far into the future to be realistic.

After estimating size, entrepreneurs should next lay out their production process. Efficient layout requires that equipment be arranged in ways that:

☐ Minimize manual handling of materials
☐ Make best use of workers' time
☐ Offer flexibility for expansion

A flow diagram showing how raw materials would enter the plant, how these materials would change into product, and how product would leave the plant, is an especially helpful tool in the planning process.

Entrepreneurs must also determine the type and size of the equipment needed for the production process. Each piece of equipment should be sized in a way that keeps the process free of bottlenecks. Equipment suppliers generally can offer expert advice on how to go about selecting and sizing equipment.

Last, entrepreneurs should lay out their plans to control the waste, quality, and inventory of their product.

STEP 8: DEVELOPING A MARKETING PLAN

This step forces entrepreneurs to spell out in detail how they plan to create customers at a profit. If, in Step 4, the entrepreneur painstakingly dug out the facts about his or her markets, then the marketing plan is likely to be creative; if not, it is likely to be fallow.

To develop a marketing plan, entrepreneurs must prepare a marketing mix—that is, a combination of marketing tools that will work together to convince customers to buy their product or service. The mix may include:

☐ Distribution channels and servicing activities
☐ Advertising, sales promotion, and trade shows
☐ Pricing
☐ Personal selling

Properly combined, these tools generate sales revenues. As one businessperson puts it:

> The entrepreneur, as the marketing man, is a kind of cook who is continually experimenting with new blends and new kinds of ingredients. He hopes . . . to come out with the ideal combination that will produce the highest amount of sales revenues at the lowest possible cost.[3]

To clarify further what a marketing mix is, let us refer to our earlier example on computer services.

EXAMPLE

Let us assume that the entrepreneur estimates first-year revenues at $100,000. She then asks herself: How should I go about getting customers for my computer service? In other words, what marketing mix should I use?

The entrepreneur knows that, on the average, her industry spends 10 percent of revenues on getting orders. This tells her she should budget

---

3. Harvey C. Krentzman, U.S. Small Business Administration, *Managing for Profits* (Washington, D.C.: U.S. Government Printing Office, 1968), p. 6.

$10,000 for that purpose. So the next question she asks is: On what marketing tools, and in what combination, should I spend the $10,000?

Because of the importance of personal contact in providing computer services to small businesses, the entrepreneur might decide that three-fourths of her marketing mix should be personal selling and just one-fourth should be advertising. In dollar terms, she would thus spend $7,500 for personal selling and $2,500 for advertising.

■

This example is oversimplified, but at least it gives some idea of the proper approach. We will examine the marketing mix in Chapter Fourteen, which covers marketing in some detail.

STEP 9: DEVELOPING AN ORGANIZATIONAL PLAN

Entrepreneurs should now assemble, at least on paper, the team they need for their new venture. First, they should spell out:

☐ What needs to be done to carry out their marketing and production plans
☐ Who reports to whom
☐ What qualifications are required for above-average performance of each job

Having analyzed and described their needs, entrepreneurs may now prepare an organizational chart, defining who does what and who reports to whom.

The subjects of organizational planning and human relations are covered in some detail in Chapters Ten and Sixteen, respectively.

STEP 10: DEVELOPING A LEGAL PLAN

This step takes us into the legal arena. Here, entrepreneurs must decide whether to go it alone as a sole proprietor, share their venture with one or more partners, or incorporate. Each choice has its advantages and disadvantages. Which one is best hinges on a host of issues—among them, personal preference, taxes, and personal wealth.

At the first opportunity, the entrepreneur should see a lawyer for advice. The lawyer should be someone expert in new ventures, preferably with experience in the entrepreneur's industry.

These and other legal questions are dealt with in some detail in Chapter Seven.

STEP 11: DEVELOPING AN ACCOUNTING PLAN

Entrepreneurs often overlook the accounting side of their venture. They reason that records can be put off until tomorrow, except that tomorrow never seems to come. Entrepreneurs mistakenly prefer to work on more pressing matters such as marketing and production plans.

From the start, entrepreneurs must keep records in order to know how well their venture is doing and in what direction it is moving. So it behooves the entrepreneur to have an accountant design a record-keeping system before, and not after, starting the venture.

The system need not be complex. It does not have to consist of journals and ledgers and worksheets. It can be quite simple. If the system only requires that notes and figures be kept on the backs of old envelopes, so be it—as long as these notes and figures enable the entrepreneur to keep on top of the job. As a rule, the best record-keeping system is one that will:

☐ Ensure a high degree of accuracy
☐ Handle information at low cost
☐ Turn out reports quickly
☐ Minimize theft and fraud

The subject of accounting as well as the related subject of control are discussed in some detail in Chapters Eleven and Twelve, respectively.

STEP 12: DEVELOPING AN INSURANCE PLAN

Like record keeping, insurance is a step that entrepreneurs often ignore, sometimes until well after their venture has been launched. This shortsighted attitude is hazardous. Entrepreneurs must protect themselves and their venture from any unforeseen events that may threaten their very survival—such as fire and theft.

To provide for their protection, entrepreneurs should develop a program of risk management before they launch their venture. Such a program would specify:

☐ Where dollar losses may occur
☐ How severe such losses might be
☐ How to treat these risks

To make sure the risk-management program is tailored to the needs of their venture, entrepreneurs should seek the help of an insurance agent and perhaps the help of a lawyer as well.

The subject of insurance is explored in much greater detail in Chapter Nineteen.

STEP 13: DEVELOPING A FINANCIAL PLAN

A financial plan ties together all the preceding steps by translating production, marketing, and organizational plans into dollars. In other words, the financial plan is a dollar expression of the entrepreneur's operating plans, as shown in Exhibit 6-3.

Dollars provide the common denominator by means of which dissimilar parts of a venture may be added or subtracted, multiplied or divided. For example, how could an entrepreneur possibly add together trucks and hammers, land and light bulbs unless such assets were expressed in dollars? That is one reason for preparation of a financial plan.

Another reason is that dollars enable entrepreneurs to communicate better. Investors and creditors, for example, understand needs expressed in dollars far better than they do needs expressed in physical terms. Only when reduced

EXHIBIT 6-3

Translating Operating Plans into Financial Plans

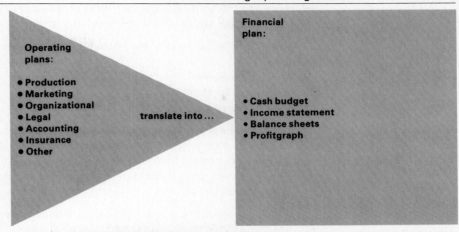

Operating plans:

- Production
- Marketing
- Organizational
- Legal
- Accounting
- Insurance
- Other

translate into...

Financial plan:

- Cash budget
- Income statement
- Balance sheets
- Profitgraph

to dollars does an entrepreneur's need for, say, 15,000 square feet of floor space and a 55-foot distillation column make sense.

However, dollars cannot paint a complete picture of a new venture. Some vital parts simply cannot be expressed in dollar terms. How can entrepreneurs put a dollar value on their managerial skills, for example? Yet it is these skills that often spell the difference between success or failure. Nor can entrepreneurs put a dollar value on such intangible things as teamwork and morale, knowledge and idea-generating ability.

Entrepreneurs should know the mechanics of preparing a financial plan. It should be made up of these statements:

☐ A cash budget
☐ An income statement
☐ Balance sheets
☐ A profitgraph (breakeven chart)

The cash budget Of these statements, the most important one is the cash budget because it tells entrepreneurs:

☐ How much money they need before they can open for business
☐ How much money they need after they open for business

The cash budget helps entrepreneurs make sure the money will be there when bills fall due. The cash budget also acts as a signaling device because it enables entrepreneurs to pinpoint future cash shortages and surpluses. A shortage, for example, signals a need to raise more money. Otherwise, marketing and production may have to be cut back to make ends meet.

As a financial tool, the cash budget is indispensable. It not only helps entrepreneurs to spot possible cash-flow problems but also gives investors and creditors precise answers to such questions as these:

☐ How much money does the entrepreneur need to carry out the business plan?
☐ When is it needed?
☐ How will it be spent?
☐ How soon can it be repaid?

The balance sheet and income statement Besides the cash budget, entrepreneurs should also prepare two balance sheets and one income statement. Though less important than the cash budget, these statements are vital parts of every business plan. Commercial banks, in particular, appreciate balance sheets because they show:

☐ The dollar amounts the entrepreneur expects to spend on such assets as inventories, machines, and land
☐ How the entrepreneur expects to finance these assets

Entrepreneurs should prepare not one but two balance sheets—one that projects the beginning of their first year of business and the other that projects the end of their first year.

They should also prepare an income statement. This statement summarizes both expected sales revenues and expected operating expenses. The difference between them, of course, equals profit or loss.

The profitgraph The last statement to be prepared is the *profitgraph*, commonly called the *breakeven chart*. We prefer the term *profitgraph* because *breakeven* suggests that entrepreneurs expect only to break even. Entrepreneurs naturally expect to do better than that.

The profitgraph shows how sales volume, selling price, and operating expenses affect profits. It also tells entrepreneurs how much product they must sell before they begin to make a profit.

Preparation of a financial plan is anything but easy, and often frustrating to the entrepreneur who lacks financial knowledge. For help, entrepreneurs should turn to their accountant or banker.

These and other financial aspects are covered in greater detail in Chapters Nine and Thirteen; the profitgraph is covered in Chapter Twelve.

STEP 14: WRITING A COVER LETTER

Though not really part of the business plan, the cover letter nonetheless plays a vital role. It is a selling tool, addressed mostly to investors and creditors. In the letter, the entrepreneur summarizes the plan in just a few words, giving special attention to its purpose and promise.

SUMMARY

As an essential step in getting their venture off the ground, would-be entrepreneurs must prepare a business plan. The business plan enables entrepreneurs to anticipate the opportunities, costs, difficulties, and requirements of deciding to go into business, establishing the business, and operating the business.

In essence, the business plan forces entrepreneurs to build their venture on paper first. It is a vital tool—to entrepreneurs because its preparation forces them to think about what they must do and how to do it; and to creditors and investors because it helps them decide whether to finance the entrepreneur.

To prepare the plan, the entrepreneur must pursue facts unstintingly. The plan will stand or fall on the completeness of the entrepreneur's fact finding. In particular, the entrepreneur must dig out the facts that bear on production and marketing, organization and legal aspects.

Help in preparing the business plan may come from accountants, lawyers, bankers, local Chambers of Commerce, and trade associations.

DISCUSSION AND REVIEW QUESTIONS

1 Why should you, a would-be entrepreneur, prepare a business plan?
2 In the business plan, which step is the most critical one? Explain.
3 Why is the cash budget more meaningful than either the income statement or the balance sheet?
4 Define these terms: *planning, business plan, market potential, marketing mix, organizational chart, cash budget, profitgraph.*
5 Why do so few entrepreneurs prepare a business plan?
6 How would you, as an entrepreneur, go about gathering facts to prepare your own business plan?
7 To what situations besides new ventures is the business plan applicable? Explain.
8 Why is the entrepreneur's forecast of sales revenues the single most important figure estimate?
9 Why is the business plan as important to creditors and investors as it is to the entrepreneur?
10 Why, in preparing the business plan, must entrepreneurs document all facts, back all assumptions, and give the authority for all opinions?
11 What questions does marketing research help to answer?
12 To prepare your business plan, whose professional help would you seek out? Why?
13 Do you agree that *profitgraph* is a better term than *breakeven chart*? Why?
14 In a business plan, how does the financial plan relate to operating plans?
15 What pitfall must entrepreneurs avoid when choosing a site for their venture? Explain.

In 1976, Richard Peabody launched his own venture—to sell motorcycle accessories. At the time, his long-range goal was to retire in ten years with an equity of $1 million. It is now 1980, and he is far short of that goal. To help achieve this goal, Mr. Peabody is wondering whether to buy out a competitor or to open a second store in a sprawling shopping mall—or do both now.

In the last 15 years, Mr. Peabody has owned 15 motorcycles. "Motorcycles are a mania with me," says Mr. Peabody. "Gas-guzzling automobiles aren't for me. Motorcycles are superior. They give me that heady feeling of freedom and gusto that I crave." Indeed, he once rode a motorcycle from coast to coast and back in 49 days in the dead of winter.

BACKGROUND

A veteran of the Vietnam War, Mr. Peabody first gave serious thought to going into business for himself when he left the U.S. Army in 1970. His war experiences had convinced him that he would be "miserable unless I were my own boss. I wanted greater control over what I wanted to do in life. And, having my very own business seemed the best way to do that."

Although taking orders annoyed him, he credits his tour of army duty with maturing him. "I went in wet behind the ears and came out a man." Trained as both an artilleryman and a wheel-and-truck vehicle mechanic, he rose from private to motor sergeant of his battery in just 14 months. "I learned some valuable lessons," says Mr. Peabody. "The Army taught me patience and how to get along with people. They also taught me how to fix almost anything that's broken."

To prepare himself for a venture of his own, one of Mr. Peabody's first acts was to enroll in a community college that featured a complete accredited curriculum in small-business management. Once enrolled, however, he decided to go after a dual degree, in accounting as well as small-business management.

Often on the dean's list, he once earned straight A's one quarter carrying a full load of courses and working 50 hours a week as a gas station attendant. With time out for cycling trips to Florida and California, he earned his dual degree in five years. A year later, in 1976, he launched his own venture. His beginning balance sheet appears in Exhibit 6A-1.

"Thank heaven for the GI Bill of Rights," says Mr. Peabody. "I never would have realized my dream without it, because no bank would help me. I knew I needed $65,000 to open my doors for business. And all I had in my name was a piddling $222 in cash and a motorcycle worth $2,800. I don't blame the banks for refusing to risk their depositors' money to help me get started."

GI BILL HELPFUL

Even so, Mr. Peabody soon found that all the GI Bill did was "open doors." Its purpose, of course, is to reward veterans by helping them adjust to civilian life. "Grateful as I am for the GI Bill, I sure wish the U.S. Veterans

Beginning Balance Sheet (February 15, 1976)

Assets			Equities	
Current assets				
Cash	$10,350		Long-term loan	$40,000
Inventory	26,000	$36,350	Owners' equity	500
Fixed assets				
Shelving & fixtures	$ 2,400			
Other	1,000	3,400		
Other assets				
Organizational cost	$ 250			
Prepaid rent	500	750		
Total assets		$40,500		$40,500

Administration had held my hand when I applied for a $65,000 loan. Instead, they sent me to the SBA because they were in charge of all veterans' loans.

"I was so naive that I thought it would be a breeze getting an SBA loan. It wasn't. The red tape, you just wouldn't believe. They fooled around for eight months before I finally got my loan.

"What really got to me was that I probably was better prepared and better qualified than anybody else for a loan. Would you believe my business plan was 44 pages long—and they still wrapped so much red tape around me that I could barely move? And, when I finally got my loan, it was for $40,000 and *not* the $65,000 called for by my business plan. You talk about frustration!"

A NOVEL SOLUTION

At one point, he was so frustrated that he went to a former professor of his for relief. After listening to Mr. Peabody's litany of complaints about government red tape, the professor suggested to Mr. Peabody that he write a special-delivery letter to the head of the SBA in Washington, Mitchell Kobelinski.

His professor's suggestion worked. Just days later, a letter came from Mr. Kobelinski himself stating that his office would look into Mr. Peabody's complaint "immediately." Then, on the very same day, Mr. Peabody received a telephone call from the SBA loan officer he had been working with. "Mr. Peabody, your loan application looks in order," said the loan officer. "I'm sure our loan-review committee will approve it in a day or so, and you'll have your check for $40,000 the day after that."

"Wow, I couldn't believe it," says Mr. Peabody. "I was so happy that I didn't even remind the loan officer that I really needed $65,000, not the $40,000 they had agreed to lend me. I wanted to leave well enough alone."

MARKETING RESEARCH

Until now, all Mr. Peabody had was a business on paper. His business plan was his blueprint, containing forecasts like those in Exhibits 6A-2 and 6A-3. He

Projected First-Year Income Statement

Sales revenues		$102,000
Cost of goods sold		
Beginning inventory	$10,000	
Delivered cost of purchases	85,000	
Merchandise available for sale	$95,000	
Less: Ending inventory	28,000	67,000
Gross profit		$ 35,000
Operating expenses		
Salaries and wages	$23,000	
Rent	10,800	
Depreciation	2,600	
Utilities	1,800	
Advertising	1,650	
Payroll taxes	1,500	
Miscellaneous	1,400	
Telephone	1,200	
Delivery and travel	1,050	
Insurance	600	
Stationery	600	
Maintenance	600	46,800
Operating loss		($ 11,800)

was sure that he had thoroughly researched the market for motorcycle accessories. He found, for example, that:

☐ On the average, motorcycle buyers belong to the middle and upper-middle income brackets
☐ They own either a so-called street or an off-the-road motorcycle, not a customized one (or "chopper")

Mr. Peabody also found that this street and off-the-road market was largely ignored by merchants in his area, which boasted a population of 1.7 million. In fact, of the 84 merchants listed in the Yellow Pages, only two served this market aggressively. Perhaps his most astonishing finding about motorcyclists was that:

☐ 59.8 percent are married
☐ 46.2 percent are college graduates
☐ $14,200 is their median income (as of 1974)
☐ $16,800 is their average income (as of 1974)
☐ 25 is their median age

These statistics belie the Hell's Angels image often depicted in the movies. "I had no idea the average motorcyclist was so well off," says Mr. Peabody. "My friends still don't believe me when I tell them who my customers are, that

Profitgraph from Business Plan

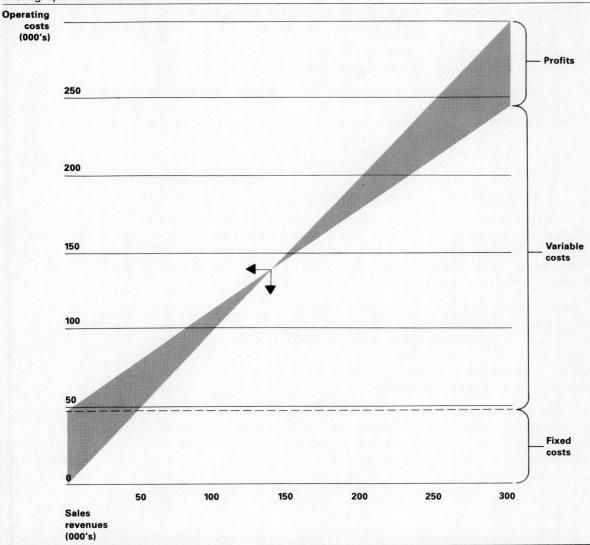

motorcyclists are better educated and make more money than the average American." Other information that he unearthed included the following:

☐ The industry is growing at a rate of 15 percent a year, with accessory sales growing at an even greater rate: 25 percent a year.
☐ Parts and accessories make up 40 percent of the money spent on motor-cycling each year.

"Clearly, I was in the right market at the right time, and I was the right person to exploit the market. The match was near-perfect. I knew motorcycling inside out; I enjoyed it more than anything else; and my market was soaring. Believe me, those facts made me confident that I would succeed."

OPENING HIS DOORS FOR BUSINESS

In March 1976, Mr. Peabody opened his doors for business in Bedford. (See Exhibit 6A-4.) He had looked at just one other site, in Twinsburg. "My business plan made it real easy for me to pick the right site," says Mr. Peabody. His business plan had specified that the right site offer:

☐ A free-standing building, 50 to 100 feet off the street, with a basement for storage of inventory
☐ Ample parking for both motorcycles and automobiles, both in front and in back of the building
☐ Cheap rent, no more than $7 per square foot of space
☐ Closeness to a freeway intersection, no more than two miles away
☐ At least 2,000 square feet of floor space
☐ A full-windowed facade, to afford ample display of motorcycle accessories

With these guidelines firmly in mind, Mr. Peabody settled on the site in Bedford. It had been empty for three years. "It was an ideal site," says Mr. Peabody. "Funny thing is, it used to be a place to make pornographic movies. There were so many complaints from nearby residents that the city fathers had to shut it down."

LEGAL FORM OF ORGANIZATION

A year before he opened for business, Mr. Peabody hired a lawyer to "make sure I was covered legally." He had known the lawyer personally for nine years; and he was impressed with the lawyer's experience in corporate law, lease contracts, and zoning law. On the lawyer's advice, Mr. Peabody decided that the Subchapter S form of legal organization would be best for his venture. Excerpts from his business plan follow:

> The attractive aspect of the Subchapter S corporation is that it allows losses incurred by a small company like mine to be distributed to shareholders on a percentage-of-investment basis. Shareholders may then treat these losses as tax deductions from their other income, up to the extent of their investment.
>
> Thus, a $1,000 loss to a shareholder in the 30 percent tax bracket would mean a $300 return on his investment because of tax savings. . . . Profits, if distributed to shareholders as dividends, are taxed, not at the corporate level, but at the shareholders' level only—thus avoiding the double taxation that shareholders of regular corporations must pay on dividends.

It cost Mr. Peabody $250 to incorporate. He pays his lawyer a $400 retainer each year. "All that means," says Mr. Peabody, "is that I can pick up the phone and get a one-sentence answer to a legal problem. It's a real comfort to know my lawyer is there for help when I need him."

MARKETING STRATEGY

Mr. Peabody's marketing research had revealed that motorcyclists complain most about service. "That's why I decided to sell accessories only and not

Views of Bedford Store

motorcycles also," says Mr. Peabody. His research had also revealed that the accessory market, although looked upon by most dealers as a sideline, was actually more profitable than the motorcycle market. (See Exhibit 6A-5.) "By specializing in this aspect of the business, I could offer my buying public more of what they wanted. That way, I could encourage them to spend more money at my store." Excerpts from his business plan follow:

I plan to offer my customers goods and services that they want, at fair prices, in an atmosphere that makes them feel comfortable. My marketing

Top 20 Motorcycle Accessories

1	Helmets	**11**	Seats
2	Luggage racks	**12**	Fenders
3	Sissy bars	**13**	Exhaust systems
4	Eye protection	**14**	Windshields
5	Apparel	**15**	Gloves
6	Tires	**16**	Footpegs
7	Safety bars	**17**	Boots
8	Handle bars	**18**	Tubes
9	Fairings	**19**	Lighting equipment
10	Saddlebags	**20**	Grips

strategy will attempt to attain a steady clientele, by being a place where shopping is pleasant and where employees are knowledgeable and courteous. My customers will *always* be satisfied that they are getting the most for their dollar, and that they have been treated *fairly.* Services will include:

- ☐ **Wheel truing and spoking** Few dealers now offer this service, which requires special tools that the average motorcyclist does not have.
- ☐ **Installation of parts** Most motorcyclists possess neither the tools nor the mechanical knowledge to install parts and accessories themselves.
- ☐ **Tire changing**

I intend to sell motorcycle parts and accessories, karts and accessories, and snowmobile accessories at the retail level. My business will be unique because it will be aimed at a specific market. And my advertising, sales promotion, pricing, and store atmosphere will be aimed at attracting that market.

The buying habits of my potential customers are varied. For example, motorcyclists who compete regularly are more likely to buy large quantities of the basic essentials, such as oil and spark plugs, and then come back to replace parts that have broken.

The average street rider, however, buys only when the need arises. On the other hand, the competition rider will buy during the week to make his or her motorcycle track-ready for weekend racing. In contrast, the road rider tends to buy only on rainy days or on weekends. Because of these buying habits, I will attempt to aim my sales at these markets:

- ☐ The replacement market created by competition motorcyclists who are incredibly hard on their equipment and who are always searching for something to make them go faster.

☐ The original market created by street motorcyclists who want to improve the appearance of their motorcycle or to equip it for touring or foul-weather touring.

As part of his marketing research, Mr. Peabody also looked at how strong his competitors were. He began by choosing 21 names at random from the Yellow Pages, which covers a county with a population of 1.7 million. Next, he visited each competitor, posing as a potential customer.

"I then recorded my impressions on 3-by-5 cards, as soon as I left their store," says Mr. Peabody. In most cases, I found that my competitors were courteous and friendly. I did find, however, two areas in which they were lacking. One was their poor display of merchandise; the other was their failure to greet me as I walked into their store."

To lure customers away from his competitors, Mr. Peabody planned to rely mostly on advertising and on his reputation as a "motorcycle pro." His business plan called for:

☐ Placing advertisements in community newspapers and the Yellow Pages
☐ Broadcasting 10-second spots on radio

In January 1981 Mr. Peabody reflected on the five years that had gone by since he first began doing business in Bedford. "I'm proud of what I've accomplished so far," says Mr. Peabody. "My careful planning has really paid off." Indeed, his sales revenues topped $660,000 in 1980. To help reach that sales level, Mr. Peabody:

Acquired another accessory store in nearby Tallmadge for its book value of $20,000. This store had rarely turned a profit. "It was ripe for acquisition," says Mr. Peabody. "The owner tried to run the store on an absentee basis, and it just didn't work out."

Mr. Peabody financed the acquisition by putting in $5,000 of his own money as a loan and by borrowing $15,000 from a commercial bank. He also incorporated the newly acquired store because of the "SBA's first-lien position with my Bedford store."

At both stores, sales have grown steadily, if not dramatically. Note in the table of sales revenues that Tallmadge sales doubled the first full year after he had taken over:

| Year | Sales Revenues at— | |
	Bedford	Tallmadge
1976	$ 87,000	$ 90,000*
1977	169,000	90,000*
1978	227,000	110,000*
1979	324,000	220,000
1980	392,000	270,000

*Under prior owner.

Typical Response to Employee Survey*

To: Employees
Subject: Survey to Help Improve Our Operations

Please do not discuss your answers with anyone else. I would like individual responses, and will collect the information and discuss it with you as a group. Be honest.

1 What five products should we expand into or carry in more depth?
        Answer: Dirt bikes more in depth
                Mini bikes
                Leather vests
                Selling ski jackets in winter

2 What five products should we drop or carry substantially less of?
        Answer: Plastic fenders
                Knapsacks
                Belt buckles
                Locks
                Most of the stuff on the shelves
                  above the spark plugs

3 What area should we place more emphasis on in 1982?
        Answer: Don't know

4 What area should we place less emphasis on in 1982?
        Answer: Touring stuff

5 What can we do to attract more customers in 1982?
        Answer: Put a sign out by the street so people can see the store better. Have Peabody's T-shirts on sale. Not real expensive but always have on sale. Everyone likes them!!

6 What can we do to sell our existing customers more products in 1982?
        Answer: Be nice to them. Show them products and explain them. Tell them your opinion about the product and just be real nice and smile a lot. Don't be grouchy!

7 How can we better serve our customers in 1982?
        Answer: Have something on sale every week. Better information on bikes. Descriptions of questionable items.

8 How can I better serve you? What means of communication can I use to better serve us all?
        Answer: We should have meetings over a pizza or something at Mama Mia's. Get to know each other better.
                You serve me good and I really can't think of how you can serve me better. Maybe a little raise. I don't really think I'm being underpaid; it's just that everyone likes raises.

* By 15-year-old employee

Mr. Peabody believes that this performance stems not only from "careful planning but also from a unique marketing strategy and unequaled customer service. Service is the key in this business," says Mr. Peabody. "That's what creates repeat customers."

He also credits his 12 employees for much of his success. Turnover, by the way, is zero. His employees are young, ranging in age from 14 to 33. "I try to make my employees feel as if they're more than just spokes on a wheel," says Mr. Peabody. "I do that by constantly asking them their ideas on how to run the two stores better." Indeed, he surveys his employees at least once a year, often getting responses like the one appearing in Exhibit 6A-6.

According to Mr. Peabody, what is unique about his marketing strategy is his monthly newsletter. "The newsletter is my most effective advertising tool. It goes only to genuine customers who have signed onto an exclusive mailing list of more than 7,000 names, all of them cyclists."

Each of the 7,000 cyclists, by the way, has met and visited with Mr. Peabody at one of his two stores. "Small wonder that my combined operation is now the largest in the state," says Mr. Peabody.

In 1980, the economy momentarily took a turn for the worse. As a recession set in, Mr. Peabody's two stores unexpectedly found themselves cash-poor, despite rising sales. That year, "a strong spring turned into a soft summer. By fall, conditions had stabilized. Yet my instincts told me to build up inventories anyway, even at the expense of my cash position," says Mr. Peabody.

He wanted to prepare for 1981 by purchasing large quantities of up-to-date, high-quality accessories. "My strategy was to seek sales opportunities while my more cautious competitors were placing their orders with suppliers. It would give me an edge. Believe me, availability of lots of high-quality merchandise is one of the keys to success in the motorcycle accessory business."

A shortage of cash ordinarily would not disturb Mr. Peabody. "I've survived in the past with little or no salary, and I could do it again," says Mr. Peabody. "But I need cash now to keep expanding, to keep improving the quality of my service to customers. Sure, my sales have been great, but I've succeeded without the benefit of a full-fledged service center.

"Not having such a facility has caused me to lose business. Why? Because, although many cyclists are do-it-yourselfers, many of them are not inclined to make repairs or to install accessories. They just don't have the time, knowledge, or tools needed to do so.

"The result is that they often purchase accessories elsewhere, or not at all. That hurts my sales. People have come to trust Peabody's. So they would welcome a single, high-quality service center to solve their repair and installation problems."

Bent on adding a service center in the spring of 1981, Mr. Peabody decided to seek a $40,000 loan from a commercial bank. His letter to the bank, justifying his request for the loan, follows:

- In Bedford, 7,600 square feet of the former Bob Kay American Motors-Jeep dealership have become available with favorable lease terms. This vacated property is less than one block from the existing store, and in a much more visible location. The large, glass-enclosed showroom that once housed new cars will now house the retail store, while a remote building that had been the body shop will become a service center.
- A third corporation will be formed in an effort to isolate the service center, with its inherent higher liability exposure, from the other two corporations.
- The service center will cost money. A comfortable estimate is $40,000. Of that sum, $20,000 will be for machinery and equipment, $10,000 for leasehold improvements and advertising, and the rest for working capital.

  Because of the poor cash-flow position created in 1980, neither the Bedford nor the Tallmadge store will have the moneys needed for this expansion. Of course, cash will also be needed to move the retail store into the vacated showroom mentioned above.
- Peabody's Cycling Systems of Tallmadge, Inc. has a very favorable position as a borrower. This corporation has a vast, unencumbered inventory and little current debt. Its debts to both Peabody's Cycling Systems of Bedford, Inc. and to Richard Peabody are long term.

  A lien position could be offered by the service center, too, on its machinery and equipment. The personal signature of Richard Peabody is also offered.
- So, we propose that a loan of $40,000 be granted immediately to Peabody's Cycling Systems of Tallmadge, Inc. The loan will be used to form Peabody's Cycling Systems Service of Bedford, Inc.
- For your review, we have attached the latest balance sheet for Peabody's Cycling Systems of Tallmadge, Inc. (Exhibit 6A-7). We will call you in a day or so to set up a meeting, either at our Tallmadge store

---

Peabody's Cycling Systems of Tallmadge, Inc.

EXHIBIT 6A-7

Latest Balance Sheet (January 1, 1981)

Assets		Equities	
Inventories	$68,000	Loan, Euclid Bank	$ 9,000
Fixtures and equipment	6,000	Loan, Richard Peabody	16,500
Goodwill	6,000	Loan, PCS* of Bedford	24,000
Cash	3,000	Common stock	500
Prepaid rent	2,000	Retained earnings	36,500
Truck	1,500		
Total assets	$86,500	Total equities	$86,500

* Peabody's Cycling Systems

or at your bank, whichever you prefer. Thank you for giving our proposal the attention it deserves.

1 What accounts for Mr. Peabody's good sales performance? What role did his business plan play, if any? QUESTIONS
2 If you were the bank, would you grant Mr. Peabody the $40,000 loan he now seeks to install a service center? Why?
3 Comment on Mr. Peabody's approach to managing his employees.
4 Could Mr. Peabody have avoided his cash crisis in 1980? How?
5 What suggestions would you make to Mr. Peabody to help him reach his goal of retiring with an equity of $1 million just ten years after he went into business for himself?

CASE 6B   URBAN LEAGUE CLIENT

The Urban League of a large southern city has a small business development center. Its purpose is to "boost the formation of new ventures among minorities." One of its business counselors, Marcia Simms, has prepared a business plan for a client who wants to expand his used-car dealership. He is seeking a $15,000 loan from the SBA, which referred him to the Urban League for help in preparing a business plan. Following are excerpts covering most of the plan as prepared for him by Ms. Simms and then submitted to the SBA.

☐ **Description of industry** Over the years, prices in the auto industry have skyrocketed to such heights that the big auto manufacturers have almost priced themselves out of the market. Despite the high prices, the public is still in the market for a car, but not so much for a new car as for a reliable used car.

In 1980, used-car dealers sold 18 million cars, which amounts to two-thirds of all cars sold that year. Moreover, the increase in used-car prices was only half of the 11 percent increase in new-car prices.

The market for used cars has been for the past decade, and continues to be, a strong and growing one.

☐ **Description of existing venture** Curtis Holmes has been in the used-car business for 20 years. He started his own business operating as Holmes's Used Car Sales in 1960. He was the first black man in the city to receive a license to sell used cars. He also maintains an auto body shop on the lot.

☐ **Competitive advantage** Used-car sales are up considerably compared to new-car sales. Prices are also up, but not so much as to hamper any possible sales. Besides used cars, Mr. Holmes offers such services as customizing of cars, spray painting, and revitalization of stripped-out cars for resale.

☐ **Marketing plan** Within Mr. Holmes's trading area, very little marketing will be necessary to expand used-car sales. Advertising spots on both radio and television will be his main marketing tools.

Yearly Estimates (Condensed)

Sales revenues	$150,000
Cost of sales	115,650
Gross profit	$ 34,350
Operating expenses*	20,200
Operating profit	$ 14,150

* Excludes salary for Mr. Holmes

☐ **Method of distribution** Mr. Holmes sells used cars from his lot, which he owns outright. He obtains his supply of cars mainly from auto auctions held in the county once a month.

☐ **Financial information** See Exhibit 6B-1.

On the strength of this business plan, should the SBA lend Mr. Holmes the $15,000 he seeks? Why?

QUESTION

CASE 6C

DECOR, INCORPORATED

Theodora Minelli has created a product she calls the *Old Mill.* To make and market the mill, Mrs. Minelli has formed Decor, Incorporated.

What is the Old Mill like? It is a decorative centerpiece—a lighted log cabin cradled in a shallow bowl against a floral background, with water splashing softly over a motor-driven water wheel.

Mrs. Minelli believes "its rustic charm will appeal strongly to homemakers who wish to enhance the look of their living rooms." She plans to sell the mill to large discount chains at a price of $30.00 each.

Materials will cost $14.00 per mill. Overhead will run about $4,000 a month. Mrs. Minelli believes her overhead will not change over the short run, regardless of volume of production.

How many mills must Mrs. Minelli sell each month before she begins to make a profit?

QUESTION

CHAPTER SEVEN

LEGAL ASPECTS

questions for mastery

how complex are the legal issues facing all small businesses?

how do you find the right lawyer?

what are the differences among sole proprietorships, partnerships, and corporations?

how do government regulations affect small businesses?

how important is it to keep up with the law?

The law is a jealous mistress.

George Sharswood

We often pride ourselves on being a nation governed by laws. So much so, that today it is all but impossible to move in many walks of life without first consulting a lawyer. Undertaking a new business venture is no exception. This chapter deals with the would-be entrepreneur's need for legal help, focusing on choosing a lawyer, deciding upon a legal form of organization, and coping with government regulations.

THE NEED FOR LEGAL ADVICE

To avoid breaking the law and to spot opportunities permitted by law, entrepreneurs need expert legal help. One of the entrepreneur's earliest acts should be to get a lawyer. Only a lawyer can help resolve the maze of legal issues raised in Exhibit 7-1, ranging from questions having to do with whether to incorporate to questions having to do with the rights of consumers.

Entrepreneurs need not necessarily consider all of the questions listed in Exhibit 7-1. The complexity of the entrepreneur's venture determines which questions must be dealt with.

EXAMPLE

An entrepreneur launching a 20-employee, million-dollar plant to make hazardous chemicals would most likely be concerned with all of the questions listed. An entrepreneur launching a part-time accounting practice working out of her own home, with herself as the sole employee, would likely be concerned with few of the questions posed.

■

Often, entrepreneurs feel they need a lawyer only when they are sued or when they sue others. This attitude is indefensible. Lawyers are by no means merely actors in tense courtroom dramas; in fact, many lawyers never set foot in a courtroom. Their more creative role is to advise entrepreneurs in such a way that it need never be necessary to go to court.

The best remedy for legal mistakes is to keep from making them. Perhaps the most apt way to describe the lawyer's role is as a kind of preventive medicine.

CHOOSING THE RIGHT LAWYER

It behooves entrepreneurs to get the right lawyer months before they plan to launch their venture. And they should choose a lawyer with the same care as they would a brain surgeon. A common mistake is to select someone recommended by friends, neighbors, or relatives whose needs for legal help may differ sharply from those of the entrepreneur. Often the personal lawyers of family or friends do not know much about new ventures, although they may be quite knowledgeable about other aspects of the law. To find the right lawyer, entrepreneurs should instead follow such guidelines as these:

☐ Seek out the names of lawyers held in high esteem by the business community. The best sources of names are usually other entrepreneurs who are

EXHIBIT 7-1

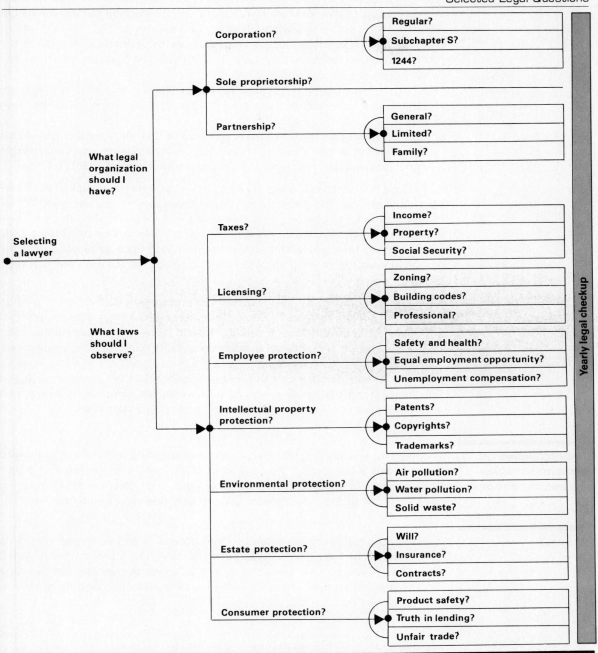

Selected Legal Questions

both seasoned and successful. As such, they are most likely to offer honest opinions about the skills of the lawyers who helped them get started.

Other good sources are the loan officers of commercial banks. They generally know firsthand which lawyers are good at helping entrepreneurs get started. Professors of law are another good source.

☐ Check the backgrounds of lawyers who are recommended to you in the *Martindale and Hubbell Directory.* This directory is updated yearly by the American Bar Association.

☐ Narrow the list of names to those whose law firms are small. Such firms are likely to be more accessible, more personal, and less expensive than large firms.

☐ Choose the right lawyer. In making a choice, the entrepreneur should be sure that the lawyer's expert knowledge "is accompanied by a reasonable match in personal chemistry. Do the parties hit it off together?"[1]

Once they choose the right lawyer, entrepreneurs are mistaken if they sit back and leave all the decision making to their lawyer. The main job of the lawyer should be to advise and to inform the entrepreneur. Only the entrepreneur should make the legal decisions, based on information provided by the lawyer. To do that wisely, the entrepreneur should become familiar with the law. In the words of Dr. Patrick R. Liles, formerly of the Harvard Business School:

> A major difficulty for the inexperienced entrepreneur is the host of strange terms and phrases which are scattered throughout most legal documents. The novice in this kind of reading should have some understanding not only of *what* is contained in such documents, but also *why* these provisions have been included.
>
> If an entrepreneur cannot find the time or take the interest to read and understand the major contracts into which his company will enter, he should be very cautious about being an entrepreneur at all.[2]

UNDERSTANDING THE LEGALITIES OF FRANCHISING AND BUY-OUTS

The need for finding the right lawyer is just as pressing for entrepreneurs who prefer to buy a franchise or buy out an existing venture as for those who start from scratch. In fact, in these two cases the need often is more pressing because many of the legal aspects have already been reduced to writing.

EXAMPLE

Franchise agreements often run into dozens of pages. Entrepreneurs as franchisees have little choice but to observe the franchisor's fine print. First, however, they need the help of a lawyer to translate the "strange terms and phrases" mentioned by Dr. Liles and discussed more fully in Chapter Five.

1. Patrick R. Liles, *New Business Ventures and the Entrepreneur* (Homewood, Ill.: Richard D. Irwin, Inc., 1974), p. 77.
2. Ibid., p. 78.

Buying out an existing venture calls for an exhaustive audit of the seller's legal documents, including deeds, sales contracts, employment contracts, purchase contracts, and the like. Chapter Four contains a more complete discussion of the factors to consider in a buy-out.

■

Legal services are expensive, although some relief is on the way. Innovations of all kinds are now sweeping the practice of law—from prepaid legal services aimed at cutting costs to computerization of legal procedures. But it will be some time before such innovations are practiced widely.

LEGAL FORMS OF ORGANIZATION

Choosing a legal form of organization—be it a sole proprietorship, partnership or corporation—ranks among the entrepreneur's most vital decisions. This choice affects a number of managerial and financial issues: for example, the amount of taxes the entrepreneur may pay, whether the entrepreneur personally may be sued for unpaid business bills, and whether the venture dies automatically when the entrepreneur himself dies.

Entrepreneurs often ask, "Is there one best form of organization?" The answer is no. The best form of organization depends on the entrepreneur's likes and dislikes, the venture's needs, and the entrepreneur's tax bracket. In the words of the SBA:

No one legal form of organization, or for that matter no combination of two or more of them, is suited to each and every small business. To try to say what is the best form for all enterprises would be like trying to select an all-purpose suit for a man.

In choosing a legal form of organization, consideration to the parties concerned must be made—their likes, dislikes and dispositions, their immediate and long-range needs and their tax situations. Seldom, if ever, does any one factor completely determine which is best.[3]

Let us now look at each of the major legal forms of organization from the viewpoint of the entrepreneur. For each one, we shall focus on the advantages as well as the disadvantages.

SOLE PROPRIETORSHIPS   Sole proprietorships are the most popular legal form of organization, accounting for 78 percent of all businesses. Because most of them are small, often employing only the entrepreneur, lay persons tend to equate small business with sole proprietorships only. However, a sole proprietorship may be as large as a million-dollar foundry or as small as a corner newsstand.

3. U.S. Small Business Administration, *Choosing a Form of Business Organization* (Washington, D.C.: U.S. Government Printing Office, 1965), p. 10.

Features Freedom is the most striking feature of a sole proprietorship. Because they own all of a venture, sole proprietors answer to no one but themselves. They alone may reap the rewards of a successful venture or, conversely, the bitter fruit of failure.

Another feature of the sole proprietorship is its simplicity. A sole proprietorship is easy to form. Often, entrepreneurs need only nail a shingle on the door telling the world they are in business for themselves. No law forces them to register with a governmental body. The lack of complex procedures is why this legal form of organization appeals so strongly to the do-it-yourself, independent-minded entrepreneur.

The sole proprietorship also offers tax benefits for new ventures likely to suffer losses before profits begin to flow. Tax laws permit sole proprietors to treat, as part of their personal finances, the revenues and expenses of their venture. They can cut taxes by deducting any operating losses from personal income acquired from other sources.

Still another attractive feature of the sole proprietorship is its low start-up cost. Legal fees are likely to be low, mostly because the entrepreneur is spared the expense of incorporating, which may run into many hundreds of dollars. But if a venture is to be called a name other than his or her own, the entrepreneur must seek legal help to make sure the name is not already being used by another business in the same state.

Drawbacks The main drawbacks of the sole proprietorship are unlimited liability, lack of continuity, and the difficulty of raising money.

☐ **Unlimited liability** Entrepreneurs are personally liable for all debts incurred by their venture. Thus, they must pay bills out of their own pocket if their venture fails to generate enough cash flow. Creditors may step in and claim the entrepreneur's savings, house, or personal possessions. Unlimited liability is perhaps the most distasteful feature of a sole proprietorship.

☐ **Lack of continuity** Legally, a venture dies when the sole proprietor dies. It can, of course, be reorganized soon after the proprietor's death if a successor has been trained to take over. But often, executors or heirs must liquidate because no heir can run the venture.

☐ **Difficulty of raising money** Sole proprietors generally find it hard to raise money not only to start up but also to expand. Commercial bankers, for example, tend to reject proprietors who are the sole strength of their venture. Bankers fear they may not be able to recover their loan if the proprietor becomes disabled.

GENERAL PARTNERSHIPS

A general partnership is really a sole proprietorship multiplied by the number of partners. It is the least popular form of organization, accounting for only 7 percent of all businesses. The most striking feature of the general partnership is its ability to grow by adding talent and money. That way, the partnership avoids one of the most serious drawbacks of a sole proprietorship, the dependence of the success of the venture on the resources of only one person.

Features There is no legal limit to the number of partners in a venture. There may be as many as 100 or more, or as few as 2. Partners may invest equal or unequal sums of money. And they may earn profits that bear no relation to their investment. For example, in a two-person partnership, a partner with no investment may get 50 percent or more of the profits.

As defined by the Uniform Partnership Act, a partnership is a "voluntary association of two or more persons to carry on as co-owners a business for profit." Like a sole proprietorship, a partnership is generally easy to organize, with few legal requirements.

Even so, all partnerships begin with an agreement of some kind. It may be written, spoken, or even unspoken. But the wise entrepreneur insists on a written agreement to avoid trouble later. This agreement should spell out such things as these:

☐ Who invested what sums of money in the partnership
☐ Who gets what share of the partnership profits
☐ Who does what and who reports to whom
☐ How the partnership may be dissolved, and in that event, how assets left over would be distributed among partners
☐ How surviving partners would be protected from the decedent's estate

A partnership agreement is a private document. The law does not require the entrepreneur to file the agreement with a government agency, nor does it regard a partnership as a legal entity. In the eyes of the law, a partnership is simply two or more persons working together. The partnership's lack of legal standing means that the U.S. Internal Revenue Service taxes partners as individuals. This feature often attracts wealthy investors seeking a tax shelter. We will say more about tax shelters in Chapter Eighteen.

In summary, the advantages of a partnership are ease of formation, a broad pool of talent, multiple sources of money, and possible tax advantages. However, there are some drawbacks to the partnership form of organization.

Drawbacks Unlimited liability is the worst drawback of a partnership. By law, each partner may be held liable for debts incurred in the name of the partnership. And if any partner incurs a debt unbeknownst to the other partners, they are all liable if the offending partner cannot pay the debt. This legal wrinkle holds even if the partnership agreement calls for all notes and bills to be endorsed by the other partners:

If one partner signs an order for 200 cases of salad oil to be delivered to a partnership's store and he cannot pay for the order, then the other partner must foot the bill—even if she disapproves of the deal, the terms, or her partner's method of operating.[4]

Another drawback is lack of continuity. When one partner dies or pulls out, a partnership legally dies also even if the other partners agree to stay on.

4. *The Time-Life Family Legal Guide* (New York: Time-Life Books, 1971), p. 187.

The liquidation of a partnership, however, need not cause a loss of revenues. If they wish, the surviving partners may quickly form a new partnership to retain the business of the old partnership.

A related drawback is the difficulty of transferring ownership. Because the law regards a partnership as a sibling relationship, no partners may sell out without the consent of the other partners. A partner wishing to retire or to transfer his or her interest to a son or daughter must get the others' consent.

The life of a partnership often depends on the ability of retiring partners to find someone compatible with the other partners to buy them out. Failure to do so may lead to forced liquidation of the partnership. If they can pay the price, the other partners may buy out a retiring partner. Surviving partners may also be faced with liquidation when a partner dies.

OTHER FORMS OF PARTNERSHIP

The entrepreneur may avoid the problem of unlimited liability by forming a limited partnership. In such an arrangement, limited partners may invest their money without being held liable for debts made by active partners on behalf of the partnership. If the business goes under, limited partners are liable only to the extent of their investment. However, limited partners may not take an active role in the operations of the venture.

More complex than general partnerships, limited partnerships require legal help to organize. All partners, for example, must register in each state in which the partnership plans to do business. Limited partners must make sure they behave as limited partners, avoiding any hint of being active in the day-to-day routine of the business. Otherwise, they risk losing their preferred status as limited partners.

Two other forms of organization have evolved to offset the defects of the general partnership. One is the *family partnership,* which enables partners to split income among members of their families to avoid high taxes. Another is the *real estate investment trust* (REIT). Managed by a trustee, REIT's enjoy both continuity of life and ease of ownership transfer.

REGULAR CORPORATIONS

As shown in Exhibit 7-2, corporations dominate the business world. They account for 87 percent of all revenues generated by the nation's businesses. Yet they make up only 15 percent of the total number of businesses.

To the lay person, the corporation is the legal form of organization used only by big business. The very word *corporation* inspires awe and respect, bespeaks bigness and power. But the tiny corner newsstand has as much right to incorporate as a giant steel mill. And, it matters not whether a venture has thousands of shareholders or just one. In short, the corporation is a versatile legal tool capable of serving the entire spectrum of business.

In the words of Chief Justice John Marshall of the U.S. Supreme Court, a corporation is "an artificial being, invisible, intangible, and existing only in

EXHIBIT 7-2

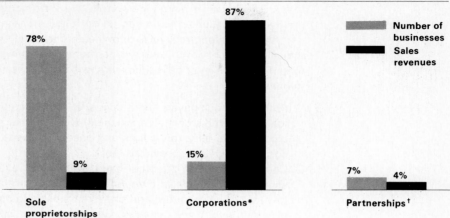

Relative Importance of Legal Forms of Organization

Most businesses form sole proprietorships, but corporations account for most of the revenues.

* Includes regular, Subchapter S, and other corporate forms.
† Includes general, limited, and other partnership forms.
Source: U.S. Department of Commerce, *Data Book, U.S.A.* (Washington, D.C.: U.S. Government Printing Office, 1980), p. 266.

contemplation of the law.''[5] By these words, the Supreme Court defined the corporation as a legal person. A corporation can therefore:

☐ Sue and be sued
☐ Buy, hold, and sell property
☐ Make and sell products to consumers
☐ Commit crimes and be tried and punished for them

Features Limited liability is the most striking feature of a corporation. It limits an investor's liability to his or her personal investment in the corporation. In the event of failure, the bankruptcy courts may seize a corporation's assets and sell them to pay debts, but the courts cannot touch the personal possessions of shareholders.

Limited liability is perhaps the major reason why lawyers often recommend the corporate form of organization. However, entrepreneurs should remember that, in some cases, limited liability may be meaningless. For example, if all of one's personal assets are tied up in a venture, then limited liability would offer little protection. Entrepreneurs should also remember that, no matter what legal form of organization they use, some personal possessions will be protected by law.

5. Quoted in Lowell B. Howard, *Business Law* (Woodbury, N.Y.: Barron's Woodbury Press, 1965), p. 332.

Another striking feature of the corporation is its continuity. Its life is independent of the lives of those who founded it. In other words, if the corporation prospers, it may outlive its founders. This feature stems from the fact that a corporation is a legal person. As the state's creation, it is independent of the lives of its founders and can go on forever, at least in theory.

A related feature is ease of ownership transfer, which takes place through the sale of stock. Corporations raise money by selling shares of stock to investors. This stock may be either *preferred* or *common.* The two kinds differ as follows:

☐ Preferred stock pays a fixed dividend, much like the interest payment on a loan. Preferred stockholders also enjoy priority, or preference, over common stockholders as to dividends and assets if a venture liquidates. Few small corporations issue preferred stock.

☐ Common stock, on the other hand, is issued by every corporation. Common shareholders enjoy an ownership interest in profits and assets, though below that of all creditors and preferred stockholders. Common stock may be issued in two forms, either par value or no-par value:

☐ Par value stock appears in the corporation's books at a fixed amount per share—for example, $1, $10, or $100—as specified in the entrepreneur's corporate charter from the state. Except by chance, the par value of the stock bears no relation to either its market value or its book value once a corporation gets underway.

☐ Stated value is the amount fixed by the board of directors for no-par value stock. The stated value governs the amounts to be entered in the corporation's books just as if it were par value stock. The difference between par value and no-par value stock is of little practical significance.

Each common shareholder owns part of the corporation, as evidenced by stock certificates. These certificates give common shareholders certain rights:

☐ To elect the directors of the corporation
☐ To cast one vote per share at shareholders' meetings
☐ To receive dividends in proportion to the number of common shares they hold
☐ To sell their shares to anyone who wants to buy them—unless the certificates say that shareholders must offer to sell them to the corporation first. Moreover, before new common stock is offered for sale, shareholders usually have the right to buy the new shares in proportion to the amount of stock they already own.

However, ownership interest does not give common shareholders the right to act for the corporation or to share in its management. American Telephone and Telegraph, to cite an extreme example, has three million shareholders; only a handful of them have any voice about the way the company is run. Shareholders may influence the running of the corporation by casting their vote for directors once a year. In most cases, though, voting is meaningless because corporate managers tend to offer just one slate of directors for election.

Drawbacks Although ease of ownership transfer is one of the corporations chief attractions, it may nevertheless complicate the life of the entrepreneur. For example, if one or more disgruntled shareholders sell their stock to someone undesirable, the entrepreneur may then be at the mercy of a person bent on overthrowing him or her. One way of sidestepping this problem is for entrepreneurs to keep the right of first refusal on all sales of stock by shareholders.

The death of a major shareholder may pose similar problems. For example, an heir or executor might well insist upon direct control, possibly resulting in a takeover. To avoid such problems, entrepreneurs should buy insurance to make sure they have the money to buy out the decedent's shares.

Forming a corporation costs more than forming either a sole proprietorship or a partnership. The main reason is that legal help is needed to make sure that all state requirements are met. To begin with, a new corporation needs a charter, which is granted by the state. Legal requirements differ from state to state in many vital matters, including:

☐ Taxes
☐ Business fees
☐ Minimum number of directors
☐ Liabilities for debts
☐ Minimum capitalization
☐ Rules for issuing stock

We now see clearly why lawyers tend to favor the corporation. No other legal form offers these advantages:

☐ Limited liability
☐ Ease of raising money
☐ Ease of ownership transfer
☐ Continuity of business life

Exhibit 7-3 compares the regular corporation with the sole proprietorship and general partnership forms of organization. Note that the regular corporation is the most attractive in all ways except freedom from government regulations. Corporations are heavily regulated by law; partnerships and sole proprietorships much less so.

Exhibit 7-3 omits, however, the greatest potential drawback of the corporate form: double taxation. A corporation must pay income taxes on its profits, and then shareholders must pay income taxes on dividends. Dividends are not a tax-deductible expense for a corporation; they come out of after-tax profits. So dividends are taxed twice.

SUBCHAPTER S CORPORATIONS

However, entrepreneurs may avoid double taxation by forming a Subchapter S corporation. This corporate form first appeared in 1958 with the enactment of Subchapter S of the U.S. Internal Revenue Code. It soon became a popular

EXHIBIT 7-3

Relative Advantages and Disadvantages of Main Legal Forms of Organization

	Sole Proprietorship	General Partnership	Regular Corporation
Ease of transfer of ownership	Medium	Low	High
Ease of raising money	Low	Medium	High
Continuity of business life	Low	Low	High
Protection against liability for business debts	Low	Low	High
Freedom from government regulations	High	High	Low
Ease of formation	High	High	Medium

form of organization because it not only avoids double taxation but also keeps such corporate advantages as limited liability.

A Subchapter S corporation enjoys the advantages of a corporation without any of its drawbacks. And because shareholders are taxed as if they were partners, a Subchapter S corporation may also serve as a tax shelter for wealthy investors during the early years of a venture.

There are, however, some strings attached to these advantages. To qualify as a Subchapter S corporation, a venture must meet some stiff legal requirements:

☐ It must be a domestic corporation that is not part of another corporation. In other words, it must be independently owned and managed.
☐ It may have no more than 25 shareholders.
☐ Only individuals or estates are permitted as shareholders. This requirement keeps other corporations from buying shares of its stock.
☐ Nonresident aliens are excluded as shareholders.

Once the venture gets underway, the entrepreneur must make sure that:

☐ No more than 20 percent of sales revenues come from dividends, rents, interest, royalties, annuities, or stock sales
☐ No more than 80 percent of revenues come from foreign nations

Many lawyers question whether the Subchapter S corporation really differs from the regular corporation. They argue that it simply is a corporation that limits size and capital structure. Even so, we believe its ability to avoid double taxation qualifies it as a separate legal form of organization, blending the regular corporation and partnership forms.

1244 CORPORATIONS

To encourage investors to risk their money in small business, Congress in 1958 also enacted Section 1244 of the Internal Revenue Code. Under this section, persons whose investments in a small business become worthless may treat that loss as an ordinary rather than a capital loss.

This tax break now permits investment losses of up to $50,000 a year to be deducted from ordinary income. In contrast, investment losses in regular corporations can be no more than $1,000 a year. To qualify as a Section 1244 corporation, a small business must meet these tests, among others:

☐ For a new venture, no more than $1 million may be raised from sale of common stock.
☐ For an existing venture, with common stock already outstanding, the combined value of that stock and any additional stock issued under Section 1244 must not top $1 million.
☐ The stock must be issued for cash or property, not in exchange for services.
☐ The tax break applies only to men or women—not to corporations, estates, or trusts.

As with Subchapter S corporations, 1244 corporations appeal strongly to the entrepreneur seeking money to launch a risky venture. Investors in high tax brackets are more likely to invest in the entrepreneur's venture if they know that losses, if any, will be tax-deductible as ordinary losses.

EXAMPLE

An entrepreneur has just won a franchise to install a cable-television system in a small suburb of Atlanta. She needs to raise $600,000, half from commercial banks and half from private investors. She plans to attract 30 wealthy investors, selling them $10,000 blocks of stock each. All would fall in the 50 percent income-tax bracket. If the entrepreneur fails, the most that each investor could lose would be $5,000, because $5,000 of the loss ($10,000 $\times$ 50%) would be tax-deductible from each investor's other income. Without Section 1244, the most that they could deduct would be $1,000.

■

GOVERNMENT REGULATIONS AND PAPERWORK

Few subjects spark more complaints among entrepreneurs than the rising tide of government regulations and the avalanche of paperwork they create. In the federal government alone, there are now more than 90 regulatory agencies issuing hundreds of new rules each year. The force of these rules is felt by every business, big or small, and by every American. For example:

The rules of regulatory agencies affect the food that people eat, the cars they drive, the fuel they use, the clothes they wear, the houses they live in, the investments they make, the water they drink, and even the air they breathe.[6]

6. "Federal Regulators: Impact on Every American," *U.S. News & World Report,* May 9, 1977, p. 61.

In fact, one of the fastest growing enterprises in America is the federal regulation business. According to the Center for the Study of American Business at Washington University:

> The growth of the federal regulation business would be the envy of any business executive tracking a company's sales, rising sixfold from $1.2 billion in 1971 to $7.2 billion in 1980.[7]

Exhibit 7-4 shows the growth of the federal regulatory budget.

REGULATIONS AT THREE GOVERNMENT LEVELS

Regulatory agencies exist not only at the federal level but also at the local and state levels. The complex details with which the entrepreneur must comply are exemplified below:

EXAMPLE

In Houston, a small real-estate developer wants to build a number of housing units in a local subdivision. To do that, the developer must first

EXHIBIT 7-4

Growth of Federal Regulations

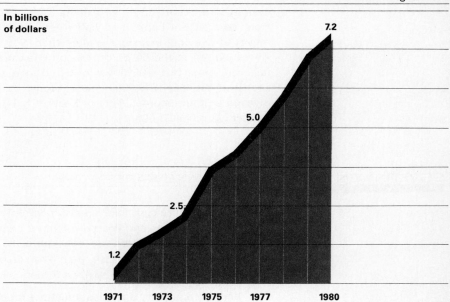

Federal regulatory budget

Between fiscal years 1971 and 1980, federal regulatory budgets went up sixfold, from $1.2 billion to $7.2 billion a year.

Source: Murray L. Weidenbaum, "Public Policy: No Longer a Spectator Sport for Business," *The Journal of Business Strategy* (Summer 1980), p. 47. Reprinted by permission from the *Journal of Business Strategy*, Volume 1, Number 1, Summer 1980, Copyright © 1980, Warren, Gorham and Lamont Inc., 210 South St., Boston, Mass. All Rights Reserved.

7. Adapted from John Cunniff, "Small Firms Devastated by Federal Regulations," Cleveland *Plain Dealer* (March 16, 1980), p. 1-E.

get clearance from a local zoning board and must also file for a local construction permit.

At the state level, the developer must comply with state environmental protection laws and state housing codes.

At the federal level, the developer must comply with various U.S. Housing and Urban Development regulations and U.S. Environmental Protection Agency requirements. Federal regulations differ, depending on the size and location of the subdivision and whether the homes are planned for low, middle, or upper income buyers.[8]

■

Small wonder, then, that so many entrepreneurs complain about federal regulations. According to the White House Conference on Small Business, "Many Americans see their government as too big, too remote, and too overbearing. Nowhere is this view more widely shared than in the small-business community. Small business suffers the effects of government regulations and paperwork on:

☐ Competition and productivity
☐ Innovation and technology
☐ Growth and capital formation

"The cost of regulation is . . . staggering to small business because it is so vulnerable to economic fluctuations and has the fewest resources. Total cost to all business of federal regulations alone is estimated at $100 billion, with small business paying 60 percent of that sum."[9] In the words of Vernon L. Weaver, who headed the SBA in 1980:

Regulatory agencies make rules when they have General Motors in mind; and they forget that the tiny corner grocery store has to fill out the very same forms.[10]

Filling out forms and handling paper have become a way of life for all businesses, including the tiny grocery store mentioned by Mr. Weaver. The SBA's Office of Advocacy surveyed 1,000 small businesses and found that those businesses had to fill out 305 million federal, state, and local government forms asking 7.3 billion questions.[11]

Some relief may be on the way, at least on the federal level. For example, two of the major recommendations to come out of the White House Conference on Small Business in 1980 were:

☐ To require all federal agencies to analyze the cost and relevance of regulations to small business

---

8. Adapted from U.S. Small Business Administration, *The Regulatory and Paperwork Maze: A Guide for Small Business* (Washington, D.C.: U.S. Government Printing Office, 1980), p. 8.
9. White House Conference on Small Business, "Issue Paper on Regulations and Paperwork" (Unpublished, January 1980), p. 140.
10. Excerpted from Mr. Weaver's talk at the White House Conference on Small Business in Washington, D.C. (January 13, 1980).
11. U.S. Small Business Administration, "Government Paperwork and Small Business" (Unpublished, December 1979), p. 3.

☐ To permit so-called two-tiering for all regulations. This means that, besides exempting small business, regulatory agencies would draft one set of rules for small business and another set for big business.[12]

To balance our discussion of regulations, we should underscore the fact that many regulations benefit both society and the entrepreneur. Few entrepreneurs would disagree, for example, with the need to:

☐ Ban monopolies that undercut competition
☐ Regulate banking practices and protect savings
☐ Protect the environment from pollutants
☐ Give both women and minorities equal employment opportunities
☐ Help the old, the poor, and the physically handicapped lead meaningful lives
☐ Protect irreplaceable natural resources from exhaustion

Without government regulations, these needs and others most likely would never be met. We tend to forget, for example, that 8-year-old newsboys worked 16-hour days at the turn of the century for just $1 a day. At the time, the courts gave only grudging acceptance to laws designed to make working conditions more humane for both children and women.

Because regulations and the paperwork they create will continue to be a fact of business life, entrepreneurs should make every use they can of the results of the government forms they file. For example, data compiled by the U.S. Bureau of Census can help entrepreneurs research their markets, as did this entrepreneur:

EXAMPLE

In Boston, a manufacturer of paneling who wanted to widen his market used census data to discover which areas would be best for franchising local contractors. These contractors used the paneling materials to convert basements into finished rooms.

First, the manufacturer used census data to learn what types of homes predominated in different areas, and whether they were built on concrete slabs or full basements. Ruling out the areas where the houses had no basements, he looked at data on family income, number of children, and number of cars for the remaining areas.

He looked at families that owned more than one car—an indication that they had discretionary income to spend for home improvement. As a result of his study of census data, he then was able to grant franchises in areas that had good market potential.[13]

■

12. White House Conference on Small Business, *Report to the President: America's Small Business Economy* (Washington, D.C.: U.S. Government Printing Office, April 1980), p. 31.
13. Adapted from U.S. Small Business Administration, *The Regulatory and Paperwork Maze: A Guide for Small Business* (Washington, D.C.: U.S. Government Printing Office, 1980), p. 29.

All new ventures require a lawyer's services, and would-be entrepreneurs should not make the mistake of neglecting the legal aspects of their venture. They should see a lawyer months before they plan to launch their venture and they should seek knowledgeable recommendations before they finally select a lawyer. The lawyer they choose should preferably have experience in new ventures.

Entrepreneurs should look upon such legal help as a kind of preventive medicine. The real value of a lawyer is his or her ability to solve problems by not letting them arise in the first place.

One of the entrepreneur's first decisions should be to choose a legal form of organization. The choice of a corporation, partnership, or sole proprietorship will strongly affect how much taxes are paid, whether the entrepreneur may personally be sued, whether the venture dissolves automatically upon the founder's death, and a host of other financial and managerial issues. Lawyers generally favor the corporate form for these reasons:

- ☐ It offers limited liability.
- ☐ It lends itself to raising money.
- ☐ It outlives the venture's founders.
- ☐ It lends itself to ownership transfer.

The main drawback of the corporate form is that it suffers from double taxation. This drawback, however, may be overcome by forming a Subchapter S corporation.

All businesses, big or small, are regulated at three government levels: local, state, and federal. Although the paperwork such regulations generate may be burdensome, entrepreneurs should turn the paperwork to their own advantage—to research their markets, for example.

DISCUSSION AND REVIEW QUESTIONS

1 Which legal form of organization do you prefer? Why?
2 Why does the public often equate big business with the corporate form of organization?
3 Interest on loans is a tax-deductible expense. Should dividends on corporate profits be treated the same way? Why or why not?
4 Define these terms: *sole proprietorship, partnership, corporation, limited liability, corporate charter, double taxation, two-tier regulations.*
5 Why do commercial bankers prefer not to lend money to sole proprietors?
6 Why might you, as a would-be entrepreneur, need legal help early on?
7 Is there one best legal form of organization, applicable to all entrepreneurs? Explain.
8 How do regular corporations differ from Subchapter S corporations? From 1244 corporations?

9 How do general partnerships differ from limited partnerships?

10 Why should partners draw up a written partnership agreement?

11 What is the basic difference between a corporation and other legal forms of organization?

12 How would you go about getting the right lawyer for your venture?

13 Who should make the legal decisions, the lawyer or the entrepreneur? Why?

14 Why are government regulations and paperwork often a burden to entrepreneurs?

15 How do government regulations benefit the entrepreneur?

In March 1980, Penelope Wadsworth received a business plan from Frank Manfredi. Ms. Wadsworth presides over Creative Ventures, a venture-capital firm; Mr. Manfredi presides over Manfredi Enterprises, a manufacturing company. Its sole product is a patented automotive device that boosts gas mileage and cuts air pollution. The purpose of Mr. Manfredi's business plan is to raise $100,000.

You have just joined Ms. Wadsworth's firm, and she has asked you to go over Mr. Manfredi's business plan. By tomorrow morning, Ms. Wadsworth wants you to recommend whether the plan merits a closer look—and why.

BACKGROUND

Mr. Manfredi was born into a family of entrepreneurs. His father and uncles all ran their own businesses in Italy. Mr. Manfredi spent the first 12 years of his life in Italy and then emigrated to this country.

At the age of 18, Mr. Manfredi began his first business in Los Angeles. With mixed success, he ran a dry cleaning and shoe repair shop for three years.

Then Mr. Manfredi headed east, where he married, started a family, and worked on General Motors' assembly line. Like millions of others, he soon fell into the rhythmic lifestyle of daily work from 8:00 to 4:00, weekly paychecks, and monthly mortgage payments.

The entrepreneurial spirit that once burned bright inside him was all but dead. Then something happened to rekindle that spirit. In 1970, on a late night drive through Pennsylvania, he observed that his Chevrolet sedan ran better in the moisture-rich mountain air. When he returned home, he made up his mind to recreate "these ideal weather conditions" under the hood of his own car.

Mr. Manfredi worked on his idea in the basement of his home for seven years. The product of his labors was a booster that not only increased gas mileage but also cut air pollution. A drawing of the booster appears in Exhibit 7A-1.

CREATES OWN VENTURE

In February 1977, at the age of 51, Mr. Manfredi gave up the security of his job with General Motors for the insecurity of entrepreneurship. His immediate goal was to "raise $250,000 to make and market the booster."

A full year went by before the first booster rolled off the production line. It took that long to raise money, lease factory space, hire talent, and build production equipment. Mr. Manfredi did indeed create a company capitalized at $250,000, though only a fraction of that sum reflected paid-in cash, as explained below. Authorized to issue 100,000 shares of common stock at a par value of $2.50 each, the company:

☐ Gave Mr. Manfredi 51 percent of the shares in exchange for the rights to his patent

Drawing of Manfredi Fuel Booster

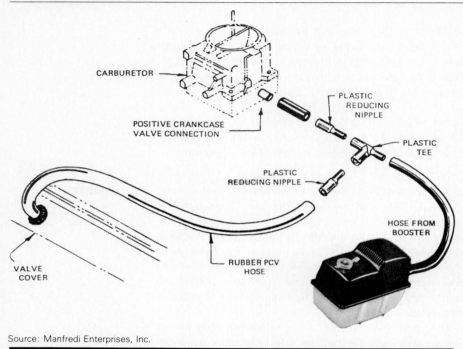

CARBURETOR

POSITIVE CRANKCASE
VALVE CONNECTION

PLASTIC
REDUCING
NIPPLE

PLASTIC
TEE

PLASTIC
REDUCING NIPPLE

HOSE FROM
BOOSTER

VALVE
COVER

RUBBER PCV
HOSE

Source: Manfredi Enterprises, Inc.

☐ Gave officers and suppliers 29 percent of the shares in exchange for their services and supplies
☐ Sold 20 percent of these shares for cash

So, cash sales of stock represented just $50,000. Such sales were mainly to members of Local 1005 of the United Automobile Workers Union, of which Mr. Manfredi had been a member. His beginning balance sheet appears in Exhibit 7A-2.

FINANCIAL PROBLEMS

By early 1978, the company was ready to make and market the booster. Despite reams of free publicity in magazines and newspapers, sales failed to meet expectations by a wide margin. The company soon found itself in financial trouble.

With its cash dwindling to zero, the company turned to a local bank for help in early 1979. The bank responded by lending the company $22,000. Of that sum, $7,000 was a personal note guaranteed by the company's board of directors.

At the same time, the company tried to float a second issue of 100,000 shares of stock, this time at a par value of four dollars a share. But because the

Manfredi Enterprises, Inc.

Balance Sheet (February 1, 1978)

Assets		Equities	
Patent	$127,500	Accounts payable	$ 3,100
Organization costs	36,000	Owners' equity	250,000
Dies and forms	30,400		
Inventories	18,700		
Experimental costs	18,200		
Equipment	17,200		
Prepaid expenses	2,700		
Cash	2,400		
Total assets	$253,100	Total equities	$253,100

company had suffered heavy losses, investors bought few shares of stock. The income statement in Exhibit 7A-3 shows how the company had performed.

By October 1979, the company once again found itself on the edge of failure. The bank threatened to call its loan and shareholders doubted the company's ability to exploit the booster's potential.

In spite of these difficulties, Mr. Manfredi refused to give up. Moving quickly, he persuaded his city to test the booster—with a promise that if the test succeeded, the city would have the booster installed on each of its 2,200 vehicles. Next, he convinced the bank to stretch repayment of its loan to April 1980.

The company's fortunes soon took a turn for the better. The test with the city gave these favorable results:

☐ On the 10 vehicles tested, the booster increased the mileage per gallon by an average of 22 percent.
☐ On a vehicle assigned to the city's Air Pollution Control Division, the booster cut the carbon monoxide emission by 93 percent.

This success spurred Mr. Manfredi to go after venture capital. But before he could do so, he needed a business plan. "All venture-capital firms ask for one,"

THE FUTURE

Manfredi Enterprises, Inc.

Income Statement (for year ending June 30, 1979)

Sales revenues	$18,100
Operating expenses	76,800
Operating loss	($58,700)

says Mr. Manfredi. "Without one they won't give you the time of day." Within three months he had completed a plan. He sought $100,000 of venture capital—enough to carry his company through April 1981—and a venture-capital firm capable of investing its *managerial* know-how as well. "That's our most pressing need," says Mr. Manfredi.

Confident of raising the $100,000, Mr. Manfredi mailed his business plan to 15 venture-capital firms in March 1980: Excerpts appear in the following exhibits:

Exhibit 7A-4—Product Technology

Exhibit 7A-5—Rating of Booster

Manfredi Enterprises, Inc.

EXHIBIT 7A-4

Business Plan Excerpt—Product Technology

Since 1887, when William Maxwell of England invented a rotary exhaust pump, people have tried to use water to get better performance from engines. In Maxwell's case, it was a gadget for condensing water vapor for use in steam engines.

Some 36 inventions and 93 years later, Mr. Manfredi has created a device that puts moisture to good use in an automobile engine. What is so unique about it?

The booster is similar to many of these other devices in its use of manifold suction to draw water into the engine. But there the similarity stops. It injects moisture-rich air rather than a liquid spray. That is the key to its performance. The explanation has to do with molecular availability.

If water is injected as a spray of droplets, only those molecules at the surface of each droplet become available for the gas-air reaction. In a droplet containing perhaps a million molecules, as few as a thousand molecules—or 0.1 percent—would be exposed to reaction.

If water is injected as moisture-rich air, the percentage of water molecules exposed to reaction would jump to as high as 10 percent. The result is more complete combustion, which brings with it such benefits as these:

☐ Greater mileage per gallon of gas
☐ Reduced carbon monoxide and hydrocarbon emission
☐ Reduced buildup of carbon in the engine

At work here is a centuries-old chemical principle, namely, the use of a catalyst (water) to quicken the rate of a reaction (gas and air). In its role as catalyst, the water molecule does not lose its individuality. Rather, it acts a little like the justice of the peace who joins couples in marriage; it helps create the union of gas and air molecules but it never becomes part of the union.

So each water molecule attracts gas and air molecules and holds them together for combustion. And the more molecules of water available, the faster and more complete the combustion.

Rating of Manfredi Fuel Booster

Criterion	Rating		
	Good	**Fair**	**Poor**
1 Marketability			
Merchandisibility	Has performance characteristics that lend themselves to promotion.		
Price	Priced low enough to enable most buyers to recover their investment through gas-cost savings in less than one year.		
Marketing strategy			Will have to set up distribution channels and marketing organization.
Number of sizes and grades	One size and grade can be used on all vehicles except diesel trucks.		
2 Durability			
Profit opportunity	Booster will have uses long enough to recover initial investment and return profits.		
Breadth of market	A national market and a potential foreign market.		
Exclusiveness of design		Protected by a patent, but it might be circumvented.	
3 Productive ability			
Equipment necessary		Company owns dies to produce booster parts but will have to buy equipment to assemble them on mass-production basis.	

Criterion	Rating		
	Good	Fair	Poor
3 Productive ability (cont.)			
Production know-how and personnel necessary	Good production know-how; more personnel needed to make booster.		
Availability of raw materials	Company can buy raw materials from wide variety of suppliers.		
4 Growth potential			
Place in market	New kind of product that will fill a pressing need not now being filled.		
Expected competitive situation			Low value added—thus enabling large, medium, and smaller companies to compete.
Expected availability of end-users	Number of end-users runs into the millions and will increase moderately.		

Exhibit 7A-6—Marketing Strategy

Exhibit 7A-7—Latest Balance Sheet

Exhibit 7A-8—Cash Budget

Exhibit 7A-9—Latest Income Statement

Exhibit 7A-10—Reorganization

Exhibit 7A-11—Organizational Chart

Business Plan Excerpt—Marketing Strategy

We have already begun to redirect our marketing strategy. Until mid-1979, our marketing efforts were directed mainly at the individual car owner. That was a mistake. The individual on the street may endorse the goals of gas economy and clean air—but not if it means dipping into a pocket and paying dollars.

On the other hand, big fleet owners *are* cost-conscious. They are interested in economy. They are interested in saving dollars. Avis Rent-A-Car, for example, estimates savings of $5 million a year on just a 20 percent increase in gas mileage. What better incentive to buy the booster?

The shift to big fleet owners as our main sales target is the most important change in marketing strategy. Other changes include:

- Building a strong regional marketing base by focusing our selling efforts on fleet owners in this state only
- Applying a marketing mix that has pricing and personal selling as its main ingredients

This strategy is working, as evidenced by two major breakthroughs—with the city and with Avis Rent-A-Car. Thanks to marketing research done by the trade magazine, *Commercial Car Journal,* we now have the names and addresses of all 182 fleet owners in this state with 10 or more vehicles.

However, our strategy lacks the one ingredient capable of bringing it to full flood—namely, a competent marketing manager.

Manfredi Enterprises, Inc.

EXHIBIT 7A-7

Balance Sheet (December 31, 1979)

Assets			Equities		
Current assets			**Current liabilities**		
Inventory	$ 31,200		Note payable, bank	$ 14,500	
Cash	1,000		Note payable, officer	4,600	
Accounts receivable	900	$ 33,100	Other notes payable	1,700	
Fixed assets			Accrued taxes payable	100	$ 20,900
Dies and forms	$ 24,300				
Equipment and fixtures	12,100	36,400	**Owners' equity**		
Other assets			Common stock	$282,000	
Patent	$127,500		Deficit	(82,300)	199,700
Experimental costs	18,200				
Organization costs	3,400				
Prepaid expenses	2,000	151,100			
Total assets		$221,000*	Total equities		$221,000*

* Rounded to nearest thousand.

Cash Budget (April 1980 through March 1981)

	April	May	June	July	August
Budgeted volume, units	0	100	200	400	600
Budgeted revenue, at $40/unit	0	$ 4,000	$ 8,000	$16,000	$24,000
Cash balance at start of month	0	$18,400	$ 7,120	$17,060	$23,520
Plus collections from credit sales	0	0	4,000	8,000	16,000
Total collections plus cash balance	0	$18,400	$11,120	$25,060	$39,520
Less payments for operations					
Purchases of materials	$ 1,200	$ 2,400	$ 4,800	$ 7,200	$ 9,600
Salaries of officers	1,000	1,000	1,000	5,250	5,250
Other salaries and wages	1,500	1,900	2,300	2,700	3,100
Welfare	500	580	660	1,590	1,670
Advertising and promotion	—	2,000	1,000	1,000	1,000
Legal and accounting	1,000	1,000	1,000	500	500
Rent	700	700	700	700	700
Utilities	300	200	200	200	200
Office supplies	200	200	200	200	200
Insurance and local taxes	200	200	200	200	200
Subtotal payments for operations	$ 6,600	$10,180	$12,060	$19,540	$22,420
Less other payments					
Loan repayments		$19,100			
Equipment and experimental costs		5,000	$ 5,000	$ 5,000	$ 5,000
Outside consultants		2,000	2,000	2,000	2,000
Subtotal other payments		$26,100	$ 7,000	$ 7,000	$ 7,000
Total payments	$ 6,600	$36,280	$19,060	$26,540	$29,420
Cash-flow summary					
Total collections plus cash balance	$ 0	$18,400	$11,120	$25,060	$39,520
Less total payments	6,600	36,280	19,060	26,540	29,420
Surplus or deficit at month's end	($ 6,600)	($17,880)	($ 7,940)	($ 1,480)	$10,100
Investment by venture capital firm	25,000	25,000	25,000	25,000	—
Cash balance at month's end after investment	$18,400	$ 7,120	$17,060	$23,520	$10,100

Upon completing the test with the city, Mr. Manfredi offered to equip its 2,200 vehicles with the booster. Unfortunately, he was turned down because the city itself was now cash poor.

Currently, Mr. Manfredi is running another large-scale test, this one with Avis Rent-A-Car. This test covers 20 vehicles. Mr. Manfredi believes that the results of this test, coupled with those of the city test, should "remove any doubts about the booster's performance."

1 What are Mr. Manfredi's prospects?

QUESTIONS

September	October	November	December	January	February	March
800	1,000	1,200	1,400	1,600	1,800	2,000
$32,000	$40,000	$48,000	$56,000	$64,000	$ 72,000	$ 80,000
$10,100	$ 6,800	$ 9,140	$16,500	$28,980	$ 46,580	$ 69,500
24,000	32,000	40,000	48,000	56,000	64,000	72,000
$34,100	$38,800	$49,140	$64,500	$84,980	$110,580	$141,500
$12,000	$14,400	$16,800	$19,200	$21,600	$ 24,000	$ 26,400
5,250	5,250	5,250	5,250	5,250	5,250	5,250
3,500	4,300	4,700	5,100	5,500	5,900	6,300
1,750	1,910	1,990	2,070	2,150	2,230	2,310
1,000	1,000	1,000	1,000	1,000	1,000	1,000
500	500	500	500	500	500	500
700	700	700	700	700	700	700
200	200	300	300	300	300	300
200	200	200	200	200	200	200
200	200	200	200	200	200	200
$25,300	$28,660	$31,640	$34,520	$37,400	$ 40,080	$ 43,060
$ 2,000	$ 1,000	$ 1,000	$ 1,000	$ 1,000	$ 1,000	$ 1,000
$ 2,000	$ 1,000	$ 1,000	$ 1,000	$ 1,000	$ 1,000	$ 1,000
$27,300	$29,660	$32,640	$35,520	$38,400	$ 41,080	$ 44,060
$34,100	$38,800	$49,140	$64,500	$84,980	$110,580	$141,500
27,300	29,660	32,640	35,520	38,400	41,080	44,060
$ 6,800	$ 9,140	$16,500	$28,980	$46,580	$ 69,500	$ 97,440
—	—	—	—	—	—	—
$ 6,800	$ 9,140	$16,500	$28,980	$46,580	$ 69,500	$ 97,440

2 Does Mr. Manfredi's business plan merit a closer look by the venture-capital firm?

3 If Mr. Manfredi were to seek $100,000 from you, and you had the money, would you invest in his venture? If not, why? If yes, on what basis?

4 Comment on Mr. Manfredi's business plan. Is it thorough and precise? Has he backed up his assumptions? What additional information might you desire—and why?

5 What should Mr. Manfredi do if he fails to raise the $100,000 he seeks from venture-capital firms? Explain.

Manfredi Enterprises, Inc.

Income Statement (for six months ending December 31, 1979)

Sales revenues		$ 3,600
Cost of goods sold		3,200
Gross profit		$ 400
Expenses		
Rent	$3,000	
Salaries and wages	2,800	
Insurance and local taxes	1,600	
Supplies	1,500	
Utilities	1,400	
Advertising and promotion	700	
Legal and accounting	600	
Interest	600	
Other	200	12,400
Loss		($12,000)

Manfredi Enterprises, Inc.

Business Plan Excerpt—Reorganization

Too busy keeping the company's head above water, Mr. Manfredi has had little time to reorganize his management team. But he has recently added two persons who are production and product-development experts. Working part time, they brought the booster to its present level of quality. Until their arrival, the booster's performance had been far from flawless. Now, it is trouble free.

Ideally, the company's organization should look like the one charted in Exhibit 7A-11. Note that the key managerial jobs, besides the presidency, would be those of:

☐ Marketing
☐ Production
☐ Administration

At present, Mr. Manfredi is both president and administrative manager. But because his skills lie mainly in research and development, he would rather delegate the day-to-day administration of the company to a person better talented in this area.

As to the other two managerial jobs, some progress has been made toward filling them. Either of the two persons mentioned earlier would be capable of filling the production manager's job. But the marketing manager's job is far from being filled. This job is critical, since a major reason for the company's failure to reach its potential was its failure to plan its marketing. So no effort will be spared to hire a talented individual as marketing manager.

Business Plan Excerpt—Organizational Chart

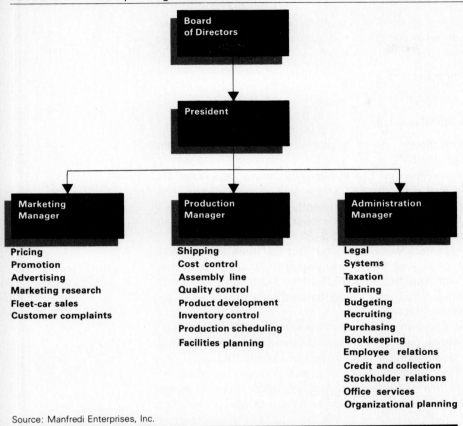

| Board of Directors |
| President |

Marketing Manager	Production Manager	Administration Manager
Pricing	Shipping	Legal
Promotion	Cost control	Systems
Advertising	Assembly line	Taxation
Marketing research	Quality control	Training
Fleet-car sales	Product development	Budgeting
Customer complaints	Inventory control	Recruiting
	Production scheduling	Purchasing
	Facilities planning	Bookkeeping
		Employee relations
		Credit and collection
		Stockholder relations
		Office services
		Organizational planning

Source: Manfredi Enterprises, Inc.

CASE 7B

CAR REPAIR SHOP*

I may be wrong, but I think partnerships are dangerous unless one draws up definite articles of copartnership that each partner understands. For example, I've seen a sailor and a southern gentleman in a trailer sales partnership. Before too long, the gentleman got the business and the sailor got experience.

But that could not happen to François, Henri, and René because nationality bound them together. All three were French.

Moreover, what could happen when they ventured into the car repair business just off Main Street? To get to their shop, at the first light going north

* Source: Adapted with permission from Henry M. Cruickshank and Keith Davis, *Cases in Management* (Homewood, Ill.: Richard D. Irwin, 1962), pp. 47–49.

on Main Street, you turned left, took another left, and then took a third left—which brought you back almost to Main Street. And all that stood between you and Main Street was someone's private lawn and an attractive 8-foot picket fence.

The three men plunged all their savings into a three-way partnership, agreeing orally that everything would be split equally. All three were convinced they had the talent to succeed:

François was an expert mechanic.

Henri had painted hundreds of cars.

René could take the dent out of any car.

At the end of the first month, the three partners proudly drew up their first balance sheet (see Exhibit 7B-1).

On a Monday morning, Henri arrived at the shop deeply depressed. He needed some money. He had nine children and a wife to feed, clothe, and house. So far, everything had been outgo. Reluctantly, the two other partners agreed to let Henri take $400 out of their bank account. After all, if he owned a third of the partnership, then he really owned $420 of the cash.

That incident was repeated two weeks later. But this time, Henri could get no cash. True, many repair jobs had been done and accounts receivable were growing. But cash had dwindled to $240. So Henri quit the partnership and demanded that his third of the total assets be paid to him in a week. He would go to work in a nearby factory.

Soon after, François and René drew up a balance sheet for a two-way partnership. The two remaining partners assumed they would pay Henri out of accounts receivable. The new balance sheet appears in Exhibit 7B-2.

Things looked good on paper. And in the next few days, $2,000 of the accounts receivable were converted into cash. And still better, René's cousin, Alfred, offered to pay off Henri and replace him as a partner with a one-third interest.

Car Repair Shop

Balance Sheet (at end of first four weeks)

Assets		Equities	
Cash	$ 1,260	Liabilities	$ 0
Accounts receivable	6,500	Owners' equity	
Tools	2,000	François	$ 5,920
Repair parts	2,200	Henri	5,920
Supplies	400	René	5,920
Paint	600		
Repossessed old cars	4,800		
Total assets	$17,760	Total equities	$17,760

Balance Sheet (at end of first six weeks)

Assets		Equities	
Cash	$ 240	Liabilities	$ 0
Accounts receivable	8,800	Owners' equity	
Tools	2,000	François	$10,120
Repair parts	2,200	René	10,120
Supplies	400		
Paint	600		
Repossessed old cars	6,000		
Total assets	$20,240	Total equities	$20,240

1 What main error was made in the formation of the original partnership? How could this error be prevented by the new partnership of François, René, and Alfred?
2 Comment on the location of the car repair shop; on the partners' personal qualifications; and on the original balance sheet.
3 Is the second balance sheet accurately prepared? Explain why, using figures if necessary. How much should Alfred pay Henri for his share of the shop?
4 What should the new partnership do now to avoid future difficulties?

CASE 7C

When Richard Dosk died, his young widow became the major stockholder in his building-maintenance supplies firm—and his executive vice president, Paula Cooke, stepped up to the top job.

For 10 years, Mrs. Cooke had piloted the marketing end of the business—soliciting customers mainly by direct mail. By the time Mr. Dosk passed on, Mrs. Cooke's department—at a substantial cost—had accumulated 20,000 names of customers. Those names were in a locked file in Mrs. Cooke's office.

The widow remarried, and her husband moved into the Dosk Company. It was apparent that *he* wanted to be kingpin. Soon, Mrs. Cooke was out.

Mrs. Cooke immediately set up a rival company in which she solicited the same market—limiting it to commercial buildings. *Some* of the customers were those of the Dosk Company—which sought to protect its expensively compiled list by running to court for an injunction.

* Source: Adapted from case prepared by *The Businessman and the Law* (a newsletter), edited by Dr. Lawrence Stessin; Business Research Publications, Inc., 817 Broadway, 3rd Floor, New York, NY 10003.

"We want Cooke stopped from soliciting any customers of the Dosk Company," the former Mrs. Dosk cried. "Those names are highly confidential, as Cooke knows. They cost us over a half million dollars to collect."

"I'm not using that list," Mrs. Cooke insisted. "I don't have a copy. Naturally, I know some of them. I dealt with them."

"We don't believe it," replied the former Mrs. Dosk. "Here is a list of 47 of our customers that you solicited."

"Only 47 out of 1,100 commercial customers?" retorted Mrs. Cooke. "That's pure coincidence. Or maybe casual memory. Besides, anybody could pick out prospective customers. They're all listed in real estate directories."

"Not *our* list," protested the former Mrs. Dosk. "It cost Dosk Company plenty to compile it."

If you were the judge, how would you decide this issue? Explain.   **QUESTION**

CHAPTER EIGHT
LOCATION

questions for mastery

is site selection important?

how should you select a site?

what is the role of marketing research in
   site selection?

how does site selection differ in importance
   among industries?

what are the trends in shopping centers and
   industrial parks?

Locality seems but an accident.

Elizabeth Coatsworth

A saying common in retailing circles is that "the three most important factors in retailing success are location, location, and location." Though an exaggeration, this saying underscores the need for entrepreneurs to research their market thoroughly. Although location is indeed critical in retailing, it also plays a varied but vital role in manufacturing, services, and wholesaling as well. And only with marketing research does the entrepreneur in any industry have the information needed to choose the right location.

VARYING IMPORTANCE OF LOCATION

CHARACTERISTICS AFFECTING LOCATION CHOICE

Location is more vital in some industries than others. Certain characteristics of businesses determine the importance of location: whether customers must travel to the business or the entrepreneur travels to the customer is a key factor; whether a business is offering a special product or service with little accessible competition is another; and whether convenience is a key selling point in what the business offers to customers is yet another consideration.

In services like accounting and management consulting, the question of location is often trivial. It matters little, for example, where a management consultant locates her office. The building may be within walking distance of prospective clients or an hour's drive away. Neither distance nor accessibility affects the consultant's ability to land clients, because generally a consultant must visit clients to solve their problems and not the other way around.

Location is also trivial for ventures that offer a unique service, such as antique-furniture repair. Customers are usually willing to travel many miles to have a precious piece of antique furniture repaired or restored. The only consideration the entrepreneur must make is whether the location is accessible by automobile.

At the other extreme are industries where location may make or break a venture. It matters a great deal, for example, where a grocer locates a supermarket. Generally, it should be within walking distance for neighborhood residents, and no more than perhaps a five-minute drive for most residents in the trading area, with ample parking space available. Finally, the supermarket should not be near another supermarket.

THE ROLE OF SHOPPING CENTERS AND INDUSTRIAL PARKS

Even in those industries where it matters, however, the choice of location is becoming less and less within the domain of the entrepreneur. The main reason is the market trend toward shopping centers and industrial parks. This trend began just after World War II and, although slowing down, shows few signs of stopping. In 1980, more than 22,000 shopping centers and more than 4,500 industrial parks dotted the country.

As a result of this trend the developer, rather than the entrepreneur, selects the location. The developer of a shopping center studies the market and decides on the mix of shops based on the needs and potential discovered in the market research. The strength of the shopping center idea is evidenced by the fact that within a generation or two, most consumers will probably be shopping at shopping centers. Just as developers of shopping centers often decide the location issue for entrepreneurs in retailing or services so too do the developers of industrial parks often decide where the manufacturing entrepreneur may locate. Often, the location of the industrial park is dictated by ecological concerns as well as by such factors as access to transportation or markets. In fact, many communities have passed laws forcing developers to meet such requirements as the following:

☐ No discharge of smoke into the air
☐ No despoiling of land around a plant
☐ No discharge of refuse, acid waste, or other pollutants into a stream
☐ Sufficient off-street parking concealed by landscaped and grassy areas
☐ Recessed loading docks so that trucks are not visible from the street

Developers of shopping centers as well as developers of industrial parks must now go to great lengths to justify their proposals. Gone are the days when developers had only to make a marketing study, buy up some vacant land, and build a complex of air-conditioned shops. Many communities are now trying to stem the unbridled growth of shopping centers, often resulting in conflicts between developers or entrepreneurs claiming their right to free enterprise and communities claiming their right to remain residential. The outcome of the conflicts will no doubt affect the pace of changes in the American landscape.

MARKETING RESEARCH IN SITE SELECTION

As mentioned earlier, developers of shopping centers and industrial parks—and not the entrepreneur—often decide where the entrepreneur may locate. Still, entrepreneurs can exercise their freedom of choice in areas uncontrolled by developers. For example, as depicted in Exhibit 8-1, entrepreneurs are still free to choose:

☐ A geographical region
☐ A city within that region
☐ An area within that city
☐ A specific site within that area (except for shopping centers)

Few entrepreneurs go through a logical process of site selection. Instead, they often permit personal preference to influence their decision on where best to locate. Entrepreneurs who enjoy warm weather the year round, for example, may choose to locate in the Deep South or the Southwest. Entrepreneurs who enjoy the four seasons may prefer New England or the Midwest. Others may prefer not to move at all but to locate in the very same neighborhood they were born in.

EXHIBIT 8-1

Selecting a Location

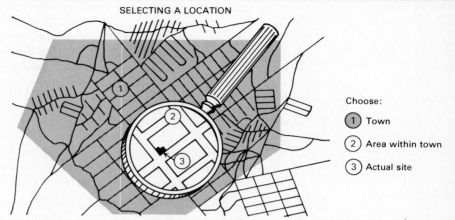

SELECTING A LOCATION

Choose:

① Town

② Area within town

③ Actual site

Source: Wendell O. Metcalf, Small Business Administration, *Starting and Managing a Small Business of Your Own* (Washington, D.C.: U.S. Government Printing Office, 1962), p. 16.

Personal preference is a vital factor to be weighed in choosing a location. But entrepreneurs should not permit their biases to take the place of sound, objective research.

SELECTING A RETAIL OR SERVICE LOCATION

In addition to personal preference, entrepreneurs need to get and analyze the facts about their potential market before they choose a location. For example, an entrepreneur who wants to open a drugstore should seek answers to such questions as these:

On the city

☐ Is the city growing? If so, how fast? What parts of the city are growing most?
☐ What is the city's population breakdown by age, income, and occupation?
☐ How many drugstores are there now in the city? Where are they located? How well are they doing?
☐ What is the civic spirit like? Is the city up-and-coming? Do residents work well together on civic projects?
☐ What is the quality of the city's schools, churches, parks, and culture?

On an area within the city

☐ What do area consumers buy when they go to a drugstore?
☐ What is the area's population? Is it growing? Are the people chiefly native-born or foreign?
☐ How do people make their living? Are they mostly white-collar workers, laborers, or retired persons?
☐ Are there people of all ages or are they mainly old, middle-aged, or young?

☐ What is the average family income? What is their total buying power?

☐ How many other drugstores are located in the area? How successful are they?

On a specific site within the area

☐ Are neighboring businesses healthy?

☐ How close is the nearest competing drugstore?

☐ Is the site surrounded by well-kept homes?

☐ Is there plenty of parking space available next to or near the site?

☐ Is the site accessible by bus?

☐ What zoning requirements must be met?

☐ How far will customers travel to shop in the drugstore?

☐ Is there a steady flow of foot traffic by the site?

☐ What is the floor area? Is there any room to expand?

☐ Can deliveries be made from the rear?

☐ Are there stores nearby that will draw customers to the site?

☐ Is the appearance of the site pleasing so that customers will want to shop there?

☐ Is there a divider on the road that may discourage some potential customers?

Choosing the best location calls for painstaking attention to detail. No fact should be ignored. As depicted earlier in Exhibit 8-1, entrepreneurs should narrow their choices down to the most likely sites and then dig out the facts about each one. The following example shows how entrepreneurs may narrow their choices:

EXAMPLE

An entrepreneur, Paula Lynne Berke, is thinking about opening a children's apparel store in the Dallas, Texas, area. Miss Berke prefers to locate in the Dallas area because it offers "just the continuity of life I'm looking for." She went to college there, worked as a manager in a local department store, and is an enthusiastic supporter of the Dallas Cowboys. As part of her business plan, Miss Berke must decide which county offers her the best chance of success.

Miss Berke's marketing professor suggested that she look at the "Survey of Buying Power" prepared yearly by *Sales and Marketing Management* magazine. This survey, the professor pointed out, gives data on population, income, and certain categories of retail sales for major metropolitan areas like Dallas. Since this survey is updated yearly, it furnishes needed statistics between the 10-year censuses made by the U.S. Bureau of Census.

Grateful for the professor's advice, Miss Berke visited the local library and examined their copy of the "Survey of Buying Power" for the various suburbs that are part of the Dallas area. She then narrowed her choices down to three suburbs, using the data shown in Exhibit 8-2.

Of these three suburbs, Arlington looks the most favorable to Miss Berke. It has a younger population than Collin and, although it is not quite

Dallas Suburb	Age Groups 18 to 24	25 to 34	Population	Median Household Effective Buying Income
Denton	24.8	15.8	99,900	$15,021
Arlington	18.5	21.1	119,100	19,468
Collin	11.7	19.6	105,300	16,532

as young as Denton, the median income is much higher. Having chosen Arlington, Miss Berke next will collect data on specific sites within the area that look the most promising.[1]

■

The example describes the process of marketing research, which will be discussed in greater detail in Chapter Fourteen. Marketing research is perhaps the entrepreneur's most important marketing activity. It helps satisfy the entrepreneurs' thirst for knowledge about their markets and continues to provide vital information after a venture begins as well as before.

GETTING AND USING INFORMATION

How do entrepreneurs get the information they need to do marketing research? How do they get answers to questions like those posed earlier in the drugstore example? We have already mentioned one source, the "Survey of Buying Power" by *Sales and Marketing Management* magazine. There are many other sources. Among the most fertile are the federal government, trade associations, and Chambers of Commerce.

The U.S. Bureau of Census, for example, provides population characteristics by census tract for all cities of 50,000 or more inhabitants. Each census tract has an average population of four to five thousand. Let us go through an example to see how entrepreneurs may use census tract data to select a site for their venture:

EXAMPLE

In Tacoma, Washington, an entrepreneur plans to launch a venture that replaces and repairs warm air furnaces. He narrowed his search for a site to two census tracts, shown in Exhibit 8-3. Data for each tract appear in Exhibit 8-4. Which tract offers the better site for such a venture?

---

1. Adapted from Robert F. Hartley, *Retailing* (Boston: Houghton Mifflin, 1980), pp. 136–137.

EXHIBIT 8-3

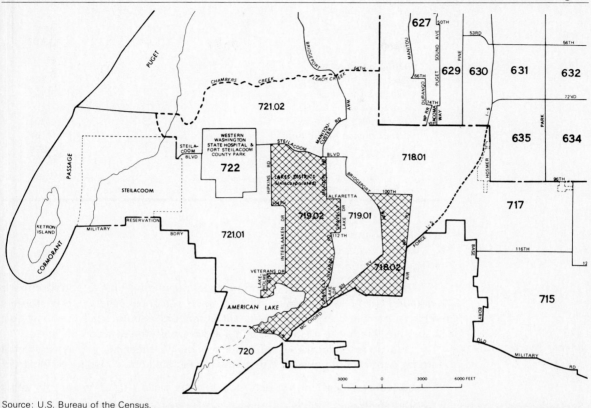

Source: U.S. Bureau of the Census.

Tract 719.02 would be better because it has many more warm-air furnaces than Tract 718.02. Replacement and repair opportunities would be much greater in Tract 719.02.[2]

■

**LOCATING A
MANUFACTURING PLANT**

So far, discussion has centered on locating a retail store or a service firm. The process of deciding where best to locate a manufacturing plant is more complex, also requiring a painstakingly thorough job of marketing research.

To find the right location for their plant, entrepreneurs generally should seek to balance three site factors:

2. Louis H. Vorzimer, U.S. Small Business Administration, "Using Census Data to Select a Store Site," *Small Marketers Aid No. 154* (Washington, D.C.: U.S. Government Printing Office, 1976).

EXHIBIT 8-4

Selected Census Tract Data for Tacoma, Washington

	Tract 718.02	Tract 719.02
Heating equipment		
Steam or hot water	23	206
Warm-air furnace	394	1,132
Built-in electric units	1,209	296
Floor, wall, or pipeless furnace	105	101
Other means or not heated	532	194
Total housing units	2,263	1,929

Source: Louis H. Vorzimer, U.S. Small Business Administration, "Using Census Data to Select a Store Site," *Small Marketers Aid No. 154* (Washington, D.C.: U.S. Government Printing Office, 1976), p. 9.

☐ Sales revenues
☐ Manufacturing costs
☐ Transportation costs

These site factors vary in importance, depending on the entrepreneur's marketing area. For example, if planning to sell their product to customers within a narrow geographic area, entrepreneurs should seek the least-cost location in relation to customers and should ignore the location of rivals.

Questions of markets and costs are by no means the only ones that entrepreneurs should answer. The following factors should also be considered:

☐ **Labor force** Does labor supply possess the skills I need to run my plant productively?
☐ **Community size** Should I locate in a nonmetropolitan area? What is the standard of living in the area? What is the quality of life?
☐ **Transportation** Will I have quick access to an interstate highway that enables me to make overnight delivery to markets, at least 400 miles distant from the site?
☐ **Water pollution** What minimum levels of water-pollution control must I adhere to?
☐ **Air pollution** What kind of equipment must I install to treat emissions of air pollutants?
☐ **Land** How much land will I need not only for making my product but also for parking and for air-pollution control equipment? Should I buy more land than I need at present in order to provide for future expansion and as a hedge against the upward trend in land prices?
☐ **Fuel and power** Will there be ample sources of energy available now and in the future?
☐ **Taxes** What effect will state and local tax structures have on my cost of manufacture?

☐ **Financing opportunities** Will the community or the state help me to finance my plant?[3]

This list of questions is by no means complete. But it does underline the complexity of picking the right location for a manufacturing plant. An example will show how the process of site selection might work:

EXAMPLE

Glenn Myers, an entrepreneur, wants to build a small plant to make ammonia. A chemical engineer and a former plant manager, Mr. Myers has already done some homework on basic problems:

☐ Because ammonia is made by reacting natural gas with air, Mr. Myers wanted to make sure there would be an ample supply of natural gas in the future. The gas company assured him there would be.
☐ Because the manufacture of ammonia requires high pressures and temperatures, Mr. Myers wanted to make sure he could build such a plant. The State Development Department assured him he could do so, as long as the plant was located at least one mile from the nearest family residence. That way, if an explosion did occur—a remote possibility—the lives of residents would not be endangered.
☐ Since hot water and other pollutants would foul the environment if discharged by the plant, Mr. Myers had to assure himself that all pollutants would be neutralized. The designer of the plant assured him that pollution-control equipment spotted strategically throughout the plant would, indeed, neutralize all pollutants.

Mr. Myers has already received promises from five fertilizer manufacturers that they will buy ammonia from him if his price is lower than that of competitors. There are no competing manufacturers in the state, and Mr. Myers is sure he can underbid out-of-state competitors. Manufacturing costs will be the same regardless of location. So, Mr. Myers's main concern is to locate the plant in a place where the cost of transporting ammonia to the five fertilizer manufacturers is minimized.

To help him decide, Mr. Myers studies the map in Exhibit 8-5, which reveals that the five fertilizer manufacturers are located almost symmetrically about the state. The solution to Mr. Myers's location problem now becomes apparent. He should locate the ammonia plant in an area roughly equidistant from the five customers, as shown in the exhibit. Because the manufacture of ammonia requires a lot of water, Mr. Myers should also place the plant near the river shown.

■

In this example, Mr. Myers chose his plant site by inspection. In the real world, symmetrical markets and purchase areas are the exception. With asymmetry, choosing a site by inspection becomes more difficult. Instead entrepre-

3. Adapted from Maurice Fulton, "New Factors in Plant Location," *Harvard Business Review,* May–June 1971, p. 4.

EXHIBIT 8-5

Location of Ammonia Plant in Relation to Customers

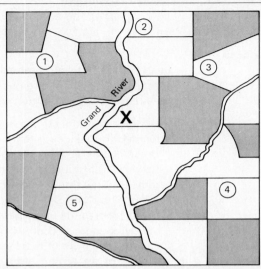

neurs should do an exhaustive analysis to measure the attractiveness of several likely sites, using two yardsticks:

☐ **Return on investment** What is the effect on both revenues and costs of each plant location? How do any changes affect potential profits?
☐ **Cost** If revenues stay the same, how does each location affect manufacturing costs?

Note the differences between locating a plant and selecting a store or office location. One major difference is that the choice of a region or community is far more important to manufacturers than the choice of a site within the community. Another difference is the lasting effect of plant location. Once a plant is built, the entrepreneur is committed to the manufacture of a certain line of products for some time. If the entrepreneur has made a poor location decision, to shut down and begin anew elsewhere would probably mean financial collapse. Thorough research is imperative before building a plant.

SUMMARY

Location is a critical factor in many industries. However, because of the strong trend toward shopping centers and industrial parks, the decision where best to locate is often made, not by the entrepreneur, but by the developer. Today, more than 22,000 shopping centers and more than 4,500 industrial parks dot the country.

Still, entrepreneurs do have some freedom of choice in areas uncontrolled by developers. In selecting a site, they should proceed in this order:

☐ A geographical region
☐ A city within that region
☐ An area within that city
☐ A specific site within that area

Entrepreneurs often permit their personal likes and dislikes to influence their selection. But they should never permit such personal biases to blind them to the realities of a poor location.

Entrepreneurs should research their markets before deciding where best to locate. They need to get and analyze the facts about the potential market.

Locating a manufacturing plant differs in two important ways from locating a retail store or a service. First, the choice of a region or city outweighs the choice of a site within the city. Second, the effects of a poor plant location are harder to undo than those of a poor retail or service location.

DISCUSSION AND REVIEW QUESTIONS

1 Why is location more vital in some industries than in others? Give two examples.

2 Since World War II, how has the rapid growth of shopping centers and industrial parks influenced the question of where best to locate a venture?

3 Do you believe that within a generation or two, most manufacturing will take place in industrial parks? Explain.

4 Define these terms: *industrial park, developer, ecological concerns, marketing research, buying power, census tract*

5 How would you go about selecting a site for your own venture?

6 What role does marketing research play in locating a venture?

7 If you were thinking about opening a retail store, why might you prefer to locate it near other retail stores that are healthy and prosperous?

8 Describe some of the ways you might get outside help in locating your venture.

9 In what ways is locating a manufacturing plant perhaps more critical than locating a retail store or service?

10 What role should personal preference play in locating a venture? Explain.

11 Do you believe there should be local laws inhibiting the growth of shopping centers or industrial parks? Why?

12 In locating a manufacturing plant, what site factors should the entrepreneur try to balance?

13 In site selection, what are some of the questions that a retailing entrepreneur should ask in selecting a city? An area within the city?

14 Under what conditions might locating a venture in a declining city be attractive to entrepreneurs?

15 What is meant by a "least-cost" location for a manufacturing venture?

Robert Kasper runs the only do-it-yourself automobile repair shop on the west side of town. Although in business a year and a half, Mr. Kasper's unique service has yet to show a profit in any month. He is now wondering whether to go on, sell out, or liquidate.

BACKGROUND

Mr. Kasper is an accidental entrepreneur. He did not think of becoming an entrepreneur until he read about an auto repair shop for do-it-yourselfers in *Popular Mechanics* magazine. "It seemed so unique," says Mr. Kasper, "that I drove the next day to Washington, D.C., to investigate the shop mentioned in the magazine. It really excited me."

In Washington, Mr. Kasper talked to the owners, who turned out to be "close-mouthed." But armed with pencil, pad, and purpose, he refused to be brushed aside. Somehow, he would get the information he had traveled 500 miles for. And he did—by talking to customers, making drawings, and interviewing neighboring businesspersons. By the time he returned home, his dream had begun to take shape.

So it was that in 1978, Mr. Kasper, at age 27, decided to go into business for himself. Until then, he had lived aimlessly, not knowing what to do or what to be. For example, he studied mechanical engineering at one college, then left to study philosophy at another. But neither subject held his interest for long. "I became bored," says Mr. Kasper.

He became equally bored with each job he held. A tool maker by trade, he describes his machine shop experience as "dull and repetitious." "But the idea of setting up an auto hobby center was something else," says Mr. Kasper.

There was one problem, among others, that bothered him. He knew little about automobiles, and even less about how to repair them. So, he decided to take on a partner, William Fabo, who was handy around cars. "Bill wasn't a mechanic," says Mr. Kasper, "but he could sure talk the language."

PREPARE BUSINESS PLAN

It took the two partners a year to organize their venture. Meanwhile, they had prepared a business plan, leased a 10,000 square-foot garage for $815 a month, incorporated their business for a lawyer's fee of $300, and raised $19,000 in cash. Their beginning balance sheet appears in Exhibit 8A-1.

"I never would have gotten the $15,000 loan without a business plan," says Mr. Kasper. "The bank wanted one. So I sat down and worked one out. It wasn't easy." He agreed to repay the loan in five years at 18 percent interest. See Exhibit 8A-2 for excerpts from his business plan.

For a week before he opened, Mr. Kasper placed a 3- by 4-inch advertisement in the local newspaper each day. Costing $240 a day, this advertisement played up two consumer benefits: saving money by "fixing it yourself" during "hours convenient to you."

Balance Sheet (December 1, 1979)

Assets			Equities			
Cash	$ 7,500		Bank loan			$15,000
Tools and supplies	4,200		Owners' equity			
Fixtures and furniture	5,000		Common stock	$ 500		
Deposits	1,800		Paid-in capital	3,500	4,000	
Prepaid expenses	500					
Total assets	$19,000		Total equities			$19,000

Mr. Kasper also bought 18 30-second spots beaming the same message on a local AM radio station, WIXY. These spots cost $480. Directed at teenagers, WIXY features rock music and ranks third in popularity in its listening area.

IN TROUBLE EARLY ON

"It was important to get off to a good start," says Mr. Kasper. Still, he and Mr. Fabo handicapped themselves by promising more than they could deliver. Neither of them qualified as an expert mechanic, so they could not help do-it-yourselfers who ran into unexpected problems.

This problem lasted just one month. The solution was Wayne Glover. An expert mechanic who happened to be jobless, Mr. Glover walked in one evening looking for a place to fix his truck. When he began to help others work on their cars, Mr. Kasper hired him on the spot to run the shop—at a salary of $12,000 a year. Mr. Kasper himself drew no salary.

After five months, business began to perk. Sales revenues tripled to $1,700 a month by May 1981. However, revenues did not yet meet expectations. To break even, Mr. Kasper needed revenues of $2,600 a month. His breakeven chart appears in Exhibit 8A-3.

With expenses outrunning revenues, Mr. Kasper soon found himself cash-poor, and he missed two monthly payments on his loan. The bank began to press for payment. At this point, he decided to seize the initiative and seek another loan of $15,000. This sum would enable him to attract more customers by adding more services. In presenting his case for the new loan, Mr. Kasper worked up Exhibits 8A-4 and 8A-5.

He also gave the bank his estimate of before-tax profits at different occupancy levels (see Exhibit 8A-6). At present, his garage has 19 bays, each operating with less than 10 percent occupancy. A typical scene at the garage appears in Exhibit 8A-7.

HELP FROM CHAMBER OF COMMERCE

The bank rejected his application for the new loan. No reason was given. He then turned to the Chamber of Commerce for help. Within weeks, they approved an emergency loan of $4,000, payable within five years at 15 percent interest.

The loan gave Mr. Kasper time to analyze why his repair shop had failed to grow. The Chamber of Commerce offered to help with the analysis.

Excerpts from Business Plan

Need for an Auto Hobby Center

Consumers pay about $15 billion yearly for needless auto repairs. Studies show that this figure will rise with more apartment living and more licensed drivers. Today, mechanics make needless repairs at a high cost of $25.20 an hour.

Definition of Service

Auto Hobby Center will provide consumers with a much-needed service—a professional garage with tooling and facilities where anyone can repair his or her own auto.

The Center will also provide a place where young persons can customize or repair their autos. In addition, men and women, unskilled in auto repair, can attend classes to protect themselves against dishonest auto-repair shops.

The Center will offer savings of up to 70% on repair costs. Consumers will have access to a complete line of professional tooling for jobs ranging from oil to engine changes. Also available will be auto-repair manuals for all foreign and domestic autos.

License

A vendor's license will be required. It can be obtained, in one afternoon, at the County Courthouse. It costs $60 and has no expiration date.

Estimated Sales Revenues

Average: $7,900 a month.

Estimated Expenses

Average: $3,400 a month.

Insurance

The insurance policy needed will be a composite of that needed by parking lot operators and garage keepers. This composite policy is offered at reduced rates by Travelers Insurance Company. The rate is $1,500 a year.

This policy will cover theft, vandalism, sprinkler damage, and so on. It will also include liability coverage of $300,000 for bodily injury or property damage. Travelers Insurance will also write Workmen's Compensation and employer's liability coverage.

Breakeven Chart

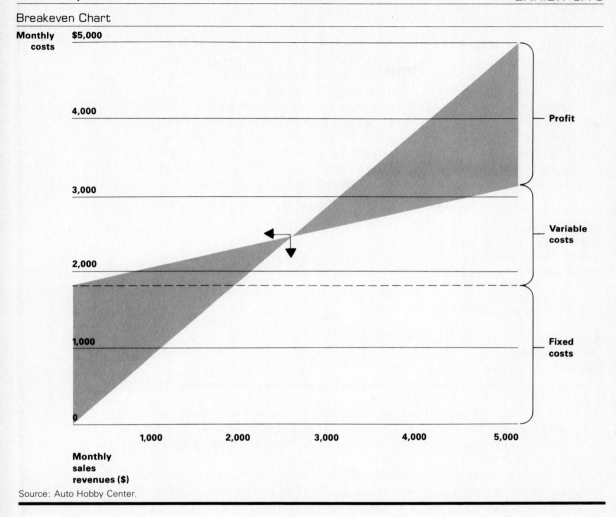

Source: Auto Hobby Center.

Working together, they found that many other entrepreneurs were succeeding spectacularly as owners of do-it-yourself repair shops. Failures were the exception. So, the Auto Hobby Center's poor performance was something of a mystery. There were two similar do-it-yourself shops on the east side of town. And both were doing well. Why had the Auto Hobby Center failed to match their performance? "That's the $64 question," says Mr. Kasper.

Even free advertising failed to boost revenues. A magazine cover story and several newspaper articles highlighted the Auto Hobby Center. One article said:

Excerpt from Justification for Additional $15,000 Loan from Bank

Location is a major factor, because the Auto Hobby Center is the only do-it-yourself shop of its type on the west side of town. This situation creates a captive clientele. The median income level for the census tracts surrounding the Center falls into the income range needed to support it.

The need for an Auto Hobby Center is there and the demand for it is there. But at present this need and demand is only half fulfilled. The space is available and consumers want to use it, but a few more ingredients are necessary to fulfill their needs. These ingredients include the addition of a parts inventory, a paint booth, and a lift. The table below compares the range of services provided by the Center to the range it should provide to be successful.

Customer Services	Provided	Not Provided
Provide savings on parts and labor		x
Conduct classes in auto repair		x
Provide a safe, clean place to work	x	
Provide convenience of location	x	
Keep open seven days a week	x	
Provide free use of tools	x	
Have available specification manuals for guidance	x	
Have available vending machines for light foods and refreshments	x	
Provide a meeting place for auto enthusiasts	x	

The Center is the biggest in town with 19 bays. There is a lift, plenty of jacks and stands, an air system and tools, including metric wrenches for working on foreign cars. At the same location, they have a Ryder truck-rental franchise.

The rates are $4.00 an hour, $32 a day, and $125 a week—and they are getting some weekly action. They are open 7 days a week from 10 a.m. to 10 p.m., and a courtesy lube job goes with each bay rental.

One recent Saturday, Sue Smith was tuning up her own car while husband Don was putting headers on his. She's the mother of a 17-month-old daughter and races on drag strips.

HIS BIGGEST MISTAKE

His analysis showed Mr. Kasper that "my biggest mistake was money. I should have gone after a $30,000 loan instead of the $15,000 I actually got when I started out. That's why I'm in trouble now. You can't succeed in a business like mine unless you're equipped to offer a full service. To do that, I've got to get $15,000 somehow."

Shortly after Mr. Kasper completed his analysis, the Chamber of Commerce helped persuade the bank to make the $15,000 loan Mr. Kasper had "prayed for." Backed by the SBA, this loan would now enable him to offer a

Location of Center

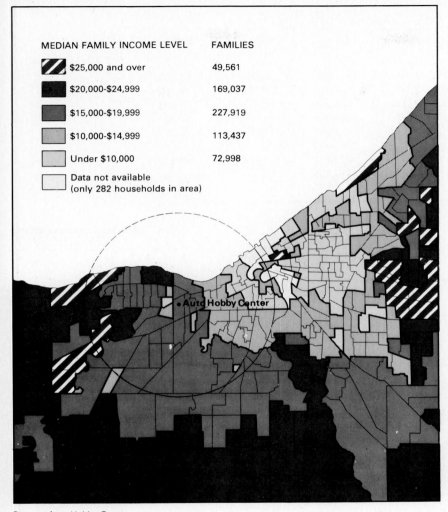

MEDIAN FAMILY INCOME LEVEL	FAMILIES
$25,000 and over	49,561
$20,000-$24,999	169,037
$15,000-$19,999	227,919
$10,000-$14,999	113,437
Under $10,000	72,998
Data not available (only 282 households in area)

Auto Hobby Center

Source: Auto Hobby Center.

full range of services he felt was necessary for success. Financial statements appear in Exhibits 8A-8 and 8A-9.

Nine months later, in July 1981, monthly revenues were no better than before the $15,000 loan. Again cash-poor, Mr. Kasper had fallen two months behind on his loan repayment schedule.

1 What should Mr. Kasper do? Why?   **QUESTIONS**
2 Had you been Mr. Kasper, how would you have established the need for a

Estimated Yearly Profit at Different Occupancy Levels

	Occupancy Level			
	20%	30%	40%	50%
Sales revenues				
Bay space rental	$32,640	$48,960	$ 65,280	$ 81,600
Parts (net)	13,380	13,380	26,760	26,760
Ryder truck commission	6,000	6,000	6,000	6,000
Lift	4,720	6,800	9,430	10,400
Paint booth	1,950	2,600	3,900	4,500
Total	$58,690	$77,740	$111,370	$129,260
Operating expenses	49,840	49,840	49,840	49,840
Operating profit	$ 8,850	$27,900	$ 61,530	$ 79,420

An Inside View

do-it-yourself auto-repair shop? In the same way as Mr. Kasper? Or differently? If so, how?

3 If Mr. Kasper were to seek money from you, would you invest in his venture?
Explain.

4 Comment on Mr. Kasper's marketing strategy.

5 Comment on Mr. Kasper's entrepreneurial traits.

Income Statement (for three months ending November 30, 1980)

Sales revenues		
Bay space rentals	$3,690	
Parts sales	1,650	
Ryder truck rentals	1,410	
Miscellaneous sales	420	$7,170
Cost of goods sold		
Parts	$1,260	
Miscellaneous	450	1,710
Gross profit		$5,460
Operating expenses		
Rent	$2,700	
Salaries	1,440	
Contract labor	780	
Advertising	560	
Supplies	540	
Legal and audit	510	
Depreciation	310	
Utilities	220	
Delivery	210	
Maintenance and repairs	210	
Telephone	160	
Organization	130	
Personal property tax	120	
Payroll taxes	120	
Insurance	60	
Office supplies	40	8,110
Operating loss		($2,650)

Balance Sheet (November 30, 1980)

Assets			Equities		
Current assets			**Current liabilities**		
Cash on hand	$1,220		Accounts and notes payable	$10,120	
Cash in bank	1,550		Accrued taxes	340	$10,460
Inventory	9,350		Note payable, bank and C of C		19,000
Prepaid insurance	40	$12,160			
Fixed assets			**Owners' equity**		
Equipment, tools	$9,290		Common stock	$ 4,000	
Accumulated depreciation	(1,180)	8,110	Due corporate officers	1,720	
			Deficit	(9,640)	(3,920)
Other assets					
Deposits	$1,850				
Organization costs	3,420	5,270			
Total assets		$25,540	Total equities		$25,540

After 13 years as an executive with two major chemical corporations, James Parrie has decided to go into business for himself. His business plan completed, Mr. Parrie has tentatively made two decisions:

☐ To manufacture nitrogen chemicals
☐ To locate his plant on the shores of Lake Erie, near Buffalo, New York

    Mr. Parrie chose nitrogen fertilizers because he knew the product line thoroughly. He had managed a plant that made nitrogen chemicals such as urea and ammonia, which were sold mostly to fertilizer manufacturers. Before that, he had worked as a marketing researcher in agricultural chemicals. "I really have a gut feeling for the fertilizer industry," says Mr. Parrie.

    Mr. Parrie chose upstate New York "not because I'm a lifelong New Yorker but because I'm sure I can adequately serve the midwestern farm belt from the region." He plans to ship fertilizer throughout the Midwest, mainly through distributors who supply farmers.

    He chose Buffalo "because I grew up there. But that's not the only reason," adds Mr. Parrie. "Rail and water facilities are good, and there's also a large supply of semiskilled workers. Too, my contacts in Buffalo are good. The banks have offered to help finance my plant, and the city fathers have agreed to give me some tax advantages if I locate there."

    Mr. Parrie's prospects looked good except for one major problem. "The city fathers suddenly became concerned about the wastes my plant would be discharging into Lake Erie," says Mr. Parrie. "Several chemical companies were already facing criminal prosecution from the state of New York for dumping pollutants into the lake."

Somehow, Mr. Parrie had ignored this problem until now. So it was back to the drawing boards for Mr. Parrie, to design special equipment that would neutralize the wastes from his proposed plant. He found that the additional pollution-control equipment would cost $120,000, which would bring the total plant cost to $720,000. He also estimated that additional energy, labor, and maintenance would cost $10,000 a year.

Because before-tax profits would average about $70,000 a year, Mr. Parrie began having doubts about locating in his home town of Buffalo. He decided to speak to a plant-location consultant, who suggested he look at plant sites in certain other midwestern states where "they're eager to attract new industry and aren't as worried about pollution." He also spoke to one of the city fathers, who suggested that he pass the added cost on to customers.

QUESTIONS

1 What should Mr. Parrie do now?
2 What alternatives, if any, does Mr. Parrie have?
3 What additional information would help Mr. Parrie decide what to do?

CASE 8C   WOOLLEY APPLIANCE STORE*

The Woolley Appliance Store is a locally owned home appliance outlet that has been in business for 18 years. It is located in Pelham, a town of 20,000 people. For the last five years, the store's yearly sales revenues have topped $500,000.

Its owner, Sarah Woolley, has controlled the business since she founded it. Recently, she has considered expanding her business by opening a new outlet in Emmett, a town not far from Pelham. Emmett has a population roughly equivalent to that of Pelham, but it does not have an appliance store.

Ms. Woolley is eager to enter this new market before someone else does. During the past several months she has been compiling buying power information for the Emmett market. Using the data in Exhibits 8C-1, 8C-2, and 8C-3, she has compared the buying power of the two markets for last year and this year.

QUESTIONS

1 Indicate the relevance, if any, of each of the exhibits to Ms. Woolley's decision.
2 What recommendation would you make to Ms. Woolley concerning the opening of an appliance store in Emmett? Give specific reasons for your recommendation.
3 What factors other than buying power should Ms. Woolley evaluate before making her decision?

*Source: Adapted from William M. Pride and O. C. Ferrell, *Marketing: Basic Concepts and Decisions,* 2nd ed. (Boston: Houghton Mifflin, 1980), pp. 611–612. Used by permission.

Disposable Income, Savings, and Discretionary Purchasing Power

	Pelham		Emmett	
Items	**Last Year**	**This Year**	**Last Year**	**This Year**
Per capita	$5,450	$5,200	$3,025	$3,500
Personal savings (as percent of disposable income)	0.06	0.07	0.03	0.04
Discretionary purchasing power (as percent of aggregate consumer purchasing power)	0.40	0.45	0.20	0.25

Percent of Families in Selected Income Classes

(Last Year)

Income	Pelham	Emmett
Under $10,000	10	25
$10,000–$15,000	25	35
$15,000–$25,000	30	20
$25,000–$35,000	20	15
Over $35,000	15	5

Patterns of Consumer Spending for Selected Products

(as percentage of total consumer expenditures)

Expenditure	Pelham	Emmett
Housing	14.5	13.7
Food for home consumption	16.1	18.2
Household appliances	1.4	0.9
Recreation	6.3	5.5
Clothing	10.3	8.6

CHAPTER NINE

FINANCING

questions for mastery

why does one need a financial plan?

**how does one estimate the amount of
money needed to launch a new venture?**

**what is the difference between equity
capital and debt capital?**

what are the various ways of raising money?

**what role do federal agencies like the SBA
play in helping entrepreneurs to finance
their venture?**

Money is the seed of money.

Jean Jacques Rousseau

ike many works of art, a business begins on a piece of paper. The would-be entrepreneur may sit down and design a small electronics plant to meet customer needs and make a fine product. But unless backed by money, the entrepreneur's plant may never become a reality. That is why entrepreneurs should understand how to estimate the amount of money they need and then how to go about raising that money.

This twin problem fascinates the entrepreneur, perhaps more so than any other part of launching a new venture. This fascination may stem from a romantic view of how some multi-million-dollar businesses have begun on shoestrings of just a few thousand dollars. Henry Ford, for example, began with only $28,000 in 1908.

Despite its romantic aspects, financing a new venture frustrates many entrepreneurs. Often, they do not know where to begin. Or if they do know, they go at it haphazardly. It is one purpose of this chapter to help relieve that frustration.

ESTIMATING MONEY NEEDS

Before they can estimate how much money they need, entrepreneurs must know what they plan to do. Unfortunately, many entrepreneurs do not, often because they have failed to work out a business plan. Yet the very act of preparing such a plan enables entrepreneurs to crystallize their thinking on how best to launch their venture. It forces them to move logically and systematically from the stage of dreams and ideas to that of concrete action. It is the concreteness of the business plan that assists entrepreneurs in determining their financial needs.

The centerpiece of the business plan is the *cash budget,* which translates operating plans into dollars. Without a cash budget, entrepreneurs have no way of estimating their financial needs. So vital are cash budgets that few investors or creditors will entertain a request for money without one. More than any other way, the cash budget enables them to decide intelligently whether to finance the entrepreneur. The cash budget, for example, helps the banker get answers to such questions as these:

☐ How much money do you need?
☐ How will you spend the money?
☐ How soon will you pay us back?

ENTREPRENEUR'S RELUCTANCE TO BUDGET

The process of budgeting has many guises. Some individuals divide the money from their weekly income into piles that they then place in envelopes earmarked for groceries, clothes, entertainment, and so on. The federal government engages in a lengthy procedure of debate and compromise between the Congress and the president. Many giant corporations proceed in an orderly system that reflects both long- and short-range goals.

What they are all doing is budgeting, or financial planning. Yet, although such planning is widely practiced among individuals, government, and big business, it is little used by entrepreneurs. One reason for their reluctance to budget may be their discomfort with numbers. To many entrepreneurs, financial skill is something best left to Wall Street. In commenting on this attitude, the Bank of America says:

> Running any business today demands certain technical skills. Purchasing demands technical skill. Production demands another technical skill; selling . . . still another technical skill. You feel at home with these skills—they are tangible evidence that you are in business.
>
> But there is another skill that plays a big part in how you do—and sometimes, whether you do—business. And that is financial skill. It is not a tangible, see-in-action skill, like the others. But rather, it is a "think" skill . . . The biggest problem with this particular "think" skill is that it intimidates most people. The mere language of finance . . . sounds so official, important, and difficult that many businesspersons automatically assume it is beyond their understanding. They feel that anything so obviously "textbookish" is better left to the professionals.[1]

With this attitude, it is hardly surprising that so many entrepreneurs find themselves in trouble from the start. Yet they often blame investors and creditors for their plight, not themselves. For example, an entrepreneur may say: "If only I had $10,000, I could really make my idea work." Generally unprepared, such entrepreneurs make little effort to convince potential investors and creditors of their need for money. But the odds favor the prepared entrepreneur. As Branch Rickey, former owner of the old Brooklyn Dodgers, once said, "Luck is the residue of design."

BUDGET PREPARATION

We introduced budget preparation in Chapter Six. Let us now discuss the details of how to work up a cash budget. Before they can begin to develop a cash budget, entrepreneurs must first spell out their operating plans, defining their production, marketing, staffing, accounting, and legal goals. Note that these are all key parts of the business plan.

Before we describe the process of translating these plans into dollars, let us first point out two limitations of budgeting:

☐ All budgets depend on estimates of what entrepreneurs think will happen in the future. But lacking a crystal ball, they do not know what will happen. Their budgets can be no better than their estimates of what the future holds, so entrepreneurs should be as thorough as possible in their efforts to prepare workable operating plans.

☐ Budgets cannot account for the effects of intangible qualities or unpredictable events. Budgets cannot, for example, reflect how skilled and able the

1. Reprinted with permission from Bank of America, NT&SA, "Understanding Financial Statements," *Small Business Reporter,* Vol. 14, No. 6, Copyright 1980.

entrepreneur may be. Nor can they reflect teamwork and morale. Budgets can only deal with future events that can be expressed in dollars.

Still, budgeting represents a remarkable achievement. It provides a way of summarizing the future in a single statement and in a language that investors and creditors understand. Let us now show how operating plans may be translated into a cash budget:

An entrepreneur plans to open a home furnishings store and she has estimated her sales revenues for the first three years (see Exhibit 9-1).

This revenue forecast is a result of the marketing plan that the entrepreneur worked out as part of her business plan. Although it is rough, the revenue forecast is the single most important estimate an entrepreneur can make. Most of the other estimates the entrepreneur must make are based on it. For example, a store with revenues of $1,000,000 rather than $200,000 may call for:

☐ Five times as many salespersons
☐ Four times as much floor space
☐ Three times as much inventory of home furnishings

Having forecast her revenues, the entrepreneur next estimates the cost of the fixed and current assets she will need to support those revenues. Before we proceed with our example, we will describe and differentiate fixed and current assets.

Fixed assets Fixed assets are resources whose use will benefit the entrepreneur for more than one year. An example is a building bought for $75,000. If the entrepreneur expects the building to last 25 years, then he or she would receive $75,000 worth of shelter benefits over the next 25 years—or $3,000 worth of benefits a year. Other examples of fixed assets include machines, land, trucks, desks, and even ash trays.

These examples are resources the entrepreneur can touch and see, but fixed assets may also be intangible. For example, an inventor may sell an entrepreneur the patent rights for a new pollution-control device for $40,000. The entrepreneur might expect to benefit from the patent rights for the next 10 years. These rights cannot be touched or seen, but they are a long-lived asset that will provide benefits to the entrepreneur's business for more than one year. Other examples of intangible assets are licenses and goodwill.

Current assets In contrast to fixed assets, current assets are resources whose benefits will last less than one year. Commonly, current assets are cash, accounts receivable, and inventories. Accounts receivable are bills owed by customers who buy on credit. These bills represent a current asset because the entrepreneur may expect to collect from customers within a short time, such as a month. Similarly, inventory is a current asset because entrepreneurs usually expect to recover their investment in inventory by selling it within a short period after purchasing it from a supplier.

EXHIBIT 9-1

Year	Sales Revenues
1	$120,000
2	160,000
3	200,000

1st month	$10,000*
2nd month	5,000
3rd month	6,000
4th month	7,000
5th month	8,000
6th month	9,000
7th month	10,000
8th month	11,000
9th month	12,000
10th month	13,000
11th month	14,000
12th month	15,000
	$120,000

* Assumes revenues will be relatively high the first month because of store's "grand opening."

EXAMPLE

Returning to our previous example, let us now assume that the entrepreneur's store will sell furniture of Scandinavian design. She has made the following estimates of start-up costs. She will:

☐ Construct a one-story, free-standing building with 5,000 square feet of floor space to display and store furniture. Cost: $75,000 at year zero.

☐ Keep a base inventory of furniture high enough to support twice the average monthly budgeted (or forecast) revenues; in addition, buy enough inventory monthly to cover the following month's budgeted revenues. She plans to pay for all inventory purchases in the same month made. Cost: $18,000 at year zero.

☐ Put an asphalt surface on a parking lot next to the building. Cost: $8,000 at year zero.

☐ Finance those customers who buy on credit. She is assuming that all sales will be credit sales, with customers taking a month to pay, on the average.

☐ Buy fixtures, office equipment, and a half-ton delivery truck. Cost: $13,000 at year zero.

☐ Incorporate the venture with a lawyer's help. Cost: $1,000.

☐ Design a record-keeping system with the help of an accountant. Cost: $500.

☐ Buy a three-year prepaid insurance policy. Cost: $3,000.

☐ Buy city, county, and state licenses. Cost: $500.

☐ Promote the store's grand opening. Cost: $1,000.

She now groups these cost items into three categories—current assets, fixed assets, and other assets—to arrive at the total cost of assets at year zero:

Current Assets:		
Accounts receivable	$ 0	
Inventory	18,000	$ 18,000
Fixed Assets:		
Building	$75,000	
Equipment & fixtures	13,000	
Parking lot	8,000	$ 96,000
Other Assets:		
Prepaid insurance	$ 3,000	
Professional fees	1,500	
Promotional costs	1,000	
Licenses	500	$ 6,000
Total Assets		$120,000

Instead of constructing the building, the entrepreneur could lease a building and its parking lot, thus reducing the asset costs from $120,000 to $37,000. If she did lease, she would probably have to pay prepaid rent covering at least the first month or two.

So far, the entrepreneur has estimated what it would cost just to open for business. She now must go one step further and estimate what it would cost to stay open through the first year, by month:

Monthly Cash Expenses (excluding cost of goods sold):	
Entrepreneur's salary	$1,200
Part-time employee wages	600
Advertising	300
Electricity, heat, telephone	200
Delivery	200
Accounting, legal	200
Supplies	100
Other	400
Total	$3,200

Note that these monthly expenses are unlikely to change with revenues. That is, first-year revenues could be double the $120,000 forecast—and yet monthly expenses would not be significantly greater than $3,200. In fact, the only expense item likely to increase significantly is part-time wages. As revenues increase, the entrepreneur will probably add more part-time salespersons to wait on customers.

To these costs, the entrepreneur should add the purchase cost of furniture sold. These purchase costs, as mentioned earlier, would vary with revenues. Assuming a profit margin of 40 percent, the entrepreneur would realize a gross profit of $40 on every $100 sales of furniture:

$100 paid by entrepreneur's customers (Revenues)
60 paid to entrepreneur's suppliers (Cost of Goods Sold)
$ 40 contribution to all other expenses and to profit (Gross Profit)

Having collected the cost figures, the entrepreneur may now go ahead and draft a cash budget for the first year. One way of doing this appears in Exhibit 9-2. Note that this budget shows:

☐ Expected *inflows* and *outflows* of cash
☐ The amount of money needed to finance the venture
☐ The cash balance at the end of each month

As shown in Exhibit 9-2, the entrepreneur needs $131,400. This estimate assumes, of course, that things will go as planned. They rarely do. So the entrepreneur adds a cushion of 10 percent to the $131,400 to allow for unevenness in the flow of money in and out of the venture and to absorb any unexpected bills. Rounding the figure to the nearest $1,000, the entrepreneur arrives at $145,000 as the total amount she must raise to launch the venture.

Besides a cash budget, the entrepreneur should prepare beginning and ending balance sheets plus an income statement. These financial statements would appear as shown in Exhibits 9-3 and 9-4. Note that most of the figures come from the cash budget and that the balance sheets assume that all the entrepreneur's assets would be financed through the sale of common stock. This assumption is unrealistic. Shortly, we will discuss other, more realistic ways of financing new ventures. Note also that the income statement shows that the venture will be profitable during its first full year of operation.

■

EQUITY CAPITAL VERSUS DEBT CAPITAL

Once entrepreneurs have estimated how much money they need to finance their venture, they must then decide what fraction of this money should come:

☐ From investors, as *equity* capital
☐ From creditors, as *debt* capital

The ratio of debt to equity capital is a controversial topic. At one extreme are commercial bankers who generally recommend that entrepreneurs and their investors put in at least one dollar of their own money for every one dollar they borrow. At the other extreme are entrepreneurs who prefer to put in as little of their own money as possible and still keep 100 percent control of their venture.

Differences arise because bankers generally are not risk takers. They are in the business of renting depositors' money, not risking it. So they tend to shun ventures backed by little investors' money, because it is the investors'

EXHIBIT 9-2

	Before Start-Up	Month After Start-Up				
		1	**2**	**3**	**4**	**5**
Expected sales revenues		$ 10,000	$ 5,000	$ 6,000	$ 7,000	$ 8,000
Cash inflow						
Collections from credit customers		0	10,000	5,000	6,000	7,000
Cash outflow						
Purchasing inventory	$ 18,000	$ 3,000*	$ 3,600	$ 4,200	$ 4,800	$ 5,400
Paying operating expenses		3,200	3,200	3,200	3,200	3,200
Subtotal	$ 18,000	$ 6,200	$ 6,800	$ 7,400	$ 8,000	$ 8,600
Buying fixed assets	$ 96,000					
Buying other assets	6,000					
Subtotal	$120,000					
Total cash outflow	120,000	6,200	6,800	7,400	8,000	8,600
Cash-flow summary						
Total cash inflow		$ 0	$ 10,000	$ 5,000	$ 6,000	$ 7,000
Total cash outflow	$120,000	6,200	6,800	7,400	8,000	8,600
Surplus or shortage	($120,000)	($ 6,200)	$ 3,200	($ 2,400)	($ 2,000)	($ 1,600)
Cumulative shortage	(120,000)	(126,200)	(123,000)	(125,400)	(127,400)	(129,000)
Money needs						
Maximum shortage	$131,400					
10% allowance for contingencies	13,140					
Total money needs	**$145,000‡**					
Cash balance at start of month	$145,000	$ 25,000	$ 18,800	$ 22,000	$ 19,600	$ 17,600
Surplus or shortage	(120,000)	(6,200)	3,200	(2,400)	(2,000)	(1,600)
Cash balance at end of month	$ 25,000	$ 18,800	$ 22,000	$ 19,600	$ 17,600	$ 16,000

* Obtained by multiplying the next month's revenues by 60 percent (60% × $5,000 revenues in *second* month = $3,000 purchase cost in *first* month).
† Assumes expected revenues of $15,000 in *thirteenth* month after start-up.
‡ Rounded.

EXHIBIT 9-2 (cont.)

6	7	8	9	10	11	12
$ 9,000	$ 10,000	$ 11,000	$ 12,000	$ 13,000	$ 14,000	$ 15,000
8,000	9,000	10,000	11,000	12,000	13,000	14,000
$ 6,000	$ 6,600	$ 7,200	$ 7,800	$ 8,400	$ 9,000	$ 9,000†
3,200	3,200	3,200	3,200	3,200	3,200	3,200
$ 9,200	$ 9,800	$ 10,400	$ 11,000	$ 11,600	$ 12,200	$ 12,200
9,200	9,800	10,400	11,000	11,600	12,200	12,200
$ 8,000	$ 9,000	$ 10,000	$ 11,000	$ 12,000	$13,000	14,000
9,200	9,800	10,400	11,000	11,600	12,200	12,200
($ 1,200)	($ 800)	($ 400)	$ 0	$ 400	$ 800	$ 1,800
(130,200)	(131,000)	(131,400)	(131,400)	(131,000)	(130,200)	(128,400)
$ 16,000	$ 14,800	$ 14,000	$ 13,600	$ 13,600	$ 14,000	$ 14,800
(1,200)	(800)	(400)	0	400	800	1,800
$ 14,800	$ 14,000	$ 13,600	$ 13,600	$ 14,000	$ 14,800	$ 16,600

EXHIBIT 9-3
Home Furnishings Store, Inc.

Beginning and Ending Balance Sheets

Assets				Equities			
	Beginning	Ending			Beginning	Ending	
Current assets				Liabilities	$ 0	$ 0	
Cash	$ 25,000	$ 16,600[a]					
Accounts receivable	0	15,000[b]		Owners' equity			
Inventory	18,000	21,000[c]		Common stock	$145,000	$145,000	
Subtotal	$ 43,000	$ 52,600		Retained earnings		500[f]	
				Subtotal	$145,000	$145,500	
Fixed assets							
Building	$ 75,000	$ 72,000[d]					
Equipment	13,000	11,700[d]					
Parking lot	8,000	7,200[d]					
Subtotal	$ 96,000	$ 90,900					
Other assets	6,000	2,000[e]					
Total assets	$145,000	$145,500		Total assets	$145,000	$145,500	

[a] Obtained directly from Exhibit 9-2 (cash balance at end of twelfth month).
[b] Obtained directly from Exhibit 9-2 (all revenues in twelfth month will be owed by customers at month's end).
[c] Assumes a base inventory ($12,000) plus enough inventory ($9,000) to support the thirteenth month's budgeted revenues of $15,000.
[d] Reflects depreciation of fixed assets during year (see Exhibit 9-4).
[e] Reflects write-off of prepaid expenses during year (see Exhibit 9-4).
[f] Obtained directly from Exhibit 9-4 (assumes profits will be plowed back into the venture).

money that protects the banker when adversity strikes. As losses occur, investors' money bears the first impact of loss, and so the greater the amount of investors' money, the greater the likelihood that the bank will recover its loan.

On the other hand, entrepreneurs are risk takers. Many are willing to risk their life savings in their venture, if they have to. But before they do so, they may try to sell stock in their venture to investors. By doing so, they may raise all the money they need and still keep control of their venture:

EXAMPLE

The entrepreneur in our earlier example needs $145,000 to finance her venture and has only $20,000 in savings. Her first choice is to float 2,000 shares of common stock at a par value of $20 each.

She buys 1,000 shares herself at $20 each, and then persuades friends to buy the remaining 1,000 shares at $80 each. That gives her a total of $100,000.

The rest—$45,000—she may readily borrow from a commercial bank. With $100,000 of investors' money behind her, most banks would be willing to lend her the $45,000. The $100,000 she has raised accounts for nearly 70 percent of the total needed to finance her venture, and banks

EXHIBIT 9-4

Income Statement (for first year of operations)

Sales revenues		$120,000[a]
Cost of goods sold		72,000[b]
Gross profit		$ 48,000
Operating expenses		
Administrative and selling	$38,400[c]	
Depreciation	5,100[d]	
Write-off of prepaid expenses	4,000[e]	47,500
Operating profit		$ 500

[a] Obtained from Exhibit 9-2 by adding monthly budgeted revenues.
[b] Obtained by multiplying total budgeted revenues of $120,000 by 60 percent (because the gross margin is 40 percent).
[c] Obtained from Exhibit 9-2 by adding monthly operating expenses.
[d] Obtained as follows:
Building depreciation   = $75,000 ÷ 25-year life = $3,000
Equipment depreciation =   13,000 ÷ 10-year life = 1,300
Parking lot depreciation =   8,000 ÷ 10-year life =   800
                                                     $5,100

[e] Obtained as follows:
Professional fees = $1,500
Insurance   = 1,000 (one-third of $3,000 prepaid insurance policy expires
                              during year)
Promotional costs = 1,000
Licenses   =   500
                     $4,000

are generally satisfied if the ratio of equity capital to total capital is 50 percent.

■

The prior example demonstrates a method of beginning a venture on a shoestring. With just $20,000 of her own money, the entrepreneur was able to raise $145,000 and still keep 50 percent control. There are other ways as well, as the following example illustrates:

EXAMPLE

A youthful entrepreneur, Terry Allen learned that a 180-student schoolhouse on four acres of land was about to be sold at a sealed-bid auction. With visions of a skiers' lodge, he turned in a bid of $12,790. He based his bid on the news that a nearby schoolhouse one-third the size had sold for $4,260. Multiplying $4,260 by 3, he came up with $12,780, and he added an extra $10 so that he would outbid anyone else using the same logic.

Mr. Allen won the bid. And he had seven days to raise the money. A recent graduate of the Harvard Business School, he had little money of his own. After going over the idea with friends, he raised the entire $12,790 in one day and kept 50 percent of the equity as his reward for putting the venture together.

Mr. Allen spent his nights and weekends changing the old schoolhouse into Chateau L'Ecole, a 140-bed skiers' dormitory. To make the changes, he needed $35,000 more. And, he got it by borrowing on the strength of his friends' signatures. His beginning balance sheet appears in Exhibit 9-5.

Without putting in a single penny of his own money but by investing his ideas and energies, Mr. Allen created a skiers' lodge and owned 50 percent of it. Incidentally, he broke even the first ski season.[2]

■

The fact that Mr. Allen had no money did not discourage him. As his Harvard professor had told him:

Money is no obstacle . . . since money could always be found to back a venture because so many people have it who do not have the ideas or energy to invest it. Furthermore, having any money at all could limit the imagination. For example, if a person had $5,000, he would look for a business he could buy with that amount. But if he had no money, he would not be confined by financial limitations, and could look for a much larger business to buy.[3]

For the entrepreneur, it is generally safer to finance a new venture with more investors' money than creditors' money because:

☐ Creditors' money involves a definite promise to repay the lender. Almost all loans require the borrower to meet a repayment schedule that demands not only repayment of the loan but also payment of interest—usually monthly. Failure to meet this twin obligation could force the entrepreneur's venture into bankruptcy.

EXHIBIT 9-5 — Chateau L'Ecole

Beginning Balance Sheet

Assets		Equities		
Improvements	$35,000	Bank loan		$35,000
Schoolhouse	12,790	Owners' equity		
Organization costs	12,790	Mr. Allen	$12,790	
		Others	12,790	25,580
Total	$60,580	Total		$60,580

---

2. Adapted from Patrick R. Liles, *New Business Ventures and the Entrepreneur* (Homewood, Ill.: Richard D. Irwin, 1974), p. 129.
3. Ibid.

☐ Investors' money, on the other hand, does not involve a definite promise to repay investors. Investors buy shares of stock at their own risk. Later, if they want to sell their shares, they cannot force the entrepreneur to buy them back. Investors are on their own to find somebody who may be willing to buy their shares. Nor are investors entitled to a return on their investment—unless, of course, the venture makes a profit and declares a dividend.

The lack of a sharply defined financial obligation makes investors' money attractive to entrepreneurs. However, some entrepreneurs prefer to run their venture with *no* investors' money except their own. Such a man was entrepreneur H. L. Hunt:

> [When Mr. Hunt died in 1974] at the age of 85, he had amassed an estimated personal fortune of $2 billion, putting him on a par with J. Paul Getty and Howard Hughes as one of the world's richest men. The exact extent of his wealth is unknown because Mr. Hunt *never* invested in anything that he could not own outright, and he had *no* outside stockholders in the businesses he did control.[4]

Unlike Mr. Hunt, some entrepreneurs who want 100 percent ownership of their venture try to put in as little as they can and borrow as much as they can. Such entrepreneurs generally want to answer to nobody but themselves. But they may be deluding themselves. The entrepreneur's freedom to act may be as limited with creditors as with investors. With a large stake in the entrepreneur's venture, for example, creditors may threaten to take over if the entrepreneur fails to pay bills or to repay loans.

SOURCES OF MONEY—EQUITY CAPITAL

One of an entrepreneur's most puzzling questions is where best to raise money. As shown in Exhibit 9-6, a bewildering variety of sources awaits the entrepreneur. The sources range from private to governmental. We will begin by looking first at sources of equity capital (or investors' money); later, we will examine sources of debt capital (or creditors' money).

VENTURE-CAPITAL FIRMS
Venture-capital firms generally invest in entrepreneurs whose ventures promise to grow rapidly. They tend to favor manufacturing ventures, especially in idea-rich, high-technology industries like electronics. Typically, a venture-capital firm receives more than 1,000 requests for money each year, many of which stand little chance of success. Out of every 100 requests:

☐ 80 are dropped after less than a day's study
☐ 10 are dropped after a week's study

---

4. "Entrepreneurs: Just a Country Boy," *Time,* December 9, 1974, p. 44 [Reprinted by permission from TIME, The Weekly Newsmagazine; Copyright Time Inc. 1974]

EXHIBIT 9-6

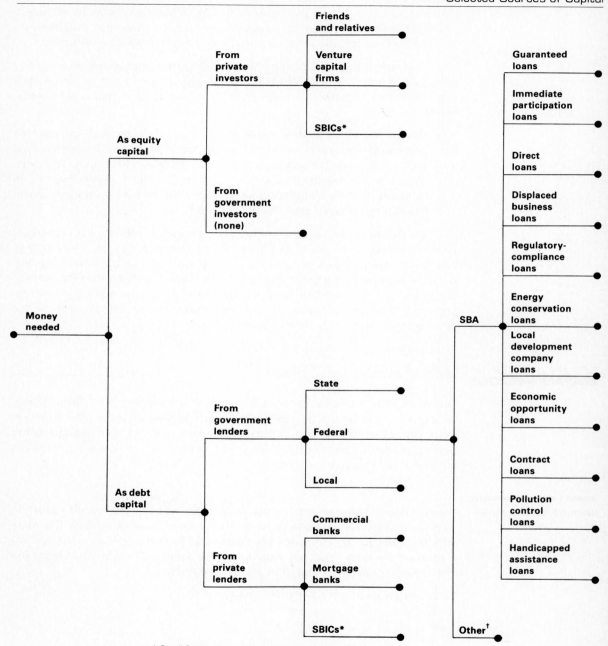

* Small Business Investment Companies.
† Including the U.S. Departments of Commerce, Housing and Urban Development (HUD), and Transportation (DOT).

☐ 8 are dropped after a month's study
☐ 2 are accepted after one or more months of detailed study

Most of the requests that are dropped within a day lack a business plan. Most venture-capital firms will not even look at a written request for money unless it is accompanied by a business plan.

There are many types of venture-capital firms, among them:

☐ **Traditional partnerships** These are often established by wealthy families to aggressively manage a portion of their money by investing in small businesses.
☐ **Professionally managed pools** These are formed from institutional money and operate like traditional partnerships.
☐ **Investment banking firms** Such firms occasionally form investor syndicates for venture proposals.
☐ **Insurance companies** These tend to be more conservative and often require a portion of equity capital as a condition of their loans to smaller businesses as protection against inflation.[5]

SMALL BUSINESS INVESTMENT COMPANIES

Small Business Investment Companies (SBICs) are another source of equity capital. SBICs began to form in 1958 after Congress passed the Small Business Investment Act. The purpose of this legislation was to encourage private investors to finance entrepreneurs. The act gave such investors an incentive to form SBICs, which they would run as private, profit-motivated businesses. Two other features of the act follow:

☐ Investors would invest only in small businesses, especially in high-risk ventures boasting a new product with promising market potential, an unusually favorable competitive position, the possibilities of growth through favorable acquisition, and an outstanding, aggressive management.
☐ The SBA would oversee the SBICs, including their licensing and regulation.

In 1981, there were more than 400 SBICs scattered throughout the nation. Some are run by commercial banks; some by engineers, scientists, or experts in technical fields; others by lawyers, accountants, or other specialists. They all have one thing in common: the willingness to assume risks for a share of owners' equity, though in varying degrees. Some SBICs act like commercial banks and prefer to make loans rather than buy shares of stock. But they are the exception rather than the rule.

A popular misconception about SBICs and other venture-capital firms is that they also invest in so-called mom-and-pop shops, meaning the corner drugstore or the neighborhood restaurant. They do not. Their interest lies mostly in ventures that promise to grow rapidly in revenues and profits.

5. LaRue Tone Hosmer, U.S. Small Business Administration, *A Venture Capital Primer for Small Business* (Washington, D.C.: U.S. Government Printing Office, 1980), p. 6.

SBICs traditionally have been the workhorses of venture capital, investing more in traditional businesses than in flashy new fields such as electronics. "Venture capitalists are realizing that everything is not high technology, and some of the older industries that aren't as sexy still have a lot of growth," explains Barbara Stack, vice president of Rand Capital Corporation, a Buffalo SBIC.

Of the three deals Rand has participated in this year, only one is founded in electronics. Besides investing $150,000 in an electronics company that invented an energy-control device, Rand also invested $300,000 in a manufacturer of wood furniture founded 50 years ago. Ms. Stack believes that both companies are positively affected by the economy:

☐ The electronics company benefits from a concern about controlling the use of energy.
☐ The furniture company benefits from a growing trend among homeowners to buy high-quality furniture.[6]

■

SBICs are similar to the venture-capital firms we discussed earlier. They expect precisely the same kinds of information from entrepreneurs, so entrepreneurs must have their business plan in hand when they go to an SBIC for financial help. Otherwise, they stand little chance of success.

BIG BUSINESS

Still another source of equity capital is big business. Many of the nation's major corporations have formed departments that seek out promising entrepreneurs to invest in. Their motives are mixed, ranging from a desire to put their money to work earning more money to a desire to identify candidates for acquisition later.

Regardless of the motivation, investment by big business into small business is a healthy idea; corporations can supply not only equity capital but also managerial skills. Often, it is not lack of money that plagues the entrepreneur but rather lack of managerial skills. Major corporations have such skills in abundance. A partial list of major corporations now aggressively seeking out promising entrepreneurs reads like a *Who's Who* of American business: Exxon Corporation, Ford Motor Company, Monsanto Corporation, and Standard Oil of Ohio.

OTHER SOURCES

In addition to the sources of equity capital we have already discussed—venture-capital firms, SBICs, and big business—there are many other personal sources, including:

☐ Friends and relatives
☐ Employees and business associates
☐ Professional persons including physicians, dentists, and lawyers

6. "How Venture Capitalists Share the Wealth," *Venture,* October 1980, p. 32.

According to one study, equity capital is more likely to be raised not from venture-capital firms, but from entrepreneurs themselves or from friends and relatives:

> Even if we take into account the various government programs that aid small-businesspeople and minority entrepreneurs, it is clear that formal institutions provide very little capital for new companies.
>
> Most venture capital comes from the entrepreneur's own resources or from family and friends. This "earnest money" reassures bankers who often refuse to lend until entrepreneurs have locked themselves in by mortgaging their home to the hilt and hustling everyone they know.
>
> Such personal sources accounted for 90 percent of the initial financing for the new businesses we studied in this country and Italy. The rest comes from private investors who regularly invest in new companies, men often talked about in Texas as "good old boys."[7]

SOURCES OF MONEY—DEBT CAPITAL

So far, we have discussed ways of raising equity capital. Let us now turn to ways of raising debt capital. Many entrepreneurs believe that banks often lend money to ventures that have yet to earn their first dollar. Many entrepreneurs also believe that the SBA often lends money to unborn ventures. Both beliefs are erroneous. It may be taken as an article of faith that most bankers reject the loan applications of would-be entrepreneurs unless, for example:

☐ A wealthy friend or relative guarantees repayment of the loan by co-signing the bank note.
☐ The entrepreneur offers as security for the loan such personal holdings as a house or top-rated bonds.
☐ The entrepreneur needs the loan to construct a building, which can be repossessed without loss of dollar value if the entrepreneur fails.

However, there are various ways that entrepreneurs may borrow money—before and after they launch their venture. We will look first at private lenders such as commercial banks; then at government lenders such as the SBA.

PRIVATE LENDERS

There are many private lenders, ranging from commercial banks to storefront finance companies, from insurance companies to relatives. Of these, commercial banks offer entrepreneurs the most help. Besides lending money, such banks offer a host of other services. For example, they:

☐ Give professional financial advice
☐ Serve as a financial reference
☐ Give credit information

7. Adapted from Albert Shapero, "The Displaced, Uncomfortable Entrepreneur," *Psychology Today*, November 1975, 86.

☐ Administer trusts
☐ Transfer funds

The commercial banker is as indispensable to entrepreneurs as the lawyer. So it behooves entrepreneurs to strike a working relationship with a banker months before they launch their venture. According to the SBA:

> Too many entrepreneurs go to their banker only when they need to borrow money. If the entrepreneur deals with her banker in day-to-day financial matters, the banker can get to know her and her business. Not only will the banker often give aid and advice on current financial operations, but when she really needs to borrow money, the banker will be familiar with her business and will be better able to evaluate her loan application.[8]

Commercial banks make two major kinds of loans: short-term loans and long-term loans.

Short-term loans As a rule, commercial banks like to see a fast turnover of loans. So they tend to make short-term loans—that is, loans that fall due within one year. Such loans generally are made to finance inventories or to finance customers who buy on credit. The entrepreneur then repays such loans when inventories are sold or when customers pay their bills. Take this example:

EXAMPLE

An entrepreneur opens a store to sell air conditioners. He must build up his inventory of air conditioners in the spring, just before the summer selling season. His need is only temporary, so he may take out a short-term loan to buy the air conditioners. He would then repay the loan when his inventory of air conditioners was sold and paid for by customers.

Because such loans last a short time, they often are made on an *unsecured* basis. Collateral is not required because the bank relies on the entrepreneur's credit standing. Of course, if the borrower's credit standing is poor or not yet established, the lender may require collateral as protection against possible default on the loan. Loans backed by collateral are called *secured* loans.

■

This example points up an important feature of short-term loans. They satisfy the entrepreneur's temporary need for money. Such loans are also called self-liquidating loans.

Long-term loans In contrast to short-term loans, long-term loans help satisfy the entrepreneur's permanent need for money. Long-term loans run for more than one year and enable the entrepreneur to finance the purchase of such long-lived assets as buildings and land, machinery and trucks. Such loans generally are repaid from profits.

8. U.S. Small Business Administration, *Financing . . . Short and Long Term Needs* (Washington, D.C.: U.S. Government Printing Office, 1965), p. 33.

Long-term loans may also enable the entrepreneur whose venture is growing rapidly to finance the permanent expansion of inventories and of customers who buy on credit. The following example shows how long-term loans work:

EXAMPLE

An entrepreneur who owns a small machine shop needs a $15,000 turret lathe. Lacking the necessary cash, he takes out a $15,000 loan to buy the lathe. If he continues to be successful, the entrepreneur would then repay the loan out of profits plowed back into his venture.

The entrepreneur and the bank agree to a repayment schedule that calls for the $15,000 loan to be repaid in five yearly payments of $3,000 each plus interest. Note that this kind of loan enables the entrepreneur to build up his equity over the five-year life of the loan—in the same way that a homeowner builds up equity each time he makes payment on a mortgage loan. ∎

SUPPLIER CREDIT

This source of debt capital works only for entrepreneurs who enjoy a good credit rating. Others have to pay their suppliers in cash. By allowing suppliers to finance them, entrepreneurs benefit from the cash released for other purposes. An example will show how this kind of financing works:

EXAMPLE

An entrepreneur who owns a tire supply store buys tires monthly. Her supplier offers credit terms of 30 days, meaning that payment is expected 30 days after the entrepreneur receives a supply of tires. If the entrepreneur sells out her inventory roughly once a month, then she really needs none of her own money to finance purchase of the tires. ∎

GOVERNMENT LENDERS

As with private lenders, there are many government lenders, not only at the federal level but at the state and local levels as well. At the federal level, such lenders include the SBA and the U.S. Department of Commerce. At the state and local levels, lenders generally include agencies whose purpose it is to boost economic development. Of all such lenders, federal and otherwise, the SBA offers entrepreneurs the most help. To qualify for SBA help, businesses must:

☐ Be independently owned and operated and not dominant in their fields
☐ Be unable to get private financing on reasonable terms
☐ Qualify as small under the SBA's size standards, shown earlier in Exhibit 1-2 on page 8.

In 1981, the SBA had 27 lending programs for entrepreneurs. A few are briefly described below.

Guaranteed loans Under this program, entrepreneurs may borrow from a commercial bank with the SBA guaranteeing the bank to pay back part of any loss suffered by the bank. Here, the SBA may guarantee up to 90 percent of the loan amount, not to exceed $500,000. Such loans may be made for as long as 15 years. Through this program flows most of the SBA's lending activity.

Immediate participation loans If the entire loan amount is unavailable from a bank and if an SBA-guaranteed loan is also unavailable, then the SBA may agree, virtually overnight, to finance the entrepreneur jointly with the bank. The SBA and the bank each put up a share of the money, with the SBA's share not to exceed $150,000.

Direct loans Under this program, loans may not exceed $350,000. These loans are made and serviced by the SBA itself rather than by banks.

Displaced business loans These loans enable entrepreneurs to stay in business or to relocate if the SBA determines that an entrepreneur's business has suffered financially because of a government project. Such loans may cover the purchase or construction of other property, whether or not the entrepreneur owned the original property occupied by the business.

Regulatory compliance loans Under this program, entrepreneurs may borrow money to help them comply with government laws that otherwise would cause them undue financial harm. Examples of such laws are the Occupational Safety and Health Act and the Clean Air Act.

Solar and other energy conservation loans This program offers loans to help entrepreneurs save energy. These loans cover such purposes as the production of energy from wood or grain, the use of windmills to generate electricity, and the burning of garbage to produce energy.

Local development companies (LDCs) Under this program, the SBA works through a profit or nonprofit corporation founded by local citizens who want to boost their community's economy. The SBA may lend up to $500,000 for each small business to be helped by an LDC.

SPECIAL PROGRAMS FOR MINORITY ENTREPRENEURS

Since the late 1960s, a number of special programs have surfaced to help minority persons become entrepreneurs. Spearheading these programs are not only federal agencies like the SBA and the U.S. Department of Commerce but also Chambers of Commerce and the LDCs mentioned earlier. Federal agencies, of course, supply the lion's share of such financial help. Some of their programs include:

Economic opportunity loan program Under this program, the SBA may make or guarantee loans to minority entrepreneurs only. The most that may be borrowed under this program is $100,000 for up to 15 years.

MESBIC program A MESBIC is a Minority Enterprise Small Business Investment Company, owned and run by an established industrial or financial concern that combines money and management resources for assistance to minority entrepreneurs. Its major purpose is to marshal the skills of big business, banks, and the federal government to help develop minority entrepreneurs through use of the MESBIC idea. Any individual or company may form a MESBIC by putting up at least $150,000 of their own money. After investing most of this sum in minority ventures, the MESBIC may then increase its original capital fifteenfold through a combination of federal and private financing. Like SBICs, MESBICs may either buy shares in minority ventures or lend them money. Take this example:

EXAMPLE

A MESBIC decides that a minority manufacturer who needs $50,000 to start production should be financed in this way:

☐ $10,000 would be a 15-year loan from the MESBIC
☐ $40,000 would be a 15-year loan from a commercial bank, 90 percent of which would be guaranteed by the SBA

Note that the bank's exposure to loss would be only $4,000—or 8 percent of the total loan amount of $50,000.

■

So far, our discussion has centered on federal loan programs. There are, however, many other federal programs having little to do with loans. These programs mostly help entrepreneurs to upgrade their managerial skills or to get federal contracts. Similar programs often exist at both the state and local levels as well. In the next chapter, we will look at such programs in some detail, especially those sponsored by the SBA.

SUMMARY

Financing a new venture often frustrates the would-be entrepreneur. This frustration stems from the entrepreneur's failure to estimate money needs wisely and lack of knowledge of where best to seek money.

Perhaps the best way to go about estimating money needs is to prepare a business plan. Its centerpiece is the cash budget, which translates the entrepreneur's operating plans into dollars. This budget covers the entrepreneur's money needs before and just after start-up of the venture.

Preparation of such a budget does not guarantee that entrepreneurs will get the money they need from money lenders and investors. All it does is improve their chances. Today, investors and creditors rarely entertain a request for money unless the entrepreneur has worked out a cash budget as part of a business plan.

After estimating how much money is needed to finance the venture, the entrepreneur should:

☐ Estimate what fraction of the money should come from investors (equity capital) and what fraction from creditors (debt capital)
☐ Decide where best to go to raise the money

It generally is safer to have more investors' money than creditors' money. The main reason is that creditors' money involves a definite promise to pay a debt, while investors' money does not.

There are many sources of money. Investors' money may come from:

☐ Venture-capital firms and SBICs
☐ Big business and investment bankers
☐ Professional persons and wealthy families
☐ Friends, relatives, and business associates

On the other hand, creditors' money may come from:

☐ Federal agencies, especially the SBA
☐ Commercial banks and suppliers
☐ State and local agencies
☐ Friends and relatives

DISCUSSION AND REVIEW QUESTIONS

1 Explain why the business plan plays such an important role in estimating money needs for a new venture.
2 Explain the difference between equity capital and debt capital. Which is preferable? Why?
3 Why do entrepreneurs tend to ignore budgeting as a financial tool?
4 Define these terms: *budgeting, fixed assets, current assets, secured loan, SBIC, MESBIC, long-term loan.*
5 Do commercial banks generally help to finance the entrepreneur who is just starting out? Explain.
6 What are the hazards of financing a new venture mostly with debt? Explain.
7 Why do venture-capital firms, commercial banks, and the SBA generally ask for a business plan?
8 How would you, as an entrepreneur, go about estimating how much money is needed to launch your venture?
9 In preparing a cash budget, which figure is the single most important estimate? Why?
10 How do these SBA loan programs differ: Guaranteed Loans, Direct Loans, and Immediate Participation Loans?
11 How may repayment of a long-term loan increase the entrepreneur's equity in a venture?

12 Why should an entrepreneur strike a working relationship with a commercial bank early on?

13 What services do commercial banks offer besides making loans?

14 Describe two programs designed to help minority entrepreneurs finance their ventures.

15 Do SBA loan programs compete with private lenders like commercial banks? Explain.

A five-year-old company in a centuries-old industry, Architectural Arts Foundry posted a profit of $7,800 on sales revenues of $187,900 in 1981. But its founder, Robert Miko, continues to have trouble making ends meet. In fact, the business earns much less for him than he could get with less effort and risk by working for somebody else. He wonders why he does not do better.

BACKGROUND

An artist to his fingertips, Mr. Miko began his present business in 1976 at the age of 28. His first one folded the year it started, in 1973. "I knew absolutely nothing about running a business," says Mr. Miko, "so I went back to my former employer, Smith-Baldwin, to learn as much as I could about the managing end." Shortly after he returned, he became manager of their finishing department. Two craftsmen worked under him, neither of whom needed much supervision.

Family-run for more than 80 years, Smith-Baldwin once led the state in the production of architectural arts. Its works draw praise from every architectural quarter. However, the company, strongly set in its ways, has failed to build on its reputation. In fact, it has lost ground. For instance, in three years Smith-Baldwin dropped from 30 to 15 employees. That drop was a signal for Mr. Miko to give entrepreneurship a second try.

So, in 1976 Mr. Miko struck off on his own again, this time convinced he was better prepared to succeed. He had worked in virtually every production department at Smith-Baldwin, so he knew every detail about producing architectural art of the highest quality.

SECOND THOUGHTS

One worry kept nagging at Mr. Miko, however. And that was his lack of managerial know-how. He still had "little feeling for what it takes to manage a business successfully."

His experience was lopsided. Virtually his entire career was devoted to the design and production of architectural arts. So he knew little about purchasing materials, getting things done through others, bidding on jobs, keeping track of costs, and the like.

Architectural Arts Foundry, Inc.

EXHIBIT 9A-1

Balance Sheet (May 15, 1976)

Assets		Equities	
Cash	$ 720	Liabilities	$ 0
Organizational costs	480	Owner's equity	1200
Total assets	$1200	Total equities	$1200

Equally lopsided was his education. He had never taken any college-level courses in business administration, especially courses in accounting and marketing. For two years, he studied design and drafting at an institute for architecture. He also took up metallurgy. His last stop was an institute of art, where he dabbled in sculpture and ceramics. This narrow educational background honed his artistic skills to such a fine edge that architects often sought him out while he was still with Smith-Baldwin.

When Mr. Miko left Smith-Baldwin to go on his own again, his first act was to form a verbal partnership with a sculptor 84 years old: Stephen Rebeck. "He was my angel," says Mr. Miko. They shared space together in a rundown, peeling 90-year-old house. Rent was $70 a month. Shortly afterward, Mr. Miko incorporated his business. His beginning balance sheet appears in Exhibit 9A-1.

"I had a lot of help when I started out," says Mr. Miko. "For one thing, I got married. And my wife became my other angel. She worked to support me until I got my feet on the ground. In fact, she still works."

A SLOW START

At first, Mr. Miko spent most of his time selling his services. He talked to every architectural firm in town. He got some orders, but not enough to pay himself a salary. In fact, during his venture's first year, he lived entirely off his wife's salary of $13,000. He blames this performance on himself. "I was going off in too many directions at the same time," says Mr. Miko. "I'm not a manager."

During his second year, orders picked up. One reason was his decision "not to be all things to all people." He would instead focus on creativity. "I decided to specialize in unique designs, and not in run-of-the-mill items like ash trays," says Mr. Miko. "That's the image I wanted to project." Examples of his architectural art appear in Exhibit 9A-2.

Thanks to this shift in marketing strategy, Mr. Miko's sales revenues have gone up steadily. Summarized in Exhibit 9A-3 are his income statements for five years. Recent financial statements appear in Exhibits 9A-4 and 9A-5.

Despite steady growth, Mr. Miko is dissatisfied. In 1981, his salary barely matched his wife's take-home pay as a secretary. From his viewpoint, his business has been an artistic though not a financial success. That puzzles him.

PRIDE IN CRAFTSMANSHIP

"My work is the best," says Mr. Miko, "but I can't seem to get the volume of business I should be getting. Architects applaud the unique designs I do. Maybe I don't charge enough." Mr. Miko has indeed done good work for some blue-chip clients. For example, he did all the mirror-finished lettering for a hotel at Disney World in Florida and he did a sculpture relief of Lyndon Baines Johnson for the federal government for which he won wide acclaim (see Exhibit 9A-2).

And yet, the bottom line on his income statement fails to reflect his artistic success. Not that he hasn't tried to improve the way he runs his business. For example, he has moved five times since 1976, each time to more spacious quarters. And as volume went up, he added talent. In fact, he now has seven men and women working for him: one general manager, one industrial designer, one pattern maker, one molder, one bookkeeper and pattern maker, and two finishers.

Examples of Architectural Art

Two of the seven worked with Mr. Miko at Smith-Baldwin. Except for the finishers, all excel at architectural art. "Without their talent, I never would have made it this far," says Mr. Miko.

NEW PARTNERS

Perhaps his most significant move was to team up in 1981 with a sculptor, Ron Dewey, and with Ray Tletski, who runs his own architectural arts firm. They now share the same quarters. This union, though in name only, was a stroke of organizational genius, Mr. Miko believes. "Our talents mesh so well that I can now tell clients we're a full-service shop. That's a great plus."

But this union also cost money. Mr. Miko had to go deeply into debt to provide spacious quarters to house himself and his two partners. At the time, his quarters were so cramped there was barely enough room for a desk.

After a long search, Mr. Miko settled on a vacant riverfront building within walking distance of the offices of most architects. It was an ideal site, with 13,000 square feet of floor space. The only drawback was the owner's refusal to lease the 118-year-old building. He was interested only in selling it, for the sum of $104,000. The building had been for sale for five years.

Mr. Miko was so enthusiastic about the building and site that he spent two months trying to find ways to finance the purchase. He talked to five

Architectural Arts Foundry, Inc.

Income Statements: 1976–1981

Year Ending September 30	Sales Revenues	Expenses	Before-Tax Profit or Loss
1977	$ 16,300	$ 17,000	($ 700)
1978	35,200	35,000	200
1979	54,000	49,200	4,800
1980	110,600	103,200	7,400
1981	187,900	178,000	9,900

Architectural Arts Foundry, Inc.

Income Statement (for year ending September 30, 1981)

Sales revenues		$187,870
Cost of goods sold		60,020
Gross profit		$127,850
Operating expenses		
Payroll	$67,030	
Outside labor	10,730	
Payroll taxes	5,280	
Interest	5,180	
Telephone	4,880	
Rent	4,600	
Supplies	4,100	
Utilities	3,390	
Advertising	2,470	
Insurance	2,450	
Freight postage	1,580	
Vehicle	1,500	
Miscellaneous	1,030	
Other taxes	840	
Dues and subscriptions	770	
Legal and accounting	720	
Maintenance	530	
Travel and entertainment	410	
Office supplies	290	
Licenses	120	117,900
Operating profit		$ 9,950
Federal income tax		2,190
Net profit		$ 7,760

Architectural Arts Foundry, Inc.

Balance Sheet (September 30, 1981)

Assets			Equities		
Current assets			**Current liabilities**		
Cash in bank	$ 1,080		Accounts payable	$9,890	
Accounts receivable	20,780		Taxes payable	910	$ 10,800
Inventory	14,640				
Work in process	8,760	$ 45,260	Long-term loan		187,820
Fixed assets			Owners' equity		100,540
Land and building	$199,200				
Equipment and furniture	48,000				
Automobile	6,700	253,900			
Total assets		$299,160	Total equities		$299,160

commercial banks. All turned him down flat. "They said my business was too risky," says Mr. Miko. "Two things bothered them most: my profit performance and the building's old age. I guess banks are just not in the business of risking money."

Rebuffed by the banks, Mr. Miko then turned to the SBA for help. It took them four months to approve his request for money. What convinced them were the following factors:

☐ Mr. Miko's dedication to his business, as evidenced by the small salary he drew.

☐ The quality of the architectural works he designed, as evidenced by praise from his clients.

☐ His new marketing strategy of supplying a full spectrum of architectural art services. This strategy would give him an edge over competitors in bidding on big jobs. For example, on a new building, he could now offer to do all the statuary, all logos, all directional systems, and the like as *one* package. No competitor could boast such a capability.

To put his marketing strategy to work, Mr. Miko found that he needed much more than just the $104,000 to buy the building. He really needed $210,000:

$104,000 for the building
65,000 for working capital
41,000 for leasehold improvements
$210,000

This total is the estimate that his accountant and the SBA came up with. The SBA also insisted that Mr. Miko raise at least $18,000 of it himself. And he

Purpose of Loan	Amount	Payment Period	Interest Rate	Percentage Backed by SBA
To purchase building	$104,000	20 years	20.00%	40%
To supply working capital	65,000	7	21.75	90
To make leasehold improvements	41,000	20	20.50	60

did, by dipping into his wife's savings for $4,000 and by convincing friends to invest $14,000. Loan terms appear in Exhibit 9A-6.

THE FUTURE

So far, Mr. Miko's cash flow has been enough to cover interest and to pay down the loan each month. Still, he worries about the future. Unless sales jump, his business will do no better than break even. "I have to get out and sell," says Mr. Miko. "I'm not as good a salesman as I ought to be." To correct this shortcoming, he has enrolled in a salesmanship course at a local community college.

And for the first time, he has set goals for himself:

☐ A sales revenue goal of $1 million by 1986
☐ An immediate legal merger with his two partners-in-name-only: the sculptor, Mr. Dewey, and the entrepreneur, Mr. Tletski

"I hope I can pull it off," says Mr. Miko. "No one does a better job than we do. I'm proud that my firm is the only one in town that also guarantees performance. We always deliver. If a client doesn't like what we give them, we do it over at our own expense."

QUESTIONS

1 If you were Mr. Miko, what would you do now to boost revenues? Explain.
2 Comment on the way Mr. Miko has been financing his venture.
3 In your opinion, is Mr. Miko's marketing strategy sound? Explain.
4 Comment on Mr. Miko's entrepreneurial traits.
5 How well has Mr. Miko performed so far? Explain.

CASE 9B   SWISSHELM DEPARTMENT STORE, INC.

John Carollo bought a small department store for $120,000. He paid the sellers $30,000 cash and gave them a 5-year note on the remaining $90,000 at an interest rate of 20 percent a year.

A graduate of Stanford University with honors, Mr. Carollo had worked for 11 years with the Sears, Roebuck Company. His experience there included:

□ Selling men's suits and appliances on the floor
□ Managing a men's clothing department
□ Serving as assistant branch manager

All along, his ambition was to have his own department store. Sears, he believed, would be a good place to learn every aspect of department-store operations. After all, Sears is the nation's biggest retailer.

Mr. Carollo gave himself 10 years to learn the business. Then he would start a search for a small department store in a small city.

A year went by before Mr. Carollo learned from a banker that a department store was for sale in New Philadelphia, a city of 16,000 persons. Three months later, he and the sellers agreed on the purchase price of $120,000.

One week after he took over, Mr. Carollo and his accountant sat down to prepare a cash budget. It was now early August. Mr. Carollo knew that he would need a short-term loan to build up his inventory in anticipation of high consumer demand in September, when schools start, and again in December, when Christmas buying is in full swing.

The cash budget would help Carollo decide how much to borrow and when to borrow. After analyzing past records, he came up with these estimates:

Sales Revenue Forecast		Monthly Expenses	
June (actual)	$24,000	Rent	$3,000
July (actual)	20,000	Depreciation	500
August	28,000	Other expenses	900
September	52,000	Wages and salaries:	
October	44,000	August	$2,800
November	76,000	September	3,200
December	96,000	October	3,200
January	22,000	November	3,600
February	32,000	December	3,600
		January	2,800

□ Sales would be:
  30 percent for cash
  70 percent for credit
□ Of the credit sales:
  80 percent would be paid within *one* month of purchase
  20 percent would be paid within *two* months
□ Credit sales outstanding on August 1 consisted of:
  $14,000 from July
  $ 3,360 from June
□ Gross profit on sales would be 25 percent.
□ Enough inventory would be purchased monthly to cover the *next* month's budgeted sales.
□ All inventory purchases would be paid for in the *same* month they were made.
□ A *minimum* cash balance of $8,000 would be maintained.
□ The cash balance was $19,000 on August 1.

☐ All borrowings would be in multiples of $1,000 and would be made or repaid on the *first* of the month.

☐ Interest at 1 percent a month would be paid when borrowings are *repaid in full.*

1 How much should Mr. Carollo borrow to meet seasonal demand? When should he repay his borrowings? (Prepare a cash budget on a *separate* piece of paper, using the worksheet in Exhibit 9B-1 as a guide.)

2 How profitable does Mr. Carollo expect the store to be during the six months covered by his budget? (Prepare an income statement).

3 Why is the cash budget useful to both Mr. Carollo and his banker?

Swisshelm Department Store, Inc.

EXHIBIT 9B-1

Cash Budget Worksheet

	August	September	October	November	December	January
Cash inflow						
Sales revenues						
Credit sales						
Collections from						
One month before						
Two months before						
Subtotal						
Cash sales						
Total cash inflow						
Cash outflow						
Inventory purchases						
Wages and salaries						
Rent						
Other expenses						
Interest						
Total cash outflow						
Cash gain or loss						
Borrowings						
Opening cash balance						
Balance before borrowing						
Borrowings						
Ending cash balance						
Cumulative borrowings						

According to a newspaper editorial, "each day in this country 1,000 firms are formed, more than 900 change hands, and another 930, on the average, are discontinued."

So what chance have I to start a business? True, the SBA supplies all sorts of information in the way of conferences and pamphlets. And it offers many types of loans. Its loan-guaranty program, for example, offers loans up to $500,000. But I don't need that much money.

Sure they say that the federal government, the world's largest buyer of supplies and services, will buy anything from paper clips to battleships. There are bids and many sources of help, such as these:

☐ U.S. Senate Select Committee on Small Business
☐ U.S. House Select Committee on Small Business
☐ Small Business Division of the U.S. Department of Justice

Well, that's all well and good. But what about the little guy?

We don't want the early headaches that go with big and middle-size businesses. We want a challenge, an opportunity to use our little business, a chance to leave our own mark of achievement in this work-a-day world. Here are a few samples of what we think is the right ideology of small business in the democratic sense, a way of life, possibly a hearkening back to the good old days:

☐ A one-room pizza kitchen that blossomed into a block-long semiautomatic frozen pizza factory for former restaurateurs.
☐ Milady's Wigs, a small shop that cannot keep up with the demand. Women who have lost their hair because of sickness or after some operation, as well as bald men, are eager to pay $100 for wigs made by an entrepreneur.
☐ New England's lusty ski resorts, which started with the Nansen Ski Club and prospered in every New England state. For the small-businessperson, these, along with summer cabins and motels, spell out entrepreneurship and a certain prestige.

One could go on telling of ventures that began small and prospered:

☐ The coffee vending machine
☐ A wiping cloths firm that grew out of a rag business
☐ An unknown detergent venture that got the jump on the soap giants in this country
☐ The Irish bubble gum, a cure for a surplus beet crop
☐ A shamrock farm to catch St. Patrick's Day patriots

But they have to get started. And that's where *New-Venture Financiers* could help. Small-businesspersons cannot always qualify for bank or SBA

*Source: Adapted with permission from Henry M. Cruickshank and Keith Davis, *Cases in Management* (Homewood, Ill.: Richard D. Irwin, 1962), pp. 26–29.

loans. But they have an idea, and they should have the opportunity to start their own venture and leave their memorial to free enterprise.

1 Is there a need for New-Venture Financiers—an agency, public or private, to help those "little guys" who cannot qualify for financial help from banks or the SBA?

2 When young people seek their first job, they are asked, "What experience do you have?" Is the entrepreneur with an idea but no money or credit in the same box? Explain.

CHAPTER TEN

ORGANIZATIONAL PLANNING

questions for mastery

why is organizational planning important?

how does one define skill needs?

how important is the help of such
  professionals as accountants, bankers,
  lawyers, and insurance agents before
  launching a venture?

how does one go about fulfilling skill needs
  and building a staff?

what kinds of counseling help are available
  from both private and government
  sources?

Good order is the foundation of all
good things.

Edmund Burke

M ajor corporations employ hundreds of knowledge workers. In contrast, would-be entrepreneurs generally cannot afford the luxury of such expert help. They often have no recourse but to stand alone.

How can entrepreneurs fill their needs for skilled, knowledgeable support? Help does exist, often for no fee. To make the most of such help, entrepreneurs should first ask themselves two questions:

☐ What skills do I need to launch my venture successfully?
☐ How can I get the help of men and women armed with those skills?

NEED FOR ORGANIZATIONAL PLANNING

In this complex age, few entrepreneurs are equipped with all the business skills they need to survive on their own. Until World War II, entrepreneurs worked in a business world of few regulations, few taxes, few records, few big competitors, and no computers. Since that time, simplicity has given way to complexity. No longer can entrepreneurs be their own troubleshooter, lawyer, bookkeeper, financier, tax expert, and systems analyst.

To survive and grow, entrepreneurs need help and should be able to identify precisely what kinds of help they do need. To do so, they need to plan their organization before they launch their venture. The organizational plan has a key role in the business plan because it is the organization that carries a venture, its goals and all its personal and operating relations.

Despite the need for it, organizational planning is ignored by many entrepreneurs. They fail to see how powerful a planning tool it really is. But its value was recognized even in Biblical times:

> The Bible tells of the advice Moses received from his father-in-law, Jethro. Feeling that Moses was making too many decisions himself in governing his people, Jethro said, "The thing that thou doest is not good. Thou wilt surely wear away, both thou, and this people that is with thee; thou art not able to perform it thyself alone."
>
> Moses followed this advice and did a better job of organizing. In the words of the Scripture: "Moses harkened to the voice of his father-in-law and did all that he said. And Moses chose able men out of all Israel, and made them heads over the people, rulers of thousands, rulers of hundreds, rulers of tens. And they judged the people at all seasons: the hard causes they brought unto Moses, but every small matter they judged themselves."[1]

DEFINING SKILL NEEDS

An organization is any team of persons who work together to meet common goals. For example, a professional football franchise may hire 45 players, each

1. Marvin Bower, *The Will to Manage* (New York: McGraw-Hill, 1966), p. 123.

with different skills, to fill its cavernous 80,000-seat stadium. Whether they fill it depends largely on how well they play as a team. Losses usually mean empty seats. That is why, each year, coaches spend so much time scouting college players.

A football franchise is about to lose an all-pro defensive tackle to retirement. The coach is looking hard for a replacement who earned at least all-conference honors as a defensive tackle, weighs at least 260 pounds, towers at least 6 feet 4 inches, sprints 40 yards in less than 5.0 seconds, bench-presses at least 450 pounds, and plays with the "hurts."

■

This is a tall order to fill. But note that the coach knows precisely what he needs to win. Equally important, he knows precisely what kind of player he is looking for to meet that need.

Entrepreneurs should define their skill needs in a similar way. There is a catch, though. Usually they cannot afford to hire, for example, a fulltime marketing researcher or a fulltime accountant. Even so, entrepreneurs should plan their organization as if they *could* afford them. Only by going through such a procedure can they assure themselves that needed skills have not been overlooked.

Entrepreneurs should thus define their organization in terms of skills rather than in terms of persons. For example, if a chemical engineer were about to go into plastics manufacture, he might begin defining his organization by asking himself: What skills do I need to earn a net profit of $10,000 on sales revenues of $200,000 by the end of my first year in business?

Note how precise this goal is. It gives the entrepreneur a target to aim for as well as a measure of performance. He might have said: "My goal is to make a profit." But such a fuzzy goal is meaningless. How much profit? By when? More will be said about goals in Chapter Twelve.

Let us assume that this particular chemical engineer has worked at nothing but engineering since graduating from college. A resourceful person, he has just invented a new process to make fiberglass-reinforced plastic for sports cars like the Corvette. This process is faster and cheaper than the present one. For the past two years, he has worked nights and weekends in his garage workshop perfecting the new process.

Our chemical engineer is now ready to exploit his invention by creating a new venture. He has set a first-year goal of $200,000 of revenues and now needs to define the specific skills he needs to make his venture a reality.

A good place to begin is with the business plan. Following the outline of the business plan presented in Chapter Six, he might set up a table like the one in Exhibit 10-1 to identify the skills he needs.

The engineer decides that he is the one best qualified to complete six of the steps shown in the exhibit. For the rest, however, he recognizes that he must rely on outside experts. To find those experts he turns to the Chamber of Commerce. Its members come from every walk of business life and are usually aware of which professionals are competent and reputable.

EXHIBIT 10-1

Identifying Skill Needs

Step Number	Description of Step	Skill Needed	Expert Best Suited to Meet Need: Entrepreneur	Other
1	Decide to go into business	Knowledge of self	√	
2	Analyze yourself		√	
3	Pick product or service		√	
4	Research market	Knowledge of marketing research		Marketing researcher
5	Forecast sales revenues			Marketing researcher
6	Pick site			Marketing researcher
7	Develop production plan	Knowledge of chemical engineering	√	
8	Develop marketing plan	Knowledge of marketing		Advertising account executive
9	Develop organizational plan	Knowledge of skill needs	√	
10	Develop legal plan	Knowledge of law		Lawyer
11	Develop accounting plan	Knowledge of accounting		Accountant
12	Develop insurance plan	Knowledge of insurance		Insurance agent
13	Develop financial plan	Knowledge of finance		Loan officer
14	Write cover letter	Knowledge of venture	√	

Commercial bankers are another good source of information about professionals—often a better source than the Chamber of Commerce. Bankers see the work of professionals at first hand; Chambers of Commerce often do not and are thus judging professionals on the basis of reputation alone.

GETTING THE RIGHT PROFESSIONALS

In his quest for help, the engineer in our example should seek professionals who also work in his industry. For example, there often are accountants who specialize in chemicals or lawyers who specialize in musical recordings. By using such specialists, the engineer may profit from the professional's experience with similar problems in other businesses in the same industry.

Before opening for business, the entrepreneur generally needs the following kinds of professional help:

☐ An accountant to set up books
☐ A lawyer to advise on legal matters
☐ A banker to advise on financial matters
☐ An insurance agent to make sure the venture is protected from dangers that the entrepreneur can neither foresee nor control

But the work of these professionals does not stop when entrepreneurs make their first pound of product or close their first sale. Rather, the need for their services continues throughout the life of the venture. Entrepreneurs have an ongoing need for:

- □ An accountant to prepare monthly income statements and quarterly balance sheets
- □ A banker to help finance expansion or renewal
- □ A lawyer to do legal checkups at least once a year and to bring the entrepreneur up to date on such things as tax, labor, and worker-safety laws
- □ An insurance agent to make sure the growing venture is safely covered against the unknown.

BUILDING A STAFF

Accountants, bankers, lawyers, and insurance agents provide an entrepreneur with outside professional help. But the entrepreneur also needs inside help. In some ventures, getting such help poses few problems because the entrepreneur may choose to be the venture's only employee. For example, entrepreneurs who start their own employment agency may need only themselves and a telephone answering service to start out. After business begins to perk they may then have to add a receptionist or an interviewer.

But many entrepreneurs do not choose to begin as one-person ventures. The chemical engineer mentioned earlier is one such entrepreneur. He expects revenues of $200,000 the first year in his fiberglass-reinforced plastic business. Based on his experience in the field and his intuition, he realizes that to support that level of revenues, he will need two chemical operators, one foreperson, and one secretary-bookkeeper besides himself.

JOB DESCRIPTIONS

The engineer's experience with other chemical companies serves him well in defining what work needs to be done. He does not need an organizational planning expert to make a study for him. Still, it behooves the entrepreneur to prepare an organizational plan, complete with job descriptions that spell out:

- □ Who does what
- □ Who has what authority
- □ Who reports to whom

Such job descriptions need not be fancy. They may be as simple and straightforward as the one for a retail salesperson shown in Exhibit 10-2.

Job descriptions spare entrepreneurs the disease that attacks many ventures, especially as they grow and add more men and women. The disease is called organizational muddle. It generally is caused by the entrepreneur's failure to plan the organization. Typically, entrepreneurs allow their organizations to evolve naturally, with everybody reporting to them or with some employees reporting to two or more bosses.

The resulting mix-ups often lead to anger and frustration, waste and duplication of work. As Marvin Bower puts it: "Like a good golf swing, an

EXHIBIT 10-2

Job:	Retail salesclerk
Supervisor:	Store manager.
Duties:	Greets and waits on customers; discusses merchandise; rings sales; makes change; writes up charge slips; wraps for shipping and bags items; keeps shelves stocked; directs deliveries; and follows procedures on opening and closing store when manager is away.
Requirements:	Applicants must be good at arithmetic; have previous sales experience; be available to work nights and weekends; be able to learn use of cash register and other store procedures as taught; and be bondable.
Personal Requirements:	Must have an easy manner with people, like retailing, and be able to withstand long hours on the sales floor.

Reprinted with permission from Bank of America, NT&SA, "Personnel Guidelines," *Small Business Reporter,* Vol. 15, No. 3, Copyright 1978, 1981.

organization should become so well grooved that people can go about their jobs without thinking twice about who does what."[2]

Job descriptions are one aspect of the organizational plan. The entrepreneur should also define the personal qualifications needed for above-average performance in each position. To expect less from one's employees could result in merely an average venture. Earlier, we defined an organization as a team of men and women working together to meet common goals. It follows, then, that the more qualified the team, the greater the likelihood of success.

ORGANIZATIONAL CHARTS

No organizational plan is complete without an organizational chart. Such a chart traces the lines of responsibility and authority between jobs. In a new venture, an entrepreneur may have to wear several hats, as would be the case with the chemical engineer in our earlier example. His organizational chart might look like the one in Exhibit 10-3.

This kind of organization is called *line-staff*. Note in the exhibit that each jobholder reports to a single boss, represented by a solid line connecting their boxes. There is no overlap. But note also that those holding the staff jobs of accounting and personnel have some control over those holding the line jobs of production and marketing, represented by shaded lines connecting their boxes. Although this may seem like an overlapping of authority, it is not. To see why, let us define what we mean by line and staff:

☐ **Line authority** Line positions give the people in them the right to lead those

2. Ibid., p. 153.

EXHIBIT 10-3

Organizational Chart

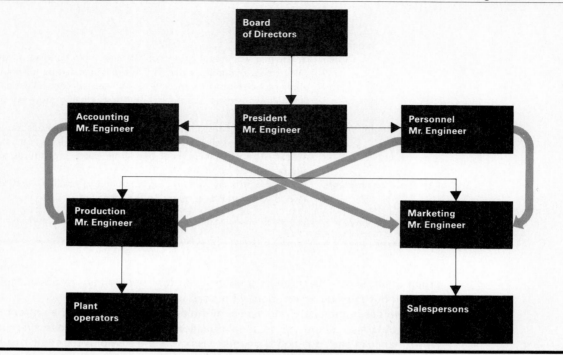

under them. They are the ones who may say "do it and do it now." The strength of their authority usually stems from their power to hire and fire.

☐ **Staff authority** Staff positions possess power that is subtler than line authority. People in staff positions have the right to exercise their expert knowledge in the solution of marketing and production problems. As line managers may say "do it and do it now," staff managers say "you *ought* to do it in this way because it's the best way."

In other words, line authority is the power of authority that one person has over another, and staff authority is the power of knowledge that one person has over another.

Another way to distinguish between line and staff is to say that line is charged with getting out the product and with closing the sale. Staff, on the other hand, is charged with getting out ideas to keep the venture profitable as well as abreast of competition. It is not enough for staff to generate ideas, however; they should also be adept at putting their ideas to work.

So far, we have focused on the line-staff form of organization. There are others, among them:

☐ **The line organization** Every jobholder reports to a single boss; no one has a staff function. This form of organization is common to ventures with fewer than 10 employees.
☐ **The functional organization** A jobholder may report to two or more bosses. With this kind of organization, a production foreperson may report directly to the accountant, the purchasing agent, and the researcher as well as to the production manager.

The functional kind of organization usually leads to chaos. With two or more bosses, a jobholder may never know where to turn when a problem comes up, nor is there any single boss on whom to fix responsibility for the way jobholders perform. Entrepreneurs naturally should drop this form of organization from their list of choices.

Attitudinal problems The line organization is a practical choice for ventures that start small. But once they begin to grow beyond 10 employees entrepreneurs should consider switching to a line-staff form of organization.

This switchover, however, often brings with it some knotty problems, especially in ventures that have grown quickly. When entrepreneurs give up one of their many hats to a newly hired accountant or to a marketing researcher, veteran jobholders are likely to resent the change. Veteran jobholders tend to treat such staff persons as intruders. Their attitude often is reflected in such statements as:

> We got along without them before, so why do we need them now? Besides, what do they know about the way we do things around here? They never even get their hands dirty. They're just overhead. Why, they don't even know how our products are made. Who needs them?

The best way to solve this attitudinal problem is not to let it arise in the first place. Before they open for business, entrepreneurs should plan their organization as if they could afford to hire persons to fill each staff job. They should do the kind of organizational planning done by the engineer in our earlier example who:

☐ Drafted descriptions for each job, both line and staff
☐ Defined the qualifications of persons to fill those jobs
☐ Prepared an organizational chart showing who reports to whom, with the engineer himself filling most of the job slots at the start

With such an organizational plan, each jobholder would know from the start how the entrepreneur plans to run the venture. They would also know that the entrepreneur is wearing many hats only temporarily. Later, as the venture grows, knowledge workers would be hired to wear those hats, thus enabling the entrepreneur to spend more time charting the venture's future.

Limitations Entrepreneurs should also be aware of the limitations of organizational charts. Although they do symbolize how an entrepreneur plans to get out the work, they often impress more than they express. Few ventures run precisely the way their organizational charts indicate. In a growing venture, organizational charts soon become dated; unpredictable events often change the course of an entrepreneur's plans. For this reason, wise entrepreneurs update their organizational charts at least once a year.

One of the values of an organizational chart is that the very act of putting one together forces entrepreneurs to crystallize their thinking beforehand on:

☐ What work should be done to make their venture profitable
☐ How the work should be done

Without such thought, however, organizational charts may have no more value than doodles on a scratch pad.

A chart is also limited in that it cannot show how all the jobs within a venture tie into one another. To try to do so would result in a chart with solid and broken lines crisscrossing the page in undecipherable confusion. A good organizational chart is a simple one that highlights only those jobs and lines of authority that are key to the goals of the company. A good organizational chart must communicate if it is to be effective.

However, to bring an organizational chart to life, entrepreneurs generally need help, especially those entrepreneurs who begin with few employees. In Chapter Nine we discussed the need for financial help. We will now discuss the need for management as opposed to professional help, focusing on these sources:

☐ Boards of directors
☐ Management consulting firms
☐ The federal government, especially the SBA
☐ Chambers of Commerce and small-business organizations

Exhibit 10-4 contrasts management with professional help.

FULFILLING SKILL NEEDS—BOARDS OF DIRECTORS

Potentially, boards of directors offer the entrepreneur a wealth of help, especially as problem solvers. Elected by shareholders, the directors are legally responsible for the venture and are given full authority. In theory, they do such things as these:

☐ Choose the president of the venture
☐ Delegate power to run the day-to-day affairs of the venture
☐ Set policy on paying dividends, on financing major spending, and on executive pay, including the entrepreneur's salary

3011

77% OFF

Special student offer
includes FREE Newsweek On Campus subscription.*

FOR STUDENTS ONLY.
CHECK ONE.

- 26 weeks
- 34 weeks
- 52 weeks
- 104 weeks

- Payment enclosed.
- Bill me.

Name _____

Address _____

City _____ **State** _____ **Zip** _____

College _____ **Year of Graduation** _____

Signature _____

Offer good in U.S. Subject to change.

$1.75	75¢	40¢
NEWSWEEK'S COVER PRICE	REGULAR SUBSCRIPTION PRICE	SPECIAL STUDENT PRICE

EXHIBIT 10-4

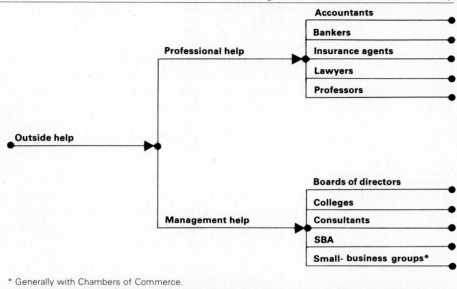

Management Versus Professional Help

Professional help:
- Accountants
- Bankers
- Insurance agents
- Lawyers
- Professors

Outside help

Management help:
- Boards of directors
- Colleges
- Consultants
- SBA
- Small- business groups*

* Generally with Chambers of Commerce.

If the venture is a sole proprietorship or a partnership, entrepreneurs do not have to form a board. However, if the venture is a corporation, they must. Every state requires that a corporation have a board to protect shareholders. This requirement holds even if the entrepreneur is the sole shareholder.

BOARD MYTHS

Studies show that more than 90 percent of all boards fail to perform, mostly because entrepreneurs tend to ignore their board. In a study, Professor Myles L. Mace of Harvard University found that:

> The generally accepted roles of boards—that is, selecting top executives, determining policy, measuring results, and asking discerning questions— have taken on more and more of the characteristics of a well-established myth, and there is a considerable gap between the myth and reality.[3]

One myth exploded by Professor Mace's study is that the board selects the president. He found that in most corporations the directors do not, in fact, pick presidents—except when faced with their unexpected death. Commenting on this function of the board, one executive said:

3. Myles L. Mace, "The President and the Board of Directors," *Harvard Business Review,* March–April 1972, 38.

The old concept that the stockholders elect the board, and the board selects the management, is fiction. It just doesn't apply to today's corporations. The board does not select the management; the management selects the board.[4]

Another myth exploded by Professor Mace's study is that board members set goals and ask wise, probing questions. He found, instead, that board members generally are passive. Like puppets, they dance to strings pulled by entrepreneurs. Since they are chosen by entrepreneurs, board members tend to act as their representatives, not as their challengers. Rarely do they ask sharp questions about falling profits, for example. Nor do entrepreneurs encourage such questions. Their attitude is: "It's my money and my company, so I'll do as I please." Friendly board members share this attitude and ask, "Why bother interfering?"

GETTING THE RIGHT BOARD MEMBERS

Of course, some boards do perform well, especially as problem solvers. How should entrepreneurs select people to serve on their boards who will contribute to the success of the venture? Preferably, board members should be drawn from the community's ranks of:

☐ **Successful entrepreneurs** Ideally, any such candidates should be familiar with the entrepreneur's industry. For example, an entrepreneur about to create a computer services venture might appoint to the board a retailer who sells small-business computers.
☐ **Professionals** Generally, these would include accountants, bankers, lawyers, or professors. For example, the same entrepreneur might appoint to the board a professor of computer sciences.

Not everyone agrees that it is wise to put professionals on boards of directors. One dissenting voice belongs to entrepreneur William Wayne, who writes:

Never put an attorney on the board of directors. Attorneys know the legal considerations, but they don't know the business considerations. You will find yourself with a lot of nit-picking questions which have legal implications but contribute in no real way to the business. You will have a lot of conversation, high bills, and slow progress.[5]

Entrepreneurs should also keep their board small. A board with more than five members may become unmanageable and unproductive. It is better to spend some time selecting five problem-solving members than to hastily assemble ten members incapable of anything but idle talk.

4. Ibid., p. 43.
5. William Wayne, *How to Succeed in Business When the Chips Are Down* (New York: McGraw-Hill, 1972), p. 107.

**THE VALUE OF
MANAGEMENT
CONSULTANTS**

Outside consultants may also play a role as sources of help to the entrepreneur. Management consulting has often been a much-maligned profession. Giving advice to management about management has grown into a four-billion-dollar-a-year industry. Yet opinions vary widely about the worth of management consultants. Entrepreneurs, in particular, seem unhappy with consultants. A typical criticism follows:

> In most cases, outside consultants simply don't solve the problem. They may be fully qualified and can give endless technical advice, but they can't tell us how to put their knowledge to practical use. Quite often I have had to take off my own coat and work with such fellows, doing more explaining of our problem to them than they do explaining their special knowledge to me.[6]

If clients complain about their consultants, consultants also complain about their clients. For example, consultants claim that their clients:

☐ Wait too long before seeking help
☐ Want someone to hold their hand rather than an unbiased analysis of the problems plaguing them

Despite the complaints from both sides, however, management consulting continues to thrive. Perhaps the best proof of its acceptance is its rapid growth. As C. Northcote Parkinson puts it, "There must be a great demand for efficiency experts since they are in such large supply."[7]

What should entrepreneurs do to ensure that they get their money's worth from a consultant? First, entrepreneurs should know what it is they want to know. The sharper the focus of their questions, the better the answers they will get. Instead of asking broad questions such as, "What advertising method should I use to reach my prospective customers," they should first ask well-focused questions such as these:

☐ Who are my customers and where are they, in what census tracts?
☐ How do they buy, at what price, in what quantities?
☐ What motivates them to buy?

**GETTING THE RIGHT
CONSULTANT**

How can entrepreneurs check a consultant's credentials? Testimonial letters generally are worthless. Reputations belong only to the big firms, whose high

6. Perrin Stryker, "What's Your Problem," *Fortune,* March 1953, 107.
7. C. Northcote Parkinson, "A Hard Look at Efficiency Experts," *New York Times,* Sunday Magazine Section, April 3, 1960, p. 31.

fees are beyond the reach of most entrepreneurs. And, unlike medicine and law, management consulting is hardly a profession.

In fact, anyone can print name cards claiming to be a magician of the entrepreneurial world. There is no law that says, for example, that men or women must have a masters degree in business administration, five years of industrial experience, and passing grades on a comprehensive test administered by the state before they can become practicing consultants.

The big firms have formed a group called the Association of Consulting Management Engineers (ACME). Its purpose is to raise the standards of consultants to the level of a profession. ACME suggests, for example, that entrepreneurs should watch for such unprofessional practices as these:

☐ High-pressure salesmanship that promises quick, sure results
☐ Preliminary surveys offered cold at a fixed fee
☐ Requests for fees in advance
☐ Offers to consult at a low fee until results are shown

Despite ACME's efforts, consulting still has a long way to go before it reaches the status of a profession. Entrepreneurs must therefore do some investigating of their own before they decide upon a consultant. Questions they should ask are:

☐ How long has the consulting firm been in business?
☐ What is the background of their consultants?
☐ What entrepreneurs has the firm served?
☐ What do these entrepreneurs say about the quality of the firm's work?
☐ Has the firm had experience applicable to the entrepreneur's problem?

FULFILLING SKILL NEEDS—FEDERAL GOVERNMENT

Let us now look at the sources of help offered by the federal government. Since the 1950s, the idea that entrepreneurs need management help to survive and grow has spread like a spider's web, stretching virtually to every corner of the country. Exhibit 10-5 shows the many sources of management help now offered at little or no fee to entrepreneurs either before or after they go into business for themselves. Different services are available to entrepreneurs who go into a high-technology business than to those who go into a low-technology business because of the greater level of management sophistication required to launch a high-technology venture such as computer manufacture.

Note that Exhibit 10-5 covers not only federal help but also help from such other sources as community colleges and universities, Chambers of Commerce, and organizations made up of small businesses.

Entrepreneurs would err not to exhaust this long list in their efforts to get the right help. Heading the list is the SBA. Since it was founded in 1953, the SBA has helped hundreds of thousands of entrepreneurs.

Most entrepreneurs have the mistaken view that all the SBA does is lend money or guarantee repayment of loans made by commercial banks. Even

EXHIBIT 10-5

Sources of Help for Entrepreneurs

Management Help Offered by—	Where Available	For Entrepreneurs—			
		BEFORE they go into a business whose technology is—		AFTER they go into a business whose technology is—	
		High	Low	High	Low
• U.S. Small Business Administration					
Counseling by:					
Staff	N				✓
Service Corps of Retired Executives	N				✓
Active Corps of Executives	N				✓
Small Business Institutes	N			✓	✓
Small Business Development Centers	S	✓	✓	✓	✓
Prebusiness workshops	N		✓		
Nonaccredited courses and seminars	N				✓
Publications	N		✓		✓
• U.S. Department of Commerce					
Seminars and workshops	N			✓	✓
Publications	N	✓	✓	✓	✓
• Other federal agencies (Example: IRS*)					
Seminars and workshops	N				✓
Publications	N				✓
• State, county, and local governments					
Counseling	S				✓
Seminars and workshops	S				✓
Publications	S				✓
• Local development corporations and the like					
Counseling	N				✓
Seminars and workshops	N				✓
• Universities					
Accredited courses	S	✓	✓	✓	✓
Nonaccredited courses and seminars	S				✓
Publications	S	✓	✓	✓	✓
Counseling	S				
• Community colleges					
Accredited courses	S				✓
Nonaccredited courses and seminars	N				✓
Counseling	S				✓
• Small-business groups (Example: NFIB†)					
Seminars and workshops	S				✓
Counseling	S				✓
Publications	N				✓
• Large corporations (Example: Bank of America)					
Publications	N		✓		✓
Counseling	S				✓
• Trade associations					
Publications	N			✓	✓
Seminars and workshops	N			✓	✓

*U.S. Internal Revenue Service
† National Federation of Independent Business

N = Nationally
S = Some parts of nation

more important, however, are the SBA's efforts to help entrepreneurs prepare themselves better for the job ahead. Any entrepreneur can spend money. The SBA's programs try to help entrepreneurs spend it wisely. As one small-business expert puts it:

> No small business ever failed because of a lack of funds. The supply of funds and the availability of cash to meet obligations is merely a thermometer that measures the wisdom and discipline with which the entrepreneur has committed his funds. When and if he runs clean out of working cash, his thermometer reading is zero. It indicates his inability to live within his means.[8]

Though obviously an exaggeration, Mr. Allen's comments underscore the central importance of management skills in any venture, big or small. What counts most is the entrepreneur's skill at managing resources, of which money is only one. The SBA offers entrepreneurs four major management-counseling programs to upgrade their management skills and to help them get federal contracts. These are:

☐ SCORE (Service Corps of Retired Executives)
☐ ACE (Active Corps of Executives)
☐ SBI (Small Business Institute)
☐ SBDC (Small Business Development Center)

SCORE PROGRAM

If entrepreneurs need help in launching a venture, they can get it free through SCORE. All of its members are retired executives who enjoyed successful careers in either small business or big business. All are volunteers.

Under this program, the SBA tries to match the expert to the need. For example, if an entrepreneur needs a marketing plan and does not know how to put one together, the SBA will pull from its list of SCORE counselors a person with marketing experience and knowledge.

ACE PROGRAM

As with SCORE, ACE is designed to help the entrepreneur who cannot afford expensive consultants. The SBA recruits ACE volunteers from virtually every industry. All ACE members currently enjoy successful careers, generally as entrepreneurs themselves.

Together, SCORE and ACE have about 11,000 counselors working out of 330 chapters throughout the country. In 1980 alone, they counseled more than 104,000 entrepreneurs about their problems and opportunities.

SBI PROGRAM

This program draws on the talents available at colleges and universities. It involves not only professors of business administration but also students work-

---

8. Louis L. Allen, *Starting and Succeeding in Your Own Small Business* (New York: Grosset & Dunlap, 1968), p. 28.

ing for their masters or doctoral degrees. Under a professor's guidance, students work with entrepreneurs to help solve their problems.

Earning degree credit for their work, students are graded on how well they solved the entrepreneur's problem. In 1980, 470 colleges and universities took part in the program, counseling more than 8,000 entrepreneurs.

SBDC PROGRAM

This is the newest of SBA's management-counseling programs. Established in 1976, it is still in the pilot stage. SBDCs are designed to draw together all the various disciplines—including technical and professional schools—of a university and make their knowledge available to new and existing small businesses. In 1980, there were 16 universities taking part in this program.

In a way, the SBDC program parallels the widely acclaimed Research and Extension Service of the U.S. Department of Agriculture. This agricultural service mobilizes through state universities all of the nation's latest technical and management advances in farming and makes sure that such knowledge reaches all farmers.

COOPERATION AMONG PROGRAMS

These four counseling programs often merge, if it is in the best interests of the entrepreneur. It is not uncommon, for example, for both SCORE and ACE counselors to work closely with an SBI professor to solve an entrepreneur's pressing problem. These programs also work together to offer:

☐ Pre-business workshops
☐ Small-business management courses
☐ Seminars on special topics such as taxation

Often, these programs are called upon to give special workshops throughout the country to deal with unique problems. One such workshop deals with encouraging women to consider small business as a career option. Another deals with Vietnam veterans and their problems as entrepreneurs.

Minorities are also benefiting from special workshops as well as from the SBA's Minority Enterprise Program. The main goal of the Minority Enterprise Program is to help close the gap between minority entrepreneurs and other American entrepreneurs. The SBA has joined with local communities, commercial banks, and major corporations to increase the number of minority entrepreneurs.

Under this program, the SBA tries to match minority persons desirous of becoming entrepreneurs with sound business opportunities. The SBA then works closely with the minority person, often helping with financial statements. Occasionally, the SBA helps the minority person to prepare a business plan.

Deeply involved in this effort are SCORE, ACE, SBI, and SBDC counselors.

Of the many programs offered by the SBA, the foregoing are the most helpful to the man or woman about to launch a venture. These same programs are also helpful to those already in business for themselves.

Besides the SBA, there are many other groups that help entrepreneurs. One that stands out is the Bank of America. Ten times a year, it publishes the *Small Business Reporter* on topics as diverse as:

☐ Retail nurseries
☐ Cocktail lounges
☐ Bookstores
☐ Sporting goods stores
☐ Shoe stores
☐ Apparel manufacture

Each issue focuses on just one industry. For example, the issue devoted to shoe stores contains 20 pages packed with well-researched information on 25 topics, among them:

☐ Choosing a location and buying a store
☐ Initial inventory and pricing
☐ Business records and store design[9]

Such information costs the entrepreneur just two dollars. Similar information is also available from the SBA and from many trade associations.

We have barely scratched the surface. There is help available everywhere if only entrepreneurs will look for it. They may not be able to hire a $30,000-a-year marketing researcher or a $500-a-day consultant. But surely they can use the many free services available from such sources as the SBA.

SUMMARY

Generally, entrepreneurs stand alone. They cannot afford the expert help that large corporations have at their disposal. So entrepreneurs must be resourceful, taking what help they can get—especially free help from organizations like the SBA. To benefit from such help, entrepreneurs should first answer such questions as these:

☐ What skills do I need to launch my venture successfully?
☐ How can I go about getting men and women armed with these skills?

In defining their skill needs, entrepreneurs should think in terms of skills rather than persons. To do that, they should begin with the business plan, identifying all the skills needed to complete each step and then identifying who has those skills.

The organizational plan should have two parts, one dealing with inside help and the other with outside help. In determining inside help, entrepreneurs should take pains to define:

---

9. "Shoe Stores," *Small Business Reporter* (San Francisco: Bank of America, 1974), pp. 1–20.

☐ Who does what
☐ Who has what authority
☐ Who reports to whom

In assessing their need for outside help, entrepreneurs should take equally great pains to define what kinds of professional and management services they can use. One source of management help often ignored is the board of directors.

There are many organizations dedicated to giving entrepreneurs a helping hand, among them:

☐ The federal government, especially the SBA
☐ Chambers of Commerce and organizations made up of small businesses
☐ Universities and community colleges
☐ The Bank of America
☐ Trade associations

DISCUSSION AND REVIEW QUESTIONS

1 Explain the need for organizational planning.
2 Explain how skill needs should be defined, using as an example an entrepreneur you know.
3 How helpful are organizational charts? Explain.
4 Define these terms: *organization, job description, organizational chart, line authority, staff authority, board of directors, ACME*.
5 Why do boards of directors tend to be ineffectual? Can they be made to work well? How?
6 If you were about to start a venture, what skills would you prefer to have on your board of directors? Explain.
7 Why don't sole proprietorships and partnerships have boards of directors? Should they?
8 How would you, as an entrepreneur, go about estimating the skills needed to launch your venture successfully?
9 Describe how entrepreneurs can get help at little or no fee.
10 How do the SCORE, ACE, SBI, and SBDC programs differ? Do they overlap? How?
11 How would you go about getting the right consultant?
12 What is "organizational muddle" and how can it be prevented?
13 Describe the line-staff kind of organization. When should you use such an organizational structure?
14 Why is preparation of a business plan so vital in planning your organization?
15 Which is more important, management skill or money? Explain.

In June 1980, Michael Wieland completed his studies in entrepreneurship at a western college. His goal was to launch a record-and-tape store soon after graduation. To better prepare himself for such an opportunity, Mr. Wieland wrote the following business plan.

"On the strength of my business plan, I know I can raise the $275,000 to start up my own record shop in a shopping mall," says Mr. Wieland. "There's no question that with my experience in retail record and tape buying, store management, and education in entrepreneurship, I can successfully open, own, and run a retail record store."

MR. WIELAND'S BUSINESS PLAN

I, Michael Wieland, desire to own a retail venture of my own. The industry I have chosen is record and tape retailing because:

ABOUT THE ENTREPRENEUR

☐ I enjoy music very much.
☐ I have the knowledge and experience to go out on my own and build a better store than my current employer, for whom I have worked these past three years.

My employer's record store is part of a large chain. At the time I was hired, the chain was expanding rapidly, thus offering opportunities for immediate promotions. After discussing the requirements for these promotions with the managers, I started to learn the aspects of buying and selling records as fast as I possibly could.

In just six months, I became a night manager, passing over many other employees with more seniority. Six months later, I was promoted to assistant day manager. In that job, I learned the financial and marketing aspects of the record business. After three months, I was promoted again, this time to my current position of product and personnel manager. As such, I am in charge of the inflow and outflow of products along with the hiring and firing of employees.

All together, I have been with my current employer for three years.

The products I wish to sell are records, tapes, and accessories. There is nothing unique about these products. In fact, they are readily available in almost every city and are also available by mail order for those who find it more convenient not to leave their homes.

ABOUT THE PRODUCT

I elected to sell products that have such fierce competition because of my belief that I can offer my customers something special, such as:

☐ Consistently good service
☐ A better selection than all my competitors combined

☐ Prices that are fair and equitable
☐ A shopping environment that enhances the enjoyable pleasure of listening to music

My store will appeal to all different tastes, ranging from the classics to rock-and-roll and disco. Customers will have the chance to learn more about their favorite recording artists, and often to meet them and get their autographs. My store will be much more than a record store; it will be a major record store, like the one shown in Exhibit 10A-1, carrying the widest selection of records and tapes as well as accessories. There are many accessory items such as posters, books, recording tape, and even miniature bubble gum records that have high markup and require little space to market.

With a broad record selection to choose from, with prices that are affordable, and with an environment that is as pleasing to the eye as it is to the ear, I am sure that I can develop a successful venture in which both the customer and I may profit.

The basic question to be answered in any kind of marketing research is: Who are my customers? In my case, the answer is virtually everybody. The scope of potential customers is limited only by the customers' unawareness that the store exists. Almost everyone enjoys music and has some type of stereo system at home, in their car, or at work. I intend to have something to please every customer, from young children to senior citizens. I will also carry foreign records.

MARKETING RESEARCH

Because I plan to locate the store in Seattle, my fact finding focused on that city. To get a good grasp of the Seattle market and its potential, I searched out the estimates appearing in Sales and Marketing Management's *Survey of Buying Power* (1978). What I found appears in Exhibits 10A-2, 10A-3, and 10A-4.

I also learned from another source where 25-to-45-year-olds, who make up the most affluent record-purchasing group, buy their records (Exhibit 10A-5). This exhibit is broken down into such categories as sex, age group, education, marital status, and geography.

In a survey made by the National Association of Recording Merchandisers, it was found that, in the 19-to-25-year-old age group:

☐ Specialty stores received 38 percent of shopper visits as opposed to discount stores with 23 percent, even though the retail price of records in discount stores is lower.
☐ The higher the shoppers' educational level, the greater their inclination to shop in specialty stores.

Competition seems strong and diversified. But with the proper market analysis, I can keep up with trends in my markets. Knowing who my main customers are and the changes evolving in the market, I can better equip my store with the proper product mix to get the best possible return on investment. Keeping up with economic changes will tell me what type of product should be advertised more extensively.

Views of a Model Record Store

At present, the record industry looks highly promising. Record companies have worked hard to make the record industry both reputable and profitable. But what about the future? By making certain assumptions and following certain trends in the record industry, I have attempted to reasonably predict the path that the industry will take in the future. Turning to Exhibit 10A-6, note that all facets of the record industry showed a steady increase over the past five years.

City of Seattle, Washington

1978 Estimates*

| Total Population (000) | % of U.S. | Median Age of Pop'n. | % of Population by Age | | | | Households (000) |
			18–24 Years	25–34 Years	35–49 Years	50 and Over	
503.3	0.2290	33.2	17.2	16.5	15.1	31.9	222.8

* Source: Sales and Marketing Management, Survey of Buying Power (1978).

Retail Sales by Store Group

1978 Estimates*

Total Retail Sales ($000)	General Merchandise ($000)	Percent of Total
2,875,670	374,456	13.02

* Source: Sales and Marketing Management, Survey of Buying Power (1978).

Effective Buying Income (EBI)

1978 Estimates*

| Total EBI ($000) | Median Household EBI | % of Households by EBI Group | | | |
		$8,000– $9,999	$10,000– $14,999	$15,000– $24,999	$25,000 and Over
4,268,475	16,550	6.0	15.4	29.8	25.1

* Source: Sales and Marketing Management, Survey of Buying Power (1978).

Given its ability to come up with innovative ideas, the record industry is as strong as ever, and will continue to grow stronger. One recent innovation has been the use of digital devices in making albums. These devices improve the quality of recordings by minimizing the surface and background noises that are found in the recording of a record.

Another recent innovation has been the introduction of the video disc. A video disc looks like an everyday record except that it is thicker and is coated with an electrostatic metal. The video disc uses a laser beam as opposed to a tone arm to reproduce a picture on a screen along with quality sound coming out of the speaker system. It is too early to tell what impact the video disc will

Where 25-to-45-Year-Olds Buy Their Records*

	Record Stores	Discount Stores	Department Stores	Mail Order	Variety Stores	All Others
All Buyers	32.5	24.7	21.8	11.9	3.7	5.4
Sex						
Male	38.2	24.5	18.6	9.8	2.0	6.9
Female	28.4	24.8	24.1	13.5	5.0	4.2
Age						
25–29	38.0	22.8	19.0	12.7	5.1	2.4
30–34	29.3	32.8	19.0	12.1	3.4	3.4
35–39	38.0	23.8	23.8	2.4	4.8	7.2
40–45	25.4	20.6	27.0	17.5	1.6	7.9
Education						
Completed college	46.2	20.0	20.0	4.6	3.1	6.1
Some college	31.5	24.1	22.2	20.4	1.8	—
Completed high school	33.0	28.4	19.3	9.1	5.7	4.5
Some high school	9.3	25.0	28.1	21.9	3.1	12.6
Marital Status						
Single	57.1	17.1	11.4	2.9	8.6	2.9
Married	26.9	26.4	24.7	13.2	2.2	6.6
Geography						
West	48.8	19.2	19.2	1.8	3.8	7.2
North Central	31.1	25.7	25.7	12.2	1.4	3.9
South	30.5	24.7	24.7	8.2	5.9	6.0
Northeast	29.3	25.9	13.8	22.4	3.4	5.2

* Source: National Association of Recording Merchandisers, *Chain Store Age Executive,* November 1979.

have on the record industry, especially if it revolutionizes the industry as claimed.

Record companies have set up new, stricter guidelines to prevent the bootlegging of live concerts by persons who print the concerts on cheap vinyl with a white cover. Such bootlegging is a liability to retailers and also to the artists themselves because they do not receive any royalties for any bootlegged albums sold.

Record companies have recently been able to stop the playing of complete albums by the radio stations. This practice was common with new releases. When radio stations got a popular new release, they would play it in its entirety. Listeners caught on and started to tape the albums at home, thus avoiding purchase of the record. Today, however, radio stations are permitted to play only two songs at a time with a break in between.

The future of the record industry looks good. But what about Seattle? Will it grow, too? Will it be able to keep up with the record industry? The answers appear in Sales and Marketing Management's *Survey of Buying Power* (October

U.S. Record Industry Sales at List Price (millions)*

Retail Sales	1978	1977	1976	1975	1974	1974–1978 Compound Annual Growth Rate
Singles	260	245	245	211	194	6.5%
Albums	2,263	2,021	1,517	1,328	1,179	14.2
Tapes	1,157	859	665	539	507	15.3
Total LP's and tapes	3,420	2,871	2,182	1,867	1,686	14.6
Record clubs and mail order	451	385	310	310	320	8.2
Total retail	3,680	3,116	2,427	2,078	1,880	13.1
Industry total	4,131	3,501	2,737	2,388	2,200	13.1

* Source: Recording Industry Association of America.

29, 1979). Projections for the Seattle-Everett area appear in Exhibits 10A-7, 10A-8, and 10A-9.

Despite falling somewhat short of the national average in projected EBI and retail sales in 1983, Seattle is still expected to rank twenty-fourth among the top twenty-five areas in the country for buying power and retail sales.

SITE SELECTION

I have decided to place my record store in the Seattle area for two reasons. The first criterion I used in choosing a site was whether I would enjoy the climate and surroundings. I would like to live near trees, mountains, and lakes. The second criterion was the business factor: Is the city growing? Will it accommodate a venture like mine? Will my venture prosper there?

After extensively researching many possibilities, I focused my attention on the one place I felt best met the criteria above—Seattle.

I have never been to Seattle, so I am not sure that I would like to live there. I plan to go there next month to see what it is like. I will keep an open mind and if Seattle does not work out, I will check out other sites such as Boston, Houston, or Portland, Oregon.

I plan to locate my record store in a shopping mall in a growing suburb. Most large shopping malls have two different record stores resembling nothing more than holes in the wall with an average floor space of 2,000 to 2,700 square feet. I plan to negotiate with the owner of a mall to rent space to only one record store, which would be mine, and to put the store in a prime location in the mall with 6,000 to 8,000 square feet. I realize that rent is high in shopping malls, but I believe the expense is worth the high traffic and exposure that a mall provides.

Seattle-Everett Area Population Projections—1983*

12-31-78 Total Pop'n. (000)	12-31-83 Total Pop'n. (000)	% Change 1978– 1983	12-31-83 Total Households (000)	% Change 1978– 1983
1,474.8	1,475.8	.1	604.1	7.9

* Source: Sales and Marketing Management, *Survey of Buying Power,* October 29, 1979, p. 88.

Effective Buying Income (EBI)*

1983 Total EBI ($000)	% Change 1978–1983	Average Household EBI 1978	Average Household EBI 1983
17,454,333	49.4	20,877	28,893

* Source: Sales and Marketing Management, *Survey of Buying Power,* October 29, 1979, p. 88.

Retail Sales*

1983 Total Retail Sales ($000)	% Change 1978–1983	Retail Sales per Household	
		1978	1983
10,024,181	44.1	12,430	16,594

* Source: Sales and Marketing Management, *Survey of Buying Power,* October 29, 1979, p. 88.

Two other vital factors that influenced my decision to locate in a suburban mall are the higher educational level and slightly higher income level of the population surrounding a mall. As shown earlier in Exhibit 10A-5, the more educated the buyer, the more likely he or she will shop in a specialty store like mine. Also, with a higher income level, consumers will have more income available to spend on nonessential goods such as records and tapes.

The retail record industry averages $150 of sales per square foot of floor space.* Using this figure and multiplying it by a minimum square footage of 6,000, I would need yearly sales of $900,000 to meet the industry average. I believe that with the proper product mix and marketing techniques, along with a good location in a shopping mall, I can meet the industry averages and easily surpass them. My forecasts for the first three years appear in Exhibit 10A-10.

EXHIBIT 10A-10

Sales Revenue Forecasts

First Year		Second Year		Third Year	
January	$ 115,000	First Q	$ 302,000	Yearly	$1,360,000
February	90,000	Second Q	283,000		
March	75,000	Third Q	326,000		
April	75,000	Fourth Q	385,000		
May	75,000				
June	115,000				
July	115,000				
August	100,000				
September	75,000				
October	75,000				
November	90,000				
December	200,000				
Total	$1,200,000	Total	$1,296,000	Total	$1,360,000

Assumptions Underlying the Forecasts Above

First Year: There are two peak selling periods for the retail record industry. One is at Christmas, when records are an ideal gift to give; the other one is during the summer months of June, July, and August, when people have more spare time than usual and like to spend it listening to music.

Second Year: Sales revenues for the second year reflect an 8 percent increase over the first year, for two reasons:

☐ Customers will be more familiar with the store, its operations, its policies, and its products.
☐ Word-of-mouth advertising will bring in new customers, as will conventional advertising that reaches out a little more than in the first year.

Third Year: For this year of operations, sales are forecast to go up 5 percent over the prior year. This increase is lower than the second year's increase of 8 percent over the first year, because I believe the introduction factor will be reduced. After two years in operation, people will be familiar with my store and so there will not be a significant number of new customers.

*Source: National Association of Recording Merchandisers, *Chain Store Age Executive* (November 1979).

In the record industry, record companies pay for advertising based on the purchase of record albums by the retail store from the record company. Using a simplified example, record companies budget a certain amount to advertise their product, which they then divide among their accounts. The advertising dollars are usually split up according to the percentage of business each account does with the record company. So large accounts get most of the advertising money.

With a larger store in a shopping mall, I plan to sell a large volume of product, thereby receiving a sizable amount of advertising money in return. I am sure I can use the money to advertise product where it is most effective, be it radio, magazines, or newspapers.

To start off, I will have a week-long grand opening sale. This promotion would be coupled with the advertising the mall would do for the opening.

I will also work closely with other vendors to set up promotions and contests giving away such prizes as records, concert tickets, stereo systems, and musical instruments. This combination of advertising and promotion should make my grand opening highly successful. I also plan to maintain a continual schedule of advertising, either radio or the printed word, in addition to having contests and promotions.

Record companies often need the help and support of a record store when they are developing or breaking in a new artist. That support usually involves participating in promotions when a band plays in town. My store would give each concertgoer a discount off the purchase price of that band's album. The day after their concert, the band would appear at my store to sign autographs, meet, and answer questions from their fans.

By helping the record companies to develop their artists, I would also be helping myself. I would be selling more records, bringing more people into my store, and developing good relations with record executives who would reciprocate by supplying advertising moneys and by giving out promotional records and concert tickets. My cooperation with the record executives also ensures that they will keep me in mind for future promotional events.

Personal selling is as important as advertising. I will make sure that there will be adequate service to help customers find what they want. My salespersons will be helpful without being pushy. They will be knowledgeable and considerate. I will have weekly meetings to keep employees informed about new products, updated on policy changes, and warned about safety hazards and theft. Employees will help customers over the phone, hold certain records for them, and even mail the record to the customers in special cases.

My store will also be an information center. Customers will be able to find out information such as concert schedules and ticket availability or release dates of their favorite artists' new albums. Customers will be able to spend an enjoyable, comfortable afternoon listening to all types of music—the unusual as well as their favorites.

I will be the product and personnel manager, overseeing all areas in the day-to-day operation of my store. Responsibilities in the product area will consist of all new release buying, which is vital to the success of my store. Record companies usually offer special discounts that, if taken advantage of, may benefit both the store and the customer.

The person second in charge will be the day supervisor. We will work together closely. He or she will have the authority to do anything that I normally do with the exception of signing checks, unless under special authorization. This person should have good product knowledge as well as a good knowledge of the day-to-day operations of the store. Equally important, the day supervisor should be able to motivate employees to work efficiently and effectively.

Next in the line of command will be two night supervisors, who will be in charge of store operations in the evenings. They will be responsible for any cashiers' shortages and for making sure that employees wait on customers, inventories are taken, bins are stocked, products are checked in, and so on. These supervisors should be self-starters who can tell when something needs to be done and then take proper action.

I will also need a shipping and receiving person who enjoys responsibility. This person must meet deadlines in shipping out products and be prompt in receiving products. He or she must check in each product, price it properly, and make sure it gets put onto the floor promptly. This person must also be knowledgeable in other areas such as cashiering and stocking.

In addition, I will need about six salespersons. Their job will be to help customers courteously, stock bins, take inventory, and write up tentative orders to be submitted to the product manager. These persons need to be polite, prompt, dependable, and knowledgeable.

Last, I will need four cashiers. Their main job will be cashiering, answering telephones, and serving as lookouts for shoplifters. They must have a sense for handling money. They must also be courteous to customers, because they will be the last impression that customers will have of the store. My organizational chart appears in Exhibit 10A-11.

LEGAL PLAN

I plan to organize my store as a sole proprietorship, rather than as a partnership or a corporation. I realize that the biggest disadvantage in being a sole proprietor is the risk of unlimited liability to the entrepreneur. However, with the proper insurance and because of the nature of my product, which does not depreciate, I will be well protected if anything should happen that would cost me money. Putting our house and valuables into my wife's name may help to protect me if a disaster occurs and forfeiture of my house would be at stake.

A sole proprietorship would allow me and my employees to profit from the good job that we were doing. I am sure that I can get enough start-up money to succeed by combining the money I have already saved with the money I am able to borrow because people believe in me and my business plan.

ACCOUNTING PLAN

I will work closely with an accountant to set up a system that will report my store's financial condition in a way that will enable me to make good decisions.

I will need to know daily sales figures and cash receipts. The daily sales figures will be broken down into certain categories so that I can tell which products are the most profitable. Keeping such records will enable me to see

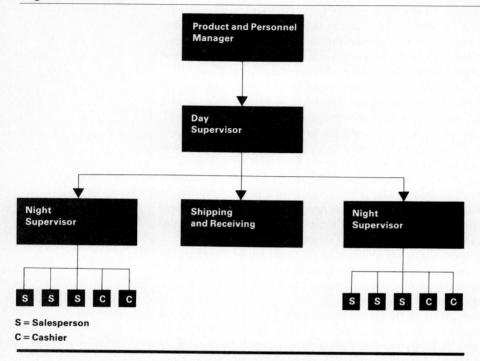

Product and Personnel Manager

Day Supervisor

Night Supervisor

Shipping and Receiving

Night Supervisor

S S S C C

S S S C C

S = Salesperson
C = Cashier

which products are popular and which are not, thus helping me to decide on where best to advertise and to sell aggressively.

I will need to keep a purchase-order log telling me how much money I have spent with what distributors. Deducting this amount from my budget will show me how much money I have left to spend. I will need to keep daily watch on the checkbook, making sure I will always have enough cash to pay my bills. A cash-flow chart will enable me to see when bills fall due.

I will have to keep a record of those customers whose checks bounce and set up a file so that cashiers do not accept additional checks from them.

I will also have to study how well actual expenses match projected expenses, especially payroll.

I will review and study monthly income statements thoroughly, so that I can spot problems early enough to avoid disaster.

Following is the list of accounts from whom I will purchase products for my store:

Capitol	WEA
Columbia	60-D
MCA	90-D
Polygram	Cut-outs
RCA	Accessories

Up to this point in my business plan, I have discussed my operating plans, focusing on marketing. What follows is a translation of those plans into dollars. I estimate that I will need about $275,000 to start up my store. The breakdown is as follows:

Inventory	$216,000	
Equipment	50,000	
Supplies	500	
Other	500	$267,000
Rent	$ 3,500	
Payroll	2,100	
Accounting	1,500	
Utilities	750	
Insurance	150	8,000
TOTAL		$275,000

The rest of my financial plan appears in the exhibits that follow:

☐ *Exhibit 10A-12* which contains my cash budget for the first year of operations, broken down on a monthly basis.
☐ *Exhibit 10A-13* which shows my income statement for the first year of operations.
☐ *Exhibit 10A-14* which shows my projected balance sheet as of the day I open my store.
☐ *Exhibit 10A-15* which shows my projected balance sheet as of the end of my first year of operations.

1 Should Mr. Wieland leave his current job to open a retail record store in Seattle? What are his prospects for success? What risks do you see? What are the key factors for making such a venture successful?
2 Evaluate Mr. Wieland's business plan as a tool to raise money. Is it thorough and complete? What suggestions, if any, would you make to improve it?
3 Is Mr. Wieland likely to become a successful entrepreneur? Why?
4 What additional information, if any, would you advise Mr. Wieland to get before making a move? How?
5 What additional alternatives, if any, should Mr. Wieland consider?

Cash Budget for First Year

Vendor	Jan.	Feb.	March	April	May	June	July	August	Sept.	Oct.	Nov.	Dec.
Capital	$ 20,000	$ 10,000	$ 8,000	$ 5,000	$ 5,000	$ 7,500	$ 7,500	$ 5,000	$ 5,000	$ 5,000	$ 8,000	$ 7,500
CBS	50,000	25,000	20,000	15,000	15,000	17,500	17,500	15,000	15,000	15,000	20,000	17,500
MCA	15,000	8,000	5,000	3,000	3,000	3,500	3,500	3,000	3,000	3,000	5,000	3,500
Polygram	40,000	17,500	15,000	10,000	10,000	12,500	12,500	10,000	10,000	10,000	15,000	12,500
RCA	15,000	8,000	5,000	3,000	3,000	3,500	3,500	3,000	3,000	3,000	5,000	3,500
WEA	50,000	25,000	20,000	15,000	15,000	17,500	17,500	15,000	15,000	15,000	20,000	17,500
60-D	8,000	5,000	3,500	2,000	2,000	2,500	2,500	2,000	2,000	2,000	3,500	2,500
90-D	8,000	5,000	3,500	2,000	2,000	2,500	2,500	2,000	2,000	2,000	3,500	2,500
Cut-outs	5,000	3,000	2,500	1,000	1,000	1,500	1,500	1,000	1,000	1,000	2,500	1,500
Accessories	5,000	3,000	2,500	1,000	1,000	1,500	1,500	1,000	1,000	1,000	2,500	1,500
Inventory at Cost	$216,000	$109,500	$ 85,000	$57,000	$57,000	$ 70,000	$ 70,000	$57,000	$57,000	$57,000	$ 85,000	$ 70,000
Inventory at Selling Price	$295,000	$150,225	$116,750	$77,750	$77,750	$105,000	$105,000	$77,750	$77,750	$77,750	$116,750	$105,000

Total Inventory at Cost: $990,500

Total Inventory at Selling Price: $1,382,475

First-Year Income Statement

Sales		
Sales revenues	$1,200,000	
Cost of sales	990,500	
Gross profit		$209,500
Fixed expenses		
Payroll	65,000	
Rent	45,000	
Utilities	9,300	
Insurance	1,800	
Total fixed expenses		121,100
Variable expenses		
Equipment	50,000	
Notes payable	30,000	
Legal	1,500	
Supplies	500	
Miscellaneous	500	
Total variable expenses		82,500
Total expenses		203,600
Operating profit		$ 5,900

Beginning Balance Sheet

Assets			**Equities**		
Current assets			Current liabilities		
Inventory	$216,000		Accounts payable	$216,000	
Prepaid rent	3,500		Bank note payable	23,650	$239,650
Cash	2,500				
Supplies	1,000		Owner's equity		35,000
Prepaid insurance	150	$223,150			
Fixed assets					
Equipment		50,000			
Other assets					
Organizational costs		1,500			
Total assets		$274,650	Total equities		$274,650

Ending Balance Sheet

Assets			Equities		
Current assets			**Current liabilities**		
Inventory	$163,075		Accounts payable	$172,550	
Prepaid rent	4,000		Interest payable	3,800	$176,350
Cash	2,000				
Prepaid insurance	175	$169,250	Owner's equity		
			Initial investment	$35,000	
			Retained earnings	5,900	40,900
Fixed assets					
Equipment	$ 50,000				
Less: Depreciation	2,000	48,000	Total equities		$217,250
Total assets		$217,250			

HOBSON MANUFACTURING COMPANY, INC.

A year ago, Charles Hobson launched a one-man machine shop in an abandoned service station. Orders have just begun to pick up and Mr. Hobson now wants:

☐ To devote most of his time to marketing
☐ To hire a machinist full time

So far, Mr. Hobson has received help from his wife, who keeps the books, and from moonlighting machinists. Recently, he placed an advertisement for a machinist in the local newspaper. One of the applicants was George Benson. Selected information from his application appears below:

Age	27
Marital Status	Married
Dependents	3
Own home	Yes
Kind of work desired	Machinist
Hobbies	Music, swimming
Previous experience	Machinist—Cole Manufacturing
	Machinist—Ward Manufacturing
Education	Graduate of West Tech

References   Mr. Ray Moon, Cole Manufacturing
                   Mr. Ira Mack, Ward Manufacturing

When he interviewed the applicant, Mr. Hobson was impressed. The applicant appeared to be clean-cut and ambitious. Mr. Hobson then checked his references. Mr. Benson's former boss gave this information:

Reason for leaving	Fired
Would you rehire?	No
Additional information	Mr. Benson was unhappy with company policies

If you were Mr. Hobson, would you hire Mr. Benson? Why?   **QUESTION**

CASE 10C   WILLIS HUDLIN

Willis Hudlin grew up in the automotive industry. His father owned a service station for 15 years, and later ran a tire store for 5 years. Now Mr. Hudlin is ready to follow in his father's footsteps—but with a difference.

"My dad was a slave," says Mr. Hudlin. "You know, he worked just about every day. Boy, he used to open that gas station at seven almost every morning. And he wouldn't come home until late at night, his clothes caked from sweat and his hands stained with grease. It was a tough life."

"I've been out of college now for six years, and I'm ready to make my move. I've worked for a department store and also a discount store learning all I could about mass merchandising."

At first, Mr. Hudlin was unsure about the type of business to go into. One obvious choice was the automotive industry. So, for eight months, he searched for a profitable business formula in that industry—and he believes he has found such a formula in the auto parts business.

In his search, Mr. Hudlin studied how auto parts dealers operated and found that they gave spotty service:

☐ Some sold a good product but offered poor service.
☐ Some sold a poor product but offered good service.

Many dealers overpriced their products. And most did not stock hard-to-get items such as rear-window vent shades. Mr. Hudlin concluded that he could succeed by pursuing this formula:

☐ Buy the best-made auto parts in high volume in order to offer them at competitive prices
☐ Staff his shop with men and women who were expert at helping customers decide which part they need

During his search, Mr. Hudlin found that high costs were forcing more and more persons to do their own repairs. It was this fact, coupled with the spotty performance of existing parts dealers, that convinced him to become an entrepreneur.

Now 27 years old, Mr. Hudlin is still working as a buyer with a discount store. However, he has already made up his mind to go into business for himself. His goals are vague, although he recently told a friend, "I'd like to establish a chain of auto parts stores, opening one new store a year. I'd never be satisfied with just one store."

At this point, Mr. Hudlin is not at all sure how and where to start. That's why he has come to you for advice.

1 What should Mr. Hudlin do now? What talents would he need to get his venture off the ground—and when?
2 What are Mr. Hudlin's entrepreneurial qualifications?
3 Comment on Mr. Hudlin's search for a venture.

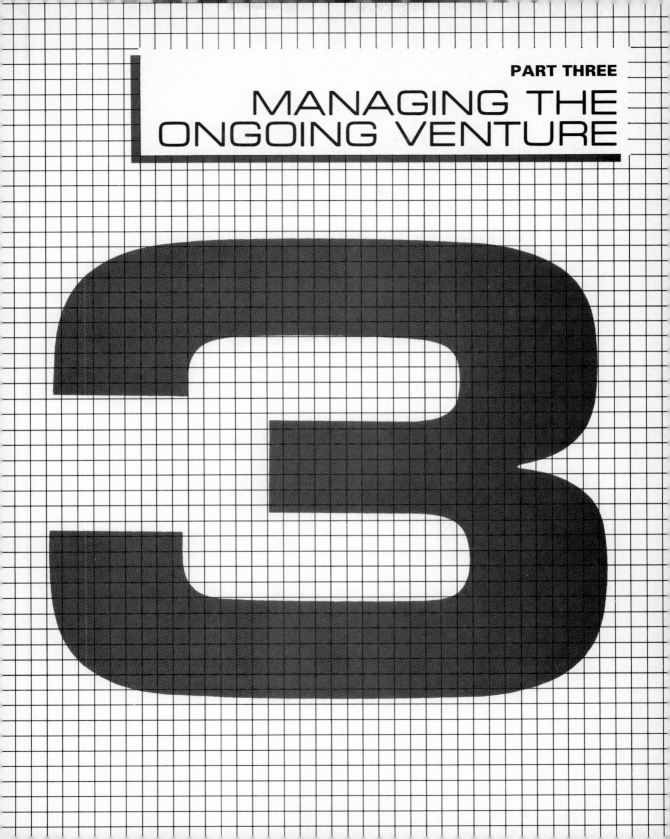

PART THREE

MANAGING THE ONGOING VENTURE

3

questions for mastery

how important is accounting?

what are the uses of accounting?

how do income statements and balance sheets differ?

what are the limitations of accounting?

what is the importance of cash flow?

Frequent accounting makes for lasting friendship.

Lucas Pacioli

The entrepreneur is accountable for the performance and health of a venture. How profitable is my venture? How wisely have I invested the moneys entrusted in my care by shareholders or creditors? What is my venture worth, at least on paper? These are just a few of the questions that an accounting system should help answer. We have already touched on accounting in earlier chapters. In this chapter, we will focus on the ways entrepreneurs can use accounting to give them the information they need to act and decide.

THE USES OF ACCOUNTING

Perhaps because accounting raises images of green eye shades, yellow paper pads, and red ink, entrepreneurs often think that accounting is something better left to accountants only. Although it is the accountant who designs the entrepreneur's accounting system, it is the entrepreneurs who need the information supplied by such a system in order to plan and control their venture. Failure to recognize that need may explain why some ventures make little headway or fail.

Entrepreneurs often blame their failures on such problems as these:

☐ Low sales revenues
☐ Wrong mix of inventory
☐ High operating expenses
☐ Insufficient working capital
☐ Too much money tied up in fixed assets

Yet, with a well-designed accounting system, entrepreneurs can spot such problems early, or even head them off. It is not enough for an accounting system to be well designed and carefully run, however. The entrepreneur must also take action based on the information generated by the system. Otherwise, the system is useless. Three different entrepreneurs, for example, may use precisely the same accounting system—the same set of records and reports, the same means of collecting data—but with wholly different results:

☐ In one venture, the system may be useless because the entrepreneur never acts on the information collected—and his employees know it.
☐ In the second venture, the system may be helpful because the entrepreneur uses the information as a general guide for planning and control and has educated her employees to use it in the same spirit.
☐ In the third venture, the system may be worse than useless because the entrepreneur overemphasizes the importance of the figures and therefore takes unwise actions.

ELEMENTS OF A GOOD ACCOUNTING SYSTEM

What should a good accounting system do? An accounting system is more than journals and ledgers and worksheets. The best system is one that:

☐ Generates reports, tax returns, and financial statements quickly

- [ ] Ensures a high degree of accuracy and completeness
- [ ] Collects and processes information at low cost
- [ ] Minimizes the incidence of theft and fraud[1]

There is no such thing as one best accounting system applicable to all businesses, big or small. Any system will work as long as it meets the goals listed above. For example, the owner of a fruit stand may use the back of an envelope to keep records. And if that is all he needs to stay on top of the job, it is enough. Or, take the entrepreneur who runs a women's dress shop with the help of one salesperson. Her accounting system may consist of just these parts:

- [ ] Daily cash register receipts
- [ ] A checkbook
- [ ] Monthly bank statements
- [ ] A file of unpaid bills
- [ ] A file of charge slips

Armed with the information yielded by this system, the entrepreneur's accountant may readily prepare her tax returns. She may know the dress shop so well that no other financial statements are needed. But if the shop joined a chain of 100 shops, some changes would have to be made. For one thing, the figures that the entrepreneur now keeps in her head, such as daily receipts, would have to be recorded in order to communicate them to persons not on the spot.

- [ ] These figures would be used by the chain to make decisions about both her shop and the chain as a whole.
- [ ] Her performance as a manager would be measured by these figures, and then compared with that of other shop managers in the chain.

The entrepreneur's accounting system would become more formal, complex, and time-consuming than before. And to enable the chain to make valid comparisons among shops, it would be the same system used by all other shops.

The bigger the venture, the more complex the accounting system. When the dress-shop entrepreneur was managing alone, with just one salesperson to look after, her need for records was slight. She could see things on the spot that executives of a 100-shop chain must find out about from written reports. For example:

EXAMPLE

The dress-shop entrepreneur scarcely needs detailed records on her inventory of dresses. She simply can look at her inventory position any time she needs to and reorder accordingly. But, if her shop belonged to a 100-shop chain, all reorders would be handled by purchasing agents at

---

1. Robert N. Anthony and James S. Reece, *Accounting* (Homewood, Ill.: Richard D. Irwin, 1979), p. 108.

headquarters or perhaps by computer. These reorders would be based on inventory information that she would give the chain weekly.

■

Regardless of the simplicity of their venture, entrepreneurs should call in an accountant to help design their accounting system. Designing a good system, especially as a venture begins to grow, takes professional skill. Long gone are the days when entrepreneurs could do it all themselves:

> A Greek restaurant owner in Montreal had his own bookkeeping system. He kept his accounts payable in a cigar box on the left side of his cash register, his daily cash returns in the cash register, and his receipts for paid bills in another cigar box on the right.
>
> When his youngest son graduated as a chartered accountant, he was appalled by his father's primitive methods. "I don't know how you can run a business that way," he said. "How do you know what your profits are?"
>
> "Well, son," the father replied, "when I got off the boat from Greece, I had nothing but the pants I was wearing. Today, your brother is a doctor. You are an accountant. Your sister is a speech therapist. Your mother and I have a nice car, a city house, a country home. We have a good business, and everything is paid for. So, you add all that together, subtract the pants, and there's your profit."[2]

Today, no entrepreneur should launch a venture without an accountant's help. Their services are vital. As with their choice of a banker or a lawyer, entrepreneurs should take pains to get the right accountant. Often, however, entrepreneurs view the accountant's role as a passive one. However, accountants can do much more than merely prepare tax returns. Their more creative role is to:

☐ Design an accounting system that best suits the management needs of the entrepreneur
☐ Suggest changes in the accounting system as a venture grows
☐ Help the entrepreneur analyze the financial statements both to spot problems and to spy trends
☐ Help the entrepreneur raise money by preparing special financial statements for prospective investors or creditors
☐ Help chart the future by translating the entrepreneur's operating plans into cash budgets
☐ Help the entrepreneur save taxes at the federal, state, and local levels

Entrepreneurs should look for and obtain the right accountant months before they plan to launch their venture. In their search for an accountant, entrepreneurs should use guidelines such as these:

2. Attributed to Walter J. Cross in Montreal *Gazette* by *Reader's Digest,* May 1973, p. 151.

☐ Get the names of experienced, reputable accountants from other entrepreneurs
☐ Narrow the list to those who work mostly with small businesses, preferably in the same industry as the entrepreneur's
☐ Choose a certified public accountant (CPA)

A CPA designation means that the accountant is a college graduate who passed a qualifying state test. The CPA designation helps assure the entrepreneur that the accountant is a professional. Let us also add that only a CPA can certify—or *legally* guarantee—the truth of the entrepreneur's financial statements.

ACCOUNTING FOR A PURPOSE

Accounting is not an end in itself. It should never be done for its own sake, as some entrepreneurs seem to believe. Rather, accounting exists to serve some worthwhile purposes, such as these:

☐ To help solve problems
☐ To help pursue opportunities
☐ To help express future plans
☐ To keep track of what is happening

These purposes all add up to planning and control, which are discussed in the next chapter. Any accounting system should help entrepreneurs answer such key questions as these:

☐ **Is my venture earning a profit?** If the answer is "no," then entrepreneurs should find out why, so that they can do something about it. And even if they are earning a profit, they should find out if it is as high as it should be—and what part of the venture is producing the profit.
☐ **What is my venture worth?** Entrepreneurs and their shareholders invest their money in the hope of earning some return. So entrepreneurs should know whether their equity in the venture has gone up or down, and why.

Answers to these two questions and others are available only after accountants have put together two important financial statements: the income statement and the balance sheet, discussed in the next section.

FINANCIAL STATEMENTS—THE INCOME STATEMENT

DEFINITION

The income statement tells entrepreneurs how well they are doing, whether they have earned a profit or not. Entrepreneurs should prepare an income statement at least every three months, if not once a month. Lucas Pacioli, who wrote the first accounting textbook in 1494, had this to say about the frequency of income reporting: "Books should be closed each year, especially in a partnership, because frequent accounting makes for lasting friendship."[3]

What does an income statement look like? In its simplest form, an income statement looks like the one in Exhibit 11-1. Note that profits are what remain after operating expenses have been deducted from sales revenues. Profits are the net effect of two opposing flows of money:

☐ Money flowing into the venture from sales made to customers, either for cash or for credit (generally called *sales revenues*)
☐ Money flowing out of the venture from costs earned in connection with making those sales (generally called *operating expenses*)

The breakdown in Exhibit 11-1 is typical only for ventures in the service industries, which do not sell a product. For those industry groups that do—retailing, wholesaling, or manufacturing—the income statement should also include an item called *cost of goods sold* (see Exhibit 11-2).

For retailers, cost of goods sold generally represents what they paid wholesalers for the products they sold to customers. For wholesalers, it represents what they paid to manufacturers for the products they sold to retailers. For manufacturers, it represents, for just those products sold to customers, the cost of converting raw materials into finished product plus the cost of raw materials.

Exhibit 11-3 shows how financial flows differ depending on whether a venture deals with a product or a service.

EXHIBIT 11-1   Computer Services, Inc.

Income Statement (for year ending December 31, 1981)

Sales revenues	$100,000
Operating expenses	90,000
Operating profit	$ 10,000

EXHIBIT 11-2   Atlas, Inc.

Income Statement (for year ending December 31, 1981)

Sales revenues	$100,000
Cost of goods sold	60,000
Gross profit	$ 40,000
Operating expenses	30,000
Operating profit	$ 10,000

---

3. John J. Geijsbeek, *Ancient Double-Entry Bookkeeping* (Denver, Colo.: John J. Geijsbeek, 1914), p. 27.

EXHIBIT 11-3

Basic Financial Flows

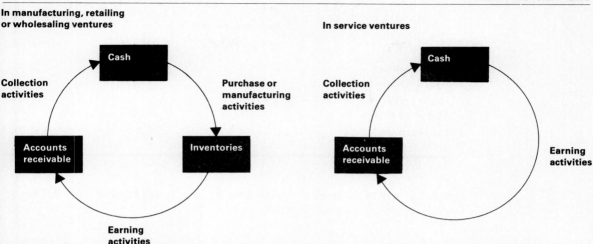

In manufacturing, retailing or wholesaling ventures

In service ventures

CONTROL

As in all businesses, control is simply a means by which entrepreneurs may check their progress against their goals. The following example shows how the income statement may help entrepreneurs exercise control:

EXAMPLE

In December 1980 an entrepreneur set a profit goal of $9,000 on revenues of $95,000 for the year 1981. She budgeted her cost of goods sold and operating expenses at $57,000 and $29,000 respectively. How well did she do? To answer that question, turn to Exhibit 11-4, which compares actual with budgeted performance.

It appears that the entrepreneur performed well. Profits and revenues both topped expectations. She ran her venture not only more efficiently than expected but probably also more effectively.

☐ She was more *efficient* in the sense that she earned more profit for each dollar of revenues than expected
☐ She was more *effective* in the sense that she probably earned a greater dollar return on investment (not shown in exhibit) than expected
■

Note that this example traces the entire cycle of planning and control. The entrepreneur began the year by translating her operating plans into dollars (budget). The entrepreneur ended the year by measuring her actual performance (income statement) and then comparing it with budgeted performance.

Such comparisons give the entrepreneur reliable signals, often triggering an investigation. In our example, the entrepreneur did well. But if she had fallen

EXHIBIT 11-4

Atlas, Inc.

Performance Report

	Performance		
	Actual	**Budgeted**	**Difference**
Sales revenues	$100,000	$95,000	+$5,000
Cost of goods sold	60,000	57,000	+ 3,000
Gross profit	$ 40,000	$38,000	+$2,000
Operating expenses	30,000	29,000	+ 1,000
Operating profit	$ 10,000	$ 9,000	+$1,000

short of her profit goal of $9,000, that fact alone would have signaled her to find out why, then take remedial action.

FINANCIAL STATEMENTS—THE BALANCE SHEET

PURPOSES

As the income statement summarizes how well a venture has done over time, the balance sheet summarizes its financial health at one point in time. The balance sheet tells entrepreneurs:

☐ What their venture is worth, at least on paper
☐ What they have invested in such assets as inventories, land, and equipment
☐ How these assets were financed, that is, where the money came from to buy them
☐ Who has what claims against these assets

These are just a few of the questions that balance sheets help the entrepreneur answer. To clarify our understanding of the balance sheet, let us go through an example:

EXAMPLE

An entrepreneur is about to lease space in a shopping center to sell men's shoes. On February 1, he deposits $10,000 in a bank account opened in the name of his venture: Kuong Men's Shoes, Inc. His beginning balance sheet appears in Exhibit 11-5.

This balance sheet says the venture has assets of $10,000 cash, with Mr. Kuong, as the sole shareholder, having a 100 percent claim against that cash. On February 2, he borrows $5,000 from a commercial bank. His new balance sheet appears in Exhibit 11-6. This balance sheet says the venture has assets of $15,000 cash. But now the bank has a one-third claim against total assets and the entrepreneur a two-thirds claim. On

February 3, the entrepreneur buys 200 pairs of shoes from a supplier for $5,000 cash. His new balance sheet appears in Exhibit 11-7.

Note that the right-hand side of the balance sheet did not change between February 2 and 3. Only the left-hand side changed. The entrepreneur simply exchanged one asset, cash, for another, inventory, getting as much as he gave up. The key point here is that he really is no better off today than yesterday, because his equity of $10,000 remains unchanged. On February 4, the entrepreneur sells 10 pairs of shoes for $500 cash. His new balance appears in Exhibit 11-8.

Note that the entrepreneur's equity has increased by $250, to $10,250, because he made some profitable sales. He sold shoes for $500 that had cost him $250—a 100 percent markup. That gave him a profit of $250. Let us now put together an income statement (see Exhibit 11-9).

Turning to Exhibit 11-10, note how the income statement in Exhibit 11-9 ties into the February 4 balance sheet in Exhibit 11-8. The income

EXHIBIT 11-5

Kuong Men's Shoes, Inc.

Balance Sheet (February 1, 1981)

Assets		Equities	
Cash	$10,000	Owners' equity	$10,000

EXHIBIT 11-6

Kuong Men's Shoes, Inc.

Balance Sheet (February 2, 1981)

Assets		Equities	
Cash	$15,000	Bank loan	$ 5,000
		Owners' equity	10,000
	$15,000		$15,000

EXHIBIT 11-7

Kuong Men's Shoes, Inc.

Balance Sheet (February 3, 1981)

Assets		Equities	
Cash	$10,000	Bank loan	$ 5,000
Inventory	5,000	Owners' equity	10,000
Total	$15,000	Total	$15,000

EXHIBIT 11-8

Kuong Men's Shoes, Inc.

Balance Sheet (February 4, 1981)

Assets		Equities		
Cash	$10,500	Bank loan		$ 5,000
Inventory	4,750	Owners' equity		
		Common stock	$10,000	
		Retained earnings	250	10,250
Total assets	$15,250	Total equities		$15,250

EXHIBIT 11-9

Kuong Men's Shoes, Inc.

Income Statement (for four days ending February 4, 1981)

Sales revenues	$500
Cost of goods sold	250
Gross profit	$250

EXHIBIT 11-10

How Income Statement Ties into Balance Sheet

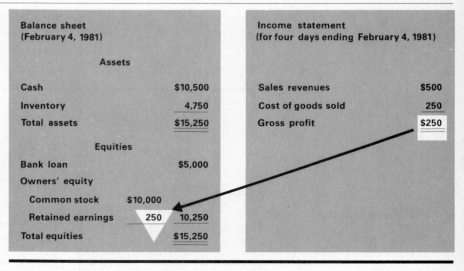

statement gives the details behind the changes that have taken place within the category of the balance sheet called retained earnings.

Without the income statement, the entrepreneur might never know what his sales revenues and operating expenses are. He also might never know what his profits are. For example, he paid himself a $250 cash dividend on February 5, and his new balance appears in Exhibit 11-11. At first glance, this balance sheet suggests that the entrepreneur made no profit. As we know, his profits were $250 on revenues of $500. The net change in retained earnings is recorded as zero because he paid himself a $250 cash dividend, as shown by his new income statement (see Exhibit 11-12).

Although the balance sheet tells the entrepreneur that his worth is $10,000, this is true only on paper. The true worth of his venture cannot be known until he tries to sell out. His venture could be worth more or less than $10,000, depending on what a prospective buyer is willing to pay. This is an important point, because entrepreneurs often believe that the balance sheet reports the real worth of their venture. Accountants do not even try to measure what a venture is worth, unless the entrepreneur wants to sell out.

■

EXHIBIT 11-11

Kuong Men's Shoes, Inc.

Balance Sheet (February 5, 1981)

Assets		Equities		
Cash	$10,250	Bank loan		$ 5,000
Inventory	4,750	Owners' equity		
		Common stock	$10,000	
		Retained earnings	0	10,000
Total assets	$15,000	Total equities		$15,000

EXHIBIT 11-12

Kuong Men's Shoes, Inc.

Income Statement (for five days ending February 5, 1981)

Sales revenues	$500
Cost of goods sold	250
Gross profit	$250
Dividends	250
Added to retained earnings	$ 0

Accountants generally define a balance sheet as a statement that lists assets on one side and liabilities and owners' equities on the other side. This definition is accurate but incomplete. It does not describe, for example, the messages that balance sheets try to convey. Among these messages are the following:

☐ The right-hand (equities) side of the balance sheet tells how entrepreneurs have financed their venture
☐ The left-hand (assets) side tells how entrepreneurs invested the funds entrusted to their care

Assets and equities always balance, because all assets of a venture must be claimed by someone—either by investors or by creditors. And because the total dollar amount of these claims cannot exceed the total dollar amount of assets to be claimed, it must always follow that:

$$\text{Assets} = \text{Equities}$$

The term *balance sheet* is an unfortunate one. It suggests that there is something good about the balance between assets and equities. On the contrary, the balance tells nothing about the financial health of a venture. In fact, accountants now recommend such terms as *position statement* or *statement of financial condition*. But the term *balance sheet* is so firmly rooted that few companies have adopted either of the two recommended terms.

FINANCIAL STATEMENTS—THE CASH BUDGET

So far, discussion has focused on the income statement and the balance sheet. Important as these two financial statements are, however, they fall short in one vital respect. They tell little about cash flow—the lifeblood of any venture. To be sure, the income statement measures operating results during a certain period; and the balance sheet measures the assets carried forward into the next period and the equities in those assets.

Yet neither statement measures cash flow. This fact escapes many entrepreneurs. They assume that if their venture is earning a profit, it must be financially sound. But this is not necessarily so. In fact, even in the midst of soaring profits, entrepreneurs often have to scurry for loans to pay bills. What they soon learn is a fact that seems paradoxical: when it comes to paying the bills, profits are not the same thing as cash in the bank. An example may help explain this seeming paradox:

EXAMPLE

A wholesaler begins a venture on January 1 with a $7,500 inventory and $12,000 cash. She pays her bills promptly and she bills customers 30 days net. She keeps an inventory equal to sales expected during the next 30 days.

One month later, the wholesaler looks at her first income statement with pride. "A $2,500 profit isn't bad for a beginner," she says. Her

January income statement appears in Exhibit 11-13, along with her projected income statement for February.

One day later, her banker calls to say she has run out of cash. "How come?" replies the wholesaler. "I made a profit of $2,500 in January. How can I possibly be out of cash?"

The missing cash is tied up in inventory and in bills owed by customers. The wholesaler had plowed her profits of $2,500 back into the business to build up inventories in anticipation of February sales of $16,000. And she had used up the $12,000 cash on hand as of January 1 for the same reason.

■

How might the wholesaler have avoided this cash-flow problem? One way would have been to forecast how much cash would flow in and out of the venture by preparing a cash budget, as discussed in Chapters Six and Nine. The cash budget answers the vital question, Are we likely to pay our bills on time? The wholesaler's cash budget appears in Exhibit 11-14.

EXHIBIT 11-13

Income Statements

	Actual January	Projected February
Sales revenues	$10,000	$16,000
Expenses	7,500	12,000
Profits	$ 2,500	$ 4,000

EXHIBIT 11-14

Cash Budget

	January	February	March
Sales revenues	$10,000	$16,000	$20,000
Cash inflows			
From sales	0	10,000	16,000
Cash outflows			
For inventory	12,000	15,000	15,000
Cash gain or loss	($12,000)	($ 5,000)	$ 1,000
Beginning cash	12,000	0	(5,000)
Ending cash	$ 0	($ 5,000)	($ 4,000)

Had she prepared such a cash budget, the wholesaler would have noted that she would run out of cash by the end of January, unless she raised more cash.

The lesson the wholesaler learned is that the sales dollar does not necessarily return when the entrepreneur needs it. That, in essence, is what creates the drain on cash. In accounting terms, the lag is called *accounts receivable.* This lag may tie up cash for weeks or even months, depending on credit terms. What really matters in a cash budget is not the volume of sales at any given time, but how soon the entrepreneur gets paid for products sold.

But even when the dollars do come in, the entrepreneur may find that they must be plowed right back into the venture to carry inventory.

Accounts receivable and inventory are the heart of the cash-flow problem. Offsetting them are *accounts payable,* that is, what the entrepreneur owes suppliers but does not have to pay today. It is the balance and timing between these two sets of items that determines just how much cash the entrepreneur will have available at any particular time.

Depreciation is another item that complicates the cash-flow problem. Many entrepreneurs believe that depreciation is a source of cash. They are mistaken. Actually, depreciation is merely a faucet by which the entrepreneur may tap the flow of cash as it goes from sales down to net income. It enables the entrepreneur to pay less taxes because it reduces net income. But, unless there *is* a cash flow to tap, depreciation is just another accounting item on paper.

LIMITATIONS OF ACCOUNTING

As mentioned earlier, accounting does not measure what a venture is worth. It has other limitations that bear mention also. A common belief, for example, is that accounting figures are precise and exact. They are not. In fact, neither the income statement nor the balance sheet gives a precise picture of a venture. The figures in them are rough. The main reason for their imprecision is that all ventures are highly complex bodies, made up of highly dissimilar parts such as cash and policies, materials and incentives, buildings and morale, equipment and human beings.

It is impossible to add all these dissimilar parts together to form a precise picture of a venture. Accounting is limited to recording only those facts that can be expressed in dollars, such as the $10,000 purchase of inventory or the receipt of a $1,000 bill from a lawyer. Note that these are hard, objective, verifiable facts. But accounting cannot put a dollar value on teamwork, for example. Nor can it report that a competitor has come out with a better product. It follows, then, that entrepreneurs should not expect to find in financial statements all the vital facts about their venture. Nonfinancial information is often as vital, if not more vital, than financial information.

Still another limitation is that assets are recorded at the price the entrepreneur paid for them, that is, at cost. This cost stays on the books even though the value of the asset may increase.

If an entrepreneur were to buy a plot of land for $10,000, this asset would be recorded at $10,000. If one year later a buyer comes along and offers the entrepreneur $20,000 for the land, the entrepreneur now has strong evidence that it is really worth $20,000 and not $10,000. Yet recommended accounting practice disallows changing the records to reflect the $10,000 gain in value.

∎

So the values at which assets are listed in the balance sheet do *not* always reflect what they could be sold for. As a rule, the older an asset, the lower the probability that its book value matches its value to a prospective buyer.

Yet another limitation is that the balance sheet reflects dollars of differing purchasing power. For example, the balance sheet may show:

☐ Cash that reflects purchasing power today
☐ Inventory stated in dollars that reflect purchasing power of a month ago
☐ Machinery stated in dollars that reflect purchasing power of 5 years ago
☐ A building stated in dollars that reflect purchasing power of 10 years ago

To reinforce our understanding of this limitation, let us go through an example:

Assume that an entrepreneur bought a 2½ ton truck for $12,000 in 1978 and another 2½ ton truck, just like the first one, for $15,000 in 1980. The entrepreneur's balance sheet would show both trucks at their *original* cost, unadjusted for price inflation:

> First 2½ ton truck = $12,000 (in 1978 dollars)
> Second 2½ ton truck =   15,000 (in 1980 dollars)
> $27,000

Accountants have suggested several ways of solving this problem. The most promising one is to apply a price index that reflects changes in the purchasing power of the dollar. That way, each asset on the balance sheet would be valued in dollars that reflect the same purchasing power.

Thus, if the first truck was purchased when the price index was 100 and the second truck when the index was 120, the dollar value of the first truck would go up 20 percent:

> First 2½ ton truck = $15,000 (in 1980 dollars)
> Second 2½ ton truck =   15,000 (in 1980 dollars)

∎

But, despite its limitations, accounting does enable entrepreneurs to compress many complex events into just a handful of financial statements: the income statement, the balance sheet, and the cash budget, among others. That, indeed, is a remarkable achievement.

Accounting enables entrepreneurs to make better decisions, supplying them with the information they need to keep on top of their venture. Among other things, accounting enables entrepreneurs to see how profitable they are and whether they have invested wisely the money entrusted in their care by investors and creditors.

Accounting systems need not be elaborate. There is no such thing as one best system applicable to all businesses, big or small. In fact, the best system is one that:

☐ Generates reports quickly and ensures a high degree of accuracy
☐ Collects and processes information at low cost

Generally, the end product of an accounting system is a set of financial statements. Among them are:

☐ The income statement, which reports how profitable a venture has been over a given period of time
☐ The balance sheet, which reports the financial health of a venture at one point in time
☐ The cash budget, which is a forecast of all cash inflows and cash outflows, and helps ensure that bills will be paid on time

To design an accounting system, the entrepreneur should call in an accountant. And the entrepreneur should retain the accountant to do such creative things as:

☐ Suggest changes in the accounting system as the venture grows
☐ Help the entrepreneur raise money by preparing special financial statements for prospective investors or creditors

Accounting has its limitations. It cannot, for example, measure what a venture is really worth; it can only report its paper value. Nor can it measure such things as teamwork, morale, incentives, and the entrepreneur's health. In short, accounting cannot give a precise and complete picture of the entrepreneur's venture. Still, accounting is a remarkable tool.

DISCUSSION AND REVIEW QUESTIONS

1 Why would you, as an entrepreneur, have need for an accountant?
2 What are the main objectives of a good accounting system?
3 Why is *balance sheet* a poor term?
4 Define these terms: *accounting system, income statement, profit, control, CPA, cash budget, depreciation.*
5 Explain some of the limitations of accounting. Can they be corrected? Explain.

6 Is it enough for an entrepreneur to have an accounting system that is well designed and carefully run? Explain.
7 How would you, as an entrepreneur, use the information generated by your accounting system?
8 Which financial statement is most important to the entrepreneur: the income statement, the balance sheet, or the cash budget? Explain.
9 When it comes to paying the bills, are profits the same thing as cash in the bank? Explain.
10 Explain why you, as an entrepreneur, should take at least two basic courses in accounting—one course dealing with principles of accounting and the other with management accounting.
11 How does the income statement tie into the balance sheet?
12 What procedure would you follow to get the right accountant?
13 How often should income statements and balance sheets be prepared? Why?
14 What generally is the heart of the cash-flow problem? Explain fully.
15 Why is accounting so remarkable an achievement?

CASE 11A **SUBURBAN AUTO WASH**

Joseph and Raymond Milas run the only full-service auto wash in a city of about 100,000 people. In 1980, their auto wash made a before-tax profit of $2,200 on sales revenues of $141,400. This success led them, in 1981, to seek a $150,000 loan to make these purchases:

☐ The land and building they now lease for the auto wash
☐ Half an acre of commercial property surrounding the auto wash
☐ A hookless convéyor capable of handling 200 cars an hour automatically

Because local banks had turned down their loan request, the two brothers went to the SBA for help. They had heard that the SBA is the "small business-man's friend."

BACKGROUND

There was little in Joseph Milas's early years to suggest that he would someday be an entrepreneur. In fact, the idea never crossed his mind until the day he walked off his job in a huff and "vowed never to work for anybody else again." He felt that his boss had "bugged me something terrible." The year was 1973.

Luck was on his side when, soon afterward, Mr. Milas met someone who was buying out a mortgage-servicing firm. This firm wrote VA- and FHA-insured mortgage loans. Mr. Milas's new friend offered to make him an equal partner. This meant they would share equally in all profits. To Mr. Milas, it seemed a good deal. After all, none of his own money would be tied up in the venture. So they shook hands and agreed verbally to work as equal partners.

The partnership prospered, though unequally. It seems his friend got more pay and all of the profits, while Mr. Milas got less pay and none of the profits. After two years, Mr. Milas quit the partnership. "I was taken to the cleaners," says Mr. Milas.

A NEW OPPORTUNITY

This experience left him shattered, though not for long. A friend called to ask if he would like to buy some auto-wash equipment housed in a vandalized building. His friend was an attorney for the bank that had repossessed the auto-wash equipment. Mr. Milas agreed to take a look.

But what he saw when he got there all but turned his stomach. Vandals had stripped the building of all valuable items. Every window had been shattered. Only equipment too heavy to move was left standing—including an air compressor and a leaky water heater. "It was a wreck," says Mr. Milas. "Nobody in his right mind would buy it."

But buy he did. At first the bank offered him the equipment for $3,000 in cash. That was the amount still owed them by the former owner. Mr. Milas then made a counter offer. "Lend me the $3,000 on my signature," he told them, "and I will give you $1,000 for the equipment and keep the rest for working capital to get started."

The bank accepted. "I made them an offer they couldn't refuse," says Mr. Milas. So again he was in business for himself, this time as a sole proprietor. His beginning balance sheet appears in Exhibit 11A-1.

Mr. Milas immediately went to work teaching himself the auto-wash business. He read everything he could get his hands on. He and his brother, Raymond, also visited owners of auto washes out of town. "I was surprised at how eager they were to tell me what they knew about the business," says Mr. Milas. They gave him advice on:

☐ How best to attract customers
☐ Who sells the best kind of auto-wash equipment
☐ What kinds of employees to hire and how to keep them happy
☐ How to manage such a business

Single and still living with his parents, Mr. Milas worked from dawn to dusk patching up the place. He hauled out three truckloads of rubbish; added a 7½ horsepower, hookless auto conveyor bought from another auto wash for $100; replaced all broken glass; and so on. When he opened three weeks later, his freshly painted auto wash bore faint resemblance to the wreck he had taken over.

On opening day, business was so slow that Mr. Milas thought he had made a colossal mistake. He washed just one car that sun-splashed day. "Boy, that really got me down," says Mr. Milas. "I should have had a grand opening and advertised in the paper. Instead, all I did was paint a sign that said: 'We're open for business.'"

A SLOW START

But Mr. Milas stuck it out. Meanwhile, he married. He and his wife moved into a peeling, two-story frame house 150 feet behind the auto wash. This move enabled him to ward off burglars and vandals round the clock. In fact, he kept a .38 revolver on hand at all times for that purpose.

The first year, Mr. Milas rang up revenues of just $8,000—hardly enough to keep body and soul together. "It's a good thing I got married," says Mr. Milas. "It was my wife's salary as a secretary that put meat and potatoes on the table. Without her, I'm not sure I could have held on with little or no salary."

In the second year, things began to break in his favor. He went after, and got, contracts to wash daily the police cars of three suburbs. "What really

Suburban Auto Wash

EXHIBIT 11A-1

Balance Sheet (June 30, 1975)

Assets		Equities	
Cash	$2,000	Bank loan	$3,000
Equipment	1,000	Owner's equity	0
Total assets	$3,000	Total equities	$3,000

helped," says Mr. Milas, "is that I went to school with some of the policemen. We were acquaintances."

When the second year ended, his books showed revenues of $31,000—more than triple the first year's revenues. This improved performance made him surer than ever that he could turn his auto wash into a money maker. The question was, How?

One answer, he believed, was to offer customers a full range of services. This meant not only cleaning the outside and inside of a car but also offering such options as spraying hot wax to protect the paint finish and selling gasoline.

Another way of boosting sales would be to mechanize the auto wash. From the start, Mr. Milas and his coworkers washed cars by hand—a time-consuming chore. It takes 15 minutes to wash a car by hand, while it can be done mechanically in 3 minutes. Because they seek fast service, customers are more likely to go to a mechanized auto wash. "It's a good selling point," says Mr. Milas.

RAISING MONEY A PROBLEM

But mechanizing the auto wash and offering a full range of services would take money—more money than Mr. Milas could possibly raise from friends and relatives. He had estimated that he would need a $12,000 loan to make these changes. But every bank in town turned him down. Bankers had soured on auto washes because most of them had lasted less than a year.

So he decided to go out of state to a small country bank in a Pennsylvania town. "My mother was born and raised there," says Mr. Milas. "Those country bankers sure were friendly, and I got the $12,000 on just my signature and my brother's." The year was 1978.

Mr. Milas immediately put the $12,000 to work mechanizing the auto wash. He installed such equipment as a power-wash machine and five brushes. He also carpeted the customer waiting area and paneled the walls in knotty pine.

Thanks largely to these changes, revenues again increased in 1978, to $82,000. Mr. Milas's new customers were mostly women, who looked for comfort and convenience along with quick service. And for the first time, Mr. Milas paid himself a salary: $400 a month.

BROTHER JOINS VENTURE

In the same year, he incorporated the business. In addition, his brother, Raymond, quit his job with General Motors to work full time at the auto wash.

Working as a team, the two brothers made some more changes, the most important of which was to tie in gasoline sales with the auto wash. They persuaded Gulf Oil Company to install gas tanks and pumps and then to lease these facilities to the two brothers.

"That really helped business," says Joseph Milas. "Our revenues went up to $96,000 in 1979, and I was now able to pay myself a salary of $800 a month."

In 1980 the two brothers made still another change. They installed a hot liquid-wax dispenser that sprays hot wax to protect a car's finish. "It gives that new-car look," says Joseph Milas. "Women, especially, go for it." Revenues climbed to $141,000 in 1980.

And revenues continued to spiral upward in 1981, as word spread that the two brothers offered a "high-quality, courteous auto wash." In fact, of the eight auto washes in town, theirs was now the only one that offered full service. "That makes us feel proud," says Joseph Milas. "So does our rapid sales growth." See Exhibit 11A-2.

"Not bad for a guy who never graduated from college and who never even washed a car before, not even his own," says Joseph Milas. "But it wasn't easy. Believe me, it's tough. You have to be a politician's politician to get along in this dog-eat-dog business."

A look at the brothers' customer profile points to high-quality service as the underlying reason for their success. In fact, many of their customers are professional men or their wives. "I know 80 percent of them by name," says Joseph Milas. "They're the backbone of our business, because they can afford to wash their cars every week."

BRANCHING OUT

Their success spurred the Milas brothers to branch out. In 1981, they thought of becoming real estate developers. "I was sure there was money to be made in real estate for anyone who knows what he's doing," says Joseph Milas.

A logical place to begin, the two brothers reasoned, would be to buy the half-acre lot next to their auto wash as well as the land and building they were now leasing. Located on that lot was a beauty salon and a convenience food store.

The owners wanted $120,000 for the lot. To help raise the money, the two brothers prepared a business plan. This plan included a request for $30,000 to buy a hookless conveyor capable of handling 200 cars an hour automatically. That brought the brothers' total loan request to $150,000.

The Milas brothers brought the completed business plan to several local banks. But each bank turned them down. "It's too risky," said one banker.

Refusing to give up, the two brothers decided to approach the SBA for help—with the backing of one of the banks that had turned them down. When they gave the SBA their business plan, the SBA thanked them and promised to call in 30 days. Meanwhile, an SBA loan officer was assigned to look into:

☐ The brothers' record as entrepreneurs
☐ The worth of their request for a $150,000 loan

EXHIBIT 11A-2

Suburban Auto Wash

Year	Sales Revenues
1976	$ 8,000
1977	29,000
1978	82,000
1979	96,000
1980	141,000
1981	200,000 (projected)

Excerpts of the brothers' business plan appear in the following exhibits:

☐ **Exhibit 11A-3** Purpose of loan request.
☐ **Exhibit 11A-4** General information about the auto wash and about Joseph and Raymond Milas.
☐ **Exhibit 11A-5** Recent income statements
☐ **Exhibit 11A-6** Latest balance sheet
☐ **Exhibit 11A-7** Inside and outside views of the auto wash

QUESTIONS

1 If you were the SBA loan officer, would you approve the Milas brothers' request for a $150,000 loan? Explain.
2 Comment on Joseph Milas's entrepreneurial traits.
3 Do you think it is wise for Joseph Milas to expand into real estate development? What would you do if you were Mr. Milas? Explain.
4 Comment on the Milas brothers' marketing strategy.
5 Why do many entrepreneurs believe, as the Milas brothers heard, that the SBA is "the small businessman's friend"?

Suburban Auto Wash

EXHIBIT 11A-3

Purpose of Loan Request

Proposal: To borrow $150,000
Purpose: To buy property and equipment, in these amounts:

Building, land, and house*	$120,000
Hookless conveyor	23,700
Installation	6,300
Total	$150,000

* The house is currently a rental unit. If purchased, however, it will be demolished. The auto wash will then be expanded to the rear. The Sun Oil Company will provide the additional gasoline pumps that would be needed to handle increased volume.

The widening of Route 254 will cause the new road to be closer to the auto wash in front, requiring a shift to the rear in the area now occupied by the house. A suit has been filed with the state for damages.

General Information from Business Plan

History:	Now starting its sixth year of business, Suburban Auto Wash was formed in the summer of 1975 with the purchase of the former Jet Auto Wash.
Business:	Washing cars, selling gasoline and auto-related merchandise
Officers:	Joseph M. Milas, President Attended Bowling Green State University Lorain County Community College Admiral King High School
	Raymond J. Milas, Vice-President B.S., Business Administration, Kansas State University General Motors Training Program Griswold Institute, Electronics Certificate Lorain High School
	Mrs. Raymond J. Milas, Secretary-Treasurer B.S., Education, Kansas State University Olsburg High School
Bank:	City Bank Company
Accountant:	Mitchell Zunich
Attorney:	Joseph Grunda

Recent Income Statements

	1979	1980	1981*
Sales revenues	$96,100	$141,400	$61,000
Cost of sales	70,800	102,600	37,300
Gross profit	$25,300	$ 38,800	$23,700
Operating expenses	27,100	36,600	18,500
Operating profit	($ 1,800)	$ 2,200	$ 5,200

* First four months only.

Suburban Auto Wash

Balance Sheet (April 30, 1981)

Assets			**Equities**		
Current assets			Current liabilities		
Cash	$23,800		Notes payable	$ 2,100	
Other	2,000	$25,800	Payroll taxes payable	1,300	
			Income taxes payable	1,300	$ 4,700
Fixed assets					
Machinery and equipment	$11,800		Other liabilities		
Other	1,500	13,300	Deferred income	$20,500	
			Shareholders' loan	4,600	25,100
Other assets		300			
			Owners' equity		
			Common stock	$ 1,000	
			Retained earnings	8,600	9,600
Total assets		$39,400	Total equities		$39,400

Suburban Auto Wash

Exterior View

After a slow start, Henry Mercer's venture grew to the point where the simple records on which he had depended for information became inadequate. So he sought help in designing a set of accounting records that would help him to manage his venture.

Mr. Mercer got the idea for his venture while serving as a pharmacist's mate in the U.S. Navy. In his off-duty hours, he carried on experiments in the pharmaceutical laboratory on his ship. And although he had only a high school education in chemistry, he developed several chemicals that seemed to have commercial possibilities. Of these, the most promising seemed to be a liquid which, when sprayed into the air, tended to neutralize foul odors.

After his discharge from the Navy, he worked in a drugstore and continued his experiments in his spare time. To test the market potential of his spray, he bottled a small quantity under the trade name of *AirNu*—and then went after customers.

Several competing products were already on the market. At first, he had a hard time convincing anyone that *AirNu* was in any way superior to them. Some of his prospects—principally hospitals, jails, and other institutions— agreed to try *AirNu,* however. And several of these trials resulted in sales.

Gradually, business increased to the point where, two years after he left the Navy, Mr. Mercer quit the drugstore to devote full time to his venture, which he named the Mercer Chemical Company.

At first he carried on alone, with help from his wife on the paperwork. Mrs. Mercer had studied bookkeeping at a business college. His records consisted of:

☐ A checkbook
☐ A file of unpaid bills
☐ A file of paid bills
☐ A memorandum record of sales to, and sums owed by, customers

Mr. Mercer kept company funds in a separate bank account. And each week he drew a check for $200 on this account and deposited it in the Mercer family account. The original capital of the venture came from savings Mr. Mercer had accumulated during his Navy days. It totaled about $2,000. At the end of another year, Mr. Mercer decided to hire:

☐ A person part-time to help manufacture *AirNu*
☐ A full-time salesperson to visit drugstores and supermarkets in an effort to break into the consumer market

The manufacture of *AirNu* was simple. Operations were carried out in the basement of the Mercer home. But storage space there was getting so crowded

* Source: Copyright © 1947 by the President and Fellows of Harvard College. Reproduced by permission. This case was prepared by R. G. Walker and C. A. Bliss.

that Mr. Mercer thought he would soon have to move his venture into more spacious quarters.

At about this time, Mr. Mercer became concerned about the adequacy of his records. He discussed the matter one evening with James Finnerty, controller of a large chemical company. Mr. Finnerty was a friend of Mr. Mercer's father.

Mr. Finnerty listened to the story of Mercer Chemical's birth and growth with interest and some surprise—and then offered these observations:

The favorable response of tough-minded industrial buyers to *AirNu* should please you. It indicates your product has merit. A successful business requires more than a good product, however. It also requires good management.

To manage the business, you need, among other things, records. The records for your business do not need to be as elaborate as those used in the large company I work for.

The need for good records is especially important in view of your decision to hire people. Furthermore, as your business grows, you likely will need to borrow from a bank. And the bank will surely want to study the facts about your progress before lending you any money.

If, as you say, you plan to introduce other products, records showing cost and profit by product will become increasingly important. In fact, good figures on your experience with *AirNu* might turn up some valuable information that would help you make your company more profitable.

QUESTIONS

1 Describe as completely as you can the kinds of information that you think Mr. Mercer needs to have in order to manage his business.
2 How would you go about preparing a balance sheet for the Mercer Chemical Company? What items would probably be shown on such a balance sheet— and how would you obtain the dollar amounts for each item?

CASE 11C   **MELISSA'S HEALTH FOOD STORE, INC.**

Tomorrow, Melissa Moran will open a new health food store. She plans to sell "foods the way nature made them." In preparing for the opening, she has already spent these sums of money:

$11,000	for equipment
10,300	for inventory
700	for advertising and publicity
400	for legal and accounting services
400	for lease deposit
200	for licenses and permits

The company's bank balance is $2,000.

Prepare a beginning balance sheet, assuming that Mrs. Moran and her coinvestors bought $25,000 worth of common stock.

QUESTION

A month later, Mrs. Moran took pride in her performance. Her revenues reached $8,000 and her expenses totaled $7,600. An expense breakdown follows:

$5,400	for cost of health foods sold
1,200	for salaries (including Mrs. Moran's)
400	for rent
200	for advertising
200	for utilities
200	for other expenses

Prepare an income statement for Mrs. Moran's first month of business.

QUESTION

CHAPTER TWELVE

PLANNING AND CONTROL

questions for mastery

what are the problems of growth?

how does one set goals?

how do planning and control interact?

what is the best way to plan and control performance?

what are such planning and control tools as management by objectives, budgets, and profitgraphs?

Planning and control go together like love and marriage.

Marvin Bower

I n creating their venture, entrepreneurs are both thinkers and doers. They are thinkers when they think through the steps of their business plan, and they are doers when they carry out these steps. The two processes, thinking and doing, are actually parts of one inseparable process. Thinking leads to doing; then doing leads to rethinking; and rethinking leads again to doing—until finally the venture is created.

Called planning and control, this circular process is as vital to the health of a venture after its birth as it is before. In this chapter we shall discuss planning and control for the ongoing venture, focusing on coping with the problems of growth, setting goals, budgeting, and using the profitgraph (or breakeven chart).

PROBLEMS OF GROWTH

Almost all entrepreneurs want their venture to grow. Often, though, growth takes place haphazardly because entrepreneurs forget the lessons they learned before launching their venture, namely, that planning and control help keep their venture on track.

Before the birth of their venture, entrepreneurs tend to plan their moves carefully before they take action. Later, the results of their actions may force them to rethink their moves, leading in turn to better actions. But, once their venture gets underway, entrepreneurs often ignore planning and control. One reason may be that planning and control are easily put off until a tomorrow that never seems to come.

Some entrepreneurs are like the climber who, after scaling the mountain, slips off the peak. They contribute to their own failure by not continuing to plan and control their progress. To them, planning takes place only before, not after, the birth of their venture. This failure to continue planning is often the reason that so many ventures grow haphazardly, stand still, or go under.

FOUR STAGES OF GROWTH

New ventures rarely take off like an Olympic sprinter. Generally, they start slowly, sometimes inching along at a snail's pace.

EXAMPLE

Without some contracts in hand, an entrepreneur who leases factory space to make vinegar expects the first few months to be lean. It most likely will take some time to:

- ☐ Debug the vinegar-making equipment, to make sure it makes vinegar that meets uniformly the quality standards of prospective customers
- ☐ Make vinegar with negligible waste and at low cost
- ☐ Convince prospective customers, especially food chains, to buy the vinegar, generally on a trial basis

Meanwhile, with sales limping along, the cash drain becomes severe as bills and wages must be paid. There is little relief until the marketplace begins to accept the entrepreneur's vinegar. Then, and only then, do cash inflows begin to match and finally overtake cash outflows—perhaps months after startup.

■

Many ventures follow the pattern of growth shown in Exhibit 12-1. Generally, however, entrepreneurs fail to handle the later stages of growth as well as they do the earlier stages. They tend to do well in bringing their venture through the *prebirth* and *acceptance* stages, despite the fact that progress in these stages is often impeded by obstacles. It is in the acceptance stage, for example, that entrepreneurs may struggle to break even as they introduce a unique product. But usually entrepreneurs in this stage are so close to their venture that they can spot obstacles and act quickly to remove them.

The *breakthrough* stage follows. Until now, the rate of growth has been slow—so slow that it often passes unnoticed. But in the breakthrough stage, the rate of growth is so fast that entrepreneurs often cannot keep up with it. Caught unprepared, they often blunder. Sales revenues continue to spiral upward as problems begin to surface that cry out for attention, for example, problems having to do with:

☐ **Cash flow** Will we have the cash when it comes time to pay bills?
☐ **Production** Are we keeping costs down in a way consistent with making a high-quality product?

EXHIBIT 12-1

Stages in the Growth of a Venture

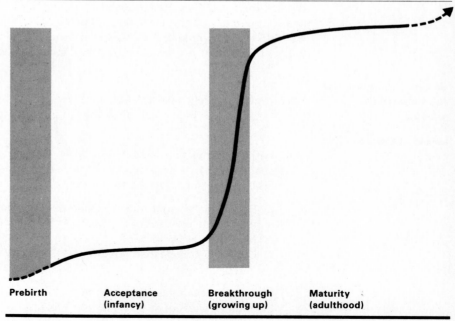

| Prebirth | Acceptance (infancy) | Breakthrough (growing up) | Maturity (adulthood) |

□ **Quality** Are we handling customer complaints by guaranteeing uniformly high quality?

□ **Delivery** Are we delivering promptly on all customers' orders?

At the same time, competition may become more severe. In the face of all these pressures, entrepreneurs often react rather than respond. They apply band-aid measures to problems. Suddenly, revenues may begin to level off or slip. In haste, they may add such specialists as an accountant, a quality-control analyst, or a customer-services representative to relieve their problems. Costs go up momentarily, squeezing profits further. Meanwhile, entrepreneurs may regain the flexibility they lost shortly after breakthrough; and the cycle of growth may begin to repeat itself as they pass through the *maturity* stage.

ENTREPRENEURS AS MANAGERS

Some entrepreneurs tend to be good at creating and nursing a venture through infancy but not so good at carrying its growth through to maturity. Other ventures never even survive infancy. Why do some ventures take off and others not? One answer may be that all the qualities that enable entrepreneurs to succeed during the venture's infancy may not be helpful at the breakthrough stage. At that point, they should change hats and work at being managers as well as entrepreneurs by:

□ Surrounding themselves with men and women who know more than they do about many aspects of the venture

□ Orchestrating the skills of such persons into efficient production

□ Keeping abreast of the latest management methods

In becoming managers they should not give up their entrepreneurial bent. On the contrary, they should continue to seek out new opportunities, at the same time striking a balance between exploiting such opportunities and solving problems. Otherwise, their venture may top out with little prospect for future growth.

SETTING GOALS

To help keep their venture alive and well, entrepreneurs should set goals, just as they did before launching their venture. The act of setting goals is especially vital once a venture begins to grow rapidly and more workers are added. That's when the entrepreneur as manager must lead others toward meeting the venture's goals. As Robert Townsend, former board chairman of the Avis Rent-A-Car Corporation, puts it:

> One of the important functions of a *leader* is to make the organization concentrate on its goals. In the case of Avis, it took us six months to define goals, which turned out to be: We want to become the fastest-growing company with the highest profit margins in the business of renting and leasing vehicles without drivers.

This goal was simple enough so that we didn't have to write it down. We could put it in every speech and talk about it wherever we went. And it had some social significance, because up to that time Hertz had a crushingly large share of the market and was thinking and acting like General Motors.

It also included a definition: renting and leasing vehicles without drivers. This let us put the blinders on ourselves and stop considering the acquisition of related businesses like motels, hotels, airlines, and travel agencies. It also showed us that we had to get rid of some limousine and sight-seeing companies that we already owned.

Once these goals are agreed on, the leader must be merciless on himself and on his people. If an idea that pops into his head or out of their mouth is outside the goals of the company, he kills it without a trial.[1]

As Mr. Townsend points out, the key to such single-minded pursuit of goals is concentration. Once they set goals, entrepreneurs should make sure that every employee understands and pursues them. In the words of Peter F. Drucker, noted author-lecturer-consultant:

No other principle of effectiveness is violated as constantly today as the basic principle of concentration. . . . Our motto seems to be: "Let's do a little bit of everything" . . . we scatter our efforts rather than concentrate them. . . .[2]

THE TIMING OF GOALS

In setting goals, entrepreneurs need to determine what requires immediate attention and what requires long-range planning. With tongue in cheek, *The New Yorker* draws this distinction between immediate and long-range goals:

☐ Long-Range Goals:
　　Health—more leisure
　　Money
　　Write book (play)—fame///??
　　Visit India
☐ Immediate Goals:
　　Pick up pattern at Hilda's
　　Change faucets—call plumber (who?)
　　Try yoghurt??[3]

Would that it were as easy to set goals for an ongoing venture. If asked what their goals are, entrepreneurs are most likely to say, "To make a profit, of course!" But entrepreneurs must learn to be as precise about their business goals as *The New Yorker* list is about personal goals.

---

1. Adapted from Robert Townsend, *Up the Organization* (New York: Alfred A. Knopf, 1970), pp. 129–130.
2. Peter F. Drucker, *Managing for Results* (New York: Harper & Row, 1964), pp. 12, 13.
3. Quoted by H. Igor Ansoff, *Corporate Strategy* (New York: McGraw-Hill, 1965), p. 43.

It is true that a venture must make a profit if it is to survive and grow. But, as mentioned in Chapter Two, profits are simply a reward for a job well done—the sale of a product or service that customers need or want. In this view, profits are a yardstick that measures how well entrepreneurs are satisfying their customers. Generally, the higher the profits, the better their customer satisfaction. Conversely, the lower the profits, the poorer their customer satisfaction. So stating only that profits are the goal of the venture is to be vague and to provide little benefit to the growth of the venture.

BUILDING ON STRENGTHS

To set meaningful rather than vague goals, entrepreneurs should look first at their own strengths and skills. What can their venture do best? Self-examination is perhaps the most creative step in goal setting, for it may lead the entrepreneur to exciting challenges: to invade wholly new markets, to drop a product, or to add a product. The approach of setting goals based on one's strengths is built on these assumptions:

☐ In a highly competitive economy such as ours, success generally favors the venture that does its job with superior skill. Being an average performer may be almost as risky as being a poor one, especially in fast-moving markets like electronics and chemicals.

☐ A venture may create new buyer demand by the job it does if it does the job well.

☐ A venture's product or service may be outdated quickly, but its profile of special skills will tend to continue for years to come.

One board chairman had this to say about the cardinal importance of building on strengths:

> Investors, financial people, and others from time to time ask about us. What's our productive capacity? How many tons will we ship? How do we figure depreciation? What profit will we make three years from next Michaelmas? And so on. All useful questions—no doubt.
>
> But rarely, if ever, do they ask the one, real, gutsy question—which is—what have you got for an organization? What sort of people are they? How do you recruit and train them? Who is going to run the business—and do the thinking for it—5 years from now, 10 years, 20 years? This is the business. The rest is spinach.[4]

MANAGEMENT BY OBJECTIVES

One method of translating the insights gained from identifying a venture's strengths into concrete goals is *management by objectives* (MBO). Practiced widely among giant corporations, MBO is a powerful tool. Its power lies in the simplicity of its premises:

---

4. David W. Ewing, "Corporate Planning at a Crossroads," *Harvard Business Review*, July–August 1967, 86.

□ The clearer the entrepreneurs' idea of what they want to do, the better the odds that they will succeed—if their intent is to make the most of their venture's skills and talents.

□ True progress can only be measured in relation to entrepreneurs' goals.

MBO is simple to grasp, yet the literature teems with articles and books about it. Most of them deal with goal-setting methods or with the propriety of one kind of goal as opposed to another. Few deal with what one author calls the hierarchy of goals:

In some orderly way, we must relate the grand-design type of goal with the much more limited goals lower down in the organization. And we have to examine how one type of goal can be derived from another.[5]

Let us now examine how MBO might work in an ongoing venture, focusing first on long-range goals and then on immediate goals:

EXAMPLE

An entrepreneur owns a Buick dealership. His hierarchy of long-range goals looks like this:

□ To rank each year among the top ten Buick dealerships in the nation as measured by the number of new models sold yearly and the ratio of after-tax profits to sales revenues.

□ To be known in the community as a dealership that offers equal employment opportunities for minority persons and the physically handicapped.

□ To be always mindful of our responsibilities to our employees and to the community in which we work, in order to create a climate of warmth in which people may give their best to the dealership and to the community.

□ To sell quality Buicks at reasonable prices, backed by excellent customer-oriented services. To meet strong competition from other dealerships, we must always give our customers superior service. Above all, we must be marketing-minded.

□ To base our decisions on information collected and analyzed in light of the latest management tools. To compete profitably, we must be able to reach decisions and take action promptly and accurately. Our margin for error is wafer-thin. For example, less than two cents of every dollar we took in last year was left for dividends and for financing our future growth.

The entrepreneur's immediate goals look like this:

□ To increase new-car sales to 2,000, up from 1,600 last year

□ To increase our return on sales to 2.0 percent of sales, from 1.8 percent last year

5. Charles H. Granger, "The Hierarchy of Objectives," *Harvard Business Review,* May–June 1964, 64.

□ To increase our return on investment, to 9.0 percent annually, from 8.0 percent last year
□ To establish a pension plan for all employees
□ To beautify our grounds by planting elm trees
■

Note how these two lists of goals descend in order of importance, giving the entrepreneur a clear idea of how much attention he should give to each item. And by separating the goals into short- and long-run lists, he also clarifies what needs to be done immediately.

Not only are the goals clear to the entrepreneur, but they are also explicit enough to be shared directly with employees. To make sure he has their support, the entrepreneur should set his goals with the help of such key employees as his new-car sales manager, service manager, and controller.

GUIDES TO ACTION

Note the balance among the goals listed in the example. Not only are these the goals of the dealership itself but also those of all its employees. When managers have a voice in setting goals, commitment is more likely to filter through each layer of the organization, from the entrepreneur to the floor sweeper. The deeper the commitment, the greater the likelihood that the goals of the organization will be met. As Dr. Douglas McGregor, the eminent behavioral scientist, puts it:

> The central principle . . . is that of integration: the creation of conditions such that the members of the organization can achieve their own goals *best* by directing their efforts toward the success of the enterprise.[6]

Finally, note that all of these goals are really guides to action. For example:

□ They facilitate decision making by helping the entrepreneur and his employees to choose the best course of action in the solution of a problem or the pursuit of an opportunity.
□ They are clear enough to suggest specific courses of action. For example, "to make profits" is a vague guide to action, but "to rank each year among the top ten dealerships" is a precise guide.
□ They suggest ways of measuring the dealership's performance. For example, the entrepreneur can tell how close he comes to the top ten by comparing his new-car sales with those of other dealers throughout the nation. This measure is much more useful than such an empty statement as "to compete in the new-car field."
□ They are challenging enough to excite the entrepreneur and his employees. Without such goals, the venture may lose its tone and risk stagnation. Goals should not be too demanding, of course. Rather, they should be challenging but achievable. It is such goals that best spur performance, as suggested in Exhibit 12-2.

6. Douglas McGregor, *The Human Side of Enterprise* (New York: McGraw-Hill, 1960), p. 49.

EXHIBIT 12-2

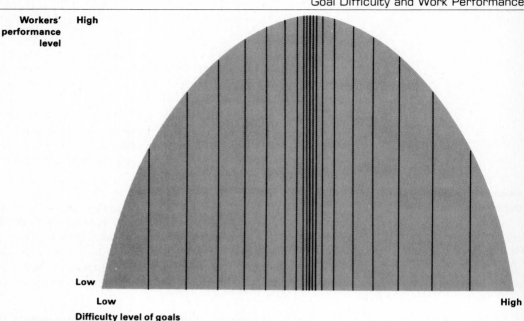

Goal Difficulty and Work Performance

Workers' performance level — High ... Low

Low — High
Difficulty level of goals

ACTION PLANS

Setting goals is just the beginning. Next, the entrepreneur must decide how best to meet those goals. This calls for the development of action plans that:

☐ Lay out in precise detail the steps necessary to achieve each goal
☐ Fix the responsibility for each step, be it the entrepreneur or a key employee
☐ Set deadlines for each step

Action plans should be designed to make things happen. Without such plans to breathe life into them, goals become meaningless. One example of an action plan is the business plan, described in Chapter Six.

CONTROL

It is not enough, however, just to set goals and draft action plans to meet them. Entrepreneurs should also measure their progress at frequent intervals. To do that, they need information that tells them whether their goals are being met.

Called *control*, this process of measurement helps assure entrepreneurs that their own actions, as well as those of employees, are on target. The key element of the control process is information that permits entrepreneurs to compare actual performance with planned performance. This information allows entrepreneurs to measure not only their performance but also the propriety of their goals and action plans—and if need be, to adjust them.

The entrepreneur in our earlier example worked out the following action plan with his new-car sales manager:

To help meet our goal of increasing new-car sales from 1,600 to 2,000 Buicks a year, you should:

☐ Send all salespersons to a salesmanship course at a local college to improve their ability to close a sale
☐ Work with our advertising agency to create eye-catching television commercials with an appealing message
☐ Invite all old customers by letter and then by a follow-up telephone call to visit our showroom
☐ Meet with me and our controller each Monday at 10 A.M., to review our sales performance for the previous week

■

Action plans may be simple. They need not be fancy and elaborate, although it is a good idea to put them into writing. The spoken word is no substitute for the written word, which provides a permanent record. It leaves little room for argument later, because presumably the entrepreneur and his employees worked out the action plan together.

BUDGETING

Earlier, in Chapters Six, Nine, and Eleven, we discussed the cash budget. We said it was the centerpiece of the business plan because it translated the would-be entrepreneur's operating plans into dollar terms. And it was this translation that best enabled entrepreneurs to talk about their plans with such outsiders as bankers and venture capitalists before launching their venture.

Budgets play an equally vital role after entrepreneurs get their venture underway, as a tool for both planning and control. Again, the focus is on dollars, though not always. To see how budgeting might work in an ongoing venture, let us go through this example:

EXAMPLE

The entrepreneur in our earlier example expressed his new-car sales in units, as shown in Exhibit 12-3. This unit budget would be used by the new-car sales manager to control the performance of her salespersons. Units, not dollars, have real meaning to salespersons and are an effective way of communicating goals to them.

But at the sales manager's level, dollars assume importance as a control. To meet her unit goal of 2,000 new-car sales, the sales manager might over-react and tell her salespersons to sell at discounts or accept trade-ins that erode profit margins. To avoid that problem, the entrepreneur would prepare another budget, this one translating units into dollars (see Exhibit 12-4).

EXHIBIT 12-3

New-Car Sales Budget—Units

Model	Quarter				Total
	First	Second	Third	Fourth	
Small	200	300	300	200	1,000
Medium	100	150	150	100	500
Large	100	150	150	100	500
	400	600	600	400	2,000

EXHIBIT 12-4

New-Car Sales Budget (net of trade-in)

Model	Quarter				Total
	First	Second	Third	Fourth	
Small	$ 600,000	$ 900,000	$ 900,000	$ 600,000	$3,000,000
Medium	450,000	675,000	675,000	450,000	2,250,000
Large	600,000	900,000	900,000	600,000	3,000,000
	$1,650,000	$2,475,000	$2,475,000	$1,650,000	$8,250,000

This control system is still incomplete, because the sales manager may overspend in her efforts to meet her unit goal of 2,000 new-car sales. So the entrepreneur would prepare a third budget, this one dealing with selling expenses (see Exhibit 12-5).

Armed with these three budgets, the entrepreneur can now control the performance of his new-car sales department. By providing them with the information they need to make sound decisions these budgets encourage the sales manager and her salespersons to do their best. These budgets also enable:

☐ The entrepreneur to evaluate the performance of his sales manager
☐ The sales manager to evaluate the performance of her salespersons

Such evaluations of performance may result in promotions, merit increases in salary, remedial action, and even dismissals. However, budget figures should never be the only way to judge a person's performance.

For example, suppose an unexpected recession hits the nation and causes unemployment to rise sharply. New-car sales slump nationwide. As a result, the sale manager fails to meet the goal of 2,000 new-car sales. Should she be penalized? No. Her failure was due to events beyond her

EXHIBIT 12-5

New-Car Selling Expense Budget

| Item | Quarter | | | | Total |
	First	Second	Third	Fourth	
Salaries	$100,000	$100,000	$100,000	$100,000	$400,000
Commissions	50,000	75,000	75,000	50,000	250,000
Advertising	10,000	20,000	30,000	20,000	80,000
Telephone	500	500	500	500	2,000
Total	$160,500	$195,500	$205,500	$170,500	$732,000

control. In any case, it would be the responsibility of the entrepreneur, not the sales manager, to foretell such a slump and to adjust the budget accordingly.
■

RETURN ON SALES VERSUS RETURN ON INVESTMENT

So far, we have touched on ways the entrepreneur can control the performance of his new-car salespersons and their manager. But what about the entrepreneur himself? Because he alone is accountable for the dealership's efficiency and effectiveness, he should be evaluated for performance in these two areas. Two of his budgeted goals are:

☐ Return on sales, which measures efficiency, of 2.0 percent
☐ Return on investment, which measures effectiveness, of 9.0 percent a year

At year's end, the entrepreneur would then compare his actual performance with budgeted performance. For example, a return on investment of 9.5 percent would tell the entrepreneur that he had managed his dealership well.

Never confuse the two yardsticks of performance above. Often, entrepreneurs say, "My return is just 2 percent," creating the impression that their return on investment is 2 percent. They more likely are talking about return on sales. Learn to distinguish between them.

EXAMPLE

An entrepreneur buys a product in the morning for 99 cents and sells it in the afternoon for one dollar. She does business this way 100 days a year. What are her return on sales and her return on investment?

☐ Her return on sales is 1 percent, computed as shown in Exhibit 12-6.
☐ Her return on investment is 101 percent a year, computed as shown in Exhibit 12-7.

The important yardstick of performance is the return of 101 percent because it tells how effectively she used her investment of 99 cents—how

EXHIBIT 12-6

Example: Computing Return on Sales

$$\text{Sales revenues} = \$100.00 \ (\$1.00/\text{unit} \times 100 \text{ units/year})$$
$$\text{Expenses} = \underline{99.00} \ (\$0.99/\text{unit} \times 100 \text{ units/year})$$
$$\text{Operating profit} = \$ \ \ 1.00$$

$$\therefore \ \text{Return on revenues} = \frac{\text{Operating profit}}{\text{Sales revenues}} \times 100$$
$$= \frac{\$1.00}{\$100.00} \times 100$$
$$= \underline{\underline{1\%}}$$

EXHIBIT 12-7

Example: Computing Return on Investment

$$\text{Operating profit} = \$1.00$$
$$\text{Owners' equity} = \ \ 0.99$$

$$\therefore \ \text{Return on owners' equity} = \frac{\text{Yearly operating profit}}{\text{Owners' equity}} \times 100$$
$$= \frac{\$1.00}{\$0.99} \times 100$$
$$= \underline{\underline{101\% \text{ a year}}}$$

well she managed her resources to produce results. Though less important, the return of 1 percent tells how efficiently she did business—how much she has left over as profit for each dollar of sales.

■

More will be said about return on sales and return on investment in Chapter Thirteen.

REPORTING PERFORMANCE

To make the best use of budgets, entrepreneurs should establish some means by which actual performance may be compared with budgeted performance. Such comparisons may be made on the back of an envelope or even on scraps of paper, but an organized chart of comparison provides a clear and concise picture, like the one in Exhibit 12-8.

Note how this quarter-to-quarter comparison gives off immediate signals. For example, in the first quarter, actual performance topped budgeted performance for both small and medium models. This signals the entrepreneur that

EXHIBIT 12-8

Report on Actual and Budgeted Sales—Units

	Small Model			Medium Model			Large Model		
Quarter	Budgeted	Actual	Difference	Budgeted	Actual	Difference	Budgeted	Actual	Difference
First	200	220	+20	100	110	+10	100	80	−20
Second	300	280	−20	150	150	—	150	120	−30
Third	300	310	+10	150	140	−10	150	130	−20
Fourth	200	180	−20	100	110	+10	100	90	−10
Total	1,000	990	−10	500	510	+10	500	420	−80

the new-car sales department performed well with those models. But the sales department did poorly with large models, falling 20 cars short of the budgeted goal. Because this is 20 percent off budgeted performance, the entrepreneur must now find out what happened and then take remedial action.

PROFITGRAPH

USES OF THE PROFITGRAPH

Another helpful planning and control tool is the profitgraph.[7] Few entrepreneurs make use of this tool. Yet it is remarkably versatile. For example, the profitgraph may give entrepreneurs visual answers to such questions as these:

☐ How many pounds of product must I make and sell before I begin to make a profit?

☐ At what percentage of capacity must I run my plant before I begin to make a profit?

☐ By how much must my sales revenues increase to justify hiring another salesperson? Or a receptionist?

The profitgraph may also give entrepreneurs visual answers to *what-if* questions, such as, what would happen to my profits if:

☐ Fixed costs increase 10 percent but volume, prices, and variable costs stay the same?

☐ Sales volume drops off 10 percent but prices, fixed costs, and variable costs stay the same?

☐ Sales volume goes up 10 percent but prices, fixed costs, and variable costs rise 5 percent?

7. As mentioned in Chapter 6, the profitgraph is often called a breakeven chart, which mistakenly suggests that the entrepreneur's goal is to break even rather than to make a profit. That is why *profitgraph* is suggested as a better term.

These sample questions underscore how handy and versatile a tool the profitgraph can be. Entrepreneurs may apply this tool not only to the venture as a whole but to parts of the venture as well.

An entrepreneur has been profitably operating a restaurant in a shopping center for six years. Her success has encouraged her to think seriously about leasing space in another shopping center for a second restaurant. One question she feels she must resolve is how many customers she must average daily before she begins to make a profit.

To answer that question, the entrepreneur and her accountant have estimated that:

☐ Variable costs will be $.40 on each $1.00 of sales.
☐ Fixed costs will be $18,000 a month.
☐ The average customer will spend $5.00 for a meal.

Using this information, the entrepreneur may now construct a profitgraph like the one in Exhibit 12-9. As shown, the new restaurant would begin to make a profit when its monthly revenues top $30,000—or at least 6,000 customers a month. Note that in constructing the profitgraph, the entrepreneur:

☐ Drew a straight line parallel to the horizontal axis to show that fixed costs ($18,000 a month) would be the same regardless of the number of customers patronizing the new restaurant
☐ Drew a second straight line beginning at $18,000 on the vertical axis and increasing at the rate of $.40 per $1.00 of sales or $2.00 per average customer to show total costs
☐ Drew a third straight line beginning at zero and increasing at the rate of $5.00 per average customer to show total revenues

The point at which the revenue and total-cost lines intersect is the point at which revenues match total costs. In other words, it is the point at which the entrepreneur would make neither a profit nor a loss, but would break even.

■

One word of caution about profitgraphs like the one above: the volume-price-cost relationships are valid only within relevant ranges of volume. For instance, if monthly volume in our example were to drop to 4,000 customers, then the entrepreneur would undoubtedly slice her fixed costs by taking such actions as these:

☐ Eliminating the job of hostess and permitting customers to seat themselves
☐ Closing the restaurant on Sundays because volume is lowest that day

Instead of constructing the profitgraph, the entrepreneur could have found the point at which she would begin to make a profit through the following calculation. First, she would estimate the contribution to fixed costs made by

EXHIBIT 12-9

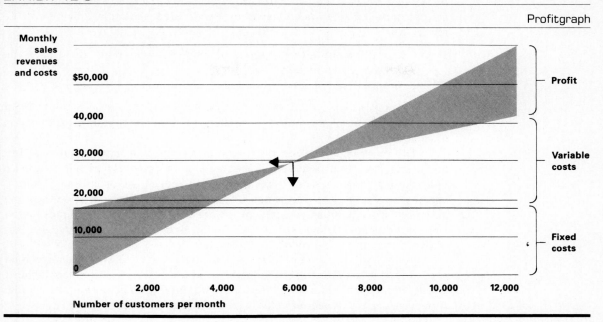

Profitgraph

Although this computation gives the entrepreneur her breakeven point, it does not have the versatility of the profitgraph. The latter is especially useful as a tool for visualizing the answers to a host of *what-if* questions. The entrepreneur can anticipate a number of possible scenarios and see the effects of changes in sales volume and costs on profits.

each customer ($5.00 selling price − $2.00 variable cost = $3.00). This means that $3.00 out of each $5.00 sale is left over to cover fixed costs. Then she would divide this unit contribution into monthly fixed costs:

$$\frac{\$18,000/\text{month}}{\$3.00/\text{customer}} = 6,000 \quad \left\{ \begin{array}{l} \text{customers a month} \\ \text{needed to cover fixed costs} \\ \text{and begin to make a profit} \end{array} \right.$$

SUMMARY

A venture often passes through four stages of growth: prebirth, acceptance, breakthrough, and maturity. Entrepreneurs tend to be good at launching and bringing their venture through the acceptance stage. But they are not as good at managing their venture through breakthrough and maturity. One reason is that entrepreneurs ignore a lesson they learned before they launched their venture—that planning and control help keep a venture on target.

As elements in a circular process, planning and control are as vital to the health of a venture after its birth as before. This process begins with setting precise goals, both immediate and long-range. Goal setting is critical for these reasons:

☐ The clearer the entrepreneur's idea of what should be done, the greater the chances that it will be done.
☐ True progress can only be measured in relation to the entrepreneur's goals.

The second step requires that entrepreneurs draft action plans to meet their goals. These plans should be similar to the business plan, which itself is an action plan.

The third step requires entrepreneurs to measure their progress at frequent intervals. This process is called control. It helps assure entrepreneurs that their actions, as well as those of their employees, are progressing according to plan. The key to any system of control is information that enables the entrepreneur to compare actual with planned performance. Such information lets entrepreneurs know where they stand, and more importantly, in what direction they may be moving.

Budgeting and profitgraphs are two tools that help entrepreneurs plan and control more effectively. Budgets generally serve as a standard against which actual performance may be compared. Profitgraphs, on the other hand, show visually the impact of volume, price, and costs on profit.

DISCUSSION AND REVIEW QUESTIONS

1 Explain the process of planning and control in a venture. Why is this process circular?
2 Why do entrepreneurs tend to avoid the process of planning and control in their own venture?
3 Why is it vital to set precise goals? Give two examples of precise goal setting.
4 Define these terms: *immediate goals, long-range goals, action plans, return on sales, return on investment, efficiency, effectiveness*.
5 What is meant by MBO?
6 Which is the better measure of venture performance, return on sales or return on investment? Explain.
7 How would you, as an entrepreneur, go about setting goals for your venture?
8 In your opinion, why do so many entrepreneurs fail to plan and control their ventures in the ways suggested in the chapter?
9 Why is budgeting a vital tool for both planning and control?
10 Why is the profitgraph so versatile a planning and control tool? Give two examples of how this tool may be used.

11 Why is it vital for small-businesspersons to be managers as well as entre-preneurs?

12 Does an entrepreneur's venture necessarily stop growing when it reaches the maturity stage in its growth cycle? Explain.

13 What is the most important principle in the pursuit of goals? Why?

14 What is meant by the hierarchy of goals? Give an example.

15 What do profits measure? Explain fully.

GRAND VALLEY ENTERPRISES, INC.

Founded in 1976, Grand Valley Enterprises has grown to sales revenues of $601,000. Its co-founder and president, Jerry Lisiecki, is disappointed in the lack of profit so far but is confident that Grand Valley is "on the brink of black ink." The company sells mostly bluegrass sod and muck soil. At the company's last board meeting, a director, Richard Sabo, told Mr. Lisiecki that "good company presidents conceptualize and do not perform physical work."

BACKGROUND

Before 1976, Jerry Lisiecki had not even dreamt that someday he would preside over 1,211 acres of gently rolling farmland in the Midwest. Rather, he expected to work for somebody else for the rest of his life. As a teenager, he became so intrigued by nature that he made up his mind to seek a career in biology.

This ambition carried him through eight years of intensive study at Ohio State University and Michigan State University. At the latter, he earned a Ph.D. in limnology, which is the study of the chemical, physical, and biological properties of fresh water.

Mr. Lisiecki knew that the demand in private industry for limnologists, especially for Ph.D.'s like himself, was slim. He also looked at jobs with state and federal governments, but he soon ruled them out because "seniority, not talent, counts in government work." Nor did he like the idea of becoming a professor, because he wanted to avoid "always scrambling for grants to survive."

LOOKS HOMEWARD

Near graduation, married and the father of a four-year-old son, Mr. Lisiecki was pressing hard to find something to do in his specialty. He decided to try his luck back home. Home was Orwell, a small farming town of just 988 inhabitants. On a visit home, he called on the Ruetenik Gardens. He had worked there summers and liked the Ruetenik family.

Mr. Lisiecki suggested to the Rueteniks that they hire him to raise fish in ponds that he himself would build. The Rueteniks agreed, although for the past 89 years they and their ancestors had raised nothing but vegetables on their land. "At last," thought Mr. Lisiecki, "I can put my talents to use."

Then fate intervened. For two growing seasons, bad weather had damaged the vegetable crops so severely that cash flow was reduced to a trickle. So much so that Mr. Lisiecki's fish venture had to be shelved indefinitely. Soon after, the Rueteniks casually told Mr. Lisiecki they wanted to sell their farm. Excited at the idea of owning so much land, Mr. Lisiecki immediately called his insurance agent, Glenn Rex, to see how much he could borrow against his life insurance policies, which he had bought while still in college. Although they had never met before, Mr. Lisiecki and Mr. Rex soon recognized each other's talents and saw the opportunity to buy Ruetenik Gardens and run it profitably together. Several meetings later Mr. Rex agreed to help raise the $600,000 purchase price and Mr. Lisiecki agreed to invest in, as well as to manage, the takeover of Ruetenik Gardens.

The Rueteniks gave them a 60-day option to raise the purchase price of $600,000. First, however, they had to put up $10,000 as evidence of the seriousness of their intentions; Mr. Lisiecki put up $8,000 and Mr. Rex $2,000. "It took all my resources," says Mr. Lisiecki. "But I couldn't help myself. The opportunity was too good to miss."

After they put up the $10,000, Mr. Lisiecki and Mr. Rex immediately went to work raising the $600,000. First, they wrote a business plan, giving the purpose of their partnership, product descriptions, personal qualifications, an organizational plan, and a financial forecast. Excerpts appear in Exhibits 12A-1, 12A-2, and 12A-3.

As part of their market research, the partners drew up a list of possible users of muck soil, which they planned to remove and sell in order to create ponds for the fish-farming operation they planned to develop later in their venture. Mrs. Lisiecki designed a direct-mail advertisement which they sent out to test the potential market. "The response was terrific," says Mrs. Lisiecki. "The response rate was over 30 percent, and experience shows that the national average for such a mailing is less than 5 percent." From this mailing, the two partners concluded that the sales potential for muck soil was large enough to justify investing some of their cash flow in this part of their business.

What was it that encouraged potential muck soil customers to respond to the advertisement in such numbers? "It was a lesson I learned when I worked for an advertising agency," says Mrs. Lisiecki. "That lesson was to differentiate

---

Grand Valley Enterprises, Inc.

EXHIBIT 12A-1

Purpose of Proposed Partnership

During the first year following purchase of the Ruetenik Gardens, we will harvest and sell sod, sell equipment not needed, and develop markets for bulk distribution of muck soil. As the muck soil is stripped to levels that reveal blue clay, we will build ponds to raise a variety of fish, including rainbow trout, brown trout, large and small-mouth bass, yellow perch, northern pike, and walleye.

It will take five to fifteen years to build these ponds, depending on customer demand for muck soil. Eventually, as we run out of sod and muck soil, the entire 1,211 acres of land will be developed as follows:

☐ 503 acres for hunting and preserving wildlife
☐ 400 acres to raise fish
☐ 175 acres for sale to private individuals in five-acre plots each
☐ 100 acres for an 18-hole golf course
☐ 33 acres for social activities by families of members using the fishing or hunting facilities

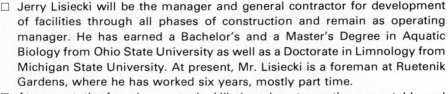

Initial Organization

☐ Jerry Lisiecki will be the manager and general contractor for development of facilities through all phases of construction and remain as operating manager. He has earned a Bachelor's and a Master's Degree in Aquatic Biology from Ohio State University as well as a Doctorate in Limnology from Michigan State University. At present, Mr. Lisiecki is a foreman at Ruetenik Gardens, where he has worked six years, mostly part time.

☐ At present, the farm has enough skilled workers to continue vegetable and sod production. Four to six more workers will be hired to run the soil-processing facilities. A secretary will also be hired.

☐ An outside accounting firm will be used to prepare year-end financial statements and reports for financial institutions and for government agencies. Inside bookkeeping will be done by both the secretary and the manager.

---

your product, make it stand out from the others. So we sent some dirt wrapped in cellophane along with the ad, and we called the ad 'Dirt Cheap.'"

Mr. Lisiecki had already worked with the sod part of the Ruetenik Gardens operation and knew that the muck soil found on the farm raised a fine quality sod. He also knew that his chief competitors were located in Michigan. By concentrating on a regional market and thus holding down transportation costs that his competitors would have to bear, he knew that he could improve the profitability of his sod operation.

Because of the time needed for muck removal, pond construction, and fish growth, Mr. Lisiecki did not expect the fish operation to produce significant cash flow for at least five years.

Meanwhile, Mr. Rex had been busy contacting commercial banks throughout the region. Upon completion of their business plan, he and Mr. Lisiecki called on the banks. They were turned down by all but one. That bank, Farmer's National, agreed to lend them $250,000 of the $600,000 purchase price, mostly because of their respect for Mr. Rex as a sound businessperson. Mr. Rex had this to say about their experience with the banks:

MONEY-RAISING DIFFICULTIES

> Every bank we went to said it's no problem financing us. Then they would try to tie us up for weeks. They didn't want the other banks looking at our financial needs. In fact, they even wanted a commitment from us not to talk to the other banks. Yet they still turned us down.

After this experience, Mr. Rex and Mr. Lisiecki realized that their dream of total control was impractical and they would need investors and not lenders. Mr. Rex then went to see one of his clients, Richard Sabo, who was a manager at a major manufacturer of welding equipment. Mr. Sabo visited the farm and met Mr. Lisiecki. Soon after reviewing the business plan with Mr. Rex, Mr. Sabo

Grand Valley Enterprises, Inc.

Projected Finances

	1977*	1978*	1979*	1980*
Sales Revenues				
Muck soil	$125,000	$500,000	$525,000	$551,000
Vegetables and sod	325,000	341,000	358,000	—
Field crops	—	—	—	20,000
Equipment	—	—	—	30,000
Total revenues	$450,000	$841,000	$883,000	$601,000
Expenses				
Fixed expenses	$175,000	$183,000	$192,000	$201,000
Equipment mortgage	55,000	55,000	55,000	55,000
First mortgage	50,000	50,000	50,000	50,000
Second mortgage	44,000	44,000	44,000	44,000
Vegetables and sod	40,000	42,000	44,000	—
Muck soil	17,000	70,000	74,000	77,000
Other	15,000	60,000	63,000	—
Total expenses	$396,000	$504,000	$522,000	$427,000
Profit	$ 54,000	$337,000	$361,000	$174,000
Cash flow	$ 54,000	$391,000	$752,000	$926,000

* Year ending May 31

agreed to invest in Mr. Lisiecki and to help find others who would. So impressed was Mr. Sabo by what he saw, that he asked but two questions:

☐ What is the smallest investment I can make and still become a partner?
☐ Who owns the mineral and oil rights on all this land?

No longer able to form a simple partnership, Mr. Rex and Mr. Lisiecki hired a lawyer to advise them on how best to organize their venture. After discussion of various legal forms of organization, they formed a Subchapter S corporation.

In 1976, Subchapter S corporations were limited to no more than ten shareholders. The lawyer told the partners that investors often prefer investing in Subchapter S corporations because any losses pass through directly to investors, thus cutting their taxes on other income. Moreover, investors pay only personal taxes and not corporate taxes on any profits. The lawyer, by the way, once told Mr. Rex that, at the time, he had given them "just one chance in 10,000" to make a success of their venture.

Once they had organized their venture, Mr. Rex began approaching prospective investors. With only five days left on the 60-day option, Mr. Rex had raised $567,000 of the purchase price but had also exhausted his list of investors. "A

A CLOSE CALL

near-miss would have been as bad as not raising a single penny," says Mr. Lisiecki. "The Rueteniks were absolutely firm in their demand that we raise all of the $600,000 in just 60 days. There were others who wanted to buy them out. Also, if we failed to raise the money, we would lose our $10,000 deposit."

"In near panic," Mr. Rex called Mr. Sabo to ask if he knew of any other potential investors. Mr. Sabo called a coworker at his company. After reviewing the business plan with his coworker, Mr. Sabo called Mr. Rex with the news that they had their final investor.

On May 18, 1976, the two partners went to the Rueteniks and completed the purchase with the help of their lawyer. The partners had raised $350,000 from ten private investors, including themselves, and had also borrowed $250,000 from Farmer's National Bank. The loan agreement called for the loan to be repaid in 5 years at an interest rate of 12 percent. To swing the loan, the two partners gave the bank a mortgage on the market value of Ruetenik Gardens. In addition, Mr. Rex and Mr. Lisiecki personally pledged their assets to guarantee repayment of the loan.

At the age of 28, Mr. Lisiecki found himself the president of his own venture, Grand Valley Enterprises, Inc. The fact that he had worked with the Rueteniks stood him in good stead. He felt at home with all farm operations, and he knew all of the employees he inherited. The day he took over as president, Mr. Lisiecki called his 14 employees together. He assured them of their jobs and asked for their help to make Grand Valley a success. He also informed all customers of the change in ownership.

IN BUSINESS FOR HIMSELF

Just before they took over, Mr. Rex arranged a line of credit of $50,000 with Farmer's National Bank. Such a credit arrangement would allow Grand Valley to meet cash needs as they arose. The beginning balance sheet appears in Exhibit 12A-4.

Mr. Lisiecki's first priority was to put into effect his ideas of what best to sell. The Rueteniks had concentrated on vegetables. In contrast, Mr. Lisiecki wanted to concentrate on selling bluegrass sod and muck soil, as mentioned earlier in Exhibit 12A-1.

When he took over, Mr. Lisiecki saw that his two biggest problems were marketing and production. Because he already had a small inventory of sod and because bulk soil operations could be initiated easily, he decided to focus his attention on marketing first.

Mr. Lisiecki drew up a list of landscapers, greenhouse operators, and gardeners in his region and sent them flyers and price lists on the bluegrass sod and bulk soil. Business grew steadily the first summer and fall. But looking ahead to the long winter, Mr. Lisiecki convinced his nine partners that additional products should be developed to maintain cash flow.

MARKETING STRATEGY

Mr. Sabo had recommended that he concentrate on basic products, so Mr. Lisiecki investigated the market potential of his muck soil further. He found that Michigan farmers packaged their soil in 40-pound polyethylene bags and sold them through large retail chains. Because Mr. Lisiecki was unsure how best to approach the chains, Mr. Rex made contact with a broker through one

Grand Valley Enterprises, Inc.

Beginning Balance Sheet (May 18, 1976)

Assets			Equities	
Current assets			Owners' equity	$730,000
Cash	$130,000			
Inventory	11,500	$141,500		
Fixed assets				
Land	$368,900			
Buildings	150,000			
Equipment	52,800			
Vehicles	16,800	588,500		
Total assets		$730,000	Total equities	$730,000

of his friends. After a visit to the farm, the broker agreed to represent the new product line and also help in designing the new production line.

Thanks to the broker's efforts, sales orders began to come in. The large chains and discount houses saw the 40-pound bag of soil as a "loss leader" item, often selling the bags for a few cents above or below their purchase price to generate store traffic. With their marketing strategy now in place, the partners' next challenge was to boost production.

PRODUCTION CHANGES

The farm equipment inherited from Ruetenik Gardens was adequate to produce more sod but incapable of processing soil for bags or delivering sufficient volume to customers. To reach his first-year forecast, shown earlier in Exhibit 12A-3, Mr. Lisiecki needed a one-shift capacity of 500,000 40-pound bags a year by 1982.

"I knew nothing about the special problems of packaging soil. If I had, I could have designed the process equipment we needed and then had my employees build it. They're handy with tools and equipment. All farmers are." The broker who helped with marketing helped with designing the new production line. "The broker was most helpful," says Mr. Lisiecki. "He knew precisely what equipment we needed to process both bagged and bulk muck soil and who the best equipment suppliers would be."

Seven months after he took over, the new production line was in place and ready to go for the spring. (See photographs in Exhibit 12A-5, p. 340.) "It really does the job," says Mr. Lisiecki, "and we have few breakdowns. There still are some minor bottlenecks, although we keep upgrading the equipment every year. Our production line is smoother than ever, because we have more experience with soil handling and more cash flow." The new process is described in Exhibit 12A-6 (p. 341) and flow-charted in Exhibit 12A-7 (p. 342).

FINANCIAL PERFORMANCE

By September 1980, four and one-half years had elapsed since Mr. Lisiecki and his fellow investors took over Ruetenik Gardens. These years had been unexpectedly lean. Only in 1979 did Grand Valley realize a profit, and then it was

Three Views of Operations

only $200. Condensed income statements for the first four years of operation appear in Exhibit 12A-8; the 1980 income statement is detailed in Exhibit 12A-9 (p. 343). In Exhibit 12A-10 (p. 344) appears the 1980 balance sheet.

"Our sales in 1980 were almost exactly what I had forecast them to be," says Mr. Lisiecki, "but it's hard to admit we're still losing money." However, he believes that the farm has been unprofitable because of:

☐ The costly start-up of two new product lines, one for bulk soil and the other for bagged soil

☐ The $225,000 purchase of additional equipment to process and deliver all products smoothly

☐ His "humane" policy of keeping all employees on the payroll even though there was little work for them to do

Description of How Bluegrass Sod and Bulk Muck Soil Are Produced

Bluegrass sod is grown on the same type of soil that we sell in bagged and bulk quantities. The soil is found in deposits 1 to 8 feet deep of a drained river-bed swamp covering more than 500 acres of the 1,211 acre farm. This soil is classified by the U.S. Department of Agriculture as muck humus, equivalent to 80 percent of organic material.

To produce bagged and bulk soil products We excavate the soil using a 2 cubic-yard backhoe bucket and then transport it to the main building complex in single-axle dump trucks. Here, bulldozers and the backhoe are used to pile the soil. This piling helps dry the soil and keep it from becoming wet again in the spring. A description of each production line follows:

☐ **Bagged soil production** To produce 40-pound bags of soil, we take soil from the stockpile and process it through a hammer mill and a rotating screen to remove large waste. Next, we reprocess it in a shredder, and then move it by trough conveyor to a surge hopper. From there, the soil moves by a bagging conveyor to a weight-activated bagger and is placed in polyethylene bags. The bags then travel an L-Belt conveyor through a continuous heat sealer and onto a bag flattener.

   After flattening, we stack the bags on pallets, using glue between the layers to prevent sliding. Later, after allowing the glue to dry, we load the pallets on a truck-and-trailer for shipment to customers.

☐ **Bulk soil production** To produce bulk soil, we take soil from the stockpile and process it, as above, through a hammer mill and a rotating screen. At this point, instead of reprocessing the soil, we place it in a hopper where lime, sand, Perlite, topsoil, and peat moss are added as needed.

   This mixture is then run through another hammer mill and dropped into dump trucks for delivery to greenhouses, golf courses, and homeowners.

To produce bluegrass sod We plow, disc, fertilize, and lime the fields during the summer. Then we plant the seed during early September so that it germinates that fall. The next year, we treat the fields as if they were a lawn. We fertilize and spray for weeds, for example. We also roll and mow at least once a week. Clippings are swept up.

   The spring following the second winter after planting, we continue to exercise care until harvest. Harvest requires specialized equipment. We then deliver the sod to customers using semitrailers.

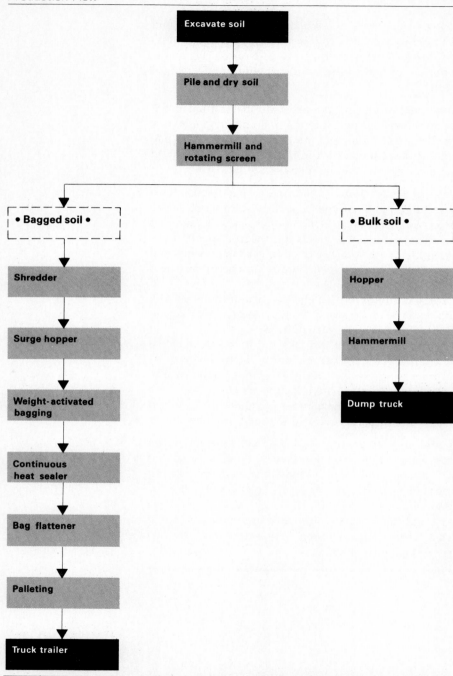

Grand Valley Enterprises, Inc.

Condensed Income Statements: 1977–1980*

Year	Sales Revenues	Cost of Goods Sold	Gross Profit	Operating Expenses	Profit or (Loss)
1977	$223,700	$172,700	$ 51,000	$105,400	($54,400)
1978	298,800	235,700	63,100	137,200	(74,100)
1979	622,000	408,900	213,100	212,900	200
1980	601,100	402,800	198,300	243,700	(45,400)

* Year ending May 31

Grand Valley Enterprises, Inc.

1980 Income Statement*

Sales revenues		$601,100
Cost of goods sold		402,800
Gross profit		$198,300
Operating Expenses		
Interest	$51,400	
Depreciation	45,500	
Gas, diesel fuel, maintenance	44,600	
Local taxes	35,000	
Chemicals, fertilizer, slag	18,700	
Subcontract labor	17,000	
Hospitalization	10,500	
Insurance	4,900	
Vehicle licenses	3,700	
Telephone	3,300	
Office supplies	2,800	
Electricity	2,600	
Advertising & promotion	1,600	
Subscriptions and dues	600	
Miscellaneous	1,500	243,700
Operating loss		($ 45,400)

* Year ending May 31

Grand Valley Enterprises, Inc.

Latest Balance Sheet (May 31, 1980)

Assets			**Equities**		
Current assets			Liabilities		
Cash	$ 1,300		Accounts payable	$ 68,300	
Accounts receivable	14,100		Line of credit	112,500	
Inventory	17,200		Mortgage loan payable	200,000	
Other	4,200	$ 36,800	Loan payable (Mr. Rex)	39,900	
Fixed assets			Truck loan payable	12,600	
Land	$377,200		Bank loan payable	6,400	
Equipment and vehicles	225,000	602,200	Loan payable (foreman)	5,800	
Loans receivable			Other	16,200	$461,700
From Mr. Lisiecki	$223,000				
From Mr. Rex	91,200		Owners' equity		
From others	25,000	339,200	Shareholders' advance	$357,100	
			Common stock	365,000	
			Retained earnings	(205,600)	516,500
Total assets		$978,200	Total equities		$978,200

"These were all enormous drains on our young company," says Mr. Lisiecki. "Also the cost of fertilizer, polyethylene bags, and fuel went up sharply because of petroleum price hikes." Seasonality is still another problem. Note in Exhibit 12A-11 how seasonal the markets for both bluegrass sod and muck soil are. Only 2½ percent of sales take place in the first quarter of the year, but 50 percent occur in the second quarter.

OPTIMISTIC OUTLOOK

Although disappointed to date, Mr. Lisiecki is optimistic about the long-term future of Grand Valley. To move the company into the black, he is considering several possibilities. One is to boost sales by concentrating on basic products. Another is to reduce transportation costs "to the bone." Still another is to adjust his managerial style. At the last board meeting, Mr. Sabo told Mr. Lisiecki that "good company presidents conceptualize and do not perform physical work." Although he sees the wisdom of Mr. Sabo's words, Mr. Lisiecki feels he cannot cease entirely his working with employees. "When employees fail to show up or when rush orders come in," says Mr. Lisiecki, "we just don't have the surplus labor to cover all production points. Everyone must work to satisfy the customer." His latest organizational chart appears in Exhibit 12A-12 (p. 346). And in Exhibit 12A-13 (p. 347) appear his suggestions on how best to move Grand Valley into the black.

Mr. Lisiecki recently recalled that soon after he took over in 1976, a geologist had told him that the farmland was ripe for oil and gas exploration. "Drilling for oil is largely a gamble," says Mr. Lisiecki. "We could drill, I'm told, as many as 30 wells on our property. But if we came up with a dry well, we'd be out $150,000. That's what it costs today to drill just one well."

Seasonality of Sales Revenues

	Percentage of 1980 Sales Revenues	
Month	Monthly	Quarterly
January	0.6%	
February	0.2	
March	1.7	2.5%
April	16.6	
May	20.1	
June	13.4	50.1
July	16.3	
August	9.5	
September	5.3	31.1
October	5.8	
November	4.0	
December	6.5	16.3
	100.0%	100.0%

QUESTIONS

1 Is Grand Valley soundly financed? Explain fully.
2 How well has Grand Valley performed financially since its beginnings in 1976?
3 What is Grand Valley's most critical problem? How would you suggest they solve it?
4 Comment on Mr. Lisiecki's managerial qualities.
5 If you were on Grand Valley's board of directors, what would be your analysis of Mr. Lisiecki's long-range plan (see Exhibit 12A-13)?

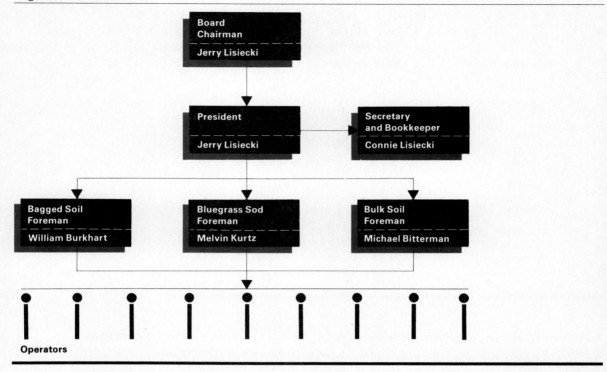

Operators

During the four years since Grand Valley Enterprises was formed, we have developed in several new areas. Initially, we contemplated a bulk soil business, immediate termination of the sod segment, and initiation of a food fish segment. But we soon found that a change of such magnitude and speed was impossible. Therefore, we have developed several new areas that will enable us to make a more gradual transition.

At present, Grand Valley Enterprises sells mostly products with a low value per ton. Because of the high cost of fuel, driver wages, and maintenance, I do not wish to expand our truck fleet. To enable us to grow without further capital investment, I believe several changes in our strategy should be made, among them:

☐ To promote custom packaging or smaller bags at a higher value per ton
☐ To bag for customers willing to do their own pick-ups
☐ To increase the use of local haulers to deliver bluegrass sod and bulk mucksoil
☐ To concentrate our marketing efforts in the region to reduce delivery costs
☐ To sell sod through pick-up brokers, especially during May and June, to reduce competition between sod and soil for our trucks

We believe our present mix of products, with the strategic changes suggested above, offers a strong base for our future growth.

James Stanton took his savings and some money his parents had left him—and started in business for himself. It wasn't a large business. But it did give him the pleasure of being his own boss.

Mr. Stanton's product was a painted wooden toy train priced at $20.30 each. It was a well-built toy, designed like the hand-made toys of his grandfather's day.

An energetic person, Mr. Stanton soon had production rolling. His only start-up problem was paint. But he soon solved the problem by finding a supplier who promised him the quality of paint needed.

At the end of his first six months in business, Mr. Stanton took pride in his first income statement, shown in Exhibit 12B-1.

He hoped it would be the first in a long series of reports showing business "in the black." His balance sheet appears in Exhibit 12B-2.

Comment on Mr. Stanton's performance to date and on his prospects for the future.   **QUESTION**

James Stanton

EXHIBIT 12B-1

Income Statement (for six months ending December 31)

Sales revenues			$11,620
Cost of goods sold			
Beginning inventory		$ 210	
Purchases of materials	$ 7,010		
Labor	11,340		
Rent of machines and space	2,930	21,280	
		$21,490	
Ending inventory		16,090	5,400
Gross profit			$ 6,220
Other expenses			
Advertising and selling		$ 2,120	
Interest		70	2,190
Operating profit			$ 4,030

James Stanton

Balance Sheet (December 31)

Assets		Equities	
Cash	$ 430	Note payable	$ 4,200
Inventory	16,090	Accounts payable	3,840
		Owner's equity	8,480
Total assets	$16,520	Total equities	$16,520

CASE 12C   KIRK'S KAMERA KORNER, INC.

Georgia Kirk is a California entrepreneur whose hobby is also her life work. She owns a camera specialty store, selling mostly photographic equipment and supplies. She herself is an avid camera enthusiast.

Mrs. Kirk has posted a profit in each of the past five years. Her last two income statements appear below:

	1980	1981
Sales Revenues	$320,000	$330,000
Operating Expenses	305,000	314,000
Before-tax Profit	$ 15,000	$ 16,000

According to the Bank of America in San Francisco, camera stores, on the average, post before-tax profits of about 3.5 percent on revenues.

QUESTIONS

1 How well has Mrs. Kirk performed?
2 Would you desire any other information in order to better judge Mrs. Kirk's performance? If so, what other information?

CHAPTER THIRTEEN

FINANCIAL ANALYSIS AND COMPUTERS

questions for mastery

how does financial analysis fit into the
pattern of planning and control?

what are the methods of analyzing financial
statements and interpreting results?

what are the ways of evaluating investment
opportunities?

how may computers be used to improve
performance?

what should you consider in selecting a
computer?

When you can measure what you are
speaking about, and express it in
numbers, you know something
about it.

Lord Kelvin William Thomson

As their growing venture strives toward maturity, entrepreneurs often fail to strike a balance between being entrepreneurial and being managerial. As mentioned in Chapter Twelve, entrepreneurs who excel at launching a new venture often do poorly at managing its growth. This is not because they lose the spark of entrepreneurship, but rather, because they fail to plan and control well.

Such entrepreneurs generally fail to use their financial statements to spot problems before they occur; or they make unwise investment decisions; or they refuse to consider computers to help them plan and control. In this chapter, an extension of Chapters Eleven and Twelve, we shall focus on analyzing financial statements, evaluating investment opportunities, and selecting and using a computer.

ANALYSIS OF FINANCIAL STATEMENTS

To plan and control their venture well, entrepreneurs should become skilled at analyzing the numbers in their financial statements. Many, if not most, entrepreneurs believe that financial analysis should best be left to their accountant. Although it is the job of accountants to design accounting systems and to prepare financial statements, it is not their job to analyze the numbers in the statements and to interpret them. That is the entrepreneur's responsibility.

Doing business is certainly not all numbers. In fact, few business problems can be solved solely by the collection and analysis of numbers, financial or nonfinancial. Often, there are important factors that merit equal consideration but cannot be reduced to numbers, such as teamwork and the entrepreneur's management skills.

Even so, analysis of financial statements can help the entrepreneur make sound decisions, especially in the areas of planning and control. As advice to entrepreneurs who may put their trust in numbers alone as well as to entrepreneurs who put their trust in intuition alone, this quotation bears mention:

> The real trouble with this world of ours is not that it is an unreasonable world, nor even that it is a reasonable one. The commonest kind of trouble is that it is nearly reasonable, but not quite. Life is not illogical; yet it is a trap for logicians. It looks just a little more mathematical and regular than it is; its exactitude is obvious, but its inexactitude is hidden; its wildness lies in wait.[1]

THE ESSENCE OF FINANCIAL ANALYSIS

Comparison lies at the heart of all analyses of financial statements. For example, the statement that "a venture earned a profit of $10,000" is, by itself, meaningless. The $10,000 becomes meaningful only if compared with some

1. Quoted by Robert N. Anthony and James S. Reece, *Accounting* (Homewood, Ill.: Richard D. Irwin, 1979), p. 470.

standard, say, with last year's profit or this year's budgeted profit—as discussed briefly in Chapter Twelve.

Note that such comparisons are precise and concrete. Comparisons, however, may also be imprecise and intuitive. For example, if the venture had sales revenues of $10 million, we would know intuitively that a $10,000 profit is a poor return—a return of just one-tenth of a penny for each dollar of sales.

The comparisons that are most meaningful to entrepreneurs are those that relate to the goals entrepreneurs set for themselves, as described in Chapter Twelve. The comparisons are intended to tell entrepreneurs how well they are meeting their goals. As we have discussed before, entrepreneurs usually have both financial goals, such as sales revenue and return-on-investment targets, and nonfinancial goals, such as psychic satisfaction, workers' satisfaction, and social awareness. Entrepreneurs should, of course, balance the two kinds of goals in measuring their venture's performance. Of the goals that can be reduced to numbers, the most meaningful one is to earn a satisfactory return on the moneys invested in a venture consistent with maintaining its financial health. Note the two-sided nature of this goal:

☐ To earn a satisfactory return
☐ To maintain financial health

We shall now discuss how entrepreneurs should analyze financial statements, in their efforts to shed light on how well they have done financially.

**EARNING A
SATISFACTORY RETURN**

The best yardstick to use in assessing return is called *return on investment* (ROI). It is computed by dividing net profit by investment. ROI tells entrepreneurs how many cents they earn in a year for each dollar of investment, in the same way that interest tells savers how much they earn for each dollar of savings at a bank. Investment may be defined in three different ways:

☐ Total assets
☐ Owners' equity
☐ Permanent capital

That means entrepreneurs may compute three different ROIs. Which yardstick is best? The answer depends on what entrepreneurs want to measure, as described below:

☐ **Return on total assets** This yardstick should be used if entrepreneurs want to measure how well they have invested all the money entrusted in their care, regardless of where it came from. Therefore, they should include as sources of money not only shareholders but also short-term creditors, such as suppliers, and long-term creditors, such as mortgage banks.
☐ **Return on owners' equity** This yardstick should be used if entrepreneurs want to measure how well they have invested only that money entrusted in their care by shareholders. This yardstick appeals especially to existing and prospective shareholders, because it is the entrepreneur's duty to run the venture in the shareholders' best interests.

☐ **Return on permanent capital** This yardstick should be used if entrepreneurs want to measure how well they have invested all the long-term money entrusted in their care. It takes into account not only the investment made by shareholders but also any long-term loans made by commercial banks, mortgage banks, bondholders, and the like.

The sum of owners' equity and long-term debt is called *permanent capital* because it reflects the total amount needed to finance fixed assets and that fraction of current assets not otherwise financed by short-term creditors.

MAINTAINING FINANCIAL HEALTH

Besides desiring a satisfactory return on investment, shareholders also expect their investment to be protected against excessive risk. For example, entrepreneurs could boost their return on owners' equity if they financed an expansion solely by borrowing from a commercial bank.

Such an action might boost the shareholders' return, but only at the shareholders' increased risk of losing their investment. By financing the expansion with a loan, entrepreneurs must both repay the loan and pay interest. Failure to do both could throw a venture into bankruptcy.

To measure their degree of protection against risk, entrepreneurs may use any one of several yardsticks. One yardstick relates total debt to total assets; another omits current debt and relates just long-term debt to permanent capital. These yardsticks and others are described in an upcoming section of this chapter called "Tests of Financial Health."

RATIO ANALYSIS

To evaluate their financial performance, entrepreneurs should use a technique called *ratio analysis.* Although dozens of ratios may be computed from just one set of financial statements, generally only a handful will be helpful to entrepreneurs. In the discussion that follows, we have grouped the ratios into two categories:

☐ Tests of profitability
☐ Tests of financial health

We shall compute ratios for the various yardsticks of performance based on the financial statements of a fictitious venture. These statements appear in Exhibit 13-1.

TESTS OF PROFITABILITY

RETURN ON INVESTMENT

As explained earlier, entrepreneurs may estimate their return on investment by using any one of three ratios, depending on whether they see investment as being total assets, owners' equity, or permanent capital. Computations follow.

EXHIBIT 13-1

Micro Products, Inc.

Balance Sheet (December 31, 1981)

Assets

Current assets
Cash	$ 20,000	
Accounts receiv.	50,000	
Inventories	80,000	$150,000

Fixed assets
Land	$ 20,000	
Building	120,000	
Equipment	160,000	300,000

Total assets	$450,000

Equities

Current liabilities
Accounts payable	$ 40,000	
Notes payable	20,000	
Accrued expenses	10,000	$ 70,000

Long-term liabilities
Loan payable (12% interest)		150,000

Owners' equity
Common stock	$100,000	
Retained earnings	130,000	230,000
Total equities		$450,000

Income Statement (1981)

Sales revenues	$500,000
Cost of goods sold	350,000
Gross profit	$150,000
Operating expenses	82,000
Operating profit	$ 68,000
Less: interest on loan	18,000
Profit before taxes	$ 50,000
Income taxes (30%)	15,000
Net profit	$ 35,000

$$\text{Return on Assets} = \frac{\text{Net Profit} + [\text{Interest} \times (1 - \text{Tax Rate})]}{\text{Total Assets}} \times 100$$

$$= \frac{\$35,000 + [\$18,000 \times (1 - 0.30)]}{\$450,000} \times 100$$

$$= \underline{10.6\% \text{ a year}}$$

$$\text{Return on Owners' Equity} = \frac{\text{Net Profit}}{\text{Owners' Equity}} \times 100$$

$$= \frac{\$35,000}{\$230,000} \times 100$$

$$= \underline{15.2\% \text{ a year}}$$

$$\text{Return on Permanent Capital} = \frac{\text{Net Profit} + [\text{Interest} \times (1 - \text{Tax Rate})]}{\text{Owners' Equity} + \text{Long-Term Liabilities}} \times 100$$

$$= \frac{\$35,000 + [\$18,000 \times (1 - 0.30)]}{\$230,000 + \$150,000} \times 100$$

$$= \underline{12.5\% \text{ a year}}$$

Note that in estimating the return on assets or on permanent capital, we added the after-tax expense of interest to net profit. It is common practice to do so because assets are financed by both shareholders and creditors and the ratio should reflect the return to both. Had we not done so, these returns would have been understated. In arriving at net profit, interest on debt is subtracted as expense, but earnings on owners' equity are not. So, net profit should be adjusted upward to reflect its value as a return not only on the investment made by shareholders but also on the loans made by creditors.

Note also that the adjustment is made by multiplying the interest expense by the complement of the tax rate. This is done because interest expense is tax-deductible and thus partially offset by the effect of taxes. For example, if a venture's tax rate is 30 percent, every dollar of interest costs only 70 cents after taxes. See the example in Exhibit 13-2 for a detailed explanation of how the actual cost of interest is reduced by taxes.

RETURN ON SALES REVENUES

Also referred to as profit margin, return on sales revenues measures how efficiently entrepreneurs are managing their operations. It tells them how many

EXHIBIT 13-2

Example: Effect of Taxes on Interest Expense

	Without Interest	With Interest
Sales revenues	$300,000	$300,000
Operating expenses	240,000	240,000
Operating profit	$ 60,000	$ 60,000
Interest expense	0	20,000(c)
Profit before taxes	$ 60,000	$ 40,000
Income taxes (30%)	18,000(a)	12,000(d)
Net Profit	$ 42,000(b)	$ 28,000(e)

Note that interest expense of $20,000 (c) reduces net profit not by $20,000 but by only $14,000 (b − e). This venture pays $6,000 less in taxes (a − d) with interest expense than it does without interest. Thus, the effective cost of interest is only $14,000 (b − e) or simply [c × (1 − tax rate)] because of the effect of taxes.

cents are left over for each dollar of sales. To apply this yardstick, entrepreneurs should divide net profit by sales revenues, as follows:

$$\text{Return on Sales Revenues} = \frac{\text{Net Profit}}{\text{Sales Revenues}} \times 100$$

$$= \frac{\$35,000}{\$500,000} \times 100$$

$$= \underline{\underline{7.0\%}}$$

This yardstick enables entrepreneurs to compare their operating efficiency with that of other ventures in the same industry. Public figures are available for most industries so that entrepreneurs can rate themselves. If their return on sales is low, it means they are inefficient, an unhealthy sign that the venture needs attention.

As mentioned in Chapter Twelve, a common mistake is to consider return on sales the best measure of financial performance. However, return on investment holds the greater significance because it takes investment into account—the resources that are the foundation of both sales revenues and profits.

<table>
<tr><td>**ANOTHER LOOK AT
RETURN ON INVESTMENT**</td><td>Intuitively, we know that the more we make for each dollar of sales and the more sales we make for each dollar of investment, the greater will be our return on investment. These relationships may be expressed as follows:</td></tr>
</table>

$$\frac{\text{Net Profit}}{\text{Investment}} = \frac{\text{Net Profit}}{\text{Sales Revenues}} \times \frac{\text{Sales Revenues}}{\text{Investment}}$$

In short, this equation suggests that entrepreneurs may improve their return on investment in two ways:

☐ By improving the efficiency of their operations, resulting in more profit for each dollar of sales
☐ By making better use of their assets, resulting in more sales for each dollar of investment

INVENTORY TURNOVER

Inventory turnover measures how well entrepreneurs are managing their inventories. Whether inventories are large or small depends mostly on the kind of industry and the time of year. A fertilizer dealer, for example, with a large inventory in early spring is in a strong position to satisfy farmers. But that same inventory in the late fall spells trouble. One way to tell whether inventories are high or low is to relate inventory to cost of goods sold, as follows:

$$\text{Inventory Turnover} = \frac{\text{Cost of Goods Sold}}{\text{Inventory}}$$

$$= \frac{\$350,000}{\$80,000}$$

$$= \underline{\underline{4.4 \text{ times a year}}}$$

On the average, therefore, Micro Products is selling out its inventory 4.4 times a year. If their industry is seasonal, entrepreneurs should make sure they relate average inventory to cost of goods sold. To do so they should take the average of the beginning and ending inventories or even the average of monthly inventories, rather than simply the year-end inventory.

TESTS OF FINANCIAL HEALTH

So far, we have discussed only those yardsticks that measure how well entrepreneurs manage their operations and their assets. We shall now look at those yardsticks that measure how well they manage the finances of their venture, focusing on:

☐ Solvency
☐ Liquidity
☐ Customer credit

SOLVENCY

The term *solvency* refers to a venture's ability to repay long-term debts when due, including interest. Naturally, the more solvent a venture, the better protected its shareholders are from possible bankruptcy. To measure such protection, entrepreneurs should use such yardsticks as *debt ratio* and *times interest earned,* as follows:

$$\text{Debt Ratio} = \frac{\text{Total Liabilities}}{\text{Total Assets}} \times 100$$

$$= \frac{\$70,000 + \$150,000}{\$450,000} \times 100$$

$$= \underline{48.9\%}$$

Note that this yardstick simply measures the degree to which a venture's assets are financed by creditors. Generally, a debt ratio of less than 50 percent is considered favorable. A variation on this yardstick is to omit current assets and to relate just long-term debt to permanent capital, as follows:

$$\text{Debt Ratio} = \frac{\text{Long-Term Liabilities}}{\text{Owners' Equity} + \text{Long-Term Liabilities}} \times 100$$

$$= \frac{\$150,000}{\$230,000 + \$150,000} \times 100$$

$$= \underline{39.5\%}$$

Though widely used, these yardsticks do not, by themselves, measure financial soundness. To complete their analysis, entrepreneurs should also apply this yardstick:

$$\text{Times interest earned} = \frac{\text{Operating Profit before Interest}}{\text{Interest Expense}}$$

$$= \frac{\$68,000}{\$18,000}$$

$$= 3.8 \text{ times}$$

This yardstick measures how low profits may drop without straining a venture's ability to pay interest when due. Here, with operating profit exceeding interest 3.8 times, the venture seems financially sound, its shareholders amply protected against financial ruin.

LIQUIDITY

Another yardstick that measures exposure to debt is the *current ratio.* Estimated by relating current assets to current liabilities, this yardstick measures a venture's ability to pay short-term bills when due:

$$\text{Current Ratio} = \frac{\text{Current Assets}}{\text{Current Liabilities}}$$

$$= \frac{\$150,000}{\$70,000}$$

$$= 2.1 \text{ to } 1$$

The rule of thumb is that a current ratio of 2 to 1 is good, because it means that current assets could shrink 50 percent in value and still cover short-term bills. An even tougher test of liquidity is the *quick ratio,* which omits inventories, computed as follows:

$$\text{Quick Ratio} = \frac{\text{Cash} + \text{Accounts Receivable}}{\text{Current Liabilities}}$$

$$= \frac{\$20,000 + \$50,000}{\$70,000}$$

$$= 1 \text{ to } 1$$

This yardstick measures a venture's ability to pay short-term bills if a real crisis strikes, by assuming that inventories would be worthless. Generally, a quick ratio of 1 or better is considered good.

CUSTOMER CREDIT

Collection period is the yardstick that measures the degree to which a venture finances those customers who buy on credit. The entrepreneur should determine whether the actual amount of uncollected sales—or accounts receivable—closely matches the amount expected to stay uncollected, given the entrepreneur's credit terms. For example, if a venture gives its credit customers 30 days to pay up, it normally would expect to have only the last month's sales owed it.

To apply this yardstick, entrepreneurs should make two computations:

$$\text{Receivables Turnover} = \frac{\text{Credit Sales}}{\text{Accounts Receivable}}$$

$$= \frac{\$500,000}{\$50,000}$$

$$= \underline{\underline{10 \text{ times}}}$$

$$\text{Collection period} = \frac{\text{Days in the Year}}{\text{Receivables Turnover}}$$

$$= \frac{360}{10}$$

$$= \underline{\underline{36 \text{ days' sales owed}}}$$

In this example, the "36 days' sales owed" means that a venture carries its credit customers for 36 days, on the average. If its credit terms call for customers to pay up in 30 days, then a collection period of 36 days is considered good. The rule of thumb is that a collection period should not exceed $1\frac{1}{3}$ times the expected payment period.

EVALUATION OF INVESTMENT OPPORTUNITIES

So far, we have discussed how entrepreneurs should evaluate their financial performance, focusing on how best to spot problems. In this section, we shall discuss how entrepreneurs should evaluate investment *opportunities* such as these:

☐ Whether to lease or buy
☐ Whether to expand a plant
☐ Whether to make or buy a product
☐ Whether to add another retail outlet
☐ Whether to acquire another venture in order to diversify
☐ Whether to replace a machine with one that reduces operating costs

Each of these questions involves a choice that may make or break a venture, because the decision may commit the entrepreneur to a way of doing business that allows little opportunity for change.

Perhaps no other area is as critical to success as making the right investment decision. Let us now look at some yardsticks that would help entrepreneurs to measure their investment opportunities, among them:

☐ Cash payback
☐ Return on original investment
☐ Return on average investment

The most popular yardstick of investment worth is simple to understand and easy to apply. *Cash payback* may be defined as the time required for the cash produced by an investment to equal the cash required by the investment. An example will show how this yardstick works:

An entrepreneur owns a machine shop that makes many kinds of nuts and bolts. He carries a large inventory of steel stock as well as finished product. In an effort to cut costs, he is now mulling over an opportunity to buy a fork lift for $15,000 that may save him $5,000 cash a year in inventory-handling costs.

Should the entrepreneur buy the fork lift? To help answer that question, he estimates that it would take 3 years to recover his investment ($15,000 investment ÷ $5,000 savings per year). Whether this payback period is short enough depends upon his own criteria. He may, for example, have decided:

☐ To accept all investment opportunities with cash-payback periods of less than four years
☐ To reject all those with payback periods of four years or more

In this example, the entrepreneur decides to buy the fork lift.
■

As a yardstick of investment worth, cash-payback period has a serious flaw. It fails to take into account savings earned after the payback period. In other words, it ignores what happens after the fork lift has paid back the $15,000 investment. If the fork lift's useful life were just three years, then the return on the $15,000 investment would really be zero, and the entrepreneur would have made the wrong decision. If savings in the after-payback period are zero, then the investment is worthless no matter how short the cash-payback period may be.

To offset this drawback, entrepreneurs should measure the size and duration of cash return beyond the payback period. Another example will show how entrepreneurs might do that.

The entrepreneur must choose between two kinds of fork lifts, each of which has the same payback (see Exhibit 13-3).

Which fork lift should the entrepreneur buy? The two fork lifts would be equally desirable as investments if he looks only at payback. But it is clear from Exhibit 13-3 that the entrepreneur should choose Model A, because it not only recovers his cash investment of $20,000 but also promises to earn a return beyond the second year.
■

Cash payback has another flaw. It fails to take into account the fact that a dollar received today is worth more to the entrepreneur than a dollar received a year or more from now. Other investment opportunities may be available for today's dollar. If he has cash tied up for many years in a fork lift, the entrepreneur loses the opportunity to invest that money in more profitable ways.

EXAMPLE

The entrepreneur must again choose between two kinds of fork lifts, this time with the cash flows shown in Exhibit 13-4.

Which fork lift should the entrepreneur buy? Each fork lift pays back its initial investment in two years. And each one earns the same total cash savings of $30,000. Yet Model B is better than Model A because it promises to earn more savings earlier. In fact, with Model B the entrepreneur would have $5,000 more to reinvest at the end of the first year—a fact that the entrepreneur might neglect if he looks only at payback. As the saying goes, a bird in the hand is worth two in the bush.

■

RETURN ON INVESTMENT

Let us now look at another yardstick of investment worth. Called *return on investment* (ROI), this yardstick tells entrepreneurs how much they may earn yearly on each dollar invested, as discussed earlier in the chapter. ROI is a helpful guide because it enables entrepreneurs to compare their estimate of return with their cost of money.

EXHIBIT 13-3

Example: Payback on Fork Lifts

| | | Cash Savings | | | Cash |
Fork Lift	Cash Outlay	First Year	Second Year	Third Year	Payback Period
Model A	$20,000	$10,000	$10,000	$10,000	2 years
Model B	20,000	10,000	10,000	0	2

EXHIBIT 13-4

Example: Payback on Fork Lifts

| | | Cash Savings | | | Cash |
Fork Lift	Cash Outlay	First Year	Second Year	Third Year	Payback Period
Model A	$20,000	$10,000	$10,000	$10,000	2 years
Model B	20,000	15,000	5,000	10,000	2

An entrepreneur who owns a chain of frozen-custard stands is thinking about building another outlet. Her chain is now earning an ROI of 10 percent a year—each dollar of investment earns ten cents a year, after taxes.

Here, the 10 percent reflects the entrepreneur's cost of money, if we assume that is what she and her shareholders expect in the way of a return. Every dollar they take from the venture and apply toward another investment opportunity costs them ten cents of lost return, so any opportunity they consider must at least recover that ten cents for it to be worthwhile.

The entrepreneur is looking at two possible sites for the new frozen-custard stand. Both sites would require the same investment of $50,000. But sales revenues, expenses, and profits would differ (see Exhibit 13-5).

Which site should the entrepreneur choose? If her cost of money is 10 percent, she should choose Site A, because its ROI would be 20 percent a year:

$$ROI_A = \frac{\$10,000 \text{ a year}}{\$50,000} \times 100 = 20\% \text{ a year}$$

The entrepreneur should not choose Site B, because its ROI would be only 10 percent a year:

$$ROI_B = \frac{\$5,000 \text{ a year}}{\$50,000} \times 100 = 10\% \text{ a year}$$

Now let us assume that Sites A and B are in neighborhoods that do not overlap but instead are ten miles apart. In that case, the entrepreneur might consider building a frozen-custard stand at both sites, since Site B also promises to earn at least 10 percent a year. The reasoning here is that the entrepreneur should make as many investments as possible that promise to return at least 10 percent a year, which is her cost of money.

■

EXHIBIT 13-5

Example: Choosing a Site

| | Site | |
	A (yearly)	B (yearly)
Sales revenues	$110,000	$100,000
Operating expenses	90,000	90,000
Operating profit	$ 20,000	$ 10,000
Taxes	10,000	5,000
Net profit	$ 10,000	$ 5,000

Note that the entrepreneur estimated her ROI by relating net profit to original investment. Another widely used approach is to relate net profit to average investment. With this approach, the entrepreneur assumes that the frozen-custard stand would wear out gradually over its estimated useful life.

EXAMPLE

If expected to last 10 years, the $50,000 frozen-custard stand would depreciate at the rate of $5,000 a year. At the end of the tenth year, the investment would shrink to zero. Thus, the average investment outstanding would be $25,000 ($\frac{1}{2} \times$ $50,000). Note that the ROI at both sites would be much higher:

$$\text{ROI}_A = \frac{\$10,000 \text{ a year}}{\$25,000} \times 100$$

$$= 40\% \text{ a year (versus 20\% using original investment)}$$

$$\text{ROI}_B = \frac{\$5,000 \text{ a year}}{\$25,000} \times 100 = 20\% \text{ a year (versus 10\%)}$$

CONFLICTING RESULTS

So far, we have touched on three yardsticks for measuring investment worth:

☐ Cash payback
☐ Return on original investment
☐ Return on average investment

These three yardsticks give highly different results. In fact, one yardstick may give figures twice those given by another. An investment that shows a return of 10 percent on original investment may show as much as 20 percent on average investment.

To resolve such confusion, since the mid-1950s many large corporations have switched to a yardstick called *present value*. It is beyond the scope of this textbook to explain this yardstick in detail. However, it measures the true rate of return offered by an investment opportunity by taking into account the timing of cash returns and outlays over the entire useful life of an investment opportunity. The other yardsticks do not.[2]

ANOTHER APPLICATION

To reinforce our understanding of investment analysis, let us review still another example.

EXAMPLE

An entrepreneur who owns a laundry needs a new dryer. Two competing suppliers have submitted bids:

2. A good book on present value is Harold Bierman and Seymour Smidt, *The Capital Budgeting Decision* (New York: Macmillan, 1975).

☐ Dryer A requires a cash outlay of $10,000 and promises to return $12,000 the first year.

☐ Dryer B requires a cash outlay of $15,000 and promises to return $17,700 the first year.

Each dryer has a useful life of one year and the entrepreneur's cost of money is 10 percent. Which dryer should he buy? He would estimate the ROI as follows:

$$ROI_A = \frac{\$12,000 - \$10,000}{\$10,000} \times 100 = 20\% \text{ a year}$$

$$ROI_B = \frac{\$17,700 - \$15,000}{\$15,000} \times 100 = 18\% \text{ a year}$$

At first glance, it may seem to the entrepreneur that Dryer A is the better investment because its ROI is higher than Dryer B's. But if he takes a closer look, he will find that Dryer B is better. The $5,000 of extra cash required by Dryer B promises to return $700 more cash than Dryer A. And the ROI on that extra $5,000 is 14 percent:

$$ROI_{B-A} = \frac{[(\$17,700 - \$15,000)]_B - [(\$12,000 - \$10,000)]_A}{\$15,000_B - \$10,000_A} \times 100$$

$$= \frac{(\$2,700)_B - (\$2,000)_A}{\$5,000_{B-A}} \times 100$$

$$= \underline{\underline{14\% \text{ a year}}}$$

Because the 14 percent exceeds the entrepreneur's 10 percent cost of money, he would buy Dryer B.

■

The foregoing barely scratches the surface on how best to measure the worth of investment opportunities. It is a complex subject. We wish merely to stress the need for weighing carefully the desirability of an investment opportunity by use of the yardsticks mentioned.

In Chapters Four and Nine, we approached investment analysis from the viewpoint of entrepreneurs about to launch their venture. In this chapter, however, we have approached investment analysis from the viewpoint of entrepreneurs whose venture is established and growing. These viewpoints differ sharply. In this chapter, for example, we looked at bits and pieces of an expanding and changing investment puzzle. In Chapters Four and Nine, we looked at the whole investment puzzle with all the pieces already in place as designed by the entrepreneur.

.

COMPUTERS

Until the late 1970s, entrepreneurs largely ignored computers as a way to help them do a better job of planning and control. One deterrent was the high cost of computers. That situation has changed. With the invention of the microchip, a computer the size of a fingernail, the cost of computers has dropped dramatically.

As a result, both computer hardware and software are today well within the budgetary reach of many entrepreneurs. *Hardware* has to do with the computer equipment itself; *software,* with the written instructions that tell computers what to do.

As shown in Exhibit 13-6, the computer revolution has already begun to engulf small business. By 1990, experts predict there will be a computer on almost every entrepreneur's desk. They likely will be as common as typewriters. Presently, computers already enable entrepreneurs to do bookkeeping tasks such as these:

☐ Prepare income tax returns as well as financial statements on the basis of continuous records of revenues, costs, assets, liabilities, and so on
☐ Process customer orders and keep track of cash balances, accounts receivable, accounts payable, and inventory levels

JUST A BEGINNING

The foregoing is only a sampling of the uses to which entrepreneurs may put the computer, both now and in the years to come. Just how fast the computer revolution has moved, and still is moving, may be gleaned from this quotation:

> In 1950, a computer with the same capacity as a human brain would have had to be the size of New York City and would have used more power

EXHIBIT 13-6

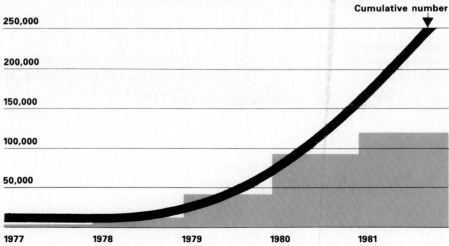

Estimated Number of Small Businesses Buying Computers

Source: Data General Corporation, *The Insider's Guide to Small Business Computers* (Westboro, Mass.: 1980), p. 2.

than the subway system. In 1980, that computer would be the size of a television set. By 1990, it will be smaller than a human brain and will run on a transistor radio battery.[3]

Few entrepreneurs can afford not to consider the use of a computer in their own venture. The computer's ability to do the old bookkeeping tasks more efficiently is undoubted. Much more important, however, is its ability to help entrepreneurs plan and control their venture more effectively. That means using the computer for tasks such as these:

☐ Managing projects such as plant expansion or introduction of a new product
☐ Analyzing financial statements, which we discussed earlier in the chapter
☐ Analyzing sales by product and by customer
☐ Scheduling production to minimize downtime
☐ Analyzing what-if situations, such as those posed in our discussion of the profitgraph in Chapter Twelve

Exhibit 13-7 summarizes some of the benefits of using a computer. Here is an example of how a computer helped an entrepreneur to plan and control his venture more effectively:

EXAMPLE

Donald Hoover is a partner in a painting contracting firm in Strasburg, Pennsylvania. His firm employs 20 persons. Mr. Hoover uses a computer to run the company's payroll, accounting, and job estimating operations.

Mr. Hoover says that their initial investment in the computer was about $3,000. "I do the programming with some help from a software consultant," says Mr. Hoover. His sales revenues have grown from $50,000 to $500,000 a year. "The computer is probably what has helped us gain a competitive edge in this business, as well as maintain our growth without additional overhead costs," asserts Mr. Hoover.[4]

■

SEEKING COMPUTER HELP

When entrepreneurs first consider using a computer, they often are in a puzzle about how best to go about it. Generally, three options are open to entrepreneurs:

☐ Service bureaus
☐ Time sharing
☐ Use of in-house computers

Service bureaus This option generally appeals to entrepreneurs who are about to use a computer for the first time. The computer is physically located at the service bureau, so that entrepreneurs must carry their raw data to the service

3. Adapted from Christopher Evans, *The Micro Millennium* (New York: Viking Press, 1979), p. 55.
4. Adapted from Jonathan Dover, "A Systematic Approach to Get On-Line," *Inc.*, September 1980, p. 90.

EXHIBIT 13-7

Some Benefits of Using a Small Business Computer

Applications	Reduce labor expense	Shorten billing cycle	Carry less inventory	Increase sales	Control costs	Manage cash	Plan and control growth
Accounts payable	●				●	●	●
Accounts receivable	●	●	●	●			●
Business modeling				●	●	●	●
General ledger	●			●	●		●
Inventory control	●	●	●	●	●	●	●
Order entry	●	●	●	●		●	●
Payroll	●				●		●
Word processing	●			●			

Source: Data General Corporation, *The Insider's Guide to Small Business Computers* (Westboro, Mass.: 1980), p. 8.

bureau for processing. Several days later, the service bureau returns the data to the entrepreneur. As a rule, entrepreneurs should seek out service bureaus that will:

☐ Do a feasibility study of the entrepreneur's need for computer help—mostly to identify and define problems and opportunities that lend themselves to solution by computer
☐ Help entrepreneurs tailor their collection of raw data in a form suitable for acceptance by the computer
☐ Train entrepreneurs and their employees in the smooth operation of their computer system, focusing on the timely and accurate collection of data

In essence, when entrepreneurs hire a service bureau, they are hiring the services of computer experts. As such, they are always available to help entrepreneurs run their system smoothly. A disadvantage, however, is that service bureaus focus mostly on bookkeeping tasks like payroll, not on tasks having to do with planning and control.

Time sharing This option generally appeals to the more sophisticated entrepreneur, mostly because time sharing enables the entrepreneur to make fuller use of the computer. Where service bureaus are largely limited to bookkeeping tasks, time sharing enables the entrepreneur to store mountains of data in the computer's memory, update the data continuously, and recall any of the data instantly. Among the sophisticated applications available to entrepreneurs are:

☐ Preparing a company history of financial information, focusing on income statements and balance sheets
☐ Preparing forecasts of sales revenues, operating expenses, and profits
☐ Computing such financial ratios as return on investment
☐ Tracking inventory, production, and quality control data

As with service bureaus, time sharing enables entrepreneurs to use a computer without having to buy or lease their own system. Time sharing does, however, require entrepreneurs to install a computer terminal in their office. A telephone line connects the terminal to an outside computer, thus enabling entrepreneurs to ''talk'' to their computer, or vice versa.

One disadvantage of time sharing is that it costs more than does a service bureau. A terminal, for example, requires entrepreneurs to install either a teleprinter or a keyboard and television-like screen called a *CRT* (cathode ray tube).

Customer service is an advantage that time sharing shares with service bureaus. Time-sharing companies generally help entrepreneurs to identify and define where a computer can best help them manage their venture more efficiently. These companies also help train entrepreneurs and their employees in the smooth use of a time-sharing system.

In-house computers This option generally appeals to the entrepreneur whose venture has grown to a size that may justify the leasing or purchase of an in-house computer. Generally, such entrepreneurs have already been exposed to computers, either through service bureaus or time sharing. Before leasing or buying a computer, however, entrepreneurs should first study:

☐ Precisely what their needs are and what they are projected to be
☐ At what costs these solutions would be justifiable

The better the study, the better the chances that entrepreneurs will have an in-house computer best able to serve their needs. They should expect their computer to do not only the routine bookkeeping tasks but also special tasks, especially in the areas of planning and control. As they master computer technology, entrepreneurs may also program their computer to do tasks tailor-made to their own needs, such as helping them to:

☐ Decide whether to add a new product
☐ Decide whether to expand their venture
☐ Decide which products to keep and which to drop
☐ Decide whether to lease or buy a piece of equipment

Whether to lease or buy a computer is a hard question to resolve. Most entrepreneurs lack the time or knowledge to get and sift the facts to make such a vital decision. *Inc. Magazine* offers entrepreneurs this advice:

A logical step might be to consult a systems house. Systems houses employ experts who are well-acquainted with hardware, software, and all aspects of servicing. There are also attorneys and law firms that deal exclusively with the growing area of computer law, particularly ensuring a tight client-vendor contract.[5]

The advantages and disadvantages of the three options open to entrepreneurs who are considering the computer are summarized in Exhibit 13-8.

Computers are now an unshakeable fact of life, first in big business and now in small business as well. As mentioned earlier, few entrepreneurs can afford to ignore this marvel of modern technology. It can help entrepreneurs in a variety of ways, from routine bookkeeping tasks to complex analyses. And with correctly prepared input data and programs, computers do not make mistakes.

SUMMARY

Analysis of their financial statements can help entrepreneurs make sound decisions, especially in the areas of planning and control. In their analysis, entrepreneurs should keep in mind that their main financial goal is to earn a satisfactory return on the money invested in a venture consistent with maintaining its financial health.

Ratio analysis is the technique used to analyze financial statements. Among the more important ratios are return on investment, return on sales, debt ratio, and current ratio. By themselves, ratios are meaningless, but when compared with some standard they can give entrepreneurs valuable insights into their performance.

Investment decisions involve choices that may make or break a venture. Such decisions often commit the entrepreneur's resources for years to come. So entrepreneurs must evaluate their investment opportunities wisely, using such yardsticks of investment worth as these:

EXHIBIT 13-8

Advantages and Disadvantages of Three Computer Options

	(1) Service Bureaus	(2) Time Sharing	(3) In-House Computers Leasing	(3) In-House Computers Purchase
Hardware costs	None	Some	Some	High
Software development costs	None	Some	High	High
Computer training needed	None	Some	Much	Much
Availability of applications	Poor	Fair	Good	Good
Privacy of records	Poor	Fair	Good	Good

5. Ibid., p. 110.

☐ Cash payback
☐ Return on original investment
☐ Return on average investment

Each of these yardsticks has its drawbacks, so it is vital that entrepreneurs be aware of them and adjust their decisions accordingly.

The computer revolution has overtaken small business. A remarkably versatile tool, the computer can help entrepreneurs not only with routine bookkeeping tasks but also with creative tasks such as deciding whether to acquire another venture or to add a product.

In selecting a computer, entrepreneurs generally have three options open to them:

☐ Service bureaus
☐ Time sharing
☐ In-house computers

DISCUSSION AND REVIEW QUESTIONS

1 How does analysis of financial statements help entrepreneurs to plan and control better?
2 What is the main financial goal of a venture? Why?
3 Can problems or opportunities be solved solely by the collection and analysis of numbers? Explain, using examples.
4 Define these terms: *ratio analysis, permanent capital, cash payback, cost of money, average investment, computer software, time sharing.*
5 Explain the three ways of estimating return on investment. Which way is best? Why?
6 If a venture makes a profit of $15,000, is its performance good or bad? Explain.
7 What are the best ways to measure the financial health of a venture? Explain fully.
8 Why is the *after*-tax cost of interest used in estimating the return on permanent capital or the return on total assets?
9 How do solvency and liquidity differ? Which one is more vital to a venture's financial health? Why?
10 Explain the pitfalls of cash payback as a way to measure the worth of an investment opportunity. How might you avoid these pitfalls?
11 What is meant by the saying, "A bird in the hand is worth two in the bush"?
12 Why would investment decisions be critical to you as an entrepreneur?
13 Besides routine bookkeeping tasks, what creative tasks can computers perform for the entrepreneur?
14 What advantages do service bureaus have over time sharing and in-house computers? Disadvantages?
15 How should entrepreneurs go about selecting a computer?

DAVID HALL COMPUTER CORPORATION

David Hall created his company in January 1973. By July 1974, he had not made a profit in any month. In an effort to finance his losses, he sought and received a $25,000 bank loan backed by the SBA. Mr. Hall then wondered how best to reach his market in the year's time that "the loan will carry me."

Why did Mr. Hall go into business for himself? "My father inspired me to do it," says Mr. Hall. "He struggled hard, working nights in a factory most of his life, often 12 hours a day. That's a tough way to earn a living. My father believed that working for somebody else was not the way to make it. So he urged me to think about going on my own. And I did just that." **BACKGROUND**

Mr. Hall began his venture at age 24 after he lost his job. He had been in charge of a computer department for a chemical company at a yearly salary of $14,000. The company let him go because it was about to fold up. Jobless, Mr. Hall looked at two options: either going to work for somebody else again or fulfilling his dream of creating his own venture.

Mr. Hall chose the latter. And for good reason. Overnight, a used $42,000 UNIVAC computer became available for just $13,000. Its original cost was $52,000. The story behind its availability tickles him to this day. It seems his old company had been leasing the computer from UNIVAC (a division of Sperry Rand, Inc.) for $19,000 a year. But when they decided to go out of business, the company found it could not break the lease, which still had more than a year to run. The lease, however, did give the company the option to buy the computer at a reduced price: $32,000 rather than its current market value of $42,000.

When Mr. Hall got wind of the problem, the idea popped into his mind that he could make a deal with his old company. He would offer to buy the computer for $13,000 if the company would *first* buy it from UNIVAC for $32,000. That way, both the company and Mr. Hall would benefit as follows:

☐ The company would save $5000[1] on its lease.
☐ Mr. Hall would own a $42,000 computer at a cost of just $13,000.

And it did work out to the benefit of both parties. But not before Mr. Hall overcame some obstacles. First, he had only $50 in his savings account. Second, his old company gave him just ten days to scrape together the $13,000. Third, his wife hated the idea.

---

1. Explanation of savings:
   (a) $24,000   still owed on lease payments
   (b) $32,000   to be paid for computer by the company
         13,000   to be paid the company by Mr. Hall
       $19,000   net cost of computer to the company
   (c) $ 5,000   savings to the company (a − b)

Clearly, Mr. Hall had some scrambling to do. And scramble he did. He knocked on the doors of virtually every bank in town. All marveled at the prospect of his purchase of a $42,000 UNIVAC computer for just $13,000. But would they lend him the money he needed?

At the time, Mr. Hall had only the foggiest idea about the kind of computer services he would create and market. "There simply was not enough time to think about such things," says Mr. Hall. "I had just *ten days.*" So he could hardly afford to spend his time preparing a business plan.

Besides, Mr. Hall had never heard of a business plan—not until he met his first banker, who turned him down for that reason. As he made the rounds, he found that not only bankers but also the SBA demanded a business plan before they would entertain a loan request.

Mr. Hall's relatives and friends had never heard of a business plan, either. So they agreed to:

☐ Lend Mr. Hall $12,500 at 6 percent interest
☐ Buy $1,000 worth of common stock when Mr. Hall incorporated his venture

"They sure had a lot of faith in me," says Mr. Hall.

Still $500 shy of the computer's purchase price of $13,000, Mr. Hall revisited the biggest bank in town—and deposited the entire $12,500 in his own name. In the next breath, he spoke to a loan officer, one of the bank's 90 vice-presidents. This time, the loan officer met him with only token resistance. And there was no talk about a business plan. In fact, Mr. Hall's determination to become an entrepreneur left the loan officer speechless. For in just eight days of whirlwind activity, Mr. Hall not only raised $12,500 but also hired a lawyer to incorporate the venture and came up with an idea about cutting the time it takes the state to pay physicians and dentists who serve welfare patients.

Meanwhile, his old company offered him use of the building that housed the abandoned computer if he would agree to keep the building in "good condition."

Impressed, the loan officer told Mr. Hall he would call an emergency meeting of the bank's loan committee. Mr. Hall had asked for $13,000. On top of the $12,500 loan from relatives and friends, that would give him $25,500 with which to begin the venture.

But time was running out. The ninth day passed with no word from the loan officer. Repeated telephone calls drew such responses as "I'm sorry, but Mr. Cline is in conference." "No, I don't know when the conference will be over. May I have him call you?"

As the tenth and last day unfolded, Mr. Hall decided not to wait for the loan officer to call. Instead, he drove to the bank, sat himself at the loan officer's desk, and awaited word. At 10 A.M. the loan officer walked in—with good news. The loan committee had approved Mr. Hall's request for a $13,000 loan, using as collateral the resale value of the computer.

An hour later, the bank deposited $13,000 in Mr. Hall's account. Now armed with a $25,500 checking account, he raced back to his old company with the happy news. They were astonished at his success. He closed the deal that

View of UNIVAC 9200 System

Source: Print courtesy of Sperry Univac, a Division of Sperry Corporation, and reproduced with permission of David Hall Computer Corporation.

very day, writing them a check for $13,000. Mr. Hall now owned a computer in search of a business. See Exhibit 13A-1 for a photograph of the computer.

Although the 10-day flurry of activity had left him breathless, he kept on running. In just 10 days more, he got word from his lawyer that the state had approved his request for incorporation. Mr. Hall's beginning balance sheet appears in Exhibit 13A-2.

Mr. Hall gave himself 60 shares of common stock booked at a par value of five dollars a share. Forty shares went to others. The state had authorized him to issue 250 shares, so he still had 150 shares of unissued stock. He planned to sell them later at $500 each.

Now on his own, Mr. Hall believed he had a lot going for him. After all, he had graduated from the International Data Processing Center with a certificate in computer programming. He had also taken every data-processing course offered at a local community college. And he had put this training to use as manager of a computer department with a chemical company.

DESIGNS COMPUTER SERVICE

Equally important, Mr. Hall found his niche in the marketplace. It would be in the design of a system enabling the state to pay, in *one* month, physicians and dentists who serve welfare patients. It then took 6 to 36 months.

Working alone, Mr. Hall designed such a system within seven months. But he soon realized that designing the system and marketing it are not the same thing. In fact, selling physicians and dentists on his idea would be all but

Balance Sheet (January 1, 1973)

Assets		Equities	
Cash	$10,500	Bank loan	$13,000
Supplies	500	Friends' loan	11,500
Computer	13,000	Owners' equity	1,000
Organization costs	1,000		
Prepaid expenses	500		
Total assets	$25,500	Total equities	$25,500

impossible without the state's approval. So he flew to the state capital, talked to the state Director of Public Welfare, and convincingly demonstrated his system's power to speed up payments. He did all that in just three months.

A month later, the state gave its approval. Mr. Hall now had his foot in the door of every dental and medical office. No doctor could now doubt his claim that "I am the only one in the state authorized to supply such a service."

And in a sense, Mr. Hall also added the state to his marketing staff—at no expense. For, on its own initiative, the state began to refer complaining doctors to Mr. Hall "if they want to get paid faster and if they want to get their records straight."

But Mr. Hall was hardly ready to exploit his opportunity. His business was still a one-man operation, so there was no one to mind the shop while he was out selling. It was not until six months after start-up that he hired a computer programmer, computer operator, and keypuncher to help out. Meanwhile, his operating expenses soared while his sales revenues continued to limp along.

MARKETING STRATEGY

Now backed by three new employees, Mr. Hall found time to map out a marketing strategy to persuade doctors to hire his service. This strategy consisted of three parts:

☐ A message emphasizing the idea that the doctor would be "buying an employee rather than a service." As such, Mr. Hall would take over *all* accounts, not just those of welfare patients. Depending on the size of the practice, the doctor would pay $100 to $1,000 a month for such a service.

☐ An approach that focused on clusters of doctors rather than individual doctors. This meant that Mr. Hall would direct his marketing efforts at clinics, laboratories, and hospitals where he could pick up as many as 10, 20, or more doctors at once. At the same time he would not rule out individual doctors with practices large enough to justify his servicing their accounts.

☐ Mailings to all doctors describing how they would benefit from Mr. Hall's service. See Exhibit 13A-3 for an example.

This strategy seemed sound to Mr. Hall. "My only problem was to make this baby go," says Mr. Hall. Indeed, the total market potential was enormous.

Dear Dr. Adams:

David Hall Computer Corporation is now in its second year of business, and is looking forward to many more years of serving customers. The following are a few of the services that are provided:

Billing

General ledger

Payroll processing

Accounts receivable

Mailing list preparation

Aid to dependent children

The corporation specializes in serving dental, medical, legal, accounting, and other professional organizations.

David Hall Computer Corporation is the only data processing organization with state approval to process your state welfare billing and enter it directly into the Welfare Department's computer system. Our services permit your office to be more organized, to maintain accurate, up-to-date information, and to receive faster processing from the state through quicker payment of your invoicing.

Thank you for your interest in David Hall Computer Corporation. Please contact us if you have any questions. We look forward to serving you.

Sincerely yours,

David C. Hall

In 1973 alone, the state paid doctors $400 million. "I know I can capture half of it," said Mr. Hall. "And when I do, it means I'll be doing $10 million a year in volume. I'm already thinking about expanding into neighboring states." Mr. Hall assumed his fees would average 5 percent of the doctors' fees. So ($400,000,000 × 50%) × 5% fee = $10,000,000.

It took Mr. Hall six months to land the 10 doctors whom he services. Meanwhile, he got another loan from his bank, this one for $25,000. Backed by the SBA, the loan helped him finance his losses and "gear up for the future." To do that, Mr. Hall expanded his staff to eight computer specialists, six of them working full time. Financial statements appear in Exhibits 13A-4 and 13A-5.

QUESTIONS

1 What were Mr. Hall's prospects for success? Explain.
2 Comment on how Mr. Hall financed his venture.

Income Statement (for six months ending July 1, 1974)

Sales revenues		$ 9,160
Cost of sales		320
Gross profit		$ 8,840
Expenses		
Employee	$12,990	
General	13,420	26,410
Operating loss		($17,570)

Breakdown of general expenses

Machine leases	$ 3,950
Rent	1,500
Automobile	1,310
Interest	1,240
Depreciation	1,080
Auto rental	730
Miscellaneous office	650
State unemployment tax	620
Telephone	490
Miscellaneous	480
Office supplies	370
Office maintenance	230
Postage	180
Personal property tax	170
Accounting and legal	160
Automobile insurance	140
Multipolicy insurance	120
Total	$13,420

Breakdown of employee expenses

Payroll	$11,700
Contract services	730
Hospital insurance	370
Life insurance	190
Total	$12,990

David Hall Computer Corporation

Balance Sheet (July 1, 1974)

Assets			Equities		
Current assets			Current liabilities		
Cash	$ 1,620		Accounts payable	$22,180	
Accounts receivable	11,730		Taxes payable	3,840	$26,020
Other	1,860	$15,210	Long-term loans		57,820
Fixed assets		10,400			
Other assets		4,800	Owners' equity		
			Common stock	$ 500	
			Deficit	(53,930)	(53,430)
Total assets		$30,410	Total equities		$30,410

3 If you were Mr. Hall, would you have pursued the same marketing strategy? If not, how would you change it? Why?

4 Comment on Mr. Hall's entrepreneurial traits.

5 If you were Mr. Hall, would you have been "thinking about expanding into neighboring states"? Explain.

CASE 13B   **PETE'S GARAGE**

Unincorporated, this garage operates as a gasoline station and repair shop. Its owner is Peter Bingham. In business for himself for 10 years, Mr. Bingham has always paid his bills promptly.

Most of his repair work comes from small truckers. He also overhauls school buses under contract with the local school district.

It is now September and Mr. Bingham would like to borrow $10,000 to buy antifreeze and tire chains. He believes his current customers will need these goods in the winter to come. He has always lacked the cash to stock such goods and he is still cash poor.

Mr. Bingham has never borrowed from a bank before. But he knew that his banker would ask for his latest financial statements. So Mr. Bingham had his accountant prepare the financial statements shown in Exhibit 13B-1.

When he sat down with his banker, Mr. Bingham told him he would earn a 35 percent gross profit on the sale of antifreeze and tire chains. He also promised to repay the $10,000 loan by February 1, for customers usually buy such goods during October, November, and December—and not later.

1 If you were the banker, what other information would you like before making a decision? Why?   **QUESTIONS**

2 Where would you get the additional information?

3 On the information given, does this loan look like a sound investment? Why?

Pete's Garage

Balance Sheet (August 31)

Assets		Equities	
Cash	$ 500	Accounts payable	$ 1,000
Accounts receivable	6,000	Owner's equity	36,000
Inventory	4,500		
Building and fixtures	26,000		
Total assets	$37,000	Total equities	$37,000

Pete's Garage

Income Statement (for year ending August 31)

Sales revenues		$100,000
Cost of sales		61,000
Gross profit		$ 39,000
Operating expenses		
Salary	$ 9,000	
Other	27,000	
		36,000
Operating profit		$ 3,000

CASE 13C **POLYCHEM SPARTAN INDUSTRIES (PSI)**

Nicholas Charles, founder of PSI, has just received from his accountant the financial statements appearing in condensed form in Exhibits 13C-1 and 13C-2. Mr. Charles has asked you to help him analyze these statements. To do so, calculate the following ratios:

☐ Return on assets
☐ Return on owners' equity
☐ Return on sales
☐ Asset turnover
☐ Days' receivables
☐ Inventory turnover
☐ Current ratio
☐ Quick ratio
☐ Times interest earned

What questions would you ask Mr. Charles, based on these ratios? **QUESTION**

Polychem Spartan Industries

1981 Income Statement

Sales revenues	$852,500
Cost of goods sold	667,600
Gross profit	$184,900
Selling and administrative expenses	144,200
Operating profit	$ 40,700
Interest expense	2,400
Profit before taxes	$ 38,300
Income tax expense	10,800
Net profit	$ 27,500

Polychem Spartan Industries

Balance Sheet (December 31, 1981)

Assets

Current assets
Cash	$ 82,700	
Accounts receivable	148,000	
Inventories	257,000	
Prepaid insurance	10,800	$498,500

Fixed assets
Manufacturing plant	$744,000	
Less: Accumulated depreciation	252,000	492,000
Total assets		$990,500

Equities

Current liabilities
Notes payable	$ 76,800	
Accounts payable	32,400	
Income taxes payable	6,000	$115,200

Owners' equity
Common stock	$804,000	
Retained earnings	71,300	875,300
Total equities		$990,500

CHAPTER FOURTEEN
MARKETING

questions for mastery

what is marketing?

how important is marketing research?

how should marketing research be carried
   out?

how do the various marketing activities fit
   together to form a marketing mix?

how can one take advantage of the
   opportunities available in export markets?

You can tell the ideals of a nation by
its advertisements.

Norman Douglas

The entrepreneur's main goal is to create satisfied customers at a profit. Marketing is one tool that helps do that by moving products or services out of the hands of the entrepreneur and into those of customers. A many-sided activity, marketing consists mostly of:

☐ Marketing research
☐ Advertising and sales promotion
☐ Personal selling
☐ Pricing
☐ Distribution and servicing
☐ Packaging

In this chapter, we shall focus on each of these marketing activities, paying special attention to marketing research and the preparation of marketing plans. The final section of the chapter will explore the special field of export marketing.

MARKETING RESEARCH

Many experts claim that marketing research is the most important marketing activity of all. Why? Because it helps satisfy the never-ending need for knowledge about markets, including:

☐ What products or services to sell
☐ Where to sell them, in what quantities, at what prices
☐ What competitors are selling, where they are, how strong they are

A venture's survival and growth depend largely on the quality of its marketing research. And it is just as vital after a venture begins as it is before. Yet marketing research tends to be ignored by entrepreneurs. To many, it is an activity that only giant corporations can afford. This belief is erroneous. Marketing research falls within reach of every entrepreneur, no matter how small. Defining, finding, and analyzing the facts about markets are activities any entrepreneur is capable of mastering. There are fancier definitions, but this one should suffice. To show what marketing research is like, let us go through an example:

EXAMPLE

One of the simplest fulltime ventures is the corner newsstand in big cities like New York. If the entrepreneur is doing a successful job selling newspapers and magazines, he is doing marketing research. Before telling his supplier how many newspapers he wants each day, the entrepreneur has settled some important marketing matters.

He knows how many newspapers he usually sells on each day of the week. So that is one fact he has on tap from his own experience.

But then our entrepreneur checks the weather each day and considers what effect it may have on the number of persons in town and in the mood to stop and buy a newspaper. This is a second fact that he uses in deciding how many papers to buy each day.

The two facts are not enough, though. Our entrepreneur next checks to see if there are any special events, conventions, or meetings that might bring additional customers by his corner. He might even go so far as to check to see what stores are having special sales. This is a third fact that he uses in his decision-making process.

Because our entrepreneur is really on his toes, he may check the early edition to see if there are any special news events that may add extra customer interest. And when his newspapers arrive, he may make a quick survey to see if there is any news item of special interest that he may be able to exploit for extra sales. So this is a fourth fact he has in his possession.

Our entrepreneur goes through this process before he tells the supplier how many papers he wants. This process is called marketing research—in short, getting all the facts available on:

☐ Customer interest
☐ Market potential
☐ Market mood
☐ Environmental conditions[1]

■

A MISTAKEN ATTITUDE

This example shows why marketing research falls within reach of every entrepreneur—and why it bears strongly on success. Chances are that most entrepreneurs do marketing research before beginning their venture. For example, decisions about where to locate their venture, what sales revenues to expect the first year, and how much money they need to finance their venture—all are usually based on facts, not opinions. After start-up, however, entrepreneurs often fail to get new facts, mistakenly assuming that their market will not change.

This attitude is dangerous. Unless they remain in tune with their markets, entrepreneurs may soon find themselves without customers. Today, buying habits change so fast that success belongs largely to those entrepreneurs who keep a close watch on their markets and, if necessary, quickly change their line of products or services to keep pace. For example, public taste has shifted away from the hot dog toward the gyro, the taco, and the pizza:

☐ The gyro, a Greek creation of lamb, tomato, and onion, has replaced the hot dog in many eastern cities.
☐ The taco, a Mexican concoction of ground meat and spices, has become a short-order favorite in the Southwest.

1. Adapted from U.S. Small Business Administration, *Marketing Research* (Washington, D.C.: U.S. Government Printing Office, 1968), p. 2.

☐ The pizza is now the most popular snack among 21- to 34-year-olds, according to the Gallup poll.

KINDS OF FACTS

So far, we have touched on the purposes of marketing research. Let us now examine the kinds of facts it can generate. Consider an entrepreneur who is about to make pocket calculators. With the help of marketing research, the entrepreneur can uncover many facts about the market by asking such questions as these:

☐ **Nature of product** What is the product like, both physically and chemically? How is it used? How is it made?
☐ **Nature of market** How big is the industry? What is the industry like? Where are customers concentrated?
☐ **Market size and outlook** How many can be sold yearly? How many have been sold yearly in the past five years? What factors affect the outlook for the market?
☐ **Pricing** How have prices changed over the past five years? What influences price? What will future prices be like?
☐ **Production** What product specifications should the production process meet? How should the product be packaged? What patent rights should be purchased?
☐ **Competition** Who are competitors? Where are they? What is their production capacity? What are their strengths and weaknesses? What is the outlook for capacity?
☐ **Marketing** Through what channels are products sold? Out of each marketing dollar, roughly how much is spent for advertising, sales promotion, personal selling, and servicing?

Although this set of questions applies specifically to manufacturing, much of it also applies to retailing, services, and wholesaling.

MORE RESEARCH QUESTIONS

The foregoing list of questions helps to expand our understanding of marketing research. To clinch our understanding, let us now explain it in another way. Again using pocket calculators as our example, we can see that marketing research helps entrepreneurs to answer such questions as these:

☐ Who is buying or will buy
   What pocket calculator in
      What quantities of
         What specifications at
            What price in
               What kind of package against
                  What competitors?
☐ What competitors are supplying pocket calculators with
   What capabilities at

What plant sites with
What capacities?
☐ What opportunities are there for us with
What calculators of
What quality at
What price under
What marketing conditions in
What quantities at
What future periods?

USES OF MARKETING RESEARCH

Marketing research replaces opinion with fact. Getting the facts helps offset the risks of doing business in today's fast-changing markets. All too often, however, entrepreneurs ignore facts they can readily obtain, facts that bear heavily on their success. Instead, they make decisions on the basis of opinion or impulse. Working without facts, entrepreneurs may decide to take such actions as these:

☐ Add a new product because their nearest competitor just did
☐ Draft a new plan to build revenues because they think it will work
☐ Add a new service because they hear that customers like it

Small wonder, then, that so many entrepreneurs fall by the wayside. They lose sight of the fact that their success begins and ends with the *customer*; their one key to success is to know better than competitors what attracts customers.

It is the entrepreneur's unique job to anticipate, adjust to, and capitalize on the sweeping changes that mark our times. In this regard, Professor Theodore Levitt of Harvard University has this to say:

An essential starting point is always to ask oneself: "What kind of society will we have in, say, five, ten, or twenty years? What does it mean for my company and its orientation?" Had the railroads asked themselves these germinal questions fifty years ago, they might now be making less frequent trips to Washington with tin cup in hand.[2]

SETTING REALISTIC GOALS

Entrepreneurs should be futurists, always looking ahead. And the more facts they have available, the better they can:

☐ Identify which markets are the most profitable to go after
☐ Identify soft spots in market coverage
☐ Choose new products or services that customers want
☐ Find out why existing products or services are selling well or poorly
☐ Set realistic market goals

Setting realistic market goals is the logical end product of marketing research. If they fail to set such goals, entrepreneurs are unlikely to know where

2. Theodore Levitt, *Innovation Marketing* (New York: McGraw-Hill, 1962), p. 120.

they stand and, equally important, in what direction they are moving, as in this example:

A tire dealer sold 10 percent more tires than he did the year before. "It's the best year I've had so far," he said. But what he did not realize was that his growth was not keeping up with the growth of his market area. The area's population had grown by 30 percent.

Even though his sales went up 10 percent, the tire dealer was not getting his share of the market. Instead, he was falling behind. But that fact had escaped him entirely.[3]

■

HOW MARKETING RESEARCH IS DONE

In giant corporations, the president may draw on many in-house resources for marketing research. Such corporations have marketing research departments staffed with high-powered professionals, many with a master's degree in business administration. Du Pont, for example, has more than 500 professionals in its marketing research department.

But few entrepreneurs can justify hiring a marketing researcher, let alone establishing a marketing research department. So how do entrepreneurs get the facts about their markets? They can get the facts by:

☐ Tapping information already available at public libraries and trade associations, Chambers of Commerce and the U.S. Department of Commerce, suppliers and the marketing research departments of local daily newspapers (see Exhibit 14-1 for an example of the kinds of information available).
☐ Buying the services of a marketing research firm
☐ Organizing a part-time marketing research effort within their own venture

Perhaps the best way to begin is by using statistical data already worked up by Chambers of Commerce, trade associations, and the U.S. Department of Commerce. Often available at no fee, such information yields the greatest return on the time and effort spent by the entrepreneur. For example, as already mentioned in Chapter Eight, entrepreneurs may use U.S. Census Bureau data to draw a profile of their market by estimating, for example:

☐ The percentage of persons in their marketing area who are under 10 years old, 10 to 19, 20 to 30, and so on
☐ The average yearly income per family
☐ The percentage of families who own their home
☐ The percentage of families who own automobiles

From such statistical data, entrepreneurs may draw all kinds of useful conclusions about their markets, as this example shows:

3. Adapted from Arthur W. Cornwell, U.S. Small Business Administration, "Sales Potential and Market Shares," *Small Marketers Aids* No. 112 (Washington, D.C.: U.S. Government Printing Office, 1972), p. 1.

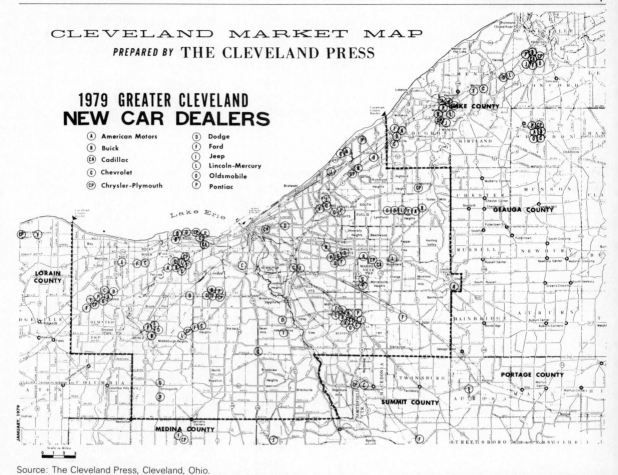

Source: The Cleveland Press, Cleveland, Ohio.

EXAMPLE

An entrepreneur who owned a supermarket could readily measure her market potential as follows:

20,000	Population of Dover (from U.S. Census Bureau)
× $5,000	Per capita income yearly (from U.S. Census Bureau)
$100,000,000	Gross income per year
× 0.15	Percentage spent on groceries (from trade association)
$ 15,000,000	Total market potential

The entrepreneur might then go one step further and estimate her share of market. Her yearly sales revenues are $3,000,000, so her share of market would then be 20 percent:

$$(\$3,000,000 \div \$15,000,000) \times 100 = 20\%$$

The entrepreneur might now carry her analysis another step further and compare her store's performance with that of other supermarkets in the area. There are three competing supermarkets. She computes that her competitors are averaging sales of $4,000,000 a year:

$$(\$15,000,000 - \$3,000,000) \div 3 = \$4,000,000$$

Clearly, our entrepreneur's work is cut out for her. Competitors are doing 33 percent better than she is:

$$[(\$4,000,000 - \$3,000,000) \div \$3,000,000] \times 100 = 33\%$$

Of course, such analysis does not explain why her performance falls short. But it does raise such pertinent questions as these:

☐ Why are competing supermarkets attracting more customers?
☐ What are they doing that I am not doing to attract customers?
☐ What changes should I make in advertising, sales promotion, and personal selling to boost sales?
☐ Am I offering the right mix of food products?

Answers to such questions may lead to further marketing research. Our entrepreneur may, for example, decide to do a consumer survey to find out:

☐ What homemakers in her marketing area want in a supermarket
☐ How they choose a supermarket
☐ Their general feelings about supermarkets

■

NEED FOR PROFESSIONAL HELP

If initial marketing research leads entrepreneurs to the decision to do a consumer survey, they might design and do the consumer survey themselves, with help from employees. But they would be wise to hire the services of a marketing researcher instead. Consumer research is not for beginners. It takes the skills of a professional to work up a questionnaire free of bias—the basic requirement for a survey.

Designing a questionnaire, for example, requires more than simply asking questions. Questions should be designed in ways that produce the most accurate replies. The very wording of a question may imply a bias and thus influence the reply.

Besides helping to draft bias-free questions, marketing researchers may also be helpful in designing the survey itself. In consumer surveys, for example, it would be impractical and costly to interview all homemakers. A better approach would be to select a representative sample of homemakers. Selecting a sample requires skill and ingenuity.

The Gallup poll uses a random sample of only 1,500 voters to learn the political preferences of a nation of more than 225,000,000 people. This sample is called *random* because every voter in the nation has the same chance of being chosen for the sample.

On a random basis, Gallup picks 300 sections of the nation and chooses 5 voters in each one. Then Gallup sends interviewers to poll them.

How accurate have Gallup's readings of the voters' likes and dislikes been? Remarkably accurate. Its national election polls have erred only 1.5 percent.

■

Sampling is not a job for amateurs. Entrepreneurs need professional help to make sure their sample is representative. Otherwise, the results will be misleading and worse than no research at all.

Although some aspects of marketing research, such as sampling, require some professional advice, entrepreneurs should do much of the research themselves. They might begin by keeping a file of marketing facts. Into it would go data from trade publications and articles from magazines and newspapers. Taken singly, these facts may seem trivial. But when filed and studied over the years, they can be a fertile source for marketing research. For example:

☐ *The Wall Street Journal* may carry information on marketing trends, alerting entrepreneurs to changes in customer needs and tastes in their market.
☐ The local newspaper may publish data on population shifts, alerting entrepreneurs to opportunities emerging outside their immediate marketing area.
☐ Trade publications may publish articles on highly successful ventures, alerting entrepreneurs to production, financial, or marketing methods they might try.

Exhibit 14-2 diagrams the approach to finding facts we have just described.

MARKETING MIX

We have been using the word *market* without defining it. There is no one best definition. Depending on how it is used, the word *market* may have many different meanings, for example:

People sometimes use it to refer to a specific location where products are bought and sold. A large geographic area also may be called a *market*. Sometimes it refers to the relationship between the demand and supply of a specific product or service. It has this meaning, for example, in the

EXHIBIT 14-2

General Approach to Finding Facts

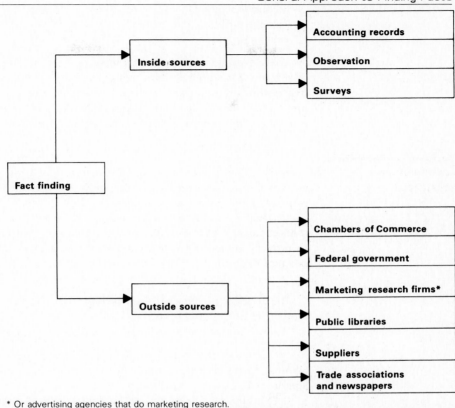

* Or advertising agencies that do marketing research.

question, "How is the *market* for diamonds?" At times, it also is used to mean the act of selling something.[4]

As used in this book, however, the word *market* refers to groups of individuals or organizations seeking products or services in the entrepreneur's industry. It is assumed that such groups also have the desire, the buying power, and the willingness to buy the entrepreneur's products.

**ELEMENTS OF A
MARKETING MIX**

After identifying and researching their market, entrepreneurs are ready to decide how best to create new customers and to keep those they already have. To the layperson, all that is needed is selling. But selling is merely the last step in a series of marketing steps, including:

4. William M. Pride and O. C. Ferrell, *Marketing: Basic Concepts and Decisions,* 2nd ed. (Boston: Houghton Mifflin, 1980), p. 140.

□ Distribution channels
□ Pricing
□ Advertising
□ Personal selling
□ Sales promotion
□ Packaging and servicing

For example, when a customer goes to a drugstore to buy toothpaste, this is the last step in the marketing process. The drugstore entrepreneur and the toothpaste manufacturer have already spent huge sums on the other steps just to convince customers to buy that particular brand of toothpaste at that drugstore. Let us now look at each marketing step.

DISTRIBUTION CHANNELS

What is a distribution channel? Every manufacturer, wholesaler, retailer, and service firm is part of a distribution network. The network's purpose is to move products from producers to users.

Distribution channels are controlled mostly by manufacturers. It is the manufacturer, not the retailer or the wholesaler, who usually decides how best to move products from the plant to the final user. No matter how good the product may be, the entrepreneur who produces a product or service may fail if:

□ The product reaches the user too late
□ Distribution costs are too high
□ The product is not distributed as widely as competing products

So, to market their products profitably, manufacturers should decide whether to sell directly to users or through middlemen such as manufacturers' agents, wholesalers, distributors, or retailers.

Exhibit 14-3 shows the various channels of distribution open to the entrepreneur. In the manufacturer-to-user channel, for example, the entrepreneur sells directly to the user and no middleman is involved. Manufacturers may use this channel when:

□ They sell from their plant
□ They sell through the mail
□ They have salespersons who sell door to door

Entrepreneurs often begin by selling their products through manufacturers' agents, because they cannot afford to hire fulltime salespersons. Only after they have grown can they justify hiring salespersons.

PRICING

Entrepreneurs and other businesspersons are more mysterious about pricing than about any other aspect of their business. Few reveal how they go about setting prices. In many cases, setting a price poses no problem—especially when the entrepreneur's product is identical to that of competitors. No rational customers will pay a higher price than they know is being charged elsewhere

EXHIBIT 14-3

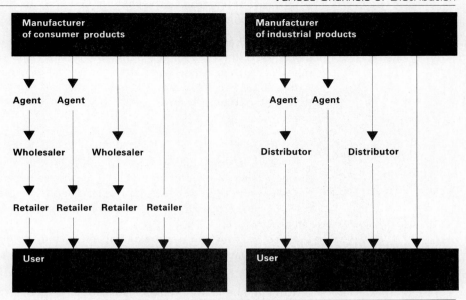

for a product they regard as identical. In such cases, all that the entrepreneur can do is follow competitors—and hope to keep costs within the price figure.

But in other cases, setting a price does pose a problem, especially to entrepreneurs with new products. Such entrepreneurs often charge what the market will bear—and so they should—for often it is the promise of high profits on their innovations that encourages them to risk money on research. This pricing practice is called *skimming.* It generally works well if:

☐ It is most likely that a high price will discourage few customers from buying the new product.
☐ The cost of developing the new product is high and the product may become obsolete in a short time.
☐ The entrepreneur's patent position on the product is strong.

High prices and high profits also tend to fire up competitors, who then may invade the market with innovative products of their own. Another pricing practice for new products is called *penetration pricing.* With this practice, the entrepreneur sets a low initial price in an effort to capture customers quickly. It generally works well if:

☐ Customers are more likely to be sensitive to the price of the new product. That means a lower price would boost total revenues to levels higher than they would be with a higher price.
☐ The low price is likely to discourage competitors from invading the market.

Both practices generally lead to the same profit picture in the long run. With either pricing practice, the entrepreneur's goal is to maximize profits:

☐ With skimming pricing, by charging a *high* price for low volume
☐ With penetration pricing, by charging a *low* price for high volume

Pricing mechanics How are prices computed? The entrepreneur generally needs more than the simple arithmetic of costs and profits to set prices. Yet many entrepreneurs seem to price on a cost-plus basis. This approach is a natural one, because entrepreneurs cannot survive unless they take in more than they pay out. So the easiest formula for the entrepreneur to use is this one:

$$\text{Price} = \text{Costs} + \text{Fair Profit}$$

But this simple formula cannot guarantee the entrepreneur a profit. Why? Because cost and profit estimates hinge on volume estimates—and volume hinges on the right price, among other things. For example, an entrepreneur with idle plant capacity and a growing market may temporarily cut prices to boost revenues.

To improve our understanding of pricing, let us look at some noncost questions that each innovative entrepreneur should answer before setting a price:

☐ How unique is my product? Is it different enough to command a premium price?
☐ How will distribution channels influence my price? What is the normal industry practice on discounts at each level of distribution? What is the industry practice on prices, credit terms, and volume discounts?
☐ How will competitors react to my price? Will they cut prices, improve old products, increase service?
☐ What market conditions will influence my price? What role do inflation, employment level, and federal tax policies play? What role do rate of technological change, excess capacity in the industry, and foreign suppliers play?
☐ Are there any legal restrictions that may influence my price?

Even psychology may enter into the pricing decision. We need only look at the reluctance of some firms many years ago to raise the price of a candy bar above five cents to see an example of psychological influences on pricing. For a long time, it was deemed wiser to reduce the size of the bar instead of raising the price. At some point, however, the psychological benefits of a stable price were outweighed by the psychological benefits of a larger candy bar and prices began to rise.[5]

Deciding upon a price for a new product is obviously a complex process. But for old products, the entrepreneur generally has no pricing decision to make. The entrepreneur need only decide whether to make and sell the product at its current market price.

5. John C. Lere, *Pricing Techniques for the Financial Executive* (New York: Wiley, 1974), p. 1.

Pricing for wholesalers and retailers Setting prices may pose a problem not only for innovative entrepreneurs who manufacture new products but also for wholesalers and retailers who sell established products. To be sure, many of the retailer's prices are set by competitors. On many products, though, retailers are free to set their own prices. How do they do it? They generally use a *markup* approach. Markup is simply the difference between selling and purchase cost:

$$\text{Markup} = \text{Selling Price} - \text{Purchase Cost}$$

For retailers, the overall markup of all products should be high enough not only to cover expenses but also to earn a profit. In practice, markup is expressed not in dollars but as a percentage of either selling or purchase cost. The simple formulas are:

$$\text{Markup percentage on retail price} = \frac{\$\,\text{Markup}}{\$\,\text{Retail Price}} \times 100$$

$$\text{Markup percentage on purchase cost} = \frac{\$\,\text{Markup}}{\$\,\text{Purchase Cost}} \times 100$$

Let us now go through an example to show how a retailer may apply markup percentages in order to set prices:

EXAMPLE

An entrepreneur runs a camera shop located in a suburban shopping center. In anticipation of the spring selling season, she has just purchased a line of cameras for $60 each. She would like to get a 40 percent markup on retail price.

At what price should she sell these cameras? The entrepreneur sets her price by using this simple formula:

$$\text{Retail Price} = \frac{\text{Purchase Cost}}{100\% - \%\ \text{Markup on Retail}} \times 100$$

$$= \frac{\$60}{100\% - 40\%} \times 100$$

$$= \underline{\$100}$$

So the entrepreneur would price her new line of cameras at $99.95 each (just below the $100 figure).

■

ADVERTISING

Entrepreneurs use advertising to communicate to customers about their product or service, focusing mostly on benefits to customers if they buy. Entrepreneurs may also try to convince customers that their product is superior to those of competitors. Their message may take any one of several forms:

☐ A two-column, 5-inch advertisement in a local newspaper, describing the product the entrepreneur is offering. The advertisement may also dramatize the ideas that surround the product—ideas that may lead customers to think well of the entrepreneur's venture; that make it clear that it is an honest venture to buy from; that build confidence in the venture's name among customers, suppliers, investors, and the press; and that publicize the venture's role in bettering the quality of life in the community.

☐ Multicolored posters splashed across storefronts heralding the specials of the day.

☐ Thirty-second spots on television or radio telling customers why they should buy a certain product.

☐ Large neon signs flashing above a building, inviting customers to stop in for a look at the latest products.

As a rule of thumb, advertising offers the cheapest way to get a message across. It can build revenues at a lower cost per sale than any other way. Few entrepreneurs can afford not to advertise. At the same time, few can afford to spend $400,000 for 60 seconds of prime time on national television. Entrepreneurs should make every advertising dollar count through careful planning. That means entrepreneurs should create advertising that:

☐ Communicates the desired message
☐ Reaches customers a sufficient number of times
☐ Sells the product
☐ Earns a return on the advertising dollars spent

These goals are easy to set down on paper. To measure progress against them, however, is extremely hard. Even giant corporations with million-dollar advertising budgets find it hard to measure how well their advertising message gets across. Still, it behooves entrepreneurs to keep these goals in mind when mapping their advertising campaign, striving always to deliver the right message to the right audience at the right time.

Many entrepreneurs, however, do not plan. For example, during a recession, some may drop advertising in the mistaken belief that it is an unnecessary cost. Or some may advertise only when a media salesperson drops in with an attractive deal. But astute entrepreneurs plan their advertising, mainly by the following methods:

☐ **Budgeting the advertising expenditures** Entrepreneurs should tie expenditures to goals. For example, an entrepreneur may be introducing a new line of products for the youth market. Her goal may be revenues of $100,000 for the first year. How much should she spend on advertising to reach that goal?

This decision should be made, however, only after two other questions have been answered: What should my advertising message be? What media should I use?

☐ **Preparing the advertising message** Before writing their message, entrepreneurs should examine their market, estimating its size, income, age, and so on. Only by getting the answers can entrepreneurs prepare messages that appeal directly to their audience.

Note that getting the answers is really doing marketing research. Without the facts, the advertising message is likely to misfire. While writing their advertising message, entrepreneurs should place themselves in the customer's shoes and ask:

☐ What is so unique about my product?

☐ What can it do for customers that competing products cannot? Will it save them money? Will it last longer? Is it of better quality?

☐ How can I convince prospective customers that my product is better?

Examples of attention-getting messages appear in Exhibit 14-4.

☐ **Selecting media** Because few entrepreneurs are advertising experts, it behooves them to work with an advertising agency. Agencies can be especially

EXHIBIT 14-4

Examples of Advertisements

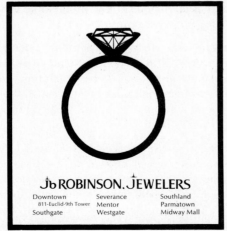

Sources: Top left, created by Carr Liggett Advertising, Inc., for Don's Lighthouse Inn. Top right, Marcia M. Polevoi. Left, Intercontinental Advertising.

helpful in mapping out advertising campaigns. They are also adept at preparing messages of professional quality, be they newspaper or magazine advertisements, radio or television commercials.

Advertising agencies are also qualified to recommend what media entrepreneurs should use to get their message across. Media account for about 90 percent of advertising costs. So entrepreneurs can ill afford to pick the wrong medium. Advertising agencies can help them to decide among such media as these:

☐ Radio or television
☐ Newspapers or magazines
☐ Handbills or direct mail
☐ Yellow Pages or outdoor signs

EXAMPLE

Several years ago, Cleveland homemaker Marion Landis had a problem—dirty windows. There was no product on the market that would make the grimy film on her windows disappear. She solved the problem in her laboratory—her kitchen—by inventing Mr. Glass, a nontoxic window cleaner that really works.

It works so well that Ms. Landis has set up her own firm, Ultra-Fine Products, Inc., to market the product. It is now sold nationally and has a national trademark. She credits much of her success to talk-show interviews on television. "Following one interview, people were lined up outside stores . . . waiting for them to open so they could buy Mr. Glass," she recalls.[6]

PERSONAL SELLING

This marketing step takes over where advertising leaves off. Advertising coaxes the customer to buy; it stimulates interest. But advertising rarely closes the sale. So entrepreneurs must also rely on personal selling—meeting customers face to face to help them make up their mind.

Interaction between advertising and personal selling Because their goal is to create loyal customers, entrepreneurs should strike the right balance between advertising and personal selling. To put it another way, entrepreneurs should decide how best to mesh their *push* strategy with their *pull* strategy. Take this example:

EXAMPLE

A customer is looking for a new, low-priced, two-door automobile. An advertisement in the local newspaper catches her eye. A dealer is offering a $200 rebate on the purchase of any automobile in a certain low-priced model. Her interest whetted, the customer decides to visit the dealer's showroom. That is *pull strategy,* because it was the dealer's advertisement that stimulated the customer to take a look.

6. "The Entrepreneurial Woman," *Cleveland Woman,* May 1981, pp. 38–39.

As the customer steps into the showroom, a salesperson offers to show her new models and to answer any questions. The salesperson reminds her that the $200 rebate is offered for a limited time only. So the customer had better act quickly. Two days later, she decides to buy—in part because the salesperson was knowledgeable, helpful, and courteous. That is *push strategy*.

■

Note how these two strategies reinforce each other. Without advertising, the customer might not have set foot in the dealer's showroom. And without personal selling, the dealer might not have sold the customer an automobile.

Finding the right salespersons Personal selling varies in importance by industry. In retailing, for example, personal selling is indispensable. It is the salespersons who give a store its personality; they help mold its image; and they help keep its customers from going elsewhere. That is why each salesperson's attitude should always be to satisfy the needs of customers. The true test of a good product is a satisfied customer.

To build a nucleus of loyal customers, entrepreneurs should find the right salespersons. One way to do that is to hire an employment agency that specializes in placing salespersons. But before going to such an agency, entrepreneurs should first decide:

☐ What the salespersons are expected to do
☐ What their salary and fringe benefits will be
☐ What their prospects for promotion are

In industries other than retailing, the requirements for salespersons vary widely. In manufacturing, for example, the salesperson is usually a highly educated expert in the field:

EXAMPLE

Sales engineers for a manufacturing company may sell lathes to machine shops. As technical experts, they may also train their customers' machinists on how to run and care for the lathes. And they may even help design lathes that better satisfy their customers' special needs.

■

Similarly, salespersons in wholesaling must be deeply knowledgeable about their products. Take this example:

EXAMPLE

Salespersons for a hardware supplier may sell to hardware retailers as many as 10,000 different items made by dozens of manufacturers. They must know all the items, their strengths and weaknesses, so that they can help satisfy customer needs. On top of that, they must keep their customers posted on supply and price trends. Besides closing sales, these salespersons must also:

☐ Answer complaints
☐ Keep daily records

☐ Prepare sales reports
☐ Help draft new sales-getting programs
■

As these examples illustrate, salespersons often qualify as managers. For it is they who manage the relations between a venture and its customers. Success or failure often depends on their performance.

SALES PROMOTION

Sales promotion makes both advertising and personal selling more effective. It may take many forms, such as:

☐ Contests to spur salespersons to sell more. Automobile dealers, for example, may offer their top salesperson a two-week, all-expenses-paid vacation in Hawaii.
☐ Special price discounts to introduce a new product. Discounts may also be used to sell slow-moving or obsolescent inventory.
☐ Free samples to introduce a new product. A cosmetics manufacturer, for example, may give away tubes of a new face lotion at shopping centers.
☐ Piggyback premiums to introduce a new product. In such a promotion, an unrelated item is attached to a product. A manufacturer, for example, may attach plastic flowers to a box of detergent.
☐ Exhibitions to build up a product's image. A manufacturer, for example, may buy a booth at a trade show in order to demonstrate a product to many potential customers.

Let us now see how one entrepreneur used sales promotion to solve a summer problem:

EXAMPLE

A clothier, Stuart and Burns, each summer offers customers $25 off on a new, tailor-made suit for each old suit the customer brings in. This promotion has worked so well that sales during the normally slack summer months of July and August almost match sales during May and June, traditionally peak months for the sale of suits.

The promotional flyer the clothier mails to customers appears in Exhibit 14-5. Note how persuasively the clothier gets the message across.
■

PACKAGING AND SERVICING

So far, we have discussed the five main marketing steps: distribution channels, pricing, advertising, personal selling, and sales promotion. Two other steps bear discussion:

☐ **Packaging** For some products, the package can be almost as important as its contents. An aerosol can of hair spray, for example, does a better job than a squeeze bottle of spray. In packaging their product, entrepreneurs should also consider:

EXHIBIT 14-5

Charity begins at home.

Retire your tired suits.

Clean out your closet of those — "I'll wear it when it rains" suits and get $25.00 off on a new suit or sport coat and slack combination for each old suit you bring in.

Your tired suit will be donated to a charity of your choice.

This charitable offer must end June 28th so don't wait for a rainy day to see our exciting summer and fall fabrics and fashions.

Stuart & Burns
Five Investment Plaza
1801 E. Ninth at Chester

Source: Stuart & Burns.

- ☐ Whether the package protects the product against damage under normal shipping conditions.
- ☐ Whether the package combines attractiveness with sales appeal. This question is especially important in such industries as cosmetics and perfumes, wines and jewelry.
- ☐ **Servicing** This marketing step deals with keeping customers satisfied. An appliance dealer, for example, may stock spare parts and repair appliances if they break down unexpectedly. Without such a service, the customer may become frustrated and never buy another appliance from the dealer.

Servicing is directed not only at products but also at customers. Some department stores, for example, now provide for the care of babies while mothers shop.

Servicing is indispensable in manufacturing industries. In fact, manufacturers often send their engineers to a customer's plant to help cure machine breakdowns or solve production bottlenecks. By doing so, the manufacturer keeps the customer satisfied and, at the same time, helps assure future orders.

PREPARING A MARKETING MIX

After learning what it takes to create customers, entrepreneurs are ready to prepare their marketing mix. Its ingredients, of course, are the marketing steps discussed above:

☐ Distribution channels
☐ Pricing
☐ Advertising
☐ Personal Selling
☐ Sales promotion
☐ Packaging and servicing

Because these steps—either singly or in combination—create customers, it is helpful to think of them as ingredients forming a marketing mix. It is up to the entrepreneur to mix the ingredients in amounts that will give the most for each marketing dollar. As one management consultant puts it:

(The entrepreneur), as the marketing man, is a kind of cook who is continually experimenting with new blends and new kinds of ingredients. He hopes ultimately to come out with the ideal combination that will produce the highest amount of sales at the lowest practical cost. In a sense, he is balancing a number of variables in which the contribution of each element to the total result is often extremely difficult to measure.[7]

Marketing mix varies widely from industry to industry. Even within an industry, marketing mix may vary among competitors. And it will also vary during the life of a venture:

EXAMPLE

Just before launching a men's shoe store, an entrepreneur places a three-column advertisement in the local newspaper heralding the store's opening. He also hires a model to pass out circulars in front of the store for three days before the opening. So his preopening marketing mix consists of advertising and sales promotion.

7. Harvey C. Krentzman, U.S. Small Business Administration, *Managing for Profits* (Washington, D.C.: U.S. Government Printing Office, 1968), p. 6.

But once the entrepreneur opens the store, advertising diminishes and personal selling becomes the main ingredient in his marketing mix. Generally, customers are unsure about the style and size of the shoes they want. A salesperson is needed to help customers make up their mind.

After peak selling seasons like Christmas and Easter, the entrepreneur offers discounts to sell old inventory. At these times, his marketing mix consists of personal selling as well as some advertising and sales promotion.

■

MARKETING IS AN ATTITUDE

The goal of marketing is to find a mix that creates satisfied customers at a profit. But often, entrepreneurs avoid deciding which ingredients are likely to work best. Why? Because they believe that the marketing mix is the exclusive province of sophisticated, billion-dollar corporations. Yet the principle of a marketing mix is simple. In fact, it may be easier to apply in small ventures than in large corporations.

After preparing their marketing mix, entrepreneurs should take pains to keep accurate records of marketing costs. Their records should enable them to compare, for example, each salesperson's salary with the revenues he or she generates, in order to single out those who are doing well and those who are not.

Because marketing is also largely an attitude toward goals and their achievement, it is vital that entrepreneurs keep their venture market-oriented at all times. Some entrepreneurs, for example, tend to take their existing markets for granted. That is a mistake. Although products may seem to remain unchanged from year to year, markets are in fact changing. It is a delusion to believe otherwise.

Entrepreneurs should also keep in mind that new products are the lifeblood of a vigorous venture. New products exploit changing markets, open new vistas, spark new investment, and charge a venture with excitement and vigor.

EXPORT MARKETING

Our discussion of marketing would be incomplete without touching on the vitality of export markets, although since 1955 the U.S. share of world export sales has dropped sharply. Such markets generally are overlooked or ignored by entrepreneurs. Yet foreign markets often offer a fertile source of sales opportunities. In fact, billions of dollars worth of products and services are exported yearly to virtually all 135 countries in the world. Of that total volume, less than 5 percent is accounted for by small business. The reasons that entrepreneurs tend to shun export markets are threefold.

☐ **Their fear of the unknown** Many entrepreneurs believe that their lack of knowledge about export markets is an insurmountable barrier. They reason that it is hard enough doing business locally where information about markets is at their finger tips, let alone trying to do business abroad where information may be much less accessible, if at all.

☐ **Their fear of long-distance relationships** Many entrepreneurs believe that any relationship with a foreign country would be too hard to control smoothly. Such entrepreneurs may be used to exercising on-the-spot control over markets locally. But in their view, foreign markets that may be thousands of miles away would be all but impossible to control. They often perceive any such relationship as unstable, untidy, and more than likely to unravel—with unhappiness all around.

☐ **Their fear of the complex** Many entrepreneurs believe that the very act of initiating a relationship abroad is too complex even to think about. Such entrepreneurs believe that it is beyond them to grasp the complexities of language, legal systems, and money matters that often differ sharply from those at home.

ABUNDANT HELP AVAILABLE

These fears are real, yet healthy. For no entrepreneur should ignore the risks involved in exporting. Yet such fears may quickly dissolve once entrepreneurs avail themselves of the professional help, much of it free, available within the federal government and Chambers of Commerce. For example, the first question asked by an entrepreneur who is considering foreign markets may be: How can I find out if there really is a market for my product or service abroad?

And thanks to the computer, answers to this question may take just minutes to get by tapping the information stored in a computerized file kept by the U.S. Bureau of International Commerce (BIC).[8] BIC, by the way, has information on more than 150,000 foreign importing organizations in 135 countries. Largely through its computerized file, BIC enables entrepreneurs to:

☐ Find agents or distributors in virtually every country of the world.

☐ Get up-to-the-minute direct sales leads and representation opportunities from overseas. Some business in Paris, for example, could be instantly spotted by an entrepreneur, say, in Denver.

☐ Get a detailed profile on an individual foreign company. A typical report, for example, would cover background information on the company, kind of organization, years in business, number of employees, size of company, sales area, method of operation, products handled, names of officers, general reputation in financial circles, and names of the company's trading connections.

OTHER FEDERAL SERVICES AVAILABLE

Besides these computerized services, BIC also offers the entrepreneur a host of personal services, among them:

☐ **Free counseling** In Washington, for example, BIC offers guidance, in-depth counseling, and scheduling of appointments with knowledgeable officials in

8. BIC is a division of the U.S. Department of Commerce.

other federal agencies. This is a one-step service designed to give the entrepreneur the most amount of information in the least time.

☐ **Publications** Thousands of government reports and booklets are available to entrepreneurs describing the sales opportunities available abroad. One example is a report that surveys the sales opportunities for suppliers of machine tools in Australia, Germany, Mexico, and Sweden. For each country, this report lists the major users of machine tools, along with other vital marketing information such as which machine tools are the most salable.

☐ **Promotional events** In 1980 alone, the U.S. Department of Commerce scheduled 170 promotional events, including trade fair exhibitions, international marketing shows, and trade missions to such fertile markets as the Republic of China. Each year, this federal department publishes a calendar listing each promotional event by product and by service.

☐ **Workshops** The U.S. Department of Commerce also conducts workshops throughout the country on export marketing. They also hold seminars and organize mini-courses on export marketing, generally in cooperation with local universities or community colleges.

The foregoing describes help available from the federal government. Equally helpful are local Chambers of Commerce. Many have special departments devoted to spurring and helping local businesses to sell their products abroad. Like the federal government, they organize trade missions, hold trade shows, and publish brochures on how best to expand into foreign markets.

Yet, despite the governmental and private help, many entrepreneurs fail to consider the sales opportunities available to them abroad. And if they do, they often ignore seeking professional help. A recent true story follows:

EXAMPLE

A U.S. company launched a frozen food venture in a major country in the Far East before it realized that most homes in the market area did not have freezers. Had the company first checked with the U.S. Department of Commerce, they probably never would have made so costly a mistake.[9]

■

PREPARING A MARKETING PLAN

To best serve a foreign market, entrepreneurs should prepare a separate marketing plan. Such a plan would rely heavily on marketing research already done by others, mostly by:

☐ The U.S. Department of Commerce
☐ Local Chambers of Commerce
☐ The foreign countries themselves

Only after collecting and analyzing all available information should entrepreneurs prepare their marketing plan. To do that well, entrepreneurs should follow a procedure much like this one:

9. Adapted from "Doing Business Abroad," *Boardroom Reports,* December 1, 1980, p. 6.

☐ Identify the most desirable market for their products or services
☐ Identify potential buyers within that market
☐ Prepare a proposal describing their products
☐ Develop terms of sale that would satisfy the foreign buyer while protecting the entrepreneur's best interests[10]

To prepare such a plan, entrepreneurs should seek the help of a lawyer versed in drafting international sales contracts. An experienced lawyer, for example, can help entrepreneurs describe what they have to offer in plain and concise language. For it is vital that the foreign buyer have a clear and precise idea of the entrepreneur's proposal. The lawyer can also help protect the entrepreneur's best interests when it comes time to negotiate a sales contract with the foreign buyer by determining what kind of legally enforceable contract will help the entrepreneur in his or her quest to maximize profit while minimizing risks in the foreign market.

SUMMARY

Selling often is equated with marketing, but selling is just one end of the marketing spectrum. At the other end is marketing research. In between fall such activities as pricing, distribution, advertising and sales promotion, packaging and servicing. Thus, marketing is a many-sided activity, involving all the steps entrepreneurs must take to get their product or service into the hands of customers.

Marketing research is perhaps the most important of these activities. Before preparing their marketing plan, entrepreneurs should first search out the facts about their markets, facts that help answer such questions as these:

☐ What products to sell, where, in what quantities, at what prices
☐ What competitors are selling, where they are, how strong they are

The answers to such questions provide entrepreneurs with solid information on which to build their marketing plan. It is these answers that suggest, for example, advertising in trade magazines as the best way to stimulate demand for a particular product. Without such direction, entrepreneurs are likely to miss their market.

To prepare their marketing plan, entrepreneurs should seek the help of such experts as advertising agencies and marketing research firms. Advertising agencies, for example, can help entrepreneurs prepare professional copy. Agencies can also help them choose the proper media for getting their advertising message across to customers. Marketing research firms can provide the expert help needed to design consumer surveys and to select representative samples.

10. D. Mark Baker and Glade F. Flake, U.S. Small Business Administration, "Negotiating International Sales Contracts," *Management Aid No. 247* (Washington, D.C.: U.S. Government Printing Office, 1979), p. 2.

Entrepreneurs should take pains to prepare their marketing plan in the form of a marketing mix. This means blending advertising, personal selling, and the other marketing activities into combinations that are likely to produce the highest amount of revenue at the lowest cost.

Export markets offer entrepreneurs a fertile source of sales opportunities. To capitalize on such opportunities, entrepreneurs should first seek help from the U.S. Department of Commerce or local Chambers of Commerce. Next, they should prepare a separate marketing plan for their foreign markets. It is also important that they seek help from a lawyer to make sure their best interests are protected when a sales contract is negotiated with a foreign buyer.

DISCUSSION AND REVIEW QUESTIONS

1 Why is marketing research one of the most important marketing activities? What questions does it help answer?
2 Describe the various ways that marketing research may be done.
3 Describe the steps needed to develop an advertising message that stimulates customer interest.
4 Define these terms: *marketing, random sampling, advertising, market, markup, servicing, BIC.*
5 Why is the marketing mix so vital to the success of a venture? How is it prepared?
6 How would you, as an entrepreneur, seek the facts before introducing a new product?
7 How do advertising and sales promotion differ? Give examples.
8 How do pull strategy and push strategy differ? How do they reinforce each other? Give two examples.
9 What kinds of professional help do entrepreneurs generally need to prepare their marketing plan? Explain fully.
10 Why is personal selling so critical to entrepreneurial success in most industries?
11 How do penetrating pricing and skimming pricing differ? Under what conditions would it better to use one rather than the other?
12 How would you, as an entrepreneur, go about exploring sales opportunities in foreign countries?
13 Do the words *selling* and *marketing* mean the same thing? Explain fully, giving an example.
14 A small manufacturer of outdoor, portable swimming pools has the problem of choosing his channel of distribution. What are his alternatives? Which alternative would you recommend he pursue? Why?
15 Compare a manufacturer's marketing mix for a product sold to other manufacturers with the mix for a product sold through retailers to consumers.

CASE 14A

In 1978, Alfred Brickel founded Newe Daisterre Glas (*new dawn glass* in Old English) to create stained-glass windows and other works of glass art. His fledgling company has already designed and built the world's biggest kaleidoscope, mostly out of glass. But sales revenues have failed to match Mr. Brickel's reputation for artistic excellence. In fact, he has laid off half his workforce, cutting it from eight to four employees. He is wondering what to do to build up demand for his unique service.

BACKGROUND

The son of a physician, Mr. Brickel qualifies as a dyed-in-the-wool entrepreneur. Although only 25 years old, he has worked on and off as an entrepreneur for 11 years. At 14, he set up his own landscaping business in the summer. Then at 16, bored with school, he left home for Bloomington, Indiana. There, he did odd jobs while earning his high school diploma.

Mr. Brickel's next stop was college, where the dean promptly expelled him for poor attendance and even poorer grades. After a brief stint clerking in a grocery store, he enrolled at another university to study art. This time he stayed four years, graduating with a bachelor of arts degree. In his junior year, he earned most of his living by painting houses on his own.

In his senior year, Mr. Brickel decided to go into the glass art business— by accident. As he sat in his parents' living room one December day, his eye caught a replica of a stained-glass window, used as a Christmas decoration. Its beauty fired his imagination. And that was the unlikely beginning of a hobby that led him three months later to set up his own business turning out works of glass art.

Still a senior at college, Mr. Brickel worked at his new venture part time and also moonlighted in a bar four hours a night. All told, he was putting in 90 hours a week studying and working. After graduation he gave up his job as a bartender to work full time at organizing his new venture and researching his market. His beginning balance sheet appears in Exhibit 14A-1.

Newe Daisterre Glas

EXHIBIT 14A-1

Balance Sheet (June 1, 1978)

Assets		Equities	
Cash	$ 500	Liabilities	$ 0
Supplies	400	Owner's equity	3,000
Equipment	1,200		
Organization costs	550		
Prepaid expenses	350		
Total assets	$3,000	Total equities	$3,000

Although he himself put up the entire $3,000 out of savings, Mr. Brickel took in Dale Mitchell as an equal partner. With the help of a lawyer, they drew up articles of copartnership which specified that:

☐ The two partners would share equally in the firm's profits.
☐ Mr. Brickel would oversee all design, production, purchasing, financial, and employee relations activities.
☐ Mr. Mitchell would oversee all marketing and public relations activities.

On the advice of his lawyer, Mr. Brickel also hired a certified public accountant (CPA) to design a simple bookkeeping system. "Every day I set aside time to make entries in my books," says Mr. Brickel. "Every three months the CPA picks them up to prepare an income statement and a balance sheet. He also does my tax returns for the city, county, state, and federal governments."

But Mr. Brickel finds such financial statements unhelpful. "My business is so small, I can easily keep on top of things," says Mr. Brickel. "There's little that goes on that I don't know about. I'm here day and night. Besides, my people and I are like a close-knit family. Each of us is interested in doing what's best for the others in the family."

From the start, Mr. Brickel's education stood him in good stead, especially in design. And what he did not know, he quickly picked up through trial and error and from a 77-year-old glasscutter. "There are only eight left in the whole country," says Mr. Brickel. "In the 1930s, there were more than 1,500. It's really a dying art."

Mr. Brickel's business is indeed unique. His creations range from a stained-glass jack of diamonds to a turn-of-the-century ticket booth, from individualized Christmas ornaments to custom-made fiberglass kayaks. He also does such unique things as slicing a beer bottle in half, glueing the bottom slice to the neck, and creating beer-bottle goblets for drinking. But his bread-and-butter trade comes from original stained-glass windows. Photographs of his creations appear in Exhibit 14A-2.

Perhaps his proudest creation is a kaleidoscope that may be the world's biggest. Ordered by a night club appropriately called The Kaleidoscope, it weighs 425 pounds and measures 12 feet in length and 3 feet in diameter. Mr. Brickel made it out of pulleys, rocks, glass, posters, and plywood. Today it sits unappreciated in his downtown studio waiting for a buyer with $3,000 to spare. He had to repossess it from the night club owner because "the guy couldn't pay."

Mr. Brickel's business is unique in other ways too. For example, he turns down repeat orders. "Everything I do is a one-of-a-kind handmade thing," says Mr. Brickel. "I don't like to repeat myself. I'm not a mass producer." Although in business to make a profit, he regards himself more as an artist than a businessman. He aims to bring back the esthetics of hand craftsmanship, an "ancient craft that some people think is dead." Clearly, he has no illusions about becoming the Tiffany's of the Midwest.

Examples of Glass Art and Equipment Used

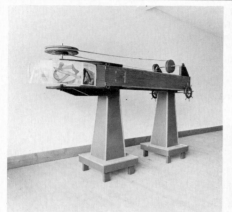

All of his four coworkers echo his business philosophy. For example, his vice president, Delbert Morrow, says: "The important thing is that we love what we do. We have ambitions only to the point of comfort, but we do get good money for what we do." Indeed, no item sells for less than $40, with most items selling at prices in excess of $200.

Unit prices may be high, but revenues have failed to take off. In May 1979, revenues peaked at $6,400. But by June 1980 monthly revenues had dropped off to half as much. This sharp drop forced Mr. Brickel to reduce his workforce from eight to four employees. "I hated to do it," says Mr. Brickel, "but I had no choice. There wasn't enough work for them."

All his coworkers exhibit an artistic bent. In fact, Mr. Brickel recruited them from classes he gives in glass art at his alma mater. None of them draws more than $100 a week in wages. And Mr. Brickel himself often draws less.

"It's a labor of love," says Mr. Brickel. "We could all be making much more working for some big outfit."

Mr. Brickel has looked for ways to boost revenues to levels that would enable him to rehire the artists he laid off. "I feel a responsibility toward them," says Mr. Brickel. "If I could drum up more sales, I could also increase their wages. Let's face it, $100 a week doesn't go very far these days." To boost revenues, Mr. Brickel has already taken these steps:

□ He replaced Mr. Mitchell with Mr. Morrow, whose main charge is to find new customers and, equally important, to come up with new product ideas. One idea he came up with was the manufacture of custom-built kayaks.
□ He incorporated his business. It had been a two-way partnership. The new company was capitalized at $500, the minimum allowable in the state. Mr. Brickel put up the entire $500 himself, getting in return 80 percent of the stock. He gave Mr. Morrow and another coworker each 10 percent of the new company. Mr. Brickel's reason for doing so was his belief that "one way to make the company grow is to have employees with a vested interest."
□ He installed a cost-accounting system to keep closer tabs on the cost of each job as it passes through production.
□ He applied for a three-year $5,000 loan from a local bank, telling them he needed the money to increase wages, promote the company and its products in a wider market, purchase more materials, and expand into new product lines.

Mr. Brickel was sure these steps would lead to "much higher revenues." His financial statements, dating from the time he incorporated his business to July 1980, appear in Exhibits 14A-3 and 14A-4. A photograph of his workshop appears in Exhibit 14A-5.

Newe Daisterre Glas, Inc.

EXHIBIT 14A-3

Balance Sheet (July 31, 1980)

Assets			Equities		
Current assets			**Current liabilities**		
Cash	$ 20		Accounts payable		$ 1,620
Accounts receivable	1,190		**Other liabilities**		
Inventory	1,980		Loan payable, officer		8,060
Work in process	2,120	$ 5,310			
Equipment and fixtures		8,500	**Owners' equity**		
			Common stock	$ 500	
			Retained earnings	3,630	4,130
Total assets		$13,810	Total equities		$13,810

Income Statement (for four months ending July 31, 1980)

Sales revenues		$9,570
Cost of sales		
Purchases	$2,980	
Less: ending inventory	1,970	
Materials used	$1,010	
Labor	3,230	
	$4,240	
Less: Work in process	2,120	2,120
Gross profit		$7,450
Operating expenses		
Rent	$1,820	
Utilities	500	
Automobile	390	
Insurance	330	
Office supplies	230	
Maintenance	230	
Advertising	120	
Legal and audit	80	
Travel	60	
Telephone	50	
Rubbish	10	3,820
Operating profit		$3,630

QUESTIONS

1 If you were Mr. Brickel, what would you do to boost sales revenues?
2 Comment on Mr. Brickel as an entrepreneur.
3 How well has Mr. Brickel done so far?
4 Comment on the way Mr. Brickel organized and financed his venture.
5 If you had the chance, would you invest in Mr. Brickel's venture? Why or why not?

View of Workshop

CASE 14B

MID-TEXAS HELICOPTER*

After retiring as an Air Force helicopter pilot, Eric Berke returned to his home town in mid-Texas to open a helicopter charter service in partnership with his wife. They spent two years researching the local market. As part of their fact finding, they talked to:

☐ Chambers of Commerce
☐ Major pipeline companies
☐ Oil-well suppliers
☐ Oil-well drillers

So favorably did they respond that the Berkes were convinced their new service would fill a need. Fortified by such knowledge, they then took these steps:

☐ Opened an account with a local bank
☐ Applied for credit with an oil company
☐ Established a line of credit with a major helicopter supplier

* Source: Adapted from a case prepared by the SBA.

The Berkes also rented a house, moved their family, and rented hangar and office space. In addition, Mr. Berke negotiated a rental contract for a four-seat helicopter.

Staffing posed no difficulty, for Mrs. Berke joined her husband as an equal partner in the venture. She would run the office, keep books, and help land new clients while Mr. Berke did the flying. But there was one nagging problem: they weren't sure what price to charge.

They knew that similar helicopter services in Dallas were charging $60 to $70 an hour. And yet, they weren't sure whether they could charge that much in their own area. However, they did have some information on fixed costs that could help them set a price:

☐ $1200 monthly rental on helicopter, including insurance
☐ $600 monthly rental for office and hangar
☐ $200 monthly advertising expenses
☐ $200 monthly office expenses

In addition, the Berkes found it would cost them:

☐ $8.40 per engine hour for aviation fuel
☐ $8.00 per engine hour for helicopter use
☐ $1.00 per engine hour for oil
☐ $.60 per engine hour for repairs

The Berkes also estimated that each would need to take out $600 a month to supplement their retirement income and maintain their standard of living.

During their fact finding, the Berkes learned that other operators kept their helicopters busy for about 60 percent of normal business hours, or about 120 hours a month. They already had promises of work that they believed would enable them to meet this average.

QUESTIONS

1 If we assume that the Berkes intend to add 10 percent of expenses for profit, what is the lowest price they should charge for each hour of helicopter service? What price should they *actually* charge? Why?
2 Prepare a profitgraph on the basis of at least two other prices than the one above (use graph paper). For each assumed price, when would the Berkes begin to make a profit?

CASE 14C   THE ITALIAN RESTAURANT*

The Italian Restaurant is owned and run by John and William Barboni, whose father and uncle began the restaurant in a medium-sized city in 1936. Their

---

* Source: William M. Pride and O. C. Ferrell, *Marketing: Basic Concepts and Decisions,* 2nd ed. (Boston: Houghton Mifflin, 1980), pp. 366–367. Used by permission.

business philosophy is to offer friendly service, good food, and drinks while keeping costs and prices as low as possible.

The products sold by the restaurant include sandwiches, complete meals, pizza, beer, and cocktails. The sandwiches include hamburgers, steak sandwiches on Italian bread, and bratwurst sandwiches. The product line of beer and liquor includes all premium brand beers and most hard liquors that can be purchased in an average tavern. The meal menu is dominated by steaks and chicken.

The restaurant's most glaring example of low price is the $6.00 charged for a choice T-bone steak, which includes tomato juice, salad, American or French fries, and bread and butter. Other representative prices include $2.50 for spaghetti and meatballs, $2.75 for a three-piece chicken dinner, and $3.00 for a twelve-inch pizza with sausage.

The advertising program of the restaurant is limited. A 2- by 2-inch advertisement appears every Saturday in the local newspaper; it features a picture of the owners and advertises the business as "The Original Italian Restaurant Where Friends Meet." John Barboni strongly believes that word-of-mouth recommendations are the best type of advertising for his restaurant.

Either John or William Barboni is usually at the restaurant from ten in the morning to one the next morning. The brothers, who are partners in the venture, try to get to know as many of their customers as possible. When familiar faces come through the front door, the brothers greet them with a friendly hello and usually take a few minutes to talk about sports or community activities.

One of the most unusual aspects of the Italian Restaurant is its clientele. It is hard to define its "average customer." When John Barboni was asked about this, he said: "Turn and look around." He pointed to a couple in the far corner and said they were retired. At another table were several teachers from a local high school. Two tables of laborers who had been working on a construction project were in the middle of the room. Also among the customers were bearded college students looking for companionship, as well as several local lawyers. John Barboni said that this particular crowd was typical.

THE RESTAURANT'S UNIQUENESS

The somewhat archaic interior of the restaurant creates a certain atmosphere. The exterior and interior of the building have changed little in the past 45 years. Many customers comment that the atmosphere reminds them of an old neighborhood tavern. Various sports symbols—pennants, pictures, and autographed bats—decorate the walls. Many sports enthusiasts frequent the restaurant, and conversation about baseball or the latest local sports events can often be heard. Although the atmosphere is relaxed, John Barboni believes that the furniture should not be *too* comfortable, or else people will stay too long.

John Barboni does not foresee any major change in the operation of his restaurant. He says that his son occasionally makes pizza at night and might someday take his place as one of the managers. Because the restaurant has survived and apparently been successful since 1936, the present philosophy of holding the line on costs while offering good food and friendly service will continue.

1 How does the atmosphere of the Italian Restaurant contribute to its many years of retailing success in one location?
2 If the Italian Restaurant moved to a modern facility in a local shopping mall, what do you think the volume of business would be? Would the same customers patronize the restaurant?

CHAPTER FIFTEEN

CREDIT AND COLLECTION

questions for mastery

what is credit?

what types of credit are there?

**what are the advantages and disadvantages
   of credit?**

**how important is it to age accounts
   receivable?**

what are collection procedures?

Words pay no debts.

William Shakespeare

This is the age of mass credit. Although mass marketing began about 75 years ago with department stores, mail-order houses, and chain stores, mass credit did not begin until 40 years ago. And it has grown dramatically since World War II. The short-term debts of individuals—personal loans, service credit, installment-purchase loans—soared from $8 billion in 1946 to $181 billion in 1980 (Exhibit 15-1 depicts the rapid rise).[1]

In most industries, entrepreneurs must give credit or lose customers. Although credit helps to create customers, it also creates risk. The risk, of course, is that customers may not pay. So it is vital that entrepreneurs understand how to give credit without risking failure. In this chapter, we shall give entrepreneurs the tools to understand and use credit to their advantage.

USES OF CREDIT

Today, consumers are bombarded with invitations to enjoy all manner of products and services right now and pay for them later. And most consumers accept freely, without feelings of guilt. No longer is it shameful to go into debt. In fact, the nation's prosperity depends on widespread use of charge accounts, mortgage loans, bank loans, credit cards, and other means by which customers get products before they can fully afford them. So deep is this dependence that any outbreak of resistance to credit would most likely afflict the nation with joblessness if not economic paralysis.

Credit is a way of life. To survive and grow, entrepreneurs should learn how best to give credit and, at the same time, how best to avoid nonpaying customers. If we look at each industry group, we find that credit supports:

☐ About 95 percent of all sales by manufacturers
☐ About 90 percent of all sales by wholesalers
☐ About 50 percent of all sales by retailers and by service firms

These high percentages mean that entrepreneurs will probably find themselves in the financing business as well. Whenever customers buy on credit, entrepreneurs are, in essence, advancing them the money to buy. To do so means that entrepreneurs must have large sums of money tied up in accounts receivable. Clearly, entrepreneurs should manage their use of credit carefully or they may find themselves in financial trouble, as did this entrepreneur:

EXAMPLE

Jack Woolson, owner of Woolson Filling Stations, developed a serious credit problem. Expanding from two to six stations in a three-month period, he personally hired all employees and trained them in the handling of credit.

Within another three months, he found a very large number of old accounts receivable that were uncollectible. It took Mr. Woolson's ac-

1. U.S. Department of Commerce, *Statistical Abstract of the United States* (Washington, D.C.: U.S. Government Printing Office, 1981), p. 461.

EXHIBIT 15-1

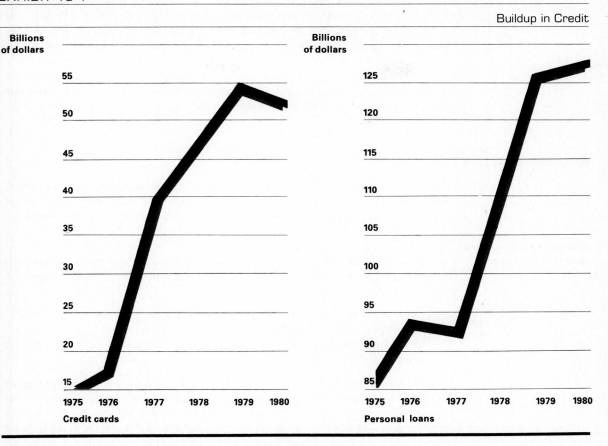

Billions of dollars

55
50
45
40
35
30
25
20
15

1975 1976 1977 1978 1979 1980

Credit cards

Billions of dollars

125
120
115
110
105
100
95
90
85

1975 1976 1977 1978 1979 1980

Personal loans

countant an additional two months to determine that two of the new station attendants, who worked evenings only, were granting credit to customers unauthorized to receive it. They had, in fact, given credit to customers on the firm's list of poor credit risks.

The firm's credit procedures called for having all credit sales checked at the home office every day. But because of the overload of work in the office, this important procedure had been bypassed and the resulting losses had occurred.

Mr. Woolson could have avoided his losses had he maintained the original procedures that worked so well. His lack of planning and poor credit discipline proved to be costly.[2]

■

2. Harvey C. Krentzman, U.S. Small Business Administration, *Managing for Profits* (Washington, D.C.: U.S. Government Printing Office, 1968), p. 106.

Entrepreneurs do have the right to charge their customers interest for financing their purchases. And many entrepreneurs do just that. In some industries the sale of credit brings in more profit than the sale of product. One example is the automobile industry: "According to *The Wall Street Journal,* more than half the dealers' average profit per new car comes from the financing charges."[3]

Credit is a source of profit that few entrepreneurs can afford to ignore. However, product should not be used as a tool for credit. Remember, the main purpose of credit is to help sell products, and not the other way around.

KINDS OF CREDIT

There are two kinds of credit. One is called *commercial credit,* which is credit that one entrepreneur may give to another. Equally important is *consumer credit,* which is credit that entrepreneurs may give to individual customers.

COMMERCIAL CREDIT

In retailing or services, entrepreneurs often can choose whether to sell for cash or credit. But they usually do not have that choice in wholesaling or manufacturing, mostly because of:

□ The buyer's desire to scan the delivered products before paying the seller
□ The buyer's need to have the purchase financed by the seller
□ The buyer's dependence on the seller to deliver the product to points distant from the seller's site

Entrepreneurs cannot be too careful in their credit decisions. Selling to the more stable industries such as the chemical industry rarely poses a credit problem. Corporations like Du Pont, for example, are almost as solid as the U.S. Treasury. But in many industries the reverse is true, especially in so-called fragmented industries, which are marked by ease of entry. Examples are housing construction and dress manufacture.

The key question How can entrepreneurs protect themselves from bad credit risks? How can they tell whether buyers will make good on their promise to pay? Naive entrepreneurs rely on blind trust. But astute entrepreneurs put their trust in the buyer's known credit reputation. The key question is: Will the buyer pay promptly?

To answer this question, it is wise for entrepreneurs to turn to credit-rating firms like Dun & Bradstreet for help. This well-known firm reports on how promptly businesses pay their bills. Their files have up-to-date credit ratings on over 3.5 million businesses. Here is what they have to say about credit:

Credit is based on confidence. Confidence in what? It is confidence in two things: Integrity, or willingness to pay, and ability. When we say a man is a good businessman, we generally mean he has been a good busi-

3. Quoted by Hillel Black, *Buy Now, Pay Later* (New York: William Morrow, 1961), p. 112.

nessman in the past. Our only guide, imperfect though it may be, to what a man is today, or what he may be in the future, is a study of his past. Hence, the painstaking, often time-consuming effort . . . to gather the facts concerning past business performance.[4]

Through a system of letters, numbers, and symbols, Dun & Bradstreet may give entrepreneurs such vital information as this:

☐ What kind of business the buyer is in and how it is managed
☐ The buyer's latest income statement and balance sheet
☐ An estimate of the buyer's financial strength
☐ A record of the buyer's promptness in paying bills

Sample credit report On the basis of this information, entrepreneurs may better judge whether the customer will pay promptly. A sample Dun & Bradstreet credit report appears in Exhibit 15-2. Note these features:

☐ The business has a credit rating of CC2, which means it has a financial strength of $75,000 to $125,000 and a good credit rating.
☐ The business pays its bills promptly, taking advantage of cash discounts.

In the Payments section, note such terms as *2-10-30.* This shorthand means that customers get a two percent discount by paying within 10 days. Customers who fail to take advantage of the discount must pay their bill within 30 days. Commonly used credit terms are explained in Exhibit 15-3.

The purpose of cash discounts is to persuade credit customers to pay their bills faster, thus reducing the entrepreneur's investment in accounts receivable. As borne out by Exhibit 15-4, credit customers also benefit substantially.

CONSUMER CREDIT

Especially vulnerable to financial loss are entrepreneurs who sell directly to individual customers on credit. To screen such customers, entrepreneurs should first settle two vital questions:

☐ How much credit can the customer safely absorb?
☐ Does the customer have a history of paying bills promptly?

To get the answers, a good place to begin is with the credit applicants themselves. Entrepreneurs should have them fill out a credit application. Next, entrepreneurs should get a credit report on each applicant from the local credit bureau. This report enables entrepreneurs to:

☐ Verify the information volunteered by the applicant
☐ Determine whether the applicant pays promptly

After comparing the application and the credit report, entrepreneurs can decide whether to give credit. What really counts is the promptness with which applicants pay their bills.

4. *Ten Keys to Basic Credits and Collections* (New York: Dun & Bradstreet, 1972), p. 11.

EXHIBIT 15-2

Estimated Financial Strength			Composite Credit Appraisal			
			High	Good	Fair	Limited
5A	Over	$50,000,000	1	2	3	4
4A	$10,000,000 to	50,000,000	1	2	3	4
3A	1,000,000 to	10,000,000	1	2	3	4
2A	750,000 to	1,000,000	1	2	3	4
1A	500,000 to	750,000	1	2	3	4
BA	300,000 to	500,000	1	2	3	4
BB	200,000 to	300,000	1	2	3	4
CB	125,000 to	200,000	1	2	3	4
CC	75,000 to	125,000	1	2	3	4
DC	50,000 to	75,000	1	2	3	4
DD	35,000 to	50,000	1	2	3	4
EE	20,000 to	35,000	1	2	3	4
FF	10,000 to	20,000	1	2	3	4
GG	5,000 to	10,000	1	2	3	4
HH	Up to	5,000	1	2	3	4

Credit bureaus have such information on virtually every person who at one time or another has bought on credit. Some idea of the size of the credit-checking industry may be gleaned from the following: The Associated Credit Bureaus of America, the largest trade association of its kind, has a membership that includes 2,200 credit bureaus, serving 400,000 businesses in 36,000 communities. The association also has 1,300 collection bureaus.

Let us end our discussion of credit by listing some of the advantages and disadvantages of giving credit to customers:

CREDIT ADVANTAGES

☐ Credit customers are likely to become repeat customers.
☐ Credit enables customers to buy products or services they might otherwise have to go without.
☐ Credit customers tend to overspend.
☐ Credit customers pay less attention to prices.
☐ Credit sales require less selling effort.
☐ Credit customers tend to buy products of higher quality.
☐ Credit is a convenience to customers who dislike carrying cash on their person.

CREDIT DISADVANTAGES

☐ Credit forces entrepreneurs to finance their customers, thus tying up money in accounts receivable.

EXHIBIT 15-2 (cont.)

1. Summary
Digests important facts detailed in the report: business name and address; chief executive; product and function; D&B Rating, reflecting estimated financial strength and composite credit appraisal; and the concise facts that back up that rating.

2. Payments
How a business pays its bills as reported by suppliers: millions of trade experiences, both computerized and manual.

3. Finance
Financial condition; trend of sales and profits.

4. Banking
Relations with bank, balances, loans, and amounts owing.

5. History
When business started; background of the principals, including specific dates.

6. Operations
What a business does; where it's located; premises.

(Reprinted by Permission of Dun & Bradstreet, a Company of The Dun & Bradstreet Corporation.)

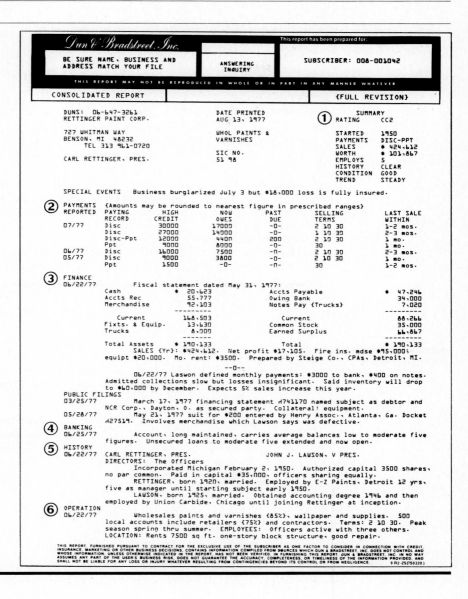

EXHIBIT 15-3

Terms	Meaning
2-10-30	2 percent discount for first 10 days; bill due net on day 30. Sales date coincides with date of shipment, not when sale is closed.
2-10-30 E.O.M.	2 percent discount for first 10 days, bill due net on day 30— but both days are counted from the *end* of the month in which the sales are made.
2-10-30 M.O.M.	2 percent discount for first 10 days, bill due net on day 30— but both days start from the fifteenth of the month *following* the sales date.
2-10-30 R.O.G.	2 percent discount for first 10 days, bill due net on day 30— but both periods start from the date of receipt of the product, not from the date of sale.
C.O.D. (Cash On Delivery)	Bill due upon delivery of product.
C.B.D. (Cash Before Delivery)	Product is prepared and packaged by seller, but shipment is not made until buyer pays in full.

EXHIBIT 15-4

If Entrepreneur Offers Credit Terms of	Then Credit Customers, by Taking Advantage of Cash Discounts, Can Earn an Annual Interest Rate* of
1-10-30	18%
2-10-30	36
3-10-30	54
1-10-60	7
2-10-60	14
3-10-60	22

*FORMULA: $I = \dfrac{D}{(G - D)(T \div 360)} \times 100$

where I = annual rate of interest earned by credit customer
D = amount of cash discount offered to credit customer
G = amount of bill owed the entrepreneur
T = the days' difference between the discount and net payment dates
360 = the number of days in a year (rounded)

☐ Credit refusal may cause ill will.

☐ Credit customers are more likely to abuse the privilege of returning products.

☐ Credit may cause entrepreneurs to borrow and repay with interest.

☐ Credit adds to the cost of doing business, because of investigations and because of the bookkeeping needed to keep records, bill customers, and collect payments.

COLLECTION POLICIES AND PROCEDURES

At one time or another, most entrepreneurs have some trouble collecting from credit customers. Slow or nonpaying customers can severely strain the entrepreneur's financial resources.

EXAMPLE

The owner of a women's dress shop makes a $100 sale on credit. Unless the customer pays, the entrepreneur may lose at least $70 and possibly more. Why? Because it cost her $70 to buy the dress from a wholesaler, and the $30 markup is designed to cover other expenses, such as rent, utilities, and the salaries of salespersons, as well as profit.

■

As the saying goes, a sale is not a sale until the customer pays in full. Otherwise it is a bad debt. Often, all it takes is a little prodding to get a customer to pay. But sometimes, entrepreneurs are saddled with bad debts that could have been avoided had they looked into their customers' credit history. Besides investigation, a good way to avoid bad debts is to design a collection system that:

☐ Traces accurately the history of each customer, until the account is closed

☐ Alerts the entrepreneur the moment a customer is past due

☐ Separates credit customers into three categories: current; past due; and suspended, meaning the customer's account has been turned over to a collection agency or to a lawyer

☐ Updates customer accounts daily, meaning that cash from customers is posted daily

☐ Protects account files from theft, fire, or destruction

These principles underlie all sound collection systems. Details will vary from venture to venture, especially regarding the use of forms and files, office machines and computers. It behooves entrepreneurs to follow these principles to the letter. They can ill afford to be lax. After all, uncollectible accounts erode profits, and in some cases may even cause failure.

AGING OF ACCOUNTS RECEIVABLE

Perhaps the backbone of any collection system is the analysis of accounts receivable—the amounts owed by customers. Entrepreneurs should prepare an aging schedule that enables them to measure the quality of their receivables.

Such a schedule helps entrepreneurs to spot overdue accounts that demand extra attention. An example of an aging schedule appears in Exhibit 15-5.

Note that the aging schedule works as a control device. It not only tells entrepreneurs the make-up of their receivables but also directs their attention to accounts that may be severely overdue. Aging schedules may be prepared for individual customers as well as commercial customers.

COLLECTION PROCEDURES

No matter how well designed a collection system may be, it is worthless unless it spurs action. Entrepreneurs should pursue each past-due customer promptly and doggedly. To be effective, follow-up procedures should move through a series of collection steps. And each step should be more pressing than the one before until customers have either paid their bills or been written off the books as bad debts. Generally, collection action should follow the sequence below:

☐ **Reminding the credit customer** As mentioned above, the entrepreneur's aging schedule should flag past-due customers who need a reminder. Reminders should normally go out after a grace period of 5 to 10 days following the day that payment fell due. The best reminder is warm and gentle. Why? Because so far, the failure to pay reflects neither unwillingness nor inability to pay. There could be any number of reasons why an account is past due. The customer may have overlooked the bill, for example. Or the customer may have been troubled by an emergency that delayed payment.

☐ **Seeking a response** This step should be taken only after the gentle reminder produces no response. Stronger in tone, the second reminder asks customers why they have not paid. There may still be some good reasons why delinquent customers have not yet paid. For one, the entrepreneur may have made a billing error. Or customers may be dissatisfied with the product they purchased. Or they may be temporarily short of cash.

☐ **Pressing for payment** If gentle persuasion fails, then entrepreneurs have no recourse but to press for payment. They have reminded delinquent custom-

---

EXHIBIT 15-5

Aging Schedule

Age	Amounts Owed by Customers (Receivables)
Not overdue	$ 6,800
01 to 30 days overdue	2,700
31 to 60 days overdue	600
61 to 90 days overdue	400
More than 90 days overdue	200
Total owed	$10,700

ers twice of their promise to pay. And these customers have twice failed to respond. So entrepreneurs must now assume that these customers do not intend to pay.

In pressing for payment, entrepreneurs have several avenues open to them. They may continue to write letters, each one more severe in tone. Or they may turn the account over to a collection agency or to a lawyer. Both are expert at coaxing past-due customers to pay their bills. Often, the mere threat to sue or to repossess a product gets results. Such recourse, however, invariably leads to unhappiness on both sides. And it reflects on both the entrepreneur and the customer:

☐ On the entrepreneur for misjudging the customer's willingness to pay
☐ On the customer for breaking the promise to pay promptly

☐ **Taking final action** When this step is reached, all else has failed. At this point, entrepreneurs have no choice but to write off the amount owed them. They now know it is unlikely that they will ever collect. The delinquent customer may have skipped town or disappeared to another address in the same city, leaving no forwarding address. Or the customer may simply be a deadbeat.

COLLECTION PERIOD

So far, discussion has focused on collection of individual past-due accounts. Another question that merits discussion is: How may entrepreneurs measure their total credit-and-collection performance? One yardstick is the collection period. Discussed earlier, in Chapter Thirteen, collection period tells entrepreneurs how many days' revenues are tied up in accounts receivable. In other words, how long does it take, on the average, to collect from credit customers?

EXAMPLE

A women's fashion shop rang up revenues of $900,000 in 1981. Of this amount, $730,000 reflects charge-account sales. The shop's year-end balance sheet shows accounts receivable of $100,000. What is its average collection period? It is computed as follows:

$$\text{Daily credit revenues} = \frac{\$730,000}{365 \text{ days}} = \$2,000 \text{ per day}$$

$$\text{Collection period} = \frac{\$100,000}{\$2,000 \text{ per day}} = 50 \text{ days}$$

How good a job of credit and collection is the shop doing? We cannot tell without also knowing its terms of sale. On net selling terms of 30 days, a collection period of 50 days might mean the shop is performing just below par. But, on net selling terms of 60 days, it would mean the shop is performing well.

■

Another way to measure credit-and-collection performance is for entrepreneurs to compare their collection period with that of others in the same industry. For many industries, such information is unavailable, although Dun & Bradstreet does compute the collection period for nearly a hundred industries.

Entrepreneurs should keep a sharp eye on credit customers. The older a bill becomes, the tougher it gets to collect, as shown graphically in Exhibit 15-6. And in extreme cases, the loose granting of credit may even lead to bankruptcy, as it did for this entrepreneur:

EXAMPLE

Robert Richards once owned a service station. Unlike many owners, Mr. Richards had planned his venture carefully. He and his wife had saved almost $24,000, and he had waited until he found what he considered an almost ideal site for a filling station. With eight years' experience as a mechanic behind him, Mr. Richards bought all new equipment for which he paid $16,000 in cash. With $8,000 left over for working capital, he was confident that he would succeed.

By all accounts, the business should have succeeded. Sales increased during every one of the 13 months that Mr. Richards was in business. Moreover, all his bills were paid, and he was getting the business into a position where he could have made "some good money real soon."

However, Mr. Richards's actual financial situation was far worse than the sales record indicated, because much of his capital was tied up in accounts receivable which he could not collect. Despite good intentions and a big "No Credit" sign at the door, Mr. Richards was soft hearted. As he put it: "See that sign? I mean what it says. You can't afford to get started in a credit business because you can never pinpoint the deadbeats.

EXHIBIT 15-6

Diminishing Returns on Slow-Paying Customers

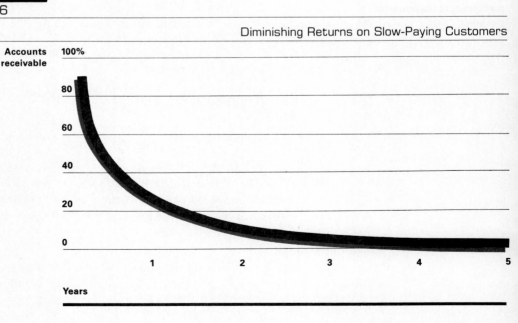

I don't want to extend credit to anyone, but the problem is to say so in a nice way. You know what I mean—so I won't lose their business."

Apparently, Mr. Richards never acquired that knack, for he lost over $8,000 in bad debts in less than a year. In desperation, he stopped giving credit altogether. But the result was that his revenues dropped almost to half. This drop so discouraged Mr. Richards that he sold the station for just $10,000.[5]

■

THE FUTURE ROLE OF CREDIT

Credit will continue to play a prominent role in the economy. Thanks to electronic wizardry, a checkless, cashless society may evolve by the year 2000. In such a society, money would transfer electronically, and the use of cash and checks would be largely unnecessary.

Credit cards are likely to play a vital role in this new era of instant money, forming the nucleus around which consumers would organize their financial dealings. In the future, for example, consumers could use their credit cards to:

☐ Get cash from commercial banks or from other businesses
☐ Charge purchases of products internationally as well as nationally
☐ Pay bills automatically
☐ Receive monthly financial statements profiling their complete family budget

From a technological viewpoint, such a system is more feasible than many entrepreneurs may realize. If there are delays in putting it into effect, they are due to social, not technological, problems. Still to be resolved, for example, are such questions as these:

☐ How should credit customers be identified? Some alternatives are by fingerprint or by voiceprint. Identification is perhaps the thorniest problem. There must be a way to make credit cards fail-safe so that their loss or theft does not result in electronic robbery.
☐ Who, and under what circumstances, should have access to a customer's credit file? The question of privacy is a major issue in the relatively simple process of determining who is eligible for credit and how much.

If it becomes a reality, the cashless society will probably handle money more cheaply, more quickly, and more efficiently. Already, many industries besides banking are studying the possibility of a cashless society and what it will mean to them. There are three reasons for believing that such a society may be just around the corner:

☐ Most of the electronic technology needed to make it possible is already available.

5. Adapted from Kurt B. Mayer and Sidney Goldstein, U.S. Small Business Administration, *The First Two Years: Problems of Small Firm Growth and Survival* (Washington, D.C.: U.S. Government Printing Office, 1961), pp. 128–129.

☐ In the years to come, the nation's financial system will need the cashless society to avoid being overcome by the sheer volume of paper.

☐ The federal government supports the idea of a cashless society because it suspects that some persons—from gamblers and racketeers to white-collar professionals and blue-collar moonlighters—receive payment in cash so that there is no record.

SUMMARY

Today, credit is a way of life. To survive and grow, entrepreneurs should learn how best to grant credit and, at the same time, avoid the problem of nonpaying customers. When they grant credit, entrepreneurs are advancing to customers the money they need to buy products or services.

There are two kinds of credit. One is commercial credit, which entrepreneurs grant to other ventures. The other is consumer credit, which entrepreneurs grant to individuals such as homemakers.

Because they are likely to have large sums of money tied up in accounts receivable, entrepreneurs cannot be too careful in screening credit applicants. For each applicant, they should find out whether the applicant has a history of paying bills promptly. Credit histories are available from local credit bureaus on individuals and from Dun & Bradstreet on businesses.

At one time or another, most entrepreneurs have some trouble collecting from credit customers. Slow or nonpaying customers can severely strain the entrepreneur's financial resources. Besides investigation, a good way to avoid bad debts is to design a collection system that alerts the entrepreneur the moment an account is past due. Entrepreneurs should pursue each past-due account promptly and doggedly; for the older a bill becomes, the tougher it gets to collect.

Credit will continue to play a prominent role in our economy. And chances are that a cashless society will evolve by the year 2000. This dramatic change will help solve the paperwork problems now plaguing the nation's financial system. It also will make it easier for customers and entrepreneurs to do business.

DISCUSSION AND REVIEW QUESTIONS

1 Explain why credit is so vital an activity in our economy.
2 Explain the difference between commercial credit and consumer credit.
3 How would you, as an entrepreneur, go about avoiding bad debts?
4 Define these terms: *credit, credit report, 2-10-30, past-due account, aging schedule, collection period, cashless society*.
5 Do you believe we soon will have a checkless, cashless society? Why?
6 How would you, as an entrepreneur, benefit from granting credit to customers?

7 What is the best measure of an entrepreneur's performance in credit-and-collection activities? Explain.

8 Explain why entrepreneurs who grant credit are also in the financing business.

9 Why do manufacturers make almost all their sales on credit?

10 Describe the steps an entrepreneur should take in collecting an overdue bill.

11 How does the aging schedule help to minimize bad debts?

12 If you owned a theater or a bowling alley, why might you be reluctant to grant credit?

13 Do you agree with the statement: "Credit is a source of profit"? Explain your answer fully.

14 If an entrepreneur has an average collection period of 28 days, is that good or bad? Explain fully.

15 At what point should entrepreneurs write off a past-due account as a bad debt?

Nolan Williams began his fabricating business in 1975. Six years and four expansions later, his business had expanded from a one-man operation to 40 employees. In 1981, sales revenues topped $1.3 million. He is wondering whether to reorganize his company for future growth—and if so, how?

BACKGROUND

A native of Texas, Mr. Williams came to Cleveland at age 18. At the time, becoming an entrepreneur was the furthest thing from his mind. He wanted only to get a job, any job. But he soon found that Cleveland employers wanted men with skills. And he possessed none.

Upon hearing from a friend that welding paid high wages, Mr. Williams enrolled in a 9-week welding course. He did well in the course. Soon afterward he got his first job, working in a metal-fabricating company as a welder. While there, he acquired a second skill: tool and die design.

After changing jobs several times—but always observing and learning—Mr. Williams decided to strike off on his own. He had been thinking about it for several years. He saw how others ran their metal-fabricating companies and he became convinced that he could do as well if not better. "I wanted to do something on my own," he says. "I knew I had the ability to get things done and the self-confidence that I could make it."

GETS HELP

Only three months passed from the moment Mr. Williams made his decision until he opened for business. He was 28 years old. The year was 1975.

But before he got underway, Mr. Williams talked to successful entrepreneurs like Julian Madison, one of Cleveland's best-known architects. Mr. Williams made mental notes of the advice he received. For example, he was told to form relationships with a banker, a lawyer, and an accountant, in that order. And he did.

Mr. Williams wasted little time assembling a management team. Together, they picked a plant site, ordered welding equipment, set up a bookkeeping system, raised cash, and moved in. His beginning balance sheet appears in Exhibit 15A-1.

Mr. Williams's corporate charter authorized him to issue 500 shares of stock at a par value of $10 each. He issued 100 shares to himself and 150 shares to others, leaving 250 shares unissued. Mr. Williams paid just $200 for his shares; the others paid nothing. It was Mr. Williams's way of paying them for their help in getting his business started.

Although he spent $3,000 for welding equipment and hand tools, he really needed "at least $25,000 to equip the plant properly to compete for customer orders." After struggling for three months, he received a $20,000 loan from the Central National Bank to finance purchase of additional equipment. Meanwhile, to survive, he had "borrowed two welding machines from another company, which had idle capacity."

American Steel Fabricating and Machinery Company, Inc.

Balance Sheet (July 1, 1975)

Assets			Equities		
Cash	$ 100		Loan payable		$3,000
Equipment	3,000		Owners' equity		
Organization costs	2,000		Williams	$1,000	
Prepaid expenses	400		Others	1,500	2,500
Total assets	$5,500		Total equities		$5,500

LONG HOURS

During the first year, Mr. Williams found himself working 14 hours a day, 7 days a week. "It was quite a change from my old job," says Mr. Williams. "My family rarely saw me. My business became my life."

He found that his lack of managerial experience was a real drawback. Until then, he had never tried to get things done through others. "I had never supervised anyone before," says Mr. Williams. "But I was in it, so I soon learned. In fact, I haven't stopped learning." What had pulled him through in the early years was his knowledge of shopwork and his "desire and determination to succeed."

One major mistake still bothers him. Early in the business, he formed an alliance with a friend. Their talents appeared to mesh. Mr. Williams's strong suit was production; the friend's was marketing. But soon after learning the business and moving up to a vice presidency, the friend resigned to form his own venture. Not wishing to have a competitor as a shareholder, Mr. Williams bought back his friend's shares of stock for $20,000. "That was my biggest mistake," says Mr. Williams. The friend had received his shares without paying a single penny for them.

FINANCIAL PERFORMANCE

Mr. Williams ended his first year—1976—with a loss of $5,000. Although he also lost money in succeeding years, in 1981 he turned the corner with before-tax profits of $170,000 on revenues of $1.3 million. His 1981 income statement appears in Exhibit 15A-2. Mr. Williams is proud of the statement, mainly because he still shoulders a heavy burden of debt. He borrowed heavily when he began. And he has continued to borrow, mostly to finance four expansions. So, he watches his "profit position closely—and more importantly, cash flow." A recent balance sheet appears in Exhibit 15A-3.

Mr. Williams continues to expand. This year he acquired 51 percent control of another steel-fabricating company in Solon, Ohio. And he is searching for still another company to buy into, one that makes rather than welds machinery.

Mr. Williams's lawyer was especially helpful in the Solon acquisition, as were his accountant and banker. The lawyer handled negotiations and the legal aspects of acquisition, the accountant audited the books of the seller, and the banker helped him finance the purchase.

Income Statement (for year ending July 31, 1981)

Gross sales revenues	$1,300,700	
Less: returns and discounts	71,600	$1,229,100
Cost of goods sold		856,800
Gross profit		$ 372,300
Operating expenses		
Office salaries	$ 84,300	
Taxes*	39,400	
Interest	17,900	
Insurance	14,300	
Freight	12,100	
Hospitalization	10,200	
Accounting	5,800	
Truck and auto	5,500	
Telephone and telegraph	4,900	
Selling	4,900	
Maintenance	4,100	
Office supplies	3,600	
Auto leasing	2,400	
Legal	1,200	
Depreciation	1,200	
Advertising	1,000	212,800
Operating profit		$ 159,500
Other income		11,400
Before tax profit		$ 170,900
Federal income taxes		0
Net profit		$ 170,900

* Includes city income tax, franchise tax, personal property tax, real estate tax, and other taxes.

To achieve growth, Mr. Williams has weathered some rugged competition. There are roughly 200 other metal-fabricating companies in Cleveland, 20 of which employ more than 100 persons. So, the industry is highly fragmented—a fact that he believes works to his advantage.

MARKETING STRATEGY

To wean customers away from competitors, Mr. Williams focuses on big business. In fact, his clients read like a *Who's Who* in manufacturing: Xerox, Westinghouse, General Motors, Cummins Engine, Warner and Swasey, Otis Elevator, Harris-Intertype, and Thompson-Ramo-Wooldridge.

To snare new customers, he uses a marketing mix made up almost solely of personal selling. Neither advertising nor sales promotion plays a role. Instead, he calls on purchasing agents himself—but only after determining whether they need his services. "I always do my homework before I pay them a visit," says Mr. Williams. "And it has paid off."

American Steel Fabricating and Machinery Company, Inc.

Balance Sheet (July 31, 1981)

Assets			Equities		
Current assets			**Current liabilities**		
Cash	$ 55,600		Accounts payable	$140,300	
Accounts receivable	144,700		Notes payable	54,800	
Notes receivable	2,600		Accrued taxes	22,900	
Raw material inventory	55,700		Other	6,300	$224,300
Work in process	67,400		Long-term loans		135,900
Prepaid expenses	21,500	$347,500	Deferred federal taxes		6,500
Fixed assets			**Owners' equity**		
Plant and equipment	$267,300		Common stock	$ 17,900	
Accumulated depreciation	79,600	187,700	Paid-in capital	7,200	
Other assets		4,900	Retained earnings	148,300	173,400
Total assets		$540,100	Total equities		$540,100

Only one salesman helps Mr. Williams. The salesman's job is to retain existing customers, while Mr. Williams's is to land new customers. Customer complaints are handled by Mr. Williams alone.

Mr. Williams is sensitive to complaints of any kind. He personally answers each one the day it is received. "We sell quality and service," says Mr. Williams, "so we can't afford to fall short." To help ensure quality, he employs only skilled welders who qualify as craftsmen.

This philosophy affects his entire organization. For example, his foremen have a combined work experience of 45 years, his accountant is a Certified Public Accountant, and his layout person is a graduate mechanical engineer. His organizational chart appears in Exhibit 15A-4.

Mr. Williams enjoys a rapport with employees that is rare in metal-fabricating circles. So good are his relations with employees that none of them belongs to a union. Recently, the Teamsters Union tried to organize all plant workers. But the workers turned the union away.

PRODUCTION CAPABILITY

Mr. Williams's Cleveland plant is equipped to deliver the full range of welding services demanded by his clients. "We sell our capabilities to do a job," says Mr. Williams. "That's what customers look for." The plant covers 50,000 square feet, which is roughly the size of a football field. When he first went into business, his plant covered just 1,000 square feet. A photograph of the plant appears in Exhibit 15A-5.

The plant houses such equipment as welding machines, brake presses that bend steel, a shear to cut steel, a burning machine to cut steel patterns, and a punch press. There is no inventory problem because Mr. Williams runs a job shop, meaning work starts only after a customer orders it. And he never produces in anticipation of orders. His backlog of orders averages three months. "I begin to worry when it gets down to one month," says Mr. Williams.

Organizational Chart, July 1, 1981

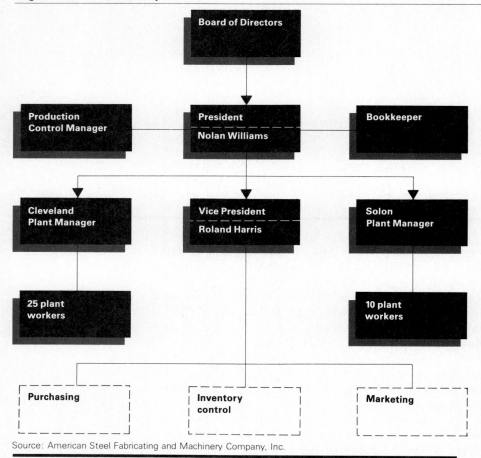

Source: American Steel Fabricating and Machinery Company, Inc.

"My door is always open to employees," says Mr. Williams. "If they have a problem, they're free to come in and discuss it with me." Indeed, his turnover among welders and fitters is so low it excites envy among competitors. But among laborers, turnover is high.

Besides being fair and open with employees, Mr. Williams also looks after them. For example, he offers such fringe benefits as Blue Cross and Blue Shield. And he will soon introduce life insurance at low group rates.

As for himself, Mr. Williams avoids estate planning of any kind. He does not even have a will. "My lawyer is after me about that," says Mr. Williams, "but I'm too young to think about it seriously." Nor has he groomed anyone to take over if he should suddenly become physically incapable of running the business.

Currently, Mr. Williams is spending much of his time merging his Solon

View of Cleveland Plant

acquisition into the company. "We've had lots of problems out there," says Mr. Williams, "problems we never found out about until after we bought 51 percent control." He is also considering how best to reach his sales goal of $10 million a year by 1987. In 1981, his revenues stood at $1.3 million. "That's an ambitious goal," says Mr. Williams.

QUESTIONS

1 What accounts for Mr. Williams's success?
2 Comment on Mr. Williams's entrepreneurial traits.
3 Do you believe it was wise for Mr. Williams to acquire a second plant? Explain.
4 Comment on Mr. Williams's relations with his workers.
5 If you were Mr. Williams, would you, too, have gone deeply into debt to achieve your sales goals? Explain.

CASE 15B

CHARLANE'S FASHIONS, INC.*

An entrepreneur owned a pair of small but highly profitable stores specializing in women's wear. For years she had placed orders only for her normal needs,

* Source: Case adapted from Sol Barzman, *Everyday Credit Checking*, by permission of Thomas Y. Crowell Company, Inc., publisher.

usually in the $500 to $1,000 range. She bought most goods from the top ready-to-wear manufacturers in New York, always without difficulty. Her credit reputation was excellent, for she paid her bills on time; never made unauthorized returns; and always behaved, from the suppliers' point of view, in a most exemplary way.

She had started from scratch. So it was with some pride that she went over her latest financial statements (see Exhibit 15B-1). She had indeed come a long way in the five years she had been in business for herself.

Heady with success, she decided to open nine new stores the next year, without investing additional money. She planned instead to rely solely upon the good will of her current suppliers to finance her expansion, and to act as references for her new suppliers.

She kept her suppliers, new and old, in the dark about her ambitious plan to expand. She was sure suppliers would never suspect that she planned to add as many as nine stores in *one* year.

Her credit rating was excellent so she aroused little suspicion when, the following spring season, she flew to New York and began placing orders larger than previously. By June 20, she had placed more than 200 orders with suppliers, totaling more than $230,000. And most of these orders were placed with new suppliers.

The day of reckoning soon arrived. On August 8, she called a meeting of her creditors, to report that her company was in troubled financial straits (see Exhibit 15B-2).

Charlane's Fashions, Inc.

EXHIBIT 15B-1

Balance Sheet (July 31, 1980)

Assets		Equities	
Current assets	$41,000	Current liabilities	$ 5,100
Fixed assets	4,300	Owners' equity	40,200
Total assets	$45,300	Total equities	$45,300

Charlane's Fashions, Inc.

Income Statement (for six months ending July 31, 1980)

Sales revenues	$100,500
Operating expenses	89,300
Operating profit	$ 11,200
Federal income tax	2,400
Net profit	$ 8,800

Balance Sheet (July 31, 1981)

Assets			Equities			
Current assets			Current liabilities			
Cash	$ 900		Accounts payable	$503,100		
Inventory	314,400	$315,300	Payroll tax	23,300		
Fixed assets		5,500	Bank loan	3,800	$530,200	
			Owners' equity		(209,400)	
Total assets		$320,800	Total equities		$320,800	

Less than a month later, the referee's office in the Central District of California judged her to be bankrupt. The new stores she had managed to open went down the drain along with her original two.

1 What really caused the entrepreneur's bankruptcy? If you had been the entrepreneur, what would you have done differently? Why?
2 Could the entrepreneur's creditors have prevented their losses? If so, how?
3 What was the company's operating loss in the past year?
4 What should the entrepreneur do now? Why?

CASE 15C

BINGHAM ELECTRICAL PARTS, INC.

Norton Bingham owned an electrical parts and supplies store in Los Angeles. Modestly successful over the years, Mr. Bingham sold his electrical products on credit terms of 2-10-30.

In 1980, Mr. Bingham's sales revenues were $480,000. On December 31, 1980, his accounts receivable were $60,000.

According to Dun & Bradstreet, collection periods for the electrical parts and supplies industry vary as follows:

Range	Collection Period
Top Fourth	38 days
Median	47
Bottom Fourth	60

QUESTIONS

1 On the average how long does it take Mr. Bingham to collect from his customers?
2 How good is Mr. Bingham at managing his credit-and-collection activities?

CHAPTER SIXTEEN

HUMAN RELATIONS

questions for mastery

what is human relations?

how important is group management?

what are the needs of workers and how can one satisfy those needs?

why are wage and salary policies important?

how important are safety and health on the job?

After all, there is but one race—
humanity.

George Moore

F ar from being a mysterious science, human relations is often nothing more than good will and applied common sense. Much of an entrepreneur's success in human relations depends on simple things, such as making a store a friendlier place to work in or making a plant more comfortable.

Entrepreneurs often ignore these simple things, especially when their venture begins to grow. When they start their venture, entrepreneurs often have only themselves and perhaps a few employees to manage. A strong sense of purpose binds owner and employees together. But the addition of new workers tends to loosen that bond unless entrepreneurs pay attention to so-called people problems. In this chapter, we shall discuss such problems by focusing on the responsibilities of entrepreneurs to recognize the needs of their workers and to manage their workers in ways that help bring out their best.

THE IMPORTANCE OF HUMAN RELATIONS

So massive are many businesses today that workers lose all sense of human contact with their employers. In many manufacturing industries, for example, the high degree of mechanization robs workers of their sense of personal pride and often their self-identification with the product they help make. Many workers do not even know how customers use the product. And the robotlike nature of much of their work thwarts their sense of self-respect. In the words of Fyodor Dostoyevsky, the famed Russian author:

> If it were desired to reduce a man to nothingness, it would be necessary only to give his work a character of uselessness.[1]

A character of uselessness is often imposed on much of the work done in plants, stores, and offices. Many workers feel they have been swallowed by a big impersonal machine that robs them of their self-respect and identity. Out of this betrayal of the human spirit, the science of human relations was born to find ways to give workers a sense of usefulness and thus improve their performance on the job. One of the tenets of human relations is that life can be made more enjoyable by making work more meaningful.

Often, however, entrepreneurs lose sight of the importance of meaningful work in their rush to boost revenues. Such entrepreneurs soon find themselves saddled with workers who do poorly. Why? Because they are unhappy. The entrepreneur can buy:

☐ A worker's time
☐ A worker's physical presence at a given place
☐ A measured number of skilled muscular motions per hour

But the entrepreneur can*not* buy:

☐ The worker's enthusiasm

1. Fyodor Dostoyevsky, *The House of the Dead* (London: William Heineman, 1915), p. 20.

☐ The worker's initiative or idea-getting ability
☐ The worker's loyalty

Entrepreneurs must earn these valuable contributions from their employees. They can do so by recognizing that workers need to feel that the work they do really matters, that the entrepreneur is interested in them and appreciates what they do. Workers generally do better, for example, when they are singled out for individual attention. The recognition makes them feel they no longer are nameless cogs. In return for their loyalty and enthusiasm, workers expect entrepreneurs to:

☐ Protect their right to work continuously, as long as they perform honestly and productively
☐ Give them a chance to advance as the venture grows
☐ Treat them as human beings, with dignity and respect

Entrepreneurs should keep in mind that every worker, regardless of abilities, has the right to be treated with respect and dignity. In fact, entrepreneurs have a moral obligation to grant their workers that right.

GROUP MANAGEMENT

One way for entrepreneurs to instill a strong sense of purpose in workers is to share decision making with them. The practice of shared decision making is called *participative* or *group management*. Its message is this:

☐ Entrepreneurs should recognize the social needs of workers as well as their need for money.
☐ Workers will respond with better performance and will help shape the venture's changing goals.

In essence, group management encourages entrepreneurs to seek out their workers' ideas and, in addition, to organize work around jobs broad enough to have meaning. Group management also encourages entrepreneurs to:

☐ Share decision making with workers
☐ Share authority and responsibility with workers
☐ Communicate openly and candidly—up, down, and sideways within the venture

This approach, however, may not work well with all employees. In fact, studies show that happy workers are sometimes merely happy—and not productive. Some workers, for example, can take only limited responsibility. They prefer to let others shoulder the main burden of responsibility.

So entrepreneurs should exercise care in unlocking the talents and energies of their workers. Group management is not for every venture. But there is an impressive body of evidence to suggest that it works well, especially among ventures that are struggling to keep pace with shifting markets or are growing at a fast pace.

Group management may not be for every entrepreneur, however. An entrepreneur with an authoritative style may find it hard to adapt to the expectations of a participative approach. How may entrepreneurs determine whether their managerial style is authoritarian or participative? One way is to use the chart in Exhibit 16-1, developed by Dr. Rensis Likert at the Institute of Social Relations of the University of Michigan.

Although the idea of group management has been known for decades, only recently has it made some headway in the United States. Entrepreneurs here still tend to be more authoritarian than democratic. The Japanese, on the other hand, use group management almost exclusively.

EXAMPLE

Troubled by increasing costs and the three to six months' time that it took to ship zippers from Japan to the United Kingdom, Y.K.K. in 1969 invested $3.5 million in a British plant. The gamble . . . has been a mighty success. The plant has never been hit by a strike or a slowdown. There is basically no difference in performance between British workers and those in Japan.

Inside the plant, pop music throbs from loudspeakers while a multi-national collection of American, West German, British, and Japanese machines turn out 6,000,000 zippers a month . . . . All men employees wear Y.K.K.'s jackets, which have the company initials proudly displayed on the breast pocket and no fewer than six zippers on the front, the pockets, and the cuffs.

Japanese-style corporate paternalism is strong. Y.K.K. provides cut-rate bus service for employees and . . . is forever throwing morale-boosting, all-hands-welcome parties at [a local motel]. After work on Fridays, the Japanese make a point of dropping [into a pub] near the plant to socialize.

John Davies, who represents the employees on the plant's Japanese-style works committee, renders the final verdict: "We asked to finish at 4:30 p.m. instead of 5 on Friday; they gave us that. We asked for a Christmas holiday; they gave us that. We asked for a sickness scheme; and they gave us that, too. These Japanese seem to understand us. I wouldn't want to work for an English firm again."[2]

At best, the Japanese style creates group unity through which entrepreneurs may achieve efficiency and a sense of teamwork. Recently, the Japanese style has made some inroads in the United States, especially among major corporations.

---

2. "Making Zippers: All the Way with Y.K.K.," *Time,* August 13, 1973, p. 76. [Reprinted by permission from *Time,* The Weekly Newsmagazine; Copyright Time Inc. 1973]

EXHIBIT 16-1

Analysis of Managerial Style

Check your appropriate answers. For example, on the first question, if you answer "almost complete," put a check mark almost to the "complete" end of the continuous gray line.

When you have answered each question, draw a line from the top to the bottom of the chart through the check marks. The result will be a profile of your managerial style.

		System 1 Exploitive Authoritative	System 2 Benevolent Authoritative	System 3 Consultative	System 4 Participative Group
Leadership	How much confidence is shown in subordinates?	None	Conde-scending	Substantial	Complete ✓
	How free do they feel to talk to superiors about their job?	Not at all	Not very	Rather free	Fully free
	Are subordinates' ideas sought and used, if worthy?	Seldom	Sometimes	Usually	Always
Motivation	Is predominant use made of 1 fear, 2 threats, 3 punishment, 4 rewards, 5 involvement?	1, 2, 3, occasionally 4	4, some 3	4, some 3 and 5	5, 4, based on group set goals
	Where is responsibility felt for achieving organization's goals?	Mostly at top	Top and middle	Fairly general	At all levels
Communication	How much communication is aimed at achieving organization's objectives?	Very little	Little	Quite a bit	A great deal
	What is the direction of information flow?	Downward	Mostly downward	Down and up	Down, up, and sideways
	How is downward communication accepted?	With suspicion	Possibly with suspicion	With caution	With an open mind
	How accurate is upward communication?	Often wrong	Censored for the boss	Limited accuracy	Accurate
	How well do superiors know problems faced by subordinates?	Know little	Some knowledge	Quite well	Very well
Decisions	At what level are decisions formally made?	Mostly at top	Policy at top, some delegation	Broad policy at top, more delegation	Throughout but well integrated
	What is the origin of technical and professional knowledge used in decision making?	Top management	Upper and middle	To a certain extent, throughout	To a great extent, throughout
	Are subordinates involved in decisions related to their work?	Not at all	Occasionally consulted	Generally consulted	Fully involved
	What does decision-making process contribute to motivation?	Nothing, often weakens it	Relatively little	Some contribution	Substantial contribution

Source: Adapted from *The Human Organization: Its Management and Value,* by Rensis Likert. Copyright © 1967 by McGraw-Hill, Inc. Used with permission of McGraw-Hill Book Company.

Today, the job of managing often is looked upon as the job of getting work done through others. Managing means much more, however. It really means making it possible for others to work easily and productively, and at the same time bringing out the best in them. How do entrepreneurs help workers achieve their best?

First, entrepreneurs must want to help their workers become achievers. Some do not, holding fast to the idea that workers do not crave satisfaction from their jobs. This attitude may cause such problems as absenteeism and high turnover, shoddy workmanship and a weakening of the will to work.

What many entrepreneurs lack is an understanding of just how deeply their managerial style may affect the survival and growth of their venture. So entrepreneurs need to analyze their managerial style, using as a guide the questions shown earlier, in Exhibit 16-1. By answering such questions, entrepreneurs may learn a good deal about themselves as well as about the way they treat their workers.

As humorist Josh Billings once said: "It's not only one of the most difficult things to know yourself, but one of the most inconvenient ones, too." Although it may be an uncomfortable task, the more realistic the entrepreneurs' view of themselves, the better will be their performance as managers; for insights are the building blocks of personal growth. Growing entrepreneurs change because they want to and because they must, in response to insights gained on the job.

SELF-IMAGE AN IMPORTANT FACTOR

Entrepreneurs cannot begin to know their workers without first knowing themselves. All entrepreneurs, whether aware of it or not, have a self-image. They may, for example, see themselves as quick or slow, neat or sloppy, busy or lazy. Everything they feel, hear, or do is filtered through their self-image. This means that entrepreneurs are what their self-image allows them to be. So in order for entrepreneurs to grow as managers they must know—and change— their self-image. To twist an old saying, it is not what the entrepreneur knows that counts, but rather who he or she is.

Mainly through these processes of self-discovery and change of self-image, entrepreneurs learn how people work better. These processes go on continuously. Yet many entrepreneurs ignore them in themselves and in their workers. When entrepreneurs do not understand how their employees see themselves and what motivates them, and cannot give their employees the tools they need to change, the result often is a poor product or slipshod service that jeopardizes survival and halts growth. Entrepreneurs cannot isolate themselves from their workers. At a conference of business leaders, Robert Townsend, former head of the Avis Corporation, offered these prescriptions:

> The boss should be constantly with the workers. So important is this that the paraphernalia of the boss should be entirely removed. He shouldn't have a mahogany office. He shouldn't have a limousine. He shouldn't have a space reserved outside for his car. He shouldn't be addressed by

anything but his first name. And he shouldn't receive a salary more than five times that of the least of his employees. For all intents and purposes, that means his salary should not be in excess of [$50,000].

What happens then? Well sir, morale is very high, workers have a sense of participation in the business, absenteeism all but disappears, and the problem is pretty well solved.[3]

A CREATIVE WORK ATMOSPHERE

Entrepreneurs can learn the art of bringing out the best in their workers by observing the model presented by successful athletic coaches.

Just as athletic coaches must be close to their players, so must entrepreneurs be close to their workers. Topflight coaches generally have teams that win consistently, mostly because the coaches know their job and have a knack for communicating that knowledge to their players:

☐ Players see their assignments with clarity because their coach helps them see.
☐ Players understand how to carry out their assignments because their coach has meticulously laid out the game plan and the plays necessary for use against competition.
☐ Players execute their assignments with West Point precision because their coach has created an atmosphere of fairness, confidence, and camaraderie, which generates the will to win.

Creating such a work atmosphere is difficult. No two players, or workers, are precisely alike. What appeals to one worker may repel another. Each worker is uniquely complex; so to help workers achieve their best, entrepreneurs must understand each worker's needs. According to psychologists, needs are what makes all of us tick. Workers are motivated to behave in certain ways because of their need for certain things, among them money, security, and status.

Work helps satisfy all these needs. Weekly paychecks, for example, enable workers to buy food, clothes, and a house. Besides security, workers may also seek status through:

☐ A promotion
☐ A merit salary increase
☐ The learning of new skills
☐ The invention of a new product

THE HAWTHORNE EXPERIMENT

Work helps satisfy a worker's physical and emotional needs. Workers want entrepreneurs to treat them as individuals, craving recognition for a job well done. A classic example of what happens when workers are treated as individuals was demonstrated by the now-famous Hawthorne Experiment.

3. Updated from William F. Buckley, Jr., "How to Stimulate Will to Work," Cleveland *Plain Dealer*, November 18, 1972, p. 11-A.

In the 1920s, Professor Elton Mayo of Harvard University asked 2,000 workers at the Hawthorne plant of the Western Electric Company how they felt about their jobs, their bosses, and the company. The professor and his interviewers used checklists that carefully itemized every feature of the work situation. The lists included the lights, the materials used, the handling of equipment, rest periods, product knowledge, and so on. The workers, however, wanted to talk about other things. Surprisingly, the interviews themselves seemed to improve production.

However, the results were so inconclusive that the research teams decided to try some experiments. They increased and decreased lighting, temperature, and rest periods. They changed room colors. They isolated groups from each other.

No matter what the change, production improved. The Harvard scholars were stumped. Finally, they asked the workers, "What's happening?" "Oh, don't you know?" the workers replied. "We're something special."

They did not know why, but they knew they had been distinguished from all other employees. They were now something more than cogs in a machine. The special treatment had made these workers feel different about themselves and about their work. They recognized that their jobs were important, and so did their coworkers. They had achieved that something special which we may call status. And status is the importance or prestige placed upon a work position by the workers themselves as well as by entrepreneurs.[4]

■

GIVING RECOGNITION TO WORKERS

How can entrepreneurs help workers to earn status, to gain a better opinion of themselves and their job? Entrepreneurs may do it in a variety of ways, among them:

☐ Sharing decision making with workers, as mentioned earlier in our discussion of group management.
☐ By applying the Golden Rule: "Behave to other people as we wish people to behave to us."
☐ By giving workers greater responsibility as soon as they are ready for it.
☐ By taking workers' ideas and suggestions to heart.
☐ By judging workers rigorously on merit and rewarding them accordingly.

Entrepreneurs who follow these suggestions are likely to succeed. By building up their workers' self-image and improving their status, entrepreneurs are likely to keep growing in stature themselves. The process feeds on itself. As the venture grows, talented men and women will be attracted to it. They

4. Adapted from U.S. Small Business Administration, *Human Factors in Small Business* (Washington, D.C.: U.S. Government Printing Office, 1965), p. 12.

generally prefer to work in a growing venture because growth creates opportunities for promotion. And the possibility of promotion is one of the strongest incentives known for improved performance and for personal growth.

ADDITIONAL GUIDELINES FOR SHARING

Entrepreneurs who want to keep their venture growing must share the venture with their workers. To foster that sharing, entrepreneurs should have:

☐ A set of precise goals, shared by all workers, as discussed earlier in Chapter Twelve
☐ An atmosphere of orderly growth that stimulates and rewards achievement of goals
☐ Challenging, exciting work to do
☐ Opportunities for personal growth
☐ A self-image that generates a sense of pride in a job well done

In managing their venture, how do entrepreneurs earn their workers' respect and loyalty? Of course, there is no one best way to manage a venture. Each entrepreneur has a unique style of managing. But chances are that successful entrepreneurs are those who:

☐ Ask the right questions—questions that generate thinking, initiate action, and spawn improvement
☐ Weave old ideas into new patterns
☐ Have a knack for reducing a problem quickly and accurately to its barest elements, thus laying the groundwork for solutions that are simple and clean
☐ Communicate clearly
☐ Have a drive for quality and a vision for results
☐ Act vigorously
☐ Seek excellence day in and day out[5]

PURSUIT OF EXCELLENCE

Of these traits, perhaps the last is the most critical one: the pursuit of excellence day in and day out. For it is the entrepreneur who must set the tone in his or her own venture. As the famed football coach, Vince Lombardi, put it: "You don't try to win some of the time. You don't try to do things right some of the time. You do them right all of the time."[6]

Generally, excellence occurs as a result of expectations. If entrepreneurs expect excellence from their workers, it often will occur. If they do not, it rarely will occur. Only highly motivated workers are likely to make and sell superior products that cause customers to return again and again.

Entrepreneurs crave worker loyalty. Some entrepreneurs, however, believe that their workers should be blindly loyal to them. They expect workers

5. Adapted from Rohrer, Hibler and Replogle, *Managers for Tomorrow* (New York: New American Library, 1965), p. 175.
6. From a film produced by the U.S. Small Business Administration, *The Habit of Winning* (1972).

to stick by them through good times and bad. And they expect workers to stick by them regardless of how the workers are treated.

Such false loyalty weakens rather than strengthens a venture. True loyalty means working up to one's capabilities, doing the best one knows how. True loyalty is to the job, not to the entrepreneur.

MASLOW'S HIERARCHY OF NEEDS

Our discussion of human relations would be incomplete without some mention of Dr. Abraham Maslow and his widely quoted study of human needs. Dr. Maslow classified all human needs in order of importance to the individual and presented them as a pyramid of five levels:

☐ Physiological
☐ Safety
☐ Belongingness and love
☐ Esteem
☐ Self-actualization[7]

According to Dr. Maslow, workers strive to satisfy these needs in ascending order. Once a lower level is satisfied, workers will strive to satisfy the next level of need, as shown in Exhibit 16-2. Note that the first level is the satisfaction of *physiological* needs—air, water, and food. Once these needs have been satisfied, the worker needs protection from hostile environments such as criminals and cold weather. These needs form the second level, called *safety.*

The third level, called *belongingness and love,* refers to the worker's need for affection and the acceptance of others. The fourth level, *esteem,* refers to the worker's need for self-respect, self-esteem, and the esteem of others.

The fifth, and loftiest, level has to do with *self-actualization* needs. Activated only when all other needs have been satisfied, this level reflects the worker's desire to fulfill his or her highest potential as an individual. Self-actualization refers to the worker's need to do what he or she is best suited to do, as athletes must compete and entrepreneurs must create.

WAGE AND SALARY POLICIES

Good human relations help motivate employees to cooperate fully and to work at their best. But a human relations policy must be supported by attractive wage and salary incentives. In fact, motivation and pay go hand in hand. Generally, highly motivated workers produce at a higher rate and hence merit more pay. Naturally, they expect their pay to reflect the skills and energy they put into their jobs.

To attract and keep good workers, entrepreneurs should make sure their pay scale compares favorably with those offered by competitors or they may soon find themselves stripped of talent. So entrepreneurs must draft wage and

7. Abraham H. Maslow, *Motivation and Personality* (New York: Harper & Row, 1970), pp. 35–47.

EXHIBIT 16-2

Maslow's Hierarchy of Needs

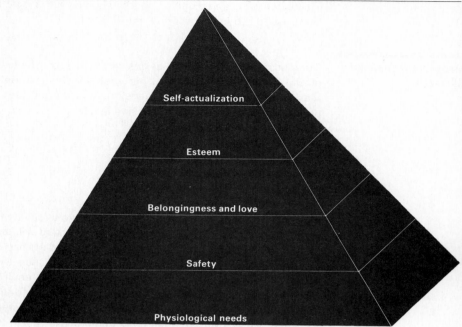

Self-actualization

Esteem

Belongingness and love

Safety

Physiological needs

Source: Data for diagram based on Hierarchy of Needs in ''A Theory of Human Motivation,'' in *Motivation and Personality,* 2nd Edition, by Abraham H. Maslow. Copyright © 1970 by Abraham H. Maslow.

salary policies that promote good human relations. One sound policy is to pay workers on merit, gearing their pay to performance.

LEGAL OBLIGATIONS

No matter how wages and salaries are set, the entrepreneur must meet certain legal obligations to workers. For example, entrepreneurs who pay more than $50 in quarterly wages must pay Social Security taxes. These payments require entrepreneurs to:

☐ Withhold a certain percentage of wages from each worker's paycheck
☐ Contribute a matching amount themselves
☐ Deposit withheld amounts and their own contributions in a bank, either monthly or quarterly depending on the amount

Entrepreneurs need legal and accounting help to make sure they honor all legal obligations. New obligations are added from time to time, and old ones keep changing. Besides Social Security taxes, entrepreneurs must meet these legal obligations:

☐ **Federal income taxes** If they pay salaries and wages or have workers who report tips, entrepreneurs must withhold a certain amount from each worker's paycheck.

☐ **Workmen's compensation insurance** If they have full-time workers, entrepreneurs must protect workers from loss of income because of injury on the job.

☐ **State unemployment insurance** If they pay wages, entrepreneurs must contribute to a fund that will be drawn upon when any of their workers are laid off but are willing and able to work.

☐ **Federal unemployment taxes** If they have four or more workers who put in 20 or more weeks a year, entrepreneurs must pay federal unemployment taxes that serve the same purpose as state unemployment insurance.

☐ **Federal wage and hour laws** If they sell across state lines, hold federal government contracts, or have revenues in excess of $500,000, entrepreneurs must abide by these laws, whose purpose is to help ensure a livable income by setting a minimum hourly wage. These laws also regulate child labor and worker health and safety.

☐ **Civil Rights Act, Title VII** If they have workers who are covered under the federal wage and hour laws, entrepreneurs must also abide by the Civil Rights Act. Its purpose is to help ensure that all job applicants and employees are treated fairly and equally, regardless of race, color, religion, sex, age, or ethnic origin.

FRINGE BENEFITS

A form of pay, fringe benefits strongly influence the lives of workers. These benefits have given the average worker not only peace of mind but also a standard of living higher than ever before. The average worker, for example, now receives the following benefits:

☐ Paid vacations and holidays, including his or her birthday
☐ Life, unemployment, and medical insurance
☐ Company pension plans and Social Security
☐ Paid leave periods for illness or jury duty

A moment's reflection will show that these are not really fringe benefits at all but are, in fact, a significant part of the entrepreneur's payroll. These benefits today cost the average employer about 37 percent of the yearly payroll—and the percentage keeps rising almost every year. In contrast, fringe benefits in 1930 cost the average employer just 3 percent of the total amount paid for wages and salaries. Generally, entrepreneurs must offer fringe benefits in order to:

☐ Attract and hold good workers
☐ Help upgrade their quality of life
☐ Keep pace with benefits offered by competitors
☐ Meet legal obligations imposed by local, state, and federal governments

Of these reasons, the most important one is to attract and hold good workers. Other things being equal, workers seek employers who offer a complete package of fringe benefits. This attitude often puts the entrepreneur at a disadvantage. Many entrepreneurs cannot afford to offer the same package of benefits as a giant corporation. So they often are forced to compete for talent on other terms, such as the appeal of contributing to the growth of a promising venture.

But sooner or later, most workers come to expect the same fringe benefits no matter whom they work for. Fringe benefits are so common today that workers look upon them as a right rather than a privilege. So much so, that they often equate fringe benefits with cash pay. If entrepreneurs fail to recognize worker expectations, they may be faced with governmental action forcing them to comply with workers' rights.

SAFETY AND HEALTH ON THE JOB

Convinced that business was not doing enough to make workplaces safe and healthful, the federal government in 1970 passed the Occupational Safety and Health Act (OSHA). This law requires that all businesses make sure their operations are free of hazards to workers. Although initially praised, this law has come under heavy fire from workers and businesspersons alike:

> Some workers have complained that the new work rules cramp their work styles. Others fear the federal government's power to shut down their workplace if it is considered unsafe.
>
> Businesspersons have complained that the law has added severely to their equipment costs and has vastly complicated their paperwork. They have also complained that many of the rules are petty.[8]

Lending weight to their complaints are these examples of the enforcement of OSHA's regulations:

☐ Businesses were ordered to take down guardrails 41 or 43 inches high and replace them with rails exactly 42 inches high.
☐ Businesses were ordered to replace round toilet seats with ones shaped like horseshoes.
☐ Mom-and-pop grocery stores and variety stores were ordered to provide separate rest rooms for men and women.[9]

Especially plagued by OSHA are small entrepreneurs. In fact, the National Federation of Independent Business has charged OSHA with using small business as "guinea pigs to establish legal precedents and to build up a record of successful cases."[10]

8. "Protecting People on the Job: ABC's of a Controversial Law," *U.S. News & World Report,* November 24, 1975, p. 70.
9. Ibid., p. 71.
10. Ibid., p. 71.

Even so, most businesspersons acknowledge that they have become more safety conscious, to the benefit of workers. The cost, however, is high. In 1980 alone, business spent more than $5 billion to comply with OSHA. Most of this sum was spent on equipment with safety or pollution-control features.

The lesson here is that entrepreneurs should make sure their operations comply with OSHA. In designing a new plant, for example, the entrepreneur must make sure the plant will be free of high noise levels, toxic substances such as carbon monoxide, clutter, and a host of other health or safety perils. Entrepreneurs would be wise to consult with their lawyer to make sure they observe the letter and spirit of the law.

SUMMARY

The best human relations are founded on good will and applied common sense. Entrepreneurs need not have extensive psychological training to have good human relations with employees. Entrepreneurs who practice good human relations treat their workers with dignity and respect. Above all, they recognize that every worker is uniquely complex.

To keep their venture running smoothly, entrepreneurs should instill in their workers a strong sense of purpose. One way to do that is by sharing decision making. This attitude generally yields high dividends, mostly because it helps satisfy the worker's desire for recognition.

There is no one best way to manage workers, for each entrepreneur has a unique managerial style. But entrepreneurs will probably succeed if they seek excellence day in and day out and treat their workers with respect. It is these two attitudes that best set the tone for a venture.

Entrepreneurs should support good human relations with attractive salary and wage policies. Motivation and pay go hand in hand. Highly motivated workers expect their pay to reflect the skills and energies they put into their job. A policy that gears wages to individual merit should satisfy workers and promote good human relations.

Entrepreneurs must also be mindful of their legal obligation to workers. They need legal and accounting help to make sure they meet such obligations as federal income taxes on salaries and wages, workmen's compensation insurance, and state unemployment insurance.

To attract and hold talent, entrepreneurs must offer fringe benefits. Today, fringe benefits are so common that workers look upon them as a right rather than a privilege. Many entrepreneurs, however, cannot afford to offer the same attractive package of benefits that giant corporations do. This puts the entrepreneur at a disadvantage in the competition for talent.

The federal government also plays a role in improving human relations. In 1970, it passed the Occupational Safety and Health Act (OSHA), requiring businesses to make workplaces safer and more healthful for workers.

1 What does the term *human relations* mean to you? Cite some personal examples of good human relations.

2 Describe one way in which an entrepreneur may create a work atmosphere that brings out the best in workers.

3 What kind of entrepreneur is likely to earn the respect and loyalty of workers?

4 Define these terms: *group management, managerial profile, managing, needs, self-actualization, fringe benefits, OSHA.*

5 Why are attractive salary and wage policies so vital to the success of a venture?

6 Are fringe benefits a right or a privilege? Explain.

7 What is the best way to measure the quality of human relations in a venture? Explain.

8 Describe the entrepreneur's legal obligations in the area of human relations.

9 Do you believe that OSHA discriminates against entrepreneurs, as some claim? Explain.

10 Does it always follow that happy workers are also productive workers? Explain.

11 How would you, as an entrepreneur, compete for topnotch talent if you cannot afford to pay the same salaries as large corporations can pay?

12 Why has group management made less headway in the United States than in Japan?

13 Dr. Maslow classified human needs in a hierarchy of five distinct levels. Describe the characteristics of each level.

14 Comment on the following statement made by an entrepreneur: "We really need to take a hard look at behavior in our venture. Our workers are totally unmotivated. So nothing gets done when it should or in the way that it should be done."

15 Is there one best way to manage a venture, one best way that works for all entrepreneurs? Explain.

CASE 16A   **NATIONAL ROLLED THREAD DIE COMPANY**

Founded in 1946, this company has had just two losing years in its lifetime. Yet William Mau, who inherited the company from his father, is concerned about its future. Why? Because for the past 17 years, Mr. Mau has been working under a "rain cloud." In each of these years, the city fathers have suggested he move out to make way for urban renewal. And each year they have come back to tell him to wait another year. "That's city hall for you," says Mr. Mau.

Mr. Mau's father created the company because he found it hard to work for somebody else. "He was a bull-headed man," says Mr. Mau. "My dad was the classic entrepreneur—a driver. Never taking no for an answer. Always running a one-man show. He was quite a guy. I had a hard time getting along with him but I respected him."

BACKGROUND

    Mr. Mau is hardly a chip off the old block. He is a mechanical engineer. "I never had what it takes to start up a business," says Mr. Mau. "By training, I'm more a professional manager than an entrepreneur. When I left the Army in 1946, my dad couldn't find room for me in the Mau empire. So I went to work for somebody else."

    Then, in 1953, Mr. Mau's father became disabled. For years he had suffered from Parkinson's disease. By 1953 the disease had so consumed him that he could no longer market his products aggressively. He turned to his son for help, asking him to quit his job and join the company. And young William Mau did just that, because he "felt a family responsibility to help out."

Despite his illness, Mr. Mau's father remained in control of the company almost until his death in 1966. Meanwhile, Mr. Mau worked hard to hold the company together and to introduce new managerial techniques. His work eventually earned him two promotions:

**EARNS SEVERAL
PROMOTIONS**

☐ In 1953, Mr. Mau started as company secretary, working mostly in marketing.
☐ In 1962, he moved up to a vice presidency.
☐ In 1966, he became president when his father died.

    When Mr. Mau joined it in 1953, the company's after-tax profits were $9,000 on sales revenues of $264,000. For the company's 1952 balance sheet, see Exhibit 16A-1.

As soon as he became president, Mr. Mau proceeded to remold the company in his own image. Where his father had been a driver, Mr. Mau would be permissive. Where his father had been a doer, Mr. Mau would be both thinker and doer. Where his father had fired incompetent employees, Mr. Mau would carry them, "matching their skills with available tasks." In short, he would humanize the company's work practices.

**INTRODUCES NEW
MANAGERIAL STYLE**

Balance Sheet (December 31, 1952)

Assets			Equities		
Current assets			Current liabilities		
Cash	$33,000		Accounts payable	$ 1,500	
Accounts receivable	10,000		Other	4,500	$ 6,000
Inventory	17,000	$60,000			
Fixed assets			Owners' equity		
Machinery and tools		27,000	Common stock	$68,000	
Other assets		2,000	Retained earnings	15,000	83,000
Total assets		$89,000	Total equities		$89,000

This managerial style was really a reaction to the way big business operated. Before joining his father, Mr. Mau had worked as an industrial engineer for a big steel company. "You tried to improve a worker's productivity in a way that was dehumanizing," says Mr. Mau. "You didn't consider the man. Only the productivity."

To this day, Mr. Mau talks eloquently about the "dehumanizing practices of big business." He deplores big business errors that make drudgery out of work and reduce workers to little more than robots cranking out bolts all day. Mr. Mau has described the cycle toward boredom in this way:

☐ Increasing work productivity requires work simplification.
☐ Simplification means specialization.
☐ Specialization means each worker does one thing, day in and day out.
☐ The end is a stifling work atmosphere and an unhappy work force.

HUMANIZING PERFORMANCE

Mr. Mau's philosophy of treating workers as human beings has paid off. In the past 28 years, he has had no layoffs, no strikes, and no work stoppages. Says Mr. Mau: "You've got to know each man; know his flexibilities; let him see where he's going; know what he's doing; and give him a feel for the product he's making.

"For some workers," says Mr. Mau, "this means letting them shift from one machine to another and from one operation to another. For others, it may mean keeping them assigned to one job. I have two men running milling machines—a job that is considered monotonous work by some. Yet, one man is completely satisfied, doesn't want to do anything else, and is doing an exceptional job. The other man needs the mantle of confidence the highly repetitive job allows him to wrap around himself. He is, however, unhappy at whatever job he is assigned."

Why doesn't Mr. Mau fire the latter employee? "I inherited him from my father's regime," says Mr. Mau. "I feel he's a kind of legacy, and I won't let him go."

He has other problem employees, one of whom he considers an irritant. "He wants things run his way," says Mr. Mau. "He wants more efficiency, more foreman control, but only as it relates to the other workers, not to himself." Spurning ultimatums that can turn small disagreements into stormy battles, Mr. Mau deals with this employee simply. "I don't talk to him because we don't operate on the same wave length. He will do what he feels he has to do. And in his own way he is highly conscientious and trustworthy."

Stressing the importance of giving workers a free hand, Mr. Mau says of one of his machinists: "He lays out his own work schedule under the guidance of a lead man, decides what steel to start with, what machine he'll be running. The important thing is that no one pays any attention to him. That's the way he wants it. He wants to be left to himself.

"Rarely does he find himself with nothing to do. I've seen him keep as many as five or six machines running—a planer, shaper, circular grinder, end miller, butt miller, and sidewheel grinder. Each machine does a different operation. And their operations must be coordinated to get our die blanks out to meet schedules."

NO POLLYANNA

In trying to avoid the pitfalls of many big manufacturers, Mr. Mau does not profess to be any management Pollyanna. "This isn't entirely unselfish," says Mr. Mau. "We recognize that we won't get the best out of the men unless we keep them in a good state of mind. Being small, we can't pay top wages. The average hourly rate is about $7.50. Surveys show that the worker's desire to be treated as a human being ranks with wages as a top priority. Those are the facts behind our approach."

All of the 18 workers on his payroll agree with this approach. One machinist, for example, says he prefers working for Mr. Mau because of the job security. During eight years with much bigger companies he was laid off for periods equal to three years. "Maybe the pay here is a little less than in a union shop, but I've been here 13 years and I've never been laid off," says the machinist.

His remarks are echoed by his fellow workers. Another machinist, for example, says he prefers his present job to work he did for a Detroit automobile plant where "you had to get a relief man if you wanted to go to the washroom."

Mr. Mau punches a time clock along with his factory workers. Why? Because it helps him maintain his perspective "at a time when the badge of success in some big companies is the key to the executive washroom."

These views may not win him high marks in Chamber of Commerce circles, but they have helped him run a stable business. In fact, revenues have gone up steadily (see Exhibit 16A-2).

Clearly, stability is the company's strongest characteristic. When Mr. Mau came in 1953, there were 15 employees; in 1981, there were 18. And in that 27-year span, revenues have tripled. "I'm proud of that record," says Mr. Mau.

MARKETING STRATEGY

But it would be a mistake to credit that record solely to his humane treatment of employees. Much, if not most, of the credit really belongs to the product he

Sales Revenues and Profits

Year	Sales Revenues	Operating Profit
1976	$568,000	$33,000
1977	642,000	39,000
1978	735,000	59,000
1979	848,000	63,000
1980	840,000	71,000

makes. So good is his product that Mr. Mau now ranks as the nation's biggest independent manufacturer of flat thread-rolling dies. Most of his customers belong to the fastener industry, which uses his dies to make screws and bolts.

Except for his nephew, Mr. Mau has no sales force to speak of. "Word-of-mouth advertising is how we get most of our new business," says Mr. Mau. "The word has gotten around that we do what few other die shops do. We make dies to a customer's specifications. Custom-made dies are our bread and butter. We tailor them to fit hand-in-glove with a customer's operations." See Exhibit 16A-3 for photographs of thread-rolling dies, and see Exhibit 16A-4 for a photograph of Mr. Mau's plant, where the dies are made.

To be sure, there are other die shops in the country that are much bigger, but they mass-produce dies. "They sell their dies off the shelf," says Mr. Mau. "We don't. We're too small to compete with them in their markets. And they're too big to compete with us in our markets." Thirty-five percent of his revenues stem from foreign markets. In fact, he has sold 50 pairs of custom-made dies to a Russian company.

Thread-Rolling Dies

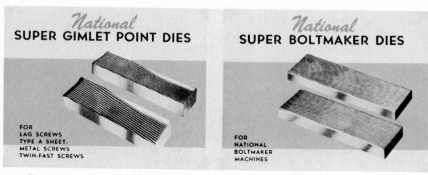

Source: The National Rolled Thread Die Company.

Inside View of Plant

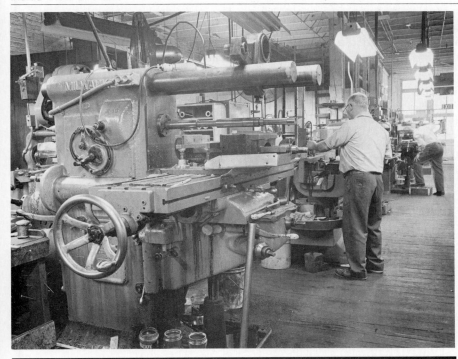

Although his past performance pleases him, Mr. Mau worries about the future. For one thing, he worries about himself, especially about his managerial skills. "I don't set goals and budget my company's future," says Mr. Mau.

THE FUTURE

"I read all those high-sounding articles about goals, and I begin to wonder what's wrong with me. But I've read enough articles to know that even experts are at odds about them. Many techniques are tried today and discarded tomorrow, such as management by objectives. It leaves me confused. What do I do?

"You know, I don't even know what my costs are, by item. But as long as I satisfy my board of directors and shareholders, I guess I'm doing OK." Mr. Mau's board consists of just three persons: himself, his brother's widow, and the vice president of a local steel company.

Another thing that worries him is urban renewal. "I've been under the gun on urban renewal for 17 years," says Mr. Mau. "Every year the city fathers tell me I'll have to move. Then they come back telling me to hold up on plans to move. I don't have a concrete plan, though maybe I should have one at all times, because I know I'll have to move some day. In any case, I've found it to be a study in futility to draw up a new plan each year to meet the ever-changing business scene. When the time comes, I'll establish a plan."

Still another problem is that his machinery is getting old. "I should replace most of my machinery with newer models and methods," says Mr. Mau, "but I don't have the money to do it. I could borrow the money, but I've never worked with debt. In fact, I've never believed in debt. What I like is a clean balance sheet. My board feels the same way. We've always expanded with retained earnings. But new techniques require capital outside our means."

Employee absenteeism also bothers him. "We used to have little absenteeism," says Mr. Mau, "but among the recent hires it's really gotten out of hand. I guess it's a way of the life these days, and you have to put up with it."

Mr. Mau has just called a special meeting of his board to go over these problems. Recent financial statements appear in Exhibits 16A-5 and 16A-6.

National Rolled Thread Die Company

EXHIBIT 16A-5

1980 Income Statement

Sales revenues		$840,000
Cost of goods sold*		612,000
Gross profit		228,000
Other expenses		
Salaries†	$91,000	
Other	66,000	157,000
Operating profit		$ 71,000

* Includes raw materials, direct labor, utilities, and depreciation.
† Covers salaries of four men, including Mr. Mau.

National Rolled Thread Die Company

EXHIBIT 16A-6

Balance Sheet (December 31, 1980)

Assets			Equities		
Current assets			**Current liabilities**		
Cash	$ 20,000		Accounts payable	$ 14,000	
Accounts receivable	98,000		Other	36,000	$ 50,000
Inventory	96,000				
Marketable securities	175,000	$389,000	**Owner's equity**		
Fixed assets			Common stock	$ 68,000	
Plant and equipment		$104,000	Retained earnings	417,000	$485,000
Other assets		42,000			
Total assets		$535,000	Total equities		$535,000

1 What should Mr. Mau do now? In the long run?
2 Comment on Mr. Mau's philosophy on human relations with employees.
3 Is Mr. Mau more a manager than an entrepreneur? Explain.
4 Comment on Mr. Mau's reluctance to go into debt.
5 How well has Mr. Mau performed as head of the company? Explain.

CASE 16B — MARKHAM LUMBER COMPANY*

Ralph Twining has just graduated from college and has been hired as personnel manager and accountant for the Markham Lumber Company. Until now, this company had relied heavily on the talents of just one man—its owner and president, Thomas Markham.

A topnotch salesman, Mr. Markham admits to knowing little about organization and management. He needed someone who did. That is why he went out and hired young Mr. Twining.

In college, Mr. Twining had majored in accounting and minored in management. And equally important, he had worked for the company two straight summers—once as a yard worker and once as a salesman. So he knew the company, its lumber products, and its employees.

His first day on the job, Mr. Twining was asked by Mr. Markham to design an accounting system for the company and suggest a new and better way of setting up the company.

In recent years, Mr. Markham has been too busy with administrative matters to call on some of his major customers. As shown in Exhibit 16B-1, he now employs 23 persons.

The company owns two lumber yards. Yard 1 is the major yard. And Yard 2 is about four miles away. Both yards carry the same line of lumber.

Salesmen in each yard sell mainly to customers who visit the yard to place their orders or who place their orders by telephone. In some cases, salesmen may leave the yard to talk with a customer. But this is not ordinarily true.

Mr. Markham is worried about his salesmen. They do not seem highly motivated, even though they are paid partly on commission.

1 If you were Mr. Twining, what organizational changes would you recommend? Why?
2 Prepare an organization chart.

---

* *Source*: Case taken from Donald C. Mosley & Paul H. Pietri, Jr., *Management: The Art of Working with and through People*. Copyright 1975 by Dickenson Publishing Company, Inc. Reprinted by permission of the publisher.

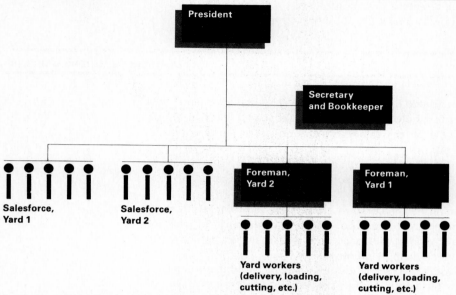

Source: From *Management: The Art of Working With and Through People,* by Donald C. Mosley and Paul H. Pietri, Jr. Copyright 1975 by Dickenson Publishing Company, Inc. Reprinted by permission of the publisher.

CASE 16C

THE DISGRUNTLED EMPLOYEE*

For the past eight years, Brian Taft has worked as a machinist for Roy Regan, the founder and sole owner of a small machine shop. Mr. Taft is an uncommonly moody person, but never before had he been in one of his sullen moods for more than one week.

When his latest moody period began about six weeks ago, Mr. Taft simply quit speaking to Mr. Regan. He also quit speaking to the other six employees of the machine shop.

Another strange thing about the matter is that Mr. Taft's work has not suffered at all, in either quality or quantity.

Mr. Regan does not know how to handle the problem. He has tried talking with Mr. Taft to find out what is troubling him, but Mr. Taft refuses to say

* Case written by Kenneth H. Killen of Cuyahoga Community College.

anything. His long silence is beginning to have a bad effect on the morale of the whole machine shop.

Yet Mr. Regan is afraid to take any kind of corrective action for fear Mr. Taft's performance may drop. Mr. Regan keeps reminding himself that Mr. Taft is much more efficient and knowledgeable than anyone else who has ever worked for him. In fact, when Mr. Taft goes on vacation, two persons are needed to replace him.

What should Roy Regan do?

CHAPTER SEVENTEEN

PURCHASING AND INVENTORIES

questions for mastery

what is purchasing?

why is efficient purchasing important?

how can one control inventories?

what is the relationship between purchasing and inventories?

why are records necessary to plan and control inventories?

The buyer needs a hundred eyes, the seller not one.

Anonymous

$\mathbb{S}$ hopping for best buys should rank high on the entrepreneur's list of priorities. Just as homemakers compare brands and prices at the supermarket to get the most for the least, so should entrepreneurs look sharply at markets and prices to get the best value for each dollar.

How well entrepreneurs do their buying may spell the difference between profit and loss. So they cannot afford to overlook the management of purchases or of inventories.

THE IMPORTANCE OF PURCHASING

THE EFFECT OF PURCHASING ON PROFITS

The goal of purchasing should be to improve a venture's profits. That is why entrepreneurs should make every effort to choose those materials, services, and sources of supply that best meet their needs at the lowest possible cost without sacrificing quality for price. To some entrepreneurs, the idea that purchasing may make or break a venture may seem far-fetched. It is not. A look at the following ratios underscores its importance:

☐ Wholesalers spend 80 to 85 cents out of every sales dollar to purchase materials from suppliers for resale later.
☐ Retailers spend 60 to 70 cents out of every sales dollar to purchase materials from suppliers for resale later to customers.
☐ Manufacturers spend 20 to 50 cents out of every sales dollar to purchase raw materials from suppliers for conversion into finished product.
☐ Service firms spend 0 to 10 cents out of every sales dollar to purchase materials from suppliers for sale as part of the service they render.

Note how widely purchasing varies in its impact. It is vital in wholesaling and retailing, less so in manufacturing, and negligible in services. But despite its impact, entrepreneurs often overlook purchasing as a major function.

Further evidence of why purchasing should rank as a major function may be gleaned from this statistic: in manufacturing alone, $878 billion was spent for materials and services in 1978.[1] Its importance can also be seen by comparing spending for purchased materials and services with spending for other items (see Exhibit 17-1). Savings in purchase costs are likely to raise profits dramatically, as shown in Exhibit 17-2. Note that if the entrepreneur's profit-to-sales ratio is just 2 percent, purchase savings of only $1,000 would be equivalent to the profit earned on a sales increase of $50,000.

Purchasing, if done wisely, offers entrepreneurs a good way to cut costs and boost profits. In short, it pays to buy efficiently.

1. U.S. Department of Commerce, "General Statistics for Industries," *1978 Annual Survey of Manufacturers,* M68 (AS)-1 (Washington, D.C.: U.S. Government Printing Office, 1978), p. 4.

EXHIBIT 17-1

Based on the Experience of 100 Representative Businesses

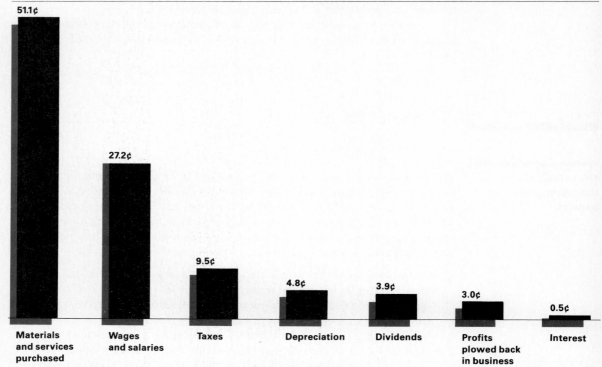

| 51.1¢ | 27.2¢ | 9.5¢ | 4.8¢ | 3.9¢ | 3.0¢ | 0.5¢ |
| **Materials and services purchased** | **Wages and salaries** | **Taxes** | **Depreciation** | **Dividends** | **Profits plowed back in business** | **Interest** |

Source: Adapted from *Purchasing Handbook,* by George W. Aljian. Copyright © 1973 by McGraw-Hill, Inc. Used with permission of McGraw-Hill Book Company.

EXHIBIT 17-2

What Purchase Savings May Mean to the Entrepreneur

If Your Ratio of Before-Tax Profits to Sales Is—	Then Purchase Savings of $1,000 Would Raise Profits as Much as a Sales Increase of—
20%	$ 5,000
15	6,700
10	10,000
5	20,000
2	50,000

Purchasing covers much more ground than the act of buying. In its broader sense, purchasing also requires the entrepreneur to:

☐ Pinpoint the need for materials and services
☐ Search out and select suppliers
☐ Settle with suppliers such matters as price and payment terms
☐ Negotiate the contract or order
☐ Make sure suppliers live up to their end of the agreement

It is the entrepreneur's responsibility to buy materials and services:

☐ Of the *right* quality
☐ Of the *right* quantity
☐ At the *right* time
☐ From the *right* supplier
☐ At the *right* price

More will be said about this vital responsibility in the paragraphs that follow.

PURCHASING MANAGEMENT

Entrepreneurs should plan their purchasing with the same care they devote to other activities of their venture. Equally important, they should also measure their purchasing performance at least once a year, asking such questions as these:

☐ How do my purchasing costs measure up to those of my competitors?
☐ What are my losses from shrinkage, spoilage, and theft?
☐ Do I have too much money tied up in inventory?

The last question is especially vital. It relates to inventory turnover, the average number of times that inventory is sold out during the year. As mentioned in Chapter Thirteen, turnover generally is the best measure of how well entrepreneurs manage their purchases.

EXAMPLE

Stein Brothers Company, an eastern food wholesaler, buys most of its produce directly from farmers in various parts of the country. Buyers represent the firm in the scattered local communities. Some of these communities are on the West Coast, and delivery to the East takes about eight days—a considerable time for perishable products. Because of this long lag between purchase and delivery, the company is forced to speculate a great deal on prices.

Practice varies with the season of the year and with the current habits of customers, but purchases must usually be made long in advance of sales. Stein Brothers sells to grocery supermarkets, institutions, and other wholesalers. Demand for any particular produce commodity varies continuously—depending on the quality of the product when it arrives in the East and on the amount of the same commodity available from other suppliers.

Daily closing inventories must be taken because each salesperson must know how much of specific lots and items is available for sale the next morning. The inventory is used to check out the sales for every case or bushel received in each railroad car or truck. Stein Brothers knows exactly how much profit is made on any given purchase. With an inventory turnover every two or three days—or more than 100 turnovers a year—the Stein Brothers office staff must always be on its toes to keep pace with changing market conditions.[2]

■

A yearly turnover of 100, for example, is the average for wholesale grocers. A lower turnover, say 90, would be a signal that the entrepreneur is carrying slow-moving or spoiled produce. On the other hand, a higher turnover, say 110, would be a signal that the grocer is carrying fast-moving produce. Now, if the level of revenues remains the same, the entrepreneur's investment in inventory is less with a turnover of 110 than with a turnover of 90. In general, the less money tied up in inventory, the better, so long as stockouts are held to an acceptable level.

The inventory turnover for wholesale grocers differs from that of most other wholesalers or retailers. Men's clothing stores, for example, have an average yearly turnover of 3; appliance stores, 4; and restaurants, 22. Manufacturers also have a broad range of turnovers. Some chemical manufacturers, for example, turn over their inventory 100 times a year. In contrast, some steel fabricators have turnovers as low as 3. An entrepreneur's goal in purchasing would be to equal or better the industry average.

So much for inventory turnover and its use as a measure of purchasing performance. Let us now look more closely at the general purchasing guidelines we mentioned earlier.

☐ **Buying the right quality** Entrepreneurs should make sure that purchased materials and services suit their needs. In manufacturing especially, entrepreneurs should make sure that raw materials meet their specifications exactly. Otherwise, the product they make may turn out to be faulty. And in retailing, entrepreneurs should see to it that the products they buy from suppliers meet their customers' standards of quality. Otherwise, customers may desert them for a competitor.

☐ **Buying the right quantity** Because they may have a lot of money tied up in inventory, entrepreneurs should make sure they buy the right amount of inventory. In retailing, for example, too small a purchase may result in a loss of customers because of empty shelves. Too large a purchase, on the

2. Harvey C. Krentzman, U.S. Small Business Administration, *Managing for Profits* (Washington, D.C.: U.S. Government Printing Office, 1968), pp. 112–113.

other hand, may mean excess inventory that hikes costs and threatens to become obsolescent.

☐ **Buying at the right time** The timing of purchases is equally critical. For manufacturers, for example, buying at the right time means buying raw materials to meet production schedules without overloading warehouses with inventory. And in times of inflation, it may mean buying raw materials just before a price rise. Entrepreneurs should study the forces of supply and demand in their markets. And they should also try to foresee what the economy will be like in the years to come. Will there be a recession or prosperity? Will there be shortages in raw materials? If so, entrepreneurs may have to look for substitute materials or stock up on materials now.

☐ **Buying from the right suppliers** Picking the right supplier is one of the entrepreneur's most challenging decisions. A bad choice may cancel out the entrepreneur's meticulous plans regarding quality, quantity, price, and time of delivery. Some suppliers, for example, may be incapable of meeting the entrepreneur's precise specifications. Others may not be able to deliver on time. And still others may not sell at the right price. It is the entrepreneur's job to find the supplier who can offer the best mix on all these points.

☐ **Buying at the right price** Contrary to popular opinion, the right price is not always the lowest price. For one thing, a lower price may not supply the entrepreneur with the product quality that customers expect. A lower price, moreover, may mean poorer service from suppliers. So in deciding on price, entrepreneurs should balance price with both quality and service. Quality must come first. Next comes service, meaning that suppliers must deliver materials of proper quality in the correct quantity on time. Last comes price. Why last? Because the entrepreneur gains little by negotiating a lower price only to lose out on quality and service.

INVENTORY MANAGEMENT

Let us begin by defining *inventory*. In manufacturing, inventory means the raw materials to make product that are stored in warehouses. In retailing, on the other hand, it means the products for sale to customers that are stored in stock rooms and on display shelves.

Note here that inventory relates only to material goods. Services are excluded. Shoes may be stored in anticipation of sales, or raw materials may be stockpiled to make product. But how could the skills of a management consultant or a lawyer be stockpiled?

Why have inventory at all? Though rarely asked, this is one question that entrepreneurs should never overlook. Its answer strongly influences how best to plan and control inventories. Here are some reasons for having inventory:

☐ To avoid the loss of customers because product is not in stock
☐ To enable customers to look over a product before buying
☐ To capitalize on discounts in the price of raw materials

☐ To keep a plant from cutting back or shutting down
☐ To make product in quantities that minimize cost
☐ To speculate against increases in price and cost
☐ To assure customers of prompt delivery
☐ To protect against strikes

This list is by no means complete, nor does each reason stand by itself. In fact, many of them overlap. Whatever their reasons, entrepreneurs should decide why they need inventory before they begin to plan and control their inventory levels.

<table>
<tr><td>**PLANNING AND CONTROL**</td><td>To plan their inventory, entrepreneurs should always begin by forecasting their revenues. At best, forecasts are intelligent guesswork. Only entrepreneurs with a monopoly in an unsaturated market can tell precisely what the future demand for their product will be and thus exercise pinpoint control over their inventory. For most entrepreneurs, however, these two questions defy precise answers:</td></tr>
</table>

☐ When should I order? Should inventory be replenished now?
☐ How much should I order? What quantity should be ordered?

Who knows, for example, what the demand will be for Valentine cards? Although the entrepreneur may forecast the demand for Valentine cards and order accordingly, the demand is sure to be zero after February 14. So the entrepreneur can ill afford to be far off in making the forecast. To decide on the right number of cards to order, the entrepreneur should rely on a tool called *inventory control*. This tool consists of a set of rules whose purpose is to strike a balance among conflicting pressures. Many of these pressures are shown in Exhibit 17-3. For example, the entrepreneur may wish to:

☐ Have an ample supply in stock at all times, so that orders can be filled promptly. That way, customers will be happy with the service and come back again and again.
☐ Keep inventories low in order to reduce the amount of money tied up in inventory. That way, more cash will be available, for, say, expansion. Return on investment will also be higher, because investment will be less.
☐ Keep inventories high in order to maintain steady production despite up-and-down demand. That way, costly shutdowns and temporary layoffs will be avoided.

To strike a balance among such conflicting goals, entrepreneurs should apply the concept of turnover, mentioned earlier. Together with the forecast, turnover analysis enables entrepreneurs to estimate roughly how many months' supply should be on hand.

<table>
<tr><td>**EXAMPLE**</td><td>A retailer of men's clothing forecasts revenues of $600,000 next year. In this industry, inventory turns over three times a year, on the average. How many months' supply should be on hand? How much investment</td></tr>
</table>

EXHIBIT 17-3

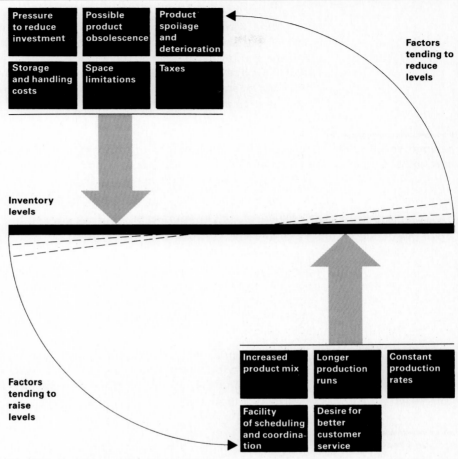

Source: James I. Morgan, "Questions for Solving the Inventory Problem," *Harvard Business Review,* July–August 1963, p. 96. Copyright © 1963 by the President and Fellows of Harvard College; all rights reserved.

should be in inventory? To answer these questions, the retailer would make the following computations:

$$\text{Months' supply} = \frac{12 \text{ months/year}}{3 \text{ turns/year}}$$

$$= 4 \text{ months' supply}$$

$$\text{Inventory investment} = \frac{\$600{,}000 \text{ revenues/year} \times 75\%\,[3]}{3 \text{ turns/year}}$$

$$= \$150{,}000$$

3. Ratio of purchase cost to selling price

These computations are only part of this entrepreneur's inventory control system. Control also involves evaluating the turnover of each item of inventory, such as shirts, ties, and topcoats.

■

As a way to judge inventories, turnover is by no means flawless. One flaw is that the very idea of turnover suggests that inventory should vary directly with revenues. That is, if revenues double, then inventory should also double. Or if revenues should drop 50 percent, then inventory should be cut 50 percent. Not so. In fact, it is more likely that turnover will increase as revenues rise and drop off as revenues fall off.

AVOIDING FORMULAS TO CONTROL INVENTORIES

As with many other aspects of managing a venture, there is no one best way to control inventories. Many books and articles have appeared recommending techniques to answer such questions as these:

☐ What is the best inventory level for a product?
☐ Where should inventories be kept?
☐ Should there be an inventory?

One technique is known as *economic order lot.* But such techniques generally do little for the entrepreneur. They result in simple formulas that may be applicable to mass production or to retail chain store operations, but not to smaller, growing ventures. What is important is not the technique itself but rather the method of reasoning by which entrepreneurs analyze their control of inventories:

If [entrepreneurs] would apply a systematic approach to analyzing their inventory problems, they would be better able to resolve their different cases, and they would have better assurance that they are using the correct formulas.[4]

RECORD KEEPING

As mentioned earlier, entrepreneurs should strive to have the right product in the right quantities at the right time in the right place. That is the goal of both purchasing and inventory management. But to meet that lofty goal, entrepreneurs must keep good records.

When they are just starting out, entrepreneurs generally can plan and control their inventories visually. They can readily see, for example, how much inventory they have on hand. And they know when and how much to reorder, the amount of time needed for delivery, and so on.

But as their venture grows, entrepreneurs need records to keep abreast of changing requirements. The need for records becomes even more pressing if the entrepreneur should delegate to somebody else the responsibility for

4. James I. Morgan, "Questions for Solving the Inventory Problem," *Harvard Business Review,* July–August 1963, p. 95.

both purchasing and inventory management. At the very least, a good record-keeping system should enable entrepreneurs to keep track of:

☐ All orders received and all shipments made to customers
☐ The rates at which purchased materials are used
☐ Suppliers' quantities and delivery cycles
☐ Names of suppliers and their price lists
☐ Order cycles and quantities ordered
☐ Products returned from customers

Such records enable entrepreneurs to handle their purchases and inventories efficiently.

EXAMPLE

An entrepreneur decides to replace old tools that are worn out with new machine tools. To buy them, the entrepreneur sets in motion a train of events. First, the foreman fills out a requisition, which states the type and number of tools needed, and gives it to the entrepreneur for approval. The entrepreneur then checks the requisition to make sure that:

☐ The cost of the tools is correct
☐ The description of the tools is adequate
☐ The quantity is sufficient
☐ The delivery date is reasonable
☐ Routing is clear

Next, the entrepreneur issues a purchase order, authorizing purchase of the tools requisitioned by the foreman. The entrepreneur sends two copies of this purchase order to the supplier. One of these copies will be later returned with the promised delivery date noted by the supplier. Other copies of the purchase order go to the entrepreneur's accountant and to the foreman.

When the shipment comes in, the foreman verifies the tools and sends his receiving copy of the purchase order to the accountant, thus completing the purchasing cycle.

■

Often, however, when a delivery date is crucial or a shipment is overdue, the entrepreneur must assume an even more active role. By every means available, the entrepreneur should negotiate with suppliers to speed up shipments. Doing so may prevent, for example, the shutdown of a plant due to shortages of vital raw materials.

To verify the accuracy of their inventory records, entrepreneurs should take a physical count of the materials on hand at least once a year. If the count differs from what the records say should be on hand, the entrepreneur should find out why. The difference could be due to theft, shrinkage, waste, or human error. When a venture is small, entrepreneurs may prevent inventory losses by their very presence. But as their venture grows, needless losses may occur because a few workers fail to exercise the same honesty or attention to detail as the entrepreneur.

INVENTORY COSTS

To buy and hold inventories is costly. Yet many entrepreneurs count only the purchase price of materials and ignore the costs incurred after their purchase. These costs include:

☐ Storage and handling
☐ Interest, insurance, and property taxes
☐ Obsolescence and spoilage
☐ Paperwork

How significant are carrying costs? One estimate puts the average carrying cost at 25 percent of the purchase cost of inventory (see Exhibit 17-4). However, carrying costs differ sharply from industry to industry.

The main reason entrepreneurs ignore carrying costs may be that they rarely appear as such in accounting records. Interest charges and property taxes, for example, are easy to isolate and identify. But the other carrying costs are extremely hard to measure, particularly the cost of money and the cost of shortages.

☐ **Cost of money** Often overlooked, the cost of money is perhaps the most critical of all carrying costs. Why? Because money not invested in inventory might be invested elsewhere, perhaps in plant expansion; the loss of the return from any such forgone opportunity is the cost of money tied up in inventory. It is especially hard to estimate this cost because it depends on an estimate of the return from other opportunities.

EXHIBIT 17-4

The True Cost of Inventory

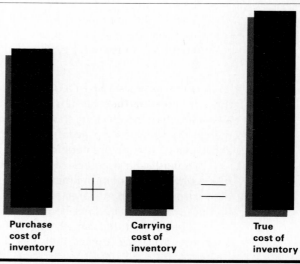

| Purchase cost of inventory | Carrying cost of inventory | True cost of inventory |

- **Cost of shortages** This cost is equally hard to estimate. Yet the costs connected with carrying too little inventory may be as severe as the costs of carrying too much inventory. Entrepreneurs often overlook this fact, because shortages are less visible than excesses. The cost of shortages may include:
  - Revenues lost because the entrepreneur could not fill a customer's order out of inventory
  - Excess costs incurred to speed up production or to break into the schedule of another product in order to avoid losing a customer's order
  - Loss of goodwill and future orders
- The costs of shortage defy computation. For example, if a $1,000 order is lost because of an inventory shortage, the cost of shortage for that order alone is precisely $1,000. But how many future orders from the same customer has the entrepreneur lost? That question is impossible to estimate with any accuracy, but is nevertheless a real cost to the entrepreneur.

SUMMARY

How well entrepreneurs do their buying and manage their inventories may spell the difference between profit and loss. Purchasing is a major entrepreneurial function along with finance, marketing, and production. On the average, more than 50 percent of every sales dollar is spent to purchase materials and services.

Entrepreneurs should plan and control their purchases with the same care they devote to the other activities of their venture. Their goal should be to buy materials and services of the right quality, in the right quantity, at the right time, from the right supplier, and at the right price.

Generally, inventory turnover is the best measure of an entrepreneur's performance in managing purchases and inventories. A turnover equal to the industry average indicates acceptable purchasing and inventory management.

In most industries, inventory and purchasing are equally important. Without sufficient inventory, customers may be lost and services compromised. To plan and control their inventories, entrepreneurs should strike a balance among such conflicting pressures as product obsolescence and longer production runs, reduced investment and better service.

To plan and control well, entrepreneurs should keep good records on all purchases and inventories. Especially vital are records of all orders received and all shipments made to customers.

DISCUSSION AND REVIEW QUESTIONS

1 Are purchasing and inventory management equally important? Why?
2 If you were an entrepreneur, what tool might you use to judge your performance in managing your purchases and inventories? Why?
3 Explain why inventories may be necessary.

4 Define these terms: *turnover, inventory, inventory control, purchase requisition, carrying costs, cost of money, cost of shortage.*
5 Explain why purchase costs are not the total cost of inventory. Give one example.
6 How may sound purchasing and inventory-control practices help you, as an entrepreneur, to boost profits?
7 Is purchasing as important a function as finance and marketing? Explain.
8 In the purchase of a product or service, which comes first: quality or price? Explain.
9 Why should entrepreneurs keep good records on purchases and inventories?
10 Would you, as an entrepreneur, try to maximize inventory turnover in order to maximize sales revenues? Explain.
11 Why is it so hard to estimate the cost of shortages? The cost of money?
12 Why should entrepreneurs take a physical count at least once a year?
13 Why is the timing of purchases so critical?
14 How do inventories differ among the manufacturing, retailing, and wholesaling industries?
15 Name some exceptions to the generalization that service industries do not carry inventories.

In his annual report, George Qua wrote that "1973 went smoothly until we were hit by the great oil fiasco. The resulting gas shortage plus high interest rates made leasing a large car a luxury few persons could afford. The last two months of 1973 were the worst I ever saw in the car-leasing business."

Even so, Mr. Qua met his budgeted goal of 207 leases in 1973. He credits this success to the "momentum built up during the early months of the year."

BACKGROUND

From the day he was born in 1930, Mr. Qua has lived in a world dominated by cars. He has worked at little else, although recently he has begun to dabble in real estate development and small-loan financing. The unveiling of new car models each autumn excites him as much today as it did when he was a ten-year-old.

Mr. Qua's life-long interest in cars is easy to understand. His father worked as a traveling service representative for the Buick and Pontiac Divisions of General Motors for 21 years. "In those days," says Mr. Qua, "they had to be able to *fix* cars as well as keep dealers happy. Today, a traveling service rep is more like a PR man."

Although the job paid well, Mr. Qua's father was dissatisfied with his lot. For years he dreamed of running his own retail automobile dealership. But not until after World War II did he attempt to do so. In 1947, opportunity knocked. General Motors offered him a Buick franchise on one condition—that he raise $37,000 of capital.

Within a month, Mr. Qua's father raised the entire sum by exhausting his savings and by borrowing from relatives. Soon after, he began selling Buicks in an old abandoned theater, using the orchestra pit to lubricate cars.

The new dealership prospered. By 1957, it was selling 1,600 new Buicks a year. Meanwhile, young George Qua earned a degree in liberal arts from the University of Michigan, served four years in the Army, and married. "I met my wife when I sold her a used car," says Mr. Qua. "It was a real courtship."

THE BIRTH OF AN IDEA

In 1957, Mr. Qua approached his father about setting up a car-leasing business. "I could see there would be a growing demand for leased cars," says Mr. Qua. "There were lots of people who needed the benefits of leasing, especially doctors."

It was vital that his father approve the idea, because Mr. Qua needed his financial help. Newly married, Mr. Qua had little money himself. At first his father resisted strongly. "He thought it was a shady business full of shady operators," says Mr. Qua, "and he couldn't see why any son of his would even entertain the idea of going into it."

But later in 1957, his father relented and gave his blessing to the new venture. "He saw that I was dead set on going into leasing," says Mr. Qua, "and wouldn't take no for an answer. He really believed I'd fall flat on my face. But I didn't."

To finance the new venture, Mr. Qua and his father agreed to form a new corporation as a subsidiary of the dealership. In essence, the dealership would supply all the financing. The beginning balance sheet of the new venture appears in Exhibit 17A-1.

Within a month, Mr. Qua received a $50,000 line of credit to buy a mix of luxury and medium-priced cars. The bank note was cosigned by the dealership.

A SLOW START

Another month went by before Mr. Qua leased his first car, a Buick convertible, to a radiologist for $105 a month. "It was kind of funny," says Mr. Qua. "When it came down to drawing up a lease agreement with the doctor, I didn't know how. So I borrowed one from a friendly competitor and copied it word for word."

Mr. Qua's first year was a near disaster. He leased only a few cars, hardly enough to support him. "I was forced to work at it part time," says Mr. Qua. "There just wasn't enough business to support one guy full time. So I had to sell used cars for my dad and at the same time drum up customers for leased cars. I worked nearly 70 hours a week, and my family life suffered. But I just had to prove to my dad that I could make it on my own."

MARKETING STRATEGY

Business picked up the second year as Mr. Qua learned more about attracting customers. He repeatedly sent flyers to physicians and to companies highlighting the benefits of leasing rather than owning a car—namely, that leasing would let them:

☐ Avoid a large initial cash outlay
☐ Deduct some or all of the leasing fee from taxable income
☐ Choose any make or model car

Mr. Qua also advertised in the Yellow Pages of the telephone directory— as he still does. A typical advertisement appears in Exhibit 17A-2. One of the "makes and models" Mr. Qua leases is a Rolls-Royce.

One of the things Mr. Qua learned is that "you have to be awfully careful whom you lease cars to." Initially, he made the mistake of leasing to "some people who turned sour during the 1957 recession." One turned out to be a nonpaying customer who abandoned his Chevrolet. Another turned out to be

Qua Lease, Inc.

EXHIBIT 17A-1

Balance Sheet (October 31, 1957)

Assets		Equities	
Cash	$ 500	Owners' equity	$20,000
Automobiles	19,000		
Organization costs	500		
Total assets	$20,000	Total equities	$20,000

Typical Advertisement

Source: Qua Lease, Inc.

a slow-paying customer who could not get liability and collision insurance on his own. He returned the car so badly damaged it needed $770 of repairs. "I learned the hard way," says Mr. Qua. "I still get lots of guys with no equity or a low credit rating or no insurability who want to lease a new car because that's the only way they can get one."

Mr. Qua was convinced that his marketing strategy would work—but only if the "public's image of lease-car operators changed." So he took it upon himself to brighten their image. In 1958, he helped found an automobile leasing association. "Too many persons were going into the business who knew less than nothing about it. Some were con artists who used teaser ads. Setting up a trade association of leasing operators was one answer to the image problem."

The main objective of the trade association was to educate members on "how best to run a car-leasing business." Mr. Qua enlisted the help of General Motors executives, insurance experts, and college professors to organize and run seminars. The association also drew up a code of ethics.

Mr. Qua's efforts paid off. He quickly earned statewide recognition as an authority on leasing cars. "That really tickled me," says Mr. Qua, "because I knew in my heart that it was really persistence, *not* know-how, that paid off for me personally."

BREAKS INTO THE BLACK

Yearly revenues began to increase. But it was not until 1964 that Qua Lease made a profit. "For seven years, I was generating tax losses for my dad's dealership," says Mr. Qua. "He wasn't too happy about that. He kept reminding me that we were eating up his money." Even after 1964, Qua Lease performed erratically, although revenues rose sharply (see Exhibit 17A-3).

Mr. Qua is not proud of that record. "We should be doing a lot better," says Mr. Qua, "but I think we turned the corner in 1973. We now have two employees working full time and one part time. All three are dedicated and hard working. The heart of our operation is Joyce Solomon. She handles all

Sales Revenues and Net Profit: 1964–1973

Year	Sales Revenues	Net Profit
1964	$ 94,000	$ 5,500
1965	41,000	(1,300)
1966	123,000	(5,900)
1967	251,000	(14,300)
1968	366,000	5,700
1969	563,000	21,200
1970	621,000	(26,800)
1971	710,000	(17,500)
1972	658,000	(19,200)
1973	751,000	14,600

lease renewals, sales calls, and office work. She's a jewel. I couldn't do without her."

Mr. Qua has yet to draw a single penny in salary from his company. But he is hardly penniless. In fact, he and his brother, Stephen, own not only the Buick dealership founded by their father but also five other ventures: a Mazda dealership, a real estate holding company, an insurance agency, a small-loan company, and an automobile financing company.

Besides managing these ventures, Mr. Qua is active in community affairs. "There are lots of people I can't say no to," says Mr. Qua. "I guess I'm too community oriented."

☐ He heads a community-wide committee to recruit more boys and adults for the Boy Scouts of America.
☐ He is vice chairman of the Council of Smaller Enterprises, a group of 750 entrepreneurs who have banded together to "fight for federal legislation that would help small businessmen compete on even terms with big business."
☐ He is president of a local Rotary Club.

Mr. Qua also accepts about 30 speaking engagements a year. In contrast, his brother has few outside activities. "He spends almost all his time on the dealership," says Mr. Qua, "and it has paid off." Indeed it has. Qua Buick ranks among the top 20 Buick dealerships in the country, selling about 2,000 Buicks and Opels a year. "My brother and I complement each other well," says Mr. Qua. "He's Mr. Inside and I'm Mr. Outside."

Although Mr. Qua is happy with his 1957 decision to go into leasing, he regrets that he wasn't able to confine himself to leasing cars only. "A friend of mine, a Harvard Business School graduate, is making a bundle of money in the

THE FUTURE

leasing business without having to worry about an automobile dealership,"
says Mr. Qua. "That's what I should have done. But it's too late now. By the
way, my Harvard friend gets most of his capital by selling notes to his lease
customers. And he pays them a *lower* interest rate than he would pay a bank.
Those Harvard guys are really bright."

Despite the up-and-down performance of his leasing company, Mr. Qua
is not about to give up. "I've been in the car-leasing business 17 years now,"
says Mr. Qua, "and I still love it. We had a good year in 1973, despite the
energy crunch, high interest rates, and double-digit inflation."

In 1973, Mr. Qua did not look forward to prospects for 1974. He foresaw
a gloomy year unless the oil crisis broke and interest rates dropped. "Our best
asset in 1974 will be our people," said Mr. Qua. "Tom Ireland, our general
manager, typifies our company slogan: 'When the going gets tough, the tough
get going'."

Mr. Ireland set a goal of 170 leased cars for 1974, down from 207 the year
before. "That may be a pessimistic goal," said Mr. Ireland, "but I don't see how
we can do better." The car-lease record for 1968 to 1973 appears in Exhibit
17A-4.

Excerpts from the 1973 annual report appear in Exhibit 17A-5. The latest
financial statements appear in Exhibits 17A-6 and 17A-7.

QUESTIONS

1 How well has Qua Lease, Inc. performed? How well is it likely to do in the
   future?
2 Comment on Mr. Qua's variety of business interests and community activities.
3 If Mr. Qua were to ask you how he might improve the performance of Qua
   Lease, Inc., what would you tell him to do? Explain.
4 Compare the managerial and entrepreneurial traits of Mr. Qua and his brother
   Stephen.
5 How has Mr. Qua financed Qua Lease, Inc.?

Qua Lease, Inc.   EXHIBIT 17A-4

Car Lease Record

Year	New Leases Written	Renewal Leases Written	Total Leases Written
1968	102	69	171
1969	118	63	181
1970*	69	47	116
1971	123	107	230
1972	74	73	147
1973	118	89	207

* In the last quarter of 1970, General Motors was on strike.

Excerpts from 1973 Annual Report

The year 1973 went smoothly for us until we were hit with the great oil fiasco. The resulting gas shortage plus high interest rates made leasing a big car a luxury that few persons could afford. Even so, our momentum carried us through our projected goal to a total of 207 leases written for the year. . . .

The last two months of 1973 were the worst I've ever seen in the leasing business. To add insult to injury, we were also plagued by an all-round ineptness by General Motors factories. Cars we ordered as replacements began to dribble in while we watched the value of the cars they were to replace come unglued. And on top of that, interest rates went through the ceiling. With a poor showing in December 1973, we still wound up the year in the black. . . .

The fact that the year ended the way it did was no fluke. The credit belongs to our dedicated employees and to Qua Buick. I have always maintained that without Qua Buick there certainly would not be any Qua Lease. . . .

I will have to be less optimistic than last year. The interest rate is only a quarter of a point off its high, and the price of cars recently went up again. People I have talked to about renewing their leases on big cars are beginning to believe that they might be better off buying a car. The difference is too dramatic from what they are paying now. Even the small cars are not exempt from some fairly ridiculous prices. . . .

In the face of all this, we will have to learn some new sales tools to accomplish anything decent in 1974—but I'm forecasting 170 cars for 1974. . . .

Tom Ireland   George F. Qua
Vice President   President
and General Manager

February 15, 1974

1973 Income Statement

Sales revenues		
Car leases	$620,900	
Gain on sales of cars	124,500	
Miscellaneous	5,100	$750,500
Operating expenses		
Depreciation	$548,800	
Interest	93,600	
Salaries and commissions	25,400	
Office rent and services	12,000	
Insurance	11,900	
Lease-car maintenance	8,200	
License and title fees	7,400	
Advertising	3,400	
Furnished rentals	3,200	
Bad debts	2,100	
Company car	2,000	
Outside services	900	
Travel and entertainment	800	
Office supplies	700	
Membership dues and magazines	500	
Telephone and telegraph	500	
Legal and auditing	400	
Delivery	300	
Other taxes	200	
Miscellaneous	100	722,400
Operating profit		$ 28,100
Federal income tax		13,500
Net profit		$ 14,600

Qua Lease, Inc.

Balance Sheet (December 31, 1973)

Assets			Equities		
Current assets			Liabilities		
Cash	$ 29,200		Notes payable	$1,332,500	
Accounts receivable	1,300	$ 30,500	Security deposits	24,800	
Fixed assets			Accounts payable	16,500	
Automobiles	$2,002,700		Interest payable	9,600	
Accumulated depreciation	659,000	1,343,700	Sales tax payable	2,400	$1,385,800
Prepaid license fees		1,500			
			Owners' equity		
			Capital stock	$ 20,000	
			Retained earnings		
			(Jan. 1)	(44,700)	
			Profit this year	14,600	(10,100)
Total assets		$1,375,700	Total equities		$1,375,700

CASE 17B   **ZEUS FABRICATED-METAL COMPANY, INC.**

George Linsenmann has watched his venture leap from 2 to 33 employees in just three years. From the start, company offices have been located in one corner of a large, musty basement in an old, multistoried factory building. Now that sales revenues are approaching $1 million a year, Mr. Linsenmann plans to move his venture to more spacious quarters in an industrial park that looks like a college campus.

In keeping with his image as a successful entrepreneur, Mr. Linsenmann plans to outfit his company's cluster of new offices with modern furniture and equipment. Four suppliers have submitted bids:

Ferrell Company	$8,000
Hildebrand Company	7,500
Hudlin Company	7,200
Pearson Company	7,000

Clearly, if all four bidders are equally capable, Pearson should be the winner. But the choice is not that simple. Two of the bidders, Ferrell and Hildebrand, are also two of Mr. Linsenmann's most important customers. In fact, his sales manager has strongly urged him to award the contract to one or both of them:

George, as I see it, you've got to choose between Ferrell and Hildebrand. I know their bids are higher than the others. But if you don't, we may lose their business. Besides, they've been loyal customers from almost the beginning. Everybody does it, George. Reciprocity is good business.

Reciprocity means that Mr. Linsenmann should place his orders with those companies that buy from him. Just how much fabricated metal have these two companies bought? Sales records show that Mr. Linsenmann sold them fabricated metal worth these amounts:

> Ferrell Company $43,000
> Hildebrand Company   32,000

QUESTIONS

1 If you were Mr. Linsenmann, how would you award the order for office furniture and equipment? Why?
2 Is reciprocity ethical? Why?
3 If you were Mr. Linsenmann, how would you explain your decision satisfactorily to the losing bidders?

CASE 17C   **SAMANTHA TEEN SHOPPE, INC.**

Samantha Martynak owned a store that specialized in clothes for teenagers. Located in a suburban shopping mall, the store was doing moderately well. Last year, the store had:

☐ Sales revenues of $234,000
☐ A gross margin of 40 percent on sales
☐ An inventory turnover of three

One day, Mrs. Martynak learned from a supplier that her yearly turnover of three was below the average in her field, which was four.

This news prompted Mrs. Martynak to take a long, hard look at the clothes she carried. She soon found that she had been carrying some slow-moving styles. So she replaced them with items that turned over more quickly—in fact, four times a year.

QUESTIONS

1 Assuming all other costs remained unchanged, by how many dollars did Mrs. Martynak improve her cash position?
2 What related costs were affected by this increase in inventory turnover? Up or down?

questions for mastery

why are taxes necessary?

what is the difference between tax avoidance and tax evasion?

why is tax planning important?

what are ways of saving or postponing taxes?

why is it vital to keep good tax records?

> **In this world, nothing is certain but death and taxes.**
>
> **Benjamin Franklin**

F ew subjects spark more controversy than taxes. Most taxpayers grumble about them; entrepreneurs are no exception. Few entrepreneurs enjoy poring over their federal income tax return, for example.

Federal income taxes are just one of many taxes that entrepreneurs must pay. Entrepreneurs must know precisely what taxes they must pay and, equally important, how taxes may affect the survival and growth of their venture.

THE NEED FOR TAXES

The English poet, Robert Herrick, once wrote, "Kings ought to shear their sheep, not skin them." He was referring to taxes and his remark strikes a responsive chord in the minds of most entrepreneurs. Even so, few entrepreneurs would quarrel with the need for some taxes. As Oliver Wendell Holmes, former chief justice of the U.S. Supreme Court, put it, "Taxes are what we pay for a civilized society."[1] Because of taxes, for example:

☐ All persons are entitled to at least a high school education, regardless of race, creed, or color, income level, or social standing.
☐ The poor, the handicapped, and the elderly are maintained at a decent standard of living.
☐ The nation is capable of defending itself against any invader.

This is but a partial list of the benefits that taxes make possible. There are many more. But despite the benefits there is often vast disagreement about who should bear the burden of taxation.

It has often been politically expedient to rake business over the coals about the taxes they pay or do not pay. Admittedly, some profitable billion-dollar corporations pay no federal income taxes. Mindful of that fact, a congressman once sponsored a bill requiring giant corporations to make public their income tax returns:

> The annual reports published by giant corporations announce to stockholders that business is better and profits are improving. The tax statements of these same companies to Internal Revenue paint a picture that reduces their profit figure, which in effect reduces their total tax figure. Like the medieval European peasant, for their stockholders they wear wedding clothes; for the tax man they wear rags.[2]

TAX AVOIDANCE NOT TAX EVASION

Are such corporations breaking the law? No. In fact, no business, big or small, has any duty to pay more taxes than the law demands. But what the public often perceives is that businesses permit their tax accountants to cut corners

1. Oliver Wendell Holmes, *Compania de Tabacos* v. *Collector,* 275 U.S. 87, 100 (1904).
2. Robert J. Havel, "Vanik Sponsors Measure to Bare Firms' Tax Data," Cleveland *Plain Dealer* February 7, 1973, p. 1-B.

in order to evade rather than avoid taxes. This erroneous perception needs correction:

☐ For one thing, tax savings boost the economy by helping to finance expansion into new products or new markets. This means not only serving customers better but also creating jobs.
☐ For another, when politicians brand business for not paying enough taxes, they generally mean federal income taxes only. But business also pays Social Security taxes, property taxes, local taxes, and possibly even foreign taxes. These taxes merit the same attention as federal income taxes.

Entrepreneurs themselves should be clear in their mind about the distinction between tax *avoidance* and tax *evasion*. Perhaps the best way to distinguish between these two practices is to say that:

☐ Tax avoidance has the blessings of the U.S. Supreme Court as well as such rule makers as the U.S. Congress and the state legislatures.
☐ Tax evasion, on the other hand, is the willful failure to live up to the spirit and letter of the tax law. In the same vein, nothing in this textbook should be understood to suggest that entrepreneurs should apply evasive tax methods to their own venture.

FOR THE GREATEST GOOD

Taxes flow in a circular direction. Money paid out in taxes has a way of coming back to entrepreneurs and other taxpayers in the form of benefits. *Time* magazine put it this way:

> The complacent observer of high taxes points out that all the money somehow comes back to the people. A fresh-water clam in the well-balanced home aquarium pumps through his voracious lungs nine gallons of water a day, yet the fish around it do not starve. Rather, the tank is purified in the redistribution. So the Government pumps it in, and pumps it out for the greatest good of the greatest number. That's the idea.[3]

TAX PLANNING

Tax laws change yearly, often in ways that strongly affect profits. Some changes may open the door to new tax savings, by hiking deductions or reducing tax rates. And some may boost taxes, by wiping out tax shelters or by shaving deductions. To keep abreast of such changes, entrepreneurs should rely on their lawyer or accountant for the latest tax information. Moreover, these professionals can help entrepreneurs to save taxes. Exhibit 18-1 shows how significant such savings may be.

3. "Cover Story: Taxes: The Big Bite," *Time*, March 10, 1952, p. 27. [Reprinted by permission from *Time*, The Weekly Newsmagazine. Copyright Time Inc. 1952]

EXHIBIT 18-1

What Tax Savings May Mean to the Entrepreneur

If Ratio of Before-Tax Profits to Sales Is	Then a $1,000 Tax Saving Will Boost Profits* as Much as a Sales Increase of
20%	$ 9,260
15%	12,350
10%	18,520
5%	37,040
1%	185,200

* Assumes a flat 46 percent corporate tax rate which is the maximum

Source: Adapted from *Key Moves to Cut Company Taxes* (Englewood Cliffs, N.J.: Prentice-Hall, Inc., 1980), p. 5.

Entrepreneurs also need tax help in areas other than federal income taxes. Equally complex are the laws covering:

☐ State, county, and municipal taxes
☐ Social Security taxes
☐ Estate taxes

We will now discuss various ways in which entrepreneurs may save or postpone taxes, focusing mainly on the U.S. Internal Revenue Code.

LEGAL FORMS OF ORGANIZATION

How much a venture pays in federal income taxes depends strongly on which legal form of organization the entrepreneur chooses. So critical is this choice that its consequences may spell the difference between profit and loss. As discussed in Chapter Seven, entrepreneurs may choose one of several legal forms, among them:

☐ The regular corporation
☐ The Subchapter S corporation
☐ The general partnership
☐ The limited partnership
☐ The sole proprietorship

Regular corporations Perhaps the first step in understanding corporate federal income taxes is to define what taxable income means. On the average, and over a period of years, taxable income equals roughly the amounts that corporations report as book profit before federal income taxes in their reports to shareholders. But in any given year, taxable income may differ sharply from book profit. This seeming contradiction comes about because the goals of *tax* accounting differ from those of *financial* accounting.

☐ The goal of tax accounting is to minimize taxes—by recognizing expenses as soon as is legally possible and by putting off recognition of revenues for as long as is legally possible. That way, tax payments are postponed to later years.
☐ The goal of financial accounting, on the other hand, is to report fairly the revenues, expenses, and profits earned.

The U.S. Internal Revenue Code, for example, permits entrepreneurs to use one depreciation method for tax purposes and another method for financial reporting purposes. Let us look first at the depreciation methods that may be used for tax purposes.

In 1981, a dramatic change took place in the tax law with passage of the Economic Recovery Tax Act of 1981. This act replaced a complex and slow depreciation system with one that is simple and fast. Called the Accelerated Cost Recovery System (ACRS), this new system now permits entrepreneurs to depreciate most equipment over just a 3- or 5-year period *for tax purposes*. In contrast, under the old system, the average depreciable life was about 10 years. Moreover, buildings now qualify for either a 10-year or a 15-year depreciable life, as opposed to 40 to 50 years under the old system. Under the new system, the depreciation rules are alike for both new and used fixed assets. The four new classes of depreciable life are described below:

☐ **Three-year asset class** This class covers automobiles, light-duty trucks, and research-and-development equipment. Also covered are special tools, molds, some materials-handling devices, and racehorses.
☐ **Five-year asset class** This class covers almost all other equipment not covered under the 3-year class. So, 5-year assets would include heavy-duty trucks, motors, lathes, office furniture, machines, and equipment, aircraft, drill presses, and a host of other equipment.
☐ **Ten-year asset class** This class covers mostly railroad tank cars and public utility equipment. Some buildings may also qualify.
☐ **Fifteen-year asset class** This class covers mostly buildings and other real property. It also includes some public utility equipment.

Shown in Exhibit 18-2 are the yearly rates at which entrepreneurs may now depreciate their cost of fixed assets for each of the first three classes described above. Note that the percentage of the asset's cost that can be depreciated each year will depend on the year the asset is put in service.

Note also that Exhibit 18-2 omits the 15-year asset class. The reason is that buildings and other real property are the exception to the principle that a single depreciation method and period apply to all assets within an asset class. Here, both the depreciation method and the period are determined on a property-to-property basis, using special tables prepared by the U.S. Internal Revenue Service.

EXAMPLE

To estimate his depreciation expense, an entrepreneur plans to use two methods. To save taxes, he must use the ACRS method described earlier. But to report his financial performance to shareholders, he uses the

EXHIBIT 18-2   Depreciation Rates Under ACRS System

Depreciation Rates if Fixed Asset Is Put in Service

	Before 1985* with a Depreciable Life of			During 1985 with a Depreciable Life of			After 1985 with a Depreciable Life of		
Year	3 Years	5 Years	10 Years	3 Years	5 Years	10 Years	3 Years	5 Years	10 Years
1	25%	15%	8%	29%	18%	9%	33%	20%	10%
2	38	22	14	47	33	19	45	32	18
3	37	21	12	24	25	16	22	24	16
4		21	10		16	14		16	14
5		21	10		8	12		8	12
6			10			10			10
7			9			8			8
8			9			6			6
9			9			4			4
10			9			2			2
	100%	100%	100%	100%	100%	100%	100%	100%	100%

*And after 1980
Source: U.S. Congress, *H.R. 4242* (Washington, D.C.: U.S. Government Printing Office, July 30, 1981), Section 201, pp. 61–62.

straight-line method. This method assumes that his depreciable assets will provide equal benefits throughout their years of service.

To show why these different methods might be used for different purposes, let us assume that the entrepreneur in his first year has sales revenues of $200,000 and operating expenses of $150,000 before depreciation. Depreciable assets cost $100,000; their average useful life is 10 years. How would the entrepreneur's book profit differ from taxable income? They would differ as shown in Exhibit 18-3. Note that taxable income is $10,000 less than book profit. That means, of course, that taxes would also be less. However, the entrepreneur would end up paying the *same* total taxes over the life of his depreciable assets, regardless of depreciation method.

There is no deceit here. The entrepreneur is merely postponing some taxes until later years. This gives the entrepreneur more cash flow in the early years, as shown in Exhibit 18-4. And, of course, cash received this year is worth more than cash received in later years, because entrepreneurs may reinvest it sooner.

■

Also influencing the tax picture in this situation is the fact that corporations are the only legal form of organization that the U.S. Internal Revenue Code recognizes as being a so-called legal person, separate and distinct from the owners. As a result, income tax rates for corporations differ from those applicable to either sole proprietorships or to partnerships. The only exception

EXHIBIT 18-3

How Book Profit Differs from Taxable Income

	First Year	
	Book Profit	**Taxable Income**
Sales revenues	$200,000	$200,000
Operating expenses before depreciation	150,000	150,000
Operating profit before depreciation	$ 50,000	$ 50,000
Depreciation	10,000*	20,000**
Operating profit	$ 40,000	$ 30,000

* Using the straight-line method: $100,000 asset cost × 10 percent depreciation rate = $10,000.
** Using the ACRS method: $100,000 asset cost × 20 percent depreciation rate (after 1985) = $20,000.

is the Subchapter S corporation, which is taxed as if it were a partnership. As shown below, corporations get a tax break of up to $100,000 of their taxable income:

Taxable Income			**1982**	**1983 and After**
$	0 to	25,000	16%	15%
	25,001 to	50,000	19	18
	50,001 to	75,000	30	30
	75,001 to	100,000	40	40
	More than	100,000	46	46

This tax break recognizes the need to help small ventures survive and grow. To show its impact, let us now go through an example:

EXAMPLE

Assume that a small corporation has a taxable income of $66,000. How much would it save in taxes with the tax break? Computations follow:

With tax break
Taxable income		$66,000
Less: Federal income taxes		
On first $25,000 (× 15%) = $3,750		
On next $25,000 (× 18%) = 4,500		
On next $16,000 (× 30%) = 4,800	13,050 ←	
Net profit	$52,950	

Without tax break
Taxable income	$66,000
Less: Taxes ($66,000 × 46%)	30,360 ←
Net profit	$35,640

EXHIBIT 18-4

How Choice of Depreciation Method Affects Cash Flow

The ACRS system yields much more cash flow in the early years than does the straight-line method.

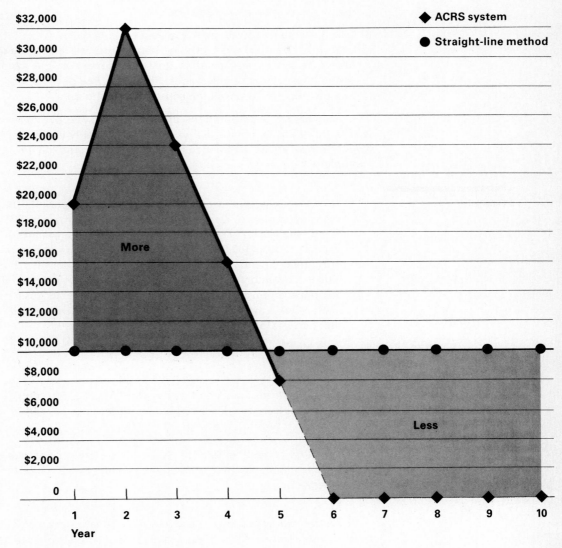

Cash flow* made available by depreciation, before taxes

◆ ACRS system

● Straight-line method

More

Less

Year

*Assumptions: (1) Asset cost = $100,000 (put in service after 1985)

(2) Depr. life = 5 years under ACRS system
= 10 years under straight-line method (which assumes asset will be in service for 10 years)

Thus, with the tax break, this corporation would save $17,310 in taxes ($30,360 − $13,050). Note, too, that net profit would be much higher: $52,950 versus $35,640.

■

Subchapter S corporations As mentioned in Chapter Seven, a Subchapter S corporation is a hybrid form of organization, a cross between a regular corporation and a general partnership:

☐ Like a regular corporation, it enjoys limited liability.
☐ Like a partnership, it is not subject to corporate federal income taxes. Instead, its profits are taxed to the entrepreneur in the same way as the entrepreneur's salary and wages. Thus, it is free of the double taxation that plagues regular corporations and their shareholders.

Subchapter S corporations are especially attractive to wealthy persons who prefer to invest in high-risk ventures. In the early years, losses incurred by a venture may shelter other income they have from the full impact of taxes. An example will show how such tax shelters work:

EXAMPLE

An entrepreneur is forming a Subchapter S corporation to open a small machine shop. He needs $250,000, 60 percent of which will come from a 5-year bank loan. The rest will be raised from wealthy individuals. He expects to lose $50,000 during the first two years of operation.

To help finance his venture, the entrepreneur has been talking to wealthy investors in the 50 percent income-tax bracket. How might he convince them to invest, even though he expects losses the first two years? One way is to demonstrate the high return they will receive in the first two years:

	First Two Years
☐ Return from investment tax credit (10% × $250,000)* =	$25,000
☐ Return from loss flow-through (50% × $ 50,000) =	25,000
☐ Total return to investors	$50,000

Investors benefit by $50,000 because they are able to reduce their other taxable income by that amount, thus paying less in taxes than they would otherwise.

■

As the example shows, investors may benefit personally even though a venture loses money if the venture is organized as a Subchapter S corporation. Personal losses, however, may be claimed only up to the amount that each individual has invested.

---

*To stimulate investment in machinery and equipment, tax laws permit a credit against income taxes—here 10 percent of the shop's cost. This investment tax credit is discussed later in the chapter.

Partnerships and sole proprietorships These two legal forms of organization fall under almost precisely the same tax laws as the Subchapter S corporation. In a partnership, it is the partners themselves who are taxed, not the partnership. The partnership merely serves as a kind of pipeline through which profits or losses flow straight to the partners. So to compute federal income taxes, each partner must report his or her share of the partnership's profit, even though some or all of it was plowed back into the partnership. In contrast, corporate shareholders must report only the cash dividends they receive.

Similarly, tax laws do not recognize the sole proprietorship as a separate and distinct legal entity, so sole proprietors are also taxed as individuals. In contrast to corporations, sole proprietorships offer few opportunities for tax savings. Sole proprietors cannot take advantage of such corporate tax-sheltered benefits as life and health insurance. Nor can they pay themselves a tax-deductible salary.

Just two tax advantages are open to sole proprietorships. If their taxable income is low, individual tax rates may be lower than corporate tax rates; and if losses occur, sole proprietors may use those losses to offset their taxable income from other sources.

General partnerships, on the other hand, offer more tax-saving opportunities than proprietorships, though not as many as corporations. Tax law, for example, permits partners to engineer their tax consequences:

☐ Revenue and expense items can be contractually allocated to the partners so as to achieve the most favorable overall tax effect. A partner may, for example, earn 35 percent of the partnership's ordinary income and 40 percent of its capital gains, but only 10 percent of its losses.
☐ A partnership is privileged to lease or buy property or borrow money from its partners, all with predictable tax consequences. A partner may, for example, make a loan to the partnership, thus earning interest income himself or herself while at the same time creating a corresponding interest-expense deduction for the partnership.[4]

The traditional tax-shelter vehicle, of course, is the limited partnership. As mentioned in Chapter Seven, the partners are called limited because the tax law limits their personal liability to their investment, but also denies them the right to take part in management. As with sole proprietorships and general partnerships, partnership losses flow straight to the limited partners. They may then save taxes by deducting those losses from their taxable income from other sources.

So much for the legal forms of organization and their effect on federal income taxes. Let us now look briefly at some other areas that merit the entrepreneur's attention:

☐ Inventory valuation
☐ Investment tax credit

4. Adapted from Marc J. Lane, *Taxation for Small Business* (New York: Wiley, 1980), p. 54.

□ Targeted jobs credit
□ Energy tax credit
□ Estate and gift taxes

INVENTORY VALUES AND TAXES

Entrepreneurs should be aware that inventory values may strongly affect their tax bill, especially in times of fast-rising prices. The basic problem is how best to value the ending inventory. There are several ways to handle this problem, among them:

□ **FIFO (First-In, First-Out)** In this method, entrepreneurs assume that the oldest materials are sold first. Ending inventory is thus made up of those materials purchased most recently. FIFO generally corresponds to the natural flow of materials through inventory. One exception is a coal pile, where coal on the outside rather than the inside is sold first.
□ **LIFO (Last-In, First-Out)** In this method, entrepreneurs assume that the youngest materials are sold first. Ending inventory is thus made up of the oldest materials. LIFO generally corresponds to the economic flow of values through inventory.

Of the two methods, LIFO saves more taxes. With LIFO, if prices go up, taxes are lower because LIFO keeps book profits down. It matches present selling prices with present costs, which are also high. The spread is not so great. Let us now go through an example to show how LIFO yields less taxable income than FIFO:

EXAMPLE

An entrepreneur runs a retail store. To save taxes, she is thinking of switching from FIFO to LIFO, because prices are rising rapidly. What tax savings will she realize, if she estimates that next year she will have:

□ $100,000 of sales revenues
□ $20,000 of operating expenses
□ 1,000 units in beginning inventory
□ 1,000 units in ending inventory
□ 3,000 units of purchases
□ A rise in the purchase cost of inventory from $10 a unit to $20 a unit

With the help of her accountant, the entrepreneur prepares Exhibit 18-5. As shown in the upper half of the exhibit, she first estimates the cost of goods sold under FIFO, then under LIFO. Next, she prepares two income statements to see the impact on both taxes and net profit.

Note that federal income taxes would be $2,000 less with LIFO than with FIFO ($6,000 under FIFO versus $4,000 under LIFO). A qualifying word is necessary here. We purposely assumed that prices would double in one year, from $10 to $20 a unit, to simplify the arithmetic. In real life, price increases would rarely be so steep.

■

EXHIBIT 18-5

Items	Units	Unit Cost	Under FIFO	Under LIFO
Beginning inventory	1,000	$10	$10,000	$10,000
Purchases	3,000	$20	60,000	60,000
Available for sale	4,000		$70,000	$70,000
Ending inventory	1,000		20,000*	10,000†
Cost of goods sold	3,000		$50,000	$60,000

Income Statements		Under FIFO	Under LIFO
Sales revenues		$100,000	$100,000
Cost of goods sold		50,000	60,000
Gross profit		$ 50,000	$ 40,000
Operating expenses		20,000	20,000
Taxable income		$ 30,000	$ 20,000
Federal income tax‡		6,000	4,000
Net profit		$ 24,000	$ 16,000

* Obtained by multiplying the unit cost of $20 by the 1,000 units in ending inventory.
† Obtained by multiplying the unit cost of $10 by the 1,000 units in ending inventory.
‡ We assumed a flat 20 percent corporate tax rate.

The U.S. Internal Revenue Code permits entrepreneurs to use LIFO for income-tax purposes, but only if they also use LIFO in their published financial statements to shareholders, commercial banks, or other interested parties. This is the only time that the Code requires entrepreneurs to use the same accounting method for both income tax and financial reporting purposes.

INVESTMENT TAX CREDIT The U.S. Internal Revenue Code permits entrepreneurs to claim a tax credit of 10 percent of the cost of certain fixed assets. This tax credit is a direct reduction of the federal income taxes owed, as opposed to a deduction that reduces taxable income. And it applies only to such tangible assets as machinery and equipment. Excluded are buildings and such intangible assets as patents and covenants-not-to-compete.

Moreover, only assets with a useful life of three years or more qualify for the tax credit. If an asset's life is less than seven years, entrepreneurs may apply only a fraction of the maximum allowable credit, as shown below:

For fixed assets with a depreciable life of	The investment tax-credit is
3 years	6%
5	10
10	10
15	10

At present, the maximum amount of credit that entrepreneurs may claim each year is $25,000 plus a certain percentage of the tax bill in excess of $25,000. That percentage was 80 percent for 1981, and 90 percent for 1982 and thereafter. To see how this tax credit works, let us go through an example:

EXAMPLE

An entrepreneur plans to build a steel-fabricating plant in 1982. He estimates that the installed cost of all equipment will be $500,000. He also estimates that, without the investment tax credit, his tax bill will be $50,000. By how much will his tax bill be reduced in 1982 with the tax credit? Computations follow:

1982

$50,000 Total investment tax credit ($500,000 × 10%)
47,500 Total credit allowed $25,000 + [90% × ($50,000 − $25,000)]
$ 2,500 Unused investment tax credit

■

Any unused tax credits, as in our example, must first be carried back 8 years, thus resulting in a tax refund. Then entrepreneurs may carry unused credits forward 15 years.

TARGETED JOBS CREDIT

Entrepreneurs may avail themselves of the targeted jobs credit if they employ certain disadvantaged persons. This tax credit is equal to 50 percent of the first $6,000 of wages per eligible employee for the first year of employment and 25 percent of such wages for the second year. Eligible employees include:

☐ Young men and women, ages 18 to 25, who come from low-income families
☐ Vietnam veterans
☐ Handicapped men and women
☐ Ex-convicts

For each of the above categories, the employee must come from an economically disadvantaged family. These families are defined as those having an income of less than 70 percent of the minimum living standard established yearly by the U.S. Bureau of Labor Statistics. Let us now go through an example to see how this jobs credit works:

An entrepreneur hires three disadvantaged youths, each one certified to be an eligible employee for the jobs credit. Each of these employees receives wages of $9,000 during the year. If the entrepreneur takes the tax credit, her tax bill will be reduced by $9,000, computed as follows:

$$\text{Targeted jobs credit} = (\$6,000 \times 50\%) \times 3 \text{ employees}$$
$$= \underline{\$9,000}$$

■

ENERGY TAX CREDIT

Energy tax credits create incentives to save oil or natural gas. For example, the Tax Energy Act of 1978 enables entrepreneurs to take an investment tax credit of 20 percent of the cost of energy-saving equipment, which is twice the normal rate. An entrepreneur who spends, say, $50,000 for recycling equipment may deduct 20 percent, or $10,000, from his tax bill.

This credit applies only to energy-saving equipment with a useful life of at least three years. And it applies only to equipment that uses a fuel other than oil or natural gas. Recycling equipment also qualifies.

ESTATE AND GIFT TAXES

Although the focus so far has been on federal income taxes, we should also look at federal estate and gift taxes. Both taxes should be of major concern to every entrepreneur. Until passage of the Economic Recovery Tax Act of 1981, tax laws often led entrepreneurs and their spouses to follow certain tax-saving patterns, to protect their estates, such as:

☐ Putting insurance policies in each other's names to avoid paying estate taxes on the money after death
☐ Legally sharing the ownership of a home or other assets

But under the 1981 tax law, there is no longer any motivation for such sharing. Entrepreneurs may now leave everything to their spouse *tax-free.*

The estate tax changes in the law have other effects. For example, the law now makes all taxable estates of $600,000 or less entirely exempt from federal taxes by 1987, no matter whom they are bequeathed to. It also lowers the maximum tax rate on estates from 70 percent to 50 percent by 1985.

Although it may appear best to leave all of an estate to a spouse, some tax experts suggest that entrepreneurs take advantage of another tax-free exclusion that applies to all estates—namely, to pass part of their estate to children or other persons rather than their spouse. Then, when the second spouse dies, that amount has already been passed along tax-free.

This exclusion is called the unified tax credit, because it may be used to cover tax-free gifts made before death. The table below shows how the unified tax credit and the amounts exempt from taxes are increased, beginning with 1982:[5]

5. U.S. Congress, *H.R. 4242* (Washington, D.C.: U.S. Government Printing Office; July 30, 1981), Section 401, pp. 245–246.

Year of Death or Gift	Amount of Estate and Gift Tax Credit	Estate Transfers or Gift Amount Exempted from Tax
1982	$ 62,800	$225,000
1983	79,300	275,000
1984	96,300	325,000
1985	121,800	400,000
1986	155,800	500,000
After 1986	192,800	600,000

One idea for entrepreneurs to consider is that *each* spouse is entitled to a unified credit allowance. Thus, in 1982, a husband and wife may give $450,000 tax-free to their beneficiaries. This amount increases to $1,200,000 in 1987.

Moreover, the tax-free transfers, above, may be further increased by taking advantage of the annual gift exclusion of $10,000 per recipient. Thus, a husband and wife may give $20,000 a year tax-free to any individual if they agree to split their gifts.

Today, with sound planning, an entrepreneur's family may have a net worth of more than $1 million and still avoid paying any estate taxes as property passes from one generation to the next. But to achieve that result, entrepreneurs must do a sound job of planning with the help of their accountant, lawyer, or insurance agent. Planning for minimizing estate taxes should cover:

☐ Taking maximum advantage of the tax rules governing estates and gifts
☐ Making imaginative use of charities
☐ Using trust devices to prevent estate taxes from depleting capital in each generation

OTHER FEDERAL TAXES A variety of other taxes complete the federal tax structure. These are mostly employment taxes and excise taxes on the sale of certain products and services:

☐ **Employment taxes** These cover Social Security and unemployment. Social Security tax laws require entrepreneurs to match their employees' contribution. In addition to Social Security, entrepreneurs must pay a federal unemployment tax. This tax applies only if an entrepreneur employs one or more persons for 20 weeks each during the year.

We shall discuss Social Security in more detail in the next chapter, which deals with insurance.

☐ **Excise taxes** Unlike the federal income tax, excise taxes affect revenues, not profits. Excise taxes apply mostly to the sale of selected products and services. Examples include taxes on the use of highways by trucks or those on the manufacture of alcohol and tobacco products.

KEEPING TAX RECORDS

Compliance with federal, state, and local tax laws requires a staggering amount of paperwork. Yet entrepreneurs must make sure that such chores as recording and withholding taxes, as well as reporting and paying taxes, are done accurately and promptly. For some entrepreneurs, these chores cause anxiety and confusion.

The best way to relieve such anxiety is to design an accounting system that also generates tax information. For example, an accounting system that turns out income statements should also provide data for preparing federal income tax returns. In any case, tax laws require entrepreneurs to keep permanent records on such items as these:

☐ Sales revenues and sales of products subject to excise taxes
☐ Tax-deductible expenses
☐ Inventories
☐ Names, addresses, and Social Security numbers of employees

THE ENTREPRENEUR AS DEBTOR AND AGENT

In dealing with taxes, entrepreneurs must play a double role. As debtors, entrepreneurs pay federal income taxes on profits. As agents, they withhold federal income taxes and Social Security taxes from their own salary as well as from the wages of employees in order to pass them on to the proper government agency.

FILING TAX RETURNS

To make sure they meet their tax obligations, entrepreneurs should keep a tax calendar reminding them of tax due dates. Failure to file returns or to pay taxes on time may bring stiff penalties, such as fines, jail sentences, and an interest charge set each year at 100 percent of the average prime interest rate during the previous September. The prime rate is what the banks charge their most creditworthy customers.

The U.S. Internal Revenue Service (IRS) can hold the entrepreneur personally responsible for taxes owed by a venture even if it is incorporated. The IRS bears down especially hard on entrepreneurs who withhold income taxes and Social Security taxes from the wages of employees and then use these sums within their own venture instead of passing them on to the government.

Often, such illegal use of money occurs with the best of intentions. The entrepreneur fully intends to pay up, eventually. But if payment is delayed for long, the IRS may penalize the entrepreneur severely.

AUDITING

Because of computers, entrepreneurs may count on having their tax returns audited from time to time by the IRS. These government computers handle more than 130 million tax returns a year. They help the IRS to:

☐ Speed refunds
☐ Spot violators
☐ Make sure entrepreneurs file the right returns
☐ Check arithmetical accuracy
☐ Determine whether other taxes are owed before a refund is paid

There are two main reasons why an entrepreneur's tax return may be selected for audit. First, it may be selected at random. Second, and more serious, a return may be audited because it was prepared inaccurately or incompletely. When the IRS selects a return for audit, it usually examines:

☐ Whether the entrepreneur's salary is in line
☐ How revenues and expenses are determined
☐ How inventories are costed
☐ How large cash transactions are handled
☐ How travel and entertainment expenses are handled

HONEST DIFFERENCES OF OPINION

Occasionally, the IRS does uncover fraud. But often, there is honest disagreement between the IRS and the entrepreneur on how certain items should be handled. They may, for example, disagree on:

☐ How revenues and costs should be allocated between years
☐ How fixed assets such as buildings should be depreciated
☐ How intangible assets such as licenses and covenants-not-to-compete should be amortized over their useful lives

Such questions generally reflect true differences of judgment. But often, the IRS requires the entrepreneur to present proof of a questionable deduction.

Clearly, it is vital to be painstakingly thorough in all tax matters. To back their tax returns, entrepreneurs should keep good records. And they must never violate the tax law. Ignoring these precautions may trigger enormous problems.

SUMMARY

Taxes are not intended to turn entrepreneurs into paupers. Rather, taxes are intended to enhance the quality of life. As such, taxes pay for the nation's defense, its schools, its welfare programs, and a host of other vital services.

Entrepreneurs should understand the difference between tax evasion and tax avoidance. Tax laws change yearly, often in ways that affect profits. Some changes may lead to new tax savings; but others may lead to higher taxes. To avoid the complications such changes may create, entrepreneurs need the best tax advice available.

Legal forms of organization strongly influence the amount of federal income taxes an entrepreneur must pay. A venture may be organized as a sole proprietorship, a partnership, a corporation, or as some other form. The legal form selected depends mostly on the personal tax status of the entrepreneur and of those who invest in the venture.

Entrepreneurs should be aware of the many ways to postpone or to save taxes. Accelerated depreciation is one way to postpone taxes. Tax-saving opportunities include the investment tax credit, the jobs credit, and the energy credit.

Federal income taxes are just one of many taxes that entrepreneurs must pay. Others include estate and gift taxes, employment taxes, excise taxes, property taxes, and the like.

As tax managers, entrepreneurs must act as both debtor and agent. They must pay the taxes they owe and they must also collect certain taxes and pass them on to the proper government agency.

Computers enable the U.S. Internal Revenue Service to monitor closely the accuracy and completeness of income tax returns. The chances are good that an entrepreneur's return will be audited some time. So entrepreneurs must be ready to support every entry on their returns. To do that, they must keep accurate, complete, and up-to-date records.

DISCUSSION AND REVIEW QUESTIONS

1 Why should entrepreneurs keep up-to-date on changes in the tax law?
2 Do you believe it is ethical for entrepreneurs to figure their income one way for federal income-tax purposes and another way for financial accounting purposes? Why or why not?
3 Describe some of the ways that entrepreneurs may minimize their federal income taxes.
4 Define these terms: *taxable income, ACRS, straight-line depreciation, investment tax credit, targeted jobs credit, employment taxes, unified tax credit.*
5 Why is estate planning so vital? How would you, as an entrepreneur, go about it?
6 Explain how entrepreneurs act as both debtor and agent in managing the tax aspects of their venture.
7 How do you, as an entrepreneur, benefit from the payment of federal income taxes?
8 How does the legal postponement of tax payments benefit the entrepreneur?
9 Why are Subchapter S corporations especially attractive to wealthy investors?
10 Why should entrepreneurs keep accurate and complete tax records?
11 How do LIFO and FIFO differ? Why does LIFO save taxes?
12 Why does the U.S. Internal Revenue Code give small corporations a tax break?
13 How significant can tax savings be to the entrepreneur? Give examples.
14 Do you believe that the tax incentives for energy-saving equipment are adequate? Explain.
15 Explain how tax evasion and tax avoidance differ.

Located in an inner city, CWC Industries was "suffering from severe growing pains" in 1980. CWC had reached its manufacturing capacity. So cramped was its plant that little room existed for expansion. Although earning $75,000 on sales revenues of $1.6 million, CWC found it hard to raise money to expand. "Every bank in town has turned us down," said Mary Jane Fabish, executive vice president. "It just doesn't make any sense."

The two entrepreneurs most responsible for CWC's success are Ms. Fabish and **BACKGROUND** Jerry Lancaster, founder and president. They have worked as a team since 1965, when Mr. Lancaster founded CWC. Before 1965, both had worked for Brooks Chemical, Mr. Lancaster as executive vice president, Ms. Fabish as office manager. In fact, it was Mr. Lancaster who hired Ms. Fabish.

"Our talents mesh beautifully," said Ms. Fabish. "I take care of finances, marketing, and organizational planning. Jerry takes care of production, product development, and overall direction of the company. We share all of the decision making, Jerry and I. If we disagree, we hammer out the pros and cons. And every time, we end up acknowledging the strong points in each other's argument to come up with what we both agree to be a good decision." Their resumes appear in Exhibits 18A-1 and 18A-2.

Since its beginnings in 1965, CWC grew from sales of $40,000 to $1.6 million **RAPID GROWTH** in 1980. "That's a dramatic growth rate," said Ms. Fabish, "even after adjusting for inflation." She credited CWC's success to Mr. Lancaster's "sheer guts, creativity, and willingness to take risks." With Ms. Fabish's help, Mr. Lancaster built CWC in two ways:

☐ Through acquisition of small chemical companies
☐ Through expansion into new markets

The acquisitions fulfilled Mr. Lancaster's dream of someday running a "full-blown chemical manufacturing company." When he first went into business for himself in 1965, Mr. Lancaster bought outright a service company called Zero Air Filter Company. It cost him just $10,000. No manufacturing was involved, just the servicing of air filters. "It wasn't very exciting, picking up and cleaning grease filters from restaurants," says Mr. Lancaster.

Even so, it was a beginning, one which Mr. Lancaster would shortly parlay into a manufacturing company. After two years of doing nothing but cleaning filters, he found out that a "sick" company called Continental Chemical was up for sale. Losing money at the rate of $1,200 a month, this company was in the same building as Mr. Lancaster's company. The owner was asking $75,000. Seeing the acquisition as an opportunity to become at last a chemical manufacturer, Mr. Lancaster decided to buy it.

Work Experience

1965 to present

CWC Industries, Inc.

Founder and president of an analytical testing laboratory that does work in the environmental sciences. This company is also the parent company of two wholly-owned subsidiaries, Continental Chemical Company and Excelsior Varnish & Chemicals, Inc.

These two companies make and sell chemical specialties. Continental Chemical sells directly to the end user, mostly industrial and institutional. Excelsior Varnish sells mostly to jobbers who use private labels; its product line includes cleaners, floor finishes, paints, and varnish.

1949 to 1965

Brooks Chemicals, Inc.

Began as technical director developing products. Was promoted to vice president of technical operations. In 1954, was promoted to executive vice president of the entire company, including its marketing operations

Professionalism

1949 to present

Professional Engineer, licensed to practice in Ohio, Pennsylvania, and Wisconsin

Present Activities

Air Pollution Control Association
American Chemical Society
National Association of Corrosion Engineers
Water Pollution Control Federation

Education

1960 to 1965

Case Institute of Technology
Received master of arts degree in environmental engineering

1945 to 1949

Hiram College
Received bachelor of arts degree in chemistry

The owner agreed not only to accept a $5,000 downpayment but to finance Mr. Lancaster for five years at an interest rate of 7 percent a year. With the purchase of Continental Chemical, Mr. Lancaster became a manufacturer of specialty chemicals and coatings for maintenance work and water treatment. The year was 1967.

ANOTHER ACQUISITION

Two years later, opportunity knocked again in the form of another acquisition, when Excelsior Varnish & Chemicals, Inc. came up for sale. This company manufactured paints, varnishes, and cleaning chemicals. Like Continental Chemical, this company was also losing money.

Work Experience

1965 to present	CWC Industries, Inc.
	Executive vice president. Oversees accounting, financial, marketing, and organizational aspects of the company.
	This company is also the parent company of two wholly-owned subsidiaries, Continental Chemical Company and Excelsior Varnish & Chemicals, Inc.
1956 to 1965	Brooks Chemicals, Inc.
	Office manager. Handled purchasing of raw materials, did costing of products, wrote technical bulletins.
1952 to 1956	Murray Ohio Manufacturing Company
	Secretary. Worked in production, personnel, and purchasing departments.

Activities since 1970

Council of Smaller Enterprises—Executive vice chairman

Chamber of Commerce—Member of board and of executive committee

Ohio Motorist Association—Trustee

Regional Advisory Council of U.S. Small Business Administration—Board member

National Advisory Council of U.S. Department of the Treasury

Awards

1971 and 1977	Chosen Woman of the Year by American Business Women's Association

Education

1977	Dyke College Studied accounting
1970	Case Western Reserve University Studied marketing and creative writing

"The asking price of $120,000 was very reasonable," said Mr. Lancaster, "but we had to buy it on the spot, or so said the lawyer representing the seller. In fact, the lawyer was so demanding that we had to have the bank call him to tell him that under the then-prevailing 'truth-in-lending' regulations it was impossible to complete the transaction as quickly as he wanted it."

"Apparently he could understand that," said Mr. Lancaster, "and it was our bank that made the purchase possible. They loaned us the entire $120,000 we needed." For that purchase price, Mr. Lancaster received "inventory, receivables, cash, manufacturing equipment, and a customer list."

For the next ten years, through 1979, both Mr. Lancaster and Ms. Fabish PERIOD OF ADJUSTMENT dedicated themselves to "turning these acquisitions around and making them profitable." Neither hard work nor sacrifice was a stranger to either of them. When Ms. Fabish joined Mr. Lancaster in 1965, she agreed to a salary of just $200 a month. She took the rest of her salary in options to buy stock, and when she later exercised her options, she ended up owning 25 percent of CWC.

"We all reminisce about the early days of eating wieners and beans," she said. "There were many times that we never took home a paycheck, but our employees always did. There were days when you could only go in the corner and cry like a child. But the next day, you knew you'd come back fighting because the competition was right around the corner."

Did their sacrifices, coupled with hard work, pay off? The answer appears in their financial statements, shown in Exhibits 18A-3 and 18A-4. Note that both sales and profits have gone up each year.

Of course, it took more than sacrifice and hard work to achieve such sales and profit levels. "Jerry and I never would have made it without our employees. They helped us a lot, although I sometimes had to whip and scream and holler. Our philosophy was, and is, to get all our employees to feel as if they're part of the team." CWC shares its profits with employees. Every employee, including Mr. Lancaster and Ms. Fabish, receives proportionately the same bonus at year-end.

CWC's success brought with it community recognition. Word soon got around REWARDS OF SUCCESS among businesswomen that Ms. Fabish was a successful entrepreneur. Twice, she was honored as "Woman of the Year" by the American Business Women's Association. This honor later led to her being appointed to the board of the

CWC Industries, Inc. **EXHIBIT 18A-3**

Comparative Income Statements (000's omitted)

	1976	1977	1978	1979	1980
Sales revenues	$1,008	$1,105	$1,162	$1,396	$1,605
Cost of goods sold	469	511	540	681	712
Gross profit	$ 539	$ 594	$ 622	$ 715	$ 893
Operating expenses					
Factory & warehouse			$ 179	$ 162	$ 190
Selling	$ 499	$ 534	187	268	282
Administrative			186	217	302
Depreciation	12	20	25	19	14
Total operating expenses	$ 511	$ 554	$ 577	$ 666	$ 788
Operating profit	$ 28	$ 40	$ 45	$ 49	$ 105
Federal income taxes	3	6	9	10	30
Net profit	$ 25	$ 34	$ 36	$ 39	$ 75
Cash flow	$ 37	$ 54	$ 61	$ 58	$ 89

CWC Industries, Inc.

Latest Balance Sheet (December 31, 1980)

Assets			Equities		
Current assets			**Current liabilities**		
Cash	$ 89,000		Long-term debt (current)	$ 28,600	
Accounts receivable	248,900		Accounts payable	115,000	
Inventories	168,200		Accrued taxes	26,800	
Prepaid expenses	21,600	$527,700	Accrued expenses	53,000	
Fixed assets			Income taxes payable	22,200	
Land and buildings	$ 52,800		Dividends payable	3,300	$248,900
Equipment	132,200		**Long-term debt**		
	$185,000		Notes payable	$ 32,400	
Less: accumulated			Lease payable	10,100	
depreciation	130,100	54,900		$ 42,500	
Other assets			Less: current portion	28,600	13,900
Goodwill	$ 8,000				
Deposits	2,000	10,000			
			Owners' equity		
			Common stock	$ 26,300	
			Preferred stock	33,000	
			Paid-in capital	1,600	
				$ 60,900	
			Less: treasury stock	9,000	
				$ 51,900	
			Retained earnings	277,900	329,800
Total assets		$592,600	Total equities		$592,600

city's Chamber of Commerce. Only one of two women to be so recognized, Ms. Fabish now serves on the Chamber's executive committee along with members from "Fortune 500" corporations.

Moreover, in 1980, Ms. Fabish was elected by her peers as a delegate to the White House Conference on Small Business. At present, she is executive vice chairperson of the Council of Smaller Enterprises, which boasts a membership of 3,500 small businesses. This council is the largest one of its kind in the country, no small thanks to her efforts recruiting small businesses. In fact, she led the recruiting effort that nearly tripled the council's membership, from 1,200 to 3,500.

Although she bemoans the fact that she never pursued a college degree, Ms. Fabish believes she has already earned an "MBA in the school of hard knocks. I've learned through doing." She often talks glowingly about her "crashing the good old boys' network in the city and becoming one of the guys."

Ms. Fabish believes it is a myth that women in business cannot get help when they need it. "Whenever I have a problem, I call on fellow businesspersons for help. They have never let me down. Often, just by discussing a problem with another person who's been there, I can work it out. Believe me, we can all learn from our competitors' experiences and mistakes—and I have."

In 1980, CWC was faced with an acute shortage of space. Located along with other manufacturers in a rambling, 99-year-old building complex, CWC needed room to meet the increased needs of its customers. (See Exhibit 18A-5.) "The only place to expand was into the street," said Ms. Fabish.

Ms. Fabish's frustration was short-lived. At about the same time, a company called Penreco, located in 12 adjoining buildings, decided to move out. It seems that Penreco had just dropped its line of chemical products because of labor problems. "What luck," said Ms. Fabish. "Jerry and I both saw Penreco's imminent departure as the answer to all our problems and prayers as a buy-out."

The two wasted little time initiating talks with Penreco's management. "Penreco's plant was just what we needed," said Ms. Fabish. Their sprawling plant was 4 times the size of CWC's, and their equipment was more modern. Penreco's price was $900,000. But, as shown in Exhibit 18A-6, CWC really needed an estimated total of $1,410,000 to complete its expansion.

"That was a lot of money for a little company like ours to raise," said Ms. Fabish. "But with our splendid record and reputation in the community, I was sure we could raise all of it through the banks."

With the help of their lawyers, CWC and Penreco soon negotiated a buy-and-sell agreement in principle. Penreco also gave CWC one year to buy them out. "Our work was now cut out for us," said Ms. Fabish. "It's one thing to have a list of customers, and another to deliver. We had to move in a hurry, Jerry and I, to raise the entire $1,410,000."

CWC Industries, Inc.   EXHIBIT 18A-5

Views of Plant and of Chemical Laboratory

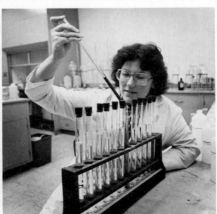

Estimate of Investment Needs

To complete the proposed plant relocation and expansion, CWC will need an estimated total of $1,410,000 itemized as follows:

$ 900,000	Purchase of Penreco plant (12 buildings with 3.10 acres of floor space; 3.04 acres of land; and equipment)
225,000	Working capital needed to expand
100,000	Boiler room equipment and installation
85,000	Dismantling and moving of existing equipment
50,000	EPA and OSHA controls and equipment
50,000	Office computer
$1,410,000	Total investment

On June 22, 1980, Penreco received from Cragin, Lang, Free & Smythe, Inc. an appraisal of $600,000 on the Penreco property. On December 1, 1978, the Industrial Appraisal Company appraised the total value of Penreco's equipment at $1,221,400. Upon their checking with the appraisers in December 1980, CWC's principals were informed that these values were still reasonably true.

Thus the total fair market value of the Penreco plant is about $1,821,400. The principals of CWC have negotiated a firm offer of $900,000 for the plant with Penreco's management.

Armed with resumes and financial statements, Ms. Fabish confidently approached the five largest banks in the city for a $1,410,000 loan. Each one turned her down. "They were so nice about it, too," said Ms. Fabish. "Many of the bank executives I knew on a first-name basis. Even so, because we were located in a 99-year-old building in the inner city, they strongly felt it would be too risky to lend us all that money."

INNER CITY LOCATION A PROBLEM

These turndowns by local banks only served to stiffen Ms. Fabish's resolve. "I knew we were a solid company, and our income statements showed lots of profits (shown in Exhibit 18A-3) and our latest balance sheets showed lots of financial strength (shown in Exhibit 18A-4).

"No doubt about it, we were solid as the Rock of Gibraltar. So I wasn't about to take no for an answer. Somehow I was going to get the money Jerry and I needed to keep growing."

At this point, both Mr. Lancaster and Ms. Fabish knew they had to be creative in their financing. "You can't go to the banks with hat in hand," said Ms. Fabish. "You sometimes have to pound on the table and not give up. Not giving up—that's the hallmark of every successful small-businessperson I know."

After numerous talks with other small-businesspersons, Ms. Fabish found that they had similar problems in the inner city. What did they do to solve their

A CREATIVE SOLUTION

financial problems? Based on the advice she received, Ms. Fabish "packaged a creative financial proposal" involving such helping hands as:

☐ The Union Commerce Bank, which was the city's fourth largest bank
☐ The U.S. Department of Housing and Urban Development
☐ The U.S. Small Business Administration (SBA)
☐ The planning commission of the city
☐ The Chamber of Commerce of the city
☐ The U.S. Department of Commerce

It took Ms. Fabish ten grueling months to prepare the proposal. "Being located as we were in the inner city, there was just no other way than to involve the government, both federal and local," said Ms. Fabish. "The red tape was unbelievable. The running I had to do from one group to another almost got me down. If I had it all to do over again, I'd be too tired." To justify CWC's request for money, Ms. Fabish's financial proposal had to show that:

☐ CWC would create a significant increase in jobs in the community
☐ A major share of the new jobs would go to residents of the surrounding community

---

CWC Industries, Inc.

EXHIBIT 18A-7

Tentative Sources of Money

To finance the proposed plant relocation and expansion, CWC's principals have obtained tentative commitments to a commercial bank loan, a HUD Action Grant and loan, and a loan from Penreco itself:

$750,000 Seven-year term loan from the Union Commerce Bank. Approval of this loan was granted subject to an SBA guarantee of two-thirds of the loan amount. In addition, CWC must obtain at least $300,000 from either investors, shareholders, or a 2 percent HUD loan, all of which must be subordinated to the Bank and to the SBA. Interest will be fixed at 12 percent.

$360,000 HUD Action Grant and loan. Of this sum, $230,000 would be a grant and $130,000 a loan payable in 10 years at 2 percent interest. Approval of both the grant and the loan are subject to firm financial commitments by private parties for the rest of the money needed.

$300,000 Penreco loan. Penreco is willing to finance this portion of the purchase price of their plant. Their loan will be payable in one year at 12 percent interest.

The principals of CWC have approached other banks and private investors, and have been turned down outright or have been offered terms that would place either an excessive drain on the company's cash flow or would force the principals to yield control of CWC to others.

Especially worrisome to Ms. Fabish was the tenuous nature of her relationship to each of the helping hands involved in the proposal. Each one had to satisfy itself that the others were equally committed. If just one pulled out, Ms. Fabish's financial proposal would collapse "like a house of cards." Excerpts of her proposal appear in:

☐ Exhibit 18A-7, which shows how and from whom CWC plans to raise the entire $1,410,000 it needs, in order to buy out Penreco and to complete its expansion
☐ Exhibit 18A-8, which shows the loan conditions set by the bank, from whom CWC seeks a $750,000 loan
☐ Exhibit 18A-9, which shows how profitable CWC expects to be, after it acquires Penreco's complex of 12 buildings
☐ Exhibit 18A-10, which shows how financially sound CWC expects to be
☐ Exhibit 18A-11, which shows how many new jobs CWC expects to add

QUESTIONS

1 Why does CWC have trouble raising money to expand?
2 Comment on CWC's written proposal to raise $1,410,000 (see Exhibits 18A-6 through 18A-11).
3 Suggest financing alternatives other than the ones proposed by CWC. Would they be better? If so, how?
4 How have the managerial styles of Ms. Fabish and Mr. Lancaster contributed to CWC's growth?
5 If CWC's request for a $1,410,000 loan is turned down, what should Ms. Fabish and Mr. Lancaster do next? Why?

CWC Industries, Inc.

EXHIBIT 18A-8

Loan Conditions Set by Bank

The $750,000 seven-year term loan from the bank will be secured by a first lien on all buildings, property, machinery, and equipment as well as on accounts receivable and inventories. It is also understood that all borrowings will be endorsed by Gerald Lancaster and Mary Jane Fabish. Reductions on the loan principal will be as follows:

Month	Monthly Reductions
1 to 12	$ 6,250*
13 to 48	8,333*
49 to 84	10,417*

The loan was approved subject to maintenance of a sound financial condition. It is further understood that all borrowings will be subject to these conditions:

☐ Minimum shareholders' equity of $686,000.
☐ Minimum working capital of $386,000.
☐ Ratio of long-term debt to shareholders' equity not to exceed 1.75 to 1.00.
☐ Quarterly financial statements and yearly audited financial statements.
☐ No additional borrowings other than trade and subordinate loans.

Finally, it is understood that CWC will maintain its major deposit relationship in the years ahead.

* Plus accrued interest

CWC Industries, Inc.

Projected Income Statements (000's omitted)

	1981	1982	1983	1984	1985
Sales revenues					
CWC Industries	$1,900	$2,270	$2,600	$3,070	$3,620
Penreco	1,020	1,500	2,000	2,500	3,000
Total sales	$2,920	$3,770	$4,600	$5,570	$6,620
Cost of sales					
CWC Industries	$ 840	$1,000	$1,200	$1,410	$1,670
Penreco	710	1,050	1,400	1,750	2,100
Total cost of sales	$1,550	$2,050	$2,600	$3,160	$3,770
Gross profit	$1,370	$1,720	$2,000	$2,410	$2,850
Operating expenses					
Administrative	$ 530	$ 570	$ 620	$ 760	$ 980
Selling	380	450	550	650	770
Factory and laboratory	290	370	430	510	610
Total operating expenses	$1,200	$1,390	$1,600	$1,920	$2,360
Operating profit	$ 170	$ 330	$ 400	$ 490	$ 490
Interest	120	110	100	90	80
Before-tax profit	$ 50	$ 220	$ 300	$ 400	$ 410
Income tax	—	80	120	160	170
Net profit	$ 50	$ 140	$ 180	$ 240	$ 240
Cash flow					
Net profit	$ 50	$ 140	$ 180	$ 240	$ 240
Depreciation	90	90	90	90	90
Total cash flow	$ 140	$ 230	$ 270	$ 330	$ 330
Debt service	$ 75	$ 100	$ 100	$ 100	$ 125

CWC Industries, Inc.

Projected Balance Sheets (condensed) (000's omitted)

	1981*	1982*	1983*	1984*	1985*
Assets					
Current assets	$ 980	$1,350	$1,730	$2,090	$2,510
Fixed assets	920	830	730	640	550
Other assets	40	40	40	70	70
Total assets	$1,940	$2,220	$2,500	$2,800	$3,130
Equities					
Current liabilities	$ 510	$ 760	$ 950	$1,120	$1,350
Long-term debt	980	870	780	680	530
Owners' equity:					
Capital stock	130	130	130	130	130
Retained earnings	320	460	640	870	1,120
Owners' equity	450	590	770	1,000	1,250
Total equities	$1,940	$2,220	$2,500	$2,800	$3,130

* Year end.

CWC Industries, Inc.

Employment Potential

To carry out its projected rise in sales, CWC must add to its workforce. CWC's most conservative estimates of the new jobs to be created follow:

Year	New Jobs to Be Added in:			Total New Jobs	Cumulative Increase in Jobs
	Plant	**Laboratories**	**Office**		
1981	4	1	2	7	7
1982	5	1	1	7	14
1983	5	1	1	7	21
1984	5	1	2	8	29
1985	5	0	1	6	35
Total	24	4	7	35	

As this table implies, within a matter of weeks after CWC acquires the Penreco plant, the principals will have to hire at least six new people to enable CWC to meet its expanding backlog of orders and its forward commitments to customers.

For the first few years after Aristotle Pappas opened his bookstore, he paid himself $8,000 a year even though his skills were worth $15,000. That had been his salary as branch manager of a bookstore chain. He worked long hours in his new venture, often seven days a week. Even so, he underpaid himself so that he could plow as much as possible back into the venture.

As the venture grew and prospered over the years, Mr. Pappas shortened his workweek. At the same time, he increased his salary to $40,000 a year. That salary, he felt, was more in keeping with his status as owner of the largest bookstore in town. Sales revenues were over $1 million annually.

The bookstore deducted his $40,000 salary as a reasonable business expense. But the IRS objected, and disallowed half the deduction. The IRS claimed that Mr. Pappas was paying himself a high salary to avoid reporting fat profits and to avoid paying dividends.

Mr. Pappas disagreed. So did his son, who was also his attorney. A week before they were to plead their case before the Tax Court, Mr. Pappas read an article that appeared in *The Wall Street Journal*:

> Small businesses that cheat on taxes will get a closer IRS look.
> Informed sources say possibly less than two-thirds of the nation's eight million small firms (generally those with assets of $1 million or less) are conscientiously paying the taxes they owe under the law. That compares with a 97 percent compliance rate for all corporate and individual taxpayers. IRS officials say small business compliance has slipped substantially over the past four years.
> To combat the problem, the IRS plans to begin next January screening all small business returns by computer. That move alone is expected to hike tax revenues by as much as $42 million next year, says John Hanlon, an assistant IRS commissioner.*

QUESTIONS

1 Is Mr. Pappas's $40,000 salary a "reasonable business expense"? Why?
2 If it were you, how would you argue your case before the Court?

Daedalus, Inc. began making golf clubs in 1981. The company prospered, posting sales revenues of $600,000 in the first year. Operating expenses came to $450,000 for cost of goods sold and $60,000 for other expenses, excluding depreciation.

Depreciable assets totaled $200,000. These assets were expected to last about 10 years. The federal income tax rate was estimated at a flat 30 percent.

QUESTIONS

1 What is the company's after-tax profit using straight-line depreciation? Using the ACRS system for 5-year fixed assets in 1981?
2 Which profit estimate best reflects the company's performance? Why?

*"Tax Report," *The Wall Street Journal,* June 14, 1972, p. 1.

CHAPTER NINETEEN

INSURANCE

questions for mastery

how do the different types of risk differ?

why is it important to develop a program of
  risk management?

what are different ways of dealing with risk?

what different types of insurance coverage
  are available?

how important is a pension program?

Oh, dry the starting tear, for they

were heavily insured.

William Schwenck Gilbert

O ur lives are fraught with risk from the very moment we draw our first breath. We can never know what tomorrow may bring, but this is especially true in business.

Entrepreneurs soon find that risk is their constant companion, and their ability to manage it depends largely on their attitude. If entrepreneurs reject risk, they are most likely to blunder. But if they accept it, they can enhance their chances of survival and growth. In this chapter, we shall discuss how entrepreneurs may protect themselves as well as their venture against risk, focusing on the use of risk management programs, insurance, and pension programs.

THE IDEA OF RISK

Risk defies easy definition. To the layperson, risk generally means the possibility of losing stamina, reputation, or self-image. But to the entrepreneur, risk means the chance of financial loss. When we mention risk in this chapter, we mean financial risk, the kind that may result in dollar losses. Such losses may show up in the balance sheet or in the income statement as:

☐ **Reduced sales revenues** For example, if a fire reduces a plant to rubble, production stops until the plant is rebuilt. Meanwhile, revenues are lost.
☐ **Increased operating expenses** For example, a disastrous fire may cause the entrepreneur to move the venture into temporary but expensive quarters.
☐ **Reduced assets** For example, inventory or equipment may be stolen. Or a major customer who owes the entrepreneur money may declare bankruptcy.
☐ **Increased liabilities** For example, the entrepreneur may fail to deliver on a contract or may lose a law suit.

Note that all of these potential losses have one thing in common: their occurrence cannot be foreseen. When such losses do occur, the entrepreneur is caught by surprise.

As shown in Exhibit 19-1, risk may be classified into three main types: pure, speculative, and fundamental.

Risks qualify as *pure* if they may result in either a loss or no loss at all but with no possibility of gain. Examples are fire, theft, traffic accidents, and the death of a key person. There is little the entrepreneur can do to avoid pure risk. For example, any venture that owns a delivery truck faces the risk of accident, or any venture that owns a building faces the risk of fire that may create a financial loss.

With pure risk, the entrepreneur can only lose or break even. With *speculative* risk, however, the entrepreneur may either gain or lose. For example, an entrepreneur may decide to invest in land on the chance that it will go up in value. Unforeseen events, however, may lower its value. Any such investment qualifies as speculative because it is the entrepreneur, not fate, who exposes the venture to loss.

Fundamental risk is the third type of risk. It differs from both pure and speculative risk in its impersonality. By *impersonality* we mean that fundamental risk plays no favorites. Fate does not single out just one venture and bypass

EXHIBIT 19-1

Types of Financial Risk

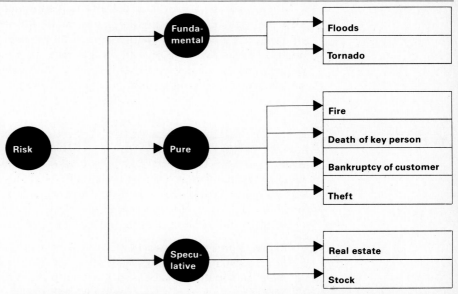

all others. On the contrary, fundamental risk touches all ventures. It arises mainly from the economic, political, social, or natural forces experienced by society. Some specific sources of fundamental risk are floods and earthquakes, inflation and war.

RISK MANAGEMENT PROGRAMS

It may seem self-evident that entrepreneurs are aware of all risks, especially those that may affect the survival and growth of the venture. Yet, entrepreneurs often ignore risk, especially risk that is not always so obvious:

> [Risk] may exist in words inadvertently omitted from a label. Or it may be born of the enthusiastic promise of a salesperson. Risk may arise from the recommendation of an architect by the building supplies manufacturer if, as part of his sales promotion, he agrees to make the architect available—even though the architect is an independent contractor in every sense of the word.[1]

In short, entrepreneurs should analyze fully their exposure to loss. Only through such analysis may entrepreneurs protect their venture against loss

1. H. Wayne Snider, *Risk Management* (Homewood, Ill.: Irwin, 1969), pp. 2–3.

from pure risk. Although easy to state, this goal—to protect against possible loss—is difficult to carry off. The main reason is that risk management is more art than science, often defying precise analysis. Expert judgment plays the key role here. So entrepreneurs should seek the expert help of an insurance agent, the better to design a program of risk management that:

☐ Pinpoints risks that may cause dollar losses
☐ Estimates how severe these losses may be
☐ Selects the best way to treat each risk

PINPOINTING RISKS

Because losses affect a venture monetarily, financial statements are a good starting point for pinpointing where losses may occur. The balance sheet, for example, may show a building valued at $100,000. The entrepreneur may then ask, "What could happen to destroy its value of $100,000?" Among many other possibilities, the entrepreneur might identify the risks of fire and a boiler explosion.

By continuing in this vein, entrepreneurs may identify all of their points of exposure to loss. But to make sure they have overlooked nothing, entrepreneurs should go through a checklist like the one in Exhibit 19-2.

For the entrepreneur, the job of pinpointing risks never ends. As a venture changes and grows, new risks arise. The manufacture of a new product, for example, may expose a venture to new risks. It is the entrepreneur's job to pinpoint such risks and gauge their possible effect on the venture.

ESTIMATING HOW LOSSES MAY AFFECT A VENTURE

This step is perhaps the hardest one to carry out, for there are no checklists to help entrepreneurs estimate the effects of losses. It generally is a good idea to seek professional help. For example, lawyers can help entrepreneurs estimate their liabilities under the contracts they sign. Lawyers can also help entrepreneurs estimate their liabilities for the hazards of a new product.

After estimating the dollar cost of each possible loss, entrepreneurs should estimate:

☐ How often the loss may occur
☐ How serious the loss may be

Such estimates are critical. They tell the entrepreneur which risks offer the greatest loss and which offer the least loss. For example, chances may be slim that a fire will break out; but if it does, it might ruin the venture. The entrepreneur cannot permit that to happen. One way to absorb that risk would be to shift it to somebody else, by buying protection, as discussed below.

SELECTING WAYS TO DEAL WITH RISK

With the help of an insurance agent, entrepreneurs should select the best combination of ways to deal with risk. There are four choices open to entrepreneurs. They may choose to:

EXHIBIT 19-2

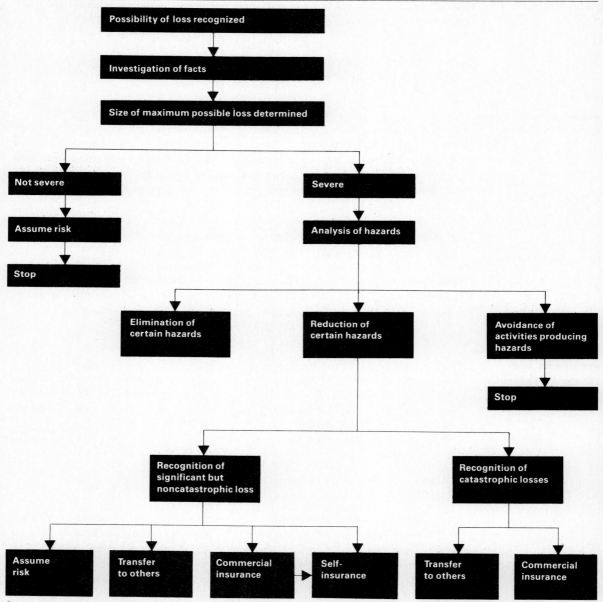

Source: Mark R. Greene, *Risk and Insurance,* South-Western Publishing Company, Inc., Cincinnati, 1968, p. 93. Reprinted by permission.

- Avoid risk entirely
- Absorb risk themselves, through self-insurance
- Prevent the occurrence of loss, cut the chances of its occurrence, or reduce its severity
- Shift risk to others, through insurance

Avoidance of risk is widely practiced among entrepreneurs. For example, entrepreneurs may choose to lease rather than buy such assets as machines and trucks, thus bypassing the risks connected with owning them. Or entrepreneurs may choose to incorporate their venture, thus avoiding many of the risks connected with the unlimited liability of general partnerships and sole proprietorships. Or they may choose to deposit at day's end all the cash taken each day, thus avoiding the risk of losing their cash to burglars after hours.

Self-insurance is rarely used by entrepreneurs, because it is too costly. Most entrepreneurs cannot possibly absorb risk by setting aside excess cash for that purpose. Generally, self-insurance makes sense only if an entrepreneur's asset values are small compared to sales revenues. One example might be the entrepreneur who runs a management consulting firm out of a rented office.

Like avoidance of risk, *prevention* is widely practiced by entrepreneurs. To minimize their exposure to risk, entrepreneurs may:

- Design their plant, shop, or office in such a way that the chances of fire and accidents to workers approach zero
- Hold safety education programs for workers
- Inspect and repair safety devices regularly
- Protect assets by hiring guards, improving burglar alarms, and screening job applicants with care

These practices help solve the problem of risk by preventing it or by lessening its impact. Even if problems do arise, losses are likely to be less severe. For example, an entrepreneur might install an automatic sprinkler system. Such a system may not prevent a fire, but it will keep the fire from spreading and causing even greater loss.

Transfer of risk is the method most widely used by entrepreneurs. Because of its unique importance, it merits more attention than the three other methods.

INSURANCE AND TRANSFER OF RISK

One way of dealing with risk is through insurance. What is insurance? In the words of a group of experts:

> Insurance . . . is the business of transferring pure risk by means of a two-party contract. In order for a particular risk technique to qualify as insurance, all of the requirements of the above definition must be met.[2]

2. Herbert S. Denenberg et al., *Risk and Insurance* (Englewood Cliffs, N.J.: Prentice-Hall, 1974), p. 149.

Thus, insurance is simply a means of letting an outside party absorb risk. For a fee, the outside party agrees to pay the entrepreneur a specified sum of money to cover losses suffered under conditions spelled out in a written contract:

☐ The fee is called a premium.
☐ The written contract is called an insurance policy.

By buying such protection, the entrepreneur is, in essence, trading the uncertainty of a major loss—say, the loss of a $100,000 building through fire—for the certainty of a minor loss called a premium.

EXAMPLE

An entrepreneur decides to protect her venture against loss of revenue that could occur if her star salesperson should die unexpectedly. To do that, she buys a $100,000 policy for $600 a year. This policy will provide her with $100,000 upon the untimely death of the salesperson. This sum of money will help the entrepreneur survive the probable loss of revenue from such a tragedy.

■

How do insurers decide whether an entrepreneur's exposure to risk—as in our example above—is insurable or not? Basically, insurers say that a risk is insurable if it meets these four tests:

☐ The risk must exist in large numbers.
☐ Insured losses must be chance happenings that are beyond the entrepreneur's control.
☐ Losses must be readily measurable.
☐ Probable losses must be so severe that the entrepreneur is incapable of absorbing them.

RISK MUST EXIST IN LARGE NUMBERS

This requirement is necessary to allow the law of averages to work for the insurer. Without this law, the insurance industry could not possibly survive. George Bernard Shaw had this to say about the workings of the law of averages:

An insurance company, sanely directed, and making scores of thousands of bets, is not gambling at all; it knows with sufficient accuracy at what age its clients will die, how many of their houses will be burnt every year, how often their houses will be broken into by burglars, to what extent their money will be embezzled by their cashiers, how much compensation they will have to pay to persons injured in their employment, how many accidents will occur to their motor cars and themselves, how much they will suffer from illness or unemployment, and what births and deaths will cost them: in short, what will happen to every thousand or ten thousand or a million people even when the company cannot tell what will happen to any individual among them.[3]

For example, because tens of thousands of ventures own trucks, insurers are willing to insure against accidents. In essence, each entrepreneur bets with the insurer on whether his own truck will have an accident—with the odds being fixed mathematically by the insurer on the basis of historical facts showing frequency of accidents by truck size, age of driver, and so on.

The odds are fixed so that the insurer runs only the slightest risk of losing financially. For when thousands of cases are considered, the probability that an accident will take place somewhere is certain; although the probability in any single case is uncertain.

INSURED LOSSES MUST BE CHANCE HAPPENINGS BEYOND CONTROL

One example of a chance happening incapable of control is a fire caused by lightning that guts a building. So great a financial loss could not have been predicted by the entrepreneur. Its timing and severity were beyond the entrepreneur's control, so such a risk qualifies as insurable.

Another example is key-person life insurance. Here the risk is not whether the key person will die but rather when that person will die. The key person cannot control the time of death except by committing suicide. Insurers do pay death claims from suicide, but only if the policy has been in force for a certain period, usually two years. This practice, of course, belies the statement that losses must be controlled by chance alone.

Let us now look at some losses that often are uninsurable, namely those from theft or shoplifting. Since the mid-1960s, shoplifting losses have become so severe that insurers charge high premiums for theft insurance. Moreover, in many of the nation's large cities, insurers often avoid selling such insurance in areas earmarked by police as high-crime areas. The chances of loss in such areas are so great that insurers can ill afford to insure the entrepreneur's exposure to risk. Burglary and fire insurance are also often denied to high-crime areas.

LOSSES MUST BE READILY MEASURABLE

Losses must be measurable in dollars and must be hard to falsify. Without such requirements, insurers would have trouble verifying losses.

EXAMPLE

An entrepreneur insures a newly constructed building against fire. The building is appraised at $100,000. A year later, an explosive fire destroys the building, leaving in its wake only rubble and ashes. Note that such a loss is readily verifiable. The insurer has no recourse but to pay the entrepreneur $100,000 to rebuild.

∎

---

3. George Bernard Shaw, ''The Vice of Gambling and the Virtue of Insurance,'' *Everybody's Political What's What* (Edinburgh: R. & R. Clark, 1944), p. 112.

Most losses, however, are not as cut-and-dried as the one above. For example, the timing and severity of losses from a burglary are often hard to verify. The insurer often may have only the entrepreneur's word on the amount lost to burglars. This is especially so for products that are portable and valuable, such as furs and jewels. Because such losses provide an opportunity for extensive fakery, insurers handle all such claims with extreme care.

Accidents on the job are another gray area, especially those injuries or ailments that defy precise diagnosis. One such ailment is the bad back. Insurance files bulge with records of persons who have collected huge sums of money because of a bad back. The problem here is that medical science cannot yet spot and measure such ailments with precision.

Physicians also cannot measure precisely how injuries upset a patient's psychological well-being. The physician has only the patient's word to go on. As a result, insurers are extremely wary of such claims.

POSSIBLE LOSSES MUST BE SEVERE

Possible losses from exposure to risk must be so great that the entrepreneur cannot absorb them. An example is the loss of a factory from fire. The factory is insurable because its loss might ruin the entrepreneur. On the other hand, the possible loss of a 15-cent pencil from fire is not insurable, because the loss is trivial.

The foregoing tests of insurability are by no means hard and fast. They vary from insurer to insurer, from situation to situation. They are only guides. Let us now look at some specific types of losses against which entrepreneurs may insure their venture.

TYPES OF INSURANCE COVERAGE

To protect their venture against fire, windstorms, and other natural disasters, entrepreneurs may buy *property insurance.* This type of insurance generally covers such assets as buildings, equipment, and inventories. To discourage deliberate destruction of such assets, insurers often keep the face value of the policy below the book value of the assets.

Another important type of coverage is *liability insurance.* It protects against losses caused by negligence. For example, a customer may sue a manufacturer because he hurt himself by using his product. Or a customer may sue a retailer because she tripped over an empty tin can and broke her leg. The liability judgments from such accidents often run into tens of thousands of dollars. With liability coverage, the insurer agrees to pay entrepreneurs for any liability claims assessed against them by the courts, but only up to the limit set forth in the policy.

Key persons are vital to the success of any venture. This is especially true in the sole proprietorship. To protect heirs from being forced to sell their venture in order to pay estate taxes, entrepreneurs may buy *key-person life insurance.* This type of insurance may also be useful in partnerships, to buy out the heirs of a deceased partner. Entrepreneurs may also insure the lives of such key persons as creative chemists or star salespersons.

To protect their venture against theft and fraud committed by employees, entrepreneurs may buy *surety bonds* from bonding companies. The face value of the policy is limited to the amount of cash, or to the value of products, accessible to employees.

EXAMPLE

A father has a son who has fallen in with bad companions. The son is caught stealing and is sent to a reformatory. Upon his release, the son cannot get a job because of his record. A satisfactory employment record is necessary, however, if the son is to be rehabilitated, become self-supporting, and develop personal pride.

The father goes to a friend and asks that the boy be given a job that will demonstrate the boy's honesty. The friend refuses, fearing that he too may suffer a loss. The father then agrees in writing to repay the friend for any loss suffered because of the dishonesty of the boy, if he is hired. On this basis, the friend hires the boy.

This agreement is a personal surety contract of the type known as a *fidelity bond.* The obligation guaranteed is the son's honesty. The parties to the contract are the father, the son, and the friend who employs the boy. The risk is the uncertainty of loss arising from the son's possible dishonesty.[4]

■

FRINGE BENEFITS

The foregoing types of insurance protect a venture from extraordinary financial loss. There are, however, other types of insurance that protect not the venture but its employees. Often called fringe benefits, these types of employee insurance include:

☐ Life insurance
☐ Social Security
☐ Health and accident insurance

LIFE INSURANCE

Life insurance protects a family from loss of income upon the untimely death of its breadwinner. The basic form of life insurance is *term insurance.* It gives pure protection, meaning there is no savings plan connected with the insurance policy. The premium is just enough to cover the insured's death claim plus the insurer's expenses and profit. Term insurance gives protection only for an agreed-upon number of years, after which the insurer can charge higher pre-

---

4. Herbert S. Denenberg et al., *Risk and Insurance* (Englewood Cliffs, N.J.: Prentice-Hall, 1974), pp. 137–138.

miums or even refuse to insure. Many ventures buy term insurance for their employees.

Another basic type of life insurance is *whole life insurance,* sometimes called straight life or ordinary life. It differs from term insurance in that premiums are paid throughout an employee's lifetime, with the whole amount of the policy payable upon the insured's death. The insurer cannot refuse to insure at any time during an employee's lifetime as long as premiums are paid promptly.

Each of the hundreds of different life insurance plans is but a variation of the two basic types of life insurance discussed above. In one variation, entrepreneurs may buy *group life insurance* if they employ four or more persons. This plan offers advantages that are denied to individuals. For one, medical examinations are usually waived. Thus employees may qualify under a group policy even if their health disqualifies them for a personal policy. Another advantage is that group premiums are low compared to individual premiums, with savings running 50 percent or more.

Most group life insurance plans are contributory. This means that an employee pays part of the premium, while the entrepreneur pays the rest.

SOCIAL SECURITY

This is another vital form of protection. Run by the federal government, Social Security is a minimum kind of insurance. It provides families with income to live on when the breadwinner dies, retires, or is unable to work. Today, Social Security covers almost all of the nation's employees.

Because it is compulsory by law, economists often refer to Social Security payments as taxes rather than premiums. In 1981, the law required entrepreneurs to withhold 6.65 percent of the first $29,700 earned by each employee in a calendar year. Note in Exhibit 19-3 the yearly rise in Social Security taxes

EXHIBIT 19-3

Rise in Social Security Taxes (1981 to 1987)

Year	Tax Rate Percent	Wage Base*	Social Security Taxes
1981	6.65	$29,700	$1,975
1982	6.70	31,800	2,131
1983	6.70	33,900	2,271
1984	6.70	36,000	2,412
1985	7.05	38,100	2,686
1986	7.15	40,200	2,874
1987	7.15	42,600	3,046

*Wage base was estimated by the U.S. Social Security Administration using a cost-of-living formula.
Source: "Social Security's Tax Bite Gets Bigger," *Business Week* (February 20, 1978), p. 116.

scheduled through 1987. The law also requires that entrepreneurs pay a sum equal to that withheld from the earnings of each employee.

It was the public desire for more financial security that led the federal government to initiate *social insurance,* with passage of the Social Security Act in 1935. Since then, the federal government has steadily expanded its social insurance programs. In fact, the government now spends tens of billions of dollars each year for such programs.

HEALTH AND ACCIDENT INSURANCE

This is still another vital form of protection. It protects employees against the high cost of hospitalization and physicians' services. The two most widely used insurance plans are Blue Cross and Blue Shield. Blue Cross pays hospital bills, whereas Blue Shield pays physicians' bills. Besides paying such bills, health and accident insurance often offers such benefits as these:

☐ Up to 26 weeks of wages if an employee cannot work because of accident or sickness
☐ A percentage of wages if an employee suffers permanent physical disability and can no longer work
☐ Lump sum payments if an employee is dismembered

PENSION PLANS

So far, our discussion has focused mostly on how entrepreneurs may protect their venture against risk, against the unknown. We shall now discuss how entrepreneurs may protect themselves against the risk of financial hardship when they retire. Such hardship is a real probability unless entrepreneurs take pains to design a financially sound pension plan.

Pension plans first appeared in the 1940s and have since grown to become a vital part of the nation's system of retirement. Today, economists often refer to this retirement system as a three-legged stool, supported by three sources of retirement income:

☐ **Social Security** As discussed earlier, almost all Americans can count on Social Security benefits when they retire. But these benefits offer no more than a bare subsistence for people who have nothing else to live on.
☐ **Personal savings** This source of retirement income is, of course, beyond the reach of many entrepreneurs and their employees. As one congressional task force concluded: "If past performance is a guide, private savings cannot be expected to contribute significantly to raising the level of income in old age."[5]
☐ **Pension plans** This third source of retirement income offers perhaps the last hope for more than the bare subsistence that many entrepreneurs and their employees can expect from either Social Security or private savings.

5. Quoted by Ralph Nader and Kate Blackwell, *You and Your Pension* (New York: Grossman Publishers, 1973), p. 93.

Unlike the major corporations, however, many entrepreneurs cannot justify the cost of a private pension plan, either for themselves or for their employees. The main reason is that private pension plans operate best with large numbers of both dollars and employees. But for small businesses:

☐ The cost of administering a pension plan would be disproportionately high.
☐ Pension moneys, set aside and put to work earning a return, would be insignificant, because small groups mean a small pension fund.
☐ Failure is so common among new small businesses that pension plans, if they exist at all, are more vulnerable to termination than those in major corporations.

KEOGH PLAN

This bleak picture is by no means unrelieved, at least not for sole proprietors and partners who own at least 10 percent of a venture. Relief came in 1974, when the U.S. Congress passed into law the Employment Retirement Income Security Act (ERISA). This act enables many entrepreneurs as well as their employees to shelter their money from taxes while accumulating a nest egg on which to retire. Popularly called the *Keogh Plan,* this act allows entrepreneurs and their employees to set aside, tax-*free,* as much as 15 percent of their taxable income—with a limit of $15,000 a year—in a retirement plan.

The Keogh Plan works in this way: An entrepreneur's taxable income is $25,000. If she puts $2,000 a year into a Keogh Plan earning 10 percent a year, her nest egg at retirement very likely will be large enough to cover her financial needs. Turning to Exhibit 19-4, note that if she begins investing at age 35, by the time she reaches 65, she will have earned $285,000 in interest, giving her a grand sum of $345,000. Exhibit 19-5 traces the growth of Keogh Plan savings at selected interest rates. The Keogh Plan has several features, among them:

☐ All of the entrepreneur's employees with three years or more of service must be included in the plan.

EXHIBIT 19-4

How Keogh Plan or IRA Builds Savings

Start Plan at Age	Total Amount You Deposit	Interest Earned	Total Savings at Age 65
25	$80,000	$848,600	$928,600
30	70,000	498,600	568,600
35	60,000	285,000	345,000
40	50,000	156,200	206,200
50	30,000	36,660	66,660
60	10,000	2,810	12,810

Note: Figures assume deposits of $2,000 a year at an interest rate of 10 percent.
Source: Data from *Thorndike Encyclopedia of Banking and Financial Tables* (Boston: Warren, Gorham & Lamont, 1980).

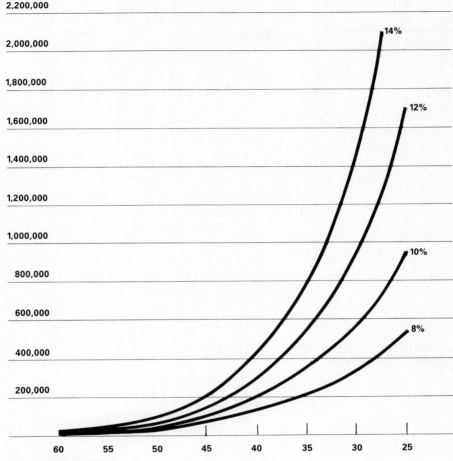

Your total savings at age 65

If you start depositing
$2,000 a year in Keogh Plan or IRA at age —

Source: Data reprinted by permission from the *Thorndike Encyclopedia of Banking and Financial Tables*, Copyright © 1980, Warren, Gorham and Lamont Inc., 210 South St., Boston, Mass. All Rights Reserved.

☐ All sums contributed to the plan are fully tax-deductible.

☐ All sums contributed are fully protected by law. In the event of a law suit, divorce, bankruptcy, or other financial problem, these sums cannot be taken away.

☐ All capital gains, interest, and dividends earned by the plan are not taxed until entrepreneurs begin to withdraw their retirement benefits. By then, entrepreneurs are more likely to be in a lower tax bracket.

To set up a Keogh Plan, entrepreneurs should approach such financial institutions as commercial banks, savings and loan associations, or insurance companies. Many of them have IRS-approved, tax-qualified master plans for investment of Keogh Plan moneys.

ANOTHER TAX SHELTER

An Individual Retirement Account (IRA) is another tax shelter available to entrepreneurs and their employees. The IRA gives *every* working man and woman in the country the opportunity to set up a retirement plan and at the same time shelter a part of their paychecks from federal income taxes. According to the Economic Recovery Tax Act of 1981, every worker may set aside up to $2,000 a year toward retirement. What is more, the worker may deduct that money from his or her taxable income.

If they like, entrepreneurs may save for their retirement using both the Keogh Plan and the IRA. Thus, a sole proprietor or a partner may invest up to $15,000 a year or 15 percent of her income, whichever is smaller, in a Keogh Plan. She may also invest up to $2,000 a year in an IRA—for a total potential deduction from taxable income of $17,000 a year.

Rather than invest in an IRA, a worker may make a voluntary contribution to his corporate pension plan of up to $2,000 a year if the plan permits it. That, too, is deductible from the worker's taxable income. Mandatory contributions to corporate pension plans are not tax-deductible, however.

Looking again at Exhibits 19-4 and 19-5, note that the growth of savings at selected interest rates applies to IRAs as well as Keogh Plans.

SELECTING AN INSURANCE AGENT

Perhaps no other industry is more carefully tailored to the needs of individual customers than the insurance industry. Insurers have something for virtually every entrepreneur. So entrepreneurs can readily buy the insurance program that best suits their own needs as well as those of their venture. To do that, however, they need the expert help of an insurance agent. Licensed by the state, agents are qualified by training and experience to design an insurance program geared to the entrepreneur's needs.

In earlier chapters, we stressed the contributions that accountants, bankers, and lawyers can make to a venture's success. No less important are those that can be made by insurance agents.

How do entrepreneurs go about selecting a competent insurance agent? One way is to ask bankers or lawyers for the names of reputable agents. They are also likely to know which agents offer insurance programs in one package. Agents who offer a one-stop service sell all lines of insurance, including fire, health, liability, and life insurance.

The alternative to a one-stop service is a piecemeal service, in which the agent specializes in just one line of service—say, fire insurance or health insurance. This alternative is less attractive than that of a one-stop service:

Agents offering a one-stop service are more likely to do a painstaking job of analyzing all of the entrepreneur's insurance needs, because they earn a commission on not just one but many lines of insurance. Thus, such agents are more likely to favor the entrepreneur's interests rather than the insurer's on any settlement claims made by the entrepreneur.

Moreover, it generally is best to select an independent agent, one who represents a number of insurers. Independence permits the agent to shop for the policies that best fit the entrepreneur's needs. For example, if one insurance company fails to offer what the agent believes to be proper coverage at a reasonable premium, the agent may well decide to go to another insurer who will.

To make sure their agent deals only with financially solid insurers, entrepreneurs should do some checking themselves. One good source of such information is *Best's Insurance Reports,* which rates each insurer's ability to pay claims promptly. Clearly, an insurer in financial straits may not honor an entrepreneur's claims—or, if it does, it may delay in paying them.

SUMMARY

Entrepreneurs should protect themselves and their venture from any unforeseen events that may cripple survival or stunt growth. To reduce their chances of loss, entrepreneurs should know how best to deal with risk. There are four ways to do that:

☐ By avoiding risk
☐ By absorbing risk themselves
☐ By preventing a damaging event from taking place
☐ By shifting risk to others

To help them decide which approach to use, entrepreneurs should analyze their exposure to risk with the help of an insurance agent. The program of risk management produced by such an analysis should:

☐ Pinpoint risks that may cause dollar losses
☐ Estimate how severe such losses may be
☐ Select the best way to treat those risks

A pension plan should be a part of every entrepreneur's master retirement plan. In particular, the Keogh Plan offers sole proprietors and partners an opportunity to tax-shelter their moneys while accumulating a nest egg on which to retire.

In selecting the right insurance agent, entrepreneurs should look for one who is independent and who offers a one-stop insurance service. Entrepreneurs should also make sure that the agent represents insurers that qualify as financially solid in *Best's Insurance Reports.*

1 What does risk mean to the entrepreneur? Give one example.

2 Explain the difference between pure and speculative risk. Give one example of each type of risk.

3 Explain the four ways of handling risk. Give one example of each.

4 Define these terms: *avoidance of risk, self-insurance, transfer of risk, premium, liability insurance, term insurance, ERISA.*

5 What is risk management? How might you, as an entrepreneur, go about setting up a program of risk management for your venture?

6 Explain why entrepreneurs should select an insurance agent with the same care they select an accountant, a banker, or a lawyer. How would you, as an entrepreneur, go about selecting an agent?

7 Why do you, as an entrepreneur, need to protect your venture against such risks as fire and theft?

8 Describe some of the ways that an entrepreneur may help employees to protect themselves against financial loss. Why are they often called fringe benefits?

9 What is fundamental risk? Give one example.

10 Describe the four tests that insurable risks must meet.

11 Describe some of the ways that entrepreneurs may minimize their exposure to risk.

12 What is insurance? How does it work?

13 What is the Keogh Plan? How does it work? Who is eligible?

14 Why is it generally best for entrepreneurs to select an *independent* insurance agent?

15 Why is key-person life insurance so vital to the survival and growth of certain ventures?

A newspaper columnist applauded Priemer, Barnes and Associates for its leadership in commercial real estate. Indeed, this five-year-old firm now owns real estate worth $9.5 million, financed mostly with debt.

The firm's meteoric rise worries the firm's three partners: Philip Barnes, Jeffrey Doppelt, and Gordon Priemer. They fear that their firm may have outgrown itself. "We must make changes to plan and control our future growth in an orderly way," says Mr. Priemer, "or else we may find ourselves in deep water." The three partners have scheduled an all-day conference to review the problem.

BACKGROUND

Mr. Priemer inherited his entrepreneurial bent from his father, who had been a successful restaurateur. "I learned the language of business when I was just knee-high to a grasshopper," says Mr. Priemer. "Dad often talked about things like taxes and profits at the dinner table. So, thanks to my dad, the seed was planted early."

Mr. Priemer's personal history sparkles with achievement—except in the classroom. "I never enjoyed studying," says Mr. Priemer. Even so, he did earn a bachelor's degree in sociology from John Carroll University. His highest marks, however, were earned on the football field. In fact, he made the Little All-America team at fullback in 1971.

Before founding his firm, Mr. Priemer worked at several jobs to pick up experience. Upon graduation from college in 1972, he profitably ran a cafeteria at Hillsdale College for one year. In 1973, he managed a women's dormitory at Indiana University on a low budget. Next, he worked as a salesman six days a week for a real estate firm in Chicago. Though exciting at first, this rootless lifestyle eventually left him bored and weary. So in 1974 he quit and returned home.

These experiences matured him. Now he knew how he would make his mark in the business world. It would be as manager of his *own* real estate firm. His interest in real estate was spurred by his uncle, who ran his own real estate business. As a teenager, Mr. Priemer had often tagged along with his uncle on business. "I often worked with him until 10 o'clock at night, soaking up trade secrets," says Mr. Priemer. "Believe me, what I learned you can't get from textbooks."

Equally important, he decided to stay out of residential real estate and to concentrate instead on commercial real estate. Since he was weak in that area, he joined Jay F. Zook, Inc., which specialized in commercial real estate. But within two years, the Mellon Bank of Pittsburgh bought out Zook, sold off its assets, and left Mr. Priemer jobless.

FORMS PARTNERSHIP

Within a week, Mr. Priemer and Philip Barnes, a friend from Zook, were working for another commercial real estate firm—Bates and Springer, Inc. While there,

Mr. Priemer and Mr. Barnes hatched their own partnership, after hours. They soon quit to strike out on their own.

Both men were mentally ready for the adventure ahead. Mr. Barnes had already traded a $20,000-a-year job with ARCO for a $12,000-a-year job with Zook. At ARCO, he was a regional real estate director, doing such things as these:

☐ Buying land on interstate highways and later selling off parcels to national chains like Holiday Inn
☐ Buying and selling service stations
☐ Pinpointing likely sites for stations

"But it was tough giving up a $20,000-a-year job. I had to get out of the corporate jungle that most men fall into," says Mr. Barnes. "Believe me, it destroyed my standard of living. I went from buying a new car every year to nothing when Gordon and I decided to set up our own firm."

Mr. Barnes graduated from Otterbein College in 1970 with a liberal arts degree in political science. A B+ student, he was much sought after by corporate recruiters. He chose to work for Phillips Petroleum, a multibillion-dollar corporation, because they made the best offer. He soon found himself in a junior executive program for promising employees. He stayed four years, leaving to join another giant oil company—ARCO. Two years later, he left to go into commercial real estate at Zook, Inc., where he met Mr. Priemer.

BUY FIRST PROPERTY

In their first act as partners, Mr. Barnes and Mr. Priemer bought a real estate corporation with assets worth $376,000 on the books. Called Starburst Home Builders, this corporation owned a 12-unit strip shopping center, 30 acres of virgin land, and 5 two-story frame houses built at the turn of the century.

How did the two partners know about Starburst? While still with Zook, they had heard a rumor that Starburst was up for sale. When the rumor turned out to be true, they moved quickly to negotiate a purchase price with the seller. The seller's financial statements appear in Exhibits 19A-1 and 19A-2.

When negotiations ended, the two partners had agreed to pay $60,000 for two-thirds of Starburst—with the seller keeping one-third for himself. Now, $60,000 was a lot of money for two young men of their age to raise in just ten days—the deadline set by the seller. Although it was touch and go, they managed to meet the deadline by borrowing the $60,000 from relatives, personal friends, and business friends.

So, in 1976, the two partners found themselves heading a corporation with assets booked at $376,000. These assets commanded a *market value* of $800,000. Proud of their achievement, the two partners later changed the corporation's name to Prebar, Inc.

A NEW PARTNER

Soon after, a third partner joined the firm: Jeffrey Doppelt. Like his two partners, Mr. Doppelt always knew that someday he would be in business for himself. In fact, he was born into a family of entrepreneurs. His father cofounded a shopping center.

Income Statement (for year ending March 31, 1976)

Sales revenues			
Rentals		$62,600	
Home sales		32,800	$95,400
Property expenses			
Home construction:			
Cost of construction	$28,600		
Cost of sale	200	28,800	
Rentals			
Interest	$19,000		
Real estate taxes	10,100		
Depreciation	7,200		
Maintenance and repairs	4,400		
Insurance	2,000		
Rental equipment	1,000		
Lease commission	900		
Utilities	600	45,200	74,000
Gross profit			21,400
Administrative expenses			
Payroll	$2,200		
Payroll taxes	1,100		
Insurance	400		
Legal and professional	400		
Real estate taxes	300		
Telephone	300		
Miscellaneous	100		4,800
Operating profit			16,600
Interest revenues			900
Profit before taxes			$17,500

"When Gordon and I formed our firm," says Mr. Barnes, "we just knew we had to have a topnotch salesman on our team. Jeff was all of that and more. In fact, I think he's the best salesman there is in real estate. Jeff has a fantastic memory about what's available for sale in 15 states in the Midwest."

A graduate of Ohio State University, Mr. Doppelt credits his education for his fast start in business. "College was a great help," says Mr. Doppelt, "especially the case studies in marketing. They were so true to life."

Although off to a flying start, the three partners held few illusions about commercial real estate. "It's a cutthroat industry," says Mr. Priemer. "I vowed that I would quit if the industry gave me a bad time. In their eyes, we were just upstarts, too young to make it."

MARKETING STRATEGY

The industry's attitude only served to steel the three partners' resolve to succeed. They took a long look at competitors, taking mental notes of what they did well and what they did poorly. They concluded that they could win by

Starburst Home Builders, Inc.

Balance Sheet (March 31, 1976)*

Assets			Equities		
Current assets			Current liabilities		$ 1,800
Cash		$11,300	Long-term liabilities		
Fixed assets			Mortgages payable	$285,200	
Commercial property	$250,700		Officers' loans	50,100	335,300
Land and buildings	71,100				
Land only	40,300	362,100	Owners' equity		
Prepaid expenses		3,200	Common stock	$ 1,500	
			Retained earnings, 3/31/75	20,500	
			Profits this year	17,500	39,500
Total assets		$376,600	Total equities		$376,600

* Just before Starburst was sold to Mr. Barnes and Mr. Priemer.

ignoring competitors, by refusing to copy them. They would substitute youth for age, innovation for tradition—in an aging city that once proudly labeled itself the "best location in the nation." They were sure that now was the time to strike out in new directions—specifically, to:

☐ Buy out ailing shopping centers owned by out-of-towners and restore them by eliminating weak tenants and substituting strong ones, sparing no expense to renovate, and responding quickly to tenant complaints and suggestions.

☐ Offer prospective clients a spectrum of services available at no other local firm—such services as searching the Midwest for likely shopping center sites; negotiating leases for major retail chains; managing shopping centers, office buildings, and apartment houses; designing, financing, and building shopping centers; and selling commercial real estate.

☐ Hire outstanding talent, people young not only in years but in ideas—in short, "people who are self-starters."

This strategy worked. Putting in 15-hour days, the three partners made one successful deal after another. Their buildup of holdings through 1981 appears in Exhibit 19A-3.

During this five-year period of meteoric growth, the three partners developed a managerial style that competitors envied. For one thing, they took risks. In fact, of the 15 major deals they put together, 8 were so risky that "nobody else wanted them." Incidentally, none of the three partners has lost any money in real estate.

RISK TAKERS

"In commercial real estate, word gets around fast if you fail," says Mr. Priemer. "If you succeed, clients will use you again and again. If you fail, you're in trouble. That's why realtors tend to be conservative like bankers. They don't

Buildup of Assets

Year	Book Value of Assets
1976	$ 380,000*
1977	1,490,000
1978	2,000,000
1979	5,790,000
1980	7,150,000
1981†	9,500,000

* All figures rounded to nearest $10,000.
† First 9 months of 1981.

like risk. But we do. And so far, it's worked for us. Customers come to us because they know we deliver.''

Chance has played little role in the partners' success. They made things happen, instead of letting them happen. For example, they saw that clients would welcome fast service, which meant:

□ Negotiating and closing a deal *in house,* without an attorney's help.
□ Doing *in house* all the things an escrow agent does.
□ Doing *in house* such work as brokering, appraising, leasing, investing, architecture, landscaping, engineering, site planning, financing, and the like.

To do all that, the three partners set up offices in a suite occupied by an architect, a landscapist, and a site planner. As a result, they are able to complete a job in one day instead of the full month required by a competitor. "Our kind of service is hard to beat," says Mr. Priemer.

Their latest acquisition offers a good example of their method of operating. A supermarket executive urged them to look into a half-empty 22-unit shopping center. Built in 1952, the shopping center had been scarred by fire allegedly set by arsonists during a barbers' union dispute. Its parking lot had craters deep as a foot. A major supermarket chain was threatening to pull out. The shopping center's 250-foot facade looked seedy. And to top it all off, the owners were New Yorkers. "They were bleeding the shopping center dry," neighbors said.

BUY SHOPPING CENTER

So what did the three partners do? They bought it. But not before they risked their reputation and a lot of money. When they first saw the shopping center, their reaction was one of revulsion. It was clear that the owners had let the shopping center go to seed. In fact, dandelions had pushed through many of the cracks and craters in the asphalt-covered parking lot. This eyesore clashed sharply with the manicured lawns of homes surrounding the shopping center.

The three partners soon discovered that homeowners living just a block or two away shopped elsewhere. Despite the inconvenience, they often drove two miles to another shopping center rather than use this one. Why? Not enough tenants; poor mix of tenants; litter, dirt, and pot holes; inconvenience; a "don't care" attitude among some tenants.

The three partners' next move was to track down the owners in New York City. Would they sell? Yes, for $1,050,000. That seemed like a lot of money for a down-at-the-heels shopping center. To determine whether it would be a good deal, they spent $30,000 to find out:

☐ What they would have to do to revive the shopping center
☐ What it would cost to do that
☐ Whether their yearly cash-flow return would be high enough to justify their investment in the shopping center

This study bore out the partners' hunch that it would be a good investment. However, their total investment would be $2,200,000, for they would have to spend $1,150,000 to restore and renew the shopping center after spending $1,050,000 to purchase it.

Even so, the return on the investment would be 19 percent a year, after taxes. The partners thought this estimated return would be high enough to attract investors. Their cash-flow and return-on-investment computations appear in Exhibit 19A-4.

Priemer, Barnes & Associates Cash-Flow and Return-on-Investment Computations for Warren Village Shopping Center (First Year)

EXHIBIT 19A-4

Cash Flow

Gross revenues		$335,000
Less: expenses		72,000
Income before debt service		$263,000
Less: interest	$173,600*	
depreciation	82,300†	255,900
Taxable income		$ 7,100
Less: federal taxes		3,600
Net income		$ 3,500
Plus: depreciation		82,300
Cash flow before debt		$ 85,800
Less: debt payment		25,200
Net cash flow		$ 60,600

Return on Investment

Net cash flow	$ 60,600
Partners' investment	$325,000
Cash-flow return on investment	19% in first year

* Based on $1,875,000, 25-year, 9.25% mortgage.
† Based on 28-year life for depreciable assets costing $1,970,000.

The partners moved quickly. They got the results of the study on a Monday morning. And that afternoon they flew to New York City to tell the owners they would buy the shopping center. The partners arrived at the owners' Wall Street offices at 4:45 P.M. An hour later, the owners agreed to sell, but only if the partners would first deposit a cashier's check for $50,000. "They wanted proof we were acting in good faith," says Mr. Barnes. "They got the check the next day. I think they were surprised."

If the deal fell through, the partners stood to lose $80,000—the $30,000 spent on the study plus the $50,000 deposit. "It was a deal that just had to be made," says Mr. Barnes. "We were playing the odds."

ARRANGE FINANCING

The partners immediately went to work to raise the $2,200,000 needed to pull off the deal. They decided that the best way would be to join up with a bank. The bank would put up $1,875,000 and the partners $325,000. And that's how it worked out.

As soon as they set up the joint venture, Mr. Priemer flew to New York City with a million-dollar check. He closed the deal over marbled steak and two-olive martinis at Luchow's, one of New York's finest German restaurants. "It was a great feeling," says Mr. Priemer, "to carry out a deal like that from beginning to end."

Note that Mr. Priemer's job was to close the purchase of the shopping center. He handled the negotiations and financial aspects of the deal. Mr. Barnes and Mr. Doppelt were equally busy. Renovation of the shopping center and later its management was Mr. Barnes's job, while leasing shop space was Mr. Doppelt's. This cooperation exemplifies their approach to all projects. Each partner has a job to do.

The shopping center turned a profit one year after they took over. And almost every square foot of space is rented. A recent photograph of the shopping center appears in Exhibit 19A-5.

STAFFING

Today, the three partners employ 35 men and women full time and 5 part time. "They're mostly self-starters," says Mr. Barnes. "In our kind of business you need people like that working for you."

Personnel turnover runs less than 10 percent a year. "One reason it's so low," says Mr. Barnes, "is that young people like to be part of a young firm that's growing. It gives them opportunities to move up. Besides, we do a lot for our people. We pay them well. And we have a big Christmas party, birthday parties, and a golf outing all at company expense. We also advance money to employees if they have an emergency. They know we care about them, and I know they care about us. Their attitude shows up in the good work they do."

THE FUTURE

The three partners are now worried that their partnership may have outgrown itself. "We're losing touch," says Mr. Priemer. "We used to be much closer to our people, but we've grown so fast that we no longer know what everybody's doing. That's bad."

They have been urged to incorporate by their attorney. At present, Priemer, Barnes and Associates is a general partnership with three equal partners.

View of Warren Village Shopping Center

"We picked the partnership form of organization because it was the simplest and also to avoid double taxation," says Mr. Priemer. "But now that we've grown so big, our attorney thinks we ought to form a Subchapter S corporation. We need a buffer against liabilities, one that limits our liability exposure as partners. When we borrow, we're now jointly and individually liable. Even banks and people we deal with want us to incorporate. Banks say they don't want *one* person jeopardizing our firm." A list of the companies controlled by the three partners appears in Exhibit 19A-6.

Another worry is debt. All 15 major deals put together by the three partners were financed mostly by going into debt. Monthly mortgage payments are so big that the three partners are forced to keep a sharp watch over cash flow. In fact, by 10 A.M. each day their controller gives them a statement of the firm's cash balance in each bank. The controller also prepares a cash-flow summary once a month for each of the firm's holdings. The firm has yet to miss a single loan payment, although Mr. Priemer once missed a mortgage payment on his *own* home.

Still another worry is client complaints. When the firm started, complaints were rare. But not now. In fact, half of Mr. Priemer's telephone calls come from complaining clients. "Maybe we've taken on more than we can handle," says Mr. Priemer. "Our organizational structure must be updated. We need a re-shuffling from top to bottom."

List of Companies Controlled by Partners

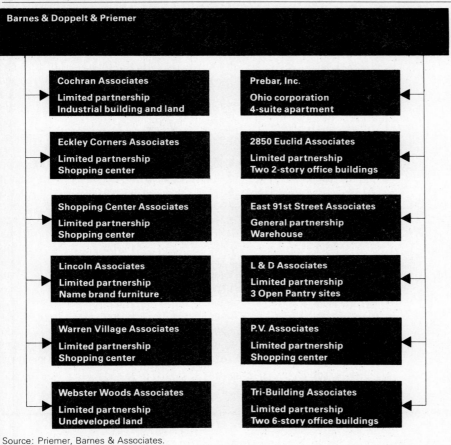

Barnes & Doppelt & Priemer

Cochran Associates
Limited partnership
Industrial building and land

Prebar, Inc.
Ohio corporation
4-suite apartment

Eckley Corners Associates
Limited partnership
Shopping center

2850 Euclid Associates
Limited partnership
Two 2-story office buildings

Shopping Center Associates
Limited partnership
Shopping center

East 91st Street Associates
General partnership
Warehouse

Lincoln Associates
Limited partnership
Name brand furniture

L & D Associates
Limited partnership
3 Open Pantry sites

Warren Village Associates
Limited partnership
Shopping center

P.V. Associates
Limited partnership
Shopping center

Webster Woods Associates
Limited partnership
Undeveloped land

Tri-Building Associates
Limited partnership
Two 6-story office buildings

Source: Priemer, Barnes & Associates.

Echoing Mr. Priemer, Mr. Doppelt believes there "may be too much fat in the organization. We're not as lean as we ought to be. When we were smaller, the three of us could do the work of six men."

To discuss these problems, the three partners called an all-day meeting at a hotel. Recent income statements appear in Exhibit 19A-7.

QUESTIONS

1 What should the three partners do now?
2 Comment on the three partners' method of financing their ventures.
3 What seems to be their main goal?
4 Comment on their marketing strategy.
5 Which form of organization best fits the three partners' operations? Why?

Income Statements for 1977 through 1980

	1977	1978	1979	1980
Sales revenues from				
Commissions	$11,900	$ 93,400	$223,200	$378,500
Gain from sale of equity*			120,000	65,800
Management of properties				38,900
Rental of properties	400	7,100	8,400	14,900
Miscellaneous		300		500
Total sales revenues	$12,300	$100,800	$351,600	$498,600
Operating expenses				
Commissions to salesmen	$ 2,800	$ 14,800	$ 59,100	$152,000
Wages	2,000	13,800	31,000	64,200
Advertising		5,400	36,500	30,600
Auto, travel, and entertainment	3,300	7,700	18,200	29,700
Rent	700	5,200	17,500	28,900
Commissions to co-brokers			26,100	20,700
Telephone and utilities	900	5,400	15,100	18,100
Office	1,500	3,700	17,800	14,600
Amortization and depreciation	100	1,400	2,600	9,900
Interest	2,300	1,600	5,500	8,600
Miscellaneous	1,500	4,200	29,400	7,500
Insurance	500	600	12,700	7,200
Taxes		1,200	2,700	5,300
Legal and professional	2,800	5,000	6,900	2,300
Total operating expenses	$18,400	$ 70,000	$281,100	$399,600
Profit before taxes	($ 6,100)	$ 30,800	$ 70,500	$ 99,000

* This is equity in partnerships sold by partners individually.

CASE 19B

BAILEY SHOES

Byron Bailey, working as sole proprietor, spent three years building up his retail shoe store. Mr. Bailey and his wife had invested their life savings of $15,000 in the store. They were the co-owners, along with the bank that held the mortgage.

The shoe store was just beginning to break even when Mr. Bailey suffered a severe heart attack. His wife was overcome with shock, for Mr. Bailey was just 30 years old, vigorous and bursting with energy. She blamed his heart attack on overwork. In her words:

> There's no doubt in my mind that Byron got sick because he tried to do everything himself. He's been carrying the entire workload himself. He'd work six and seven days a week, from dawn to dusk without any let-up.

He hasn't taken a single vacation in the three years we've been in business for ourselves.

How many times have I begged him to let me help out—even for a few hours. But he wouldn't listen. He thinks a wife's place is in the home. Now look at what's happened. If he pulls out of it, he's going to need a long rest at home. But meanwhile, who's going to run the store?

He used to tell me, "I want you to take care of our home and the baby, and look pretty for me when I get home." Then I'd say, "What's the good of looking nice when you're not home to see me?" His whole life was wrapped up in that store.

Two days after he was stricken, Mr. Bailey died. The store now faced a serious problem. George Dean, who was 63 years old and worked in the store as a salesman, kept things running. But Mrs. Bailey knew it was too much to expect him to keep doing that. Soon after the funeral, the store's accountant worked up the financial statements shown in Exhibit 19B-1.

Mr. Bailey had no will. Nor did he have much insurance—just a $10,000 G.I. life insurance policy. He had once told his wife that "wills and insurance policies are for older folk. I'm too young to think about stuff like that."

1 What should Mrs. Bailey do now? Why?
2 Had you been Mr. Bailey, what might you have done differently? Why?

QUESTIONS

Bailey Shoes

EXHIBIT 19B-1

Balance Sheet (August 31, 1980)

Assets		**Equities**	
Current assets	$27,200	Current liabilities	$18,000
Fixed assets	23,000	Mortgage loan	20,000
		Owners' equity	12,200
Total assets	$50,200	Total equities	$50,200

Bailey Shoes

Income Statement (for year ending August 31, 1980)

Sales revenues		$92,000
Cost of goods sold		64,400
Gross profit		$27,600
Operating expenses		
Mr. Bailey's salary	$15,000	
Other	12,400	27,400
Before-tax profit		$ 200

David Storm is president and sole shareholder of *13* corporations, each organized to run a taxi service. When he started out with just one cab, there was just one corporation. Each time he added a cab to his fleet, he created another corporation. "You've got to be smart to make it in this business," says Mr. Storm.

As required by local law, each of Mr. Storm's 13 corporations carries liability insurance of $25,000. This insurance enables each corporation to pay damages suffered by passengers or pedestrians injured in the negligent operation of its taxicab.

One smog-shrouded morning, one of Mr. Storm's cab drivers negligently struck a pedestrian, causing serious injury. The pedestrian sued the corporation.

The court awarded the pedestrian a judgment of $60,000. But the corporation lacked the cash to pay it. After collecting $25,000 on its insurance policy and $500 from its bank account, Mr. Storm had virtually exhausted the corporation's assets. Even the cab was beyond repair—worth only scrap value.

QUESTIONS

1 Can the pedestrian take action against Mr. Storm to recover the unpaid balance of $34,500 on the judgment?
2 Would Mr. Storm be personally liable for the pedestrian's injuries if he himself had been the driver on the day of the accident?

CHAPTER TWENTY

SOCIAL RESPONSIBILITIES

questions for mastery

why is it important to be socially
responsive?

how may property rights conflict with social
rights?

what is the public's perception of business?

what are the problems of minorities,
women, and the handicapped?

why is consumerism important?

There is a point beyond which even
justice becomes unjust.

Sophocles

f this is the age of computers and jets, it is also the age of nervousness. A vague feeling of helplessness plagues many, if not most, entrepreneurs. It is a helplessness born largely of despair. Newspapers cry endlessly about the urban crisis, the energy crisis, the crime crisis, and a host of other crises. Moreover, in the 1980s, these crises are magnified by the problem of inflation.

And who is blamed for much of society's dis-ease? Business. Giant corporations, in particular, have become a favorite target of politicians and journalists alike. "Business is cold and heartless," we hear them say. "Business isn't doing enough to solve the nation's ills. Businesspersons are socially irresponsible. They think only of profits."

Unless reversed, this popular view bodes ill for the future of business. For one thing, it tends to discourage the best and the brightest from embarking on entrepreneurial careers. It also invites governmental interference and control.

In this chapter, we shall discuss the entrepreneur's social responsibilities, focusing on the meaning of social responsibility, the issues of civil rights and employment discrimination, and the impact of consumerism.

THE MEANING OF SOCIAL RESPONSIBILITY

"What's good for General Motors is good for the country," said a former president of General Motors. That remark sums up the sentiments of many entrepreneurs. They sincerely believe that what is good for their venture is likely to be good for the community in which they invest their energies and moneys. They see their investment as sparking new products, new services, new jobs. Thus, especially as their venture prospers, entrepreneurs see themselves as benefactors to the community.

Years ago, this narrow view generated little resistance. Today this view is no longer accepted by the public. As a result, there has been a steady erosion of the ideas basic to free enterprise, ideas such as these:

☐ Individualism
☐ Personal property rights
☐ Unhindered competition
☐ Limited role of government

Today, however, property rights are fast giving way to social rights such as these:

☐ The right to equal opportunity and the right to equal justice
☐ The right to good health and the right to clean air
☐ The right to survive and the right to a decent income

Social rights are not eliminating property rights, but they are reducing their significance. In the words of Professor George Cabot Lodge of the Harvard Business School:

Your right to enjoy your property is no longer subject merely to paying your taxes and obeying the laws. It is subject as well to the needs of the people who work for you and of the entire community. . . . It's not that property rights are wiped out, it's just that they become less important.[1]

HOSTILE ATTITUDE TOWARD BUSINESS

What Professor Lodge is saying is that the good of the community should come before property rights. This is a concession that few entrepreneurs have been willing to make. Giant corporations have also been reluctant to do so. Many seem oblivious of the social ills plaguing the nation.

As a result, the public has taken an increasingly hostile attitude toward business. The degree of hostility is evidenced by the results of a poll taken by the Opinion Research Corporation of Princeton, New Jersey:

☐ Sixty percent of those questioned have a low opinion of American business.
☐ Fifty percent believe that profits run to 28 percent or more of sales revenues.[2]

The second finding underscores the public's lack of knowledge about the true role of profits. Profits actually average only 4 cents out of every sales dollar. In any case, profits play a vital role in keeping the economy healthy by attracting investors to finance new products and new markets that create new jobs.

Yet a misinformed public continues to believe that business is greedy and should somehow be punished—or at least regulated by the federal government to keep profits down. Note in Exhibit 20-1 how low major companies rank in public confidence.

RESTORING PUBLIC CONFIDENCE

As members of the business world, entrepreneurs must share the blame for the public's distorted image of business. In their rush to sell products, entrepreneurs often create the impression that their goals are purely materialistic, caring little about social problems such as these:

☐ Air, noise, and water pollution
☐ Faulty products and slipshod service
☐ Discrimination against minorities, women, and the handicapped

In fact, many businesspersons, including entrepreneurs, *are* trying to do something about such problems, but they have failed to convince the public of their sincerity. Why?

American businesspersons are respected the world over for their superior knowledge and salesmanship. They are masters at selling air conditioners, automobiles, computers, and even ballpoint pens. But when it comes down to

1. Quoted in "Radical in the Boardroom," *Forbes Magazine,* May 15, 1972, pp. 61–62.
2. John A. Davenport, "Free Enterprise's Forgotten Virtues," *The Wall Street Journal,* July 27, 1973, p. 10.

EXHIBIT 20-1   Public Confidence in Leaders of Major Institutions

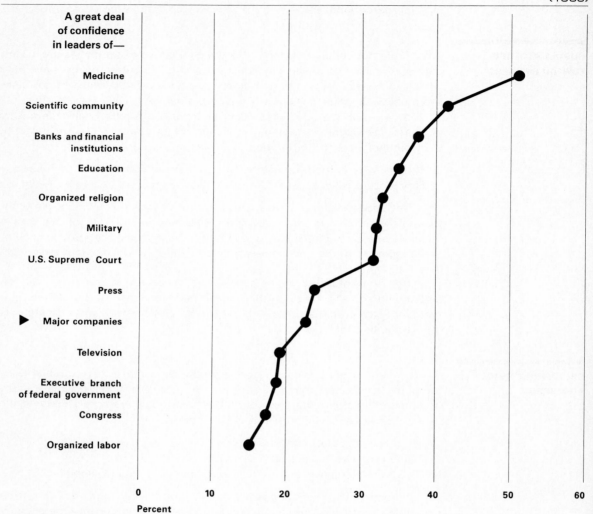

A great deal of confidence in leaders of—

Medicine

Scientific community

Banks and financial institutions

Education

Organized religion

Military

U.S. Supreme Court

Press

▶ Major companies

Television

Executive branch of federal government

Congress

Organized labor

0   10   20   30   40   50   60

Percent

Source: U.S. Bureau of the Census, *Social Indicators III* (Washington, D.C.: U.S. Government Printing Office, 1980), p. xlii.

selling themselves to society by explaining their role in society, they do a poor job. Their message rarely gets across, especially to the young.

The young are not likely to be impressed, for example, by pages of statistics on steel tonnage or kilowatt-hours generated. Rather, they are looking for meaning in this complex world of computers and electronic wizardry. It is not materialism alone that attracts the young—a fact that business still largely ignores.

In a Gallup survey, a majority of teenagers rated businesspersons very low for their honesty and ethical standards (see Exhibit 20-2). "Many teens feel that businesspersons are only interested in profits and care little for the quality of life or the well-being of the public."[3]

A FEELING OF HELPLESSNESS

A melancholy tension grips not only the young but also entrepreneurs. Few know how to overcome their sense of futility about problems such as inflation and the fouling of our environment. They know that the giant pieces of a new order are falling into place and they feel helpless. Why? Because the very size of each problem creates its remoteness from the individual entrepreneur. The

EXHIBIT 20-2

Gallup Youth Survey on Honesty and Ethical Standards of Major Occupations (1980)

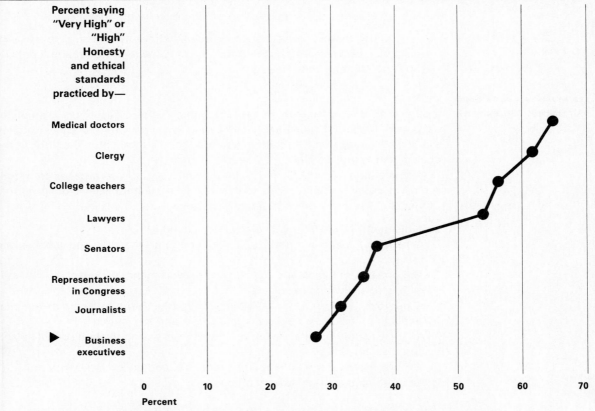

Percent saying "Very High" or "High" Honesty and ethical standards practiced by—

Medical doctors
Clergy
College teachers
Lawyers
Senators
Representatives in Congress
Journalists
► Business executives

0   10   20   30   40   50   60   70
Percent

Source: George Gallup, "Doctors, Clergy Rate Highest," Cleveland *Plain Dealer,* November 30, 1980, p. 6-C.

3. George Gallup, "Doctors, Clergy Rate Highest," Cleveland *Plain Dealer,* November 30, 1980, p. 6-C.

entrepreneur feels somehow connected to the problem but not to the means of solving it.

This feeling of helplessness can be overcome. Individual entrepreneurs may not be able to write legislation for the entire nation, but surely they can make their ideas known to those around them. And they can take an active role if they do things such as these:

☐ Help clean the air
☐ Help make the streets safer
☐ Make their plant a safer place to work
☐ Employ the handicapped, the poor, and minorities
☐ Participate in politics to help ensure the election of honest and intelligent public officials

Clearly, entrepreneurs must act in ways that enhance the community's well-being. However great their ability to innovate and to sell, if they cannot also use their skills to work for a safer and better community, they are incomplete businesspersons. In the words of Economist Irving Kristol:

> Business tends to operate too narrowly within the constraints of "economic" concern. The businessman must act within the broader contexts of the "human" community.[4]

AN OMINOUS QUESTION

Indifference is a luxury few entrepreneurs can afford. The times cry out for action to preserve the nation's vitality. One observer went so far as to pose this ominous question: "Are we as a people and as a nation on the brink of the decline and fall of the United States of America?"[5]

It seems hard to believe that the nation's plight is so great as to trigger such a gloomy question. Yet, in his highly acclaimed television program, "America," Journalist Alistair Cooke saw these signs of decline:

☐ A disregard of law by those elected to uphold it
☐ A belief by many—in and out of government—that the end justifies the means
☐ The practice of deceit and hypocrisy in government, business, unions, religion, and elsewhere in society
☐ A perilous decline in the credibility of nearly every category of national leadership, including politicians, the press, and the church
☐ An increasingly popular desire to live off the state on welfare subsidies and business subsidies
☐ A moral blackout toward vulgarity, violence, and public indecency
☐ An inordinate love of show and luxury

4. Quoted by Desmond M. Reilly, "Students View the Business Ethics Dilemma," *The Collegiate Forum*, Winter 1980, p. 10.
5. Roscoe Drummond, "Time to Deal with the National Decay Issue," Cleveland *Plain Dealer*, July 1, 1974, p. 5-B.

□ A moral indifference toward money corruption in politics and political corruption in government[6]

How does the public perceive its quality of life? To answer that question, the U.S. Department of Commerce made a nationwide survey designed to elicit feelings of alienation. Shown in Exhibit 20-3, the results of the survey suggest the "prevalence of substantial feelings of mistrust and hostility, inasmuch as over three-fourths of the respondents agreed that the 'rich get richer and the poor get poorer.'"[7]

POSITIVE ACTION

Of course, these are not necessarily the worst of times. The past, too, was pockmarked with human imperfection. What has been forgotten is the hunger of the unemployed, the despair of the aged and the crippled, the pervasiveness of violence. Nor was the past spared the problems faced today, problems such as pollution and urban blight. Still, the fact that the past was miserable does little to soften the miseries of the present.

Let us now look at one example of a small business that is responsive to the social challenges of the times.

EXAMPLE

When my partner and I bought the Kerscher Elevator Company of Toledo in 1978, its image was going down. Our building was an eyesore. It looked like a sieve, vandals attacked the property on weekly sorties, and our 23,000-foot factory was so cluttered that we could barely fit a pick-up truck on the floor.

We figured the business would be dead in less than a year if we didn't improve our image immediately. My partner and I then joined civic organizations like the Kiwanis and Rotary clubs. We did work at the city zoo, a $1,000 job for which we charged $1. The public exposure was excellent, and we met more people in the process.

Now we've budgeted about $5,000 a year for giveaways such as tickets for local sporting events, that we donate to local public television station auctions. We also help finance the college education of ghetto youth.

The result? We now employ 16 repairmen, up from just 2 in 1978, when we started.[8]

■

Similar examples have appeared all over the country. There is little doubt that, out of enlightened self-interest, entrepreneurs and other businesspersons are undertaking projects that enhance the well-being of their community. But this is just a start. Businesspersons have a long way to go before they convince

6. Ibid.
7. U.S. Department of Commerce, *Social Indicators III*, (Washington, D.C.: U.S. Government Printing Office, 1981), p. XXVII.
8. Adapted from "The Company Image: How Much Is It Worth?" *Inc.*, November 1980, pp. 44–45.

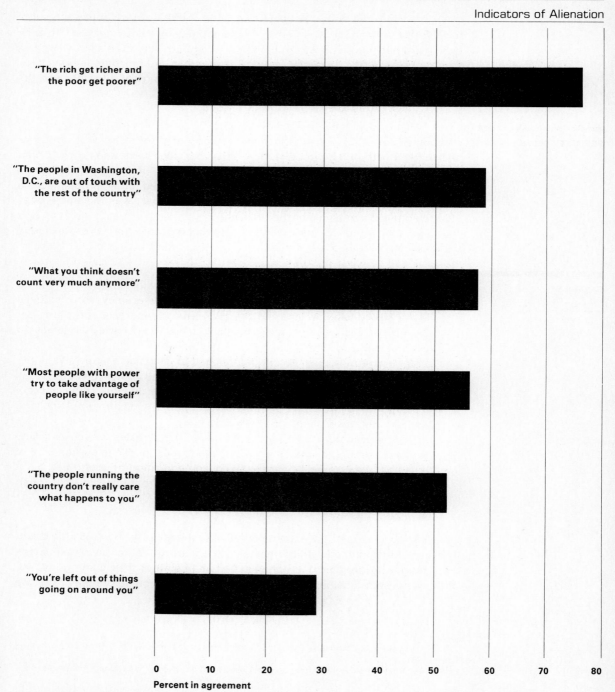

Source: U.S. Department of Commerce, *Social Indicators III* (Washington, D.C.: U.S. Government Printing Office, 1981), p. xlii.

the public that they have, indeed, developed a social conscience. In the words of Ernest Conine, a writer for the *Los Angeles Times*:

> For public consumption, at least, most companies now endorse the creed enunciated in the Caterpillar Tractor Company code of business conduct: "The law is a floor. Ethical business conduct should exist at a level well above the minimum required by law."
>
> Unfortunately, professions of noble intent frequently have no discernible effect on the actual conduct of business.
>
> It still happens that a chemical firm neglects to tell its employees that they may become sterile through repeated exposure to a given production process. Some manufacturing companies still dump deadly pollutants into a lake or river with one hand while fending off environmental orders with the other. The examples go on and on.[9]

CIVIL RIGHTS AND EMPLOYMENT DISCRIMINATION

Today, most businesspersons claim to be "an equal opportunity employer." Many are, indeed, working to erase bigotry and to provide full equality of opportunity for all men and women. Many also observe the spirit as well as the letter of the hiring practices law laid down by the federal government in 1964:

> It shall be an unlawful employment practice for an employer . . . to discriminate against any individual . . . because of such individual's race, color, religion, sex, or national origin.[10]

Good intentions do not, however, ensure good results. It is true that some progress has been made. But to many entrepreneurs, being an "equal opportunity employer" often means simply being willing to consider minorities for employment. Few minority persons move into managerial jobs, for example. Those who do often find their progress blocked in staff jobs with titles such as these:

☐ Equal employment opportunities officer
☐ Manager of community relations
☐ Director of urban affairs

The high visibility of such jobs smacks of tokenism. Few minorities find themselves in line jobs that count. Commenting on this problem, Professor Robert W. Nason of the Wharton School at the University of Pennsylvania, said:

> For most firms to date, institutional and overt racism make the commonly used claim of being "an equal opportunity employer" a mockery . . . a

---

9. Ernest Conine, "Can You Rate Corporate Consciences?" Cleveland *Plain Dealer,* October 31, 1977, p. 19-A. (Reprinted by permission of the *Los Angeles Times.* Copyright 1977. All rights reserved.)
10. Civil Rights Act, Title VII (1964).

new and subtle deterrent to black mobility is institutional racism. In this case, individuals may justifiably feel they and fellow managers hold no personal prejudice against blacks, yet there are real barriers to black mobility in management.

Most employment tests and screening criteria are standard for white subjects. A corporation often requires the black applicant to have higher qualifications than comparable whites. To the extent that seniority influences promotion, blacks newer in management are discriminated against.[11]

OTHER MINORITIES AND WOMEN

Entrepreneurs who pay only lip service to the principles of equal opportunity are surely not living up to their social responsibilities. Nor is it only blacks who are denied equal opportunities. Women, Native Americans, Hispanics, and other minorities face similar problems. All the talk about equal opportunity cannot hide the fact that business still discriminates against minorities and women either openly or unconsciously.

EXAMPLE

An executive search firm submitted the name of an exceptionally well-qualified woman for a corporate position. But she was not considered for the position. To find out why, the executive search firm questioned the corporation. Their dialogue follows:

"Why?"

"Her salary is too high."

"But women have always been underpaid; she must be outstanding to have reached that level."

"We have other candidates with pretty much the same qualifications for less pay."

"Pretty much?"

"Yes."

"Men?"

"Yes."

"Isn't it reasonable to assume that she could be better qualified than they are?"

"Maybe."

"Then you wouldn't be willing to see her?"

"No, she is too expensive."[12]

■

This dialogue bares the mask some businesspersons wear. On the surface, they seem to welcome minorities and women. They radiate equal opportunity. But too often, beneath it all, they throw up fences to keep minorities

11. Quoted in "Calls Equal Opportunity a Mockery," *The Cleveland Press,* August 31, 1972, p. B-6.
12. Frances Lear, "EEO Compliance: Behind the Corporate Mask," *Harvard Business Review,* July–August 1975, pp. 139–140.

and women out. As they go over an applicant's credentials, they often let their own stereotyped attitudes influence them:

> One company sought to employ more minority males. And it would, too, except for one "problem." Its executives say, "The minority male is fine here at corporate headquarters, but we can't control him out in the divisions. He goes to pieces."[13]

TESTING JOB APPLICANTS

Entrepreneurs are as guilty of such discriminatory behavior as their big-business counterparts. Although they may mean well, when it comes down to hiring more minorities and more women, they often fall short.

One area where entrepreneurs and other businesspersons often unconsciously discriminate is in testing. Many use tests to screen job candidates. What entrepreneurs must ask themselves is: Are the tests equally valid for all ethnic groups? Do those who perform well on tests also perform well on the job?

The best test is one that shows no bias toward any ethnic group, including minorities. A study made by New York University concludes that unbiased testing is rare. This study also points out the following:

> The circumstance that justifiably is of most concern to blacks is that members of their race may not score well on tests, even though their performance on the job is as good as that of whites. The solution, if the tests are otherwise valid, is to set a lower passing score for blacks; but this procedure, sensible and just though it may be, is forbidden in many federal and state jurisdictions.
>
> If there are two tests—one which works well for whites and one which works well for blacks, although both groups perform equally well on the job—the employer is faced with another dilemma under the present law. Which test shall he use? If he uses both tests for both groups, the effectiveness of the test that is valid for one group is diluted by adding the results of the invalid test. The logical answer is to employ one test for whites and another for blacks; but this is generally illegal.[14]

Perhaps the best solution to this dilemma is for entrepreneurs to place less emphasis on test scores and more emphasis on the other information they collect on applicants. Tests should be used only as preliminary screens to reject applicants whose scores are so low as to cast serious doubt on their ability to perform.

THE HANDICAPPED

So far, our discussion has focused mostly on minorities and women. Another group that merits attention is the handicapped. In the rush for equal opportu-

13. Ibid., p. 139.
14. Richard S. Barrett, "Grey Areas in Black and White Testing," *Harvard Business Review,* January–February 1968, p. 93.

nity, the handicapped have been largely overlooked. Yet discrimination against them is often more severe than that against minorities and women.

In recent years, however, entrepreneurs and other businesspersons have begun to realize that the handicapped are as dedicated and talented as any other group. Studies show that, to compensate for their disability, the handicapped often work harder than the able-bodied. Moreover, absenteeism among the handicapped often approaches zero.

So when they begin expanding their venture, entrepreneurs should not pass up the opportunity to hire the handicapped. The experience is likely to be mutually rewarding.

THE IMPACT OF CONSUMERISM

The coming of consumerism may be traced to 1966, when Ralph Nader began making headlines with his exposés of unsafe automobiles. Since then, he has broadened his interests and helped launch a consumer movement that now spans the continent. Thanks largely to his efforts, consumers are no longer alone in the fight against dishonest businesspersons.

The main goal of the consumer movement is to help erase private abuses of the public interest. In essence, the consumer movement tries to:

☐ Teach consumers to care
☐ Make institutions more open, accessible, and accountable to consumers
☐ Educate consumers on their opportunities and their responsibilities to make changes
☐ Teach consumers how to learn what is going on, how to make complaints, and how to seek change

Today, amost every community has a consumer group. Such groups have already made their mark on entrepreneurs and other businesspersons, and even on the federal government. For example, in response to consumerism, the Federal Trade Commission (FTC) has hired hundreds of consumer specialists to:

☐ Spot-check businesses for violations of FTC rules
☐ Investigate complaints about faulty products or slipshod service
☐ Educate consumers on how not to be taken in by dishonest businesspersons

TWO OPPOSING VIEWS OF CONSUMERISM

Traditionally, the FTC has investigated mergers and other practices that could hamper free trade. Now that the FTC is also part of the consumer movement, one FTC official had this to say about the behavior of business:

> Every business is involved in some sort of misrepresentation. They're not all doing it maliciously, though. Some of them are doing it because they have to keep up with the competition that is doing it.[15]

15. Thomas S. Andrzejewski, "Idealist Untouchables Battle for Consumers," Cleveland *Plain Dealer*, April 9, 1972, p. 1-AA.

Though exaggerated, this statement echoes the attitude of Mr. Nader and other consumer advocates. In response to such attitudes, some entrepreneurs now go to extreme lengths to please the consumer. But some believe that government—at all levels—has overreacted to consumerism. One such entrepreneur had this to say:

> The government has been pushed and badgered and harried by consumer groups, and it has acted before making a proper study of the matter under question. Some of our politicians . . . are going around the country saying all clothing should be fire-proof without regard to how much this is going to cost the consumer.
>
> When you say, "Make all clothing flame-retardant," it gets out of control. People won't be able to afford their clothes. There would be no variety, no fashion. But to argue for it makes great politics.[16]

There is more than a grain of truth in these remarks. For the price of consumer protection is often a higher cost. Automobiles are a good example. Prices rose dramatically in the 1970s because manufacturers equipped each automobile with safety belts and pollution controls.

BENEFITS OF CONSUMERISM

Despite its critics, the consumer movement has left its mark in many areas. For example, Mr. Nader and his colleagues have:

☐ Exposed the cozy relationship between some federal regulatory agencies and the industries they presumably watch over.
☐ Forced the Atomic Energy Commission to give verified assurances that back-up systems will work reliably if an atomic reactor breaks down.
☐ Drafted legislation to require federal chartering of corporations, a move that consumer advocates believe would make corporations legally accountable to consumers.
☐ Set up a group called Congress Watch to push for legislation on such matters as consumer protection and tax reform. This group follows and grades the performance of each congressman.

Although consumerism has struck fear in the hearts of many entrepreneurs, it has also encouraged tens of thousands of consumers. Remember, the only true test of a satisfactory product or service is a satisfied customer. If that test be their guide, entrepreneurs need never worry about doing the right thing.

Dr. Erika Wilson of California State University researched the question: What is the small-businessperson's stand on business responsibility in society? She found that only 12 percent of the 180 small-businesspersons she interviewed in Los Angeles felt no social responsibility at all.

The remaining 88 percent mentioned responsibilities either to their customers, employees, or community. Responsibility to the consumer seemed most important—almost half referred to responsibility to the consumer.[17]

16. Larry Barth, "Says Consumer Law Can Go Too Far," *The Cleveland Press,* September 26, 1974, p. 2-B.
17. Erika Wilson, "Social Responsibility of Business: What Are the Small Business Perspectives?" *Journal of Small Business Management,* July 1980, p. 23.

Social forces, no less than market forces, operate to influence business success. Just as the wise person must give thought to what makes for a more fulfilling life, so must entrepreneurs give thought to what makes for a better community in which to invest their energies and moneys.

The idea that businesspersons must be socially responsible is relatively new. Although some have aggressively tackled the social problems facing society, many have not. Entrepreneurs must understand that the business of business is not simply profit but also the good of the community.

Because entrepreneurs and other businesspersons have been slow to change, the public's attitude toward them has become increasingly hostile. Polls show that most Americans have a low opinion of businesspersons. They believe that businesspersons should exercise strong leadership to help solve problems such as these:

☐ Poor product quality
☐ Air, noise, and water pollution
☐ Discrimination against minorities, women, and the handicapped

One area where many entrepreneurs fall short is in the hiring and promotion of minorities, women, and the handicapped. Although well-intentioned, many entrepreneurs are hamstrung by stereotyped attitudes toward these groups.

Consumerism has left its mark on business and on the federal government. Thanks largely to consumer groups across the country, consumers are no longer alone in their fight against dishonest businesspersons in the marketplace.

Consumerism is a force whose time has come. No entrepreneur can afford to deny its power.

DISCUSSION AND REVIEW QUESTIONS

1 Define what is meant by the ''social responsibilities'' of businesspersons. Give at least one example.

2 On the basis of your own observations, do you believe that entrepreneurs in your community are living up to their social responsibilities? Why?

3 How would you, as an entrepreneur, go about pursuing the principle of equal opportunity? What guidelines for hiring and promotion would you use?

4 Define these terms: *property rights, social rights, equal opportunity employer, institutional racism, consumerism, FTC, Congress Watch.*

5 Do you believe that consumerism helps or hinders the entrepreneur? Why?

6 Explain the true role of profits.

7 Explain how you, as an entrepreneur, would go about meeting your social responsibilities.

8 What must entrepreneurs and other businesspersons do to attract the young? Explain.
9 Comment on the results of the Gallup Youth Survey. Do you agree with the majority of teenagers who rate businesspersons very low for their honesty and ethical standards?
10 On the basis of your own observations, do you believe that job barriers against minorities, women, and the handicapped have been reduced? Explain.
11 Why is the testing of prospective employees often hazardous?
12 Do you believe that the quality of life in the country is declining or improving? Explain.
13 If an entrepreneur observes the law to the letter, does it also necessarily follow that his or her behavior is ethical? Explain, giving an example.
14 How may property rights conflict with social rights? Give one example of such a conflict.
15 What is the ultimate test of a satisfactory product or service?

CASE 20A

Emil Bialic has devoted 44 years of his life to graphic arts, the last 24 years of it running his own business. Now 61 years old and financially secure, he is wondering, "Where should I go from here? The ultimate question for an individual is: What have I done? Have I had a profound influence?"

BACKGROUND

The son of a Polish immigrant tailor, Mr. Bialic completed his high school education in the depression year of 1937. Although he earned top grades, "out of necessity" he went to work rather than to college. So, at age 18, he began as an apprentice with Reliance Litho at 30 cents an hour. He stayed 20 years. During that time, he became skilled at graphic arts. Equally important, he learned how to run a graphic arts business.

Although he spent 20 years working for somebody else, the idea of having his own business came to him during his very first year with Reliance Litho. In fact, it was his boss who planted the idea, unwittingly. How? By ignoring new ideas—especially when they came from an 18-year-old apprentice—and by cutting corners to save pennies. The result was often a slipshod piece of graphic art.

His boss's style so bothered Mr. Bialic that he vowed to someday start his own business. And 20 years later he did just that. "I decided to go into business for myself because I wanted to be able to express my ideas without having shackles and handcuffs imposed upon me by other men," says Mr. Bialic.

CREATES VENTURE

So it was that in 1957, the year of Sputnik, Mr. Bialic and John Crooks started their own business. They named it Bi-Craft Litho, Inc. and they financed it out of their own savings, each putting up $5,000. Their beginning balance sheet appears in Exhibit 20A-1.

Each man got 50 shares of common stock at $100 a share as evidence of ownership and each got an equal say in running the business. Their 50-50

Bi-Craft Litho, Inc.

EXHIBIT 20A-1

Balance Sheet (July 1, 1957)

Assets		Equities	
Cash	$ 1,000	Liabilities	$ 0
Inventory	1,000	Owners' equity	10,000
Equipment	7,000		
Other assets	1,000		
Total	$10,000	Total	$10,000

share of Bi-Craft Litho lasts to this day. Meanwhile, their equity has soared to $241,000 (see Exhibit 20A-2).

Mr. Bialic credits his success to his ability to supply customers with high-quality work and to his own sense of taste. Most of his customers are artists, printing brokers, designers, and advertising agencies. "They look for reliability and quality before price," says Mr. Bialic. "And we have the knowledge, personnel, and equipment to do their work—with taste."

As mentioned earlier, Mr. Bialic belongs to the graphic arts industry. To the layperson, the phrase *graphic arts* has little meaning. Yet it is one of the nation's oldest industries, communicating ideas through words and pictures. Its products are so widespread that the public takes for granted the skills that go into their production.

GRAPHIC ARTS INDUSTRY

What is the industry like? Although the tiny village blacksmith shop has mushroomed into the giant, smoke-belching factory and the corner grocery store into the sprawling, half-acre supermarket, the graphic arts shop has stayed small. The graphic arts shop remains small because of the old-world tradition of fine craftsmanship and high fragmentation, with many shops specializing in only one or two kinds of product.

This is not to say that the graphic arts industry is unchanged since the days of Benjamin Franklin. Were he alive today, Franklin would hardly recognize his old craft. When he ran his Philadelphia shop in the eighteenth century, everything was done by hand. Since then, dramatic changes have taken place. For example, today:

☐ High-speed presses turn out tens of thousands of printed pages an hour.
☐ Computers set type for big-city newspapers.
☐ Giant four- and six-color offset presses turn out more than 100,000 color impressions an hour.

And today, the graphic arts industry makes a bewildering variety of products that includes brochures, newspapers, greeting cards, magazines, labels, catalogs, calling cards, billboard posters—and almost anything else that can be put into print.

EXHIBIT 20A-2

Bi-Craft Litho, Inc.

Balance Sheet (July 1, 1980)

Assets		Equities		
Cash	$ 10,500	Accounts payable		$ 17,700
Accounts receivable	142,600	Taxes payable		6,000
Inventory	79,900			
Equipment	31,700	Owner's equity		
		Common stock	$ 10,000	
		Retained earnings	231,000	$241,000
Total	$264,700	Total		$264,700

Out of this broad market, Mr. Bialic has carved a profitable niche in brochures and posters. And he does them so well that almost all of his customers are repeat customers. In his words, "I take what artists give me and give back more than the customer expects. And I do it cheaper and faster than they expect. My work has an eye appeal that gives a sales punch to my customers' brochures and posters." Examples of his work appear in Exhibit 20A-3.

Mr. Bialic is so sure of his skills that he relies entirely on word-of-mouth advertising to attract new customers. He neither promotes nor advertises—not even in the Yellow Pages. Instead, he lets his work do the talking for him. "I'm a craftsman, not a salesman," says Mr. Bialic. "I haven't made a sales call in 10 years."

Bi-Craft Litho, Inc.

EXHIBIT 20A-3

Two Examples of Graphic Arts

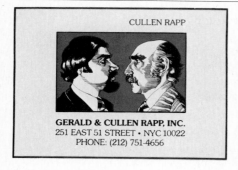

1222 Spring St., N.W., Atlanta, Ga. 30309 • 874-1634

Source: Gerald & Cullen Rapp, Inc., Bi-Craft Litho, Inc., and Swift Tom and His Electric Shop.

Most of his customers are in the Midwest. But he also has customers in Atlanta, New York City, Boston, and Indianapolis. And he landed all of them by word of mouth.

Competition is keen. His city is one of the nation's biggest graphic arts centers, boasting 1,500 companies with more than 20,000 employees and yearly sales revenues of $900 million. Almost all these companies are small. Despite such competition, Mr. Bialic has "managed to survive and even prosper." A recent income statement appears in Exhibit 20A-4. Industry operating ratios appear in Exhibit 20A-5.

ORGANIZATION

Mr. Bialic is quick to praise his partner, Mr. Crooks, and their six employees for helping keep the business above water. "I employ the best talent available, craftsmen with intelligence and know-how," says Mr. Bialic. In fact, when he started out in 1957, he combed the city to hire the "best available pressman." And he found him in the person of Clifford Vick, who still works for him.

Mr. Bialic motivates men like Mr. Vick by example. "I'm demanding of others and murder on myself," says Mr. Bialic. He appraises his workers' performance continually and rewards them by letting them share in the profits.

His plant has a distinctiveness and charm without being pretentious. Located within walking distance of the bustling downtown district, the plant occupies 7,200 square feet of floor space in an old but well-maintained, multi-story, brick building. The plant houses an 8½-by-11 press, a 41-by-54 press, a big two-color press, a big cutter, a small bindery, complete camera and plate-making facilities but no desk for a secretary. In fact, he does not employ one.

Bi-Craft Litho, Inc.

EXHIBIT 20A-4

Income Statement (for year ending June 30, 1980)

Sales revenues		$648,800
Expenses		
Salaries and wages	$273,000	
Supplies	140,300	
Outside services	78,800	
Rent	10,400	
Utilities	10,400	
Deliveries	3,900	
Depreciation	2,300	
Maintenance	2,100	
Legal, accounting fees	1,900	
Insurance	1,600	$524,700
Operating profit		$124,100
Federal income tax		37,700
Net profit		$ 86,400

Operating Ratios for a Small Graphic Arts Shop

Sales revenues		100%
Expenses		
Supplies	35%	
Salaries	12	
Wages	12	
Depreciation	7	
Outside services	6	
Equipment lease payments	5	
Rent	4	
Maintenance	4	
Utilities	3	
Deliveries	3	
Legal, accounting fees, interest	3	
Advertising and promotion	1	
Insurance	1	96
Operating profit		4%

LIFESTYLE

The cluttered, busy look of Mr. Bialic's plant contrasts with the clean, open look of his townhouse. The three-story townhouse sits amidst formal gardens that have won acclaim in several landscaping books and magazines.

Besides being an entrepreneur, Mr. Bialic prides himself on being civic-minded and socially conscious. For example, he once took on the Illuminating Company, a Cleveland-based electric utility with $3.2 billion in assets. Called by a Cleveland newspaper "a contemporary tilter at windmills," Mr. Bialic slapped a $10,000 claim against the utility for its failure to eliminate pollutants that daily blanketed his house with soot. The newspaper article appears in Exhibit 20A-6.

Last month, another graphic arts company offered to acquire Bi-Craft Litho if a "reasonable price could be set." Mr. Bialic is unsure about pursuing the offer further. He has received many similar overtures in the past, but mostly from "floundering businesses that want to bail themselves out."

QUESTIONS

1 What should Mr. Bialic do now? Explain.
2 Do you agree with Mr. Bialic that "the ultimate question for an individual is: What have I done? Have I had a profound influence?" Explain.
3 How well has Mr. Bialic's company performed? Explain.
4 Comment on Mr. Bialic's marketing strategy.
5 Do you agree with the Cleveland newspaper's comment that Mr. Bialic is "a contemporary tilter at windmills" in his $10,000 suit against a corporation with $3.2 billion in assets? Explain.

A contemporary tilter at windmills, Emil Bialic of Avon Lake, will pay his electric bill today. But it will be the first time in nine months that he has done so.

Bialic was incensed over 23 years of "false promises" from the Cleveland Electric Illuminating Company about eliminating pollutants from its Lake Road power plant.

Last August 19, he informed the CEI legal department and the utility's president, Karl H. Rudolph, of his intentions to stop paying his electric bill. Ever since then, bills sent to his home—200 yards east of the plant—have piled up, all unpaid.

Bialic had warned Rudolph in August he would refuse to pay until he got relief from the "airborne obscenities that are slowly smothering us."

The company took no action about the charges until yesterday, when a shutoff notice finally arrived. Bialic is paying the bill today, he said, because he does not want to "revert to candles or kerosene."

The total is $122. Bialic thinks it should be higher and feels CEI's billing department has "jumbled up" his account over the long period of the squabble.

Bialic said that the plant has been an annoyance since he built his home near it in 1948. He said "ugly blanketing of automobiles, humans, dogs, cats, houses, grounds, plants, and trees" regularly occurred and that every morning before his family could have breakfast, the dining room had to be cleaned of soot that came into the house during the night.

He also presented a claim for $10,000 to the company president, then invited Rudolph and his wife to come out for martinis in the Bialic yard where the dirt from the CEI smokestacks could be observed by them as the neighbors have seen it for years.

Source: Pauline Thoma, "CEI Neighbor Yields on Bill," Cleveland *Plain Dealer* (April 28, 1971) 2-D.

CASE 20B

JOHN BELL

John Bell comes from a poor family. Freshly discharged from the army, he landed a job with a manufacturing company that employs 11 persons. On his first day at work, the entrepreneur gave him 15 minutes of instruction and then told him to get busy. Asked if he understood what to do, Mr. Bell said yes.

Thirty minutes later, the entrepreneur returned. He noticed that Mr. Bell had not done the job properly. Angered, the entrepreneur yelled in front of the other workers, "I'll show you only once more how to do it. And you'd better pay attention or you're fired!"

Now Mr. Bell got the job done properly. Or so he *guessed,* because the entrepreneur came back to check several times but did not say a single word to Mr. Bell.

Next day, Mr. Bell failed to show up for work.

QUESTIONS

1 What would you have done had you been the entrepreneur?
2 To what extent must the entrepreneur use an autocratic approach when supervising relatively unskilled employees?

CASE 20C

SAM HERNANDEZ*

Sam Hernandez is a painting contractor. At present, he has six full-time crews doing both interior and exterior work. Recently, Mr. Hernandez's accountant told him that his quarterly profits had dropped by 15 percent. That information puzzled and troubled Mr. Hernandez, because he had completed a record number of jobs in recent months.

After giving it some thought, Mr. Hernandez decided to visit a couple of job sites to see if he could pinpoint the problem. First, he decided he would visit his most productive crew. Perhaps by studying the work habits of this crew he could find out why his less productive crews were eating up the profits.

Mr. Hernandez felt good as he arrived at Roy Smith's job site. Since Mr. Smith had joined the organization six months before, he had consistently accounted for more finished jobs than his fellow crew managers. Mr. Hernandez hoped that he could discover Mr. Smith's secret of success, so he could pass it along to the other crew managers.

However, after observing Mr. Smith's crew for only ten minutes, Mr. Hernandez's feelings about Mr. Smith turned to doubt. Although it was true that Mr. Smith's crew was fast, their work habits were a disaster. They completely ignored safety regulations when it came to anchoring ladders and securing scaffolds. It was a miracle that one of Mr. Smith's crew had not suffered a dangerous fall yet.

In addition, paint was spilled all over the work site, and a number of expensive brushes had been thrown aside hopelessly encrusted with half-dried paint. Expensive drop cloths were torn and dirty, and at least two ladders had broken rungs. The drop cloths and ladders would have to be replaced right away.

After passing the time of day with Mr. Smith, Mr. Hernandez jumped back into his pickup truck and drove off. His mind was filled with questions, especially about Mr. Smith. For example, was Mr. Smith really his best crew manager?

QUESTIONS

1 How does the relationship between effectiveness and efficiency enter this case?
2 Can you think of any other information Mr. Hernandez needs before taking action in this matter?
3 Do you think Mr. Hernandez is a good manager, being caught by surprise as he was?

* Source: Robert Kreitner, *Management: A Problem-Solving Process* (Boston: Houghton Mifflin, 1980), pp. 22–23. Reprinted by permission.

INDEX